P9-EDI-612

DATE DUE

			PRINTED IN U.S.A.

MAGILL'S SURVEY OF CINEMA

MAGILL'S SURVEY OF CINEMA

English Language Films

FIRST SERIES
VOLUME 1
A-EAS

Edited by

FRANK N. MAGILL

Associate Editors

PATRICIA KING HANSON

STEPHEN L. HANSON

SALEM PRESS
Englewood Cliffs, N.J.

LIBRARY OF CONGRESS CATALOG CARD NUMBER: 80-52131

Complete Set: ISBN 0-89356-225-4
Volume 1:   ISBN 0-89356-226-2

PRINTED IN THE UNITED STATES OF AMERICA

PREFACE

MAGILL'S SURVEY OF CINEMA is projected as a comprehensive examination of more than fifteen hundred outstanding motion pictures presented in three series of about five hundred films each. The first two series, devoted to English-language films, and the third series, covering foreign-language productions, comprise a general reference of representative films released after 1927. Individual articles, which vary in length from one thousand to twenty-five hundred words, offer an in-depth analysis of the film under study, stressing the importance of the various elements—production, direction, screenwriting, acting, cinematography, editing—that go into the making of a successful motion picture.

Historically, cinema has been an outstanding unifying social force in the United States. Through the medium the Western rancher could often see quite explicitly how his Eastern city cousin lived and worked; on the other hand, the Eastern city dweller has been presented with countless vicarious experiences of the Wild West—the challenge of the frontier laced with its evil and its nobility. In a similar vein, it is difficult to see how the average prairie family ever could have known what a Park Avenue drawing-room gathering was like, with its slick socialite dress and conversation (or a Hollywood Star party for that matter), unless the father had gathered his brood together on Saturday night and taken them to the nearest town with a movie house.

The educational and civilizing values of motion pictures have often been overlooked or taken for granted. Unquestionably, the primary purpose of films has been *entertainment*; nevertheless, the moral examples displayed on the screens of the nation from time to time have had a broad impact on our social mores and political persuasions. Indeed, not only have our mores been affected by the screen on occasion but also the entire nation's social conscience has sometimes been aroused by a single film (*I Am a Fugitive from a Chain Gang*; *Gentleman's Agreement*; *The Grapes of Wrath*) to establish forthwith a keen sense of community guilt requiring redress.

Much of the serious fare in cinema has been derived from world classics or from the contemporary literary output published by the print medium of the day. The choices have ranged from styles not unlike the old "penny dreadfuls" of Dickens' time to the most sophisticated novels of manners, the cleverest drawing-room comedies, and the most bizarre science fiction fantasies. (With *Gone with the Wind*, we even have our own "War and Peace.") Spectacles of splendor or squalor have been presented in their extremes but with the force of truth and conviction. Even a new kind of fiction writer was called for as cinema developed. He was required to deal with a visual dimension, and his art came to be called screenwriting. Many a successful novelist brought to Hollywood failed miserably as a screenwriter, being completely unable to adjust his talent to the requirements of the new medium.

The style of the essay-reviews covering the 515 films included in this series is formal, the work having been developed primarily as a resource for educational reference. Films are dealt with not by an episodic recital of the plot but through a smooth-flowing account of the story line, accompanied by an interpretation of the contributions of the direction, character portrayal, screenwriting, cinematography, and the various other nuances of filmmaking.

Selection of the list of films to be discussed in the two English-language series has been a major concern from the beginning. Guidelines called for the inclusion of all important names, eras, trends, and genres, noting the "firsts" as well as the "best" in the years between 1927 and 1980. In our considerations we were fortunate in having had the advice of a number of film specialists and consultants, including Dr. Timothy Johnson of the University of Southern California; Don K Thompson, Head of Reference Services at the University of Southern California Library; Bonnie Rothbart, librarian at Metro-Goldwyn-Mayer Studios and formerly head of the Academy of Motion Picture Arts and Sciences Library; Anthony Slide, Director of Film Information for the Academy of Motion Picture Arts and Sciences; Dr. Janey Place, author, film historian, and professor at the University of California, Santa Cruz; and DeWitt Bodeen, screenwriter and film historian.

Acknowledgment and appreciation for aid to our writers and staff are also due library personnel at The Academy of Motion Picture Arts and Sciences, The American Film Institute, The British Film Institute, The University of Southern California Cinema Library, and The University of California at Los Angeles Performing Arts Library. In addition, staff members at the University of California at Los Angeles Film Archive were very generous and cooperative in making rare archive films available for viewing or consultation by our writing staff.

Some 115 writers, many with outstanding careers in film history and film criticism, contributed original articles for this series, of whom Rudy Behlmer, author and member of the Director's Guild of America; Ronald Bowers, Editor of *Films in Review*; David Chierichetti, film historian; Nancy S. Kinney, of the American Film Institute Library; Ted Gershuny, director, screenwriter, and film historian; Judith M. Kass, author and film historian; Libby Slate, The Burbank Studios; Joan M. Cohen, of the Los Angeles County Museum of Art; Nick Roddick, Professor of Drama, University of Manchester, England; and Gene Stavis, Director of the American Cinematheque, Metropolitan Museum of Art, New York City, are but a few. Names of the entire writing staff are listed in the front pages of Volume One.

More than 230 directors provided the 515 films represented in this series. Some of the most active include Woody Allen (*Annie Hall*, 2 others); George Cukor (*Dinner at Eight*, 12 others); Charles Chaplin (*City Lights*, 4 others); Victor Fleming (*Gone with the Wind*, 5 others); John Ford (*Stagecoach*, *The Grapes of Wrath*, 14 others); Howard Hawks (*To Have and Have Not*, 10 others); Alfred Hitchcock (*Rebecca*, *Spellbound*, *Psycho*, 12 others); Elia Kazan (*On the Waterfront*, 5 others); and Billy Wilder (*Double Indemnity*, *Sunset Boulevard*, 8 others).

Responding to the genius of the 230 directors were thousands of performers, more than two thousand of whom this work lists by name in various roles.

One will find Katharine Hepburn with Jimmy Stewart in *The Philadelphia Story* or with Spencer Tracy in *Adam's Rib*; Ingrid Bergman with Humphrey Bogart in *Casablanca* or with Gary Cooper in *For Whom the Bell Tolls*. Others include Paul Newman and Robert Redford in *The Sting*, Bette Davis in *All About Eve*, Faye Dunaway in *Network*, Dustin Hoffman in *Kramer vs. Kramer*, Greta Garbo in *Ninotchka*, Clint Eastwood in *Dirty Harry*, Henry Fonda in *The Grapes of Wrath*, and Clark Gable in *Gone with the Wind*. Also here are Charles Chaplin in *Modern Times*, Jane Fonda in *Coming Home*, Joan Crawford in *Mildred Pierce*, Orson Welles in *Citizen Kane*, John Wayne in *The Quiet Man*, Robert De Niro in *The Deer Hunter* and George C. Scott in *Patton*. Here too are Gary Cooper and Grace Kelly in *High Noon*; Cary Grant in *My Favorite Wife* and the fourteen other Grant films included in this series; GI dream queen Rita Hayworth in *Gilda*; and undershirted Marlon Brando in *A Streetcar Named Desire*. These reminders are only a few of the great films and stunning performances discussed in these four volumes.

The format of the articles in MAGILL'S SURVEY OF CINEMA includes a quick-reference heading showing information about date released, production, direction, screenplay, cinematography, editing, art direction, and running time. Then follows a list of the principal characters along with the identification of the performer who plays the part. For convenience this individual identification is always repeated the first time the character's name is mentioned in the essay-review. At the beginning of each volume there is an alphabetical list of the films dealt with in that volume. Indexes, which appear at the end of Volume Four, include indexes of Directors, Screenwriters, Cinematographers, Editors, and Performers, as well as a chronological list of films, the latter sometimes useful in tracing developments in the techniques of filmmaking.

The American Cinema is indeed an indigenous art form, and in this work we have considered it a *serious* art form deserving to be dealt with in terms of literary criticism. The pioneers who brought the medium into being—the producers, the directors, the writers, the actors, the camera specialists—all should be recognized for their early contributions, and this work is meant as a tangible step in that direction. As the art grew it developed and improved steadily through the years, striving always to surpass itself with each new opportunity. The democratic idea of mass entertainment, begun with early motion pictures, has flowered and become a living force of major significance, often reflecting our social conscience as a nation. It is well to remember this aspect of film tradition. Perhaps what we remember most about it all, however, are those gifted performers who energized their roles, made them spring to life, and burned them into our memory for the rest of our lives. In this transfer lies cinema's special *raison d'être*.

FRANK N. MAGILL

CONTRIBUTING REVIEWERS

Charles Albright, Jr.

Ralph Angel

Lewis Archibald

Leslie Armistead

Irene Kahn Atkins

David Bahnemann

Rebecca A. Bailin

Julie Barker

David Bartholemew

Rudy Behlmer

Joel Bellman

Charles M. Berg

Debra Bergman

Douglas Blau

DeWitt Bodeen

Ronald Bowers

Pat H. Broeske

William H. Brown, Jr.

Kenneth T. Burles

Virginia Campbell

John C. Carlisle

David Chierichetti

William M. Clements

John Cocchi

Joan Cohen

James J. Desmarais

Leslie Donaldson

Rob Edelman

Linda Edgington

Daniel Einstein

Glenn Erickson

Lawrence Fargo, Jr.

F. X. Feeney

Daniel D. Fineman

Sam Frank

Bonnie Fraser

Juliette Friedgen

Roger Geimer

Ted Gershuny

Dennis L. Giles

James P. Girard

Christine Gladish

Patricia King Hanson

Stephen L. Hanson

Thomas A. Hanson

Ruth L. Hirayama

Larry Lee Holland

Sally V. Holm

Charles Hopkins

William O. Huie, Jr.

Ed Hulse

D. Gail Huskins

V. I. Huxner

Jeffry Michael Jensen

Julia Johnson

Timothy W. Johnson

Anne Kail

Cheryl Karnes

Alan Karp

Kathleen Karr

Judith M. Kass

Tanita C. Kelley

Nancy S. Kinney

Stephanie Kreps

Jonathan Kuntz

Audrey Kupferberg

Michael D. Kurtz

Elizabeth Leese

Janet E. Lorenz

Blake Lucas

Anne Louise Lynch

Carl F. Macek

Michael McCrann

Marsha McCreadie

Elaine McCreight

Connie McFeeley

Alain Silver

Libby Slate

Anthony Slide

Edward S. Small

Dennis K. Smeltzer

Ellen J. Snyder

Maria Soule

Gene Stavis

Gay Studlar

Leslie Taubman

Don K Thompson

John G. Tomlinson, Jr.

James Ursini

Mike Vanderlan

Elizabeth Ward

Carolyn Y. McIntosh

Andrew M. McLean

Frances M. Malpezzi

Gregory William Mank

Mark Merbaum

Harold Meyerson

Carl J. Mir

Robert Mitchell

Nancy Moon

Grace Anne Morsberger

Katharine M. Morsberger

Robert E. Morsberger

Rodger Nadelman

Joyce Olin

Isabel O'Neill

Gabrielle Ouellette

John-Paul Ouellette

Susan Karnes Passler

Ruth Peeples

Janey Place

Howard H. Prouty

Elaine Raines

Steven D. Robertson

Nick Roddick

Dena Roth

Lawrence J. Rudner

Dan Scapperotti

Michael Shepler

Karl W. Weimer, Jr.

Leslie Wolf

Lynn Woods

William Woods

Joanne L. Yeck

BRIEF GLOSSARY OF CINEMA TERMS

ACADEMY OF MOTION PICTURE ARTS AND SCIENCES, THE: Usually referred to simply as the Academy, this professional honorary organization founded in 1927 has nearly 4,000 members in twelve branches of the motion picture industry. Its best-known activity is the annual giving of Academy Awards, known as Oscars, for merit in many categories of filmmaking.

AMERICAN FILM INSTITUTE: Founded in 1967, this body began with a grant from the National Endowment for the Humanities and money from private sources. Its office is located in Washington, D.C., at the Kennedy Center for the Performing Arts, and its Center for Advanced Film Studies is located in Beverly Hills, California. Among its numerous activities, the American Film Institute works on film preservation, offers educational programs, and gives an annual Life Achievement Award to a prominent person in the film industry. Recipients of this award have included Bette Davis and John Ford.

ART DIRECTION: In the early days of motion pictures the art director supervised and/or designed all of the sets, costumes, and properties of films. Later, the increased sophistication of all of these elements broadened the art director's role to include such aspects of filmmaking as lighting and special effects. Occasionally the person who directs the activities of all of the visual aspects of a particular film is called the Production Designer. William Cameron Menzies was the first person to be called a Production Designer, for his careful supervision of the film *Gone with the Wind* (1939). Other notable art directors are Vincent Korda and Ken Adam.

ASPECT RATIO: The aspect ratio refers to the relationship between the height and width of the screen. The standard ratio (which is that of television and virtually all pre-1950's films) is 1:1.33, which makes a picture slightly wider than its height. Beginning in the 1950's, however, various wide screen processes were developed, some of which had an aspect ratio above 1:2.50, or a picture over 2½ times as wide as its height. Most films now have an aspect ratio near 1:1.70.

AUTEUR: What is usually called the "*auteur* theory" in cinema criticism is the basic idea that, although it usually takes hundreds of people to create a film, the one person who is responsible for the overall quality of the finished work is the director. The term is the French word for author.

B-PICTURE: A low budget film usually cast with unknown or no longer prominent actors. In the 1930's and 1940's a "B-picture" would usually accompany a main feature. In recent years television has caused a drastic reduction in the number of B-films which are produced for the theater. Occasionally a B-picture will become a success such as the 1956 *Invasion of the Body Snatchers*, but usually they fade into immediate obscurity.

BLACKLIST: In the late 1940's the House UnAmerican Activities Committee began investigating charges that the film industry contained Communists who were injecting Communist propaganda into Hollywood films. Though such charges were never proven, the publicity from the hearings made the industry so sensitive that for more than a decade studios blacklisted (refused to hire) anyone who was suspected of being "un-American" and also tended to avoid any controversial political themes in films. Despite all evidence to the contrary, the industry has always denied that any blacklisting was done.

CINEMATOGRAPHER: The person who performs as cameraman and photographer for a film. The cinematographer works in close contact with both the director and the art director to give the film the best possible visual impact for the type of film being produced. Famous cinematographers have been James Wong Howe and Gregg Toland.

CLOSE-UP: The terms close-up, medium shot, and long shot are used to indicate how much of the subject is shown on the screen. In general a close-up of a person includes little more than the head, a medium shot shows the person from the waist up, and a long shot shows the entire person and a good deal of the setting.

CROSS-CUTTING (also called **PARALLEL ACTION**): The term implies the presentation of two events happening at the same time by showing alternating shots of the two actions.

DEEP FOCUS: In "standard" filming practice only the most important parts of a scene are in sharp focus and objects in the extreme foreground or background may be slightly out of focus. With deep focus, however, everything is in sharp focus, whether it is in the foreground or background. This method can give added emphasis to a character's environment and reduce the number of separate shots needed to convey a scene.

DIRECTOR: The person who is generally regarded as the primary creative force behind a film and who oversees its entire artistic production. Although the power of the director has changed from era to era, it has usually been the case that the more important a director is, the greater control he has over all aspects of a film's production, from its initial casting to the final version of that film. Many motion pictures are known by the director's name, such as "A Frank Capra Film," with the individual director's name displayed over the title of the film in both publicity and credits.

DISSOLVE: A transitional effect in which one image slowly disappears as another appears in its place. It is used less now than it was before 1960.

DUBBING: The term usually refers to the practice of having another person supply the singing or speaking voice for an actor or actress who is not a good singer or not fluent in the language. Dubbing is easily done because the sound for a film can be recorded before, during, or after the visual portion is photographed, and the sound track for musical numbers is almost always recorded before the number is filmed.

FADE OUT: An effect in which the image becomes darker and darker until it is completely black, usually used at the end of a film.

FILM EDITOR, EDITOR: The person who assembles the individual shots and scenes of a film, working in conjunction with the director, cinematographer, and other members of the production unit to produce the final version of a motion picture which the audience sees. The role of a film editor varies from that of a skilled technician who closely follows the instructions of the director, to a high-level artist who plays an important part in the determination of what the film will look like.

FILM NOIR: A term applied to certain films of the 1940's and 1950's which were generally characterized by dark, shadowy lighting and an atmosphere of fear and violence.

FLASHBACK: An episode which interrupts the chronological continuity of a film to show a past event. Though it is usually a few minutes long, a flashback can last less than a second or more than an hour. In pre-1960's films the flashback was often indicated rather obviously: for example, a character might say, "Do you remember that day in the mountains?" and the image on the screen would become wavy before the scene from the past was shown. More recent films usually give fewer indications of a flashback, even at the risk of confusing the viewer.

GRAND GUIGNOL: A style which emphasizes horror, violence, and cruelty. The term comes from the name of a theater in Paris which featured plays of this type.

HAYS OFFICE: This office was Hollywood's self-censorship board which ruled what could and could not be shown in an American film in accordance with the Production Code. It was called the Hays Office after its president, Will Hays, who was hired in 1922 to handle the outcry over the immorality of Hollywood at that time.

BRIEF GLOSSARY OF CINEMA TERMS

HOLLYWOOD TEN: Nine writers and one director who did not cooperate with the House UnAmerican Activities Committee in 1947 (see also **BLACKLIST**) and were imprisoned for six months or a year as "unfriendly witnesses." They were Alvah Bessie, Herbert Biberman, Lester Cole, Edward Dmytryk, Ring Lardner, Jr., John Howard Lawson, Albert Maltz, Samuel Ornitz, Adrian Scott, and Dalton Trumbo.

JUMP CUT: A cut which makes the subject seem to jump from one position to another. In traditional films this is not done except by mistake because it interrupts the smooth continuity of a film, but some recent directors who desire a less polished style use the device intentionally.

LOCATION SHOOTING: This term refers to the photographing of a film (or parts of it) away from a studio. Shooting in a studio gives the filmmakers the use of a set constructed exactly for their needs as well as great control over such important factors as lighting and sound, but location shooting is often used to provide the realism of an actual setting.

MAKE MONEY: In the motion picture industry, a film is said to have "made money" only after it has taken in more than three times its production costs in box-office receipts. As of 1980, the biggest money-making picture of all time was *Star Wars* (1977).

MISE-EN-SCÈNE: This French term for the staging or directing of a play or film is usually used in cinema criticism to refer to a style of filmmaking in which the visual impact comes more from the combination of the actors, settings, and lighting than from the editing.

OUT-TAKES: For a feature film a great deal of film is shot which is not used (for both technical and artistic reasons). The portions not used are called out-takes. These out-takes are, however, occasionally used later in another film or to make the original film longer for a showing on television.

PAN, SWISH PAN, TILT: A movement of the camera to the right or left is called a pan; a movement up or down is called a tilt. A pan can be a long, slow move to show a landscape or an entire room or a shorter, quicker move from one character to another. If the movement is so quick that the image is only a blur, it is called a swish pan.

PRODUCER: The person in charge of the budget for a film and ultimately responsible for the financial success or failure of that film. The power of a producer varies from film to film with some taking only a budgetary interest in them, while others are active in all stages of the production. Some films have their origins as special projects of an individual producer, and the studio will credit the film as "Hal B. Wallis' Production of" or "A Darryl F. Zanuck Production" over the title. Early producers such as Irving Thalberg were often the head of a studio or a major production unit. It is also a common practice for the producer and the director to be the same person.

RESTRICTED POINT OF VIEW: This term refers to the techniques of showing on the screen only what one of the characters knows or can see. Thus, if a film restricts its point of view to one character, only what he or she knows is seen. An example of this type of film is *Chinatown*, in which the audience knows only what the detective knows.

REVIVAL HOUSE: A theater which specializes in showing films which are no longer in current release. Usually these theaters strive to obtain the best possible prints of the films which are rarely seen on commercial television. Today many large universities as well as museums and art centers have their own revival house theaters, often showing films which belong to their own private collections.

SCREENPLAY: The written material for a film. The screenplay of a motion picture has various stages of development from an original story to the shooting script to the final version of the film. Often the original idea for a film as well as all subsequent written material is developed by one person or one team of writers. Other films have their basis in previously published novels or plays or in original story ideas from other writers.

SCREWBALL COMEDY: This is a type of romantic comedy which developed in the 1930's and is usually characterized by main characters from different social classes, an antagonistic relationship which becomes love, and fast-paced action.

SLEEPER: A film which becomes a financial success although it had not been expected to be one. Usually these films are low-budget productions brought out with little advance publicity. *Rocky* (1977) and *Breaking Away* (1979) were highly successful examples of sleepers.

SUBJECTIVE CAMERA: This technique attempts to show exactly what the eyes of one of the characters sees. Frequently, for example, a swirling or out-of-focus image will indicate that the character's mind has been disordered by a beating or by intoxication.

TAKE: The smallest amount of film shot for a single scene. A scene may have several takes or filmings in order for it to be used in the final edited version of a motion picture. Although one take may be enough, many takes are more usual for a single scene.

TECHNICOLOR: Although Technicolor is a corporate name, it has become almost synonymous with the word "color" when used in conjunction with motion picture photography. Technicolor is a process which began in 1915 and reached its high level of development by the 1950's. Warnercolor and Metrocolor are names coined by Warner Bros. and M-G-M respectively to denote their own processing of the same Eastman Color stock used by Technicolor.

3-D: A response of the cinema industry to the competition of television was three-dimensional filming, usually called 3-D. This technique gives a lifelike illusion of depth in contrast to the standard flat image, but it must be shown by two synchronized projectors and the audience must wear special glasses. Because of these difficulties, the process was abandoned very quickly.

VARIETY, HOLLYWOOD REPORTER, THE TRADES: *Variety* and *Hollywood Reporter* are the two most important entertainment industry newspapers and are commonly known as "the Trades." *Variety*, particularly, has become internationally important since its birth in 1905. Its unique style of reporting has made it an entertainment industry institution. In addition to general industry news, the Trades also review films and give current casting information. Each year *Variety* publishes a list of the top fifty box-office successes in the United States and Canada.

WIDESCREEN, CINEMASCOPE, VISTAVISION, PANAVISION: One of the cinema industry's chief responses to the competition from television in the early 1950's was the development of various widescreen processes. The wider image, often combined with huge casts and spectacular sets and scenery, gave the public something it could not get on television. Three of the major widescreen processes which have been developed are CinemaScope, VistaVision, and Panavision, and virtually all feature films now made are in a widescreen format. (See also **ASPECT RATIO.**)

WIPE: In the most common form of this transitional effect a vertical line passes across the frame "wiping" off one clear image to reveal another. In more complex wipes the line can be diagonal, jagged, or can form any one of a large number of shapes such as a star or a spiral.

WOMAN'S FILM: "Woman's film," "weepie," and "soaper" are terms used to describe a type of film which was particularly popular in Hollywood from the 1930's through the 1950's. This type of film has a woman and her concerns at its center and tends to be melodramatic, with stories of sacrifice, affliction, and difficult choices.

LIST OF TITLES

LIST OF TITLES IN VOLUME ONE

MAGILL'S
SURVEY
OF
CINEMA

ABE LINCOLN IN ILLINOIS

Released: 1940
Production: Max Gordon for Plays and Pictures Corporation and RKO/Radio
Direction: John Cromwell
Screenplay: Robert E. Sherwood; based on Grover Jones's adaptation of the
   play of the same name by Robert E. Sherwood
Cinematography: James Wong Howe
Editing: George Hively
Art direction: Van Nest Polglase
Costume design: Walter Plunkett
Running time: 110 minutes

Principal characters:

Abraham Lincoln	Raymond Massey
Stephen A. Douglas	Gene Lockhart
Mary Todd Lincoln	Ruth Gordon
Ann Rutledge	Mary Howard
Elizabeth Edwards	Dorothy Tree
Ninian Edwards	Harvey Stephens
Joshua Speed	Minor Watson
Billy Herndon	Alan Baxter
Jack Armstrong	Howard da Silva
Judge Bowling Green	Aldrich Bowker
John McNeil	Maurice Murphy
Mentor Graham	Louis Jean Heydt
Seth Gale	Herbert Rudley

Robert E. Sherwood's biographical play opened at the Plymouth Theater in New York on October 15, 1938. Abraham Lincoln was a special hero of Sherwood (in part, perhaps, because they were both exceptionally tall men— Sherwood stood six feet, seven inches and once remarked that if he had been shorter he might have written a play about Napoleon); and the project of dramatizing Lincoln's early years was one that he had been turning over in his mind since he had read Carl Sandburg's *The Prairie Years* in 1926. For the first time, he wrote later, he was made aware of the complicated, fallible human being behind Daniel Chester French's statue. Lincoln's doubts and hesitation (as described by Sandburg) about fulfilling his great mission "could not have occurred to a lesser man," wrote Sherwood; and his triumph over his fears was "in many ways the supreme achievement of his life."

As the Depression of the 1930's ground on and democratic institutions everywhere seemed to retreat before the growing threat of totalitarianism, the drama of Lincoln's decision to fight for the moral principles upon which the American nation was founded presented itself to Sherwood with a greater urgency. When, late in 1936, he finally began to work in earnest, the first lines he wrote were Lincoln's prayer for the recovery of a sick child, lines that signaled Lincoln's acceptance of his political destiny and which were also meant as his prayer for the American people in a time of grave national peril. The characters in the play were girding themselves for the coming Civil War; but to American theater audiences of 1938, faced with the prospect of another World War, the parallel with the crisis of a century earlier was easy to see. *Abe Lincoln in Illinois* ran for a total of 472 performances and won Sherwood his second Pulitzer Prize (the first was for *Idiot's Delight* in 1936) before it was sold to producer Max Gordon and RKO for $225,000.

On the stage, Sherwood had compressed the events of Lincoln's life between 1833, when he was a struggling storekeeper in New Salem, Illinois, and 1861, when he left with his family for Washington, D.C. after his election as President, into just twelve scenes. In rewriting the play for the screen, Sherwood broke up the action into many short scenes illustrating not only Lincoln's life but the major public events of the period as well. The result only intensified the episodic quality of a drama that had been diffuse enough on the stage. John Mason Brown complained that, "instead of demonstrating Lincoln's greatness, Sherwood allowed it to overtake him during the intermissions. When, in the film, Robert E. Lee captures John Brown after the raid of Harper's Ferry, the two men barely have time to introduce themselves to each other and to the audience in the manner of actors in a historical pageant.

The film carries a credit to Grover Jones for his "adaptation" of the play, while Sherwood is credited separately as screenwriter. This may mean that Jones was responsible for the expanded treatment of events that in the play had taken place offstage; or it may mean that he was called in to rewrite and polish portions of Sherwood's completed script. It may even mean that he was a full collaborator on the screenplay, but was denied this credit because of Sherwood's contract or his prestige as the author of the original work. Sherwood *was* an experienced screenwriter whose previous credits included *The Scarlet Pimpernel* (1934), *The Ghost Goes West* (1936), and the adaptation of his own *Idiot's Delight* (1939). Much of the dialogue for the new scenes in the film comes from scenes in the play that had to be shortened for the screen; and it seems fair to assign most of the credit—or blame—for the final screenplay to Sherwood.

In the theater, Sherwood had noticed that audiences were merely polite and attentive during the first two acts and only seemed to get caught up in the drama during the Lincoln-Douglas debate scene that opened the third act. Accordingly, the film expands on the action of the play most often when depicting Lincoln's life as a poor young man and a struggling attorney in the years before his marriage to Mary Todd in 1842. In quick succession, we witness the arrival of Tom Lincoln and his family in the Illinois wilderness in 1830; young Abe Lincoln's acceptance of a job hauling a flatboat of hogs from Springfield to New Orleans; Abe's meeting with Ann Rutledge when the flatboat catches on a mill dam near New Salem; his return to New Salem to clerk in Denton Offut's store in 1831; his fight with the local bully, Jack Armstrong, which gains him Armstrong's friendship and the respect of the townspeople; the failure of Offut's store and Abe's decision to stay on in New Salem because of his growing love for Ann; and his appointment as a captain of militia during the Blackhawk Indian War in 1832.

Only at this point does the film reach the first scene of the play: a quiet conversation between Abe Lincoln (Raymond Massey) and the local school-teacher, Mentor Graham (Louis Jean Heydt), over books one night in the back room of the store that Abe has opened in partnership with another young man named Berry. Even then, the scene is given an emphasis that it lacked in the play by Sherwood's device of having Abe steal frequent glances out the window at Ann Rutledge (Mary Howard) as she walks in the moon-light with her lover, John McNeil (Maurice Murphy). McNeil tells Ann that he has to return to New York State to help his family; but that they must write each other in the meantime and that eventually he will return to marry her. Two years later, Abe, in his capacity as postmaster (a job his friends got him after his and Berry's store failed), gives Ann a letter from McNeil an-nouncing his definite intention not to return to New Salem. Abe at last gets up the courage to tell Ann he loves her and timidly suggests that if she allows him to keep company with her for awhile, it might quiet the wagging tongues of the town gossips. Ann accepts Abe's offer, even though she still loves McNeil.

In the play, Ann is never seen again after her scene with Abe over McNeil's letter. Her death from brain fever is reported by Abe, who stumbles into a friend's cabin out of the wind and rain like a messenger in a Greek tragedy. Sherwood's (or Jone's) treatment of the same event in the film is dramatically much more effective. Abe has been approached by the town squire, Judge Bowling Green (Aldrich Bowker), and a Springfield politician, Ninian Ed-wards (Harvey Stephens), with an invitation to stand as the Whig Party's candidate for the State Legislature from New Salem. Reluctantly, he has accepted; but on election night he is summoned to Ann's bedside before the ballots have been counted. Abe is at first overjoyed when Ann calls out to him tenderly; but then he draws back in horror when he realizes that Ann, in her delirium, has mistaken him for McNeil. Ann dies in his arms; and Abe walks blindly back to his cabin through the darkness, paying no attention to the voices in the background cheering his first victory in an election campaign.

In Vandalia, which was then the state capitol, Abe has his first run-in with another rising young politician, Stephen A. Douglas, as played by Gene Lockhart, who was highly praised by Otis Ferguson, among others, when the film opened, but whose performance now seems indistinguishable from any other in the gallery of smug hypocrites he played in the course of his long career. By 1840, Abe is settled in Springfield as a partner in the firm of Stuart and Lincoln, Attorneys and Counselors at Law. One day, his law clerk, Billy Herndon (Alan Baxter), conveys to Abe an invitation from Ninian Edwards and his wife (Dorothy Tree) to a party to meet Mrs. Edwards' sister, Mary Todd (Ruth Gordon) of Kentucky. Miss Todd and Mr. Lincoln are attracted to each other at once—so far as Miss Todd is concerned, in part because she sees in Abraham Lincoln the man who can fulfill her ambition to marry a future President of the United States. Over Mrs. Edwards' objections (she had hoped that her sister would be attracted to Stephen Douglas), Abe and Mary are engaged; but, on the day set for the wedding, Abe tells his friends that he cannot go through with it: "I don't want to be ridden and driven, with her whip lashing me, and her spurs digging into me!"

Abe returns to New Salem, now almost a ghost town, where Jack Armstrong (Howard da Silva) finds him contemplating Ann Rutledge's grave in the moonlight. Jack tells Abe that Seth Gale (Herbert Rudley), another old friend, had been passing through New Salem with his family on their way to join a covered wagon train headed for the Oregon Territory; but that the Gales have had to stop because their little boy has fallen ill with a fever. Abe goes with Jack to see them; and, while they all wait anxiously for the doctor, Seth asks Abe if, in the absence of a preacher, he would mind saying a prayer aloud for the boy's recovery. Abe then speaks the lines that were the first words Sherwood wrote for the play: "Oh God, the father of all living, I ask you to look with gentle mercy upon this little boy. . . ." The boy recovers; and Abe returns to Springfield to tell Mary that, if she still loves him and will forgive him, he will devote the rest of his life to trying to do what is right—"as God gives me power to see what is right."

The rest of the film follows the play closely in tracing Abe's rise to national prominence and Mary's parallel decline into hysteria and near insanity. We hear Abe speak out in Congress against the Mexican War and against slavery during the famous Lincoln-Douglas debates (skillfully condensed by Sherwood into two speeches made up of the most memorable lines uttered by each man). We also hear Mary shriek at Abe in the presence of his friend Joshua Speed (Minor Watson) when he has forgotten to tell her that a delegation of prominent Republicans will be visiting them in their home; and, on election night, 1860, after he has told her that he will not put up with any more of her hysterical outbursts. She bitterly declares: "This is the night I dreamed about when I was a child . . . the night when I'm waiting to hear that my husband has become President of the United States. And even if he does—it's ruined, for me." Ruth Gordon's performance throughout hovers just on the edge of absurdity; but it seems unfair to blame this intelligent actress for conveying the passionate intensity that Sherwood wrote into the part of Mary Todd. Sherwood drew heavily from William Herndon's biography of Lincoln for his account of the Ann Rutledge affair and of Lincoln's quarrelsome and unhappy marriage. Modern historians generally agree that Herndon was motivated by feelings of personal bitterness toward Mrs. Lincoln. She had never invited him to her home, even after he and her husband had become law partners, most likely because she disapproved of Herndon's drinking and, as a Southerner, distrusted the influence of his strong antislavery views on Lincoln's political thought. This does not, of course, detract from the artistic validity of Sherwood's portrait of Lincoln as a passive man driven to greatness by an ambitious and shrewish wife, any more than Shakespeare's portrait of Richard III as a monster of evil is artistically invalid because the playwright was influenced by the prejudices of Tudor historians. It seems odd, however, that Sherwood should have relied on Herndon so heavily (he makes much of Billy Herndon's emotional instability and alcoholism) in view of his stated determination to have no theatrical "hoke" in the play.

Abe Lincoln in Illinois was released by RKO in April, 1940, less than a year after Twentieth Century-Fox released John Ford's *Young Mr. Lincoln*, which dramatized many of the same events in Lincoln's life. Fox studio chief Darryl Zanuck, who suggested the Lincoln project to Ford, may have been hoping to cash in on the box-office success of the play by beating RKO into the nation's movie theaters with his own version of the Lincoln legend. If so, Zanuck's idea paid off handsomely: *Young Mr. Lincoln* is studied in film courses and still frequently shown today, while *Abe Lincoln in Illinois* receives only an occasional airing on late night television. This is unfortunate because the film version of Sherwood's play has much to recommend it. In spite of Otis Ferguson's objection that he "found little to look at in it, though some very fine stuff to listen to," director John Cromwell and his associates, art director Van Nest Polglase, costume designer Walter Plunkett (who had also done the costumes for *Gone with the Wind*), and cinematographer James Wong Howe, did a remarkable job of re-creating the look of backwoods and small-town American life a century before. When the Republican delegation visits the Lincolns in their Springfield home, one can practically feel the scratchiness of Mrs. Lincoln's horsehair furniture and experience the discomfort of wearing stiff clothes and being crowded into the parlor of a small, dark house. Howe received one of the film's two Academy Award nominations, as did Raymond Massey for his performance as Lincoln. Massey has become so well-known as the definitive twentieth century Lincoln—our idea of Lincoln as he may have been in life, as opposed to the backwoods lawyer of American myth portrayed by Henry Fonda in *Young Mr. Lincoln*—that it is surprising to realize that he had never played the role before he was asked by his friend, Sherwood, to act in *Abe Lincoln in Illinois* on Broadway. Massey has since played Lincoln on radio and television, in the film *How the West Was Won* (1963), and in Norman Corwin's play *The Rivalry*.

Charles Hopkins

ADAM'S RIB

Released: 1949
Production: Lawrence Weingarten for Metro-Goldwyn-Mayer
Direction: George Cukor
Screenplay: Ruth Gordon and Garson Kanin
Cinematography: George J. Folsey
Editing: George Boemler
Running time: 101 minutes

> *Principal characters:*
> Adam Bonner .... Spencer Tracy
> Amanda Bonner .... Katharine Hepburn
> Doris Attinger .... Judy Holliday
> Warren Attinger .... Tom Ewell
> Kip Lurie .... David Wayne
> Beryl Caighn .... Jean Hagen

Billed as the hilarious answer to the age-old question "Who wears the pants?," *Adam's Rib* was years ahead of its time in its portrayal of a marriage of equals. The battle between the sexes theme which dominates the film gives director George Cukor the opportunity to explore the potential conflicts and possibilities for growth in a relationship in which the husband and wife are intellectual equals. *Adam's Rib* is also notable for being the sixth in the series of nine motion pictures made by Spencer Tracy and Katharine Hepburn, considered to be one of the screen's great couples, and it is one of their best.

The story contrasts the views of attorneys Adam and Amanda Bonner and compares their relationship with that of philandering Warren Attinger (Tom Ewell) and his scatterbrained wife, Doris (Judy Holliday). Adam and Amanda Bonner move from mutually supportive husband and wife to competitors when district attorney Adam confronts defense attorney Amanda, who seeks to defend the woman (Doris Attinger) whom Adam has been drafted to prosecute for the attempted murder of her husband. Their battle soon moves out of the courtroom and into their home as each staunchly defends his or her contrasting point of view. As the trial progresses, their marriage is shaken, but eventually each learns from the experience, and the two reach a mutual understanding.

As the story opens, the audience sees Doris Attinger follow her husband Warren from his office to the apartment of his mistress, Beryl Caighn (Jean Hagen). In one of the movie's funniest scenes, Doris stands outside in the hallway holding a revolver which she has purchased that afternoon. She is so inept that she is unable to release the safety catch without consulting the instruction manual, and she seems more likely to shoot herself than anyone else. She finally shoots the lock and bursts into the apartment to find a surprised Beryl and Warren nestled together on the couch. She fires several rounds, finally wounding her husband in the shoulder. When she runs out of bullets, Beryl runs for help, while Doris looks down at Warren tenderly.

The main theme of the film, the double standard of conduct for men and women, is established when Adam and Amanda read about the incident the next morning. Amanda takes the strongly feminist stand that Doris has done exactly as any man might have done in that situation, but that social conditioning will cause her to be convicted of a crime for which a man would go free. Adam, a strict believer in law and order, believes that crime must be punished, not condoned. Complications arise later when Adam, much to his chagrin, is assigned Doris' prosecution in what seems to be an open and shut case. When Amanda hears this, she rushes to offer her services to Doris. That night, when Amanda tells Adam she has taken the case, he tries to dissuade her and they begin to bicker. Each day their feud intensifies, until it becomes all-out war. In court, they progress from friendly competitors who drop pens in order to blow kisses to each other under the table, to arch enemies, when Amanda humiliates her husband in public.

Adam and Amanda both fight the case on the basis of principle, he believing in the sanctity of the law, she defending the idea of equal justice. Adam has little sympathy for philandering Warren while Amanda has great sympathy and understanding for simpleminded Doris. We see their overreaction to this case during Amanda's initial interview with Doris. Amanda, prepared to defend equal rights, is aghast at Doris' willingness to plead guilty, and refuses to let her do so. The actual details of the trial become less and less important to the attorneys, while the principals of the case, Doris and Warren, become mere rallying points in the battle of the sexes between Adam and Amanda.

As part of her defense, Amanda calls a succession of successful women whose professions prove that they are intellectually and physically equal to men. In the movie's most farcical scene, Amanda turns the courtroom into a circus by having a female weightlifter lift a protesting Adam up over her head to demonstrate a woman's potential strength. Adam, although shaken, remains professional in the midst of this debasing treatment. It is clear that Amanda's passionate desire to win has both clouded her judgment and seriously damaged her marriage. That night, Adam moves out.

During her summation the next day, Amanda illustrates for the jury how different their reactions would be if Doris' and Warren's positions were reversed. At this point the camera shows the action through the jurors' eyes, as Amanda urges them to picture Doris, dressed as a faithful husband seeking to protect his home, and Warren, pictured as a blond woman, lured away by Beryl, the predatory male wolf. Adam's stance that every crime should be punished stands no chance against Amanda's theatrics. Doris is acquitted.

That night an ambivalent Amanda seeks companionship next door with her neighbor Kip Lurie (David Wayne). While he tries to seduce her, Amanda can think only of Adam. Just as Kip is about to kiss her, Adam bursts into the room, pointing a gun at them and declaring he has the right to defend his marriage. Panic-stricken, Amanda blurts out that no one has the right. Adam, with a triumphant smile, agrees and then places the gun to his mouth. Kip and Amanda are horrified until Adam bites off the barrel of the licorice pistol.

When Adam and Amanda meet in their law office the next day, they begin recalling times spent in their country home. Amanda is greatly touched when tears well up in Adam's eyes; they are reconciled and drive to the country house for the weekend. That night, Adam demonstrates that men can effectively use women's wiles when he shows Amanda how easy it is for him to concoct those tears. She claims that his demonstration proves there is very little difference between men and women, to which Adam replies "Vive la différence!"

Director George Cukor's use of an immobile camera during scenes containing lengthy dialogue gives the audience more of a feeling of watching a stage performance than a film. The screenplay by Ruth Gordon and Garson Kanin is lively and provides some witty dialogue, but the story is a spoof which must take the characters through some improbable antics at the end in order to resolve the plot.

The film works as well as it does primarily because of the excellence of all the performances, which met with universal praise from critics. Tracy and Hepburn have a magnetism between them which makes even the most absurdly contrived plot work. *Adam's Rib* was a box-office success which bolstered Tracy's and Hepburn's popularity and launched the film careers of Judy Holliday, Tom Ewell, and Jean Hagen. As a result of her portrayal of Doris, Judy Holliday landed her Oscar-winning role in *Born Yesterday* (1950).

Anne Louise Lynch

THE ADVENTURES OF ROBIN HOOD

Released: 1938
Production: Hal B. Wallis for Warner Bros.
Direction: Michael Curtiz and William Keighley
Screenplay: Norman Reilly Raine and Seton I. Miller; based on the Robin Hood legends
Cinematography: Sol Polito, Tony Gaudio, and W. Howard Green
Editing: Ralph Dawson (AA)
Art direction: Carl Weyl (AA)
Costume design: Milo Anderson
Music: Eric Wolfgang Korngold (AA), with orchestrations by Hugo Friedhofer and Milan Roder
Running time: 102 minutes

Principal characters:
Robin Hood (Sir Robin of Locksley) .... Errol Flynn
Lady Marian Fitzswalter .... Olivia de Havilland
Sir Guy of Gisbourne .... Basil Rathbone
Prince John .... Claude Rains
Little John .... Alan Hale
Friar Tuck .... Eugene Pallette
King Richard (Richard the Lion-Hearted) .... Ian Hunter
High Sheriff of Nottingham .... Melville Cooper
Will Scarlett .... Patric Knowles
Much the Miller's Son .... Herbert Mundin
Bess .... Una O'Connor
Bishop of Black Canon .... Montagu Love

The Adventures of Robin Hood is possibly the greatest swashbuckler ever filmed. Its chief rival for that title is *The Prisoner of Zenda* (1937), but until the final duel, that film depends more on court intrigue and characterization than on acrobatic derring-do. With *Captain Blood* (1935) Errol Flynn had almost singlehandedly revived the swashbuckler genre, which had flourished in the 1920's but had gone into eclipse in 1929. *Captain Blood* launched Flynn's career, and he consolidated his image as an adventurer with *The Charge of the Light Brigade* (1936) and *The Prince and the Pauper* (1937), but it was *The Adventures of Robin Hood* that made him legendary.

The Adventures of Robin Hood had, of course, been filmed before in a spectacular silent version of 1922, with Douglas Fairbanks as the hero and Wallace Beery as Richard the Lion-Hearted. But Fairbanks' version, for all its virtues, lacks the verve and panache of the Flynn remake. For one thing, Fairbanks' Earl of Huntington does not become Robin Hood until the film is two-thirds over. Most of the story deals with the Crusades and is closer to Sir Walter Scott's *The Talisman* than to the Robin Hood legends. The 1938 film, while taking some liberties with legend, wisely confines itself to the greenwood (with Chico, California's Bidwell Park doubling as Sherwood Forest) and to Nottingham town and castle. From Robin Hood's initial confrontation with the villainous Guy of Gisbourne until the final fight in Nottingham Castle, the film moves at a lightning though lighthearted pace, a perfect blend of action, comedy, and romance.

Curiously, Warner Bros. first intended to film *The Adventures of Robin Hood* with James Cagney in the title role. Though a fine actor, Cagney neither looks nor sounds remotely like the popular conception of what Robin Hood should be. But as soon as Errol Flynn appeared as a replacement for Robert Donat in *Captain Blood*, the studio realized that here was the perfect star for *The Adventures of Robin Hood*. Actually, though it is his best-known role, *The Adventures of Robin Hood* is not Flynn's finest performance; at times he dashes through it almost too cavalierly, and he created more subtle and well-rounded characterizations in *Gentleman Jim* (1942), *They Died with Their Boots On* (1941), and *Dawn Patrol* (1938). But *The Adventures of Robin Hood* brought out Flynn's unique combination of dash, gracefulness, impudence, athletic ability, devil-may-care humor, romanticism, and gallantry. Despite the fine supporting cast of Olivia de Havilland as Marian, Basil Rathbone as Gisbourne, Claude Rains as Prince John, and Ian Hunter as King Richard, Flynn dominates the film with his boundless energy and high spirits. As Robin Hood, he epitomizes the image of the dashing, cavalier outlaw.

The screenplay by Norman Reilly Raine (who won the Academy Award that same year for *The Life of Émile Zola*) and Seton I. Miller (who was coauthor of Flynn's *The Sea Hawk*) is unusually literate. The titles say that the story comes from old Robin Hood legends, but while some sequences (such as the meetings with Little John and Friar Tuck) do so, the scenario also borrows material from Sir Walter Scott's *Ivanhoe* (the alliance of Robin Hood and Richard the Lion-Hearted and the stress upon the tyranny of Norman over Saxon) and lifts the rivalry of Robin and Guy of Gisbourne for the hand of Marian from the 1890 light opera by DeKoven-Smith.

The film opens with news that King Richard, returning from the Crusades, has been taken prisoner in Austria and is being held for ransom. His brother John, who has just usurped the role of regent from Richard's appointed man, plots with Sir Guy of Gisbourne, the Sheriff of Nottingham, and other Norman nobles to tax the people unmercifully for the ransom, which they then plan to keep for themselves; for if Richard vanishes, John will become king. They proceed to extort exorbitant taxes by the most brutal means.

The scene then shifts to Sherwood Forest, where Gisbourne and a party of knights discover Much the Miller's son (Herbert Mundin) in the act of poaching a royal deer. When Gisbourne tells him it is death to kill the king's deer, Much indignantly replies that it is death from starvation if he does not and proceeds to denounce the rapacious tyranny of the Norman nobles. Gisbourne raises his mace to strike Much down, but it is shot out of his hand by an arrow from the bow of Robin of Locksley, who has just ridden up with Will Scarlett (Patric Knowles). When Gisbourne in turn threatens him with the death penalty, Robin smilingly asks if Normans cannot die too, draws a second arrow, and aims it at Gisbourne's heart. The latter backs down and gallops off with his retinue. The grateful Much offers himself to Robin's service.

That night there is a banquet at Nottingham Castle for Prince John and the Normans helping him extort the next taxes. With a Saxon dangling from every gallows, there are no protests. Sitting at the dais with Prince John is Lady Marian Fitzwalter, whom he tries to match in marriage to Gisbourne. She demurs and mocks Gisbourne when he tells of his encounter with Robin, but confesses his inability to take one man prisoner. At this point, the gate to the great hall bursts open, and Robin enters with the body of the slain deer across his shoulders. He throws it on the table before John, who finds his impudence amusing and invites him to share the feast. But his amusement turns to wrath as Robin boldly denounces Norman taxes, brutality, and John's treasonable plans to usurp the throne. He vows to organize a revolt, to exact a death for a death until Richard once more rules England. John signals a spearman, who hurls his weapon into the back of Robin's chair. Dodging aside in the nick of time, Robin overturns the chair, draws his sword, fights off the castle guard, and exits through a sally port from which he can send a deadly rain of arrows at the gate through which Gisbourne tries to pursue him. Robin then leaps upon a horse that Will Scarlett has waiting, and the two escape into the forest.

Now outlawed and committed to rebellion, Robin proceeds to recruit a band of followers. Through a quarterstaff fight on a log footbridge, he meets Little John (Alan Hale) who becomes a chief lieutenant. Then, discovering a fat friar sleeping by another stream, Robin steals his leg of mutton and then forces him to carry him piggyback across the stream. Halfway across, the friar flips Robin into the water, and they have a brisk broadsword fight before Robin's men break it up and introduce the friar as Tuck of Fountain's Abbey (Eugene Pallette). He also joins the band, recruited as much by the promise of feasting in the greenwood as by opposition to tyranny. Meanwhile, as John's and Gisbourne's men continue their brutal extortion, they are shot down by black arrows. One, bearing a warning, even strikes into the table between the Prince and Gisbourne as they plot more villainy.

Learning that Gisbourne and a small army are bringing the tax money through Sherwood to Nottingham, Robin arranges an ambush. His men come flying out of trees, leapfrog over bushes, and subdue the men-at-arms in a bloodless skirmish. Gisbourne and the simpering Sheriff of Nottingham are forced to dress in rags and attend a feast in the greenwood. Lady Marian, also with the party, is Robin's reluctant guest, but she changes her opinion that he is merely a Saxon hedge-robber when he has his men pledge to use the captured treasure to ransom Richard; and when he shows her the mutilated victims of John's injustice and she hears their gratitude to Robin, she gives way to her growing love for the outlaw. Bess (Una O'Connor), her peppery lady-in-waiting, and Much the Miller's son also develop a romance.

Prince John splutters with rage when his henchmen return moneyless and in rags, but he accepts the Sheriff's suggestion that they trap Robin by arranging an archery contest in Nottingham. The bait will be a prize offered by Marian, and the winner will obviously be the man they seek. Though he suspects a trap, Robin cannot resist. Disguised as a tinker, he wins the contest, splitting his opponent's shaft when the latter makes a perfect bull's-eye. Detected by John and Gisbourne, Robin puts up a spectacular fight and almost escapes but is dragged from a horse by hordes of soldiers. He is thrown into a dungeon to await execution.

Determined to save Robin, Marian learns from Bess that the outlaws sometimes meet at the Saracen's Head inn, and there she goes with a plan for rescue. On the day of the hanging, Robin's men infiltrate the crowd in disguise, shoot the hangman, and sever his rope with an arrow. His hands still bound behind him, Robin leaps on a horse and gallops towards the city gates. As planned, carts and wagons pull out in front of the pursuers and block their way. As his men gallop through the gate, Robin severs the portcullis rope, swings up with the rope to the top of the gate, slides down the other side, and vanishes into the forest.

That night in her chambers, Marian confesses to Bess that she is in love with Robin. She is startled and embarrassed as Robin enters through the window; he has climbed up the ivy on her wall to thank her for rescuing him and has overheard her confession. He urges her to marry him and come with him to Sherwood, but she insists on staying at Nottingham to provide intelligence on John's activities. It is well that she does so, for she learns that Richard is back in England and has been detected by the treacherous Bishop of Black Canon (Montagu Love). John sends an assassin to murder Richard. Marian writes a message to Robin, but Gisbourne detects it. No longer attempting to win Marian for himself, Gisbourne sends her to a dungeon to await her death. But Bess sends word to Much, who intercepts the assassin and kills him.

Meanwhile, Robin has encountered Richard and his men, disguised as monks, and invites them at sword's point to one of his forest feasts. When Much is carried in wounded with word of the attempted assassination, Robin declares that his men must search for Richard and save him. Richard then casts off his cowl and reveals himself. Learning from Much that John plans

on the morrow to announce Richard's death and have himself crowned, Robin
and his men pay a call on the Bishop of Black Canon. The next morning, his
men and Richard's enter Nottingham Castle disguised as monks, interrupt
the ceremony, and defeat John's men in a brisk battle. Robin engages Gisbourne at sword's point, and after a prolonged duel throughout the castle,
kills him. Restored to his throne, Richard makes Robin Earl of Huntington
and orders him to marry Lady Marian. "May I obey all your commands with
equal pleasure, sire," grins Robin.

A brief recounting of the plot indicates the spirited pace of the film but
fails to do justice to its critical values. Warners' first film in three-strip technicolor, boasting the studio's largest budget at that time ($2,000,000), *The
Adventures of Robin Hood* is an opulent production. The casting is flawless,
down through the supporting players, though the picture is Flynn's all the
way. Basil Rathbone excells as a sneering villain, Claude Rains is a wittily
sinister John, Olivia de Havilland (in the third of her eight films with Flynn)
a charming heroine, Ian Hunter a robust Richard, and Eugene Pallette an
engaging Friar Tuck. Repeating his role from the silent version, Alan Hale
is a hearty Little John; he was to play the part twice more, in *The Bandit of
Sherwood Forest* (1946) and *Rogues of Sherwood Forest* (1950). (There were
plans for Flynn to star in a sequel, *Sir Robin of Locksley*, but this never got
off the drawing boards.)

William Keighley, who had directed Flynn and Rains the year before in
The Prince and the Pauper, started as director of Robin Hood; but after he
completed a considerable portion of it, Warners' decided that his direction
was too lighthearted and insufficiently energetic; Michael Curtiz, who directed
most of Flynn's early swashbucklers, was brought in to replace Keighley for
the interior and action scenes. (Keighley, however, later directed Flynn's *The
Master of Ballantrae*, 1953, with an immensely vigorous style.) Whoever
deserves the credit, the film's pace never flags, the action is spiritedly acrobatic
(Flynn took pride in doing all of his own stunts, but archery expert Howard
Hill did the actual trick shooting), and the final duel, directed by Fred Cavens,
is the longest and most spectacular that either Flynn or Rathbone ever did.
It is actually too fast and furious for a fight with heavy broadswords; the
fencers wield them as if they were nineteenth century sabres, with lunges,
cuts, and parries quite anachronistic for the twelfth century. Nevertheless,
it is one of the most exciting duels on film, as the swordsmen cut and thrust
their way through the castle, past enormous pillars on which their shadows
are silhouetted, and down a winding staircase to the dungeons.

Imaginatively photographed by Sol Polito and Tony Gaudio, whose use of
color brought out all the lushness of Sherwood Forest and the pageantry of
Nottingham and whose employment of light and shadow is almost expressionistic, *The Adventures of Robin Hood* shows no sign that it is more than
forty years old. One of the strongest ingredients was the Academy Award-

winning score by Eric Wolfgang Korngold (who scored seven Flynn films and used themes from a number of them for his *Violin Concerto* and *Symphony in F-Sharp*). Incorporating variations on some old English songs, and ranging from tender love scenes to humorous scherzos to brilliant fanfares and rousing battle music, Korngold's stirring score has a symphonic richness and romanticism reminiscent of Richard Wagner and Richard Strauss.

The Adventures of Robin Hood won Academy Awards for Best Art Direction, Music, and Film Editing. It was also nominated as the Best Picture of 1938 but lost to Frank Capra's *You Can't Take It with You*. Of all the films of 1938, *The Adventures of Robin Hood* is the most enduring, and in the late 1960's, it was even hailed as a handbook for revolutionaries.

Robert E. Morsberger

THE ADVENTURES OF TOM SAWYER

Released: 1938
Production: David O. Selznick for Selznick International; released by United
   Artists
Direction: Norman Taurog
Screenplay: John V. A. Weaver; based on the novel of the same name by
   Mark Twain
Cinematography: James Wong Howe and Wilfred M. Cline
Editing: Hal C. Kern and Margaret Clancey
Running time: 93 minutes

    Principal characters:
       Tom Sawyer .... Tommy Kelly
       Huckleberry Finn .... Jackie Moran
       Aunt Polly .... May Robson
       Muff Potter .... Walter Brennan
       Injun Joe .... Victor Jory
       Becky Thatcher .... Ann Gillis
       Sid Sawyer .... David Holt
       Joe Harper .... Mickey Rentschler

During the 1930's, producer David O. Selznick had successfully filmed a
series of reasonably faithful screen versions of famous literary works, among
them *David Copperfield* (1935), *Anna Karenina* (1935), *A Tale of Two Cities*
(1935), and *The Prisoner of Zenda* (1937). It was inevitable, perhaps, that
Selznick should eventually turn his attention to Mark Twain's American classic, *The Adventures of Tom Sawyer*, which already had been filmed twice
before. Selznick planned a new production in 1937, to be filmed in the still
novel Technicolor process. A nationwide talent search to locate a young actor
to play the title role was initiated, and eventually freckle-faced Tommy Kelly,
a twelve-year-old nonprofessional from the Bronx, was cast in the role.

John Weaver's screenplay incorporates all the famous characters and incidents of the novel. Tom Sawyer and his younger brother Sid (David Holt)
live with their Aunt Polly (May Robson) in a sleepy river town on the Mississippi river, where Tom and his friends have many escapades that evoke a
humorous nostalgia for boyhood in late nineteenth century Midwestern
America. In the story's most celebrated scene, Tom shrewdly convinces his
friends of the immense pleasure and importance of whitewashing Aunt Polly's
fence, and they end up paying him for the privilege of doing it—a task
originally assigned to Tom by Aunt Polly as punishment for truancy. Tom's
pranks continually perplex and exasperate Aunt Polly and delight Becky
Thatcher (Ann Gillis), whom Tom courts throughout the story. His "goody-
goody" brother Sid, whose behavior Aunt Polly unfavorably compares to

Tom's, is often the butt of Tom's mischief.

One night Tom and Huckleberry Finn (Jackie Moran) sneak out to the graveyard with a dead cat to perform a wart-dispatching ritual, but instead they witness a terrifying sight: Muff Potter (Walter Brennan), the town drunk, and Injun Joe (Victor Jory) are robbing a grave. During a fight Injun Joe commits a murder, but he manages to convince Muff that *he* had actually done the deed in his alcoholic stupor. Later, Tom, Huck, and Joe Harper (Mickey Rentschler) run away from home and retreat to an island in the river to play pirate games. They are mistakenly assumed dead by the adults of the town, and the boys return just in time to attend secretly their own funeral. They are found out and treated to a comical blend of joy and outrage by the elders. Tom and Huck testify at Muff Potter's murder trial in order to prevent a miscarriage of justice. Injun Joe, the actual murderer, escapes, swearing vengeance. The film concludes with a picnic during which Tom and Becky become lost in a labyrinthian underground cave. They are discovered in the cave by Injun Joe, who pursues them through the cave until he falls to his death. In a melodramatic climax, Tom discovers a cache of pirate gold in the cave, and he and Becky are rescued.

Because of the motion picture censorship of the times, the story has suffered somewhat in its transfer to the screen. Twain's salty dialogue has been laundered of all its profanity. The comic episode on the island in which Huck Finn introduces Tom and Joe to the dubious pleasures of pipe smoking has also been omitted from the screenplay, presumably in deference to the censor. In a regrettable decision to augment Twain's humor of character and incident, several instances of slapstick have been added to the story, particularly in the case of young Sid. In what becomes a virtual running joke, Sid is pelted at various times with overripe tomatoes, whitewash, and cake frosting, and he piteously cries, "Aunt Poll-lee!"

The art direction of the film is typical of Hollywood's efforts in the 1930's with the exterior scenes of the town meticulously constructed on a studio back lot. The Mississippi river, however, a dominant presence in the novel, is visually slighted in the film. Only a few quick glimpses of matte paintings of the river landscape give evidence of its presence in the film. The concluding sequence in the cave was designed by long-time Selznick associate, William Cameron Menzies, whose designs provide a colorful fantasy background against which the melodrama of the finale is played out.

The Technicolor process used in *The Adventures of Tom Sawyer* has resulted in a pleasing, if somewhat bright, colored image on the screen. Attempts were clearly made, as in the concluding cave sequence, to exploit the possibilities offered by the colored medium. In a long scene in which the camera tracks along in front of the boys walking down the street, the intense level of light that was necessary to obtain proper exposure of the early color film is evident. In this scene, the brilliant principal source of light seems to be mounted with the camera and moves with it down the street.

The cast in *The Adventures of Tom Sawyer* is variable. Tommy Kelly offers a pleasing performance and is appropriately boyish and mischievous. Ann Gillis is an appealing Becky Thatcher, her performance ranging from co-quettishness to outright hysteria in the cave sequence. The adult players, generally in shorter roles, tend more toward broad caricature. May Robson's Aunt Polly, however, although suitably gruff and exasperated, does have a softer, more human side. But Victor Jory has a difficult time rising above the stereotype inherent in the role of Injun Joe.

Selznick obviously set out to produce a motion picture with wide family audience appeal, and he succeeded. Although most adult readers of Mark Twain's novel will find that the classic characters have been too vigorously scrubbed and prettified by this Hollywood treatment, the film retains a strong juvenile appeal. It also remains today as an interesting example of an early color feature film.

David Bahnemann

ADVISE AND CONSENT

Released: 1962
Production: Otto Preminger for Columbia
Direction: Otto Preminger
Screenplay: Wendell Mayes; based on the novel of the same name by Allen Drury
Cinematography: Sam Leavitt
Editing: Louis R. Loeffler
Running time: 139 minutes

Principal characters:

Robert Leffingwell	Henry Fonda
Bob Munson	Walter Pidgeon
Seabright Cooley	Charles Laughton
Brigham Anderson	Don Murray
Herbert Gelman	Burgess Meredith
President of the United States	Franchot Tone
Fred Van Ackerman	George Grizzard
Vice-President Harley Hudson	Lew Ayres
Dolly Harrison	Gene Tierney

The United States Constitution requires that the United States Senate must advise and consent to all major appointments by the President; otherwise, the designee may not serve. It is upon this premise that the 1962 film, *Advise and Consent*, drawn from the best-selling novel by Allen Drury, is based. The Secretary of State has died during the Administration of a future nameless and partyless President. The film explores the ramifications of the investigation, the hearings, and the vote on the newly appointed Secretary, Robert Leffingwell (Henry Fonda). Filmed on location in many public buildings in Washington, D.C., *Advise and Consent* has the atmosphere of a behind-the-scenes view of the inner workings of the Washington power elite.

From the opening meeting between Senate Majority Leader Bob Munson (Walter Pidgeon) and his majority whip, it is clear that Leffingwell's nomination will not be approved without a major floor fight. The opposition is centered in the venerable Senator from South Carolina, Seabright Cooley (Charles Laughton in his last picture). Cooley still carries a grudge against Leffingwell for an embarrassment suffered a few years before when Leffingwell was director of the Federal Power Commission. Leffingwell's nomination is referred to the Senate Foreign Relations Committee, which establishes a special subcommittee chaired by Brigham Anderson (Don Murray), a relatively new member of the Senate from Utah. In one of the film's many contrived turns of fate, Seabright Cooley is allowed to serve on the committee as an ex-officio member with the power to question the newly appointed Secretary—a judicial procedure which would not be allowed in the real Senate.

This movie, made only six years after the Senate censure of Joseph McCarthy for his reckless and baseless witch hunts for Communists in the federal government, had much fodder from which to extract its drama. At the hearing Mr. Leffingwell is interrogated regarding his loyalty to the United States. He replies that he is loyal, but a surprise witness shows up who claims that Leffingwell was a member of a Communist cell in Chicago years before. The witness, a pathetic weakling named Herbert Gelman (Burgess Meredith, who was nominated here for an Oscar for Best Supporting Actor), has a history of mental illness and is now a clerk in a government office. In a brief scene which does much to destroy the suspense of the hearings, we learn that Leffingwell was indeed involved with the cell temporarily, and that the one other person who knows about this also works for the government. However, the two decide that the witness can easily be discredited, and Leffingwell returns to the committee room, where he proceeds to destroy the stumbling, stuttering Gelman on the witness stand.

Leffingwell, fearing that his past will be revealed, pays a visit to the President (Franchot Tone), confesses to the recklessness of his political youth, and offers to withdraw his name from consideration. The President does not agree and convinces Leffingwell that his mistake could be hushed up. The President believes in Leffingwell and chooses to help him for the good of the nation. This scene drew considerable criticism when the film was released. Not only was it considered implausible, but critics found it un-American to suggest that a President would cover up wrongdoing by those surrounding him. In our post-Watergate world, of course, this assumption seems naïve.

Unknown to the President and Leffingwell, Seabright Cooley has discovered who the other former member of the cell is and has pressured him to reveal all he knows to Brig Anderson. With this new information the subcommittee chairman announces a delay in the vote. A hurried meeting is held between Bob Munson, the President, and Brig Anderson wherein the President acknowledges that he knows Leffingwell lied at the hearings but asks Anderson to ignore this fact for the good of the country. Anderson refuses and leaves believing that he has convinced the President to withdraw the nomination. The President, however, does not make the withdrawal, and instead sends the threatening witness out of the country. In the meantime, a young impetuous Senator named Fred Van Ackerman (George Grizzard), carried away with an irrational desire to have Leffingwell gain the office of Secretary of State, embarks upon a cruel campaign to blackmail Anderson into backing down. There are anonymous phone calls to Anderson's wife with ominous messages that they have all the facts about Hawaii. The mystery as to exactly what Anderson is being blackmailed for is dwelt upon in order to develop what little tension the film has. The mystery is resolved when Anderson flies to New York in search of a man with whom he had a homosexual relationship during World War II; this man has been well paid by Van Ackerman for his incriminating information. In another of the film's coarse stereotypes, Anderson seeks the informant out in dark, sordid dens of homosexual iniquity. When he finds the man shallow and uncomprehending of the consequences of his confessions, Anderson feels that all is lost and returns to Washington, where he commits suicide.

The film then rushes to a "surprise" climax in which Seabright Cooley agrees not to reveal the blackmailing of Anderson, and in which Munson releases all previous pledges for votes. In another quick turn of events, Van Ackerman is brusquely denounced on the Senate floor for his destructive plotting and is left in shocked dismay. The vote taken on Leffingwell is a tie, and Vice-President Harley Hudson (Lew Ayres) must cast the deciding vote. Before he does so, however, he receives a note that the President, who has been rumored to be sick throughout the film, has died. Hudson, now the President, announces that he will choose his own Secretary of State, and leaves the Senate chambers. Thus the film ends on a note of futility, although with the melodrama of a soap opera.

Advise and Consent was directed by Otto Preminger following the success of two other lengthy, large-cast epics drawn from popular novels: *Anatomy of a Murder* (1959) and *Exodus* (1962). Films such as these often lose sight of the characters in relating their detailed stories. This is certainly the case in *Advise and Consent*. It is never made clear, for example, through the characters' interactions why the President feels that Robert Leffingwell is so indispensible to the country; nor do we ever receive any insight into why Cooley hates Leffingwell so intensely. In the novel the whys and wherefores are more clearly delineated.

Undoubtedly, the most interesting casting involved in *Advise and Consent* was the one that never came to pass. Preminger offered the part of a Southern senator to Dr. Martin Luther King, Jr., although in 1962 there were no blacks in the Senate. Preminger believed that this part could be a positive suggestion to the nation that blacks could be United States Senators. King refused the part after serious consideration on the grounds that hostility might be created by his performing the role and this would hurt the cause of black equality.

The film was not well-received by the critics, nor was it a blockbuster at the box office. It did, however, earn many fine reviews in Europe where the respected French paper *Le Monde* ran a front-page story marveling that the United States government would cooperate with the filming, as well as not object to the distribution of a film ostensibly critical of the American political system. The film provoked little controversy in the United States, although one Senator from Ohio did propose legislation to prevent the film from being shown outside the country. The bill, like Leffingwell's nomination, failed to gain the necessary support for passage.

William Woods

THE AFRICAN QUEEN

Released: 1951
Production: S. P. Eagle (Sam Spiegel) for Horizon Romulus Productions; released by United Artists
Direction: John Huston
Screenplay: James Agee and John Huston; based on the novel of the same name by C. S. Forester
Cinematography: Jack Cardiff
Editing: Ralph Kemplen
Costume design: Katharine Hepburn's costumes by Doris Langley Moore
Running time: 103 minutes

> *Principal characters:*
> Rose Sayer .... Katharine Hepburn
> Charlie Allnut .... Humphrey Bogart (AA)
> Reverend Samuel Sayer .... Robert Morley

The African Queen is a tale of adventure and of an implausible love affair that develops in spite of the disparate personalities of the two main characters, Charlie Allnut and Rose Sayer. While the adventure element had already been seen in director John Huston's previous films, the technicolor and the almost continuous low humor that accompanied the development of the relationship between Charlie and Rose was new. Huston has written that the humor was not apparent in the original C. S. Forester novel, nor was it written into the screenplay, but that it evolved naturally as the stars, Humphrey Bogart and Katharine Hepburn, reacted to each other. Hepburn has stated that nothing was happening at all until Huston suggested that she play Rose like Eleanor Roosevelt.

Most of the scenes were filmed on location in what was then the Belgian Congo and the British protectorate of Uganda. Huston felt that if the actors were living under hardships on location that it would translate into their performances. Even on an English soundstage, where the swamp scenes and the early mission scenes with Robert Morley were shot, he insisted on reality. When Bogart emerges from the river covered with what look like leeches, they are real leeches.

Huston uses few cinematic devices to tell his tale. The cinematography is straightforward and beautifully done, but the camera never lingers too long on the steamy lushness of Africa. The setting and the adventure are important elements in the movie, but they are secondary to the development of the characters.

The story takes place on a partially uncharted river in Africa in 1914. Charlie Allnut, the uncouth, gin-swizzling captain of an equally disreputable mailboat, the *African Queen*, arrives to deliver mail and news to the English missionaries, Reverend Samuel Sayer and his sister Rose. The differences in personality and social station between Charlie and the missionaries are delineated as a grubby Charlie observes the high-collared, fervent twosome trying to lead a group of atonal natives in hymn singing. Charlie smiles at the din and absently tosses away his cigar. The noise reaches a crescendo as a group of natives pounce on the discarded stogie and add their yells to the singing. Samuel glares humorlessly as Charlie slyly enjoys the distraction he has caused. Their differences are further underscored when the missionaries stiffly ignore Charlie's uncontrollable stomach rumblings while at tea. Charlie proceeds to make things worse by trying to apologize. They stonily ignore him and continue their polite conversation.

Charlie leaves after giving the missionaries the alarming news of a state of war between England and Germany; World War I has begun. Rose and Samuel's fear about being aliens in German East Africa is soon realized as the Germans arrive and destroy the mission. Samuel tries to stop the destruction, but he is hit on the head, has a breakdown, and dies. Charlie returns a day later and offers to take Rose into hiding with him, as the Germans will surely return in search of the *African Queen* and her cargo: oxygen and hydrogen cylinders and blasting gelatin. Escape is impossible since the Germans are all along the river, and even the lake at the end of the river is patrolled by a German gunboat, the *Louisa*.

The adversary relationship, which is the source of much of the film's humor, begins as Rose's English patriotism is stirred by the words "explosives" and "*Louisa*." She develops a plan from which she never wavers: to go to the lake and torpedo the *Louisa*. She goads Charlie into continuing the voyage and makes him promise to sink the *Louisa*.

Later, his courage buoyed by much gin, Charlie reneges on his promise because they would have to get past a German fort in full daylight; and after the fort there are rapids, and then unknown territory. Rose archly calls him a liar and a coward. Charlie fights back by mimicking her speech, whimpering as he recalls his poor old mother, and calling Rose a "crazy, psalm-singing, skinny old maid." Rose retaliates by pouring his liquor overboard and by unnerving the sociable Charlie with the silent treatment. For all his bravado, Charlie is no match for Rose, and he gives in. The stars supply most of the humor here, but Huston also gives us a touch of his own: one of Charlie's outraged outbursts causes the entire jungle to erupt in animal roars, bellows, and screeches.

As they prepare for and stand together through the dangers of getting past the fort and shooting the rapids, their relationship evolves into one of mutual admiration and love. During the flight past the German fort, Rose witnesses Charlie's courage. As they are fired upon, the steam hose on the *African Queen* disconnects and the boat loses power in front of the sharpshooters, making them easy targets. To repair it, Charlie must expose himself and risk being shot. Huston maintains a fast, exciting pace as the *African Queen* begins its journey past the fort and through the rapids; and the pace is set with sharp editing rather than with tricks. The action jumps from long shots of the *African Queen* as seen from the fort, to close-ups of Rose and Charlie, to groups of riflemen, and finally to a single sharpshooter and Charlie as seen through the German's gunscope. Charlie is saved when the sun blinds the shooter.

At first triumphant at having made it safely past the fort, Rose's joy gives way to fear again as they rush directly into the rapids. They both struggle with the rudder to keep the boat from hitting the rocks, and miraculously, they make it. Wildly exuberant at having accomplished two seemingly impossible feats, they forget themselves completely and embrace and kiss. It is the beginning of one of the most memorable love scenes on film. At first awkward and embarrassed, they slowly succumb to each other's charms. The humor remains even here when, after their first night together, Rose asks Charlie, "Mr. Allnut—dear—what is your first name?"

The film next takes a serious turn as the *African Queen* enters the uncharted portion of the river, and Charlie and Rose are beset by bugs, leeches, and the increasingly swampy condition of the river. Here, the camera as much as the acting creates the oppressive atmosphere when it closes in on Bogart's exhausted and tense face as he pulls his boat through the muck. Finally, unable to continue, they face the fact that they are beaten and will probably die. Having done the impossible has given the feverish Charlie some pride, and he gently tells Rose that it was all worth it. As they fall asleep the camera retreats from the *African Queen* and we see that they are only yards away from their goal, the lake.

During the night, a rainstorm raises the level of the river, and the *African Queen* is freed from her swampy grave. Charlie and Rose awaken and joyfully view the lake—and the *Louisa*. With their humor and spirits restored, Charlie makes the torpedoes, and they head for the gunboat under cover of night. However, a storm arises, and Charlie and Rose are separated as the *African Queen* sinks in the choppy water. Morning finds the two on board the *Louisa* and undergoing trial as spies. When Charlie is sentenced to death, Rose decides to die with him and tells the Germans of their plans to sink the *Louisa*. She looks on with pride as Charlie tells how he made the torpedoes. The exasperated Germans hurry them on deck for the hanging. As a last request Charlie asks the captain to marry him and Rose. The captain assents, and then immediately orders the executions to proceed. Interspliced between the action of the trial, marriage, and execution preparations are scenes of the *African Queen* slowly rising from the lake until the torpedoes are above the waterline and aimed directly at the oncoming *Louisa*.

Just before the nooses are tightened an explosion erupts, and the Allnuts make their escape as the *Louisa* sinks. As they swim toward shore they find a piece of the *African Queen* floating in the water and realize that they have accomplished their goal.

While reviews were generally excellent, critics pointed out the weaknesses of a story that was too pat: the Reverend is too conveniently eliminated; the love affair is too predictable; and the ending is too melodramatic and contrived. To the audiences that flocked to see the film, however, these factors were inconsequential in comparison to the stellar acting of Bogart and Hepburn, the cinematography, and the adventure.

The film earned Academy Award nominations for Huston and Agee for Best Screenplay, Huston for Best Direction, Hepburn for Best Actress, and Bogart for Best Actor. Bogart was the only one to win, and it was to be his only Oscar in a career studded with memorable performances.

Indeed, it is the acting and charisma of Bogart and Hepburn which have given the film its lasting appeal. Hepburn's primly determined Rose is the perfect foil for Bogart's belligerent Charlie. Her very primness makes her thawing and capitulation to Charlie all the more enjoyable. Bogart's Charlie is a masterpiece of comic characterization, and even after Charlie has gained some dignity, the old Charlie, however sober, is still evident. As Rose and Charlie's relationship evolves from polite tolerance of each other to adversaries to lovers, they make the audience believe that a pious, teetotaling, iron-willed spinster really could fall for a boozy, seedy boatman.

Ellen J. Snyder

AH, WILDERNESS!

Released: 1935
Production: Hunt Stromberg for Metro-Goldwyn-Mayer
Direction: Clarence Brown
Screenplay: Albert Hackett and Frances Goodrich; based on the play of the same name by Eugene O'Neill
Cinematography: Clyde de Vinna
Editing: Frank E. Hull
Running time: 101 minutes

Principal characters:

Sid Davis	Wallace Beery
Nat Miller	Lionel Barrymore
Lily Miller	Aline MacMahon
Richard Miller	Eric Linden
Muriel McComber	Cecilia Parker
Tommy Miller	Mickey Rooney
Essie Miller	Spring Byington
Mr. McComber	Charley Grapewin
Arthur Miller	Frank Albertson
Mildred Miller	Bonita Granville
Belle	Helen Flint

When M-G-M's film version of the play Eugene O'Neill called a comedy of recollection opened in New York on Christmas Day, 1935, it was widely hailed as the perfect film for the holiday season. Movie audiences responded as appreciatively to O'Neill's genial portrait of a middle-class family living in a "large small-town" in Connecticut in 1906 as Broadway theater audiences had when the play was first produced two years earlier. This was hardly surprising. The turn of the century provided the same kind of idealized refuge from a troubled present for Depression audiences that their own period in idealized fashion provides for us today.

What *was* surprising about *Ah, Wilderness!* was that America's best-known playwright was able, temporarily, at least, to shake off the gloom that had pervaded most of his previous works and create a piece written, as Andre Sennwald noted in his *New York Times* review of the film, with "a humorous kindliness that is far more mindful of Booth Tarkington than of Eugene O'Neill." If, however, both the play and the film, by poking gentle fun at the pretensions and puppy love of an adolescent boy, recalled such light-hearted Tarkington entertainments as the *Penrod* books and *Seventeen*, O'Neill's hero nevertheless read and quoted from the Socialist Emma Goldman and the poems of Swinburne and Oscar Wilde. Furthermore, O'Neill's naturalistic evocation of the period was closer to the Tarkington who wrote *The Mag-*

nificent Ambersons, with its passages of social commentary and chapters tracing the physical evolution of a small American city.

O'Neill was describing the appurtenances of middle-class life as he remembered them in New London, Connecticut, where his family summered when he was a boy and his actor father was not on tour in *The Count of Monte Cristo*. Not that O'Neill's memories of his family bore much resemblance to the generally happy and peaceful existence of his fictional Miller family. *Ah, Wilderness!*, said O'Neill, was a picture of his boyhood as he wished it had been; the harrowing picture of his boyhood as he actually remembered it was not revealed until *Long Day's Journey into Night* (1962) received its first production after his death in 1953.

In adapting the play for the screen, the husband and wife writing team of Albert Hackett and Frances Goodrich opened up the action to show more of the town in which the story was set. Clarence Brown, the director, had also grown up in New England; and, although it was unusual for a movie company to go outside the studio in the early 1930's, Brown got M-G-M's permission to shoot the exterior scenes for *Ah, Wilderness!* on location in his home town of Grafton, Massachusetts. About two hundred townspeople were recruited as extras, and many of them dug deep into trunks that had not been opened in years for the authentic turn-of-the-century clothes they wore in the film. The interiors were shot in Hollywood on sets that art director Cedric Gibbons and his staff had carefully dressed to match the accuracy of O'Neill's recollection. The result, in such sequences as the Miller family's ride in a Stanley Steamer or a band concert in a park, was occasionally to make the audience more aware of the effort that went into staging them than to believe themselves back in 1906. In general, however, the period was not captured so faithfully on film again until Orson Welles's production of *The Magnificent Ambersons* in 1942.

The action of the play opens with the Miller family coming into the sitting room after breakfast on the morning of the Fourth of July. The film begins some two weeks earlier, on the night before Richard Miller's graduation from high school. The seniors have gathered for a farewell dance in the same upstairs assembly room where the following day they will receive their diplomas; and Richard (Eric Linden) is discovered waltzing with his "best girl," Muriel McComber (Cecilia Parker), to the familiar strains of "The Glow Worm" as pounded out on an upright piano. The music director, Herbert Stothart, relied on popular songs to set a period atmosphere as heavily, and sometimes as distractingly, as Peter Bogdanovich later did in *Paper Moon* (1973) and *The Last Picture Show* (1971). On their way home, Richard gets Muriel to agree to spend the day of the Fourth alone with him boating on the river, although she worries that her parents may not approve. In the play, Muriel was talked about but not seen until she made a brief appearance near the end of the fourth act; the increased prominence the Hacketts gave her in their script both dramatizes her importance to Richard and gives him another sounding board for his effusions about life and love.

The other members of the Miller family have been spending a quiet evening at home. We meet Richard's father, Nat (Lionel Barrymore), the editor and publisher of the local paper; his mother, Essie (Spring Byington, in a typical role); his older brother Arthur (Frank Albertson), home from Yale for summer vacation; his younger sister Mildred (Bonita Granville); and his eleven-year-old brother Tommy (Mickey Rooney, who a dozen years later was to play the part of Richard in Rouben Mamoulian's musical remake of this film, *Summer Holiday*). In the kitchen, Nat's sister Lily (Aline McMahon), an old-maid schoolteacher, is packing a box of heart-shaped brownies she has baked for Essie's brother Sid (Wallace Beery) to eat on the electric car to Waterbury, where he is about to start a new job as a reporter. Eighteen years earlier, Lily broke off her engagement to Sid because of his drinking and fondness for loose women. She still loves him; and Sid wants desperately to marry her and has promised to reform. Lily finally tells him that if he stops drinking for good this time, and succeeds on his new job, that she will consider it. According to Nat, Sid has been the best reporter ever to work for him; and the job on the Waterbury paper is a long overdue step-up in his profession.

Richard is a bright boy who has been named class valedictorian and who will be following Arthur to Yale in the fall; but his precocious taste in literature worries his mother as much as it amuses his tolerant father. Nat keeps a copy of Fitzgerald's version of the *Rubáiyát of Omar Khayyám* (from whose lines "Thou/ Beside me singing in the wilderness" the title of the play is taken) in his own office; and it bothers him not at all that Richard, in the privacy of his bedroom, eagerly devours Swinburne, Wilde, Ibsen, and Shaw. When, however, on graduation day he glances through Richard's notes for his valedictory address, and realizes that his son is about to wind up with a peroration on the evils of capitalism, Nat interrupts him before Richard embarrasses the family as well as himself. Richard's high school commencement ceremony was barely alluded to in the play; but it is a high point of the film. The audience of proud, perspiring parents and fidgety children crowded into the underventilated auditorium; the sweet, untrained voices of the school choir; the senior girls in their stiffly starched white dresses; the truly awful recitations and solo musical turns that precede Richard's address: these details were woven by Brown into a hilarious and touching piece of Americana.

On the morning of the Fourth, Muriel's father (Charley Grapewin) confronts Nat with a particularly erotic verse by Swinburne that Richard had copied and sent to Muriel. He tells Nat that he has made Muriel write Richard a letter breaking off with him, and that he expects Nat to punish Richard, too. Nat angrily orders McComber out of the house; but then, worried, he goes up to find out from Richard himself just what his intentions toward Muriel have been. Richard reassures him that he loves and respects Muriel and only sent her the verses to keep her from being afraid of life. "Well," his father tells him, "I'm afraid she's still afraid"; and gives him Muriel's letter. That evening, Richard, full of grim determination to go the pace that kills along the road to ruin, sneaks out with a school chum of Arthur to meet "a couple of swift ones" at a local hotel. While the older boy is occupied with one of the girls in an upstairs room, a circumstance that is baldly stated in the play and that easily can be inferred in the film, Richard desperately tries to match drinks with the other girl, Belle (Helen Flint), in the back room of the bar. After she has made him spend all his money, Belle has Richard thrown out for being under age when she spies a traveling salesman making eyes at her over the swinging door. The bartender throws Belle out in turn when he discovers that the boy she came in with is the son of the editor of the local paper. It is after midnight by the time Richard stumbles home to his worried family, drunkenly announcing that he comes "with vine leaves in my hair." Uncle Sid, home from Waterbury after having lost his new job, goes up to him at once and puts his arm around him. "You let me take care of him, Essie," he tells his sister. "I know this game backwards."

The next morning, Belle leaves a note for Nat at his office revealing where and with whom his son spent the previous evening. Nat comes home at noon, and, in the play's most famous scene—it had been a *tour de force* for George M. Cohan, who created the part on the stage—struggles painfully through his embarrassment to warn his son about "a certain class of women" and "whited sepulchres." In the evening, Muriel slips out to meet Richard in the moonlight. The two are reconciled; and Richard blissfully goes home to tell his parents before stepping back outside to enjoy the night's beauty a while longer. Arthur is out with his girl, Mildred has a beau, and even Sid and Lily have made up and are spooning happily on the front porch. Nat and Essie are, as he tells her, "completely surrounded by love." They kiss tenderly and go up to bed.

On the stage, *Ah, Wilderness!* lasts nearly three hours if performed uncut. The original Theatre Guild production was, of course, done under O'Neill's supervision; and there were playgoers who complained that it was inordinately long for a piece in which nothing really "happened." On the screen, even with the extra scenes the Hacketts added to the script, *Ah, Wilderness!* runs only a little more than one hundred minutes, and yet there are filmgoers who complain that the movie, too, for all its charm, is a little slow. There seems to be no satisfactory answer to this complaint, except to note that the many separate incidents with which both play and film are filled, only a few of which have been described in this summary, are really the point of the story, rather than the admittedly slender plot about Richard's difficulty with Muriel and her father. The complaint about the film, however, that seems to possess a more general validity is that if one is going to present a story that is nothing more than a series of vignettes illustrating the day-to-day life of an ordinary family, not only must the details of set and costume be impeccably "right," but the performances, too, must be "right"; and the Hollywood actors in *Ah, Wilderness!* play nearly everything a little broadly. There is no way the modern critic who never saw Cohan in the part of Nat Miller on the stage can judge whether he would have been less fraudulent, less of a foxy grandpa, than Lionel Barrymore sometimes is in the film.

However, both Elisha Cook, Jr., who played Richard in the play and Gene Lockhart, who played Sid in the play, had long movie careers; and it is easy to regret that they were not asked to repeat their performances in the film. Eric Linden was a handsome juvenile who brought to the part of Richard his good looks and a certain intensity. In 1935, Cook also could have supplied these, as well as the sensitivity that makes Richard something more than the "fresh kid" his brother Arthur calls him. Gene Lockhart also possessed a dignity that would have made Lily's affection for Sid in spite of his drinking at least credible. Instead, one must watch the invincibly boorish Wallace Beery, who, as the best-known actor in the cast, received star billing, snuggle up to the genteel Aline McMahon as if she were Marie Dressler and they were still doing *Min and Bill* (1930). McMahon gives what is the only consistently believable performance in the film. Her Lily matches O'Neill's description not only in her outward appearance ("the conventional type of old-maid school teacher") but in her whole demeanor ("one of shy kindliness"). She conveys Lily's swift transitions from hopefulness, to joy, to disappointment, to despair and back again without ever seeming to strain for her effects. Had the rest of the film been up to her level, *Ah, Wilderness!* might have been the ideal screen translation of O'Neill's play that Clarence Brown and his associates tried so hard to create.

Charles Hopkins

ALFIE

Released: 1966
Production: Lewis Gilbert for Paramount
Direction: Lewis Gilbert
Screenplay: Bill Naughton; based on his play of the same name
Cinematography: Otto Heller
Editing: Thelma Connell
Art direction: Peter Mullins
Music: Sonny Rollins
Song: Burt Bacharach and Hal David, "Alfie"
Running time: 114 minutes

Principal characters:
Alfie .... Michael Caine
Ruby .... Shelley Winters
Siddie .... Millicent Martin
Gilda .... Julia Foster
Annie .... Jane Asher
Lily .... Vivien Merchant
Carla .... Shirley Anne Field

"My understanding of women goes only as far as the pleasures. When it comes to the pain, I'm like every other bloke. I don't want to know." Thus the unscrupulous, hedonistic seducer Alfie expresses his philosophy. For Alfie, all women are "its," as in "It can cook." Based upon the London stage play of the same name by Bill Naughton, which starred Terence Stamp, this episodic film deals with the various amorous adventures of a bragging, although engaging, Cockney lothario, Alfie (Michael Caine). A sometime chauffeur, sometime photographer, who lives in a rented room in London's East End, the impeccably groomed Alfie moves from young "bird" to old, from blond to brunette, from fat to slim.

At first we see Alfie having an affair with a young married woman named Siddie (Millicent Martin), whose husband knows nothing of her extramarital exploits. Next we see him take up a relationship with a simple-minded, plain Cockney girl named Gilda (Julia Foster). When the uncomplaining girl becomes pregnant by Alfie but expects neither love nor marriage from him, she marries her devoted ex-boyfriend, a bus conductor named Humphrey. Alfie becomes a bit perturbed by this action because it means giving up his and Gilda's son, the only person he loves.

After a doctor discovers that a shadow on Alfie's lungs indicates a mild case of tuberculosis, Alfie enters a sanitorium. He is not only attracted to the woman doctor who examines him, but also seduces a pretty nurse named Carla (Shirley Anne Field) as well. Later, after leaving the hospital, he takes up with Lily (Vivien Merchant), the not-so-young wife of a fellow patient from the hospital. After she becomes pregnant, Alfie calls up an abortionist so that her husband will never learn of their affair. The offscreen operation shakes his morale, however, and Alfie's sensitive reaction after he sees the stillborn fetus on the table is the most moving scene in the film.

Though less self-confident now, Alfie continues on his promiscuous path and settles in with a lusty, voluptuous, and rich American widow named Ruby (Shelley Winters), who lives in a more fashionable side of town. When he discovers, however, that Ruby has taken up with a younger, long-haired guitar player, Alfie fears the loss of his sexual prowess and goes back to his former girl friend Siddie; but she is no longer interested in him. Acknowledging that his life is not a happy one, he says in the film's conclusion, "My life's me own—to do what I like with. But I ain't got me peace o' mind—and if you ain't got that, you ain't got nothin'."

Alfie is a successful and frank seriocomic study of a rake's progress from insolence and irresponsibility to some awakening maturity regarding the sterile and unrewarding nature of his promiscuous life, and it was considered the best British picture of 1966. A Cockney himself, Michael Caine became a star as a result of his performance in the role. With his low-key style, immobile face, and flat voice, Caine gives a deft portrayal of a contemporary antihero—a tall, blond, good-looking womanizer of bawdy humor and charm, who is alternately shrewd, weak, cynical, self-serving, and endearing.

Alfie is made even more sympathetic through the theatrical device of asides, during which the action is interrupted and he speaks directly to the audience. During these occasional asides, Alfie establishes a rapport with the viewer, chatting confidentially about his ladies and his life. Although Alfie may be an infuriating rogue, Caine makes the character irresistible. He is aided by the fine performance of Shelley Winters as a blowsy American matron, and of Vivien Merchant as the drab housewife who undergoes the trauma of an abortion.

Because the film's treatment of abortion was shocking to some, *Alfie* had trouble obtaining a seal of approval from the Production Code Office. The office's president, Jack Valenti, however, eventually consented, and *Alfie* received the stamp of approval from the Motion Picture Association of America.

Leslie Taubman

ALICE ADAMS

Released: 1935
Production: Pandro S. Berman for RKO/Radio
Direction: George Stevens
Screenplay: Dorothy Yost and Mortimer Offner; based on Jane Murfin's adaptation of the novel of the same name by Booth Tarkington
Cinematography: Robert de Grasse
Editing: Jane Loring
Running time: 99 minutes

Principal characters:
Alice Adams .... Katharine Hepburn
Arthur Russell .... Fred MacMurray
Mr. Adams ....Fred Stone
Mrs. Adams .... Ann Shoemaker
Walter Adams .... Frank Albertson
J. A. Lamb .... Charley Grapewin
Malena .... Hattie McDaniel
Mildred Palmer .... Evelyn Venable
Frank Dowling .... Grady Sutton

Alice Adams is a poignant story of a young woman's social ambitions and romantic dreams which are almost thwarted by her family's lack of money. The film is both a romance with a fairy-tale ending and a commentary on middle-class mores in a small Midwestern town in the first quarter of the twentieth century. Katharine Hepburn vividly depicts both the affectations and the vulnerability of a young woman who sees a respectable marriage as the only means to fulfillment and happiness.

The small-town milieu is quickly and indelibly established in the opening scenes, beginning with the camera moving from a sign reading "South Renford, Ind. The town with a future," past storefront signs, until it tilts down to reveal Alice Adams emerging from a department store. She stops at a florist shop to order a corsage for the dance that evening but nothing seems to satisfy her. We realize that she cannot really afford a corsage when the next scene shows her picking violets in a park to make her own. The sequence conveys perfectly Alice's poverty, affectation, and aspirations.

Alice's father (Fred Stone), who is recovering from a long illness, is content with his clerical job with the wholesale drug firm of J. A. Lamb (Charley Grapewin), but her mother (Ann Shoemaker) is not. Bitterly, she tells her husband that they have been left behind in the race for money and social position and that his refusal to start his own business has endangered Alice's chance to marry well.

Alice's brother, Walter (Frank Albertson), is not interested in society or social position and has to be cajoled by his mother into taking Alice to the dance given by Mildred Palmer (Evelyn Venable), a member of a socially prominent family. Walter does not like what he calls those "frozen-faced" society people and is rude to Alice and his mother, saying that Alice should be able to get somebody to take her since she tries so hard. Underneath his reluctance and brusque exterior, however, he does feel sorry for Alice and finally allows himself to be persuaded.

One of the most memorable sequences in the film, the Palmers' dance interweaves the romantic fairy-tale element with sharp commentary on Alice's pretensions and those of the rich and socially prominent people around her. Alice makes Walter park their old car on the street so she can pretend to the butler that their car has broken down. Once inside, she puts on her best society manners, simpering and giggling and talking breathlessly to Walter on inane topics when anyone can overhear their conversation. Walter is embarrassed by her play-acting but agrees to dance the first dance with her. Walter is an excellent dancer, but he mortifies Alice by greeting the black orchestra leader as an old friend.

Abandoned by Walter, who goes off to shoot dice with the cloakroom attendants, Alice, alone and uneasy, pretends desperately that she is having a good time. She is ignored by several men obviously searching for partners, and several of the women comment on her outmoded gown. She is finally rescued by fat Frank Dowling (Grady Sutton), an undesirable partner, who humiliates her by his awkwardness on the dance floor and bores her with his lack of conversation. Finally, even Frank is taken away by his mother, and Alice is alone, pretending she is waiting for a partner. Furtively, she pushes her now bedraggled homemade corsage under her chair and watches as Mildred Palmer greets a tall handsome stranger at the door. When Mildred and the stranger walk by, Alice goes into her act, posing, laughing to herself, and pretending she is having the most amusing thoughts as she waits for her partner.

We sympathize with Alice through this period of suffering because, despite her outward pretentiousness, snobbery, and silliness, her vulnerability—the eager, expectant look in her eyes—shines through. We realize that her pride demands this show of bravado, which reveals how she thinks a society girl enjoying herself at a party would act. At last, giving up all hope of a partner, Alice is going to sit with the old chaperones when she is rescued by the tall dark stranger, whom Mildred introduces to her as Arthur Russell (Fred MacMurray). Here is Prince Charming, but Alice, thinking Mildred has asked him to dance with her out of pity, is for once silent and natural. After the dance, she asks Russell to find Walter for her so she can go home.

The next day Alice meets Russell again just as she has worked up enough nerve to enter a business college to seek a secretarial job. Having rescued her from a horrible fate—one that would have put any chance of social advancement entirely out of her reach—Russell proceeds to tell her he has been thinking about her and wants to see more of her. Alice immediately assumes her airs and mannerisms, talking incessantly, giving little trills of laughter, fabricating a social background similar to those of the other girls of his acquaintance, and guarding herself against gossip by telling him she is not very popular with men because she shows them she is bored by them.

Russell is anxious to visit and further his acquaintance, but Alice, who is ashamed of her family's shabby house, refuses to let him come inside. Indeed, their entire courtship is conducted on the front porch of the house or at restaurants. Finally, Mrs. Adams practically forces Alice to invite Russell to dinner. Up to this point Alice's strategy has been masterly. She has already warned him against listening to gossip about herself or her family and has used her father's illness as an excuse for always entertaining him outside and not going to dinners and dances to which, unknown to Russell, she has not been invited. As she tells him, with more truth than he knows, she would not dare to be merely herself with him.

Meanwhile, her mother's constant nagging has worn her father down, and despite many misgivings, he has mortgaged the house to start his own glue factory. Virgil Adams feels it is like stealing to take a glue formula developed on company time to start his own business. He likes and trusts his paternalistic employer, J. A. Lamb (for whom he has worked for twenty-five years), and does not want to anger him. But under his wife's relentless hammering he makes the break and rents an old warehouse for his factory. On the evening of the ill-fated dinner he is worried because there has been no response to this action from Lamb, who is not a man to let someone else get the best of him.

In order to do the dinner in style, her mother hires a black maid and cook, Malena (Hattie McDaniel), for the evening. Although it is a hot, humid night, the meal is heavy and elaborate, beginning with caviar sandwiches and hot soup. The slow-moving, gum-chewing Malena, with her maid's cap askew, inelegantly removes plates and thrusts serving trays under people's noses. Everything that can go wrong, does. Virgil Adams' shirtfront keeps popping open, and when he wants more water, he cannot remember the maid's name. The smell of Brussels sprouts pervades the little house, and Russell is obviously ill-at-east as he mops his sweaty neck. Alice chatters brightly, trying to retrieve what she knows is a disaster, but Russell is politely unresponsive. When she offers a penny for his thoughts, he replies uncomfortably that he hasn't any. She takes him outside, "where we belong," and indicates her understanding of his feelings by telling him she knows it is over, that he will not be coming to see her again. After all, when "everything's spoiled you can't do anything but run away," she tells him.

If Alice's romance has reached a crisis point on this hot, humid evening, so have the affairs of her father. Walter tells him he has embezzled one hundred and fifty dollars from Lamb's firm and could be sent to jail. Lamb himself pays a visit and informs Adams he is starting a glue factory of his own, which will mean ruin for Adams. Though Alice's hopes may have been destroyed, she is determined to save her father's dreams if she can. In an emotional scene she persuades Lamb that it is the fault of her and her mother that her father defected. After her plea Lamb agrees to work something out to save both her father and her brother.

The film continues in this fairy-tale manner as Alice goes back out onto the porch to find Russell still there. She will keep her Prince Charming and have a happy ending. When Russell tells her he loves her, her response is the most natural and unaffected thing she says in the whole film—"Gee Whiz!"

Although *Alice Adams* makes some trenchant comments on middle-class society, particularly in the dance and dinner scenes, and although the arguments between Mr. and Mrs. Adams are sharply realized and almost painful to watch, the film is not wholly successful as social commentary, primarily because of the unrealistic happy ending which was tacked on by the scriptwriters. In the Booth Tarkington novel on which the film was based, Russell leaves and does not return, and Alice actually does climb the stairs to the business college to get a job. It is doubtful, however, that the moviegoing public of the 1930's would have accepted such a downbeat ending (or so the studio believed). Even Tarkington thought the novel's ending would have to be changed before it could be filmed.

Aside from the ending, the film is a perfectly realized portrait of an intelligent, socially ambitious young woman, struggling to find a foothold in a society that has left her and her family behind. At a time when a woman's only socially acceptable career was marriage, Alice looked upon a job as the last resort, and as one which would spell the end of her social aspirations.

The role is sensitively played by a luminous, tremulous Katharine Hepburn. Although Alice's mannerisms and snobbishness are tiresome, we nevertheless become emotionally involved with her and sympathize with her. This is due in no small measure to Hepburn's skill at letting the essential loneliness and vulnerability of the heroine shine through her artificial society manners. It is one of Hepburn's most memorable performances of the 1930's. The rest of the cast lends excellent support, particularly Fred Stone and Ann Shoemaker as Alice's parents, and Hattie McDaniel in a bit part as the hapless Malena. Fred MacMurray is not required to do much except look handsome and romantic, but he is certainly credible as the Prince Charming of a young woman's dreams. All in all, the film is a touching, sometimes realistic, sometimes romantic portrait of small-town life.

Julia Johnson

ALIEN

Released: 1979
Production: Gordon Carroll, David Giler, and Walter Hill for Twentieth Century-Fox
Direction: Ridley Scott
Screenplay: Dan O'Bannon; based on a story by Dan O'Bannon and Ronald Shusett
Cinematography: Derek Vanlint
Editing: Terry Rawlings
Production design: Michael Seymour
Special effects: Carlo Rambaldi, H. R. Giger, Brian Johnson, Nick Allder, and Denys Ayling (AA)
Running time: 105 minutes

> *Principal characters:*
> Dallas .... Tom Skerritt
> Ripley .... Sigourney Weaver
> Lambert .... Veronica Cartwright
> Brett .... Harry Dean Stanton
> Kane ....John Hurt
> Ash .... Ian Holm
> Parker .... Yaphet Kotto

Alien opened in 1979 after a publicity campaign which the *Wall Street Journal* said had cost almost as much as the movie. Initial showings in New York were sold out. After some mixed reviews, the lines next day were even longer. Early indications were that the film might be among the top all-time grossers. But why? The answer lies in the movie, in its marketing, and in the dynamics of mass psychology. The picture is a slick synthesis—part space opera, part horror film, part undergraduate speculation, part literary offshoot. Yet the parts are fused by director Ridley Scott's visual and tactile style into a product which is both popular and surprisingly sophisticated.

A spaceship, the *Nostromo*, is heading back to earth with twenty million tons of mineral ore when its computer, "Mother," wakes the crew prematurely from their sleep-state. A radio signal is being received from a downed space vessel on an uncharted planet; three of the seven-person crew embark in a shuttle vehicle to investigate. They find a bed of large, egg-shaped pods in the hold of the broken ship. When a crewman investigates the pods, a growth leaps out of one, pierces through his helmet, and affixes itself to his face. The man is not killed, however; somehow the gelid, pulpy mass supplies him with oxygen. Against the wishes of second-in-command Ripley (Sigourney Weaver), the three voyagers are readmitted to the home ship in violation of quarantine regulations. Thus the alien comes onboard, where it grows with astonishing speed, taking a variety of forms and living parasitically off the bodies of the crew members, then destroying them. The crew soon discovers that its true mission all along has been the recovery of this new, apparently indestructible life form. They themselves are expendable; indeed, they are mere nourishment for the beast, which now hunts them.

There is little conventional suspense in the film because there is little or no character development; the few shorthand touches could just as easily have been applied in different ways for all the impact they have. This is no Hitchcock picture. The audience is simply teased, waiting for each new appearance of the alien on the ship. Yet this simple story is more than just one shock after another. That is the triumph of Ridley Scott and his team of designers, model builders, matte artists, special effects technicians, and so forth, for it is visually and aurally that the film holds together and develops. Its sophistication lies in its visual motifs, which emerge like themes.

The first motif is technological. The commercial ore vessel looks as big as Cleveland and its satellite is the size of a nuclear aircraft carrier. Cruising through the blue-velvet space void, the ships boast a full complement of hatches, tanks, and knobs shining in the bone-white light of some nameless moon. Within these vessels is an array of control panels, doors that close soundlessly on air cushions, video systems that scan the terrain of an uncharted planet and produce computer-generated images of its peaks and valleys—and much more. The look is straight out of *2001: A Space Odyssey* (1968) via *Star Wars* (1977). It is a "given" of the space opera and as such is a huge cliché, displaying chunks of hardware floating through space like giant stereo sets, populated by humans who are, relatively, the size of pinheads. Luckily, all this is only the background for another motif which is more primitive and visceral.

Everything in space that technology does not understand and use, everything unknown, hostile, and dangerous, is, quite literally, guts. The interior of the downed spaceship suggests a huge whale belly with ribs supporting a skin of steely flesh. The alien form at first is raw, quivering, and fleshy, like the underside of some crustacean. It oozes yellow bile that eats through the floor of the big space vehicle. And its spawn, in the ship, is "born" from the guts of the first infected crewman. It actually tears through his stomach, appearing as a screaming, bloody lizard shape with rows of tiny, razorlike teeth. Guts and the tearing at guts provide the driving images in *Alien*. As the monster grows, its metallic teeth are glimpsed briefly in double and quadruple rows: mouths full of teeth, arms reaching out with teeth, all accompanied by a din of shrieks, wind, and synthesized cacophony. The monstrosity of the alien lies precisely in its otherness from the world of technology. There is no accounting for its shape(s), its power, its hunger. Yet, ironically, its shape seems more natural than the technological atmosphere in the ship.

As the alien comes to dominate the ship, the atmosphere becomes much more menacing, scenes are backlit, pierced with jets of steam, misted with planetary fog, illuminated by flickering television screens and flashing warning lamps, punctuated by musical sounds and a bit of obligatory symphonic relief. It is what you would expect, but it is done superbly. The film has antecedents in everything from Joseph Conrad (*Nostromo*) to a student picture about an alien by director John Carpenter (*Halloween*) and Dan O'Bannon, writer of the *Alien* screenplay. But the real authors of the movie are clearly Scott and his visual team.

Scott has also guided a remarkably natural acting ensemble. The crew of the *Nostromo* throw away lines as if they have been shipmates for years (or have been directed by Robert Altman). Scott avoids the "punchy," melodramatic close-ups of television. Sometimes lines blur together, which only enhances the natural feeling. The ensemble effect is completed by using character actors, not stars, although Sigourney Weaver emerges from the crew with stellar status. A tall, rangy, dark-haired beauty with fine features, she projects intelligence and a coltish independence, like a young Jane Fonda who is already miles beyond *Barbarella* (1968). It is a nice feminist touch to have her outwit and survive the alien, and it is a nice sexist touch to have her face the creature at the end in only a t-shirt and bikini pants. Such calculation is the stuff of megahits.

Alien is the right movie in the right genre, bolstered by an expensive media blitz. It cashes in on a craze but also delivers something unique. When the creature is finally ejected from the shuttle vehicle into space, we feel as if we are watching an intestinal purge. It is an ugly, primal, hypnotic image, and it emphasizes the whole disturbing quality of the movie; it is imagery designed by very sophisticated people to work on our unconscious minds in the most basic way.

As man ventures deeper into space, the terrors of microbodies and irrational hungers become more threatening to his complex life-support systems. He cannot escape such dangers. The further he probes, the more certain he is to confront his "alien." *Alien* combines its Oscar-winning high technology and barbaric terror with the implication that both are part of man's destiny in space. No audience can ignore that ominous vision.

Ted Gershuny

ALL ABOUT EVE

Released: 1950
Production: Darryl F. Zanuck for Twentieth Century-Fox (AA)
Direction: Joseph L. Mankiewicz (AA)
Screenplay: Joseph L. Mankiewicz (AA); based on the short story and radio
   play *The Wisdom of Eve* by Mary Orr
Cinematography: Milton Krasner
Editing: Barbara McLean
Costume design: Edith Head and Charles LeMaire (AA)
Running time: 138 minutes

> *Principal characters:*
> Margo Channing .... Bette Davis
> Eve Harrington .... Anne Baxter
> Addison De Witt (Narrator) .... George Sanders (AA)
> Karen Richards .... Celeste Holm
> Bill Sampson .... Gary Merrill
> Lloyd Richards .... Hugh Marlowe
> Miss Caswell (Girl at Party) .... Marilyn Monroe

The film *All About Eve* typifies an aspect of filmmaking which is uniquely suited to the genre: the flashback. As the film opens, the viewer is placed in the middle of an awards ceremony. It is quickly discovered that Eve Harrington is being honored as the youngest woman ever to win the Sarah Siddons award as Best Actress. Through the eyes of the camera the viewer can scan the participants in the ceremony and see the unmoving faces of all of the main characters in one overview. Against the background of muffled speeches and false smiles, the real action of the film—events which led to this award—begins to unfold through the thoughts of each important character as he watches the ceremony.

The film is true to its title; though the audience knows little at the beginning, by the end they do, indeed, know "all" about Eve Harrington; and along the way they also learn a considerable amount about the backstage life of the New York theater. Through a constant interplay of scenes from plays and of dressing room reality, the audience is given insights into the real drama of the Broadway stage and is reminded of the similarities between the people in this movie and people in all walks of life, especially the success seekers.

The story unfolds to show that Eve Harrington (Anne Baxter), a lovely young woman and purportedly a war widow, wants to be a success, but not just moderately so: she wants to be the biggest and the brightest star on Broadway. By cajoling her way into the confidence of several of the main characters, she is able to achieve her goal. In the beginning, she is befriended by Margo Channing (Bette Davis), one of the great ladies of the stage, an ageless, eternal success. Using her own acting abilities, Eve is able to make her fabricated image of shy helplessness believable to Margo and the others, at least for a time.

Along the way, Eve causes dissension between Margo and her fiancé, director Bill Sampson (Gary Merrill), by using many of the clichés of romantic drama, such as playing on Margo's fear of getting old, and chipping away at Bill's confidence in himself as a director. Again, watching Eve act out her part, viewers—as well as Bill and Margo—are able to get a clearer picture of what the characters are and how success and fear of failure affect them.

Gradually the audience becomes privy to the tricks which Eve plays on her newly found "friends." It comes as no surprise when Eve, who has acted as Margo's understudy, arranges for the star to be stranded out of town one night so that she herself can be seen by the top New York theater critics. Eve even enlists the aid of Karen Richards (Celeste Holm), the playwright's wife, in the scheme. At this point the audience realizes that everything has been part of Eve's plan; her ingratiating manner, her reluctant acceptance of the part as Margo's understudy, and all the rest have been calculations.

The victims of Eve's aggressive rise to stardom have varied fates. Margo and Bill marry and come to realize their own abilities and weaknesses. Margo also reluctantly accepts the fact that she will have to give way to younger stars who are on the way up. However, Karen, the dupe in many of Eve's plans, is herself destroyed by Eve's disruption of her marriage to Lloyd Richards (Hugh Marlowe). As the final conquest in her fight for stardom, Eve must win Lloyd over to her side. As the writer of her new play, he gives her his total aid and love.

Eve seems to return his love, but because of Addison De Witt (George Sanders), the acid-tongued critic who knows her past, any happiness with Lloyd is impossible. Addison has seen everything in the theater, and he is the only person who immediately recognizes Eve's calculating heart. He is willing to help her, however, because of his own designs on her. At a critical juncture in the film, Addison reveals to Eve and the audience all that he knows about her. He confronts her with the fact that she has never been the innocent Eve Harrington, but is instead an ambitious and opportunistic actress who has been acting out a part for the benefit of those who might help her. We finally see Eve for what she is and at the same time see what might become of her. Addison is now using her. She has suddenly become the victim of her own trap, and there is no way for her to get out of that trap and still become a success.

At the end of the film we are again taken back to the awards dinner. The audience gets the feeling that it has drifted off into thought while the sham of the awards ceremony has continued uninterrupted. We see Eve accept her award as Best Actress of the Year with proper humility and gratitude. She especially thanks those who helped her most, and, as the audience knows, those she hurt the most.

After the ceremony we see Eve in a final and magnificently ironic light. Eve, it seems, acquires a protégée who bears a striking resemblance to herself. Although she does not realize it yet, the audience sees that this girl, like Eve, wants success at any cost, and at the end we realize that it will not be long until another young girl is thanking all of those who helped her at a future awards ceremony.

Dramatically, this film is a masterpiece. The acting and direction are flawless. The characters are believable, and the situation of the ambitious person rising to the top without regard to scruples or feelings is universal. Even a quarter of a century later, *All About Eve* does not seem dated. When the film came out in 1950, it opened to sensational notices and wide box-office appeal; it won many of the year's industry awards including several Oscars. George Sanders won the Academy Award for Best Supporting Actor, and Joseph L. Mankiewicz took two Academy Awards, one for Best Direction and one for Best Screenplay. The movie itself won the most coveted award, Best Film of the Year.

Despite all of these awards, however, the two outstanding female stars of the movie, Bette Davis and Anne Baxter, were passed over. In typical Hollywood fashion, Anne Baxter insisted on campaigning for "Best Actress" rather than "Best Supporting Actress," and as a consequence the Academy vote was split between her and Davis. The result was that a relatively unknown actress, Judy Holliday, won the Oscar that year for Best Actress for her performance in the delightful comedy, *Born Yesterday*.

All About Eve is an excellent blend of script, direction, and acting. Without relying heavily on music, locations, or other techniques of cinema, it has become one of the all-time classics of the motion picture industry, one which has passed the test of time. The story itself was also transferred successfully to the Broadway stage in the form of the Tony Award-winning musical *Applause*, starring Lauren Bacall as Margo Channing.

Patricia King Hanson

ALL QUIET ON THE WESTERN FRONT

Released: 1930
Production: Carl Laemmle, Jr., for Universal (AA)
Direction: Lewis Milestone (AA)
Dialogue direction: George Cukor
Screenplay: Del Andrews, Maxwell Anderson, and George Abbott; based
  on the novel of the same name by Erich Maria Remarque
Cinematography: Arthur Edeson
Editing: Edgar Adams and Milton Carruth
Running time: 140 minutes

> *Principal characters:*
> Katczinsky .... Louis Wolheim
> Paul Baumer .... Lew Ayres
> Himmelstoss .... John Wray
> Gerard Duval .... Raymond Griffith
> Tjaden .... George "Slim" Summerville
> Muller .... Russell Gleason
> Albert .... William Bakewell
> Mrs. Baumer .... Beryl Mercer

Appropriately enough, Universal began production on the film which more
than any other depicted the horror and waste of war at eleven o'clock on
November 11, 1929 exactly eleven years to the day after the termination of
World War I. Carl Laemmle had originally wanted Herbert Brenon to direct
All Quiet on the Western Front, but because the salary Brenon demanded was
too high, Laemmle offered the assignment to Lewis Milestone. It was Milestone's first sound feature, the first of four films in which he examined men
at war—the others being *The Purple Heart* (1944), *A Walk in the Sun* (1945),
and *The Halls of Montezuma* (1951)—and it was without question his greatest
dramatic achievement. John Wray was initially slated for the leading role of
Paul Baumer, but then Paul Bern brought Lew Ayres, who had minor roles
in only two features to his credit, to Universal's attention, and he was assigned
the part. ZaSu Pits originally portrayed Paul's mother, but after a preview
audience in Santa Ana, California, too accustomed to her playing comedy
roles, laughed at her performance, Beryl Mercer was substituted.

Shooting was not completed until the last week of March, 1930, with Karl
Freund photographing the final moving scene after Arthur Edeson had left
for another assignment. *All Quiet on the Western Front* premiered only sixteen
days after the film version of R.C. Sherriff's *Journey's End*, a pacifist drama
concerning a group of British soldiers in the trenches, had opened. Of the
two films, it was the latter which received the better notices, but it is *All
Quiet on the Western Front* which is remembered today and which can still

inspire an audience to applaud individual scenes and performances. Without star names and with World War I fading into memory, the film did exceedingly well at the box office and received the third Academy Award for Best Picture.

Based on Erich Maria Remarque's famous 1929 novel, *All Quiet on the Western Front* tells of the war experiences of a group of German boys as they mature from students at a small-town school to weary war veterans. In the opening scenes, they are shown listening avidly to their schoolmaster talk of the glory of war, the thrill of victory. But disillusionment soon sets in; by the time they have completed their basic training under a generally disliked ex-village postman, from whom they can no longer escape, and have experienced their first night at the Front, during which one of the boys is killed, the students have learned that war is no more than constant death and destruction. Later, when the central figure, Paul Baumer (Lew Ayres), returns home on leave, he hears, through the open window of the schoolroom, the same teacher still glorifying the conflict. The teacher urges Paul to address the class, proudly displaying him like a prized trophy as "one of the first to go." When Paul is asked what it is like at the Front, he answers bitterly, "We live in the trenches and we fight. We try not to be killed—that's all." His words are wasted on the new generation of students. Through the war propaganda of their teacher and others, they have already become new fodder for the war machine.

Aside from the futility of war, *All Quiet on the Western Front* concentrates on comradeship. There is warm affection between the young soldiers such as Private Tjaden (George "Slim" Summerville) and the seasoned veterans such as Katczinsky (Louis Wolheim). Wolheim, with his bull neck and cheeky grin, gives a magnificent performance, and there can be no emptier feeling than when Katczinsky dies after Baumer has carried him over his shoulders to safety. The anguish of the young Baumer as he desperately tries to get the dead Katczinsky to drink some water is heart-rending; the scene is made even more effective by Baumer's dull response of "No, we're not related," to an inquiry from another soldier.

It is Tjaden and Katczinsky who deliver the two most simple, low-keyed, yet impassioned comments on war. When he is told that wars start because one group of people offend another group of people, Tjaden notes that nobody has offended him; he doesn't even know any Frenchmen or Englishmen personally. The ridiculousness of war is further expounded when one soldier claims that wars begin when one country gets angry at another country, soliciting the comment that there is no way a French mountain can get angry with a German field. Katczinsky's solution to war is to gather all the emperors, kings, prime ministers, and top military officials together in a field, clad only in their underwear, and have them fight it out amongst themselves with clubs.

Women play little part in the film, except when three French girls enjoy a brief romantic interlude with Baumer and two other German soldiers. There is a gentleness to the cinematography and the direction in this sequence which creates an overall mood of calm and tranquility and offers both the characters and the audience a brief respite from the horrible reality of the conflict. The only other female role of any significance in the film is that of Baumer's mother (Beryl Mercer), who appears in a brief scene when the boy returns home.

With a realistic, almost documentary quality to every aspect of the production, Milestone shows the endless sorrow of war. With Baumer and his colleagues, we experience the dying room, and as Franz dies, we see not him but his boots as they leave the room in Baumer's hands and reappear on another soldier's feet. In turn, the new owner of the boots is killed. One of the most painfully emotional moments in the film occurs when Baumer finds himself sharing a shell hole with a French soldier, superbly played by the one-time silent screen comedian, Raymond Griffith. Baumer stabs the Frenchman with his bayonet, and through the night must listen to the groans of the dying man. Desperately trying to atone for his "murder," Baumer attempts to get the Frenchman to drink some water, but it is too late. He is dead, with a half-smile and a look of accusation on his face. The message of Baumer's impassioned speech ("our thoughts are earth and our bodies clay, and we sleep and eat with death") is vividly brought home to the film's audience.

In the end, Baumer must also face death. His friends gone, he sits alone in the trenches watching a butterfly alight close by. Yearning for its beauty (we know from the scenes of his return home that Baumer had once collected and mounted butterflies), he stretches out his hand towards it. The camera then cuts to a sniper, thus juxtaposing an image of life—the butterfly—with one of death—the sniper's gun. Suddenly a shot is heard and the hand goes limp. All is finally quiet on the Western front.

In a film such as this, which is so obviously a team effort, it is difficult to single out anyone for special praise, yet one cannot but be impressed by the moving and convincing performances of two young actors, Lew Ayres and William Bakewell. Ayres was later to become an avowed pacifist; he declared himself as a conscientious objector during World War II—a courageous step at a time when so many screen actors, such as Clark Gable and James Stewart, were being lauded for their efforts in behalf of the war.

All Quiet on the Western Front has been reissued many times since 1930, most importantly in 1939, in a version which included a voice-over narration comparing the German soldiers of the film to the then-current German military. The 1939 reissue closed with a bitter attack on Nazism, including scenes of the burning of a number of books, among which was *All Quiet on the Western Front*.

Anthony Slide

ALL THAT JAZZ

Released: 1979
Production: Robert Alan Aurthur for Twentieth Century-Fox and Columbia
Direction: Bob Fosse
Screenplay: Robert Alan Aurthur and Bob Fosse
Cinematography: Giuseppe Rotunno
Editing: Alan Heim (AA)
Art direction: Philip Rosenberg and Tony Walton (AA); set decoration, Edward Stewart and Gary Brink (AA)
Costume design: Albert Wolsky (AA)
Music: Ralph Burns (AA)
Running time: 123 minutes

Principal characters:
Joe Gideon	Roy Scheider
Angelique	Jessica Lange
Kate Jagger	Ann Reinking
Audrey Paris	Leland Palmer
Davis Newman	Cliff Gorman
O'Connor Flood	Ben Vereen
Michelle	Erzsebet Foldi

Some twenty-five years ago, Bob Fosse made his debut as a Broadway choreographer by staging an innovative "Steam Heat" number for a stage production of *Pajama Game*. Since that time, Fosse's largely excessive choreographic and directorial (stage as well as screen) styles have won awards and audiences. Most of Fosse's work involves music and dance (the 1974 drama *Lenny* is an exception; however, that work is set against a mostly theatrical backdrop), and generally the works are rich in dance imagery. *Sweet Charity*, Fosse's much-ignored (at the box office) 1969 film, enticed the critics with its colorfully staged and vigorous dance numbers. In his 1972 film, *Cabaret*, Fosse heightened the musical drama format by delivering largely impressionistic staging of musical numbers on the stage of the cabaret, which served to reflect Germany's political and social mood during the 1930's, emphasizing the emergence and acceptance of Nazism. *All That Jazz* possesses many of the Fosse trademarks. It is a highly creative work, energetic, fast-paced, and colorful. Its characterizations are vivid, its dance sequences memorable.

Unlike Fosse's previous works, *All That Jazz* is marked by a highly personal tone. It is an excessive work, sometimes joyous, sometimes cynical and brooding, and very often, because of its bizarre imagery and unique staging of musical numbers, fascinating. Much of what happens to Joe Gideon, the film's central character, has happened to Fosse. The film's openly autobiographical mood divided critics of the day. Many labeled the film as blatantly self-indulgent. Still others saw the project as a brilliantly conceived tribute to show business. Many likened the film to Federico Fellini's bizarre and autobiographical *8½* (1963). In fact, the cinematographer for *All That Jazz* was Giuseppe Rotunno, noted for his work with Fellini.

As the film opens, Joe Gideon (Roy Scheider) is talking about high wires and life with a beautiful, soft-spoken woman. We see Gideon, briefly, on a high wire. Then the scene quickly shifts, and the screen is filled with a huge, bloodshot eye. Gideon is just awakening to begin his day. "It's show time, folks," he tells his mirrored reflection. The next shot is of a crowded theater stage, where legions of hopefuls are auditioning for a new musical. This opening dance sequence sets the stage for Gideon's characterization. Dressed in black, with close-cropped beard and cigarette dangling from his mouth (a habit of the real-life Fosse), he is energy personified as he moves from hopeful to hopeful asking about their backgrounds and offering advice. Gideon is thus identified as a choreographer-director; and from his dialogue with the female performers, we also see him to be a womanizer. Seated in the theater watching the goings-on are an attractive middle-aged woman and a young girl. Through their interest in what is happening onstage, we sense their interest in Gideon; later, we learn that they are Gideon's ex-wife Audrey (Leland Palmer) and his daughter Michelle (Erzsebet Foldi). A group of men, also seated in the theater, watch the proceedings with indifference, even boredom. They are the show's backers and producers, and, through these earliest moments with them, Fosse darkly underlines the differences between the artist and the businessman.

The editing of the audition number is fast-paced, moving rapidly from stage to auditorium then back to stage again. When Gideon at last selects his performers, the film's audience has a strong sense of the rigors of auditioning (that theme, of course, is the basis for the popular Broadway musical, *A Chorus Line*).

Shortly after the audition, Gideon is once again conversing in a flirtatious vein with the beautiful blonde with whom he spoke in the opening scene. It is at this point that we realize that *All That Jazz* alternates from life as it is, or reality, to life as Joe Gideon perceives it—that is, Gideon's fantasy life. In his talks with the compelling Angelique (Jessica Lange), Gideon discusses his childhood. In fact, moments from Gideon's life are acted out on a stage while Gideon watches, in fascination, along with Angelique. We have a glimpse of Gideon's mother cooking at a stove, telling us what a hard-worker her son is. Then we see young Joe himself working backstage in a vaudeville show and being playfully teased by a group of near-naked strippers. Young Joe, who is obviously both fascinated and upset by the women, next takes the stage to perform his tap dance. It is a humiliating moment for Joe, who is laughed off the stage when the rowdy audience sees the large stain that has appeared on the front of the boy's pants. Later, Gideon tells Angelique of his relationships with women, including a liaison with two women at the same time. It is an especially strange fantasy sequence involving Gideon and two attractive women posing onstage in order to suggest the relationship.

Gideon's real-life exploits, we next discover, are almost as creative as the fantasylike situation he previously detailed, for, although he seems seriously involved with Kate, a leggy dancer much devoted to him, Gideon also remains in touch with his ex-wife and colleague Audrey. Moreover, Gideon is also having a brief affair with one of his show's new dancers. When a teary Kate confronts him about his unfaithfulness, Gideon makes a vain attempt at professing a commitment to her, but the move seems half-hearted. Where women are concerned, this man is a charmer, but also unreliable.

He is also courting death—hampered by chest pains and being seductively quizzed by Angelique, who, one senses, is an enticing angel of death. But Gideon does not want to give up life; in fact, he embraces it excessively. In addition to his labyrinth of personal relationships, he is stretched to the limits professionally. Not only is he working on the new musical, but he also is editing a feature film called *The Stand-Up* (very obviously based on Fosse's *Lenny*, the "film" stars Davis Newman, portrayed by Cliff Gorman, who starred in the Broadway version of *Lenny*).

Death remains an imminent theme. It is during a reading of the play that Gideon has his first attack. It is an effective scene; as the cast of players, including Audrey, reads the lines with exaggerated humor, the seriousness of Gideon's condition becomes more and more apparent. Finally, Gideon has created a kind of detached environment for himself. The players are there, reading and laughing, but we no longer hear them, nor does Gideon. Instead, we hear the crinkling of Gideon's papers or the amplified sounds of him opening another packet of cigarettes. We also see Gideon's worried look—something the players miss. His attack follows the reading.

We now see Angelique, more seductive than ever. But two real-life women are also pulling at Gideon. At his side, as he is wheeled down the hospital corridors, Audrey and Kate are partners in an attempt to reassure him. Looking up at them from the gurney, Gideon says, first to Audrey, "If I die, I'm sorry for all the bad things I did to you," and, to Kate, "If I live, I'm sorry for all the bad things I'm going to do to you." Gideon is forever fun-loving, even in the face of death. He is also forever neglectful of his health. Despite the doctor's warnings, the hospitalized Gideon, who appears to have survived the attack, takes to smuggling cigarettes, booze, and even women into his room. He is admonished by the doctors, who are puzzled over the way he seems to try to tempt death.

It is during the hospital sequence that *All That Jazz* alternates, countless times, between real and fantasy lives. Angelique is ever-present. So is the monologue delivered by Davis Newman, who also pays a visit to the hospital.

It is a monlogue Gideon had listened to again and again while editing his film, but suddenly Newman's words about death and the acceptance of death have renewed meaning. Meanwhile, outside the hospital, the backers of Gideon's play are having serious financial discussions. How long can the show be postponed, they wonder? Should a replacement be brought in?

Gideon, who has toned down his rowdy hospital ways, appears to be on the road to recovery. His personal relationships, however, are floundering. He has been surprised to learn that the devoted Kate has recently spent a night with another man. He is also distressed at some of the critical response that greets the release of his film, *The Stand-Up*. Fosse wryly comments on the critical field by showing a television critic who rates films with a "balloon rating"—four balloons signifying approval, one balloon indicating the kiss of death.

In a hallucination sequence, Gideon sees the women in his life (Audrey, Kate, and daughter Michelle) perform in musical numbers, as they taunt and admonish him about his past doings. In one number (a rendition of "Who's Sorry Now") a bevy of chorines in white beaded outfits and holding huge feathers encircle Gideon's bed, performing a seductive dance. As the musical numbers come to a close, Gideon's three women drive off atop a hearse.

Later, a somewhat dazed real-life Gideon aimlessly wanders through the hospital. It is a cynical moment when he enters an autopsy suite; then, the mood shifts to one of understanding as Gideon, witnessing an elderly woman patient in obvious pain, bends to kiss her, murmuring, "I think you're the most beautiful thing in the world, and I love you." His action, for the moment, at least, eases the woman's pain. When finally found by hospital orderlies, Gideon is with a black janitor who, to amuse the patient, is singing "Pack Up Your Troubles." Gideon, ever the showman, looks for music, and dance everywhere.

Indeed, it is during Gideon's final moments, his death scene, that song and dance is delivered in the film's grandest, most dazzling scale. Gideon has imagined himself to be on the O'Connor Flood show. Flood (Ben Vereen), glimpsed briefly on the television screen, is a bejewelled, very hip talk show host. He is everybody's best friend, and for Gideon's big send-off, he proves to be a most appropriate host. The musical number, a jazzed-up tune called "Bye, Bye Life" (a rendition of the Everly Brothers tune, "Bye, Bye Love"), is performed by the energetic Flood and Gideon before an audience composed of people from Gideon's life. They are all there, ranging from the near-naked strippers to Gideon's women, and even including the Broadway play backers ("This must have cost a fortune," enthuses one, motioning to the opulent settings). Onstage, Gideon hams it up, then moves into the audience for embraces, especially with his teary daughter, and handshakes. Intercut with this number are vivid, detailed scenes depicting open-heart surgery. Obviously, the surgery is unsuccessful, for, as the musical number comes to a climax, Gideon races down a hospital hallway. Waiting for him at the end of the hall is the patient, lovely Angelique. In the final scene, Gideon's motionless body is zipped into a bag. Over the closing credits come the familiar lyrics to the ever-popular "There's No Business Like Show Business."

As a musical, *All That Jazz* has few equals. Not surprisingly, considering its subject matter, it was one of the most controversial films of 1979. If the theme distressed some, the feeling was fairly unanimous that *All That Jazz* was a dazzling artistic work. The film received nine Academy Award nominations, including one for Best Picture, and won four awards, including Best Editing, Best Art Direction, and Best Costume Design.

Roy Scheider also captured a Best Actor nomination, and some well-deserved notoriety, for his vigorous portrayal of the enigmatic Gideon. Up until his work in *All That Jazz*, Scheider had ranked mostly as a character actor, playing heavies and cops (*The French Connection*, 1971), as well as second banana to a shark in *Jaws* (1975) and its sequel, *Jaws II* (1978). Though Scheider dominates this film, his female costars also have effective moments. Cast as Angelique is Jessica Lange, the actress who played the Fay Wray role in the *King Kong* (1976) remake. Ann Reinking, Leland Palmer, and young Erzsebet Foldi are all convincing as the women in Gideon's life; and the dynamic Ben Vereen delivers some sly humor in the closing musical extravaganza.

Pat H. Broeske

ALL THE PRESIDENT'S MEN

Released: 1976
Production: Walter Coblenz for Wildwood Enterprises; released by Warner Bros.
Direction: Alan J. Pakula
Screenplay: William Goldman (AA); based on the book of the same name by Carl Bernstein and Bob Woodward
Cinematography: Gordon Willis
Editing: Robert L. Wolfe
Art direction: George Jenkins (AA); set decoration, George Gaines (AA)
Sound: Arthur Piantadosi, Les Fresholtz, Dick Alexander, and Jim Webb (AA)
Running time: 138 minutes

> *Principal characters:*
> Bob Woodward .... Robert Redford
> Carl Bernstein .... Dustin Hoffman
> Ben Bradlee .... Jason Robards (AA)
> Harry Rosenfeld .... Jack Warden
> Howard Simons .... Martin Balsam
> Deep Throat .... Hal Holbrook
> Hugh Sloan, Jr. .... Stephen Collins
> Bookkeeper .... Jane Alexander

Several weeks after the 1972 Watergate breakin, Robert Redford was promoting his most recent film, *The Candidate*, the story of a congressional nominee and the electoral process. Redford was intrigued with the *Washington Post*'s courageous investigation of the breakin, and four years later, his Wildwood Enterprises filmed the story of Watergate in *All the President's Men*, based on the book by Carl Bernstein and Bob Woodward. This film illuminates the techniques and persistence of these two reporters' investigation of one of the most sensitive epochs in contemporary political history. Every scene is well-researched and faithful to the facts of the Watergate scandal from the reenactment of the breakin to activities in the *Post* newsroom; there is even a small role for the original Watergate Office building security guard, Frank Wills, who first noticed and reported the breakin.

The morning after the burglars are arrested, Bob Woodward (Robert Redford), a reporter for the *Washington Post*, is called and told to investigate the burglary. Carl Bernstein (Dustin Hoffman), who is present at the newsroom when the call is placed, insists that he should receive the assignment, but the editor admonishes him to finish his other stories first. This and other humorous encounters establishes Bernstein's character as flamboyant and a little unpredictable. Woodward, on the other hand, is more levelheaded. He goes to the courtroom where the burglars are to be arraigned and stolidly does some checking. He talks with the public defenders who were originally assigned to the case and discovers that the burglars retained their own counsel and that they were caught at the scene dressed in suits and carrying surveillance equipment. Their intention obviously was to wiretap the National Democratic Headquarters; the question was, under whose orders?

Woodward's next lead is the information that "Howard Hunt at W. House" and "HH at WH" were noted in two of the burglars' address books. He traces Howard Hunt and finds that he was hired as a White House consultant and worked for the CIA until 1970. As Woodward writes the Hunt story and turns in the story page by page to the copy desk, he notices that Bernstein is surreptitiously taking each page and rewriting it. When Woodward confronts him, Bernstein insists that the stories need polishing. After Woodward reads Bernstein's version, he thoughtfully admits, to Bernstein's surprise, that the revision is better; in this way the two begin their joint authorship. They investigate each thin lead, each reluctant source to uncover information about Howard Hunt and the breakin. They are told that Hunt was doing research on Ted Kennedy for the White House in hopes of discouraging Kennedy's possible presidential campaign; in order to substantiate this rumor they root through more than ten thousand request slips that the White House made at the Library of Congress. The contrast between these unknown reporters pitting themselves against this gargantuan task is symbolized in this sequence by showing the two men seated in the main reading room perusing each slip. The camera uses a tight shot in which we can read the contents of the slip, then slowly pulls back to reveal the immensity of the Library of Congress and the two tiny figures engulfed in their investigation.

Woodward's secret source, a highly placed White House official known only as Deep Throat (Hal Holbrook)—a nickname concocted by editor Howard Simons because this source could only be used on deep background, only to confirm information, never to volunteer anything new—advises Woodward to "follow the money" and seek out the source of the burglars' payoff. They discover a check earmarked for the Committee to Re-elect the President deposited in the bank account of one of the burglars, and eventually discover the existence of a secret cash fund which they suspect financed the Watergate caper. They secure a list of CRP employees, but all the employees refuse to talk to them until Bernstein contacts a bookkeeper (Jane Alexander) who worked for Hugh Sloan, Jr. (Stephen Collins), treasurer of CRP, and who was then promoted to work for Maurice Stans, finance chairman for CRP. She also refuses to talk, until Bernstein weasels his way into her home and stalls until she loosens up and bit by bit confirms some of Bernstein's information. She acknowledges that there was indeed a slush fund and that the money was kept by Stans in his safe and that he and Mitchell doled out payments. Bernstein takes notes in the bathroom on napkins, matchbooks, toilet paper, and whatever he can find in order not to frighten the bookkeeper by taking notes in her presence.

When their investigation leads the two reporters to link the breakin with members of the White House staff, they endeavor to discover how high the knowledge of the breakin reaches. Meanwhile, Ben Bradlee (Jason Robards), executive editor for the *Post*, and editors Harry Rosenfeld (Jack Warden) and Howard Simons (Martin Balsam) are concerned that the articles are not broadcast by other newspapers or television networks. They wonder whether the two reporters, dubbed "Woodstein," are on the right track or if they are overzealous in connecting Watergate to the White House. However, when the two want to print a story about Mitchell's controlling the slush fund while he was still attorney-general and ordered the cover-up of Watergate, Bradlee gives the go-ahead to run the article on the front page. Walter Cronkite and other network reporters as well as newspapers pick up the story and give validity to the *Post*'s reporting of Watergate for the first time.

As the investigation delves deeper into the workings of the secret fund, the reporters find that Stans, Magruder, Mitchell, and Kalmbach controlled the fund, and they suspect that the fifth man who authorized payments was Nixon's closest aide, H. R. Haldeman. Because Haldeman is so closely connected with the President, the reporters find this story more difficult to confirm. Deep Throat will say nothing about Haldeman and Sloan will not make a direct statement one way or another about him although he does volunteer that if they wrote a story about Haldeman, he should have no problem with it, which they assume means that he will be testifying against Haldeman before the Watergate grand jury. After several intricate confirmations, the *Post* prints an article that Sloan's testimony before the grand jury revealed that Haldeman was the fifth man to control the fund. The White House issues its first straightforward denial since the Watergate series of stories began, which worries Bradlee. His worry is confirmed when Sloan's lawyer states to news media that Sloan did not testify against Haldeman. The two reporters are stunned and believe that they somehow misunderstood their information or they were betrayed by one of their sources. They return to talk with their sources and find that no one will deny that Haldeman controlled the fund; and Sloan tells them that he did not testify against Haldeman because he was not asked about Haldeman.

Woodward and Bernstein convince Bradlee that Haldeman was indeed connected with Watergate and the cover-up, and Bradlee issues his comment on the story which is that he stands by it. He urges the two to investigate thoroughly and find the facts because the paper's reputation is at stake. As Nixon's Oath of Office ceremonies are televised, Woodward and Bernstein are in the back of the newsroom diligently typing new stories. In the film's epilogue, we see a close-up of a teletype clacking out subsequent articles, the last one stating that Nixon resigns from the presidency and Gerald Ford is sworn in as the 38th President of the United States.

Redford's influence on this film is felt not only through his acting but in the film's conception. He wanted the film to be entertaining yet to reflect accurately the events portrayed. He is partial to the semidocumentary style used and encouraged the personal account angle of Woodward and Bernstein's book, feeling that the interest of the story lies in the way Bernstein and Woodward dig up the facts on Watergate. Redford viewed the story as somewhat of a detective thriller; presented in this way, the film is suspenseful although the audience is aware of the outcome.

The acting in *All the President's Men* is understated yet paradoxically energetic and filled with near-explosive tension. There is no competition for the spotlight between Redford and Hoffman; the two meld perfectly to create a serious and professional partnership on the screen. Although the emphasis of the film is on the art of investigative reporting rather than on characterization, Hoffman's Bernstein is colorful and eccentric. The supporting cast is excellent, especially Jason Robards, who won an Academy Award for Best Supporting Actor for his role as Ben Bradlee. Jack Warden and Martin Balsam also turned in competent performances, along with Hal Holbrook in his almost hysterical portrayal of Deep Throat, a paranoid personality who generates much of the suspense of the film. Jane Alexander was lauded by several critics for her brief appearance as the bookkeeper, for which she was nominated for an Oscar as Best Supporting Actress.

Credit for adapting a complex book full of incidents, facts, and a multitude of personalities into a viable screenplay goes to William Goldman, who won an Academy Award for his efforts. This picture was also nominated for Best Picture and Best Director, and won well-deserved awards in the Art Direction and Set Decoration categories. An exact replica of the *Post* newsroom was constructed in Burbank by George Jenkins and George Gaines. They even shipped from the *Post* old galley proofs, directories, and other clutter to be distributed on the desks. There were 1972 calendars which were changed to match the dates on which the events took place, 1972 telephone directories, and even the front pages of seventeen editions which the *Post* reset for them to place around the newsroom on the day they were printed. The film also won an Oscar for Best Sound for its realistic mixing to denote location; the background sound added color to the scenes but it also made the dialogue difficult to understand in places.

Director Alan J. Pakula coordinated the large-scale filming operation with expertise. To deal with the problem of creating a visually interesting film with no explicit sex or violence, Pakula used colors that are hard and bright and lighting that is harsh, evoking a frightening, threatening mood. The newsroom is a stark white, almost shocking against the blackness of the subterranean garage where Woodward meets Deep Throat. Pakula has commented that to provide suspense and maintain the audience's interest in a story whose ending is known ". . . depends on a certain kind of hypnotic tension to keep it going

. . . a constant sense of actually being there, an immediacy. . . ." *All the President's Men* succeeds because it achieves this tension and immediacy.

Ruth L. Hirayama

AMERICAN GRAFFITI

Released: 1973
Production: Francis Ford Coppola for Lucasfilm Ltd./Coppola Company;
    released by Universal
Direction: George Lucas
Screenplay: George Lucas, Gloria Katz, and Willard Huyck
Cinematography: Ron Eveslage and Jan D'Alquen
Editing: Verna Fields and Marcia Lucas
Sound: Walter Murch
Running time: 110 minutes

Principal characters:
Curt Henderson	Richard Dreyfuss
Steve Bolander	Ron Howard
John Milner	Paul Le Mat
Terry Fields	Charlie Martin Smith
Laurie	Cindy Williams
Debbie	Candy Clark
Carol	Mackenzie Phillips

Bill Haley and the Comets' electrifying "Rock Around the Clock" blares forth from a car radio, beginning an almost nonstop, two-hour stream of classic rock 'n' roll that accompanies and counterpoints the story of *American Graffiti*. Taking place during one eventful night in 1962, the film focuses on four buddies in a small northern California town. Two of them, Steve Bolander (Ron Howard) and Curt Henderson (Richard Dreyfuss), are scheduled to leave for college the next day; John Milner (Paul Le Mat), the local drag-racing champion, cruises the town's "strip" looking for a rumored challenger; and Terry Fields (Charlie Martin Smith), nicknamed "The Toad," given the loan of Steve's car for the evening, sets his sights on the conquest of Debbie (Candy Clark), a pretty, if somewhat bubble-headed, blonde. This is the framework for the engaging misadventures of these four and the host of minor characters who populate this amusing and sometimes penetrating look at growing up, leaving (or not leaving) home, and other postadolescent traumas.

Steve is concerned about his future relationship with his girl friend Laurie (Cindy Williams) after he goes away; Curt's conflict is within himself, as he has strong reservations about leaving. John lives for the moment, and in searching for "action" is inadvertently saddled with the company of the childish thirteen-year-old Carol (Mackenzie Phillips). Curt, tantalized by a glimpse of a beautiful blonde in a white Thunderbird (who mouths the words "I love you" to him, then vanishes around a corner) chooses to avoid his problems and spend the night looking for her. Meanwhile, Terry is occupied in trying to recover Steve's car, stolen practically from under his nose; when he finds it, he must then be rescued from the car thieves by John. Steve's rift with Laurie is exacerbated by the fact that she ends up riding with the drag-race challenger during his predawn race against John, which climaxes the film. John wins the race, and Laurie is miraculously unhurt in the crash of the other car. Curt, failing in his quest to track down the mysterious blonde, nonetheless manages to come to terms with himself and go off to college. Steve, however, decides to put off his own departure, and he and Laurie, reunited after her close brush with death, join the others in seeing Curt off at the airport in the morning. A postscript reveals the futures of the four: Steve has become an insurance agent, John was killed by a drunk driver, Terry is missing in action in Vietnam, and Curt is a writer living in Canada.

No mere summary of events can do justice to *American Graffiti*'s remarkable orchestration of its many characters and their adventures. The essence of the film is twofold: the period re-creation and the complex narrative interaction. Although the four main characters actually spend very little of the film in direct contact with one another, in a sense they are always together; the story of each is also the story of the others, so closely are they related to their environment. They represent four alternative versions of the same experience, four courses of action available to young men growing up in that time and place.

It is important to the film, however, and a tribute to all involved in its making, that the minor characters are often just as vivid and memorable as the four principals. The ensemble acting in the film is remarkable. The four leads are outstanding; among the minor performers, Candy Clark as the object of Terry's affections and Mackenzie Phillips as the bratty yet affecting Carol deserve special mention, as does legendary disc jockey Wolfman Jack, whose voice is heard over the radio throughout the film, and who appears in a brief but memorable scene near the end.

The film is most noted, and ultimately most important, for its stunning re-creation of a small American town, circa 1962. It is not a literal creation—the music, for instance, ranges over nearly a decade—but rather an evocation of the essence of the era in cinematic terms. Photographed almost entirely at night, *American Graffiti* glows like neon and flashes like chrome; its distinctive look is due largely to the contributions of visual consultant Haskell Wexler, one of Hollywood's most renowned cinematographers. Equally important to the film's effectiveness is the brilliant sound track by Walter Murch, a complicated and innovative blending of music (forty-one classic rock 'n' roll tunes) and dialogue. Even though the direction is sometimes pedestrian and the script occasionally smacks of situation comedy, the energetic visual and aural evocation of the period never falters.

American Graffiti is a watershed of the modern American cinema, one of the most influential films of the 1970's. The American film industry had suffered a serious identity crisis during the 1960's, desperately trying to adapt to a more radical consciousness, particularly among younger audiences, and still remain in touch with the traditional values inherent in any large industry. There were indications as early as 1971 that the industry might do well to abandon its awkward struggle for "relevance" and look instead to the past for filmic material. Historical settings, of course, had always been common in the movies, but most often in generic terms—the distant past of the costume epic, for instance, or the stylized worlds of Westerns or gangster films.

Summer of '42 (1971) and *The Last Picture Show* (1971), however, were not genre pieces, and notable among their strengths was a strong sense of period. The trend toward the meticulous cinematic re-creation of fairly recent periods in American history indicated by these two films simmered just beneath the surface for a few years, again most often in genre settings like gangster films (*The Godfather*, 1972) or musical biographies (*Lady Sings the Blues*, 1972). The nostalgia boom, traceable back to the 1960's, was about to take firm hold in mainstream American cinema.

The desire for a return to simpler times, when moral alternatives were clearer and life in general seemed (at least in hindsight) much better was supported by the national disillusionment over American involvement in Vietnam. The single most important catalyst was perhaps the phenomenally successful stage musical *Grease*, which hit Broadway in 1972. *Grease* discovered that the 1950's were distant enough for nostalgic celebration; since "better times" had become almost synonymous with "pre-Vietnam" in the minds of many people, the early 1960's were included by association. Significantly, *Grease*'s way into the past was through its music.

It remained for *American Graffiti* to cement these various trends and exploit them to the fullest. Not only a fine movie, it was thus also in the right place at the right time; it caught the public's imagination, and soon became one of the top-grossing films of all time. Money, as always, speaks loudly in Hollywood, and the stampede of filmmakers into the past was not far behind. The most obvious result has been the production of a multitude of films dealing specifically with the recent American past, but there has also been a corresponding return to a less pretentious, even old-fashioned, style of filmmaking. Although used more self-consciously than ever before, "entertainment" is no longer a dirty word, as it had become in the socially conscious 1960's; and the looking-backward trend has yet to abate. Even *American Graffiti* itself has been subject to one of the offshoots of this trend, "sequelitis"—*More American Graffiti*, which picks up the characters at the end of the original, was released in 1979.

The phenomenal success of *American Graffiti*, filmed on location in twenty-nine days on a shoestring budget ($750,000), also had ramifications for independent film production in America, proving as it did that a major box-office hit need not rely on a big budget, big stars, or proven production personnel. Most of the cast of the film were unknowns at the time, the writers had never written a major feature film before, and director George Lucas' only previous feature was the interesting *THX 1138* (1971), a resounding box-office flop. (Lucas' success with *American Graffiti* is also notable because of his age—only twenty-nine at the time—and his filmmaking origins—he was a graduate of the cinema school of the University of Southern California.) Support for the film came largely from coproducers Gary Kurtz and Francis Ford Coppola, the latter fresh from the triumph of *The Godfather*.

Larger influences aside, *American Graffiti* also helped to launch a number of successful careers. Two of its stars, Ron Howard and Cindy Williams, went on to star in enormously successful television spin-offs of the movie (*Happy Days* and, once-removed, *Laverne & Shirley*, respectively), and Howard has moved into feature-film direction as well. Many of the other players have also gone on to various levels of stardom—most notably Richard Dreyfuss, who won the Academy Award as Best Actor for *The Goodbye Girl* (1977). Director Lucas' next project, of course, was *Star Wars* (1977). Although equally influential in its way, it was made possible only by the success of *American Graffiti*.

Howard H. Prouty

AN AMERICAN IN PARIS

Released: 1951
Production: Arthur Freed for Metro-Goldwyn-Mayer (AA)
Direction: Vincente Minnelli
Screenplay: Alan Jay Lerner (AA)
Cinematography: Alfred Gilks and John Alton (AA)
Editing: Adrienne Fazan
Art direction: Cedric Gibbons and Preston Ames (AA)
Set decoration: Edwin B. Willis and Keogh Gleason (AA)
Costume design: Orry-Kelly; Beaux-Arts costumes by Walter Plunkett; ballet
   costumes by Irene Sharaff (AA)
Choreography: Gene Kelly
Music direction: Johnny Green and Saul Chaplin (AA)
Music: George Gershwin and Ira Gershwin
Running time: 113 minutes

> *Principal characters:*
> Jerry Mulligan .... Gene Kelly
> Lise Bouvier .... Leslie Caron
> Adam Cook .... Oscar Levant
> Milo Roberts .... Nina Foch
> Henri Baurel .... Georges Guetary

An American in Paris is a classic M-G-M musical based on George Gershwin's music. Besides the fine Gershwin score it boasts expert direction by Vincente Minnelli, lavish costumes and sets, dazzling color cinematography, and the dancing of Gene Kelly and Leslie Caron. All of these combine with one of the most ambitious ballets ever filmed in Hollywood to earn *An American in Paris* an important niche in film history and an honor seldom won by a musical—the Academy Award for Best Picture.

The film tells the simple love story of Jerry Mulligan (Gene Kelly) and Lise Bouvier (Leslie Caron). Jerry is an ex-GI turned artist who has stayed in Paris to study painting, and Lise is a French girl whom he meets by chance in a Montmarte nightclub. He is immediately attracted to her and pursues her persistently until she reluctantly agrees to go out with him. We learn that she is engaged to an older man, Henri Baurel (Georges Guetary), a French entertainer to whom she feels she must remain loyal, although she is attracted to Jerry. Lise's ambivalent attitude explains why she sometimes rebuffs and sometimes encourages Jerry. The situation is further complicated by an American heiress, Milo Roberts (Nina Foch), who tries to win Jerry's heart by buying his paintings and sponsoring him in the Paris art world.

Jerry's best friend, Adam Cook (Oscar Levant), an aspiring American concert pianist and sardonic wit, is the means by which we are first introduced to Lise. Adam is discussing Lise with his friend, Henri Baurel. As Henri tries to explain to Adam what Lise is really like, we see different aspects of Lise's personality—studious, fun-loving, sensuous—flashed on the screen. Each section is danced to "Embraceable You" and uses a striking color scheme—for example, a bright yellow dress in a completely green room. At the end the screen splits into five parts to show all five vignettes at once.

During the course of Jerry and Lise's romance, we see Jerry's exuberant and happy moments in two numbers. In "Tra-la-la" he bounds up the stairs to Adam's garret and ends up dancing on top of his piano. In " 'S Wonderful" he sings about the joys of being in love. Ironically, the song is a duet with Henri Baurel; at the time they do not suspect that they are in love with the same girl.

The best demonstration, however, of Jerry and Lise's feelings is the dance they do to "Our Love Is Here to Stay" on a quay by the Seine. It is a tender and lyrical expression of their repressed emotions in a lovely setting. In both its tentative beginning, in which Lise must be persuaded into the dance, and its building to a climax of shared emotion, it is reminiscent of the "Night and Day" number in *The Gay Divorcee* (1934). The number ends with the couple walking into the smoky-blue mist, but the moment the music stops, Lise suddenly runs away without explaining why.

Finally, Lise realizes that she must tell Jerry the truth—she is going to marry Henri. Depressed by the news, Jerry takes Milo, his wealthy patroness, to a gala ball sponsored by the art students. Lise and Henri are also there; during the evening Jerry manages to see Lise alone on a balcony overlooking Paris for a final good-bye. Afterwards Jerry's emotions are chaotic; almost absent-mindedly he draws a black and white sketch of the Place de la Concorde then tears it in half. The two pieces drift to the floor where they mingle with confetti and a red rose dropped by Lise.

The ballet begins with the two pieces of the sketch uniting and becoming the background for the opening sequence. Color is important in this transition: the costumes and set for the Ball are all in black and white, as is the sketch, providing a dramatic contrast with the color to come. The rose, which is seen with the torn sketch, provides the first note of color and leads us artistically into the ballet.

There is great stylistic variety in the ballet. The scenery, decor, and costumes for each section are done in the style of famous painters—Van Gogh, Rousseau, Renoir, Utrillo, Dufy, and Toulouse-Lautrec. The dancing and choreography range from modern dance and tap dance to ballet.

The ballet's story is that of the ups and downs of the romance of Lise and Jerry. As the painter pursues his love, the settings change from a flower market in the style of Renoir to a street scene inspired by Utrillo. This quiet, lyrical mood is followed by a spirited George M. Cohan-style strut in a Rousseau setting. In the next section the mood changes again to one of longing and passion as Jerry and Lise dance around a fountain in the Place de la Concorde. In a jazz-inspired section Jerry is a famous Toulouse-Lautrec character, "Chocolat." Then the scene returns to the fountain, the music becomes frenzied, there is a final burst of color and movement, and everyone suddenly vanishes. Jerry returns to reality and finds himself alone with his rose. But Henri, who has overheard the lovers' good-byes, releases Lise from her engagement, and Jerry and Lise have an ecstatic reunion for the traditional happy ending.

The ballet is intended to dazzle and overwhelm us with its lights, movement, color, and variety of styles of costumes and decorations. There are several breathtaking crane shots (shots made by a camera mounted on a crane so it can move and rise above the action), colored lights and colored steam, and costumes and sets which are surrealistic and impressionistic—all trademarks of director Vincente Minnelli. There is so much to see and hear that the viewer cannot assimilate it all in one viewing. The ballet is an ambitious, carefully crafted piece of work and is truly the high point of the film.

Ballets are rare in Hollywood musicals, and one of this length had not been attempted before. The artistic and commercial success of the British film *The Red Shoes* (1948), which featured a long ballet, helped to convince the studio to support the idea of a long one in *An American in Paris*. Minnelli had also done shorter ballets in *Yolanda and the Thief* (1945) and *Ziegfeld Follies* (1946). These gave him the inspiration and confidence to try something longer and more ambitious.

In addition to the ballet there are several noteworthy musical sequences. In the film's opening scene we see Jerry in his tiny Montmartre garret using mechanical contrivances to save space. His movements, as he tugs a rope to raise the bed out of the way and lets down a shelf to make a table, are as carefully choreographed as a musical number. The scene is reminiscent of a famous sequence in Buster Keaton's *The Navigator* (1924).

Two of the musical numbers feature the talents of supporting actors Oscar Levant and Georges Guetary. Levant was chosen for the role of Adam Cook because Minnelli considered him the definitive interpreter of George Gershwin. In a dream sequence he imagines himself as conductor and soloist of the orchestra as well as playing nearly every instrument in Gershwin's "Concerto in F." A popular French entertainer of the time, Guetary—in the role of Henri Baurel—performs "I'll Build a Stairway to Paradise" on a lighted staircase with statuesque showgirls holding aloft elaborate candelabra.

Another supporting role is Nina Foch as Milo Roberts, Jerry's rich patroness. She is appropriately sophisticated as the American heiress who hopes to find a way to Jerry's heart by buying his paintings, and her performance is as smooth and sleek as her appearance.

It is the performance of Gene Kelly, however, that is crucial to the success of the film; he is its star and principal singer and dancer, as well as its choreographer, and his performance is impressive. In fact, it is obvious that the part of Jerry was written for him since the exuberant vitality of his acting and dancing style is perfect for the role of the brash, optimistic American in Paris. So impressive was his contribution that the Motion Picture Academy awarded him a special Oscar that year, because of his performance as an actor, singer, dancer, and choreographer.

Leslie Caron as Lise is the fresh young French girl with whom Jerry is in love. In her screen debut, Caron's youthful, charming screen presence and delightful dancing overshadow her inexperience as an actress. Indeed, she is one of the film's chief delights.

Some critics consider *An American in Paris* director Vincente Minnelli's greatest achievement in the handling of color, design, and movement. It is perhaps the film's attempt to lift the musical to a higher plane of art and its bold conception that helped to earn it the Academy Award for Best Picture. In addition, it also won Academy Awards for Best Screenplay (original), Best Cinematography (color), and Best Costume Design.

Julia Johnson

THE AMERICANIZATION OF EMILY

Released: 1964
Production: Martin Ransohoff for Metro-Goldwyn-Mayer
Direction: Arthur Hiller
Screenplay: Paddy Chayefsky; based on the novel of the same name by William Bradford Huie
Cinematography: Philip H. Lathrop
Editing: Tom McAdoo
Running time: 117 minutes

Principal characters:
Lieutenant Charles E. Madison .... James Garner
Emily Barham .... Julie Andrews
Admiral William Jessep .... Melvyn Douglas
Lieutenant Commander
"Bus" Cummings .... James Coburn
Mrs. Barham .... Joyce Grenfell

The Americanization of Emily occupies an important niche in the history of the Hollywood war movie primarily because it runs counter to the prevailing philosophy of the genre. It is not just an atypical war movie, it is an antithetical one. Its premise is the glorification of cowardice, and its theme is one of survival, not of victory. These assertions form the basis for the film's attack upon the fundamental absurdity of war as well as upon the irrationality it instills in the men who conduct it.

Screenwriter Paddy Chayefsky has constructed a black comedy employing the common device of the wartime love story as a vehicle for a satire that questions the glorification of war and debunks the idea that the giving of one's life for one's country is necessarily a virtue. These dark insights into human behavior in time of conflict are provided through a plot structure that alternates comedy, satire, and serious drama within the context of a number of improbable or at least unusual situations. The movie is concerned only in a comparatively minor way with the "Americanization" of Emily. The heroine, as portrayed by Julie Andrews in the strongest performance of her career, does eventually become Americanized. In the beginning she views the cowardice of Charlie Madison (James Garner) as a virtue; in the end, however, in the American tradition, Emily wants her man with her even if it means that he must play the hero.

The major concern of the film, though, is the exposition of the follies of war as embodied in the preposterous misadventures of antihero Charlie Madison. He is a direct-commission naval lieutenant commander whose prewar occupation of assistant hotel manager involved the procurement of goods and services. This experience gains him a position as "dog-robber," that is, caterer, valet, social director, and general wheel-greaser for a deskbound admiral, William Jessep (Melvyn Douglas). He has special access to normally unobtainable supplies, privileges, and comforts. He also has access to a nonconformist philosophy. "As long as valor remains a virtue," says the unheroic protagonist, "we shall have soldiers. So I preach cowardice. Cowards run like rabbits at the first shot. If everybody did, we would never get to the second shot. I'm a coward, and I say that cowardice will save the world!" Heroism, according to Madison, is thus immoral because it supports and encourages war.

While Britons queue up for rations, Madison is a fat cat who, in the weeks before D-day, inhabits an Eden teeming with bourbon, sirloin, and gorgeous girls who will do almost anything for a Hershey bar or perhaps a designer gown. When Emily, a WAAF car driver, refuses to play the game, Madison terms her a "prig." But she explains that she has lost a husband, brother, and father in this war and is repulsed by the high-living, gift-dispensing Americans. Madison's reply is that Europe was a brothel long before the Yanks arrived. He woos her with his charm while his philosophy of cowardice takes advantage of her bitterness, and she gradually succumbs. "I'm glad you are yellow," she asserts. "It is your most important asset, being a coward. Every man I ever loved was a hero and all he got was death."

Even as Madison is winning Emily, however, he is losing in his efforts to avoid the war. The Admiral is more concerned about congressional hearings than he is about the Germans. "They're tryin' to scrap the Navy!" he bellows. Then one night in a manic tirade he concludes that "the first dead man on Omaha Beach must be a sailor! We'll build him a monument—the Tomb of the Unknown Sailor." Such lunacy shocks even Madison, who is further outraged when the Admiral places him in charge of the motion picture crew scheduled to film the landing and the death. When the Admiral goes insane, the Navy brass, led by Madison's buddy, Bus, the promiscuous commander played by James Coburn, decide they want the movie made anyway. The cowardly Madison, anxious to prove his philosophy to an increasingly Americanized Emily who attempts to convince him to alter his beliefs, winds up in a much different role.

Despite his best efforts, Madison, in a comic scene on D-day, is forced onto Omaha Beach at the point of his buddy's gun and winds up accidentally at the head of the assault force. It appears that the first dead man on Omaha Beach is Madison himself, and the next day finds his picture on the front page of every newspaper in the United States; he is a hero. But a week later, his "corpse" turns up alive. "Omigawd!" shouts Bus, the officer in charge of public relations. "Instead of a dead hero we've got a live coward!" This state of affairs presents screenwriter Chayefsky with some obvious satiric opportunities. He puts together some shrewd pacifist repartee in a number of biting scenes including one in which a Naval officer proudly states, "He was the first dead man on Omaha Beach!" A civilian innocently inquires, "Was there a contest?"

Ironically, in the end, Madison, in the best American tradition, accepts the erroneous mantle of a wounded hero and agrees to return to the United States to take part in a victory bond drive. Through his love for Emily, he embraces her realization that "We shall never get rid of war by pretending it's unreal. It's the virtue of war that's a fraud. Not war itself. It's the valor and the self-sacrifice and the goodness of war that need the exposing." Where she previously found Madison's cowardice a virtue, Emily now finds it a failing if it means that he will go to prison for telling the truth about his experience on Omaha Beach. Madison agrees to let "God worry about the truth" and to accept the fact of his love for Emily. In abruptly changing the characters' values to achieve this traditional heroic ending, the movie may have opened itself to the charge of stopping short or taking the easy way out. If the ending actually did weaken the film's message, however, it did so with such rapidity that the average viewer is not completely aware of it and is still left with an overall feeling that the film is pacifist in tone.

Emily's final speech concerning the fraudulent virtue of war reflects the guiding philosophy of the film's director, Arthur Hiller, who constructed the film as "a wild satiric, cynical comedy" because that type of structure was the ideal way to comment on the lunacy of the attributes we attach to war. Virtue and nobility are realistically ill-suited to the context of war. "Satiric laughter is the only logical response," he believes. Yet the quest for satiric laughter is not entirely successful since Hiller and writer Chayefsky occasionally dissipate the force of the satire through a concern for commercial success. The result is that some of the episodes are obviously directed at the audience and loom dangerously close to farce with James Garner becoming reminiscent of a stand-up comedian.

For the most part, *The Americanization of Emily* is a well-constructed film which, even at its most outrageous, is grounded in reality. Melvyn Douglas, for example, based his excellent performance as the film's eccentric Admiral upon his own military experience. He had encountered at firsthand, in his tours of duty in two World Wars, some of the excesses that were exploited in the film, and had seen living counterparts of the Charlie Madison character. James Garner plays a more sophisticated version of the character he has perfected since his days as television's Bret Maverick; this picture provides the perfect vehicle for the Garner character. Charlie Madison is a lovable scoundrel whose philosophical statements concerning the wisdom of cowardice and the spuriousness of wartime postures of nobility are delivered naturally and believably by an actor who has been delivering similar statements throughout most of his career. James Coburn gives a smooth farcical performance as the naval officer who takes charge of the film project when the Admiral goes mad; and Keenan Wynn has a brief drunk scene that is superb.

It is Julie Andrews' performance as Emily, however, which makes the film memorable. She not only provides a counterpoint to Madison, but, in contrast to the typical war movie heroine, she spices up scenes between battles. She is a major figure whose role is not subordinate to Garner's. Her portrayal makes a strong woman of Emily, who upon occasion dominates her man, ultimately convincing him to change his most dearly held tenets on her behalf. Charlie Madison emerges from Omaha Beach with a wholly unjustified reputation as a hero since the one naval officer who witnessed his cowardice is whitewashing it with a coat of public relations-oriented nobility. Charlie cannot puncture the myth without making the kind of senseless noble gesture he enjoyed denouncing in others. Emily, Americanized enough to want her man at home rather than in prison, in turn Americanizes Madison, who remains the hero.

The film when first released in 1964 suffered a mixed critical reception and stirred controversy among those who felt it ridiculed patriotism; it was not until the rise of antiwar sentiment in the late 1960's and early 1970's that it found its niche. It is now a cult film enjoying wide popularity with new audiences. It has come to be recognized by a newer generation as not an attack on patriotism or upon the military but more universally as an attack on the facile counterfeits of patriotism—the sloganeering and the false heroics. Although the film tends to reject public and social obligations for more personal and private ones, it makes an intelligent and timeless statement against the excesses of war and succeeds admirably as thought provoking entertainment as well.

Stephen L. Hanson

AND THEN THERE WERE NONE

Released: 1945
Production: René Clair for Twentieth Century-Fox
Direction: René Clair
Screenplay: Dudley Nichols; based on the book and the play *Ten Little Indians*
   by Agatha Christie
Cinematography: Lucien Andriot
Editing: Harvey Manger
Running time: 97 minutes

> *Principal characters:*
> Judge Quincannon .... Barry Fitzgerald
> Dr. Armstrong .... Walter Huston
> Philip Lombard .... Louis Hayward
> Vera Claythorne .... June Duprez
> Emily Brent .... Judith Anderson
> Detective Blore .... Roland Young
> General Sir John Mandrake .... C. Aubrey Smith
> Rogers, the butler .... Richard Haydn
> Mrs. Rogers .... Queenie Leonard
> Prince Nikki Starloff .... Mischa Auer
> Boatman .... Harry Thurston

And Then There Were None was the last of seven English-language films
that René Clair directed in the decade 1935-1945, during his exile to England
and to Hollywood. He had already earned international fame in his native
France for a series of deft, witty fantasies, gently mocking and ultimately
optimistic—works such as *Sous les Toits de Paris* (1929), *Le Million* (1931),
and *À Nous la Liberté* (1931) which had a clear enough influence on Chaplin's
Modern Times (1936), that Clair's producers sued Chaplin for plagiarism.
Clair's British and American films, however, show notably less social consciousness than those he had done in France, and are given over almost
entirely to farce and whimsy. Some have titles that unmistakably identify
their contents: *The Ghost Goes West* (1935), *I Married a Witch* (1942), and
It Happened Tomorrow (1944). *And Then There Were None* remains the most
successful of his films in English, a comedy-mystery with a generally superior
cast and an entertaining plot taken from Agatha Christie's story.

Christie's story was a magazine serial that she turned first into a novel, *Ten
Little Indians* (originally released in Great Britain as *Ten Little Niggers*), and
then into a play of the same title, produced in 1943. It involves a fanatical
scheme for retribution and belated, informal justice by one man against a
group of guilty people—an inversion of the situation in her *Murder on the
Orient Express*, in which a group in concert kills a guilty individual. The story

begins on Friday afternoon as ten people arrive to spend the weekend on Indian Island off the Cornish coast, an island thus named because it has the shape of an Indian's head. Eight are invited guests, the other two are the butler and his wife, the cook. No one knows or has ever met the host, a Mr. U. N. Owen, who remains "unknown" until the end.

That night at dinner the host, instead of appearing, makes a startling list of accusations by way of a phonograph record: all present, including the two domestics, are murderers who will now pay the maximum penalty for their crimes, even though they are beyond society's justice because those crimes cannot be proved by legal evidence. After the first death, one of the figures in a china centerpiece depicting ten little Indian boys is broken. The murders thus proceed according to the nursery rhyme, "Ten Little Indian Boys," beginning "Ten little Indian boys going out to dine,/ One choked his little self, and then there were nine." The first victim, Prince Nikki Starloff (Mischa Auer), dies gagging after being poisoned. With each death another figure is found broken. By Monday morning, when the boatman (Harry Thurston) returns, only Philip Lombard (Louis Hayward) and Vera Claythorne (June Duprez) remain alive. They have thwarted the plan of the murderer, Judge Quincannon (Barry Fitzgerald), who, pretending earlier to have been the sixth victim, poisons himself after he explains to Vera how he had planned for things to end. Since she would be left alone with nine corpses for which she had no credible explanation, she would simply commit suicide to make things easier for herself, for the blame for the murders would surely be hers: "One little Indian boy left all alone,/ He went and hanged himself . . . and then there were none."

The people assembled by Judge Quincannon form an anthology of social classes. He brings together a doctor (Walter Huston); a retired general (C. Aubrey Smith); a private detective, Blore (Roland Young); a spinster, Miss Brent (Judith Anderson); a professional house guest, Prince Nikki; and a butler and cook, Rogers and his wife (Richard Haydn and Queenie Leonard). Lombard and Vera are, as it happens, impersonating two invited guests, Lombard a friend, a soldier of fortune, Vera her own sister. In her novel Agatha Christie aptly likens the old boatman who brings this group to Indian Island to the aged Charon, boatman of the other world in classical mythology, ferrying his passengers across the River Styx. The ill-matched assortment will soon be equalized before the bar of justice, receiving the condemnation and punishment already decreed by Hades, Judge Quincannon, who numbers among them on their journey into the dark. Some have committed crimes predictable enough, as in the case of Dr. Armstrong and Prince Nikki, both drunks: the doctor killed one of his patients, Nikki two pedestrians. The judge accuses himself of having sent an innocent man to the gallows. The Rogerses murdered a former employer for his money. The crimes of the others are simply understandable, not necessarily obvious. General Mandrake sent his wife's lover on a dangerous mission from which he never returned. Emily Brent sent a nephew to reform school and consequently to his death, while Blore gave false evidence that caused a guiltless man to die in prison. The judge and Miss Brent display a mysterious iciness that makes them appear sufficiently capable of murder, but the others seem merely to be petty enough, or careless enough.

The action involves two important collusions, the first between the judge and Dr. Armstrong, narrated by the judge in a flashback at the end, the second between Vera and Lombard. By Sunday evening the judge has disposed of five of his victims: Prince Nikki with poison, Mrs. Rogers with a drug overdose, the general with a knife, Rogers with an ax, and Miss Brent with a poisoned hypodermic. He and Dr. Armstrong agree, in an excellently staged scene at the billiard table, that he, with Armstrong's connivance, should pretend to be shot, presumably to give the two of them an advantage in catching the murderer. The judge's "death" is crucial to the success of his plan, but the agreement that Vera and Lombard make at the end deprives him of his triumph. They have fallen in love, something he could not have foreseen, and thus have come to trust each other. After finding Blore crushed by a stone ornament from the roof and Dr. Armstrong drowned on the beach, they decide that neither is the murderer, even though apparently no one else remains alive. Vera pretends to shoot Lombard so that the actual murderer will show himself. Back at the house, the judge, having provided Vera with a noose, admits all to her before he swallows poison (he will soon die anyway); Lombard, however, makes known he has witnessed the judge's confession. The judge dies disappointed, mumbling "Never trust a woman."

The cast comprises an abundance of talent that Clair does not always use to advantage. The normally dependable Auer is at his worst, overacting up through his death scene. Judith Anderson merely sits about and sneers; and neither Duprez nor Hayward, ever gallant and inoffensive, has much to do except be pleasant. Huston, his considerable abilities notwithstanding, is so homespun American that he seems like a visiting chiropractor from Milwaukee. But Young and Smith are expert as usual. Smith's dignified, senile ex-general approaches authentic pathos, as he talks absently to his dead wife, asking her why she loved another man, and grimly repeats that he will never leave Indian Island alive. Fitzgerald had the year before won an Academy Award for his supporting role as the cantankerous but lovable Father Fitzgibbon in *Going My Way* (1944); yet here he skillfully plays a straight dramatic part without his "Oirish" brogue as a prop. Nonetheless, the top honors go to Haydn, a comparatively unknown actor at that time, whose stiff, adenoidal butler steals the picture singlehandedly. Of particular note is his drunk scene: after two of the others vote him the most likely suspect to have killed the three victims to date—no one else receives more than one vote—he races around the room and gulps down every cocktail in sight, then downs what remains in the pitcher, thus to prove that he has not poisoned the drinks. Hurt and drunk, he elects to spend the night in the woodshed, safe from his accusers—but not safe, alas, from the killer's ax.

Clair plays Nichols' script for comedy and mystery rather than for the fearful or the bizarre. Although he kills off eight people in a little more than an hour and a half, he maintains a lightness throughout and, generally, an adequate level of suspense. The opening sequence shows Clair's direction at its most sophisticated and sets a standard that he frequently meets during the rest of the film. Here Nichols' script calls for no dialogue at all. Clair frames each character in the boat while it tosses on the rough waters, lingering on Miss Brent as she evinces a scowling disgust for the smoke from Blore's pipe, then on Prince Nikki, obviously with a hangover, as he gets sick over the side after he sees the boatman gulping down a huge sandwich. At times Clair tries too hard to evoke atmosphere; and his attempt to play up suspense at the end becomes frankly precious when Vera walks up from the beach alone, while only the hands and torso of the judge are visible as he shoots billiards under the noose he has tied, waiting. Yet Clair quietly avoids the gruesome, showing only two deaths on camera, both by poison and both essential to the development of the plot. Some of the most effective scenes involve the discovery of a body: Rogers' feet sticking up near the wood pile, for instance, or the limp hand of Miss Brent over the arm of her chair as a cat unrolls her ball of yarn and a bee fights at the window pane ("A bumblebee stung one, and then there were five").

Clair holds his characters somewhat coldly at a distance. Vera and Lombard, however weak their roles may be, qualify as the only sympathetic ones. They are at least a generation younger than the others, they fall in love, and, of course, neither is actually the person condemned by the voice on the phonograph record. The real Lombard, recently dead, had through irresponsibility caused the death of some native bearers on a safari he was leading, while Vera's deranged sister had killed Vera's fiancé. By taking the places of Lombard and the sister the surrogates become even more admirable as defenders of the guilty; and the film's conclusion, long since predictable, enables Clair to confine the judge's actions within a positive context. Although the judge's private search for justice is demented, it rids society of seven murderers, plus the judge himself, all of them beyond the processes of the law. None of this dull, foolish little group seems unworthy of that fate. The question of who will die next, and how, quickly becomes more interesting than any of the victims themselves.

William H. Brown, Jr.

ANGELS WITH DIRTY FACES

Released: 1938
Production: Sam Bischoff for Warner Bros.
Direction: Michael Curtiz
Screenplay: John Wexley and Warren Duff; based on a screen story by Rowland Brown
Cinematography: Sol Polito
Editing: Owen Marks
Running time: 97 minutes

> *Principal characters:*
> Rocky Sullivan .... James Cagney
> Jerry Connolly .... Pat O'Brien
> James Frazier .... Humphrey Bogart
> Laury Ferguson .... Ann Sheridan
> Mac Keefer .... George Bancroft
> Soapy .... Billy Halop
> Bim .... Leo Gorcey
> Crab .... Huntz Hall
> Pasty .... Gabriel Dell
> Swing .... Bobby Jordan
> Husky .... Bernard Punsley

The fast-paced crime melodramas of Warner Bros. in the 1930's have won a special affection among movie buffs, and no film of that noble breed enjoys a better reputation than *Angels with Dirty Faces*, released in 1938. The film is a marvelous *mélange* of those facets and personalities characteristic of the Warners' output. James Cagney brings to his role all the unique mannerisms that delight impressionists; Pat O'Brien plays the tough, forceful priest; Humphrey Bogart is a snarling gangster lawyer; "Oomph Girl" Ann Sheridan plays Cagney's tough girl friend; and the "Dead End Kids" appear as slum punks. All the familiar elements are welded together by director Michael Curtiz in one of the most fondly remembered and most frequently revived movies of the 1930's.

Angels with Dirty Faces weathered an unusual production history. The story was originally the property of Hollywood's Grand National Studios, a minor lot where Cagney was working under a star contract he had signed in 1936 after suing Warner Bros. for his release (that studio had starred him in five releases of 1935 rather than the four outlined in his contract). Cagney's new studio starred him in *Great Guy* (1936) and *Something to Sing About* (1937) and was preparing to star him in *Angels with Dirty Faces* when the star suddenly opted to return to Warners' (at the promise of $150,000 per film against ten perent of the gross). Left with a property and nobody to star in it, Grand National released the rights to the film, which were quickly picked up by the victorious Warners'; Grand National went out of business within a year.

Angels with Dirty Faces tells the saga of slum kids Rocky Sullivan and Jerry Connolly, who are caught by the police in the act of stealing fountain pens from a freight car. Jerry escapes, but Rocky is caught and sent to reform school. As adults, Rocky (James Cagney) embraces a life of crime, while Jerry (Pat O'Brien) becomes a priest assigned to his old home parish. The stars, close friends offscreen, had already played together in the Warners' features *Here Comes the Navy* (1934), *Devil Dogs of the Air* (1935), *The Irish in Us* (1935), *Ceiling Zero* (1935), and *Boy Meets Girl* (1938), and had perfected a stimulating rapport that peaked in *Angels with Dirty Faces*. As the pugnacious Rocky, Cagney was never more charismatic, tapping his memories of the East Side kids he grew up with to develop the now-celebrated mannerisms of hitching his pants, twitching his neck and shoulders, jabbing his finger to make a point, and cracking "What do you hear? What do you say?" O'Brien's more subtle performance is forceful and free of specious piety. Indeed, one of the most enjoyable scenes in the film comes when O'Brien, razzed by a pool hall flunky, punches him in the mouth.

Father Jerry is delighted when Rocky begins a romance with childhood friend and parishioner Laury Ferguson (Ann Sheridan). Sheridan works splendidly with both leading men and brings a power to her part as a token love interest which never interferes with the tautness of the story. But the priest is less delighted when Rocky returns to crime, joining forces with gang boss Mac Keefer (George Bancroft) and crooked lawyer James Frazier (Humphrey Bogart). Rocky's criminal exploits soon make the headlines and fascinate the Dead End Kids (so named for their appearance in United Artists' *Dead End* of 1937). Soon regarding Rocky with almost fanatical hero worship, they begin to avoid the athletic programs that Father Jerry has formed for them and to emulate Rocky's criminal ways. As a result, Father Jerry courageously unleashes a media campaign against the community's professional hoodlums, vowing to bring them to justice, even if it means the condemnation of his friend Rocky.

The priest's campaign creates enormous controversy, and soon causes Keefer to squirm. He and Frazier decide to murder Father Jerry, but Rocky finds out and kills them both (the first of three times in cinema history that Bogart dies a screen death at the hands of Cagney). A wild police chase through an abandoned building follows, and Rocky is finally apprehended after holding off police with his empty revolver. "It's empty!" marvels a cop as he looks at the gun. "Empty as your thick skull, copper!" snarls Cagney.

Sentenced to the electric chair, Rocky is soon filling the headlines with his promises to spit in the eye of his executioners, and the slum kids are enthralled by his bravado. However, shortly before the hour of death, Father Jerry visits Rocky in his cell. The priest asks Rocky to "straighten yourself out with God" by showing a special kind of courage; he wants Rocky to pretend to be "yellow" as he goes to the electric chair. "They gotta despise your memory" says the priest of the gang which so reveres the hoodlum. Rocky refuses, and one of the most unforgettable episodes of 1930's cinema follows, tautly directed by Curtiz, beautifully played by Cagney and O'Brien as the men march the last mile to the chair. "Please!" whispers O'Brien to the doomed man as the grisly parade passes the staring prisoners on death row. "No!" barks Cagney, his eyes glaring cocky hatred as the camera examines his face, challenging the audience to perceive what is happening in his mind. Finally, Cagney passes into the chamber, and suddenly the heartrending screams of pathetic cowardice are heard, "Help me! I don't wanna die!" Out of respect for Cagney's Rocky, Curtiz never fully reveals this climactic cowardice; we see only shadows, fists clenching a radiator as the police try to drag him to the chair, and the grateful love that fills O'Brien's face. Some critics have conjectured that Rocky was probably not faking cowardice at the end, but finally allowing his true nature to show. Cagney himself later claimed that he intentionally played this famous scene so that Rocky's true motives were never fully revealed, allowing the audience to decide the actual cause of his actions.

Father Jerry returns to the gang members, who have read the headlines about Rocky's "turning yellow." They ask the priest if it is true; he replies, with obvious difficulty, that it is. Then, remembering the boyhood crime that separated Rocky and him, and made its mark on their futures, he says, "Okay, boys. Let's go say a prayer for a boy who couldn't run as fast as I could." The gang sadly and mutely follows.

Released in November of 1938, *Angels with Dirty Faces* was a critical and popular triumph. It joined Warners' *Dodge City* and *Juarez* as Hollywood's top moneymakers of the 1938-1939 season, and was a special triumph for Cagney, who won the New York Film Critics Award and his first Academy Award nomination for Best Actor (he lost to Spencer Tracy for *Boys Town*). It even spawned a "B" sequel, *Angels Wash Their Faces* (1939), starring Ann Sheridan, the Dead End Kids, and Ronald Reagan. While that film is long forgotten, *Angels with Dirty Faces* is vividly remembered and survives as a slick example of Warner Bros.' flair in its prime, as a classic credit of James Cagney's, and as an exciting, moving, and dynamic motion picture.

Gregory William Mank

ANIMAL CRACKERS

Released: 1930
Production: Paramount
Direction: Victor Heerman
Screenplay: Morrie Ryskind; based on the musical play and book of the same
name by Morrie Ryskind, George S. Kaufman, Bert Kalmar, and Harry
Ruby
Cinematography: George J. Folsey
Editing: no listing
Running time: 98 minutes

Principal characters:
Captain Jeffrey Spaulding .... Groucho Marx
The Professor .... Harpo Marx
Signor Emanuel Ravelli .... Chico Marx
Horatio Jamison .... Zeppo Marx
Mrs. Rittenhouse .... Margaret Dumont
Arabella Rittenhouse .... Lillian Roth
John Parker .... Hal Thompson
Roscoe Chandler .... Louis Sorin

No Marx Brothers film is very interesting until at least one of the brothers
appears on film, but *Animal Crackers* manages at least to be efficient in its
preparation for their entrance. In the first few minutes of the film, the audience learns the three essentials of the plot which all too often intrudes on
the comic madness to follow: Mrs. Rittenhouse (Margaret Dumont) is holding
a party at her mansion; she plans to unveil a famous oil painting, "The Hunt";
and her daughter, Arabella (Lillian Roth), is in love with John Parker (Hal
Thompson), a struggling young artist. Only the first of these seems to hold
much promise since the party is also in honor of the return of one "Captain
Spaulding, the African explorer" (Groucho Marx). The party guests partic-
ipate in a production number in which they sing the praises of the fearless
Captain, who arrives right on cue on a litter carried by natives. His first act
is to haggle over the fare with his African bearers ("What? Africa to here,
a dollar eighty-five?"); only moments later he has managed to insult both
Mrs. Rittenhouse and her home. At this point and with cheerful contempt
for the elaborate welcome, he launches into song—"Hello, I must be going.
I cannot stay, I came to say, I must be going"—and attempts to depart.
Animal Crackers, a model of plot exposition until Groucho's entrance, will
never be quite the same.

The insanity is soon accelerated by the arrival of Signor Emanuel Ravelli
(Chico Marx), one of the musicians hired for the party. He explains to
Groucho that even though he could not come tomorrow because that would

be too soon, he will only charge for not playing yesterday because his rates for not rehearsing are even higher. Harpo (announced as "The Professor," although professor of what is never made clear) arrives next, neatly attired in top hat and cape, which he hands to the butler to reveal himself clad only in an undershirt and shorts. He begins by blowing solid puffs of light smoke, turning them dark when Groucho asks "Does he have chocolate?", continues by pulling a gun and taking potshots at whatever strikes his fancy, and concludes for the moment by exiting in hot pursuit of a passing blonde.

With the Marx Brothers all present and accounted for (Zeppo was actually the first to arrive, but typically served only as a harbinger of Groucho by singing a few bars of a song to the guests), the comedy proceeds in spite of the intrusive plot. The Marx Brothers can neither ignore the plot nor use it to their advantage; they are simply stuck with it. Sometimes they are forced to deliver dull expository dialogue to further the story line, which they do with an almost subversive lack of conviction.

In addition to the silliness of the plot, *Animal Crackers* has other problems. It followed close on the heels of the first Marx Brothers film, *The Cocoanuts* (1929); and similar to it, *Animal Crackers* was adapted from one of their stage successes. In fact, the brothers were appearing on Broadway in *Animal Crackers* during the filming of *The Cocoanuts* at Paramount's studios in Astoria, Long Island. Similar to many film versions of stage productions during the early days of sound motion pictures, *Animal Crackers* is static and visually unexciting, and today seems something of an antique, although most of the comedy is verbal and is not excessively hampered by the technical crudity of the film. Despite the cumbersome plot and technical deficiencies, however, *Animal Crackers* is something of a triumph for the Marx Brothers. As the structure of the film gets more and more disorganized and the plot less and less interesting, the Marx Brothers get funnier and funnier; left to themselves, they are magnificent.

Groucho and Chico, as usual, engage in several memorable verbal battles. At one point, following the discovery of a theft, Chico suggests searching the house next door. When Groucho innocently inquires what to do if there is not a house next door, Chico replies that of course they will have to build one; there ensues an extended discussion on the design of this dwelling, followed by Chico's final deduction that the missing painting in the plot has been eaten by left-handed moths.

Groucho contributes several brilliant scenes of his own, usually running verbal rings around one of the other characters. In one scene, he combines a simultaneous proposal of marriage to both Mrs. Rittenhouse and another woman by means of a bizarre (if now somewhat dated) parody of Eugene O'Neill's *Strange Interlude*, in which he speaks in "interior monologues" directly to the audience ("How happy I could be with either of these two, if both of them just went away!"). Groucho also offers a discourse on how "the eight-cent nickel" could solve the country's economic woes, regales the guests with a hilarious blow-by-blow account of his African expedition, and dictates a letter to his lawyers, taken down by his secretary Zeppo, which deliciously lampoons legal terminology.

Harpo and Chico also contribute their specialties: a harp solo and piano solo respectively. Chico's turn at the piano is given an unusual twist when he continues playing the same notes over and over again, like a broken record. ("I can't think of the end," he says. "Funny," replies Groucho, "I can't think of anything else.") Harpo runs riot, chasing the women and continually producing the most unlikely objects from within the confines of his coat. Harpo's stage gimmicks often border on the surreal, as when an impossible amount of silverware tumbles from the sleeve of his coat as a detective shakes his hand. Harpo and Chico also team up with two ladies for a chaotic game of cards during which Harpo cheats in every way imaginable.

It is virtually impossible to catalogue the truly funny scenes in *Animal Crackers*. Even if the effect of their antics is somewhat diluted by the uninspired production, there are so many brilliant comedy passages that the Marx Brothers definitely dominate the film. It helps that much of the humor is verbal rather than visual, and credit for this must go to Morrie Ryskind, who wrote the screenplay and who had collaborated with George S. Kaufman on the book of the original musical play. Ryskind had also adapted *The Cocoanuts* for the screen, and would team again with Kaufman five years later on the screenplay of *A Night at the Opera* (1935), considered by many the Marx Brothers' finest film.

Animal Crackers was the second of the Marx Brothers' films for Paramount, the last to be taken from one of their stage successes, and the last to be filmed on the East Coast. The following year, they abandoned the theater stage for motion pictures, and Broadway for Hollywood.

Howard H. Prouty

ANNA AND THE KING OF SIAM

Released: 1946
Production: Louis D. Lighton for Twentieth Century-Fox
Direction: John Cromwell
Screenplay: Talbot Jennings and Sally Benson; based on the biography of the
  same name by Margaret Landon
Cinematography: Arthur Miller (AA)
Editing: Harmon Jones
Art direction: Lyle Wheeler and William Darling (AA)
Interior decoration: Thomas Little and Frank E. Hughes (AA)
Music: Bernard Herrmann
Running time: 128 minutes

Principal characters:
Anna Owens .... Irene Dunne
King Mongkut of Siam .... Rex Harrison
Tuptim .... Linda Darnell
Kralahome .... Lee J. Cobb
Lady Thiang .... Gale Sondergaard
Louis .... Richard Lyon
Prince (younger) .... Mickey Roth
Prince (older) .... Tito Renaldo

When Margaret Landon wrote her best-selling biography *Anna and the King of Siam*, Twentieth Century-Fox purchased film rights from galley proofs. The story, which was only slightly fictionized, had all the ingredients for a beautiful big period romance, and the studio spared nothing in its lavish production, creating anew the fantastic city of Bangkok as it had been in the second half of the nineteenth century, building sixty-seven exteriors and thirty-four ornate interiors as sets.

During the first half of the 1940's, Hollywood had not gone in for expensive escapist spectacles; but with the end of World War II, even the Orient could be looked upon once again as a mysterious land of romance. The stark realism of the recent Pacific conflict was something most Americans especially wanted to forget, and Twentieth Century-Fox opened the door again to the East as a land of mystery. They had only to turn time back to 1862, when very little was known about Siam in the West, and in *Anna and the King of Siam* they had the setting for as exotic a romance as was ever played out in real life.

The story of the film tells of a young English widow who arrives in Bangkok in 1862 with her small son. She has been engaged by the progressive-minded King Mongkut of Siam (Rex Harrison) to teach his many wives and all the many children he has fathered by them. Her real name is Anna Leonowens, but for simplicity's sake in the screenplay she becomes Anna Owens (Irene

Dunne). The King recognizes that only those who are educated are truly free, and he insists that every member of his royal house should at least know how to read and write in both his native language *and* English, for he wants them to be acquainted with the outside world as it is. King Mongkut is a curious combination of traits: he thinks and acts intelligently and is keenly aware of the changing times, yet he is also a barbaric tyrant who is instinctively savage and can be mercilessly cruel. His tolerance goes only so far, and Anna quickly realizes that she must be patient and diplomatic in her relations with him.

Theirs becomes a remarkable association, almost a conflict. For, while the King respects her, he cannot lose sight of the fact that she is a woman, and a woman's place in his eyes is not on the same level as a man's. She is not even allowed to sit or recline on the same level with him, nor, for that matter, is any man, since the King is the absolute ruler. The highest compliment he pays Anna is to address her as "sir," and she understands and is grateful, as only an intelligent Victorian widow could be. The feeling between Anna and the King is a friendly one. They need each other, and both often have to compromise as politely as possible.

Anna is aided subtly by the elder wife, Lady Thiang (Gale Sondergaard), mother of the Crown Prince (Mickey Roth). Both realize that they must sometimes bow to the whims of the King, who does not always act with a complete understanding of modern progress, and honestly complains that life is too much of a puzzlement. But his eldest son, the Crown Prince, though young, is remarkably far-seeing. His mind is eager and his quick intelligence grasps and appreciates what Anna and Lady Thiang are doing to instruct him about the world outside Siam. His father might never take the step away from the feudalism of his ancestors, but the boy prince understands what his father cannot, and the two women know that he will be the hope of a free Siam when his time comes to ascend the throne.

The relationship between Anna and the King is given a particular warmth and wit through the efforts of screenwriters Talbot Jennings and Sally Benson, who underscore most of their scenes with a sly but gentle humor. Anna is not beyond needling the King, and each tries to best the other. He has promised her in writing in his original contract that she and her son, Louis (Richard Lyon), will have a house apart from the palace, a home to call their own. When he deliberately and blithely disregards that stipulation, Anna thinks of ways to remind him of his promise. Before she teaches his children the English alphabet, she coaches them in caroling sweetly "Home, Sweet Home." This is more than a puzzlement; it is enough to drive a King mad. Thus the King and Anna become like a man and wife enjoying a friendship that transcends sex.

The King's favorite wife in all his harem is a young beauty named Tuptim (Linda Darnell), who makes the mistake of falling in love with a handsome young man at the court. They try to run away together, but are caught. He is killed, and she is burnt at the stake for her infidelity, although Anna begs clemency for the girl. The King's stubborn reversion to so barbaric a punishment repels Anna, and she almost resigns her position to return home to England.

Her own son falls ill with a fever, however, and dies. The King grieves as if the loss had been his own. Anna turns a deaf ear to even the smallest child pleading with her to stay on in Siam. It is Lady Thiang who finally persuades her not to go home yet, for the health of the King is failing, and he needs them both in his last days, as does the young prince, who will be ascending the throne.

The death of the King is as touching as any true lover's might be, and Anna's sorrow is lifted only when, with Lady Thiang, she sees the boy she has educated crowned as the new King of Siam (Tito Renaldo), and in his first speech, he frees all his people so that none can hold another in bondage. This is all based upon the actual truth, for without Anna and her wise counseling the country of Siam might have remained backward, never becoming a land where free men and women walk.

The film is directed with an enviable understanding by John Cromwell, who balances the charming scenes of comedy with very strong moments of intense personal drama, and raises the picture's final moments to a triumphant declaration of the free human spirit. His picture won two Oscars, one for Cinematography and another for Art Direction and Interior Decoration, and it gained Academy nominations in three other categories.

As Anna, Irene Dunne gives a superlative performance. The role of Anna provides her with just the right combination of gracious, feminine charm mixed with a stubborn abrasiveness of character. Anna remains one of Dunn's strongest roles, and certainly she never looked more winning than when dressed in the crinolines Bonne Cashin designed. She and Rex Harrison as the King are an ideal team, and Harrison, for all his British heritage, makes a very acceptable King in his own right, although he more frequently seems like a monarch schooled in the best traditions of Oxford rather than the royal court of Siam.

Linda Darnell is a lovely and tragic Tuptim. Ironically, accidental death by fire was to be a fate she herself was to know some twenty years later. Lee J. Cobb as Prime Minister Kralahome is memorable; and one of the strongest yet most sensitive performances in the picture is contributed by Gale Sondergaard as the eldest wife, Lady Thiang, mother of the young prince.

The elegant sets and costumes of Louis D. Lighton's production made audiences realize what they had been missing during the war years when there had been no exquisite splendor, little charm and play of wit among the characters, and nothing like the extravagant display of rich silks and rare sparkling gems that made *Anna and the King of Siam* a thing of extraordinary beauty. It surprised no one, therefore, when less than a decade later, Richard Rodgers and Oscar Hammerstein, with the aid of John van Druten, brought *Anna and the King of Siam* to Broadway as a highly successful, long-running musical, *The King and I,* and Twentieth Century-Fox also transferred that version to the screen in 1956, winning honors at Academy Award time including a Best Actor Oscar for Yul Brynner, who re-created the role he had starred in onstage. He is still playing the role continuously both as a revival in New York and London and on tour. Brynner is as perfect for the King as Irene Dunne had been for Anna in the original 1946 screening, and many have lamented that the two never costarred, either onstage or on screen, in a production of the story.

DeWitt Bodeen

ANNA KARENINA

Released: 1935
Production: David O. Selznick for Metro-Goldwyn-Mayer
Direction: Clarence Brown
Screenplay: Clemence Dane and Salka Viertel, with dialogue by S. N. Behrman; based on the novel of the same name by Count Leo Tolstoy
Cinematography: William Daniels
Editing: Robert J. Kern
Running time: 95 minutes

Principal characters:
Anna Karenina .... Greta Garbo
Count Vronsky .... Fredric March
Sergei .... Freddie Bartholomew
Alexei Karenin .... Basil Rathbone
Kitty .... Maureen O'Sullivan

It was inevitable that Greta Garbo would star in a talking film version of Tolstoy's classic novel, *Anna Karenina*. Retitled *Love* (1927), the original *Anna Karenina* had been one of Garbo's finest silent pictures, so she did not demur in any way when Irving Thalberg proposed that she remake the story and that it be a version closer to the Tolstoy novel. By 1935 she needed a picture that would really show her off. It was the custom of M-G-M to provide perfect frames for its stars, but her 1934 release, *The Painted Veil*, had been an indifferent vehicle full of imperfections. A full-valued *Anna Karenina* could restore her star luster and it was assigned to David O. Selznick to produce.

Selznick, long a Garbo enthusiast, was determined that his *Anna Karenina* would be as perfect as humanly possible. The earlier version, *Love*, had been flawed, getting off to two false production starts before what had been shot was junked, and the film started anew. By that time, the box-office returns were coming in on Garbo's preceding picture, *Flesh and the Devil*, and they were outstanding. It had been the first film to present John Gilbert and Greta Garbo as a team, although, technically, Gilbert was the star and she his leading lady. As a result of that success, the thought was to capitalize on the two of them again as a team, get rid of the literary title, *Anna Karenina*, and bill the picture as "John Gilbert and Greta Garbo in *Love*." The story was also brought up-to-date. There would be no heavy period costumes; the styles of 1927 were flattering, and adultery was as dramatic set in the present as in the past. There were two things audiences would always remember about *Love*: the impassioned love scenes between Garbo and Gilbert, who were themselves romantically involved in real life, and the exquisite poignancy of Garbo's scenes with her young son, played by Philippe De Lacy. A tragic ending was filmed for *Love* in which Anna throws herself under the wheels of a train, in keeping with Tolstoy's ending; this tragic finale was rejected, however, in preference to the happy ending, which exhibitors preferred.

Fortunately, Selznick insisted that the new *Anna Karenina* would follow the story as Tolstoy had written it. The main story would be an unhappy love affair, with Anna, her lover, and her husband as the main characters. The other story line, revolving around Kitty and Levin and his social struggle with his farm, would be played down. After all, Tolstoy himself had given them the clue to success in the memorable first sentence of the novel: "Happy families are all alike; every unhappy family is unhappy in its own way." The story of the unhappy Karenin family would be what the movie was largely about. The screenplay was brilliantly constructed by Clemence Dane and Salka Viertel, with dialogue by S. N. Behrman.

Anna Karenina is the story of an ill-starred romance. Anna has become resigned to a loveless marriage with Alexei Karenin; her only happiness she finds in her devotion to her son, Sergei (Freddie Bartholomew), the one joy she has known throughout eight years of married life. Anna (Greta Garbo) is introduced in the film at the moment her life changes, when she first meets the dashing Count Vronsky (Fredric March) on the platform of the railroad station. She steps out of a cloud of steam enveloping the train, and, as the steam clears, she and Vronsky first look upon each other. The train station figures prophetically in their story, for it is the scene also of Anna's chosen doom at the finale.

Vronsky is a nobly born officer of the guards. His life is the Russian Army. Yet he and Anna are attracted to each other, and they might have known happiness had the decadent and hypocritical society in which they lived not condemned them. Alexei Karenin (Basil Rathbone) is a cold, passionless husband. When he learns of his wife's illicit love for Vronsky, he could close his eyes to the affair and wait coolly until it burns itself out, as his peers do when their wives err. What other people think, however, is important to Karenin. He could countenance a liaison by his wife and a noble officer if it were kept secret, but Anna, swept along by passion, makes the mistake of asking for a divorce—and that her husband cannot bring himself to give her.

Blind to whatever trouble he might make for her, Anna leaves her husband and gives up everything, including her son Sergei, to go and live with Vronsky. He obtains leave from the guards, they depart from Russia, and for a few months live out their love in foreign countries where they are not known. It is only a short respite however, for Vronsky is recalled to duty, and they must return to Russia. Society scorns them both, but it is Anna who feels the full impact of being an outcast. Vronsky has the company of his fellow officers in which to revel, but Anna is always unhappily alone, an embarrassment to her family and friends. She yearns for the young son she has deserted, and plots for even a glimpse of him. On the boy's birthday, she goes to her husband's house, finds her way inside, and goes up to the boy's room, where he is ill and sleeping. She has brought him a present, and when he awakens, his eyes light up with joy as she takes him in her arms. He has been told by his father that she is dead, and he rejoices now to find her alive. But Karenin enters, and in a cold fury orders her out; she is forced to go as he berates her viciously. Karenin convinces his son that his mother's presence has been a feverish dream.

Anna languishes in her misery and finds fault with her lover, deliberately picking a quarrel with him. He is ordered to battle maneuvers and they are forced once more to part—this time with bitter words and misunderstanding. Anna lets Vronsky go to the train station alone, until it occurs to her that the only life she has is with him. She follows him, but on the platform she realizes that she has gone beyond the crossroads; there can be no reconciliation or happiness for her. A train is coming in; Anna knows what she must do to avenge herself and to make Vronsky regret his treatment of her. The train begins to pass her, and she waits, staring emotionlessly, almost hypnotically, as the lights of the passing cars light up and then shadow her eyes. When the moment is right, she falls forward beneath the wheels in a cloud of steam.

Anna's fate is uncompromising. It must be. From the start it evolves visually from clouds of steam, and in the end the clouds envelop her again. Her life and the love she holds for Vronsky are illuminated in between by a passing parade of fashionable Russian aristocrats pretending virtues they do not possess. She dances *mazurkas* at balls, pretending a gaiety she does not feel. She tries to force a great love into a life that has been lived for eight years without love. When that life becomes an open scandal, society cannot tolerate her. There is a place of sorts left for Vronsky in the army, but Anna's sin is unforgivable, and there is no place left open to her.

The role of Anna was a perfect one for Garbo. Anna's changing moods of somberness and joy, of longing and despair suit her perfectly. To view *Anna Karenina* and then to see *Love* again, it is impressive to see Garbo's talent mature, growing into a role that seemed created especially for her. She had been intriguing in the silent version, but she is hauntingly perfect in the talking film. It is almost as if the 1927 film had been a rehearsal for the one in 1935. Her scenes with her lover and those with her son are convincing and moving in both versions. John Gilbert had been an impassioned Vronsky in the silent, and she worked beautifully with him. Fredric March is stolid but nonetheless romantic as Vronsky in his scenes with her in the talking version, but Garbo's performance as Anna overshadows his role. March is competent, but the eyes of the viewer stay on Garbo; she is magnetic.

Clarence Brown directed Garbo in five of her talking films and two of her silents but he never worked better with her than in this one, where she is given every variety of emotion to express, and he allows her every subtlety. William Daniels photographed her in all but two of her fifteen talking films and in eight of her ten silent M-G-M releases, twenty-one films altogether. No man knew as much about Garbo as Daniels, and his cinematography of her reached a zenith in *Anna Karenina*.

In 1948 Julien Duvivier directed a new version of *Anna Karenina* for London Films, starring Vivien Leigh. Although it was a handsome film, it possessed none of the sense of real tragedy that had brought the Garbo version so close to perfection. Again, in 1967, the U.S.S.R., emboldened by its success with *War and Peace*, made what might have been a definitive version of *Anna Karenina*, starring Tatiana Samoilova. It was beautiful to look at, but for those who had seen and remembered Garbo, this would not be a film to remember for long.

Greta Garbo had so perfect a face for the camera and was such a natural mistress of its technical demands that her very presence illuminated everything she ever appeared in on the screen. One must see such films as *Susan Lenox* (1931), *As You Desire Me* (1932), *The Painted Veil*, and, of course, *Two-Faced Woman* (1941), several times to realize how meretricious they really were. The very fact that she was in them made them seem satisfying, to a superficial extent, on a first viewing.

But *Anna Karenina*, like *Camille* (1936) and *Ninotchka* (1939), is exceedingly good. Garbo is not only a supreme actress in it, but the picture is well-produced and authentic drama. The characters are all true to Tolstoy and to life, and Garbo's Anna is so translucent and warm and real a heroine that the screen acquires a special glow when her shadow falls upon it.

DeWitt Bodeen

ANNIE HALL

Released: 1977
Production: Charles H. Joffe for United Artists (AA)
Direction: Woody Allen (AA)
Screenplay: Woody Allen and Marshall Brickman (AA)
Cinematography: Gordon Willis
Editing: Ralph Rosenblum
Running time: 93 minutes

> *Principal characters:*
> Alvy Singer .... Woody Allen
> Annie Hall .... Diane Keaton (AA)
> Rob (Max) .... Tony Roberts
> Tony Lacey .... Paul Simon
> Allison .... Carol Kane

Woody Allen has never been one to tell a straightforward story in a straight-forward way. For example, in 1966, he took a Japanese-made imitation James Bond film and reedited it. He changed the plot into an intrigue concerning an egg salad recipe by redubbing the film in English. He called it *What's Up Tiger Lily?* In 1971 he was coauthor, costar, and director of *Bananas*, a film in which the plot about a Latin American revolution was merely a weak thread with which Allen tied together the series of physical and verbal jokes which made up the film. *Annie Hall*, for which Allen is once again coauthor, in addition to costar and director, is more disciplined than either *What's Up Tiger Lily?* or *Bananas*, but it is an obvious continuation of the spirit and style of those films. The importance of the film lies in the strength of each individual scene as it merges with others to form a bittersweet view of modern love. It is presented as memories of a romance after it is over, rather than as a chronological story of that romance. It uses a variety of techniques to explore, if not explain, the relationship between Alvy Singer (Woody Allen) and Annie Hall (Diane Keaton).

The fact that the film is not a standard narrative is obvious from the first moment, when Alvy Singer speaks, not to another character, but directly to the audience. He tells us that he has broken up with Annie Hall, that he is sifting the pieces of the relationship in his mind, and quotes a joke from Sigmund Freud in an attempt to explain his problems with women: "I would never want to belong to any club that would have someone like me as a member."

From this point on, we get a guided tour of Alvy's mind as he reflects upon himself and his romance with Annie. We find that he is a successful comedian, has been married and divorced twice, is a Jew sensitive to (or paranoid about) anti-Semitism, and has been in analysis for fifteen years. We also learn the story of Alvy and Annie: they meet, fall in love, live together, split up, get back together, then split up for good. Annie then goes to live with a record producer named Tony Lacey (Paul Simon) in Los Angeles, where Alvy tries unsuccessfully to get her back. Ultimately, they meet in New York and reminisce about old times. We learn these things in no particular order. At times one scene may have no direct relationship to the next, but at other times one scene will suggest the next. For example, Annie asks something about Allison (Carol Kane), Alvy's first wife, and we see a series of flashbacks concerning Allison.

Simple flashbacks are not the only cinematic devices used, however. When Alvy initially meets Annie, they have an awkward, exploratory conversation, consisting mostly of self-conscious, banal statements. It is funny and quite believable. The feelings which one has in such a situation are highlighted by subtitles which tell the audience what each character is actually thinking while they are talking.

In another scene Alvy asks Annie about her previous boyfriends. Rather than just hearing about them we see Annie and Alvy watching Annie as she was a few years before with each of her boyfriends. We see and hear both the younger Annie and her boyfriend as well as the present-day Annie and Alvy commenting on the scene. In another use of the same technique we see an adult Alvy visiting his grade school class.

Allen also uses a split screen technique to provide a contrast between the two characters. At one point we see Annie with her analyst saying that she is making progress, while on the other side of the screen we see Alvy with his analyst complaining about a lack of progress. Another time we see Annie's Wisconsin Protestant family side by side with Alvy's New York Jewish one.

Another device, which is perhaps the most startling, though not the most meaningful, one used in *Annie Hall*, is animation. It is used in only one short scene: Annie and Alvy are arguing and suddenly become cartoon characters as they continue the argument. A different yet equally remarkable scene shows Alvy upset by the pontifications of a man standing behind him in a theater line. When the man begins quoting the ideas of media theorist Marshall McLuhan, Alvy leaves the line and pulls McLuhan from behind a sign to tell the man he does not know what he is talking about. Then Alvy turns to the camera and says, "Why isn't *life* like this?"

Both the fantasy scene with McLuhan and the animation sequence are techniques which are amusing and attention-getting, but they fail to illuminate the characters or their situations as do most of the other devices Allen uses. What emerges, both as a result of, and in spite of, the cinematic devices used, is a comic, believable story about two people who are just right for each other on a certain level, but are unable to resolve their conflicts well enough to stay together. We especially see their compatibility with each other in a high-spirited scene in which they are trying to cook live lobsters in spite of

Alvy's fear of them. Later there is a telling contrast when Alvy attempts to re-create the mood with another woman, and she is completely unable to appreciate either his fear of lobsters or the humor of the situation.

The circumstances that eventually separate them are seen in their arguments about sex, about meeting other people, and about Annie's mind. She says that he does not think her intelligent enough to be serious about, and he buys her books and urges her to take adult education courses. Perhaps Alvy's own assessment of the relationship is correct. He compares it to a shark: "It has to constantly move forward or it dies. I think what we've got on our hands is a dead shark."

A recurrent subtheme of *Annie Hall* is Alvy's preference for New York over California. The only cultural advantage to California, he feels, is that you can turn right on a red light. He first argues against California with his friend Max (Tony Roberts), an actor who moved to Los Angeles to star in a television series. Alvy is especially upset when he finds that the series uses canned laughter. Later the issue looms larger when he and Annie break up and she goes to Los Angeles to live with a record publisher.

The faults of the film are primarily in its form. Since it is a succession of relatively isolated scenes, the weak scenes, such as the ones about driving cars, stand out more than they would in a conventional narrative, and the final section of the film, which covers in chronological order the events after Annie moves to Los Angeles, has too little direction. It only gains momentum when it reaches the reminiscences, a series of short scenes from the rest of the film with Annie's voice singing "Seems Like Old Times" on the sound track.

The keys to the success of the film are the script by Woody Allen and Marshall Brickman, and the performances by Diane Keaton and Allen. Keaton possesses an undeniable screen presence as well as the ability to make every scene interesting and believable. Allen plays much the same character he has played in several of his other films, such as *Bananas*, *Love and Death* (1975), and *Play It Again, Sam* (1972), but in *Annie Hall*, his performance is more effective because he has toned down the clumsiness which marred many of his previous roles. The script, in all of the best scenes, gives the characters lines which are witty enough to be funny, but not so funny that the characters and the situations cease to be real.

There is a good deal of autobiography in this film, even though Woody Allen may not be exactly like the character he plays. We know that Allen is a Jewish comedian who has two ex-wives and has had a relationship with Diane Keaton (whose real surname is, in fact, Hall). But to what extent Allen and Keaton are playing themselves and their own story is not important to the appreciation or enjoyment of the film itself.

The film was generally well received by critics and was a hit at the box office. It won Academy Awards for Best Picture, as well as Best Direction and Best Original Screenplay for Allen and Best Actress for Keaton. As an imaginative treatment of a romance which ends neither happily nor tragically, *Annie Hall* might be called a 1970's film about a 1970's romance.

Timothy W. Johnson

THE APARTMENT

Released: 1960
Production: Billy Wilder for the Mirisch Company; released by United Artists (AA)
Direction: Billy Wilder (AA)
Screenplay: I. A. L. Diamond and Billy Wilder (AA)
Cinematography: Joseph LaShelle
Editing: Daniel Mandell (AA)
Art direction: Alexander Trauner (AA); set decoration, Edward G. Boyle (AA)
Running time: 125 minutes

Principal characters:
C. C. (Bud) Baxter	Jack Lemmon
Fran Kubelik	Shirley MacLaine
J. D. Sheldrake	Fred MacMurray
Dr. Dreyfuss	Jack Kruschen
Miss Olsen	Edie Adams

Originally branded "a dirty fairy tale," Billy Wilder's *The Apartment* combines irony, burlesque, soap opera, and truth into a morality play whose message is "be a *mensch*," a Yiddish term for a human being. Filmed in black-and-white, Wilder's story expresses the moral ambiguities facing a hero and heroine who are neither innocent nor evil, just human. By dealing with pandering, adultery, and suicide in an often poignant, yet entertaining way, Wilder created one of the most sophisticated Hollywood movies of its time. The innovativeness of *The Apartment*, however, is due not so much to the types of activities it portrays, but rather to the fact that Wilder allows his principal characters to sin, suffer the consequences, and yet be redeemed for a happy ending.

Wilder's sharp wit and satiric sword begin by slicing into the heart of Manhattan society's immorality and callousness as seen through the corporate world. The protagonist, C. C. (Bud) Baxter (Jack Lemmon), is a basically decent young executive with an undeveloped code of morality who finds himself reacting to, rather than shaping, the events around him. Bud begins as a night school graduate relegated to Section W, desk number 861 of the Ordinary Policy Department in the home office of Consolidated Life, an insurance company in New York. His is but one of hundreds of steel gray desks lined up row upon row in a huge office filled by people with equally gray, expressionless faces. Art director Alexander Trauner and set director Edward G. Boyle exhibited their Academy Award-winning techniques in the early office scenes by enhancing the effect of a vast sea of faces with the use of tiny desks with dwarfs in the rear of the set, followed by even tinier desks with cut-out figures operated by wires.

Bud has learned that in an organization with more than 31,000 employees, a person has to have something more to offer than training, industry, and dedication. Bud stumbled onto his key to success—his apartment. Though small and rather dreary, the apartment has quickly become the favorite love nest shared by four of Bud's bosses. In exchange for providing a bed and catering service, Bud has been rewarded with glowing performance evaluations which will lead to promotions and one of the coveted glass-enclosed cubicles along the office's sidewall. Though less than enthusiastic about this arrangement, Bud is pliable whenever the fruits of society, measured in money, status, and sex, are dangled in front of him.

Throughout the first half of the movie, Bud's objections to the services he is providing are based on personal inconvenience rather than moral conviction. Lonely Bud, instead of spending his evenings eating TV dinners, watching old movies, and reading the men's fashion section of *Playboy*, often ends up spending the night in the cold, damp park, while one of his bosses shares his bed with the latest office ingenue. Wilder and Lemmon skillfully milk the laughs out of Bud's predicament as he catches an awful cold one night and then sniffles his way around the office the next day, alternating his attention between a handkerchief, nasal spray, and a thermometer.

It is on this day that Bud comes to the attention of Mr. Sheldrake (Fred MacMurray), the Director of Personnel, who, after delivering a sermon on morality, offers to trade two tickets to *The Music Man* and a future promotion for exclusive rights to Bud's apartment. As Bud's reluctance turns to elation, he finds the courage to invite the girl of his dreams, Fran Kubelik (Shirley MacLaine), an elevator operator in the building, to join him at the theater. She hesitatingly agrees to meet him at 8:30 in the lobby. That night, while Bud waits for her at the theater, Mr. Sheldrake is busy convincing Fran that if she will resume their affair, he will divorce his wife. Sheldrake prevails and Bud gets stood-up.

Throughout the next month, on Mondays and Thursdays the apartment is reserved for Mr. Sheldrake, and true to his word, he promotes Bud to one of the glass-enclosed cubicles. It is now December 24, and the wild office Christmas party serves as a dividing point in the movie. Wilder helped to capture the true spirit of office parties, where everyone forgets his inhibitions in a swirl of booze, music, and laughter, by actually shooting the scene on December 23. Until now the movie has concentrated on Bud's culpability and ambitiousness, and on his bosses' lechery. At this point, however, the human consequences begin.

During the Christmas party both Fran and Bud have their illusions shattered. First a drunken Miss Olsen (Edie Adams), Mr. Sheldrake's secretary, taunts Fran about the number of conquests, herself included, which Mr.

Sheldrake has scattered throughout the building. Then, when Bud asks her opinion of his new derby, Fran lets him look at himself in her compact's cracked mirror. Startled, Bud recognizes it as the compact he had found in his apartment and returned to Mr. Sheldrake a few weeks before.

While the disillusioned Bud drowns his sorrows in martinis at the local bar, Fran confronts Sheldrake at the apartment. Realizing that he regards her only as a mistress and not as his future wife, the despondent Fran happens to find a bottle of sleeping pills in the bathroom. Wilder uses the mirrors in the bathroom and her compact to symbolize the identity crisis with which she is suffering. Unable to cope with the reflection she sees in the glass, Fran takes the pills.

When Bud returns home, he finds Fran unconscious with the bottle of pills in her hand. He quickly summons his neighbor, Dr. Dreyfuss (Jack Kruschen), who pumps out her stomach, and, believing Bud to be responsible for her suicide attempt, delivers a lecture on being a *mensch*. Dr. Dreyfuss, an honest, straightforward human being, presents Bud with an alternative role model to the corporate connivers he has been trying to emulate. It has become clear that in the world presented in *The Apartment*, corporate success and integrity cannot coexist, and Bud will soon be forced to make a choice. Wilder, however, manages to keep the suicide attempt and the moral dilemma from becoming too bleak through the use of plenty of deft comedy.

Fran and Bud spend the next two days swapping hard luck stories and playing gin rummy while she recovers enough strength to go home. Here Wilder mixes sentimentality and light-hearted buffoonery in a classic scene where Bud dexterously uses his tennis racquet to drain their spaghetti dinner.

In the meantime, Sheldrake fires Miss Olsen, who in turn informs Mrs. Sheldrake of his philandering habits. Sheldrake, who has been more concerned with preventing a scandal than in caring for Fran, rewards Bud with a promotion to Assistant Personnel Director and the key to the executive washroom. Though still willing to accept the rewards, Bud is no longer willing to play the game. He has fallen in love with Fran and is dismayed to hear that Sheldrake, who was thrown out by his wife, now intends to marry her— eventually, but not just yet.

On New Year's Eve day, when Sheldrake asks for the apartment key, Bud symbolically renounces corporate success and becomes a *mensch* by giving Sheldrake the key to the executive washroom instead. That night at dinner Sheldrake recounts Bud's inexplicable action to Fran, who realizes that Bud really loves her. Leaving Sheldrake sitting in the restaurant, she rushes off to Bud's apartment, where they welcome in the New Year with a game of gin rummy.

The happy ending was met with surprise by some critics who did not feel that protagonists who transgressed sexually deserved to find happiness. But Wilder has created human beings, not stereotypes, and they are capable of developing some self-recognition and capacity for growth. The question the movie does not successfully answer is why five supposedly well-paid executives are so totally dependent upon using Bud's rather dingy little flat.

The performances are universally good. Jack Lemmon and Shirley MacLaine make an appealing couple, capable of evoking both tenderness and humor. Ultimately, however, it is Lemmon's performance which gives the film the vitality to remain entertaining in the face of some pessimistic assessments of the human character.

The Apartment won the Academy Award for Best Picture in 1960 and is one of the best achievements in Wilder's illustrious career.

Anne Louise Lynch

APOCALYPSE NOW

Released: 1979
Production: Francis Ford Coppola for United Artists
Direction: Francis Ford Coppola
Screenplay: John Milius and Francis Ford Coppola; suggested by the novella
 Heart of Darkness by Joseph Conrad
Cinematography: Vittorio Storaro (AA)
Editing: Richard Marks
Narration: Michael Herr
Sound: Walter Murch, Mark Berger, Richard Beggs, and Nat Boxer (AA)
Music: Carmine Coppola and Francis Ford Coppola
Running time: 153 minutes

Principal characters:
Colonel Walter E. Kurtz .... Marlon Brando
Lieutenant Colonel Kilgore .... Robert Duvall
Captain Benjamin L. Willard .... Martin Sheen
Chef .... Frederic Forrest
Chief .... Albert Hall
Lance .... Sam Bottoms
Clean .... Larry Fishburne
Freelance photographer .... Dennis Hopper
General .... G. D. Spradlin
Colonel .... Harrison Ford

Anticipation was high when producer-director Francis Ford Coppola first
announced plans to make *Apocalypse Now.* Coppola's background as director
of the stunning saga of a Mafia patriarch and his successor, in *The Godfather*
(1972) and *The Godfather, Part II* (1974), made him appear the likely candidate to deliver the definitive film about the Vietnam War.

When Coppola first revealed his intentions for *Apocalypse Now*, no other
major feature, with the exception of *The Green Berets* (1969), had examined
the war; yet, because of a much-publicized lengthy production schedule of
more than four years, Coppola's film was the last of several war films to be
released. It followed such Vietnam-theme films as Oscar-winners *The Deer
Hunter* (1978) and *Coming Home* (1978), as well as a string of exploitation
films, such as *Rolling Thunder* (1978), which also examined aspects of the
Vietnam dilemma.

A four-year wait and heavy media attention can generate great expectations. Adding to the notoriety of *Apocalypse Now* was its budget of some
$30,000,000. Because of such statistics, *Apocalypse Now* was a phenomenon
before it even arrived on the screen. Critical reaction after its release, however, has varied, ranging from accolades to anger. Considering that the film
has the look and tone of a highly personal "art film" in spite of its massive,

awesome scale, it remains unclear at this time whether the film will become a major commercial success; however, it will undoubtedly snare a cult following and be the object of debate for decades.

Scripted by John Milius and Coppola, and loosely based on the Joseph Conrad novella *Heart of Darkness*, *Apocalypse Now* uses Vietnam as a backdrop to study the madness and folly of all wars. From its opening moments which focus on the debauched Captain Willard (Martin Sheen) recovering in a sleazy Saigon hotel, *Apocalypse Now* evokes a sense of doom. Through voice-over narration, the young captain reveals that he is awaiting a mission. He is a military assassin who, when finally summoned, admits, "I was going to the worst place in the world—and I didn't even know it." During a luncheon meeting with grim military personnel, played by G. D. Spradlin and Harrison Ford, Willard is given his instructions: he must travel upriver into off-limits Cambodia and "terminate the command" of Colonel Kurtz (Marlon Brando), a once-decorated officer who, we are told, has gone mad.

Willard travels the river via a patrol boat. En route, he encounters myriad episodes which all point to the madness of war. During the journey, Willard studies the Kurtz dossier. Ultimately, the bizarre and often bloody events of the trip, together with the Kurtz enigma, make Willard deeply ponder his assignment. Through his narration, he confesses that he has never before murdered an American officer. Though the military claims that Kurtz is leading his own forces in senseless murder, Willard points out that "charging a man with murder in this place was like handing out speeding tickets at the Indy 500."

The river journey is composed of episodic adventures delivered with a mixture of near-documentary astuteness and hallucinatory vision. First we meet the young crew members of the Navy patrol boat: Chief (Albert Hall), who is black, is the boat's commander; Chef (Frederic Forrest) is a cook from New Orleans; Clean (Larry Fishburne) is a ghetto youth; and Lance (Sam Bottoms) is a famed California surfer who works on his tan and waterskis behind the boat. The crew's encounter with a well-known Cavalry unit, led by gung-ho field commander Lieutenant Colonel Kilgore (Robert Duvall), is the occasion for some of the film's most startlingly realistic battle footage, as the unit napalms a Vietnamese village. The sequence is complete with a helicopter attack set to Wagner's "The Ride of the Valkyries." The black-Stetsoned Kilgore orders the battle so that some of his men, and Lance, can surf one of the Viet Cong's best beaches. Francis Coppola is seen briefly, directing a camera crew, when Willard and the patrol crew first encounter Kilgore during the final moments of a battle.

After the episode with Kilgore, the patrol boat resumes its journey, which becomes increasingly surreal. At one point, for example, the crew comes upon a brilliantly lit nighttime USO-type show featuring a trio of *Playboy* Bunnies playing to a frenzied, uncontrolled audience. On another occasion, the crew's worn nerves cause them to imagine that a lone sampan which arouses their curiosity is smuggling supplies. When a civilian on the sampan appears to be moving for a weapon, the men respond with a barrage of bullets, cutting down all the civilians onboard except for a badly wounded woman. Chief, who wants to take her to "friendlies" for treatment, is rebuked by Willard, who solves the matter by killing her with a single bullet; he then orders the boat and its hostile crew to continue.

Before venturing into Cambodian waters, the patrol boat cruises through a bizarre night fight at a temporary bridge. Willard, who seeks information, disembarks together with a drug-drowsy Lance. This sequence of leaderless black GI's shooting recklessly into the night is hallucinatory and, for Willard, unsettling. Unable to locate a commanding officer, he and Lance return to the boat for the final stretch of the journey.

Natives, presumably commanded by Kurtz, attack the boat, resulting in the deaths of Clean and Chief; ironically, Chief is killed with a spear. When at long last the boat reaches Kurtz's strange jungle retreat, Lance is becoming increasingly primitive in action and appearance. He carries a spear, sports green and black facial makeup, and ultimately dons a loincloth. Chef is becoming increasingly paranoid, and the severed heads and hanging, mutilated bodies displayed at the Kurtz camp further unsettle his nerves. He and Willard are anxious to carry out the mission and retreat.

Greeted by a hyperactive, fast-talking freelance photographer (Dennis Hopper), Willard is finally close to meeting the baffling Kurtz. Actually, Kurtz's introduction during the film's final half hour is devoid of the kind of high-intensity drama that has led up to the meeting. Filmed in dramatic shadows as he reads passages from T. S. Eliot's "The Hollow Men," Kurtz proceeds to question Willard about his past and about his mission; and Kurtz recounts a childhood experience of traveling down the Ohio river and coming upon a gardenia plantation.

A moral battle between Kurtz and Willard now ensues in which Kurtz challenges Willard to question his commanding officers. At the same time, Kurtz, a man out of control, implores Willard to kill him. Willard finally carries out his mission after witnessing Kurtz's atrocities, including the decapitation of Chef. The scenes of Kurtz's murder are intercut with the ritualistic slaughter of a carabao by the natives. With his mission accomplished, a bloodied Willard guides Lance to the boat so they can leave. *Apocalypse Now*, which has an overabundance of lingering dissolves, closes with a dissolve sequence, over which can be heard Kurtz's words, a revelation of war's agony, "the horror, the horror."

During its initial release in 70 mm, *Apocalypse Now* was screened without any credits whatsoever, and theater patrons were issued credit booklets at film's end. Credits were added to the ending, however, for the film's 35 mm screenings, as was footage of an air raid staged at Kurtz's retreat. The fact that Coppola shot two endings—one a large-scale air attack, the other show-ing Willard's quiet departure—elicited considerable press comment. When Coppola at last decided to add the attack footage, he stressed that the infrared film showing the stronghold's obliteration is simply a visual backdrop for the credits. The scenes are not recognizable as Kurtz's jungle fortress.

Apocalypse Now seems weighted by an overly ambiguous tone as well as disappointing characterizations. Meant to be microcosms, the characters, specifically the crew of the patrol boat, capture our interest but never our concern. Though each has some potentially emotional and revealing mo-ments, we never feel deeply for these men. Willard is a paradox, as much an enigma as Kurtz. The few things we know about him emerge from the narration, but they are sketchy visions.

The film's casting is equally unsettling. Although Marlon Brando as Kurtz milks each line for dramatic intensity, the audience never understands the character's motivations; Kurtz remains a puzzling figure, bald and overweight, telling stories of wartime atrocities. Martin Sheen displays a frenzied intensity as Willard, but, like Kurtz, he remains a paradox. Robert Duvall, known, like Brando, for his work in the *Godfather* films, is effective as the crazed but courageous Kilgore, a man who loves the smell of napalm in the morning because it reminds him of victory. He earned an Academy Award nomination for his role.

Technically dazzling, *Apocalypse Now* offers stunning visuals despite an onslaught of dissolves and close-ups; the film also achieves superlative sound effects. Although visually exciting, *Apocalypse Now* has a tendency to pound in its messages too obviously, especially in its use of the voice-over narration, written by journalist Michael Herr, author of *Dispatches*, a best-selling work based on his Vietnam experiences.

If *Apocalypse Now* is a clouded effort, its artistry is nevertheless obvious. In all probability it will stand as a landmark study of men at war, but sadly, it lacks a stirring dose of the human element. Although the film received a total of eight Academy Award nominations, including one for Best Picture, it received only two, one for sound and one for Vittorio Storaro's cinema-tography.

Pat H. Broeske

THE APPRENTICESHIP OF DUDDY KRAVITZ

Released: 1974
Production: John Kemeny for Paramount
Direction: Ted Kotcheff
Screenplay: Mordecai Richler and Lionel Chetwynd; based on the novel of
the same name by Mordecai Richler
Cinematography: Brian West
Editing: Thom Noble
Running time: 121 minutes

> *Principal characters:*
> Duddy .... Richard Dreyfuss
> Yvette .... Micheline Lanctot
> Max .... Jack Warden
> Virgil .... Randy Quaid
> Uncle Benjy .... Joseph Wiseman
> Friar .... Denholm Elliott

The Apprenticeship of Duddy Kravitz is the film that launched actor Richard
Dreyfuss' career in 1974. While most moviegoers will remember his portrayal
of the nervous college-bound senior, Curt, in *American Graffiti* (1973), one
of the all-time biggest box-office moneymakers, it was in *The Apprenticeship
of Duddy Kravitz* that Dreyfuss was really able to show his range and depth
as an actor. The role paved the way for his performances in such major
productions as *Jaws* (1975), *The Goodbye Girl* (1977), and *Close Encounters
of the Third Kind* (1977). Oddly enough, however, Dreyfuss has said many
times in interviews that he considers *The Apprenticeship of Duddy Kravitz*
a bad movie and that he would prefer that it never be shown again, since he
feels his performance was poor in it.

The title of the film refers to its protagonist's apprenticeship in the job of
making it successfully in the harsh, cruel world—or, more specifically, in the
gentile world outside Duddy's Jewish Montreal neighborhood. The achievement of material success has always eluded Duddy's father Max (Jack Warden), a cab-driver who pimps on the side to bring in enough money to support
his family and an older son who is in medical school. Duddy's Uncle Benjy
(Joseph Wiseman) is an aloof, aristocratic relative who has accomplished
through patience and prudence what Max, with all his cheap hustling, could
not achieve. Uncle Benjy has built up a large garment business, and has also
maintained cultural and intellectual standards for himself and his family. He
has also managed the additional luxury of not having to sell out his principles:
at the same time he was building a small fortune in his business, he assisted
his workers in unionizing; and he remains a staunch defender of socialism.

The contrast between Duddy's father and his uncle provides the impetus

Duddy needs to launch his campaign to make as much money as possible, in any way he can. His schemes include waiting on tables at a Jewish resort, where he soon learns that the cost of bribing the cook to hurry the orders is more than offset by the increased tips; starting a film production company to make bar mitzvah documentaries; running dope across the United States-Canadian border; and going into business selling and delivering pinball machines around town. By the film's end, Duddy has achieved the material success he hoped for. He takes his elderly grandfather's words to heart—"A man without land is nobody"—and acquires his own parcel of land by a beautiful lake. But it is a Pyrrhic victory: he fails to earn his grandfather's approval (the land was partially ill-gotten), and he has lost the only girl who ever really loved him to a friend crippled indirectly because of Duddy's callousness. And he earns the scorn of the now fatally ill Benjy: "Why did I never have time for you? Because you're a *pusherke*. A little Jew-boy on the make. Guys like you make me sick and ashamed."

Nevertheless, the film treats Duddy and his aspirations with sympathy. There were fears expressed in some quarters that the film could in some way be "bad for the Jews" by encouraging perpetuation of offensive stereotypes, but an article in *Commentary* magazine correctly pointed out that "the film's materials are too much seen from the inside to be appropriated by an enemy camp." As the story reveals, it is those hustlers like Duddy who provide the sustenance that allows the rest of us to remain high-minded and pure. In this sense, Duddy is an example to the entrepreneur in all of us, for while the film takes place in a Jewish milieu—drawing on the experiences of Ted Kotcheff, the director, and Mordecai Richler, the film's primary screenwriter and author of the 1959 novel—its message is more universal and speaks to everyone.

The film does have its share of in-jokes, though they are integrated nicely into the fabric of the story. There are many hilarious scenes, such as the one in which Duddy shows his client, Farber, a documentary of Farber's son's bar mitzvah, entitled, "Happy Bar Mitzvah, Bernie!" This unimaginative title leaves the father ill-prepared for what follows: a surreal film essay on a "young Hebrew's initiation into his tribe," complete with arty cross-cuts of the bar mitzvah boy, roaring lions, primitive African rites, a circumcision operation, Hitler ranting, marching Nazis—all the products of director Friar's (Denholm Elliott) addled, anti-Semitic brain. Elliott, a fine English character actor rarely seen in the United States, is superb as the drunken, pretentious director Duddy has hired for his "Duddy Kane Enterprises" company.

There are moments of great poignancy as well. Duddy's romance with Yvette (Micheline Lanctot) has a touching spontaneity to it, although the audience knows from Yvette's growing dissatisfaction with Duddy's hustle that the affair is doomed. When Virgil (Randy Quaid), Duddy's trusting epileptic friend, has a seizure while delivering for Duddy in a truck, Yvette leaves Duddy to care for the crippled boy—who, in his simplicity, still trusts and admires Duddy for his friendship.

The role of Duddy is one that Richard Dreyfuss seems to have been born to play. In all of his movies, Dreyfuss carries a bit of that character with him; there is the same brash confidence, pushy manner, nervous energy, charming insecurity. Although his subsequent films have shown the severe limitations of his approach, Dreyfuss excelled here. *The Apprenticeship of Duddy Kravitz* could serve as a parallel for Dreyfuss' own career; it came along at just the right intersection of his personal and career growth to crystallize his style of work. The film was important for other reasons, too. It represented the first major breakthrough of a Canadian production into the international market, although, ironically, both Kotcheff and Richler were expatriate Canadians living in England at the time, and most of the cast was American. Unfortunately, it may have been one of those magical conjunctions that produced a success that neither writer, director, nor actor will be able to duplicate.

Certainly, Kotcheff's later films suggest an inability to match his previous standard. *Fun with Dick and Jane* (1976) and *Who Is Killing the Great Chefs of Europe?* (1978) were both unfunny knockabout farces, hammered out by a legion of uncredited screenwriters who could not make a coherent film out of either one. Richler, who got an Oscar nomination for Best Screenplay Adaptation for *The Apprenticeship of Duddy Kravitz*, has lately occupied himself writing a series of "roving reporter" magazine pieces, and Richard Dreyfuss' performances have declined in quality as the films' budgets have escalated, though his worst job so far was in *The Big Fix* (1978), made on a relatively small budget and produced by Dreyfuss himself.

The Apprenticeship of Duddy Kravitz, however, has an undeniable vigor and force, probably the result of Dreyfuss' dynamic characterization of Duddy more than anything else. And despite a certain unevenness in the film's continuity and somewhat patchy editing, the absorbing story and vivid portrayals render it a powerful statement on the travails of making it in a hostile environment.

Joel Bellman

AROUND THE WORLD IN 80 DAYS

Released: 1956
Production: Michael Todd for United Artists (AA)
Direction: Michael Anderson
Screenplay: S. J. Perelman, James Poe, and John Farrow (AA); based on the
  novel of the same name by Jules Verne
Cinematography: Lionel Lindon (AA)
Editing: Paul Weatherwax and Gene Ruggiero (AA)
Narration: Edward R. Murrow
Music: Victor Young (AA)
Running time: 170 minutes

Principal characters:
Phileas Fogg .... David Niven
Passepartout .... Cantinflas
Mr. Fix .... Robert Newton
Princess Aouda .... Shirley MacLaine

When Orson Welles produced Jules Verne's *Around the World in 80 Days* on the stage in the 1940's, he made the point of introducing a kitchen sink just to prove that he had put everything into the production. Although producer Michael Todd omits that particular piece of apparatus, his film is even more lavish than the stage production, with flamenco dancers, the Japanese Circus Theater, a re-created Barbary Coast saloon, the Royal Thai barge and Navy, a Mack Sennettlike cavalry with an attacking band of Indians, some dancing girls in Bombay, a huge torchlight parade in San Francisco, and more.

Filmed in 70mm (twice the size of normal Hollywood film stock), *Around the World in 80 Days* is a cinematic spectacular, an action-packed adventure, a riotous comedy, a magnificent travelogue, and even a charming love story. The enchanting story of an around-the-world jaunt has nonsense, beauty, fantasy, suspense, color, song, dance, and incredible scenic and human wonders. The film was photographed in the widescreen Todd-AO Process, which provides the illusion of three-dimensional depth and is made to be projected at thirty frames-per-second, as opposed to the usual twenty-four, on a very wide, deeply curved screen; and it used a multitrack sound system. The result of all these technical and dramatic devices is an ambitious, grandiose production.

The seven-million-dollar, almost three-hour-long extravaganza boasts a roster of fifty stars, a supporting cast of nearly sixty-nine thousand people, a wardrobe of nearly seventy-five thousand costumes, and scenes photographed in thirteen countries on 140 actual locations around the globe. Taking 127 days to shoot, the mammoth film made use of five full production crews, thirty-three assistant directors, a large number of studio sound stages in Hollywood (including RKO, Fox, and M-G-M), England, Hong Kong, and Japan, and thirty-four different species of animals—nearly eight thousand in all. At one point during the Rocky Mountain sequence, 2,500 buffalo and 3,800 sheep are seen crossing a railroad track.

Further enlivening an already lavish production are the more than forty cameo appearances by well-known stars in small parts. (Interestingly, the term "cameo" was invented by Todd for the credits of *Around the World in 80 Days*. Because he did not want to belittle such stars as Frank Sinatra or Marlene Dietrich by listing them as co-stars, he concocted the term to indicate a small part by a well-known personality. Since that time, the term has become a part of film language and is used frequently to honor stars who take small parts which would otherwise be either unavailable to them, or beneath their stature.) Some of the stars making such appearances were Charles Boyer, José Greco, Red Skelton, John Mills, Martine Carroll, and Glynis Johns. There were so many stars in the production that, as a joke, comedian Red Buttons appeared in an ad in a special issue of the *Hollywood Reporter* with the caption, "Positively the only star not appearing in '80 Days!'" Most of the guest stars appear for only two minutes, and some speak no lines; Marlene Dietrich's part, for example, includes a total of only seven lines. All of these actors, as well as the principal players, obviously enjoyed their roles, which were considerably tongue-in-check, and this enjoyment comes through to the audience. *Around the World in 80 Days* opens in London's Reform Club in 1872 as an eccentric English gentleman named Phileas Fogg (David Niven) bets twenty thousand pounds that he can go around the world in the then-incredibly fast time of eighty days. Fogg and his manservant Passepartout (Cantinflas) embark on their breathless tour of the world, getting into silly jams and overcoming monumental obstacles. On the way, an Indian Maharani, Princess Aouda (Shirley MacLaine), joins them when Fogg rescues her from a funeral pyre. At the same time Scotland Yard Inspector Fix (Robert Newton) mistakenly suspects Fogg of being the man who had recently robbed the Bank of England, and follows in close pursuit. The course of the journey is a beautiful *mélange* of fantastic modes of transportation, magnificent scenery, and wild misadventures. From the air-filled balloon which takes them over the Alps, to the final leg of the journey across the Atlantic in a steam-powered wooden ship, Fogg and Passepartout use almost every means of transportation known in the 1870's.

The film ends as Fogg wins his wager by appearing in the Reform Club just as the clock strikes 8:45 P.M. on the evening of Saturday, December 21, 1872, exactly eighty days to the minute from the time Fogg had left his whist-playing cronies. His devotion to punctuality and propriety is somewhat marred, however, by the appearance of Princess Aouda in the club. The members are aghast that a woman has entered the club for the first time, and the audience begins to realize that Fogg's life will now be irrevocably changed.

David Niven is outstanding as the staid Phileas Fogg, whist player and intrepid adventurer. "Have there been women in his life?" the princess asks Passepartout regarding the persnickety Englishman. "I assume he must have had a mother," the valet replies. In his first movie made outside Latin America, Mexico's idolized comedian Cantinflas is wonderful as Fogg's curious, ingenious servant. Like Charles Chaplin, he is a master mimic and does his own stunt work, sliding down a high wire, jumping atop a moving train, and fighting in a comic bullfight along with Luis Dominguin. There is one funny sequence in which Fogg and Passepartout ride in the rococo balloon *La Coquette* over the mountaintops across the French-Spanish border. Passepartout leans over, scoops up a pailful of snow, and chills the champagne with it; he and Fogg then ceremonially toast to their success. Robert Newton, in his last role before his death, is equally fine as Mr. Fix, the bumbling English detective who thinks Fogg is an escaped criminal, as is Shirley MacLaine as the Princess Aouda.

Cinematographer Lionel Lindon exquisitely captures all the characters' seriocomic adventures with his dazzling use of many aerial and panoramic shots and with his gorgeous color photography, especially striking in such shots as those of Oriental sunsets with temples silhouetted against a river, or the brilliant sight of the Spanish city of Chincon. Victor Young wrote the musical score which makes use of authentic international melodies, and his mock use of "Rule Brittania" is particularly humorous. Likewise, Perelman's dialogue is custom-tailored to each new location of the film, whether that location calls for stuffy Victorian phraseology or homespun American colloquialisms.

The film's opening prologue is noteworthy for the appearance of Edward R. Murrow, the famed radio and television commentator. In this, his first job in Hollywood, Murrow solemnly speaks about the "shrinking world and Man's search for new horizons" as we see shots of guided missiles and pictures of the earth from afar plus a condensation of Frenchman George Melies' *Le Voyage Dans La Lune* (*A Trip to the Moon*), also based upon a story by Jules Verne. The epilogue, designed by Saul Bass, provides a remarkable and colorful ending for the film.

Around the World in 80 Days was directed by the then-thirty-six-year-old Englishman Michael Anderson, the director of the screen version of George Orwell's *1984* (1955). The real genius behind the production, however, was veteran Broadway stage producer and showman Michael Todd. *Around the World in 80 Days* marked Todd's debut in motion pictures. He not only raised the necessary finances for the film, but also worked as impromptu director, ad lib screenwriter, location scout, and film editor. In addition, he was partly responsible for the development of the revolutionary wide screen Todd-AO Process. (*Around the World in 80 Days* was the second film to use the process;

Rodgers' and Hammerstein's *Oklahoma!*, 1955, was the first.) Todd's efforts, which at times during the filming seemed destined for failure because of the high production costs, finally paid off when the film was released. It received rave reviews and was the second-highest moneymaker of 1957, finishing just behind *The Ten Commandments*. It was placed high on all of the major lists of the ten best films of the year, and garnered five Academy Awards from its numerous nominations. This colossal film has a few minor flaws: Murrow's introduction is overly long; some sequences are inserted merely to exploit the Todd-AO Process; other scenes are static tableaux at the expense of narrative thrust; and occasionally the diverse accents are difficult to understand. Nonetheless, the movie remains a stunning aural and visual achievement and proved to be a huge international success. Ironically, Michael Todd died in a plane crash on March 22, 1958, just as the film was moving into general release on the worldwide market.

Leslie Taubman

ARSENIC AND OLD LACE

Released: 1944 (completed 1941)
Production: Frank Capra for Warner Bros.
Direction: Frank Capra
Screenplay: Julius J. Epstein and Philip G. Epstein; based on the play of the same name by Joseph Kesselring
Cinematography: Sol Polito
Editing: Daniel Mandell
Running time: 118 minutes

Principal characters:
Mortimer Brewster .... Cary Grant
Abby Brewster .... Josephine Hull
Martha Brewster ....Jean Adair
Teddy Brewster .... John Alexander
Elaine Harper .... Priscilla Lane
Jonathan Brewster .... Raymond Massey
Dr. Einstein .... Peter Lorre
O'Hara .... Jack Carson
Lieutenant Rooney .... James Gleason
Mr. Witherspoon .... Edward Everett Horton
Judge Cullman .... Vaughan Glaser

Arsenic and Old Lace was one of the biggest Broadway hits of the 1940's, a fast-paced, light-hearted treatment of murder exemplifying the black humor of the time. When Frank Capra bought the film rights to the play and began production in late 1941, it was with the stipulation that he would not release the film until it had closed on Broadway. Capra had hoped to use the income from the film to support his family while he earned the pay of a major in the Army. Unfortunately for Capra, the play was extremely popular and the movie could not be released until 1944. However, his good fortune lay in securing the talents of Josephine Hull, Jean Adair, and John Alexander of the original cast for his film version. Having signed Cary Grant, Hollywood's best *farceur*, for the lead role of Mortimer Brewster, Capra then chose some of his favorite character actors to round out his cast, notably Edward Everett Horton and James Gleason.

Translating hit Broadway plays to the screen has always been a problem for Hollywood, and it even proved a problem for a creative hand such as Capra. Critics complained then and still complain about the scenes that were added to the original play: a comment about the unorthodox behavior of Brooklynites is exemplified by a riot scene during a Dodgers game at Ebbetts Field; a scene with Mortimer Brewster, a drama critic, and his fiancée, Elaine Harper (Priscilla Lane), applying for a marriage license; the newlyweds' tryst in the cemetery next to the Brewster mansion; and a cabby waiting for Mortimer throughout the movie with the meter on and eventually presenting him with a $22.50 tab. But in spite of these additions, *Arsenic and Old Lace* remains as entertaining on the screen as it was on the stage.

Martha (Jean Adair) and Abby Brewster (Josephine Hull) are two wealthy, sweet old maids who live in the old family mansion where they take care of their nephew, Teddy (John Alexander). Teddy needs a great deal of care, since he thinks he is President Theodore Roosevelt. One delightful and famous feature of Teddy's behavior is that every time he goes upstairs, he yells "Charge!" and then charges up to the second floor. But if Teddy is strange, his aunts are even stranger. Very church-oriented, one of their charitable acts is to serve a special elderberry wine laced with a combination of arsenic, strychnine, and cyanide to unsuspecting lonely old gentlemen who come to inquire about the room they advertize for rent. That the ladies are disarmingly sentimental about their victims, remembering all their names, and are blissfully unaware that what they are doing is immoral, makes for a very amusing situation. The bodies are properly disposed of by Teddy, who thinks that they are all yellow-fever victims from Panama and must be buried quickly to avoid contagion. He digs a grave in the cellar, which he believes to be the Panama Canal, and then he and the sisters holds a proper Christian burial service. It is all quite tidy.

However, things take a turn when Teddy's brother Mortimer (Cary Grant) comes to tell his aunts that he has married. While there, Mortimer discovers his aunts' latest "charity case" in the window seat. At first he thinks the eccentric Teddy is responsible, but with some pride his aunts assure him that the dead man is their doing. With the revelation that this is their twelfth victim, Mortimer almost goes crazy himself. However, while he worries about what to do about the situation, he prevents his aunts from taking a thirteenth victim.

When Mortimer goes out to see about getting his aunts committed to an insane asylum, his older brother Jonathan (Raymond Massey), stealthily arrives at the house with his cohort Dr. Einstein (Peter Lorre), a plastic surgeon of sorts. Jonathan is a very cold-blooded killer who likewise boasts of twelve dead victims; he also bears a striking resemblance to Boris Karloff. Jonathan has eluded the police because Dr. Einstein has given him three different faces in five years. Unfortunately, the last time he operated, Dr. Einstein had recently seen a horror movie and was drunk when he operated; the result is that Jonathan has ended up with Boris Karloff's face. Jonathan is extremely unhappy about this and turns murderously angry whenever anyone reminds him of it. The two have come to the Brewster house so Dr. Einstein can operate again and correct his error. While Raymond Massey is made up to look like Karloff and his reaction to the allusions to his face is amusing, the humor loses some of its sharpness on the screen; the real Boris

Karloff played Jonathan in the original Broadway version.

Abby and Martha make it very clear that Jonathan's menacing presence is not welcome and that they would like him to leave. During the evening it becomes known that Jonathan also has a body to dispose of—that of his twelfth victim. However, he has decided to stay for a long time, since the quiet, respectable house is a perfect hiding place.

When Mortimer returns, we find that there is little love lost between the two brothers. Discovering a new body in the window seat, Mortimer realizes that this is his brother's victim and that he now has a hold on him. However, when Jonathan discovers his aunts' victim in the cellar, he realizes that he also has a trump card. Meanwhile, however, the fact that his aunts have accumulated the same number of victims as he has makes Jonathan jealous, and to beat them, he decides to make Mortimer his thirteenth victim. Jonathan and the doctor tie Mortimer to a chair so Jonathan can kill him by the "Melbourne method," a slow method which even gives Einstein the shivers. Just as Jonathan is about to strangle his brother, police officer O'Hara (Jack Carson) arrives. O'Hara has ambitions of being a playwright, and finding Mortimer quiet and unoccupied at the moment, he takes advantage of the situation to relate the lengthy plot of his play to the helpless drama critic. A stereotypal dumb cop, O'Hara is oblivious to the fact that Mortimer is bound and gagged. Mortimer, Jonathan, and Einstein are saved from being bored to death by the arrival of two more policemen who have come to see about putting Teddy away, as he is just too much of a neighborhood nuisance. Luckily for Mortimer, they *do* notice that he is tied up, and they become very suspicious of Jonathan because of his looks. When Lieutenant Rooney (James Gleason) and Judge Cullman (Vaughan Glaser) arrive to help commit Teddy, the lieutenant recognizes Jonathan right away from wanted posters and arrests him.

Seeking some sort of revenge, Jonathan tells the police officers about the twelve bodies in the basement, but none of them will believe him. When Teddy backs up the story, the police take that as evidence that it is a crazy story from two crazy men. Even hardboiled Rooney refuses to believe it when Martha and Abby offer to show him the graves in the cellar. When the sisters are told that Teddy has to go to Happy Dale they insist on going with him and happily commit themselves. One of the play's running jokes concerns Mortimer's worry about the insanity in his family. When he signs the commitment papers as next of kin, the sisters quietly take him aside and tell him that he is really not a Brewster, but the son of a sea cook. Instead of being upset, Mortimer is overjoyed that he is not part of this family. However, the strain of dealing with four insane people has driven him slightly crazy, and the judge wonders if he is not committing the wrong Brewster. While everyone is busy getting the papers signed, Dr. Einstein tries to sneak out of the house. He is stopped by Mortimer who asks him to sign the papers because a doctor's signature is needed. Everyone is so engrossed in the paper signing that Einstein is the only one who is aware that Rooney is concurrently getting a description of him as Jonathan's accomplice over the phone. His services over, Einstein quietly escapes, unable to believe his luck.

Teddy is persuaded to leave for Happy Dale when Mortimer tells him that his term in office is over. Teddy decides that now he can go on his African safari. After everyone else has left, and while waiting for Teddy to get his things together, the sisters strike up a conversation with Mr. Witherspoon (Edward Everett Horton), the head of Happy Dale. It turns out that Mr. Witherspoon is alone in the world and not very happy. As the movie ends, the sisters sweetly offer him a glass of elderberry wine.

Arsenic and Old Lace was a departure for Capra. His previous major films, such as *Mr. Smith Goes to Washington* (1939) and *Meet John Doe* (1941), were full of social commentary and the celebration of the common man. There is not a trace of either in this film; a fact, Capra has reported, that could not have made him happier. Critics have always thought of the film as one of Capra's lesser efforts. In fact, some analyses of his work have either glossed over it or omitted it completely. The critics felt that the additions to the original play broke up its fast pace and did little to heighten its humor. They criticized the great amount of overacting from everyone, especially from Cary Grant and Jack Carson. Capra unashamedly admits that he let his cast romp and mug to their hearts' content. With all its faults, even some of the critics had to admit that the film was and is rollicking good fun. Most of the lines and sight gags are still funny today, making the film a continuous favorite with audiences.

Ellen J. Snyder

THE AWFUL TRUTH

Released: 1937
Production: Leo McCarey for Columbia
Direction: Leo McCarey (AA)
Screenplay: Vina Delmar; based on the play of the same name by Arthur
   Richman
Cinematography: Joseph Walker
Editing: Al Clark
Running time: 92 minutes

> *Principal characters:*
> Lucy Warriner .... Irene Dunne
> Jerry Warriner .... Cary Grant
> Daniel Leeson .... Ralph Bellamy
> Armand Duvalle .... Alexander D'Arcy
> Aunt Patsy .... Cecil Cunningham
> Barbara Vance .... Molly Lamont
> Mrs. Leeson .... Esther Dale

The Awful Truth was one of the most admired and popular zany comedies of the 1930's, and it is still regarded as one of the best. Stylishly written, directed, and acted, it has a warmth and charm that spring both from the excellent performances of the actors and from director Leo McCarey's involvement with his material. McCarey had worked on "Our Gang" comedy shorts for Hal Roach and had directed some Laurel and Hardy films. He had also worked with Mae West, W. C. Fields, and the Marx Brothers. In *The Awful Truth*, he applied some of the slapstick visual style and comic timing he had learned earlier to the more sophisticated and romantic marital farce in order to obtain the perfect synthesis of visual and verbal humor.

At the beginning of the film, the opportunity for suspicion and distrust in the marriage of Lucy (Irene Dunne) and Jerry Warriner (Cary Grant) emerges. Jerry returns home from a supposed vacation in Florida to find his wife gone. When she returns in full evening dress with her handsome voice teacher, Armand Duvalle (Alexander D'Arcy), and a story about being out all night because the car broke down, Jerry is suspicious but tries to appear nonchalant. Then, when he gives Lucy a basket of fruit he says he has bought on his vacation and she finds that it is marked "grown in California," she has her own reasons for becoming suspicious. Though each gives lip service to the idea that they have a happy marriage free from doubts, Lucy is soon on the telephone to her lawyer to arrange a divorce.

The divorce is granted, but the focus of the film is the ninety-day waiting period before it becomes final. Although Lucy gets custody of Mr. Smith, their Airedale, Jerry gets visiting rights, so their paths often cross. They bicker, try romances with other people, become jealous, and finally find that they do not want to marry anyone else. Moments before the divorce decree would have become final, they reconcile.

Neither Lucy nor Jerry admits to wanting to get back together, but from the divorce proceedings on, both act as if they want the other back. Both embark on new romances, but without much enthusiasm. Lucy's Aunt Patsy (Cecil Cunningham) is staying with her, and, bored from sitting at home every night, she practically thrusts Lucy into the arms of a rich Oklahoma oil man, Daniel Leeson (Ralph Bellamy), so that he may be their escort. Even though Daniel is the complete opposite of Jerry and Lucy's other friends, Lucy determines to marry him mainly to show Jerry that she does not need him. This romance with a naïve homespun man who says things such as "I'm so happy I could eat three steaks" hurts Jerry, though he tries not to show it. He is jealous, especially because he thinks Daniel is not worthy of Lucy. "What kind of a line could he have that would impress you?" Jerry asks Lucy. Slyly trying to break up the romance, he pretends to encourage it. Brimming with sarcasm, he extolls the virtues of living in Oklahoma and gives Lucy a glowing recommendation when Daniel's mother (Esther Dale), upon whom Daniel relies heavily, expresses doubts about Lucy's reputation. These tactics make Lucy uncomfortable, but the romance survives until Daniel and his mother happen to be present when Jerry and Armand have a fight in Lucy's bedroom. Dumbfounded, Daniel says, "Well, I guess a man's best friend is his mother," and they leave.

Lucy returns the favor when she learns of Jerry's impending engagement to socialite Barbara Vance (Molly Lamont). Posing as Jerry's gauche sister, she crashes a dinner at the home of Barbara's parents and disconcerts Jerry by pretending to be drunk and by telling embarrassing stories about him. Jerry has to leave the dinner and take her away.

The comedy begins on a small scale and becomes generally more outrageous throughout the film. In an early scene Jerry hides behind a door and tickles Lucy as she talks to Daniel. When he encounters Lucy and Daniel at a nightclub, Jerry encourages them to dance because he can see Lucy is embarrassed by Daniel's awkward dancing style, and he prolongs her agony by paying the orchestra leader to play an encore.

Later, Armand is visiting Lucy, but when Jerry arrives, she pretends to be alone and hides Armand in the bedroom. The scene becomes hilarious when she sees Armand's hat and desperately tries to hide it while Mr. Smith, the Airedale, keeps retrieving it. Everything gets out of hand when Jerry also has to hide in the bedroom and starts a noisy fight with Armand that carries them through the living room and out into the hall, to the astonishment of Daniel Leeson and his mother.

In another slapstick scene Jerry attempts to break into a room where he thinks Armand and Lucy are alone. Armand's Oriental houseboy bars his

way, and the two engage in a wild wrestling match. Finally, Jerry eludes the
houseboy's grasp and bursts through the door, only to find Lucy giving a
recital before a group of sedate society women.

Perhaps wildest of all are Lucy's zany antics after disrupting the Vances'
dinner party. She persuades Jerry to drive her to Aunt Patsy's cabin, but
before they leave she turns the car radio up full blast and throws away the
knob. Near the cabin she deliberately causes an accident. Total chaos ensues
when Lucy and Jerry's arguing is added to the sound of the radio and the
questions of the two motorcycle policemen who have arrived on the scene.

Lucy and Jerry's second courtship is conducted largely through comic scenes
in which they try to conceal their true feelings. They do at times, however,
allow their sentiments to show. We see this especially in a scene near the end
of the film in which Lucy reminds Jerry of the first time they had champagne
together, and both become emotional.

The last sequence of the film finds Lucy and Jerry again trying to hide their
love for each other. Lucy has successfully set up the situation. Because of
the automobile "accident" they are forced to stay the night in Aunt Patsy's
cabin. They go to bed in separate rooms, knowing it is the last day of their
ninety-day waiting period; at midnight they will be officially divorced. But
there is a weak catch on the door between the rooms, and both surreptitiously
begin encouraging it to open. Above the door is a clock; on one side is a
figure of a man and on the other the figure of a woman. Every quarter hour
they come out, turn around, and go back in. In the last shot of the film the
clock strikes midnight, the two figures come out and turn around, but instead
of going back alone the man goes back in with the woman.

The casting of the picture contributes to our understanding of the romance.
Indeed, in the heyday of Hollywood one could tell by looking at the names
of the stars which two would end up together. In *The Awful Truth* Cary Grant
and Irene Dunne are the only two stars, so we expect them to remain the
romantic couple. As actors and as characters they play so well together that
we easily see why they are not satisfied with anyone else. Third-billed is
Ralph Bellamy, who made a career of playing the man who loses the woman
(often to Cary Grant).

Director Leo McCarey often had his actors improvise scenes based on a
line he had given them. Under this type of direction, Irene Dunne and Cary
Grant give inspired, perfectly timed performances, although some scenes are
allowed to go on too long (for example, Lucy's description of the Vances'
dinner party and the wild car ride that culminates in a night at Aunt Patsy's
cabin). Generally, however, *The Awful Truth* is a perfect blend of the ridiculous and the romantic, artful enough to have won McCarey the Oscar for
Best Direction.

Timothy W. Johnson

THE BAD AND THE BEAUTIFUL

Released: 1952
Production: John Houseman for Metro-Goldwyn-Mayer
Direction: Vincente Minnelli
Screenplay: Charles Schnee (AA); based on the story "Tribute to a Bad Man"
　by George Bradshaw
Cinematography: Robert Surtees (AA)
Editing: Conrad A. Nervig
Art direction: Cedric Gibbons and Edward Carfagno (AA)
Set decoration: Edwin B. Willis and Keogh Gleason (AA)
Costume design: Helen Rose (AA)
Running time: 118 minutes

> *Principal characters:*
> Jonathan Shields .... Kirk Douglas
> Georgia Lorrison .... Lana Turner
> Harry Pebbel .... Walter Pidgeon
> James Lee Bartlow .... Dick Powell
> Fred Amiel .... Barry Sullivan
> Rosemary Bartlow .... Gloria Grahame (AA)
> Victor "Gaucho" Ribera .... Gilbert Roland
> Von Ellstein .... Ivan Triesault

Long before Budd Schulberg's famous novel fictionally devastated a Hollywood producer, people had been asking the question "What makes Hollywood run?" The subject had been treated in many films—*Sullivan's Travels* (1941) and *Sunset Boulevard* (1950), for example. In these films and others like them, Hollywood was usually a mythical kingdom, flashy, romantic, humorous, and sometimes tragic. Mainly actors and actresses—the faces, voices, and lives of those before the camera—had been dealt with. No one had yet tackled the producer seriously; when he had been represented, it had been either as a figure to laugh at or as a father image, as in *A Star Is Born* (1937) and *The Goldwyn Follies* (1938). And usually, the producer was played by Adolphe Menjou, especially in the 1930's.

In 1952, Vincente Minnelli attempted to remedy this situation. He was approached by John Houseman, the well-known producer and associate of Orson Welles, about an idea for a film based on a short story by George Bradshaw called "Tribute to a Bad Man," about the rise and fall of a charming schemer in the theater. Minnelli and Houseman approached Dore Schary at M-G-M and suggested that the setting be changed to Hollywood and that the main character be turned into a film producer. When the screenplay by Charles Schnee was finished, it so fascinated Minnelli that he immediately agreed to direct it with a budget of a little over one million dollars.

The casting quickly fell into place, headlined by Kirk Douglas as Jonathan

Shields, the ruthless and opportunistic producer, based loosely on a composite of David O. Selznick and Val Lewton. Lana Turner was cast as Georgia Lorrison, a drunk who rehabilitates herself and becomes a star. Walter Pidgeon plays the slightly seedy "B" picture producer Harry Pebbel, and Dick Powell portrays the Southern novelist James Lee Bartlow who comes to know and to reject, *à la* William Faulkner, the Hollywood scene. With Gloria Grahame as Powell's flirtatious Southern belle wife Rosemary and Barry Sullivan as the director Fred Amiel, Minnelli completed his casting. His idea was to incorporate many of the well-known Hollywood legends into the film and yet, at the same time, give it a life of its own. He met this challenge successfully, and the resulting film possesses an inherent reality, even though it appears to be a cliché about the fleshpots of Hollywood. The plot involves a strange paradox: in rising to power, a gifted producer betrays all of his closest friends, who nontheless attain success and are called upon to help him when he needs it.

The film opens as director Fred Amiel, leading actress Georgia Lorrison, and prize-winning author James Bartlow are gathered together in the office of studio executive Harry Pebbel. Jonathan Shields, whose father had been one of the founders of the film industry and who is determined to rebuild the family fortune and regain possession of the Shields studio, is an old enemy of them all. He is now down on his luck and has asked for help. As the camera moves in on each of their faces while they are considering Shields's request, flashbacks of their different pasts quickly reveal that Shields has trampled each of them on his climb to success.

The audience learns that Shields, enlisting the aid of young would-be director Fred Amiel, tricked Harry Pebbel, a former employee of his father, into giving him and Amiel jobs with Pebbel's production unit. Starting with shoestring budgets, they worked their way up to bigger productions, including a film which pays homage to Val Lewton's *Cat People* (1942) and has actors prancing around in cat costumes. Finally, Shields and Amiel persuaded popular film star Victor "Gaucho" Ribera (Gilbert Roland) to play the lead in a picture written by Amiel. However, in order to persuade the studio to make the film, Shields doublecrossed Amiel and agreed to allow the famous Von Ellstein (Ivan Triesault), to be the director. Amiel and Shields parted in anger, the film became a hit, and Shields continued his rise with Pebbel eventually working for him.

In this one sequence, so many Hollywood legends and stories are incorporated that it is difficult to separate fact from fiction. Like David Selznick, who went into pictures to avenge his father's ruin, Shields is portrayed as a perfectionist. Von Ellstein is not unlike a von Stroheim-style director, and the similarities to Lewton have already been mentioned. Moreover, the appearance of the Shields studio when Jonathan Shields first comes in has the correct "poverty row" atmosphere, and looks like RKO or a "B" picture unit at

Columbia.

The next segment of the film is also heavily steeped in film lore. It is the story of Georgia Lorrison, daughter of the greatest Hamlet the stage had ever known. In the flashback, Jonathan Shields finds her in a drunken stupor listening to recordings of her father reciting Hamlet's soliloquy, and surrounded by photographs, in profile, of him. The parallel between John and Diana Barrymore could not be clearer, but in the film, Georgia Lorrison succeeds where Diana Barrymore failed, and, with Shields's help, is rehabilitated and becomes a star. Her big mistake is to fall in love with Shields and to believe he loves her in return. When Georgia finds Shields in the arms of an ambitious extra at a party, she drives home in a tear-stained frenzy and walks out of Shields's life.

Shields's next pawn is a young college professor, James Bartlow, who has written a best-selling novel. He comes to Hollywood unwillingly, but is talked into adapting the book for the movies by his wife Rosemary. Shields tries to collaborate with Bartlow in adapting his book, but their progress is constantly frustrated by interference from Bartlow's wife. In a ruse to get Rosemary out of the way, Shields induces Victor "Gaucho" Ribera, an actor with considerable Latin charm, to take her on a romantic sojourn to Mexico. Their private plane crashes and both Rosemary and Ribera are killed, causing Bartlow to leave Hollywood in disgust after discovering Shields's part in the tragedy.

When filming begins on Bartlow's script, the autocratic Shields quarrels with the director and takes over the direction himself. The film turns out to be Shields's third box-office disaster. He goes bankrupt and loses his studio. Three years later, as his four ex-colleagues are sitting in Pebbel's office, they vow not to help him. Then the phone rings and Jonathan Shields exerts his old magic; all four agree to assist him in making a fresh start.

Minnelli's precise powers of observation are everywhere evident in this picture, from the scenes of moviemaking to the blasé small talk at Hollywood parties. He elicited excellent performances from all his actors, with Kirk Douglas immediately grasping the Jonathan Shields character and playing him as an irresistible cad. Lana Turner surprised everyone by showing just how far she could stretch her acting ability when well directed. In one scene in particular, as she is driving home from the party after being jilted and collapses in a state of hysteria on the steering wheel, she demonstrates a dramatic ability not seen since *The Postman Always Rings Twice* (1946). Walter Pidgeon's studio executive, Barry Sullivan's director, and Dick Powell's writer were all believable; and Gloria Grahame's performance as the frivolous Southern belle garnered her an Academy Award as Best Supporting Actress.

Prior to the film's release, the M-G-M publicity wheels were grinding away. Here was a picture about "our town" and no one was going to forget it. A typical M-G-M blurb billed the picture as "not the Hollywood of yesterday, but Today's Hollywood, showing the working of both a great motion picture Studio and behind-the-scenes of what makes Hollywood tick." Sometime during the course of the filming, the name of the picture was changed. Since Lana Turner was getting star billing, *Tribute to a Bad Man* hardly seemed fitting, so *The Bad and the Beautiful* was settled upon—the "Bad" referring to Kirk Douglas and the "beautiful" to Lana Turner.

The film opened on Christmas Day, 1952, in Los Angeles. The critics were delighted, especially in Hollywood, where the subject matter of the film was all too familiar. John Houseman, the film's producer, summed it all up best in a *Look* magazine interview in January, 1953, in which he stated, "People like these develop in any business where the rewards are high. We made it a Hollywood story because this is a colorful industry."

Joan Cohen

BAD DAY AT BLACK ROCK

Released: 1954
Production: Dore Schary for Metro-Goldwyn-Mayer
Direction: John Sturges
Screenplay: Millard Kaufman; based on Don McGuire's adaptation of the story "Bad Time at Honda" by Howard Breslin
Cinematography: William C. Mellor
Editing: Newell P. Kimlin
Running time: 81 minutes

Principal characters:
John J. MacReedy	Spencer Tracy
Reno Smith	Robert Ryan
Liz Wirth	Anne Francis
Tim Horn	Dean Jagger
Doc Velie	Walter Brennan
Pete Wirth	John Erickson
Coley Trimble	Ernest Borgnine
Hector David	Lee Marvin

Bad Day at Black Rock is a particularly fascinating message picture for two reasons: first, because the message is set in a successful, tightly plotted suspense drama; and second, because opinion as to what its message is has changed considerably since the film was originally released. Reviewers of the time saw the film's theme as one of civic responsibility, individual integrity, and group complacency; the *Hollywood Reporter* went further, seeing in the story a specific statement about United States treatment of citizens of Japanese ancestry during World War II. No reviewers of the time, however, saw the message that seems so clear today: *Bad Day at Black Rock* is a scathing indictment of the blacklist in Hollywood.

Spencer Tracy plays John MacReedy, a one-armed veteran who comes to the town of Black Rock to deliver a medal to Kumoku, a Japanese farmer, father of the man who saved MacReedy's life in the battlefields of Italy. He finds the town sullen, hostile, and uncooperative. Led by Reno Smith (Robert Ryan), the majority of the few citizens we see seem to be protecting a secret which clearly involves Kumoku, the object of MacReedy's search. After visiting the farmer's burned-out home, MacReedy tries to telephone and then telegraph state police to report a possible crime against the missing farmer, but he is prevented from reaching the outside world by the conspiracy of silence enforced by the group of men led by Smith. Finally, MacReedy beats up one of the men who by now plans to kill him for his interference. One conscience-stricken member of the group, Pete Wirth (John Erickson), significantly the youngest, decides to help MacReedy; he breaks down and tells him the town's secret.

Seized by a "patriotic" fever after Pearl Harbor, a group of men led by Reno Smith began to harass Kumoku. Smith harbored an additional grudge against the farmer: Kumoku bought his farm from Smith and made it work after Smith had failed. One night the drunken "patriots" had set fire to Kumoku's house; and when the farmer ran out, Smith shot him. In covering up the murder, all the men became accomplices.

The boy calls his sister Liz (Anne Francis) after telling MacReedy the story, asking her to help him escape; but she tells Smith, who organizes an ambush. MacReedy manages to capture Smith, but not before Smith, as part of his ambush plan, has killed a girl who would have been a witness to his crimes. When MacReedy leaves, Doc Velie (Walter Brennan), the first man to help MacReedy, asks him to give Kumoku's medal to the whole town to remind the people of the cowardly conspiracy that nearly destroyed Black Rock.

In the climate of fear that existed during the McCarthy years in Hollywood, any criticism of the tragedies, injustices, and terrorism of the blacklist had to be carefully camouflaged. Genre films, whose established conventions offered a ready-made smoke screen, were often given a layer of meaning more relevant to the 1950's than to the subjects of the films. Westerns were most often used because of their historical distance in terms of setting: *Johnny Guitar* (1954) is an outstanding example.

Bad Day at Black Rock was called a "motorized Western" by one reviewer; although it is set in post-World War II America, its narrative conventions and isolated outdoor setting place it in the Western genre, thus providing enough distance to enable the filmmakers to state their message rather directly. On the surface, the film protests self-interest and revenge in the name of patriotism, and specifically, it attacks the ill treatment of the Japanese. It shows with bitter irony that while Smith was murdering Kumoku's father in the name of Americanism, the young Kumoku was fighting for the United States in Italy. It does not take much imagination to extend this message. Many of the "anti-Red" witnesses who appeared before the House Un-American Activities Committee during its hearings in Hollywood were taking their revenge on enemies by naming them Communists and thus ruining their careers. And, like the initially silent and uninvolved characters in the film, Doc and Liz, many people in the film and television industries were aware of the injustices done to others but did not speak out against them.

Bad Day at Black Rock demonstrates the guilt that concealment breeds. When the train stops to let MacReedy off in the opening shots of the film, the town looks isolated, desolate, uninviting. This is the first time the train has made this stop since Kumoku's death; and the very fact of someone entering from the outside represents a danger to the guilty citizens. The self-imposed isolation of the town is emphasized by long, lonely shots of

MacReedy walking down the street trying to find a car to rent, and by unbalanced compositions in which a man's suspicious face seems to hang in the corner of the frame. Black Rock's closed doors suggest a frightened populace. Those who linger around the hotel are part of the group which burned Kumoku's farm, with the exception of Doc and Sheriff Tim Horn (Dean Jagger); and their restless lack of activity as they sit and nervously speculate on MacReedy's motives and intentions suggests the unhealthy state of the town.

Two secondary characters are of particular interest as victims of guilt. One is the Sheriff, a drunken straw man set up by Smith to give his domination of the town a legal front. The Sheriff does not even fully know the secret, and has an attack of conscience when MacReedy asks him questions. Trying to use the power of his badge, the Sheriff stands up to Smith, but is easily knocked down again into the drunk he has become. When appealed to by MacReedy and Doc, he again hides in his bottle, too weak to act on his own best intentions. Also interesting is Hector David, played with his full range of sadistic violence by Lee Marvin. Turned into an unthinking bully by his power as Smith's right-hand man, he torments MacReedy verbally, trying to provoke the crippled veteran into an apparently unequal fight. MacReedy endures his insults until Hector actually lays hands on him, and then he beats the bully easily by using judo.

Bad Day at Black Rock is a fascinating film on whatever level one wishes to view it: as a suspense/action drama it is fully satisfying, and as a general message film about civic responsibility it is powerful without becoming preachy. But to appreciate fully not only the film itself but also its relationship to its frightening time, it can be seen as a powerful and effective protest against the McCarthy years in this country. Perhaps the medal MacReedy leaves for the town of Black Rock to remind them of what happened and to prevent it from happening again is what this film should be for our own time.

Janey Place

BALL OF FIRE

Released: 1941
Production: Samuel Goldwyn for RKO/Radio
Direction: Howard Hawks
Screenplay: Billy Wilder and Charles Brackett; based on the story *From A to Z* by Billy Wilder and Thomas Monroe
Cinematography: Gregg Toland
Editing: Daniel Mandell
Running time: 111 minutes

> *Principal characters:*
> Professor Bertram Potts .... Gary Cooper
> Sugarpuss O'Shea .... Barbara Stanwyck
> Joe Lilac .... Dana Andrews
> Professor Oddly .... Richard Haydn
> Professor Gurkakoff .... Oscar Homolka
> Professor Jerome .... Henry Travers
> Professor Magenbruch .... S. Z. Sakall
> Professor Robinson .... Tully Marshall
> Professor Quintana .... Leonid Kinskey
> Professor Peagram .... Aubrey Mather
> Garbage Man .... Allen Jenkins

Although Hollywood has produced a variety of characterizations of the intellectual—from Bing Crosby's crooning professor in *College Humor* (1933) to Clint Eastwood's macho, mountain-climbing art historian who is also an assassin in *The Eiger Sanction* (1975)—the image audiences seem to remember best is that of the stuffy absent-minded professor. *Ball of Fire*, directed by Howard Hawks and written by Billy Wilder and Charles Brackett, is perhaps the film which best embodies the quintessential use of that stereotype.

The film opens in the study of a group of scholars who have been living and working together for nine years. They are predominately old, white-haired, conservatively dressed, and slightly unkempt. Of the eight members, only Bertram Potts (Gary Cooper) has any youth or virility. Their housekeeper, who regards all of them as overgrown children, scolds them for sneaking into the pantry to eat the strawberry jam. The project of the group is to write all the articles for an encyclopedia financed by a rich inventor who is upset that his name is not in any other encyclopedia. Each scholar specializes in a given discipline, such as botany or history, and writes all the articles in his specific area. Potts's specialty is language.

Although the youngest of the scholars, Potts is very much the pedant. He chides the housekeeper for splitting infinitives and believes that his only concern is grammar; he is naïve, innocent, and sheltered from the world. It takes a garbage man, some gangsters, and a nightclub singer to overturn the quiet, orderly world of Potts and the other scholars. The garbage man (Allen Jenkins), having noticed that the household possesses a great many books, appears, hoping that the scholars can assist him with answers to a newspaper quiz, the only use anyone seems to have for their knowledge. Similar to all the other scholars, Potts has reached the letter "S" in his research and has just written an article on slang. Listening to the garbage man talk, however, Potts realizes that his article is very much out of date and in need of revision. Since the only place to research contemporary slang is in the outside world, he leaves the house, the only one of the scholars to do so in the nine years that they have been working on the encyclopedia. (To ensure that their script was authentic and contemporary, Wilder and Brackett made similar investigations of slang, visiting malt shops, bars, and racetracks—putting the bar bills and racetrack losses on the film's expense account.)

During his research in the outside world, Potts listens to many different people until finally he wanders into a nightclub where Sugarpuss O'Shea (Barbara Stanwyck) is singing. Potts makes careful notes on the slang she uses in her song, and after the show, goes to her dressing room to invite her to come to the scholars' house the next day to assist him in his linguistic research. Sugarpuss is totally unreceptive both to the idea and to Potts, whom she neither likes nor understands; he is totally alien to her world of nightclubs, gangsters, flashy clothes, and easy money. Later that night, however, she is forced to accept the invitation because she needs a place to hide from the police who want to question her about a murder committed by her gangster lover, Joe Lilac (Dana Andrews).

Naturally, her presence in the house completely disrupts work on the encyclopedia. Not one of the staid old scholars is immune to her vivacity and allure, and before very long she has them dancing around the room in a Conga line. Finally Potts feels he must ask her to leave so that they can continue their work: "Make no mistake, I shall regret the absence of your keen mind. Unfortunately it is inseparable from an extremely disturbing body." However, since the police are still looking for her, Sugarpuss cannot leave. In order to change Potts's mind, she stands on a stack of books to kiss him, showing she does know a good use for books.

Completely out of his realm in the world of romance, Potts falls in love with Sugarpuss, not realizing that she is merely using him until she can rejoin Joe Lilac, and a great many complications ensue. First, Lilac tricks Potts and the scholars into bringing Sugarpuss to him so that he can marry her to keep her from testifying against him. Then, when Potts learns about the deception, he is disillusioned and leaves, believing Sugarpuss wants to marry Lilac. Sugarpuss, however, now finds Lilac and his world repugnant and refuses to marry him, with Lilac responding by threatening to kill Potts if she refuses.

In the best tradition of romantic comedies, Sugarpuss comes within moments of marrying Lilac, but the scholars apply their knowledge to outwit the gangsters sent to hold them captive until the wedding is over. They use a mirror to concentrate the sun's rays in order to burn through the cord of a picture hung above one of the gangsters, causing it to fall on him. The scholars then overpower the gangsters and set off to rescue Sugarpuss. After finding out where Lilac is hiding by tickling their former captors for information, they use guns and a blackjack to capture the whole gang. In an amusing sequence Potts studies an old-fashioned book on boxing in preparation for fighting Lilac, and when the techniques in the book do not work, he tosses the book away and immediately knocks out the gangster of his own accord. He then convinces Sugarpuss that he is her man, this time by a kiss rather than reason.

The basic concepts of the film play upon caricatures—the idea that a scholar is a stodgy, ineffectual person who is isolated from ordinary concerns, and the idea that to become a "real man" it is necessary to become physically violent. Once one realizes that caricature is the style of most of the film, however, the contrasts between Sugarpuss and the encyclopedists are delightful. Picking up a book of Greek philosophy, Sugarpuss says, "I've got a set like this with a radio inside," and when she invites him to pour a couple of drinks, light the fire, and "move in on my brain," Potts can only reply, "Any hasty random discussion would be of no scientific value."

It is also a delight to watch the group (played by such accomplished character actors as Oscar Homolka, S. Z. Sakall, and Richard Haydn) progress from being stuffy pedants to "squirrelly cherubs" (as Sugarpuss calls them) to intrepid, if not very adept, heroes. Gary Cooper, who plays Bertram Potts, was usually cast as a man of action, but in this film he is completely believable as a strait-laced grammarian who is disconcerted by the sight of Sugarpuss' leg. The biggest delight of the film, however, is the performance of Barbara Stanwyck as Sugarpuss O'Shea, the worldly-wise nightclub singer who easily manipulates the scholars but does not realize that she is falling in love. Although she is appropriately flippant and cynical in her early dealings with Potts and the other scholars, she also makes the romantic scenes near the end of the film very moving.

Director Howard Hawks is noted for his films of male camaraderie, and *Ball of Fire* fits into that mold even though Hawks's men are usually men of action rather than men of thought. Two moving scenes express this camaraderie: in one, they sit around a table the night before Potts is to be married and sing songs; in the other, when they all have returned to work thinking Sugarpuss is gone forever, the housekeeper accidentally turns on the phonograph, and each pauses wordlessly and remembers the liveliness Sugarpuss had brought to the house. Hawks also paces the film well, presenting an unhurried first part to set up the quiet, orderly world of the encyclopedists in order to emphasize the later confusion when Sugarpuss is thrown into their midst.

Ball of Fire, in short, combines excellent acting, screenwriting, and directing to produce a delightful comedy. A remake of *Ball of Fire* was filmed in 1948 as *A Song Is Born*, a musical featuring Danny Kaye and Virginia Mayo. Even though the remake was also directed by Hawks, it has few of the virtues of the original, and even Hawks is said not to have cared for it.

Timothy W. Johnson

THE BAND WAGON

Released: 1953
Production: Arthur Freed for Metro-Goldwyn-Mayer
Direction: Vincente Minnelli
Screenplay: Betty Comden and Adolph Green
Cinematography: Harry Jackson
Editing: Albert Akst
Dance direction: Michael Kidd
Song: Howard Dietz and Arthur Schwartz
Running time: 112 minutes

> *Principal characters:*
> Tony Hunter .... Fred Astaire
> Gabrielle Gerard .... Cyd Charisse
> (sung by India Adams)
> Lily Marton .... Nanette Fabray
> Lester Marton .... Oscar Levant
> Jeffrey Cordova .... Jack Buchanan
> Paul Byrd .... James Mitchell

Nearly all of Hollywood's great musicals of the 1940's and 1950's were produced for Metro-Goldwyn-Mayer by the Freed unit. Headed by Arthur Freed, a lyricist who became a producer in the late 1930's, the unit created such classics of the genre as *Meet Me in St. Louis* (1944), *Singin' in the Rain* (1952), and *Gigi* (1958). Freed was the catalyst for the group of talented film artists he had assembled, a group which included not only performers, but also writers, directors, choreographers, and designers. In 1953 the unit produced one of its most outstanding films, *The Band Wagon*.

For the film Freed chose as scriptwriters Betty Comden and Adolph Green, who together had written *On the Town* (1949) and *Singin' in the Rain*; as director Vincente Minnelli, who had directed *Meet Me in St. Louis* and *An American in Paris* (1951); and as the star Fred Astaire, who, besides his 1930's musicals with Ginger Rogers had been in such Freed films as *Yolanda and the Thief* (1945) and *Easter Parade* (1948). Freed asked Comden and Green to write a film using some of the hundreds of songs written by Howard Dietz and Arthur Schwartz. Extensive discussions followed, involving not only Freed and the writers but also Minnelli, Astaire, and others in the Freed unit. Out of Astaire's cinematic past and everyone's shared theatrical experiences came a story that is very much a part of the creative lives of all those involved in shaping the film.

Though it has a happy ending, the story is essentially concerned with such uncommon themes for a musical as loneliness, failure, and the passing of time. These themes center in the character of Tony Hunter (Fred Astaire), a musical film star. In an attempt to revive his fading popularity, he returns to New York to star in a light Broadway musical that his friends Lily (Nanette Fabray) and Lester Marton (Oscar Levant) have written for him. The Martons are delighted when Jeffrey Cordova (Jack Buchanan), a highbrow director who has three hit shows on Broadway, agrees to produce and direct the show. But their problems begin when he changes the show into a modern version of Faust. Cordova wants Gabrielle Gerard (Cyd Charisse), a ballerina, to costar with Tony, and Paul Byrd (James Mitchell), her boyfriend, to choreograph the show, but he knows they are disdainful of musical comedy. When Cordova explains the idea to Paul, however, he is so intrigued that he agrees to do the show and insists that Gabrielle be Tony's costar. Unfortunately, Paul and Gabrielle, with their background in ballet and the contemporary theater, patronize Tony because they regard him as merely a popular entertainer from another era. Finally, after weeks of rehearsal, Tony explodes and walks out after telling off Gabrielle and Cordova. But after Gabrielle goes to Tony and apologizes, the two resolve their differences in a dance. Even the new rapport between Tony and Gabrielle, however, cannot save the pretentious show, which closes after its first out-of-town performance.

Dejected at first, the cast decides to save the show by changing it back to the Martons' original idea of a light musical comedy. Tony becomes the director with Cordova staying on as merely one of the cast, but Paul Byrd sees no place for himself in such a show and leaves. He is unable, however, to persuade Gabrielle to leave with him. After more weeks of rehearsals and tryouts, the new show has a smash opening on Broadway, and Tony, who by now has fallen in love with Gabrielle, finds that she also loves him. The film ends with a rousing rendition of the song "That's Entertainment."

The story and the characters are also developed in the songs and dances which display the musical talents of Fred Astaire as Tony, Cyd Charisse as Gabrielle, Nanette Fabray and Oscar Levant as the Martons, and Jack Buchanan as Jeffrey Cordova. From the very first moment, when Tony Hunter proclaims his pride and independence by quietly singing "By Myself" as he jauntily walks down the train platform ignored by reporters and photographers, to the moment in a noisy penny arcade when he reaffirms his sense of identity and self-worth by singing and dancing "Shine on Your Shoes," the Dietz-Schwartz songs carefully establish and deepen the Tony Hunter character. Both "By Myself" and "Shine on Your Shoes" are performed by Tony alone. In the first, Fred Astaire as Tony assures himself he can face the unknown and build a world of his own; he knows that he has the resiliency to bounce back from disappointment and defeat. "Shine on Your Shoes" tells us that he can also overcome depression and cheer himself (as well as others) by taking pleasure in such small details as a shine on his shoes.

When he is taken backstage by the Martons to meet Jeffrey Cordova, Tony is dubious about Cordova's abilities to direct a musical. After the Martons describe their story to Cordova and he decides to turn their light musical comedy into a modern version of the Faust legend, Tony tries to bow out of the project, feeling he is not suited for it. To convince him to stay, Cordova assures him that the barriers between musicals and the drama are unimportant. "In my mind there is no difference between the magic rhythms of Bill Shakespeare's immortal verse and the magic rhythms of Bill Robinson's immortal feet," Cordova tells Tony. (Bill "Bojangles" Robinson was a famous black American tap dancer in the 1930's and 1940's.) "Everything that happens in life can happen in a show," he adds, and, joined by the Martons, he launches into a spirited rendition of "That's Entertainment" to persuade Tony of the validity of his arguments. The song, reportedly written in a few hours by Dietz and Schwartz when producer Arthur Freed decided they needed another song for the film, has become not only an M-G-M anthem, but a classic celebration of the theater. It is performed in the film by Jack Buchanan, Nanette Fabray, Oscar Levant, and Fred Astaire with great gusto and flair. Not a big production number, it is performed backstage with only a few simple props (such as a ladder and derby hats) and relies on the professionalism and charm of the performers to make it a success. It is a rousing number with each performer entering into the spirit of the song and trying to outdo the others until by the end they are competing for space before the camera.

Later, the conflict between Tony and Gabrielle is resolved in a dance. When Tony is forced to accept the young, classically trained ballerina as his leading lady, the two appear to be irreconcilably different. "We're from two different worlds, two different eras, but we have to dance together, work together," Tony tells Gabrielle. To find out if they really can dance together they take a stroll through the soft blue shadows of Central Park, their white clothing gleaming in the darkness. Pensive, not speaking, they come to an open-air dance floor full of swaying couples but walk quietly on to a deserted space. After she takes a tentative step and he follows, there is a rapt moment when they are poised, confronting each other; then they drift into "Dancing in the Dark." The first steps are hesitant as each reacts to the other, but as they become more confident, the movements of the dance become long, smooth patterns, excitingly broken by motions symbolic of their growing emotion. Director Minnelli called it a dance "full of witchery," and by the end Tony and Gabrielle are fulfilled. As they step up into their horse-drawn carriage and are driven away, their faces are serene and contented. They know now they can dance together, and they have a new awareness and feeling for each other.

After the show fails in New Haven (a huge drawing of an egg and the somber faces and slow gait of the audience as they leave the theater convey perfectly what has happened) and Tony and the cast decide to save it, they go on tour to various cities where we see the new musical numbers they are trying out. What is now a musical revue serves as the frame for a group of short musical numbers in the middle of the film. Most memorable are "I Guess I'll Have to Change My Plans" and "Triplets." "I Guess I'll Have to Change My Plans" is in some ways the most effective because it is the simplest. It presents Astaire and Buchanan in white ties and tails with canes and top hats doing a relaxed soft-shoe routine against a plain background. The simple setting concentrates attention on the two performers. "Triplets," a cheerful song with malicious lyrics, is performed by Astaire, Buchanan, and Fabray with great verve and is the outstanding novelty number of the film. Dressed in identical baby clothes, the three are seated in high chairs, which they soon jump out of to do a little dance, daintily holding up their ruffled dresses as they sing about how much they hate each other.

Ballets were popular in Hollywood musicals of the early 1950's. "The Girl Hunt Ballet, A Murder Mystery in Jazz," is not only better than some of the more elaborate film ballets of the period, but also parodies them and the Mickey Spillane thrillers so popular at the time. As Rod Riley, a hard-boiled detective, Astaire narrates and dances the ballet. The surrealistic, stylized settings, the quick cutting from one scene to another, the sensuous dancing of Astaire and Cyd Charisse, and the skillful direction of Minnelli makes this an evocative and amusing ballet. The melodramatic events change swiftly and bewilderingly from one setting to another as Rod Riley tries to find a killer.

The opening scene of dark, deserted streets and a lonely subway platform, with Rod Riley in white suit, dark shirt, and felt hat slowly walking into the scene and pausing to light a cigarette is the perfect counterpoint for Rod's spoken words: "The city was asleep. The joints were closed. The rats and hoods and killers were in their holes." He hears the lonely sound of a single trumpet in a hotel room. Suddenly a beautiful blonde enters (Cyd Charisse in a blonde wig). She is scared, as "scared as a turkey in November," and a hood following her is blown up before Rod's eyes. Rod is left with only three clues to the killer's identity: a rag, a bone, and a hank of hair. After a slinky brunette (also danced by Charisse) tries to seduce him ("She came at me in sections. More curves than a scenic railroad. She was selling hard, but I wasn't buying"), the mood and scene swiftly changes back to the subway platform, where Rod again meets the blonde. Oblivious of their surroundings, they dance—closely, sensuously—while in the background black-suited men fight, shoot at each other, and die, all in carefully choreographed movements. In the middle of the violence the blonde disappears.

After further bizarre encounters in surrealistic settings, Rod finds himself at Dem Bones Cafe, a jazzy, smoky dive. The music stops when Rod enters, and the brunette, sitting at the bar, takes off her voluminous green coat to reveal a red sequined dress and long black gloves. She dances around Rod in an increasingly provocative manner until he accepts her challenge. The dance they do is exciting and sensual, with Rod at one point grabbing her ankle. Later, the blonde dies in his arms, leaving Rod alone again, and the scene is deserted as it was when the ballet began. A black-gloved hand then comes into the frame and lights his cigarette, and Rod walks slowly off with the brunette clinging to his arm. ("She was bad. She was dangerous. But she was my kind of woman.")

If "The Girl Hunt Ballet" has a fault, it is its length and its reliance on quick cutting and unusual camera angles rather than on the dancers to convey a mood. When Astaire and Charisse dance together, they are exciting, but they do not dance enough. Still, the ballet is a visual delight, more stylistically controlled and less excessive than some of Minnelli's other film ballets. It is an exciting climax to the show within the film and to the film itself.

Astaire's role as Tony Hunter is often considered his most complex and challenging musical role. There is both range and dimension in his performance but no self-pity. Since the screenplay both perpetuates and comments on the Astaire legend, it is natural he should feel a certain sympathy for the Tony Hunter character. The parallels between Tony Hunter and Fred Astaire are established immediately and continue throughout the film. Under the opening credits we see a top hat and cane, trademarks of Astaire. We soon see that the top hat and cane are part of the personal effects of Tony Hunter, which are being auctioned off at a Los Angeles gallery. But there are no bids, although the auctioneer touts them as perhaps the "most famous top hat and stick of our generation," worn in films such as *Swinging Down to Panama* (*Flying Down to Rio*, 1933, and *Swing Time*, 1936, are two of Astaire's best-known films). A line from the song "That's Entertainment"—"A gay divorcée who is after her ex"—refers to the title of another Astaire film, *The Gay Divorcee* (1934). And when a nervous Gabrielle tries to make conversation with Tony, she tells him she saw all of his films when she was a little girl and recently went to see a revival of them at a museum. Astaire's films were, and are, of course, frequently shown in revival houses and museums.

The clever Betty Comden and Adolph Green script also took the differences between Astaire and Charisse and incorporated them into the story, giving their roles added dimension. When Astaire, who is of only medium height, worries about the height of his leading lady (played by Cyd Charisse, a tall elegant dancer with ballet training) and her classical approach to dance as opposed to his popular, jazz-oriented approach, it strikes a true note.

One of the great delights of *The Band Wagon* is the brilliant performance of British musical star Jack Buchanan as Cordova. Buchanan was a skilled light comedian and an expert dancer. As Cordova he dominates virtually every scene in which he appears. With its sharp, witty dialogue, his role is a well-drawn, fully realized characterization which gains added resonance from the fact that it has certain resemblances to director Vincente Minnelli. We see these likenesses especially in the clothes he wears and in his penchant for elaborate scenery and colored smoke effects. The latter is humorously exaggerated in a rehearsal scene in which Cordova uses so much colored smoke that Tony and Gabrielle are obscured and then begin coughing so much that they have to stop.

Besides Astaire and Buchanan's performances, those of Cyd Charisse, Nanette Fabray, and Oscar Levant are outstanding. Any limitations Cyd Charisse may have as an actress are more than compensated for by her elegant and expressive dancing; indeed, Gabrielle Gerard is arguably her best performance on film. Nanette Fabray's vivacity is perfectly suited to the role of Lily Marton, and Oscar Levant's sardonic Lester Marton complements her pertness.

Underlying the visual style and elegance of the film is the pensive theme of loneliness and the passage of time. It is, in fact, the image of Fred Astaire striding jauntily down the train platform singing "By Myself" that sets the mood of the film and remains in the mind's eye. This theme in the witty and perceptive screenplay combined with the remarkable musical numbers and the fluid direction and feeling for the theater of Vincente Minnelli makes *The Band Wagon* a masterpiece of its genre.

Julia Johnson

THE BANK DICK

Released: 1940
Production: Universal
Direction: Edward Cline
Screenplay: Mahatma Kane Jeeves (W. C. Fields)
Cinematography: Milton Krasner
Editing: Arthur Hilton
Running time: 74 minutes

Principal characters:
Egbert Sousé .... W. C. Fields
Agatha Sousé .... Cora Witherspoon
Myrtle Sousé .... Una Merkel
Elsie Mae Adele Brunch Sousé .... Evelyn Del Rio
Mrs. Hermisillo Brunch .... Jessie Ralph
J. Pinkerton Snoopington .... Franklin Pangborn
Joe Guelpe .... Shemp Howard
Mackley Q. Green .... Richard Purcell
Og Oggilby .... Grady Sutton
J. Frothingham Waterbury .... Russell Hicks

The name W. C. Fields is synonymous with a pool cue, a stove-pipe hat, a flask of hundred-proof whiskey, and a disdain for children, animals, and wives. Fields was a masterful pantomimist, a caustic wit, a hustler, an eccentric, a windbag, a phony, and a comic genius. Decades after his death, film-goers, many of whom were born years after his demise, still respond fanatically to his characterizations of irreverent, aggressive nonconformists scheming to outwit bullying wives, hostile sheriffs, or snobbish upper-class ladies and gentlemen. *The Bank Dick*, Field's penultimate starring feature, is possibly his finest and funniest film, and one of the all-time comedy classics.

In *The Bank Dick*, Fields satirizes family life, banking practices, small-town morals, and even filmmaking. He stars as Egbert Sousé (pronounced soo-zay) an unemployed elbow bender and number-one barfly of Lompoc, U.S.A. Sousé is a classic Fields creation: whiskey-loving, child-hating, and henpecked. He wins a bank night prize but does not deposit the money into the aprons of his nagging wife Agatha (Cora Witherspoon) or grouchy mother-in-law, Mrs. Hermisillo Brunch (Jessie Ralph); instead, he drinks it away at the Black Pussy Cat café. Sousé is then hired to replace the inebriated director of a movie shooting on location in his town. His cinema debut is ruined by the arrival of his bratty younger daughter Elsie Mae Adele Brunch Sousé (Evelyn Del Rio), who demands a part in the film.

All of this is a prelude to the actual "plot." Two robbers hold up the local bank and, by chance, one literally runs right into Sousé as he rests on a bench. The no-account is credited with the capture. He overexaggerates the struggle he alleges to have put up to overcome the bandit and is rewarded with a free bank calendar and a job as the bank's special detective. Back at the Black Pussy Cat, he is hustled by con man J. Frothingham Waterbury (Russell Hicks) into purchasing shares in the worthless Beefsteak Mine. Salivating at the thought of a mansion in the country and instant wealth, Sousé imposes upon Og Oggilby (Grady Sutton), the dimwitted husband-to-be of his lovesick older daughter Myrtle (Una Merkel). Og, employed at the bank as a teller, is talked into temporarily "borrowing" the money.

The next morning, however, prissy bank teller J. Pinkerton Snoopington (Franklin Pangborn) unexpectedly arrives to inspect the books. Sousé eventually leads the virtuous Snoopington into the Black Pussy Cat and treats him to a pair of "Michael Finns." Soon the auditor is in no condition to work, even falling out of a hotel window two stories above the street. Yet the following morning, a sobered Snoopington reappears to proceed with the bank audit. After Sousé squeezes a letter press on his hand and smashes his glasses, the examiner begins to realize that the bank guard is indeed not overly anxious for him to check the books.

Meanwhile, the Beefsteak Mine has unexpectedly proved to be a bonanza. Waterbury implores Sousé to resell him the shares but before the deal can be consummated, the second holdup man returns to rob the bank again. He steals a load of cash and the mining stock, and then, using Sousé as a shield, escapes and forces Sousé to drive the getaway car. What follows is a zany car chase in which Sousé barely maneuvers the screeching auto around corners and over the heads of ditchdiggers. The robber is soon knocked unconscious by a tree branch during the chase, and Sousé brings the vehicle to a halt on the edge of a precipice. The value of the mining shares is established, and he is rewarded with $5,000 for capturing the thief; and a film company buys his story for $10,000. Sousé is last seen in top hat and tails, leaving his newly purchased mansion for a day at the Black Pussy Cat.

The mechanics of the plot are secondary to the routines and sight gags expertly played out by Fields. Sousé attempts to climb a staircase; instead, he ascends a hassock and bookcase. He dries his wet fingers with a napkin, rolls the paper into a ball, throws it into the air, catches it, and deftly kicks it away. The highlight of the film is the chase sequence finale. The visuals—three cars zooming through the roads of the city and country, barely avoiding crashing and beheading people as they circle one another—are superbly timed, and may be traced in cinematic history back to the silent antics created by Mack Sennett. Edward Cline, the film's director, had years earlier staged several Keystone Kops comedies.

The Bank Dick is filled with typical Fields humor. His younger daughter sneers and flings rocks at him; in turn, he attempts to heave a vase at her. In his capacity as bank dick, he accosts a little boy in a cowboy suit as a possible robber and the lad makes fun of his bulbous red nose. The ineffectual Egbert Sousé, ninety-nine percent hot air, takes credit for accomplishments of which he is incapable: he brags about his experiences working in the "flickers" with Mack Sennett and his physical dexterity in capturing the first bandit. Yet he is a choice sucker for the con man Waterbury. When he offers his services to assist a chauffeur toiling over a stalled limousine, he fails miserably: one twist of the wrench, and the entire motor plops to the ground. All Sousé can do is smile sheepishly and continue on his way, unchanged by the reality that his only talent is for telling tall tales and imbibing alcohol.

The dialogue is pure Fields. "I shall repair to the bosom of my family, a dismal place I admit," he explains. "Don't be a fuddie-duddie," he tells Og as he hustles the "loan" for the mine shares. "Don't be a moon-calf, don't be a jabbernowl. . . ." So are the characters' names: Elsie Mae Adele Brunch Sousé, Mrs. Hermisillo Brunch, J. Pinkerton Snoopington, J. Frothingham Waterbury, Og Oggilby, Repulsive Rogan, Loudmouth McNasty, A. Pismo Clam. The screenplay, credited to "Mahatma Kane Jeeves," was actually written by Fields. The script was published during the early 1970's; among the stage directions are: "He enters carrying a light portfolio and a heavy load of woe." Fields had total control over the film's production, and his influence effortlessly overshadows the contribution of director Cline.

The supporting players in *The Bank Dick* are expertly cast: effeminate Franklin Pangborn; dense Grady Sutton; sexless Cora Witherspoon; grumpy Jessie Ralph (who could play sentimental Irish mothers as she did in *San Francisco*, 1936, as easily as she could grouches); suave Russell Hicks; pompous Pierre Watkin (as the bank president); and perennially drunk Jack Norton (as the film director). The leading man on the film set is portrayed by Reed Hadley, years before his success on television's "Racket Squad."

As the last sequence in *The Bank Dick* is played, a melancholy arrangement of "There's No Place Like Home" fills the sound track. The image is of Sousé—Fields's alter ego, as are all his characterizations—forever relieved of financial burdens, aggressive wives, and mischievous children, and free to pursue the simple life of braggadocio and booze. This is an apt finale of a master comedian's masterful film.

Rob Edelman

BARRY LYNDON

Released: 1975
Production: Stanley Kubrick for Warner Bros.
Direction: Stanley Kubrick
Screenplay: Stanley Kubrick; based on the novel *The Memoirs of Barry Lyndon, Esq.* by William Makepeace Thackeray
Cinematography: John Alcott (AA)
Editing: Tony Lawson
Art direction: Ken Adams and Roy Walker (AA); set decoration, Vernon Dixon (AA)
Costume design: Ulla-Britt Soderlund and Milena Canonero (AA)
Music (adaptation): Leonard Rosenman (AA)
Running time: 184 minutes

> *Principal characters:*
> Barry Lyndon (born Redmond Barry) .. Ryan O'Neal
> Lady Lyndon .... Marisa Berenson
> Lord Bullington, her son .... Leon Vitali
> The Chevalier .... Patrick Magee
> Captain Potzdorf .... Hardy Kruger
> Barry's Mother .... Marie Kean

Stanley Kubrick is one of the most unpredictable directors now working in the film world. He is not only a critics' favorite, but his pictures also attract the attention of an intellectual cult which does not ordinarily attend motion pictures. Two of his most important films, *2001: A Space Odyssey* (1968) and *A Clockwork Orange* (1971) deal with the future; both reflect their maker's extraordinary imagination. In his next project, his tenth feature film, Kubrick turned in a completely new direction; instead of delving any further into the future or into space, he looked to the past for a subject, re-creating Ireland, England, and Europe as it was in the second half of the eighteenth century. The film, *Barry Lyndon*, is a remarkable and stunning visual re-creation of an historical period not often dealt with by filmmakers. The story is based on a picaresque novel by William Makepeace Thackeray, *The Memoirs of Barry Lyndon, Esq.*—the first tale of any consequence that Thackeray published, and one not well-known to most readers.

Whereas Thackeray's masterpiece, *Vanity Fair*, is subtitled "A Novel Without a Hero," *Barry Lyndon* might be described as "A Novel with an Anti-Hero." Born in Ireland, the so-called hero is a handsome dullard named Redmond Barry (Ryan O'Neal) with no wealth, background, or education; the only person tolerant of his stupidities and shortcomings is his determined peasant mother (Marie Kean). A social climber, he has fallen in love with his rich cousin more for her money than for herself. When he gets into a senseless duel with her fiancé and wounds him, he is forced either to flee or to go to jail, so he hurriedly sets out for Dublin. When his money and his horse are stolen, he joins the British Army to subsist. He fights in the Seven Years' War, but watches for a chance to desert; when he makes his escape attempt, he is captured by the German Captain Potzdorf (Hardy Kruger), who makes him serve in the Prussian Army.

Potzdorf assigns Barry to spy on an Irish Chevalier (Patrick Magee) who is thought to be a spy, but who is really only a gambler. Barry aids the Chevalier in cheating at cards, and as a team they soon amass a tidy sum. Barry next takes refuge in Belgium, where he is attracted by the beautiful Lady Lyndon (Marisa Berenson). When her elderly husband dies of an apoplectic stroke caused by jealousy, Barry loses no time in courting the widow, marrying her, and taking her surname. Thus he becomes Barry Lyndon, Esq. Returning to London, he is envied because he has a beautiful wife who lavishes her wealth upon him. His only problem is his wife's son (Leon Vitali) by her first husband. The boy sees Barry for what he is: a not-too-bright opportunist who is unfaithful to his wife and is squandering her wealth. Barry's pride and joy, however, is his own son, whom Lady Lyndon bears him. But the boy dies and Barry is disconsolate. At this point, Barry's mother arrives from Ireland to take charge of the household.

With the death of his beautiful son, Barry's fortunes take an ill turn, and his stepson, who has never ceased loathing him, bides his time, waiting for an opportunity to destroy him. Eventually, he challenges Barry to a duel and wounds him so severely that he loses a leg. Barry's downfall is complete when Lady Lyndon legally rids herself of him and exiles him, along with his mother, to his native Ireland. Barry's loss of a leg is the only event that is not in Thackeray's novel, but it enhances the ignominious end to which Barry is brought. One cannot sympathize with him since he brings every disaster upon himself through his own stupidity and evil. Men find him likable enough on a first meeting, and many women admire him until they get to know him; but he is actually totally self-serving and egotistical.

If one cannot sympathize with Barry Lyndon, however, one is soon caught up in his world. Kubrick explores every facet of the times, which are brought vividly to life against the backdrop of the lovely green Irish countryside, the baronial elegance of Prussian and Belgian castles, and the great formal town and country houses of the English aristocracy. He masterfully depicts fashions and styles in the time of Louis XIV, which in the Germanic countries were often absurdly affected. Extravagantly costumed, bewigged, and beribboned, the people in Germany and Belgium move like painted puppets around the ornate banqueting rooms and gamble their fortunes away in candlelit salons. The film becomes an elegant pageant in the midst of which the tale of the rise and fall of Barry Lyndon is played out. Kubrick maintains a leisurely pace (the movie runs for more than three hours) which effectively simulates the unrushed pace of life during the era he depicts.

Barry Lyndon is excellent in many regards. The Academy Award-winning cinematography, art and set decoration, and costume design are flawless and deserving of the honors won. Leonard Rosenman won an Oscar for his music score, which uses both classical and traditional themes to underscore the action. Music by Bach, Mozart, Handel, Schubert, and others helps establish the mood of each scene. Also noteworthy is Kubrick's use, for the first time in a motion picture, of an F:0.7 lens as developed by Zeiss. The lens enabled cinematographer John Alcott to shoot interiors at night, lit only by candles. For the first time film viewers could see what lovely rooms really look like when they are candlelit, with none of the artificial lighting previously used in film production. Colors in these scenes are subdued, and yet they glow as they do in fine old paintings. Flesh takes on a becoming soft radiance; women look seductive and men gallant in the flickering half-light.

The acting in the film is also memorable. Ryan O'Neal's performance as the unpleasant "hero" is impeccable. O'Neal plays Barry Lyndon as Thackeray designed him and as Kubrick interpreted him: as a young man physically blessed but without grace, boorish, selfish, and vain. Only once does the character show any true emotion, and that is his reaction to his son's death. Yet even that sincere cry of despair is accompanied by a senseless show of violence and destruction, as if Barry knew that the tide of his fortune was turning and that he was powerless to halt it. Marisa Berenson as Lady Lyndon is beautifully costumed and coiffured, always appearing as if she has stepped directly from the eighteenth century. The film is studded with other performances superbly realized by some of the best English, Irish, and Continental players.

Critics admired *Barry Lyndon*, as did moviegoers, and, although it did not attract a large box-office response, its many perfections are undeniable. Kubrick's followers feel certain of one thing: Kubrick will never fall into a rut or be accused of making the same picture over and over again. No other director has ten pictures to his credit which are so varied.

DeWitt Bodeen

BEAU GESTE

Released: 1939
Production: William A. Wellman for Paramount
Direction: William A. Wellman
Screenplay: Robert Carson; based on the novel of the same name by Percival Christopher Wren
Cinematography: Theodore Sparkuhl
Editing: Thomas Scott
Interior decoration: Hans Dreier and Robert Odell
Running time: 114 minutes

Principal characters:
Beau Geste .... Gary Cooper
Beau Geste (younger) .... Donald O'Connor
John Geste .... Ray Milland
Digby Geste .... Robert Preston
Sergeant Markoff .... Brian Donlevy
Rasinoff .... J. Carrol Naish
Schwartz .... Albert Dekker
Lady Brandon .... Heather Thatcher

In 1926, Paramount released its silent film version of *Beau Geste* under the direction of Herbert Brenon, with Ronald Colman, Neil Hamilton, and Ralph Forbes as the three Geste brothers who for honor's sake vanish from England to become members of the French Foreign Legion. The film quickly became one of the best-liked movies ever filmed, and for two years it held a top place among box-office winners; it also provoked a whole series of imitators. French Foreign Legion films abounded in the late 1920's and carried over into the 1930's. Finally, in 1939, Paramount released its remake of *Beau Geste*, directed by William A. Wellman and starring Gary Cooper, Ray Milland, and Robert Preston as the three Geste brothers.

Beau Geste is a melodrama of loyalty and fraternal devotion. The original film version faithfully followed the story by novelist Percival Christopher Wren, and the talking version followed the silent script almost sequence for sequence, with only minor detours. The addition of dialogue, however, proved somewhat of an encumbrance, for the story of *Beau Geste*, although complicated, is basically one of engrossing and suspenseful action which lent itself particularly well to the silent screen.

As in Wren's story, the film begins with a relief patrol in the Sahara coming upon Fort Zinderneuf only to find the entire garrison dead, with lifeless soldiers propped up on the parapets. One man, John Geste (Ray Milland), is selected to scale the walls by ladder and open the doors from the inside for the patrol to enter. John does not return, however, to rejoin his company, which has pitched camp in the nearby oasis and is waiting. There is the sound of a revolver shot, and then silence. The captain scales the wall. An eerie silence prevails in the fort, guarded by all the dead soldiers at their posts. There is no sign of John Geste. The captain goes to the gates, unbars them, and walks out to his waiting men; but before they can enter the fort, there is an explosion, a cloud of smoke rises over the towers, and the fort is soon entirely aflame. The stage is thus set for the telling and solving of the story's central mystery.

The next sequence is a flashback which takes place fifteen years previously in England at Brandon Manor, where the three Geste brothers live as wards of Lady Brandon (Heather Thatcher). Her profligate husband has long been away from home, spending the family fortune until Lady Brandon has only one source of possible income left to sell for living costs and the education of the Geste brothers—a rare gem known as the Blue Water. Beau (Donald O'Connor), the oldest of the boys, hidden in a suit of armor in the main hall, witnesses Lady Brandon's selling of the precious jewel to an Oriental buyer for a handsome price.

The years pass, and Lady Brandon's husband suddenly sends instructions to sell the Blue Water. The boys are now grown and well-educated, and only Beau (Gary Cooper) knows that the real Blue Water was sold fifteen years earlier, and that the gem which Lady Brandon has substituted for it in the safe is an almost worthless fake. On the night before Lady Brandon must bring forth the counterfeit jewel and eventually confess to having sold the real one, the boys persuade her to let them look upon the stone once again. She consents and gets the jewel, setting it on the table. Suddenly, the room is blacked out, and when the lights are turned on again, the jewel is gone. Lady Brandon is not only stunned, but angry, thinking that one of the boys is playing a joke. She turns out the lights again, after instructing whoever took the Blue Water to replace it in the darkness, promising that she will say nothing more about the incident. The lights are extinguished, but when they are turned on again, the jewel is still missing. Indignant, Lady Brandon goes up to her room, stating coldly that the thief will have his opportunity during the night to return the gem.

John Geste awakens at the first light of dawn and comes downstairs where he finds a letter from Beau admitting to taking the jewel. John, however, knows that his brother is no thief, and he also has an idea where Beau may have gone. John also quietly disappears, and several days later meets with Beau in Africa at the French Foreign Legion headquarters. The brothers are delighted to see each other, and before the newly enlisted company departs for training, the third Geste brother, Digby (Robert Preston), joins them. It becomes a great joke with them to talk about the jewel they made off with. Their hearty tomfoolery does not escape the attention of Rasinoff (J. Carrol Naish) and Schwartz (Albert Dekker), two of the legionnaires; and eventually their sergeant, a Russian brute named Markoff (Brian Donlevy), hears that the Gestes possess a rare jewel and plans to pit those who would steal it against one another and so gain the gem for himself.

Beau and Digby are assigned to one company of which Markoff is second in command, and they set out for the desert fort, while John is separated from them to join another detachment. Markoff is a tyrant, and when his commanding officer dies of the fever and Markoff, next in line, assumes command, his villainies become so outrageous that mutiny among the men is secretly planned. Markoff has spies, however, who inform him of the intended mutiny, and he and his cohorts usurp the weapons. In the light of day, Markoff faces his unarmed men with plans for torture and extreme punishment, but before he can do anything, the fort is attacked by a band of enemy Arabs.

The sequence of the fight to hold the fort marks the return to the action of the opening scene of the film. Beau dies gallantly with the fake Blue Water still in his tunic; Markoff then steals the jewel. Next, John enters the fort and finds everyone dead except Markoff. He slays the sergeant and throws his body at the foot of the funeral pyre he builds for Beau, who had always wanted a Viking funeral. John then sets it afire and escapes over the back wall of the fort; he is eventually joined by Digby, and they make their way across the desert toward Egypt. John reaches safety, but Digby is slain in an encounter with an Arab band during the journey.

Only Ray Milland and Heather Thatcher were English-born and thus have the proper accent; neither Gary Cooper nor Robert Preston sound the least bit English. The top performance of the picture is given by Brian Donlevy, who, as Sergeant Markoff, was nominated by the Academy for Best Actor in a Supporting Role. In the silent version, Noah Beery had been outstanding in the villainous part; he was called Sergeant Lejaune (as he was in the book), and was presumably French; but his nationality was changed to Russian for the talking version, because by 1939 there was no desire on the studio's part to offend the French with a brutally realistic impersonation of a legionnaire sergeant. Also noteworthy in the early flashback showing the Gestes as boys is the performance by a young Donald O'Connor, who plays an effective twelve-year-old Beau.

In more recent years, Universal, which had acquired film rights to many of the early Paramount features through its affiliation with MCA, filmed a third version of *Beau Geste*, but it was very much cut down, and one of the Geste brothers was even written out. Once again, the villain stole the show, with Telly Savalas playing a cruel and vicious sergeant at Fort Zinderneuf.

In 1977 a take-off of *Beau Geste* was made by Marty Feldman for Universal called *The Last Remake of Beau Geste*. All three re-makes have only proved one thing: the first version of *Beau Geste* was a nearly perfect film classic.

DeWitt Bodeen

BECKET

Released: 1964
Production: Hal B. Wallis for Paramount
Direction: Peter Glenville
Screenplay: Edward Anhalt (AA); based on the play of the same name by Jean Anouilh
Cinematography: Geoffrey Unsworth
Editing: Anne V. Coates
Running time: 148 minutes

> *Principal characters:*
> Thomas Becket .... Richard Burton
> King Henry II .... Peter O'Toole
> Bishop Folliot .... Donald Wolfit
> King Louis VII .... John Gielgud
> Queen Matilda .... Martita Hunt
> Queen Eleanor .... Pamela Brown
> Gwendolen .... Sian Phillips
> Brother John .... David Weston

The film *Becket*, adapted from Jean Anouilh's play of the same name, presents one of those rare instances in which the motion picture medium is better suited to the script than the stage production. Edward Anhalt, who won an Academy Award for Best Screenplay based on material from another medium, actually did very little adaptation, following Anouilh's script as closely as possible. The fact that the plot is unfolded almost entirely as a flashback is an attribute of the film version which the stage version lacks. The many outdoor scenes, especially those in which the characters are on horseback, are also better realized in the film; in the stage version, the actors gave the impression of riding by hopping around on hobby-horses. Most significantly, the film was shot on location, and the award-winning cinematography beautifully captures the pageantry and gusto of life in twelfth century Plantagenet England.

The film begins with King Henry II (Peter O'Toole) doing penance before the sarcophagus of the recently murdered Thomas Becket (Richard Burton), his erstwhile close companion. In Anouilh's version, Thomas was a Saxon and of similar age to Henry. Historically, the real Becket was fifteen years older, and although he was born in London, his parents were both Normans, the same as Henry's. The conflict in the film is a personal one, depicting Henry as a frivolous, pleasure-loving member of a foreign race opposed to an ambiguous, somewhat aloof collaborator of the conquered nation.

As the King reminisces about his relationship with Becket, the film presents a flashback showing the comradeship of the two men—how they faced down the clergy in the debate over taxes; how pleased both were over Becket's appointment as Chancellor of England; how they often went wenching or hunting together in the forest. Henry's affection for Becket is clearly shown, while Becket seems more reserved toward Henry; his language is always qualified, and the King is never sure of his love. In a very revealing scene the two take refuge during a rainstorm in a Saxon peasant's hut where the King, who conceives of all Saxons as "dogs," lecherously eyes the peasant's daughter. Becket contrives to save the girl from the King's lust by pretending that the wound he has actually received from her brother has been caused by the horses, and requesting her as his reward for protecting the King. Becket's nationalism comes before his friendship.

In another scene the drunken King asks Becket for his mistress; when Becket assents, Henry asks him whether he would take her back, and Becket says he would not. Becket's aloofness includes even her; he says to her that he does not like being loved. Before the King can take her, Gwendolen (Sian Phillips), Becket's mistress, commits suicide, and the shaken King insists on spending the night with Becket.

The crucial action of the film is Henry's appointment of Becket as Archbishop of Canterbury. Becket is fearful of the plan. He tells Henry that if he becomes Archbishop, he will no longer be able to be Henry's friend because he would be incapable of serving both God and the King. Nevertheless, Becket is made Archbishop; afterwards, he undergoes a behavioral change to live up to his appointment. He disposes of his customary material wealth and gives up the Chancellor's seal. The film's major crisis arises when Becket refuses to allow his clergy to be tried in secular courts. Henry orders Becket to trial, but Becket turns the trial into a personal victory by forbidding the court to utter the sentence under threat of excommunication. Henry admires Becket's ploy but he is taunted by Queen Mother Matilde (Martita Hunt), who suggests something "unhealthy and unnatural" about the King's obsession with his friend; indeed, the matter of Henry's homosexuality is hinted at throughout the film.

Becket takes refuge in France with King Louis VII (John Gielgud), who, for political reasons, refuses to extradite him. Pope Alexander III and his cardinals are satirized in a scene in which they hypocritically accept Henry's "contribution" and relieve Becket of the archbishopric only to reappoint him properly and send him to a French convent to live on bread and water. After Louis VII informs Becket that he must withdraw his protection, Becket announces that he had planned to return to England anyway. Louis arranges a meeting between King Henry and Becket, who attempt a reconciliation at the seashore in one of the most effective scenes of the film. They indulge in small talk in order to avoid the real issues, but Becket finally agrees to all the articles except the one dealing with his clergy, whom he says he must protect. To the King's query of whether he has ever really loved him, Becket replies that he did as far as he was capable, but that it is the honor of God that he has truly started to love.

Becket's murder by King Henry's barons is portrayed dramatically with Becket, dressed in his best finery, anticipating "the supreme folly." His alter ego, Brother John (David Weston), a Saxon monk whom he has taken under his protection, attempts to fight the barons but is immediately struck down; this is followed by the cruel and vicious murder of Becket himself.

The film closes as it began, with King Henry in the same spot where Becket has been martyred; he is being whipped by Saxon monks in retribution for his part in the crime. The King realizes that his action of proclaiming Becket a Saint as well as his orders to seek out and punish the murderers will help secure his position as King in this foreign country. Yet the main feeling the audience is left with is that of Henry's perplexity at the loss of his favored subject.

It is difficult to single out the excellent aspects of this film. In addition to the Academy Award it received, the film was also nominated for Best Picture of the Year, Best Director, Best Actor (both Richard Burton and Peter O'Toole, who lost to Rex Harrison for his role in *My Fair Lady*), and Best Supporting Actor (John Gielgud as King Louis VII). The interplay between O'Toole and Burton is universally acclaimed as a *tour de force*, while the superb settings are breathtakingly underplayed behind the drama between the two main characters. An example of this is the scene in which Henry divulges his plan to name Thomas Archbishop. Almost unobtrusively, a typical twelfth century mural allegorically portrays the fall of pride in the background.

One criticism of the film may be traced to the play from which it is adapted. For the length of the film, the script contains much dialogue and little action. Director Peter Glenville, who also directed the Broadway stage production, may not have sufficiently made the transference to the more expansive medium of film. He did, however, alter the conception of the two leads in his casting of O'Toole and Burton. (The stage version reversed the types, casting Anthony Quinn as a more masculine, gruff Henry and Laurence Olivier as Becket, although Olivier has played both roles at different times.)

In addition to the Academy Award, *Becket* was named the best English language picture by the National Board of Review, the best motion picture in the drama category by the Golden Globe Awards, which also named O'Toole the best actor; and the screenplay won the best written American drama award from the Writers Guild of America. A moving intellectual experience universally recognized as one of the better adaptations of a stage play for the screen, *Becket* has not achieved the box-office ratings of those pictures with more popular appeal. Yet, it is the type of picture which will always remain fresh and stunning for its own audience.

Roger Geimer

THE BEGUILED

Released: 1971
Production: Malpaso (Don Siegel) for Universal; released by Jennings Lang
Direction: Don Siegel
Screenplay: John B. Sherry and Grimes Grice; based on the novel of the same name by Thomas Cullinan
Cinematography: Bruce Surtees
Editing: Carl Pingitore
Running time: 109 minutes

Principal characters:
Corporal John McBurney .... Clint Eastwood
Martha .... Geraldine Page
Edwina .... Elizabeth Hartman
Carol .... Jo Ann Harris
Amy .... Pamelyn Ferdin

Of all of today's superstars, Clint Eastwood remains one of the most constantly popular. He remains at the top because the public put him there; he was not an image invented by a studio. Ironically, when he first came to films, he was unsuccessful as a contract actor. It was only after seven years as the costar and then as the star of the CBS television weekly series "Rawhide" that he found himself a movie star because of three Italian Westerns he had starred in during his annual time off from the television series. His three foreign-made movies, *A Fistful of Dollars* (1966), *For a Few Dollars More* (1967), and *The Good, the Bad, and the Ugly* (1968), made him a top European star. They were known as the Paella Trilogy because they were largely shot in Spain, and the character he consistently played was "The Man with No Name," the mysterious stranger who rides into town, sets everything right with a maximum of violence, and then rides out alone.

When his popularity was established, Eastwood formed his own company, Malpaso Productions, of which he was the principal commodity, to be loaned out as a star wherever it was profitable; he made approximately one million dollars per production, payable at $50,000 annually, plus other percentages and profits. After a highly profitable group of films released through United Artists, Universal, M-G-M, and Paramount, Eastwood concentrated his efforts at Universal; it looked as if he might remain there permanently, making *Two Mules for Sister Sara* (1970), a romantic Western directed by Don Siegel, with whom he had previously worked in *Coogan's Bluff* (1968).

In 1971 came *The Beguiled* at Universal, with Don Siegel again directing. The company went on location in Louisiana near Baton Rouge. This film told a story completely unlike any others in the Eastwood pattern. It was adapted from an overlong but intriguing novel by Thomas Cullinan, and presented

Eastwood in a different kind of role, an antihero who, as Don Siegel claimed, makes "the mistake of zigging when he should have zagged."

The Beguiled is set in the American Civil War, and the film begins with a series of battle scenes filmed in the style of Matthew Brady in an effective sepia tone. The noise of the battle dies away, and it is deathly quiet, save for the singing of a few birds. Bruce Surtees' camera moves through the woods, with their Spanish-mossed branches, to pick up a lone girl in a pinafore as she searches the ground for mushrooms. Suddenly, the color blazes into a startling red as she comes upon a wounded soldier whose blood is staining the leaves he lies upon. He is semidelirious and claims to be a Quaker who had been aiding the wounded when he was brought down by gunfire. The girl helps him to reach the gates of the young ladies' seminary where she lives. The other women take him in, although some of them are in favor of turning him over to the Confederate authorities; but Martha (Geraldine Page), the spinster who runs the school, and her assistant, Edwina (Elizabeth Hartman), decide to let him stay, and they nurse him back to health. He becomes a project in which all the girls try to outdo one another.

The wounded soldier is, of course, not a Quaker, but the Union Army's Corporal John McBurney (Clint Eastwood), known as McB, who had been in the act of deserting his company when a Confederate bullet cut him down. An opportunist, he now settles in for a lengthy recovery, waited upon by a small battalion of eager females of varying ages, all of whom are entranced by him. From the spinsterish Martha to young Amy (Pamelyn Ferdin), who found him, everyone idolizes McB. Such attention and open adoration is grist to McB's mill, and he rakishly deals out his favors to all: a smile here, a tender word there, a quick caress when he can. Of them all, McB favors Edwina, the pretty assistant, but he continues to play one girl against the other. The head mistress, Martha, is the most lustful, however, for the most passionate highlight of her sex-starved life has been the incestuous love she felt for her brother, whom McB resembles.

The most sexually experienced girl in the seminary, Carol (Jo Ann Harris), is so jealous when McB rejects her that she almost turns him in to a passing Confederate patrol, but that plan is thwarted by Martha. Although McB plainly prefers Edwina, the night comes when three women make it clear that they want to sleep with him: Martha, Edwina, and Carol. When the house is quiet, McB is tiptoeing his way to Edwina's room, when Carol opens her door. Knowing that he dare not repulse her, McB goes to Carol's bed. Their lovemaking wakes up Edwina; he tries to escape, but is cornered by her, and in a rage, she pushes him downstairs. His leg is badly fractured, and Martha, half out of her mind with frustration, decides that the only way to save him is to amputate the shattered leg. This she does in the most horrifying scene in the film.

Slowly, McB recuperates, realizing more than ever that Edwina is the only female in the seminary whose love is adult and sincere. They plan to leave and get married. Later, at the dinner table, McB explodes, exposing the quirks of all the women and revealing his intention to wed Edwina. Martha resolves that McB must die, and she has Amy, who can distinguish between a mushroom and a deadly toadstool, gather a basket of toadstools, which are lovingly prepared for McB's final going-away meal. None of the girls touches the food, but he devours the dish hungrily; he collapses, and dies in Edwina's arms. The girls, in a small funeral cortege, bury him in the woods outside the seminary gates, and Edwina stays on to continue teaching at the seminary.

This is the kind of Southern gothic-Civil War melodrama that the right audiences might have devoured with the same relish shown by McB in attacking the poisonous toadstools. Unfortunately, however, Universal did not know how to promote the picture. They had one-sheets with only one intriguing catch-phrase—"Clint Eastwood Has Never Been in a more Frightening Situation"—but they had no idea of how to exploit or distribute such an offbeat movie. The result was that Eastwood audiences, thinking it another "Man with No Name" Western, were puzzled and apathetic, while horror-picture fans, having no idea of the delights that awaited them, ignored the film. *The Beguiled* was scheduled to premiere at a first-run Los Angeles theater, the Picwood, but after the ambiguous Sunday publicity had appeared, the premiere was cancelled, and it opened several weeks later, "city-wide," on a double bill. Universal then realized its error, withdrew the film, and a month later tried to open it as the solo attraction at the Four Star, then a sometime art movie house on Wilshire Boulevard. But the damage had been done, and only later, when fans who loved horror, suspense, and gothic tales spread the word, did *The Beguiled* begin to attract the audience it should have had in the beginning. It opened in Paris and London to rave reviews—Rome loved it, and it was a movie completely tailored to Spain's taste. Clint Eastwood gained new converts.

Eastwood naturally was furious with the treatment *The Beguiled* had received through its handling by Universal. His next film which Universal/Malpaso released, *Play Misty for Me* (1971), marked his directorial debut, but when he saw how badly the studio had handled *The Beguiled*, he made sure that *Play Misty for Me*, an offbeat romantic suspense thriller with a modern setting, would not be similarly mishandled. *Play Misty for Me* was given a big build-up, and the public knew exactly what kind of a picture it was going to be when it opened in Los Angeles at the Cinerama Dome, where it received good notices and enjoyed an enthusiastic run.

Because of the treatment of *The Beguiled*, however, Eastwood felt disappointed in Universal, and when Malpaso received invitations for him to star for Warner Bros. in a melodrama about the San Francisco police, *Dirty Harry* (1971), Eastwood accepted. *Dirty Harry* had been scheduled originally to star Frank Sinatra, but Sinatra had suffered a hand injury and could not make such a physically active film. The role and the story were perfect for Eastwood, and he has since made two sequels released by Warners' which continue the adventures of the "Dirty Harry" character.

The Beguiled, however, remains Eastwood's favorite film, and it still stands high on many film critics' lists. It is the best of his pictures directed by Don Siegel, and the empathy between Eastwood and Siegel is obvious. As the head mistress Martha, Geraldine Page comes across like a Louisiana Lady Macbeth, while Elizabeth Hartman displays a winning and fragile charm as the assistant, Edwina. The film marks a definite departure for Eastwood, and working this third time with Siegel as director gave him confidence to try his own directorial skill.

Eastwood's popularity as an actor remains undisputed. He first made the Top Ten as a box-office champion in 1968, when he placed fifth in earnings. Since then he has always been in a lead spot: Number One several times, and other times Number Two, but always high on the list. He seems always to have his finger on the pulse of public taste. Even when he stars in such an outrageous and scatter-brained dark comedy as *Every Which Way But Loose* (1979), the film is an instant moneymaker; in fact, this one, which raised some critical eyebrows, may make more money than any other Eastwood film to date.

Nevertheless, it was *The Beguiled* which opened the way. Although anti-heroic, his character was noted for its "cool, threatening sexuality," and he continued with that image in his next film, *Play Misty for Me*, creating a modern amoral man who plays around with women and who very nearly gets his comeuppance. In previous films, Eastwood's cast had been predominantly male, either friends or antagonists, but in *The Beguiled* the supporting players are all female, and the figure of Eastwood becomes the male threat to their survival and supremacy. He exudes so much sexuality that if he is not tricked into death, he will mean the destruction of them all.

Eastwood knows that his days as a top star will inevitably wane. He has prepared for that day by developing his talent as a director and his knack for judging public taste. In future years our biggest box-office star may become a creative American director.

DeWitt Bodeen

BEING THERE

Released: 1979
Production: Andrew Braunsberg and Lorimar for Northstar International; released by United Artists
Direction: Hal Ashby
Screenplay: Jerzy Kosinski; based on his novel of the same name
Cinematography: Caleb Deschanel
Editing: Don Zimmerman
Running time: 130 minutes

> *Principal characters:*
> Chance .... Peter Sellers
> Eve Rand .... Shirley MacLaine
> Benjamin Rand .... Melvyn Douglas (AA)
> President "Bobby" .... Jack Warden
> Dr. Robert Allenby .... Richard Dysart

Being There is a one-joke movie based upon a fragile premise. Still, the understated delivery of the film, along with a restrained performance by the talented (and usually rambunctious) Peter Sellers, underlines the fact that *Being There* is a quiet but important parable about society.

The story line centers on a slow-witted gardener named Chance (Peter Sellers), who knows only gardening and what he sees on television, and what transpires when he is suddenly put out into the world. Because Chance speaks so simply and so directly, his words are mistaken for profundities; everything he says is mistaken for a metaphor by the media-mad society. By film's end, Chance—who has become an adviser, of sorts, to one of the world's most wealthy men—is spoken of in glowing terms by men seeking a candidate for the presidency.

The often double-edged fable, scripted by Jerzy Kosinski and based on his 1971 novel, looks at a media-obsessed society, and particularly at Chance, a man who has been literally drained by television. He is emotionless; he is unaware of his sexuality; his face forever has an empty look.

Actually, during the first fifteen minutes of the film, the viewer has no idea what is happening. We meet the deadpan Chance as he is watching television. His pace is slow, and he appears fascinated by any imagery that appears on his screen. When a bustling black woman enters the room, apparently to ready Chance for some outing, she alludes to the fact that his life is about to change. But only when Chance leaves his protective room and his familiar gardens and ventures outside of the Washington, D.C., townhouse, where he has lived and apparently been employed, do we fully understand the impact. To the strains of a jazzy (Deodato) version of "Also Sprach Zarathustra," Chance makes his way onto the streets. It is, we sense, the first time he has been out in society. It is a rebirth—this simple-minded man has, it seems, spent most of his life in service to his employer, who has only recently died.

Obviously, the streets of Washington, D.C., are no place for a "newcomer." When he finds himself harassed by members of a black street gang, Chance reaches for an appropriate means of escape by trying to press a remote control button to tune the gang members out. Chance's encounters on the street are mostly humorous, underlining his conditioned mental state. For example, because he was apparently cared for at the townhouse by the black servant woman, when he becomes hungry he approaches a black woman on the street and asks for some lunch.

Amazed by everything he is really seeing (as opposed to seeing it on the small screen), Chance is walking about very nearly in a daze. Through a mishap, he encounters Eve Rand (Shirley MacLaine), the beautiful wife of a powerful financier. It is Eve who, upon hearing him identified as Chance the Gardener, misunderstands. Thinking him to be one Chauncey Gardiner, she insists that he come with her to her palatial home, where her doctor can see to a leg injury. (Eve is hopeful there will not be legal ramifications, since she feels her car is to blame for the mishap.)

Dressed in a tailored, expensive-looking business suit (no doubt a hand-me-down from his employer), complete with a neat homburg, Chauncey takes his first ride in a car. It is the first in a string of misadventures for the apparently illiterate gardener. Upon meeting the powerful Benjamin Rand (Melvyn Douglas), Chauncey quickly secures his interest and friendship. Rand is taken with Chauncey's direct approach, and mistakenly attaches profundities to Chauncey's ramblings about gardening.

When the President (Jack Warden) meets with Rand, he, too, is affected by Rand's house guest. Surprised by Chauncey's quiet, unassuming manner (the gardener is not in awe of the world leader—he does not have the emotional capability to be excited), the President is further caught off-guard by Chauncey's remarks about current conditions. "As long as the roots are not severed, all will be well in the garden . . . there will be growth in the spring." Mistaking the words for a metaphor about the current political climate, the President remarks, "Well, that's one of the most refreshing opinions I've heard in a long time."

Chauncey goes on to attain a kind of Kissingerlike fame. Talk show hosts want him for guest spots as the populace suddenly grows interested in Chauncey's opinion. As interest in Chauncey grows, the President becomes increasingly uneasy; his sexual performance is even affected. At a Washington party, Chauncey, who has escorted a glowing Eve, is immediately besieged by opinion-makers. One anxious publisher offers Chauncey a "six-figure advance" if he will write a book; Chauncey, however, cannot read or write, and he tells the publisher so. Unruffled, the publisher is determined to work out some kind of deal.

It is, of course, Chauncey's frankness and his desire to please everyone that secures his following. As Benjamin Rand tells him, "One of the things I admire about you is your balance. You seem to be a truly peaceful man." In fact, Rand is so pleased with Chauncey that he encourages the relationship between Chauncey and Eve. Rand, who has been in ill health, is anxious to leave his wife with some purpose and happiness following his death, and he is hopeful that Chauncey can provide that.

Eve, who is enamored with Chauncey, also hopes for some sexual fulfill-ment with the prophetic visitor, but a sexual misunderstanding ensues when Chauncey tells her, "I like to watch." He means television, of course, but Eve, thinking he wants to watch her as she arouses herself, complies. It is a riotous sequence, with Eve groping and squirming about the floor while Chauncey mimics assorted scenes on the screen, even going so far as to do a head-stand during an exercise program. For Eve, the encounter is her most sexually stimulating ever.

By the film's close, Chauncey's passive state has soothed nearly all of those with whom he has come in touch. Though the Rand physician, Dr. Allenby (Richard Dysart), has come to learn that Chauncey is simply Chance the Gardener, Eve looks upon him with serenity and the President fears him as a potential candidate. (When the President's staff is unable to locate infor-mation regarding Chauncey's background, the President enraged: "What do you mean he's got no background! I quoted him on national television today—he's a very well-known man!") It is during Benjamin Rand's funeral that the pallbearers begin to see Chauncey as a potential presidential candidate.

Hal Ashby, whose credits range from cult favorites such as *Harold and Maude* (1971) to the critically and commercially successful *Coming Home* (1978), has directed *Being There* with a deliberate, slow pace. The slowed pace further amplifies the dulled emotions of the deadpan Chauncey.

Peter Sellers, known for a variety of film roles, including his slapstick portrayals of the popular Inspector Clouseau of the *Pink Panther* films, re-ceived a Best Actor Academy Award nomination for his work as Chauncey. Melvyn Douglas, at 79, received the Best Supporting Oscar, for his work as Benjamin Rand. Shirley MacLaine, who, like Sellers, has often been accused of overacting, delivers a restrained performance as the enraptured Eve.

Although *Being There* is not the first film to examine television's impact deftly, its treatment of the theme is decidedly unique. In seeing television viewers as passive, empty victims, author Jerzy Kosinski's view is in marked contrast to the "mad as hell" audiences skillfully depicted in Lumet's *Net-work* (1976).

Released in late 1979, *Being There* gained the support of most major critics, although many underlined the film's one-joke premise. Acclaimed for its subtle delivery in a year when special effects, especially in science fiction-theme films, were everywhere, *Being There* was also applauded for its fine, sensitive performances.

Pat H. Broeske

BEN-HUR

Released: 1959
Production: Sam Zimbalist for Metro-Goldwyn-Mayer (AA)
Direction: William Wyler (AA)
Screenplay: Karl Tunberg; based on the novel of the same name by Lew Wallace
Cinematography: Robert Surtees (AA)
Editing: Ralph E. Winters and John D. Dunning (AA)
Art direction: William A. Horning and Edward Carfagno (AA); set decoration, Hugh Hunt (AA)
Special effects: A. Arnold Gillespie, Robert MacDonald, and Milo Lory (AA)
Costume design: Elizabeth Haffenden (AA)
Sound: Franklin E. Milton and M-G-M Studio Sound Department (AA)
Music: Miklos Rozsa (AA)
Running time: 212 minutes

> *Principal characters:*
> Judah Ben-Hur .... Charlton Heston (AA)
> Quintas Arrius .... Jack Hawkins
> Messala .... Stephen Boyd
> Esther .... Haya Harareet
> Sheik Ilderim .... Hugh Griffith (AA)
> Miriam .... Martha Scott
> Simonides .... Sam Jaffe
> Tirzah .... Cathy O'Donnell
> Balthasar .... Finlay Currie

Ben-Hur, as novel, play, silent film, and epic sound film, has set an impressive number of records and precedents. As a novel, it was the first fiction allowed in a number of American homes and the first to be carried in the Sears catalogue, outselling everything but the Bible. It has been in print continuously since 1880. The 1899 stage adaptation set precedents both for an author's control over the rights to his works (Wallace remarked, in rejecting an initial offer, "The savages who sell things of civilized value for glass beads live further West than Indiana") and for his control over the adaptation of material. A lawsuit against the unauthorized 1907 Kalem film established the same precedents for film. Wallace insisted, for instance, that Christ not be directly represented on stage, and his heirs made a similar provision when selling the film rights to M-G-M. Both the stage version, a monumental international success for twenty years, and the 1925 epic silent film shared the distinction of being the first play or film that many Americans were allowed to see. As "A Tale of the Christ," it was a landmark in breaking down Puritan prohibitions against fiction, drama, and film.

The 1959 film version gave rise to so many superlatives as to be almost overpowering. The M-G-M publicity department was not remiss in providing the public with statistics, from the number of horses to the amount of plaster used in constructing the sets. A roster of distinguished visitors came to the set in Rome together with an impressive number of tourists (twenty-five thousand), and a large number of genuine titled Italians took part as extras in one of the most authentically aristocratic (and most sedate) Roman orgies ever filmed. Most impressive were the five years M-G-M spent in preproduction before a foot of film was shot. Critics were somewhat cynical about the advance publicity. Overall, however, the critical response was favorable, and the picture set a record (still unbroken) for winning eleven Academy Awards.

William Wyler, a director noted for intimate dramas rather than epics, whose distinguished films included *Wuthering Heights* (1939) and *The Heiress* (1949), and who won the Academy Award for Best Direction for *Mrs. Miniver* (1942) and *The Best Years of Our Lives* (1946), took on the project as a challenge to make an "intimate spectacle." He had, in fact, been one of several dozen costumed unit directors among the crowd in filming the 1925 *Ben-Hur*'s chariot race. At first, Wyler wanted to direct only the chariot race in the 1959 film, but producer Sam Zimbalist insisted that he take on the human drama and leave the chariot race to second unit directors Andrew Marton and Yakima Kanutt. Wyler decided to cast the Romans with British performers and the Jews with Americans to underscore the conflict of cultures. Charlton Heston, who had played Moses in Cecil B. De Mille's epic *The Ten Commandments* (1955) and a "heavy" in Wyler's own *The Big Country* (1958), was considered for both Ben-Hur and Messala but ended up with the lead.

Though it is a great oversimplification to call the drama of *Ben-Hur* "Christ and a horse-race," the combination has proved to have surefire box-office appeal. The story is indeed a paradox. It is both a passion play and a bloody drama of revenge, both the timeless story of Christ the healer and of the conflict between Roman and Jew, between two opposite ways of life in the pagan world. Like the novel and the stage version, the film opens with a series of tableaux of the birth of Christ and the coming of the Magi. There follows the sharp contrast of a Roman legion marching into Jerusalem, foreshadowing the fate of both Christ and Judah Ben-Hur.

Messala (Stephen Boyd), a boyhood friend of Judah Ben-Hur returning after some years in Rome, marches with the legion. The two men had been like brothers, and their reunion has a heroic intensity as they compete in hurling spears at the point where two beams cross in the ceiling of the Roman garrison. Judah is a Prince of Judea, wealthy and influential; Messala is on his way up in the imperial service. Judah, his mother Miriam (Martha Scott), and his sister Tirzah (Cathy O'Donnell) receive Messala almost as one of the family, and Judah, foreshadowing the race to come, gives him a valuable Arabian horse that he has admired. Messala in turn offers to advance Judah in the favor of the Emperor Tiberius. But the price is too high. Messala wants Judah to reveal the names of Jewish opponents of Roman rule; rebellion has been brewing. Judah previously has been apolitical, but he will not betray his compatriots and coreligionists. Messala gives him an ultimatum to be with him or against him. The sentiment, if not the words, is "He who is not with me is against me," another allusion to the contrast of Roman and Christian values. When Judah declares that he must be against him, Messala breaks off the friendship with the words "Down Eros, up Mars!"

The new Roman governor arrives shortly thereafter. As Judah and his family watch the parade from the roof of their palace, a tile breaks off when Tirzah leans forward to get a better view, and it strikes the governor on the head. At once, soldiers under Messala's command break into the palace and arrest the entire family. In prison, Judah makes a daring escape from his guards, forces his way into Messala's presence, and threatens to impale him with a spear unless he will free Miriam and Tirzah. Messala counters with a promise that they will be put to death unless Judah surrenders. In frustrated rage, Judah hurls the spear into the wall, recalling the friendly rivalry of the javelins on their first encounter, one of Wyler's many directorial touches reinforcing the dramatic relationships with parallels in action. Messala, who knows that the loose tile was an accident, nevertheless plans to make an "example" of the family to advance his own position.

Needless to say, there is no trial. Judah is condemned to the galleys for life, and his mother and sister are imprisoned. The galley slaves endure a forced march across the desert. Stopping at Nazareth for water, the slaves are permitted to drink only after the soldiers and their horses have finished. The centurion orders that Judah be given no water, but a carpenter quietly defies the centurion's order. It is Judah's first encounter with Jesus of Nazareth.

Opinion differs on the treatment of religion in the film. Certainly no pains were spared for accuracy. Professor Gottstein, Judaic historian of the University of Jerusalem, was one of the technical advisers, and a consultant from the Vatican was also called in. One sample of the technical problems encountered was that none of the experts knew exactly what the cross really looked like. A carpenter on the film crew proposed that the simplest construction was probably the most likely. Wyler concurred—a cross was not, after all, a common means of execution at that time, nor a worldwide symbol—and approved a plain T-shaped cross. Once away from the perhaps stifling tradition of Wallace's stipulation that Christ not be shown directly (the film never shows his face), Wyler presents the events of Jesus' life from the perspective of the time, particularly that of the Romans—as minor events in the life of another Jewish fanatic.

In the galleys, three years pass. Judah is now shackled to an oar of a Roman flagship, and when the new commander, Quintus Arrius (Jack Hawkins), arrives, he orders a demonstration of the rowers at increasingly punishing speeds, set by a sinister hortator hammering relentlessly on a drum. Some oarsmen die of heart attacks; all collapse at the end except Judah, who sits erect and defiant. Arrius is impressed and sends for the slave to learn his history. Though Arrius mocks the Jew's assertion that his God will free him to take revenge on his enemy, Arrius orders that Judah's leg be unchained during the coming battle to give him a chance to survive. When the ship is rammed (a series of gruesome close-ups of the effects of oars smashed and splintered in human bodies provides a less felicitous example of "intimate spectacle"), Judah breaks loose, strangles the hortator, frees his fellow prisoners, and dashes on deck to find the galley boarded by pirates. When Arrius is knocked overboard, Judah dives after him and hauls him aboard some floating planks. The rammed flagship sinks, and Arrius tries in Roman fashion to commit suicide. Judah prevents him, throwing in his face his words to the galley slaves, "We keep you alive to serve this ship. Row well, and live." Thus Judah saves Arrius' life a second time. They are rescued by another Roman ship, and Arrius finds that the fleet has gained the victory.

In gratitude, he adopts Judah and takes him to Rome as his son. Ironically, Judah learns the Roman arts of war that he once rejected and becomes, among other things, an expert charioteer. Although he is devoted to Arrius and has every advantage in Rome, he returns to Judea to look for his mother and sister and to seek revenge. On his return, he finds that Simonides (Sam Jaffe), his steward, has not only saved the family fortune but has increased it to immense wealth, despite his being crippled and nearly killed by Roman torture. Judah falls in love with Simonides' daughter Esther (Haya Harareet).

But he still must locate his mother and sister and gain his revenge on Messala. An opportunity for the former comes first. While searching for his family, he encounters an Arab, Sheik Ilderim (Hugh Griffith), the proud owner of four superb white horses, a team received into his tent like members of the family. Ilderim persuades Judah to drive the horses against Messala in a chariot race. Messala has become a very powerful figure in Jerusalem, but he is apprehensive about Judah's return. He has forgotten the fate of Miriam and Tirzah. The soldier he dispatches to find whether they are still alive in prison is horrified to discover that they have contracted leprosy after years of confinement. He frees them to go to the Valley of the Lepers, but Judah is led to believe that they are dead.

This belief increases Judah's desire for revenge. If he can beat Messala in the race, he will not only shame but bankrupt him, for Ilderim has taunted the Roman into betting his entire fortune. The race is suitably spectacular. Only eleven minutes long, it is a taut and suspenseful sequence that is the best example of "intimate spectacle" in the entire film. Wyler began with a panoramic parade around the ring to display the immense and detailed set. Once the race begins, with a false start for added drama, it is seen largely through a series of close shots which focus on the human conflict. There were very few shots with doubles. Boyd had the most difficult assignment; since a dummy looked fake, the body being dragged around the stadium at the climax of the race, was actually Boyd, covered only by some padding and protective clothing. The race alone took three months to film.

Fully aware of the stakes, Messala has his chariot outfitted with revolving blades at the end of each axle. As the race progresses, he maneuvers his chariot alongside that of one of his chief rivals, and the blades chew the spokes of the wheel. The chariot crashes, and the driver is trampled by the other teams. Messala then tries to repeat the maneuver with Judah and almost succeeds in doing so, but in the last lap of the race, his own wheel comes off. Dragged by his team, trampled and run over by following teams, he is left broken and flayed on the sands. Later, writhing in agony, Messala tells Judah what has happened to his mother and sister and dies gloating at Judah's horror.

Esther has discovered that Miriam and Tirzah are in the Valley of the Lepers and has been taking them food, but she has promised them not to tell Judah. As he searches, Judah encounters a preacher addressing large crowds but does not recognize the carpenter who brought him water at Nazareth. When he finds himself caught up in a mob taking the preacher to be crucified, he is horrified to realize that this is the compassionate young man who gave him water when he was a slave. Again, the audience does not see Christ's face. Judah goes along to Calvary and witnesses the crucifixion. In the darkness and tempest that follow, Miriam, the dying Tirzah, and Esther take refuge in a cave. Lightning flashes reveal that the lepers have been miraculously healed. A spring rain follows, renewing life, and the film ends.

Though it follows the novel in its general outline, the 1959 film departs from it in a number of details. It omits altogether the subplot about Iras, the Egyptian siren who is Messala's lover and who tries to seduce Judah. She is quite expendable, and Heston felt that the love story with Esther could have been cut as well. As Heston portrays him, Judah is older and more mature than Lew Wallace's hero. In both the novel and the 1925 film, Judah sees Jesus as the potential leader of a revolution against Rome, and like a Maccabee, he raises a legion to help him. Not until the end does he realize that Christ's kingdom is not of this world. In the 1959 film, Judah Ben-Hur is not a Jewish nationalist and pays no attention to Jesus until the crucifixion.

Although the screenplay was credited solely to Karl Tunberg, the veteran but not very distinguished scenarist who had written *My Gal Sal* (1942), and *Beau Brummel* (1954), a number of others had a hand in it, including Maxwell Anderson, Gore Vidal, S. N. Behrman, and most importantly and controversially, Christopher Fry, who was called in to work over the script when the cast was actually working on location. Wyler credits Fry with revising the dialogue to add a more classic and flowing tone, altering a line such as "Did you enjoy your dinner?" to "Was the food to your liking?"; Heston called Fry "the principal though uncredited creator of the screenplay." When the authorship came up for arbitration, however, the Screen Writers Guild awarded Tunberg sole credit. He received an Oscar nomination, but his was the only category in which the film did not win.

Heston, of course, won the Oscar for Best Actor and created some stir by publicly thanking Christopher Fry during his acceptance speech. *Ben-Hur* also won Best Picture, Direction, Supporting Actor, Musical Score, Color Costuming, Special Effects, Sound, Film Editing (over a million feet of film were exposed during the shooting), Color Art Direction, and Color Cinematography. In addition, it was named Best Picture of the Year by the British Film Academy and the Hollywood Foreign Press Association. Within the profession, Sam Zimbalist was honored (posthumously, as he had suffered a fatal heart attack two weeks before the conclusion of location shooting in Rome) by the Screen Producers Guild as Best Producer of the Year, and William Wyler was named Best Director by the Screen Directors Guild.

Equally impressive was *Ben-Hur*'s box-office success. It had the largest advance sale to date ($500,000) and made almost $40,000,000 in its first year. Of all M-G-M films, only *Gone with the Wind* (1939) surpassed it in popularity, judging by box-office receipts. On February 14, 1971, *Ben Hur* was shown uncut, on prime time television; viewers gave it the highest rating accorded any movie shown during that period on television; it was telecast again at Easter in 1972 and 1974. Arthur Knight, writing in *The Saturday Review*, observed, "Wyler has proved . . . that taste and intelligence need not be lacking in a film spectacle." It is these qualities that account for *Ben-Hur*'s durability.

Katharine M. Morsberger
and *Robert E. Morsberger*

THE BEST YEARS OF OUR LIVES

Released: 1946
Production: Samuel Goldwyn for Goldwyn Productions (AA)
Direction: William Wyler (AA)
Screenplay: Robert E. Sherwood (AA); based on the novel *Glory for Me* by
   MacKinley Kantor
Cinematography: Gregg Toland
Editing: Daniel Mandell (AA)
Music: Hugo Friedhofer (AA)
Running time: 172 minutes

Principal characters:
Milly Stephenson .... Myrna Loy
Al Stephenson .... Fredric March (AA)
Fred Derry .... Dana Andrews
Peggy Stephenson .... Teresa Wright
Marie Derry .... Virginia Mayo
Wilma Cameron .... Cathy O'Donnell
Homer Parrish .... Harold Russell
                                                           (AA Special Award)
Butch Engle .... Hoagy Carmichael

One of the most honored films ever to be made in America, *The Best Years of Our Lives* won a total of eight Academy Awards in 1946. Producer Samuel Goldwyn, who always had a keen showman's instinct, first got the idea for a film about returning World War II veterans in 1944 when he read a story in *Time* magazine. The article suggested that American men might be returning to their jobs and families with mixed emotions, and that life might not be smooth for them. Goldwyn asked novelist MacKinley Kantor to write a story treatment, but Kantor became so fascinated with the subject that his "treatment" turned into a 268-page novel entitled *Glory for Me*. Then playwright Robert E. Sherwood, winner of three Pulitzer Prizes, and speechwriter for Franklin D. Roosevelt, was hired to write the script. The result was both literate and articulate, treating the story of the confused ex-soldiers with honesty and compassion.

Next, director William Wyler was brought in. Wyler had worked with Goldwyn several times before and was one of his favorite directors. He had been in the Air Force for three and a half years and had some understanding of the problems of readjustment to civilian life. Goldwyn and his company were determined that this film would be different, not just another Hollywood product. They spared no expense to assemble the finest cast they could muster, including Fredric March, Myrna Loy, Dana Andrews, Teresa Wright, and Virginia Mayo. The most notable member of the cast was Harold Russell, a young man who lost both hands during the war when a defective fuse exploded while in his grasp. Russell had never acted before, except in a brief training film made by the War Department where he demonstrated his mastery of the prosthetic hooks he used in place of hands. Goldwyn and Wyler were both amazed by Russell's ability, and Wyler went on record to say that Russell was the best natural actor he had ever tested.

The film was shot by ace cameraman Gregg Toland in black and white, with the entire wardrobe of the cast designed in varying shades of black and white to get as naturalistic a look a possible. Sets were built life-sized instead of larger than life, as was common, so that rooms that were meant to look cramped really were small, and characters seemed actually to live in their houses. Other technical innovations included the absence of makeup on all of the male characters in the film, and the revolutionary depth of focus that Toland achieved by strapping down his camera for almost every shot.

Aside from being a well-made film, *The Best Years of Our Lives* is a moving one as well. Wyler has stated that the film in a sense was written by certain events, and therefore the filmmakers had a responsibility not to distort those events. Nothing is overdramatized; human emotions are dealt with in intimate detail and seem to be actually happening and not acted out. The unease and nervousness of people who are reunited with unreal expectations is beautifully shown by small gestures. For example, Milly Stephenson (Myrna Loy) says "I look terrible!" when she first sees her husband; and Homer Parrish's (Harold Russell) mother bursts into tears when she sees his hooks for the first time. The behavior of the characters always arises out of the situation they are in, and by the end of the film, the audience feels as if they know these people very well.

The film opens when three veterans meet on an army plane taking them home to Boone City. Al (Fredric March) is an Army Sergeant returning to his wife, two children, and his job in the Cornbelt Bank. Homer is a young sailor who lost both his hands when his boat was torpedoed, and who has already learned to use his hooks with dexterity. The third man is Fred (Dana Andrews), an ex-Bombardier Captain from the wrong side of the tracks who is anxious to see his beautiful war bride. Their homecomings are mixed affairs. Al's wife and children are glad to see him, but Al, self-conscious, suggests they go out and celebrate rather than stay at home. Fred visits his drunkard father and blowsy stepmother only to find that his wife Marie (Virginia Mayo) has left his father's house and gone to work in a night club. He sets out to find her with mixed emotions. Homer's family treats him with pity—even his sweetheart does not know how to act. All three men meet later in a bar—Al with his wife Milly and grown daughter Peggy (Teresa Wright). Before the bartender closes after sending Homer home to bed, Fred and Al are both roaring drunk. Milly and Peggy drive them home, and put Fred to bed in a guest room.

The next morning, Peggy drives Fred to Marie's new apartment. A certain sympathy has sprung up between them, for during the night, Fred had nightmares about the war, and Peggy, a trained nurse, comforted him. Fred sees Marie and finds her small talk boring after his visit with Peggy's family, but physically she still excites him. The weeks pass and all three men go through the various traumas of adjustment. Al strives to make his work at the bank meaningful; Homer tries valiantly to make a go of his life at home, but he rejects the love of his girl friend Wilma (Cathy O'Donnell) as pity and repudiates her. Fred cannot find a job and finally admits to Marie that they are penniless. He goes back to the drugstore in which he was soda jerking before the war, this time behind the perfume counter for thirty-two dollars a week. Marie becomes disgusted with pinching pennies and the two become more and more estranged. Fred's only relief comes when Peggy drops into the drug store to say hello. One day they go out for lunch and realize that they are in love. When Peggy confesses this to her parents, Al is worried, and seeks Fred out at their favorite bar, telling him to stay away from Peggy. Fred telephones Peggy in Al's presence. He tells her he will not see her again; she is heartbroken.

Later, Fred gets into a scuffle with a customer in the drugstore and is fired. Homer, who was watching, talks to Fred, who wearily advises him to marry Wilma and to take what is good in life before it is too late. When Homer gets home, he removes his hooks in front of Wilma, showing her the harness he must wear. She is neither shocked nor repelled and tells him again that she loves him. Homer, convinced at last of her affection for him, asks her to marry him. Meanwhile, Fred returns to his apartment to find Marie entertaining a man. He realizes that she has been unfaithful to him, and that he is not even remotely in love with her anymore. He tells her to see about getting a quick divorce, and leaves. Jobless and discouraged, Fred decides to leave Boone City, but at the airport he sees hundreds of Flying Fortress planes being dismantled and scrapped. He asks the foreman in charge of the salvaging operation for a job and resolves to start a new life for himself.

Homer and Wilma are married. Al and his family are among the guests and Fred is best man. He greets Peggy coolly, but as the ceremony progresses, they both discover that they are still in love. As the guests crowd around Homer and Wilma, Fred takes Peggy in his arms, and with Al's blessings they decide to face the future together.

As mentioned earlier, *The Best Years of Our Lives* won eight major Academy Awards in 1946; in addition, Samuel Goldwyn won the Irving G. Thalberg Memorial Award primarily because of the film. The acting plaudits were given to Fredric March (who had to be lured away from the Broadway stage to do the film) and to Harold Russell. Russell also received a special award "for bringing hope and courage to his fellow veterans" through his appearance in the film. The critics were rapt; they all felt that this was no ordinary film, but one that had special meaning for the millions of Americans who were living the same situation that they were seeing on the screen. The film is revived frequently in spite of its length, and has lost none of its power or its truth. It is not only quality entertainment, but is an important social document as well.

Joan Cohen

THE BIG KNIFE

Released: 1955
Production: Robert Aldrich for United Artists
Direction: Robert Aldrich
Screenplay: James Poe; based on the play of the same name by Clifford Odets
Cinematography: Ernest Laszlo
Editing: Michael Luciano
Running time: 111 minutes

Principal characters:
Charles Castle	Jack Palance
Stanley Hoff	Rod Steiger
Marion Castle	Ida Lupino
Smiley Coy	Wendell Corey
Nat Danziger	Everett Sloane
Dixie Evans	Shelley Winters
Connie Bliss	Jean Hagen

In 1949 Clifford Odets took out his bitterness and revulsion toward Hollywood by writing *The Big Knife*, a play produced on Broadway starring John Garfield and Nancy Kelly. Odets had not had a very satisfying experience writing for the motion picture industry, and, like so many others, had taken the money and run. He managed to purge himself in this tale of the guilt-ridden New York actor who compromises his ideals in the loose-living film capital. The play was moderately successful and soon became a standard piece for community and repertory theaters. Director Robert Aldrich picked it up for the screen in 1954. Aldrich had long known about Odets' story of corruption in Hollywood and saw the play as a vehicle for a film that might free him from the control of the major studios. Aldrich had become a successful director during the 1950's with such solid works as *Kiss Me Deadly* (1955), *Vera Cruz* (1954), and *Apache* (1954). He wanted to function as an independent producer, however, so he commissioned James Poe to write a screenplay based on Odets' work. Aldrich personally took the script around Hollywood, trying to get actors on a deferred payment basis. John Garfield, who would have gotten the role, was dead, so Jack Palance, in a bit of offbeat casting, was hired to play Charlie Castle, the anguished actor-protagonist, with Ida Lupino cast as his wife Marion. With a budget of $423,000, Aldrich realized he had to work fast and economically, so a nine-day rehearsal period and a two-week shooting schedule were planned, and corners were cut whenever possible. The main (and virtually only) set used was movie star Palance's Bel Air mansion, where all of the action was limited to two rooms, an entrance hall, and the patio.

During the rehearsal period, Aldrich worked with his company very much as if they were members of a repertory group. The rehearsal sessions were intense, with many of the "method" actors from New York clashing with the Hollywood-based ones. But by the time the cameras were ready to start rolling, the cast members were finely attuned to one another and worked together like a true ensemble. Aldrich had a great deal at stake personally in *The Big Knife*. Having been haunted by the story ever since he saw Garfield do the play in New York, he was determined to make the film in an uncompromising manner, despite the film industry's antagonism toward the property. Many people in Hollywood felt that *The Big Knife* was a vicious and unnecessary assault on the film industry, and that it held the filmmaking world in contempt. According to Odets, it was merely the story of an individual actor who was not strong enough to live with himself and resolve his doubts. Aldrich felt that simply because a story had a Hollywood background, it did not have to be anti-Hollywood.

The film does indeed deal with the trappings of success and how one man gets caught by them. Charlie Castle is a top box-office name who possesses all of the shiny luxuries and comforts that go with it. On the upward climb, however, the young actor has paid a price: he has suffered the loss of his integrity and self-respect. His marriage is on the verge of breaking up because of his readiness to sign a seven-year contract with a ruthless producer, Stanley Hoff (Rod Steiger). Charlie's wife Marion has put an ultimatum to him—if he signs the contract, she leaves. Charlie tries to maneuver his way out of signing, but his agent Nat Danziger (Everett Sloane) comes to warn him that Hoff and his hatchet man, Smiley Coy (Wendell Corey), are on their way to the house to secure his signature. Danziger tells Charlie that if he does not sign, Hoff will reveal to the world Charlie's part in a murder cover-up in which Charlie's publicity agent went to jail for him over a car accident for which Charlie was actually responsible. Hoff comes to Charlie's house, and the scene of the interview between the two men reveals why the film industry resented the film.

Stanley Hoff is a venal, power-crazed film producer, resorting to such tricks as turning off his hearing aid when he does not want to deal with unpleasant facts. He is a man used to having his own way, and he will stop at nothing to get it. He gets Charlie to sign the contract, and when Marion calls from a pay phone and is told, she hangs up. During the next three hours, Charlie tries to drink away his problems. He is alone in the house when Buddy Bliss's flirtatious wife Connie (Jean Hagen) drops in, but he repels her advances. For a few days he mopes about in quiet despair, until Smiley places a new weight on his shoulders. Hoff wants Charlie's help in "removing" Dixie Evans (Shelley Winters), the starlet who was in the hit-and-run car the night of the accident, and is now talking too much. Charlie refuses to help even though Smiley Coy engineers Dixie's arrival at Charlie's house. The weeks pass and Charlie is almost relaxed, thinking he is off the hook, when Coy arrives and insists that Charlie help him get rid of Dixie by poisoning the gin in her apartment. This is the breaking point for Charlie. In an angry confrontation with Coy, Hoff, and Danziger, he allows all of his accumulated bitterness to pour out, and forces Hoff out of the house. Wearily, Charlie goes upstairs to take a bath. While he is gone, Coy comes in and rushes to the phone to notify Hoff that Dixie Evans has been killed in a street accident and that all their troubles are over. As he talks, he notices water dripping through the ceiling and rushes upstairs to see that Charlie has killed himself.

Besides the unforgettable performance of Rod Steiger as Stanley Hoff, *The Big Knife* is memorable for its uncompromising look at the film industry. In spite of protests by Odets and Aldrich to the contrary, the film is very hard on the studio system. All of the people around Castle, with the exception of his wife, are shown to be corruptible, if not corrupt. Some critics felt that Odets was trying to exorcise his own personal guilt for having stayed in Hollywood for so long; others felt that the film was a savage and unwarranted attack on an industry that had treated both Odets and Aldrich very well. When the film was released in September, 1955, even the most flattering reviews did not miss the chance to dig at Aldrich and his treatment of Hollywood. Back in Hollywood, Odets was delighted; he thought that the mere fact that a film like *The Big Knife* could be made was a healthy sign, in spite of the invective heaped upon it. The picture was well thought of abroad and won the prize for the Best American Film at the Venice Film Festival of 1955. Over the years, it has gained more and more respect as one of the most interesting and provocative films ever made about the motion picture business. Perhaps its effect has been summed up best by Philip Scheuer of the *Los Angeles Times*, who said at its opening: "Its impact as drama is cumulative and wringing. One can deplore it, one cannot ignore it."

Joan Cohen

THE BIG SLEEP

Released: 1946
Production: Howard Hawks for Warner Bros.
Direction: Howard Hawks
Screenplay: William Faulkner, Leigh Brackett, and Jules Furthman; based on the novel of the same name by Raymond Chandler
Cinematography: Sid Hickox
Editing: Christian Nyby
Running time: 114 minutes

Principal characters:
Phillip Marlowe .... Humphrey Bogart
Vivian Sternwood Rutledge .... Lauren Bacall
Carmen Sternwood .... Martha Vickers
Eddie Mars .... John Ridgely
Book Seller .... Dorothy Malone
Harry Jones .... Elisha Cook, Jr.
General Sternwood .... Charles Waldron

The Big Sleep is a classic on many counts. It is a *film noir* that consistently appears on lists or retrospectives on the movement, even though as a big-budget, big-star production it violates the "B" film norm for *film noir*. It is a cult favorite on television, college campuses, and at art houses. The Bogart-Bacall relationship, not as outrageous as that depicted in their first film together, Howard Hawks's *To Have and Have Not* (1944), succeeded off screen as well as on. The film is a classic of the private detective genre and is the best example of the type of mystery in which no one knows or cares (including the director and writers) about the intricacies of who did what to whom. Finally, *The Big Sleep* is classic Warner Bros. and classic Howard Hawks and is generally regarded as a completely successful adaptation of a much-loved Raymond Chandler novel to film. Chandler himself liked the film, calling Bogart "the genuine article" and admiring Hawks's direction.

The Big Sleep opened to excellent reviews. Bogart and Bacall were already known as a "hot couple," which assured good box-office receipts, and both critics and the public loved the film. Bogart was considered perfect for the tough-yet-romantic character of Phillip Marlowe, and today, most people—since they see the film before reading the book—picture Bogart when they meet Chandler's Marlowe in the novel.

The plot of the film makes no real sense. Phillip Marlowe is employed by General Sternwood (Charles Waldron), a sick, rich old man, to deal with a man who is asking Sternwood to pay legally uncollectible gambling debts. The debts were incurred by Carmen Sternwood (Martha Vickers), the General's youngest daughter, who is spoiled, perhaps slightly retarded, and certainly sexually perverse. The General has another daughter, Vivian (Lauren Bacall), who tries to find out from Marlowe what her father has asked him to do. She and a lot of other people assume that his job is to find Sean Regan, who has disappeared. Sean was a friend and employee of the General who was actually a surrogate son. In the film it is fairly clear that he is dead, but who killed him, and who later killed the Sternwood's chauffeur, simply ceases to be an issue. In the novel, the murderess is the dangerously psychotic Carmen, who nearly kills Marlowe as well. Hawks explains that the Production Code officials suggested the ending upon which the film finally settled: Carmen will be put away and "taken care of," and Eddie Mars (John Ridgely), who is instrumental in her corruption, is killed by his own men, leaving Marlowe and Vivian to carry on their affair. The story is carried along with plenty of action (including Bacall singing a sexy song in a gambling club) and fast, witty dialogue, and is enhanced by the love story of Marlowe and Vivian. Chandler bemoaned Hollywood's insistence upon the "love angle," but the change of focus from the novelist's lonely detective always living up to his personal honor in a corrupt world to a love story between two strong adults provides much more than a "Hollywood" ending.

The Phillip Marlowe of Chandler's novel is tough, romantic, in control, and above all pure. He is untainted by the tawdry world in which he lives and the underworld characters with whom he rubs elbows. He is a romantic, always looking for a woman worthy of him, but (and this is a key to Chandler) every potential candidate lets him down. Chandler's Marlowe is at heart a misogynist whose fundamental purity is a direct result of being uncontaminated by women. Carmen elicits a declaration of his hatred of women when she comes to his room to trade her body for his silence. His room is soiled by her very presence: "But this was the room I had to live in. . . . I couldn't stand her in that room any longer." When Carmen leaves, he must cleanse the room: "I walked to the windows and pulled the shades up and opened the windows wide." The next morning: "You can have a hangover from other things than alcohol. I had one from women. Women make me sick."

Marlowe's neurotic fear of women, and especially of their sexuality, is the basis of his alienation in the novel; only in his room can he keep himself, his memories, and his future safe from them. The Marlowe of the film is very different: like all Hawks heroes, he is challenged by sexually aggressive women. His relationship with Vivian culminates in the kind of hopeful love of which *film noir* is capable, but only at the expense of her character. Before she acknowledges her love, she is feisty, strong, and equal to him. The camera follows her in their first encounter in her bedroom—she is clearly in control both of our attention (through the camera) and of the space of the frame in which she freely moves. In their verbal sparring, when she is "winning," she dominates the frame visually, but as she falls in love with him, he gains power over her and she becomes less and less the dynamic, interesting character she was. She is merely an observer in Joe Brody's apartment, sitting still on the couch while the men spar, and she continues to lose mobility until in the final scenes she must sit like a statue. The degree of space characters create around themselves is indicative of their control in any film, certainly, but even more so in a Hawks film, where physical space is so important in determining power relationships. Vivian's space decreases as Marlowe "conquers" her in this film. By the end of *The Big Sleep* she has been visually immobilized and confined and verbally reduced to a second-rate assistant for Marlowe, in sharp contrast to the aggressive, witty, and tough fighter she was in the beginning, and the independent, provocative woman she was in Eddie Mars's gambling club. This process of "taming" the strong, aggressive and independent woman is not as effective in *The Big Sleep* as in most examples of *film noir* because sexual fear is not at the heart of the film, as it is in the book. Vivian (and Carmen, as a symbol for women in general) is not the threat to Marlowe that she is in the book, so the need for her confinement and control is not so urgent, and it is accomplished with more subtlety. Vivian's taming is presented as important for its positive rewards rather than for its loss of mobility and independence for her. The film *The Big Sleep* is a more "healthy" male fantasy than those usually seen in *film noir*, but the process of controlling aggression and undercutting the independence and intelligence of the female is still very much present, though in the less urgent form that Hawks's less paranoid view of the world requires.

Janey Place

BILLY BUDD

Released: 1962
Production: A. Ronald Lubin and Peter Ustinov for Allied Artists
Direction: Peter Ustinov
Screenplay: Peter Ustinov and DeWitt Bodeen; based on Louis O. Coxe's and Robert H. Chapman's stage adaptation of the novel *Billy Budd, Foretopman* by Herman Melville
Cinematography: Robert Krasker
Editing: Jack Harris
Running time: 123 minutes

Principal characters:
Master-at-Arms John Claggart .... Robert Ryan
Captain Edward Fairfax Vere .... Peter Ustinov
The Dansker .... Melvyn Douglas
Billy Budd .... Terence Stamp
Jenkins .... Ronald Lewis
Lieutenant Wyatt .... David McCallum
Lieutenant Ratcliffe .... John Neville

Herman Melville's short novel *Billy Budd, Foretopman* was discovered when the manuscript was found in an attic trunk more than twenty years after Melville's death in 1891. Almost immediately it gained admirers, most of whom found as much to praise in it as they had in his lengthy masterpiece, *Moby Dick*. In theme it went beyond the remorseless conflict between good and evil, which had always fascinated Melville; in *Billy Budd* the thesis was that absolute good cannot live in the same world as absolute evil. One will surely destroy the other, and in so doing put an end to itself.

Hollywood had first discovered *Moby Dick* during the silent era, but it was not until *Billy Budd* was dramatized for the theater, where it enjoyed considerable success, that it was even considered as a possibility for film. A young theatrical producer, Franklin Gilbert, bought the film rights to the novel in 1956, and engaged DeWitt Bodeen to write a screenplay based upon both the novel and the stage version. Gilbert, however, could not get his proposed production off the ground, and was forced to sell out to Gabriel Katzka, who was then just entering film production. Robert Rossen came into the enterprise as producer/director and brought Bodeen to New York, where an entirely new screenplay was written, this time based more completely upon Melville's novel. Again, problems beset the production unit, and eventually the property was sold to an English producer, A. Ronald Lubin, who engaged Peter Ustinov not only to coproduce the project but to direct it and play the key role of Captain Vere. Ustinov wrote his own shooting script, basing it upon the screenplay Bodeen had written for Rossen. This final version went into production in England, with the exteriors filmed off the coast of Spain. It received excellent notices everywhere, but Allied Artists was releasing it. After its initial showings, return engagements were few, and audiences who may have wanted to see it had a hard time even finding it showing anywhere. The film won new actor Terence Stamp, who played the title role, an Academy Award nomination; but the picture found its largest audience when it was released for television, where it is often chosen as picture of the week.

Billy Budd was based upon the character of Jack Chase, captain of the foretop in a earlier Melville novel, *White Jacket*; Melville dedicated *Billy Budd* to Chase. Although a similar conflict to that which takes place in *Billy Budd* actually happened in the American Navy, the story works better dramatically in the setting Melville used: the British Navy at the time of the Napoleonic Wars, when the evil of impressment was in full sway. When a warship suffered a shortage in its crew because of either the death, disability, or desertion of some of its members, that ship could legally seek new manpower from the crews of merchant ships it passed at sea; or, if the ship docked, the officers could impress available men on land.

Such is the dilemma of *HMS Avenger*, a battleship which has sailed shorthanded and now desperately needs new men; the crew boards a merchant ship, *Rights-of-Man*, but can find only one sailor suited to their needs. He is Billy Budd (Terence Stamp), young, strong, and full of life. He is loved by all and is so innately good that all his fellow crew members lament his being taken from them. But Billy cannot protest. He knows that the *Avenger* is acting within its rights; also, because he stammers when he is emotionally upset, he is unable to state his case. As the longboat pulls away, Billy waves farewell to the ship and to the friendly mates he is leaving behind, crying out, "And goodbye to you, too, old *Rights-of-Man!*" It is a farewell that is not only prophetic, but filled with doom.

Edward Fairfax Vere (Peter Ustinov), Captain of the *Avenger*, is an intelligent officer with a fine sense of justice, although one that is perhaps too inflexible; he welcomes his new foretopman, sensing Billy's worth at once. There is an almost immediate paternal feeling between Vere and Billy, who in his young strength and honest goodness impresses Vere as being the kind of son he would have liked to have had. Almost at once, Billy encounters the ship's Master-at-Arms, John Claggart (Robert Ryan). He is too innocent to recognize the evil that coils within Claggart, who is despised by his crew, whom he treats with vile cruelty. Claggart sees at once that Billy is as different from him as night from day, but he refuses to acknowledge that a man may be entirely good and innocent. There must be a flaw, a fatal weakness, somewhere in Billy. Vere is aware of Claggart's villainy, and warns Billy not to cross Claggart, telling him that some men cannot stand too much perfection.

Claggart is driven to destroy Billy, and enlists his corporal, Squeak, to aid him in forcing Billy into error and thus into Claggart's power. But Billy blithely defeats being overpowered by Claggart and his minions. Claggart forces another foretopman, Jenkins (Ronald Lewis), who is ill, to go aloft, but Jenkins falls to his death despite Billy's attempts to save him.

There is now a growing restlessness among the crew, who not only fear Claggart but openly hate him. Captain Vere is aware of the danger Claggart poses to the ship, and when Claggart boldly confronts Vere, accusing Billy of hatching a mutinous plot among his fellow crew members, Vere, confident that Claggart is lying, confronts him with Billy, who is invited to deny the charges. Unfortunately, Billy is so unnerved by the false accusation that he cannot speak at all. Unable to assert his innocence vocally, he is driven to turn upon Claggart in physical protest, and with one blow strikes him so that he falls to the deck dead, his skull broken, a smirk in his dying eyes.

Sick at heart, Vere has only one recourse: he convenes a secret court martial. The ship's officers meet, and when they hear the complaint, hating Claggart as they do and loving Billy, they try to judge Billy as being guilty only in defense of himself. But Vere, who loves Billy more than any of his men, is bound by an unbending code of ethics and feels compelled to persuade his men to stand by the laws of maritime justice and place a sentence of death upon Billy. In the early morning hours, the crew is called to attend mass upon deck and to witness a hanging; they are almost driven to mutiny when they realize that their Billy is the one to be executed, but they are held at bay under threat of musket fire by the marines. Billy is resigned and accepts his doom; he puts the noose around his neck and turns to look straight into Captain Vere's eyes. His last words are "God bless Captain Vere!"

The crew then rushes the marines, and a mutiny takes place, which leaves the ship unprepared for the French warship hiding in a cove, which now sweeps out into the open sea to cover the foray. The French fire upon the *Avenger*, destroying the ship; a falling spar kills Captain Vere. The film's last significant shot is a close-up of the *Avenger*'s figurehead—the blind goddess of justice bearing the ship's name—floating on the troubled sea.

Billy Budd is an allegory that has been interpreted in many ways. Melville believed that the only way to live an untroubled life was to pursue the middle way, to say positively "Yes" or "No" to nothing, to let neither good nor evil triumph, because in such a triumph there is only destruction. His Billy becomes a young Christ; his Claggart, a Judas with the heart of a Herod; his Captain Vere, an unhappy, puzzled Pontius Pilate. All must meet death. Somerset Maugham has advanced an interesting explanation of the conflict besetting Claggart which drives him and Billy to their deaths. Maugham sees Claggart as a latent homosexual in possession of himself until he meets Billy and falls in love first with his goodness and then with Billy himself. Yet he realizes that if he were ever to weaken and so much as hint at his true feelings, Billy would reject him forcibly, with contempt—and it would be the end of

Claggart's power over himself and the men he controls. Billy must be killed before Claggart destroys himself. There is a scene that supports this basic conflict when Billy and Claggart meet upon deck during the midnight watch and talk, Billy with honesty, Claggart watchfully. Claggart accidentally drops his stick, and Billy quickly recovers it for him. As Claggart takes the proffered stick, his fingers touch Billy's flesh, and he withdraws at once, horrified, realizing that the hour of Billy's destruction is imminent, and afraid that he will betray himself.

Terence Stamp was chosen to play Billy; he was made into a blond, innocently beautiful in his appearance, and thus perfect for the role. Robert Ryan, as the villain who smiles with his eyes and murders with his hands, gave one of his best performances in a remarkably subtle evocation of all that is evil. Melvyn Douglas, who had retired from screen acting, came back to play the Dansker, a Dane who senses the conflict that has come aboard with Billy and knows that disaster threatens the ship. Peter Ustinov was unfortunately miscast as Captain Vere, a role which demands an actor like Laurence Olivier to evoke an aristocrat with a tortured soul. As director, producer, and screenwriter, however, Ustinov performed flawlessly.

DeWitt Bodeen

BIRDMAN OF ALCATRAZ

Released: 1962
Production: Stuart Millar and Guy Trosper for United Artists
Direction: John Frankenheimer
Screenplay: Guy Trosper; based on the biography of the same name by Thomas E. Gaddis
Cinematography: Burnett Guffey
Editing: Edward Mann
Running time: 147 minutes

Principal characters:
Robert Stroud	Burt Lancaster
Harvey Shoemaker	Karl Malden
Elizabeth Stroud	Thelma Ritter
Stella Johnson	Betty Field
Bull Ransom	Neville Brand
Tom Gaddis	Edmond O'Brien
Roy Comstock	Hugh Marlowe
Feto Gomez	Telly Savalas
Dr. Ellis	Whit Bissell

Robert Franklin Stroud is one of the most extraordinary men ever to be incarcerated for murder in an American prison. In 1909, at the age of nineteen, he shot a bartender; and later he knifed to death a prison guard. In 1920, after nursing a sick sparrow, he began studying ornithology and became one of the foremost authorities on the subject of caged birds. He wrote books and articles on the subject, as well as manuscripts on penology. Stroud was in solitary confinement for a record forty-two of his fifty-four years in prison. His biography was written by Thomas E. Gaddis. In 1963, he died of a heart attack in his sleep, a year after the release of a film based on Gaddis' book, *Birdman of Alcatraz*.

Birdman of Alcatraz is a prison film, but it is not concerned with prison life *per se* or the interrelationships between inmates, as are most films of the genre. Stroud (Burt Lancaster), who had killed a bartender in Alaska, is sentenced to twelve years in prison. When he knifes a prison guard, he loses any opportunity for parole. He is later sentenced to death for murdering a guard who refuses to let his mother (Thelma Ritter) see him, but his death sentence is commuted to life in prison when Mrs. Stroud visits the wife of President Woodrow Wilson, and the First Lady persuades her husband to alter the sentence. Stroud will spend the rest of his years in solitary confinement.

One day, while exercising in the prison yard at Leavenworth, he comes upon a wounded sparrow. He takes it back to his cell and, without the knowledge of his watchers or the warden, Harvey Shoemaker (Karl Malden), he nurses the bird back to health. When Shoemaker is replaced as warden, Stroud is allowed to construct an aviary in his cell and, after relentless study, he becomes an expert in ornithology and writes a textbook on bird pathology. After publishing his work, and after marrying a widow, Stella Johnson (Betty Field), so that he has a possibility to market his bird remedies, he is abruptly transferred to Alcatraz. Shoemaker is the warden there, and he takes away Stroud's birds. The prisoner then writes a book about caged men, which is also confiscated. But when Stroud acts as a peacemaker in a prison riot—a predictable, overtly commercial addition to what is otherwise a perceptive, original study of survival in a prison cell—he is rewarded with a transfer to a minimum security farm in Missouri. As he leaves Alcatraz at the film's finale, he is met by Tom Gaddis (Edmond O'Brien), who eventually writes Stroud's biography.

Screenwriter Guy Trosper does not completely editorialize in chronicling Stroud's story. While his ornithological accomplishments are exceptional, Stroud is, after all, a convicted murderer. This is not denied in the script: Stroud is at first depicted as a moody, desperate killer. But overall, he is presented by Trosper and portrayed by Lancaster as a man who reforms, a man whose wretched life takes on meaning when he becomes an authority on birds and writes an exhaustive textbook about them. The viewer identifies with him and feels that he is worthy of parole after his decades in solitary confinement, the length of time which has passed since his criminal activity, and his efforts to quell the prison riot. Trosper's script is an indictment of the American penal system for not acknowledging Stroud's "rehabilitation." But *Birdman of Alcatraz* is a fictionalized account of a man's life. In reality, Stroud was allegedly not the introspective character depicted in the film, but an arrogant, shameless individual.

In the film, the accomplishment of Stroud's later years clearly overshadows the murderous follies of his youth. Stroud is undeniably a remarkable man who, despite taking two lives, developed into a self-made scholar with a profound concern for tiny birds. But the viewer must remember that this depiction of Stroud's life is not objective. In retelling a story based on fact, actual events and personalities are bound to be lost in interpretation. Here, Trosper has clearly taken dramatic license. To believe that, based solely on the viewing of *Birdman of Alcatraz*, Robert Stroud was treated unfairly by the American penal system is fallacious. The film is a fictionalization of a man's life, and definitely tells his side of his story. The question of whether Stroud should have been paroled is open to endless debate, but the answer is ultimately a matter of opinion.

Beyond the facts of Stroud's life as fictionalized for the film, *Birdman of Alcatraz* is a forceful, well-acted, and well-directed account of the life of this unusual man. Lancaster, usually a physical actor whose work tends to lack subtlety, offers the most sensitive performance of his career as Stroud. His Stroud becomes a subdued individual who attains human dignity by devoting his life to scholarship. His most effective scenes are when he lovingly tends to the first sparrow, which elicits his initial interest in ornithology. Though he was nominated for an Academy Award as Best Actor, Lancaster lost to Gregory Peck for *To Kill a Mockingbird*.

Lancaster is given fine support by Thelma Ritter as his aggressive, supportive mother, Karl Malden as his warden and nemesis, Betty Field as the widow, Neville Brand as a guard who grows to appreciate Stroud's work, and Telly Savalas as an inmate who becomes Stroud's companion. Savalas, Ritter, and cinematographer Burnett Guffey were all nominated for Oscars, but lost to Ed Begley in *Sweet Bird of Youth*, Patty Duke in *The Miracle Worker*, and Jean Bourgoin and Walter Wottitz for the black-and-white cinematography of *The Longest Day*.

John Frankenheimer graphically captures Stroud's sterile, solitary existence before he finds the fateful sparrow. Carefully detailed are the prisoner's efforts to construct his first aviary: a piece of bottle is transformed into a drinking bowl; wooden crates become cages. The film's focus is mostly on Lancaster/Stroud; however, the other characters are skillfully interwoven into the story. The shooting of *Birdman of Alcatraz* began under director Charles Crichton before Lancaster appeared in Stanley Kramer's *Judgment at Nuremberg* (1961). After completing that assignment, filming was resumed with Frankenheimer.

Birdman of Alcatraz earned only $2,200,000, and was the twenty-seventh highest grossing film of its year. It received generally favorable reviews; at the Venice Film Festival, Lancaster won a Best Actor prize, and the film was awarded the San Giorgio Prize for stimulating "with artistic dignity feelings and ideas useful to civilization."

Rob Edelman

THE BITTER TEA OF GENERAL YEN

Released: 1933
Production: Columbia
Direction: Frank Capra
Screenplay: Edward E. Paramore; based on the novel of the same name by Grace Zaring Stone
Cinematography: Joseph Walker
Editing: no listing
Running time: 87 minutes

Principal characters:
Megan Davis .... Barbara Stanwyck
General Yen .... Nils Asther
Jones .... Walter Connolly
Mah-Li .... Toshia Mori
Dr. Robert Strike .... Gavin Gordon
Captain Li .... Richard Loo

When one views Capra's films, *The Bitter Tea of General Yen* and *Lost Horizon* (1937) stand apart from his usual exploration of American ideology, for they have backgrounds which are diametrically opposed to the world of Mr. Deeds and John Doe. They both take place in the Orient, but whereas *Lost Horizon* is set in the best of all possible worlds, *The Bitter Tea of General Yen* takes place amid civil war, chaos, and famine. The leaders of Shangri-La believe that harmony—through goodness, truth, and beauty—prolongs life, whereas General Yen holds his great power through a complete distrust of humanity, showing no mercy and having no regard for human life. *Lost Horizon* is a story about an Occidental missionary who creates a paradise in an isolated valley in the mountains of Tibet, but *The Bitter Tea of General Yen* is about the incongruity and futility of missionaries and their work in China. To savor fully the delightful jabs at Christianity and missionaries in China, one must realize that Capra was, and is, a devout Catholic. Not only does Capra crucify the missionary, but also his story makes Christianity a fatal pill for General Yen: the first time he shows mercy to anyone it leads to his quick destruction.

The story of *The Bitter Tea of General Yen* opens in Shanghai on a scene of utter chaos: peasants flee as an army moves amidst the turbulence of the civil war. Megan Davis (Barbara Stanwyck), a newly arrived American missionary, is being carried through the screaming crowds in a rickshaw, when the "boy" pulling it is struck and killed by an ominous black limousine. Kneeling in the crowd, Megan attempts to comfort the dying boy, then vents her fury on the driver of the limousine. The driver does not understand what she is talking about, but then the smiling, sardonic figure of General Yen

(Nils Asther) emerges from the car. Speaking in English but not understanding her concern, he tells her that life is cheap in China and not to worry, for he will take her to her destination. Although he is immaculately dressed in his general's uniform and is exotically handsome, she is repelled by his lack of concern and inhumane attitude. She curtly refuses him and turns to make her way on foot, while he looks after her with an insolent smile as if to foreshadow a future meeting between them.

Meanwhile, the missionaries have gathered for the wedding of Megan to Dr. Robert Strike (Gavin Gordon), another missionary. Dr. Strike has not arrived on the scene when Megan makes her appearance. The missionaries themselves are an unchristian lot, finding nothing good in the Chinese. The house where they have gathered is completely American; there is no Oriental design about it, nor are there any Orientals gathered for the marriage ceremony. When Dr. Strike does arrive, it is to postpone his wedding to Megan, for he says he must leave at once to rescue children left in an orphanage which is dangerously near the fighting line. Megan insists, to the horror of all the ladies present, that she will accompany him. Dr. Strike is helpless to deny her and allows her to go along.

When she tells him of her strange meeting with General Yen, Strike is amazed, for Yen is not supposed to be in Shanghai. Since Yen could give him a safe conduct pass, they go to the general's headquarters. As Megan waits outside, Strike begs Yen for the pass. General Yen scoffs at him, but he sits down and writes in Chinese calligraphy what Strike believes to be a pass. Actually, however, it is a message introducing Strike as a Christian fool who prefers rescuing a band of lowly children "without ancestors" to passing the night with his bride in his arms.

Megan and Strike get an automobile and reach the orphanage, where they assemble the children for flight. But the streets are full of fighting, and a band of soldiers commandeers the automobile. In the ensuing struggle, Megan is separated from Strike and the children and is felled by a blow.

When she regains consciousness, she finds that somehow she has been transported to the secret and distant summer palace of General Yen. She is surrounded by every possible luxury, and when she steps out on her balcony, she sees the expansiveness and beauty of her prison. When Yen enters the room to inquire about her, she asks him why she has been kidnaped. He laughs and tells her that he has saved her life. Coldly, she informs him that she must return to Shanghai, but he tells her that it is impossible at this time because of heavy fighting; however, as soon as it is safe, he will send her back in a special train. For the meanwhile, he asks if she will be his guest and whether he may expect her presence at dinner that evening. Then he gallantly bows as he closes her door. Not for one moment does Megan believe Yen. She will not succumb to his charm, nor be pleasant or agreeable in any way. She is a prisoner.

Next, Mah-Li (Toshia Mori), Yen's young mistress, enters and inquires if Megan has all she needs. Megan likes Mah-Li and attempts to learn more about Yen from her. Megan refuses, however, to associate with Yen, and as the days pass, she becomes confidential with Mah-Li. One night, while the moon is full, Megan and Mah-Li watch from the balcony as Yen's soldiers romance the local ladies. A whistle from below makes Mah-Li twitter, for it is her young secret lover, Captain Li (Richard Loo), Yen's right-hand man. Mah-Li implores Megan not to tell Yen, and smilingly Megan agrees and tells her to go meet her beau. Alone, she watches the lovely setting and then falls asleep.

Megan dreams that a sinister Yen in mandarin robes is coming towards her with long claws. She cowers on the bed in fear, but there is a beating at the door as her rescuer attempts to break in. Finally, the door is smashed. Her hero enters and with one blow destroys Yen. She opens her arms to her uniformed hero, who is also Yen, and he bends down and kisses her. She awakens with a start and is troubled, pondering her dream.

Daily, Megan rejects Yen's invitations to dine with him. Eventually she changes her mind, deciding to go down to dinner to meet Jones (Walter Connolly), who is Yen's financial adviser and a wily American whom she hopes will persuade Yen to release her. At first, she lets Mah-Li dress her in Oriental attire, and puts on makeup, but then, fearing that she is succumbing to Yen, she wipes off her makeup and dresses herself in her New England attire.

At dinner, Jones tells Yen that Mah-Li and Captain Li are betraying him, and Yen indifferently decides to exterminate them. Later, a panic-stricken Mah-Li tells Megan bluntly that her guilt has been exposed and she will die for her sins. Megan implores Yen to be forgiving and let Mah-Li live; carried away with the situation, she begs him to use his God-given privilege, promising that he will know for the first time in his life what real happiness is. She breaks off in tears, realizing that she has almost confessed that she herself loves him. This does not escape Yen, who forgives Mah-Li, not in order to show that he too can display the mercy of the Christian world, but to show Mah-Li how foolish Megan is to plead on the girl's behalf, for he will let Mah-Li go only if Megan will stand as hostage for her. He is confident that Mah-Li will betray him again, and he drives the bargain, not to gain Megan's love on those terms, but to prove to her how false her Christian beliefs are; in this circumstance they simply will not work. As Yen confides to Jones subsequently, he is "going to convert a missionary."

Mah-Li does indeed betray General Yen a second time—outrageously, mercilessly, and with utter finality. Through her treachery, Yen's treasure train is stolen, his troops desert him, and no one is left in the summer palace except Megan, Jones, and General Yen.

When Megan realizes the extent of Mah-Li's perfidy, she goes to Yen, expecting him to demand payment of her honor. Instead, he gives her complete freedom; he will not take anything the heart does not freely give. She does not understand that it was her life, not her love, she pledged when she stood as hostage for Mah-Li's loyalty. Megan is frightened, and Yen scoffs at her fear of death, which she seems to fear as much as she has life. He confesses that he had intended to go to her room and kill her, after which the two would be joined in some celestial life as free lovers.

Megan runs to her room, dresses herself in Oriental garb, and paints her face. Meanwhile, Yen prepares the "bitter tea," the poison he will take to escape the world. She returns to him dressed in rich Chinese attire to affirm her love for him, which she realizes is her truest and finest emotion. She kneels at his feet weeping, and he dries her tears with a fine silk handkerchief as he slowly drinks his "bitter tea."

In the final sequence, Megan and Jones are together on a boat going back to Shanghai. Jones, who has been drinking enough to feel more than mellow, is talking about Yen, whom he characterizes as "a great guy." Yen had believed that we never die; we only change. Maybe, even now, he is the wind pushing their sail; maybe he is also the wind playing around her hair. Jones hopes that when he dies, the "guy" in charge of changing things will send him wherever Yen is; he looks at Megan, and ventures the thought that she will be there, too.

The Bitter Tea of General Yen opened New York's Radio City Music Hall as a motion picture theater, with a live prologue entertainment. New York critics had praise for the film, but in its general release it was deemed too bizarre, too esoteric for rural America. It is still one of Capra's favorites of all his films, and he was disappointed that it did not receive any Academy Award nominations. He had filmed it carefully, lovingly, and yet it was not for the masses. Almost in resignation, expecting nothing, he selected an inconsequentially light love story, *It Happened One Night* (1934), for one of his next efforts. He was lucky enough to borrow Claudette Colbert and Clark Gable from other studios for the leads, and at Academy Awards time, he swept the boards with a five-point major winner and made a great deal of money at the box office as well. Today, however, whenever there is a Capra, Columbia, or Barbara Stanwyck retrospective, *The Bitter Tea of General Yen* rates high as a favorite.

Although critics did not consider Barbara Stanwyck's role as Megan Davis to be one of her more memorable performances, today's audiences respond to her sympathetically; as a missionary who is converted to the real meaning of life, she is very believable. The picture belongs, however, to Nils Asther as General Yen. He gives a superb performance, his very best in film, although he had also played an Oriental prince in Garbo's silent *Wild Orchids* (1929), looking very handsome and rated as one of the few actors strong enough not to be emasculated by Garbo's strength. Asther makes Yen a fully dimensional character, a pagan who loved and lost, but whose loving had made life worth-while.

The picture was denounced by Protestants as an affront to their religion and their missionaries. It was banned throughout the British Empire, making it one of the few big Capra films to have lost money.

Larry Lee Holland

BLACK NARCISSUS

Released: 1947
Production: Michael Powell and Emeric Pressburger for J. Arthur Rank
Direction: Michael Powell and Emeric Pressburger
Screenplay: Michael Powell and Emeric Pressburger; based on the novel of
   the same name by Rumer Godden
Cinematography: Jack Cardiff (AA)
Editing: Reginald Mills
Art direction: Alfred Junge (AA)
Set decoration: Alfred Junge (AA)
Running time: 100 minutes

Principal characters:
Sister Clodagh	Deborah Kerr
Sister Ruth	Kathleen Byron
Mr. Dean	David Farrar
Sister Philippa	Flora Robson
Kanchi	Jean Simmons
Young Prince	Sabu
Prince	Esmond Knight

Black Narcissus is an engrossing psychological study of five Anglican nuns who are sent to establish a convent school and dispensary in the Himalayas. For this purpose the local Prince has given them an old palace that used to house his harem. It is called the House of Women.

The film's theme is the eternal conflict between the spirit and the flesh, the sacred and the profane. It is a study in mood whose subtler nuances are conveyed by its beautiful and striking visual qualities. The fantastic, eerie House of Women with its empty birdcages, erotic wall paintings, and tattered curtains, deserted except for the continuously blowing wind and an old half-mad woman caretaker who remembers its former splendors, is an appropriately bizarre setting for both the spiritual and secular aspects of the story.

The nuns belong to the Anglican Order of St. Mary, a working rather than a contemplative order, whose vows must be renewed each year. In setting up their school and dispensary they are helped, unenthusiastically, by the agent for the Prince (Esmond Knight), Mr. Dean (David Farrar). A cynical but charming Englishman, he tells the nuns that he thinks they will fail, probably before the rains come. The nuns do not believe him, but they do feel a certain strangeness from the day they arrive. As time passes, they begin remembering events and feelings which they had long suppressed. An older nun, Sister Philippa (Flora Robson), finds her faith shaken by her surroundings. She stares into space when she should be working and plants flowers instead of the necessary vegetables. When the quietly serene Sister Superior Clodagh (Deborah Kerr) questions her, Sister Philippa voices the thought that sums up what they are all feeling: "I had forgotten everything until I came here." Sister Clodagh can only advise her to work until she is too tired to think of anything else.

Sister Clodagh herself finds the clear air, the majestic mountains, the wind, and the local Hindu Holy Man all disturbing. She, too, begins to dream of the past, and we learn through flashbacks that she entered the order because she was deserted by her lover. She is also disturbed by the presence of Dean, upon whom she must rely for help and advice in dealing with the villagers.

Sister Ruth (Kathleen Byron), a high-strung, frustrated young nun, is also disturbed by and attracted to Dean. Whenever he visits the convent to discuss business with Sister Clodagh she hovers watchfully and broodingly around corners and on staircases, always listening. Sister Ruth becomes increasingly jealous of Sister Clodagh and conceives a hatred for her that eventually leads to Ruth's destruction.

Indeed, all the nuns seem to be reexamining their emotions and their ideas about love, beauty, and human nature. They are shocked, at first, when they learn that the Prince is paying the villagers to attend their school and dispensary. Dean explains to them what a sensible idea it is: pay them until it becomes a habit, then gradually stop paying them; eventually they will not remember when they did not come voluntarily.

The Prince himself brings a beautiful, sensual young village girl, Kanchi (Jean Simmons), to the convent and persuades Sister Clodagh to let her remain in order to keep her out of trouble until she is married. Sister Clodagh is also persuaded to allow a young Prince (Sabu), the son of their benefactor, to attend the nuns' school, although it is not customary for nuns to teach young men. He is an exotic figure in his gorgeous costumes covered with jewels and his disturbing perfume, Black Narcissus, which he tells Sister Ruth he bought at an Army/Navy store in London. It is inevitable that he and the young beauty, Kanchi, will be attracted to each other, and it is surprising that the seemingly sensible, clear-sighted Sister Clodagh would have permitted such a potentially explosive situation by taking the two in. It is a further indication of how much the place has affected her. Indeed, she asks Dean if he has noticed any changes in her. When he replies that she is nicer, more human, she begins to cry and tells him the story of her broken romance. He tries awkwardly to comfort her and advises her to go away before something happens.

Disaster comes when a child, brought to the dispensary for treatment, dies after being given a bottle of castor oil by one of the nuns. The superstitious villagers then refuse to come to either the school or the dispensary, and Dean warns the nuns not to venture out of the convent because their lives might be in danger. Another blow falls when Sister Clodagh learns that the young Prince has run away with Kanchi. The nuns choose to blame their misfortunes on the environment and its effect on them, but it has only brought out their buried frustrations and fears. Beneath their strength is weakness, and beneath their religious dedication is flight from the past.

The crowning calamity comes when Sister Ruth becomes completely mad. During the film we have seen her increasing jealousy and hatred of Sister Clodagh, her frustrated attachment to Dean, and her inability to cope with her strange surroundings and the new people. In a dramatic night scene, Sister Clodagh, making her rounds, notices a light under Sister Ruth's door and finds her in a burgundy dress wearing bright red lipstick. The contrast between her former appearance in her white habit, without makeup, is startling. Sister Clodagh tries to persuade Ruth to stay when she learns that she has decided not to renew her vows. But Ruth escapes and makes her way down the mountain to Dean's house. She tells him that she loves him, but he is rude and curt; he wants no part of her. He insists that she return to the convent, and when she recovers from the shock of his rejection, she agrees, if he will let her go alone.

Meanwhile, the nuns have been searching frantically for her. As dawn approaches, Sister Clodagh paces wearily up and down before going to the chapel to pray. Startled by a noise (it is Ruth stealthily returning to her room) the exhausted nun imagines for a moment that she is being attacked by Ruth. Later, Ruth actually does attack her as she stands near the edge of a cliff, ringing the bell for prayers. The two struggle desperately until Ruth finally slips and falls to her death. In the final sequence of the film we see the nuns packing up to leave. They have not only failed to establish a school and dispensary, but also have been almost spiritually destroyed themselves. When Dean comes to say good-bye, Sister Clodagh gives him her hand in a parting gesture. As he watches the caravan move on, rain begins to fall, slowly at first, then in a downpour. In the last image of the film, Dean turns to watch the nuns out of sight, but a sheet of rain hides them from his view.

Black Narcissus is a film of great visual distinction. It is filled with images which remain in the viewer's mind: the fantastic House of Women, a place of dreams and spirits; the sunsets that paint it different shades of gold and red; the dawn mists; the masses of exotic flowers; the white habits of the nuns contrasted with the deep blue of the sky and the dark shadows of the Palace; a snowfall; and the climactic rainstorm. In 1947, when this film was made, not many films were shot on location or in Technicolor. The makers of *Black Narcissus* chose to use Technicolor and carefully painted backgrounds to evoke the atmosphere of the Himalayas instead of shooting on location. Today, however, Technicolor is no longer a novelty, and, despite the expert cinematography of Jack Cardiff, the painted backgrounds tend to be distracting. This is, however, a minor flaw in a film of beautiful pictorial images. Its visual quality was recognized by the Academy with Oscars for Best Cinematography, Best Art Direction, and Best Set Decoration.

The fine acting by Deborah Kerr as Sister Clodagh, Kathleen Byron as

Sister Ruth, and David Farrar as Dean adds to the distinction of this fascinating, intellectual film. Deborah Kerr is always quietly authoritative and believable as the proud, ghost-haunted Sister Superior. Kathleen Byron is appropriately hysterical and overwrought and makes Sister Ruth's slide into madness credible. David Farrar conveys the appropriate air of amused detachment and cynicism. Effective performances by the supporting cast, including Jean Simmons as Kanchi and Sabu as the young Prince, also contribute to the overall impressiveness of the film.

Julia Johnson

BLACKMAIL

Released: 1929
Production: John Maxwell for British International Pictures
Direction: Alfred Hitchcock
Screenplay: Alfred Hitchcock and Benn W. Levy; based on the play of the
  same name by Charles Bennett
Cinematography: Jack Cox
Editing: Emile Ruello
Running time: 96 minutes

Principal characters:
Alice White .... Anny Ondra
Mrs. White .... Sara Allgood
Frank Webber .... John Longden
Mr. White .... Charles Paton
Tracy .... Donald Calthrop
The Artist .... Cyril Ritchard

As a play by Charles Bennett, *Blackmail* was a far from successful vehicle
for Talullah Bankhead, who was cast in its leading role; one cannot imagine
anything more ludicrous than casting Bankhead as the daughter of a London
tradesman. However, as Alfred Hitchcock's first sound feature, the film version of the play proved to be a popular British success, and more than any
of the director's previous films indicated his potential as a major master of
film suspense. Hitchcock's two films previous to *Blackmail*, *Champagne* (1928)
and *The Manxman* (1929), had proved disasters; but with *Blackmail* the
director was getting back to a style he had developed still earlier in *The
Lodger* (1926).

Blackmail was initially shot as a silent film, but Hitchcock was able to
persuade the head of British International Pictures, John Maxwell, to allow
him to reshoot sections of it with sound. Thus, although the film is in no way
a full-blown talkie, it is approximately fifty percent a silent film with musical
score and sound effects and fifty percent a sound feature. (*Blackmail* is often
credited as being Britain's first talkie, but this is doubtful; several other films
also lay claim to that distinction.) One major problem that Hitchcock had
to overcome in turning *Blackmail* into a talkie was that his leading lady, Anny
Ondra, had a strong German accent. The only solution in those days prior
to the use of dubbing was to employ another actress to stand just out of
camera range and read the lines as Anny Ondra mouthed them. The problem
caused by this technique in *Blackmail* is that the actress chosen to be the
voice of Ondra, one Joan Barry, has a heavy upper-class British theatrical
accent which is totally out of keeping with the role Ondra is playing—that
of the daughter of a London tobacconist.

The opening sequences of the film are from the original silent version and are used to illustrate the operation of the London police as they apprehend a criminal in his working-class lodgings; take him to Scotland Yard; and fingerprint, photograph, and arrest him. These sequences also serve to introduce the character of Detective Frank Webber, who is the boyfriend of Alice White. These early sequences are excellent devices to set the mood and the theme for the film, and are examples of silent filmmaking at its best.

Alice (Anny Ondra) and Frank (John Longden) meet on a date, and Frank takes her to a Lyons' Corner House restaurant, once the epitome of English middle-class dining pleasure. All is not going well with the two, and Alice begins to flirt with a young man (Cyril Ritchard) at a neighboring table. She leaves with him, and he proves to be an artist who invites her back to his studio. (Cyril Ritchard is the only one in the cast who was to attain an international career as an actor.) At his studio, Alice is persuaded to remove some of her clothing in order to model for him, but it is not modeling that the artist has in mind. He tries to rape her, but in the process Alice grabs a breadknife and stabs him to death. The only witness to the act, ironically, is a painting of a leering jester. In a masterful film sequence, Alice is shown wandering the streets in despair, envisioning in her mind all the while the trailing hand of the dead artist. Suddenly she sees a sleeping beggar whose hand is lying in the same position as that of the murdered artist. As she screams, there is a sharp cut to the screaming face of an old woman, the artist's charlady, who has discovered his body.

Back at Alice's parents' shop, word of the murder has reached a local gossip, who discusses the murder and the weapon, a knife, as Alice and her parents sit down to breakfast. Every innocent mention of the word knife begins to take on a sinister implication for Alice; words become blurred and unintelligible except for one word, "knife," repeated over and over again in dialogue. One critic noted that the knife keeps emerging, stabbing and hurting Alice mentally, and here, Hitchcock shows remarkable originality in the use of sound, realizing its true worth far more than most early sound directors.

Meanwhile, Frank Webber, who has been assigned to the murder case, has discovered one of Alice's gloves left at the scene of the crime; however, rather than admit to anyone what he already suspects, he pockets the evidence. The other glove has fallen into the hands of the vaguely sinister Tracy (Donald Calthrop), who attempts to blackmail Alice, visits her at the shop, and forces her to concoct a story of friendship to persuade Alice's suspicious parents to feed him breakfast. Tracy confronts Alice and Frank, but the latter recognizes Tracy as a minor criminal who is himself a suspect in the case. In a film sequence which obviously owes much to the German cinema, Tracy is pursued by the police through the British Museum, cornered at the dome of the reading room, and falls to his death, effectively closing the case.

Alice goes to Scotland Yard to confess her guilt, but because of repeated interruptions is unable to do so, and Frank escorts her from the building free from arrest and prosecution. Hitchcock has stated that he desired the film to end with Alice's arrest and with Frank treating her as the common criminal was treated in the film's opening sequence. Frank would then meet his elder partner, who would ask, "Are you going out with your girl tonight?," to which Frank would reply, "No, I'm going straight home." It was certainly a novel manner in which to end a film, but one which British International Pictures found totally unacceptable. It should be pointed out, however, that the ending of *Blackmail* is far from morally acceptable, and would surely never have been approved of in the American film industry. Furthermore, the ending leaves Alice and Frank with guilt not only for the death of the artist but also for the death of Tracy—with which they will have to live for the rest of their lives. Even if Hitchcock's ending had been used, it is unlikely that Alice would have been found guilty of murder since her action was done to protect her honor and would, presumably, have been considered justifiable homicide.

Critical response to *Blackmail* was fairly mixed. *Variety*, while finding it the best "all-talker" yet made in England (not much of a compliment considering how few talkies had been made in England up to that time) thought it only "a fair program picture," being "draggy" and having "no speed or pace and very little suspense." However, after viewing *Blackmail*, Kenneth MacPherson wrote in *Close Up* (October, 1929), "Some of us are beginning to say that talkies are an art."

Anthony Slide

BLAZING SADDLES

Released: 1974
Production: Michael Hertzberg for Warner Bros.
Direction: Mel Brooks
Screenplay: Mel Brooks, Norman Steinberg, Andrew Bergman, Richard Pryor, and Alan Uger; based on a story by Andrew Bergman
Cinematography: Joseph Biroc
Editing: John C. Howard and Danford Greene
Running time: 93 minutes

Principal characters:
Bart	Cleavon Little
Jim, The Waco Kid	Gene Wilder
Taggart	Slim Pickens
Indian Chief/Governor Lepetomane	Mel Brooks
Hedley Lamarr	Harvey Korman
Lili Von Schtupp	Madeline Kahn
Mongo	Alex Karras

Mel Brooks is the master parodist of contemporary cinema. Unlike Woody Allen, who specializes in a more subtle brand of satire, Brooks lays it on thick, never stopping with one joke if he can think of ten more. *Blazing Saddles* is his burlesque of that time-honored cinematic genre, the Western.

If the Brooks name alone is not enough to tip off the viewer that this is no ordinary Western, the title song gives the game away quickly. "Blazing Saddles," written by Brooks and John Morris, is about a man who "made his blazing saddle a torch to light the West," whatever that means. To show that absolutely nothing is sacred, Brooks hired Frankie Laine to sing "Blazing Saddles," which is punctuated by the sound of cracking whips, *á là* Laine's Western classic "Mule Train." Thus Brooks begins firing his satirical salvoes even before the opening credits are over.

The melodic slapstick continues in the film's first scene. A group of black convicts are laying down a railroad track when Taggart, the white boss of the chain gang, played by the veteran Slim Pickens, demands to hear a "good ol' nigger work song." The laborers ponder the request for a moment, but the best they can come up with is a stunning a capella version of Cole Porter's "I Get a Kick Out of You." To show them what he had in mind, the frustrated Taggart leads the other white guards in an exaggerated minstrel show version of "Camptown Races," as the blacks struggle to muffle their laughter.

The plot of the film, such as it is, is based on a time-tested Western theme. Crooked politicians are scheming to steal land on which a railroad is about to be built, never caring whom they hurt along the way. The Marx Brothers took a jab at this hackneyed plot in their 1940 film, *Go West*. The politicians in this case are Attorney General Hedley Lamarr (Harvey Korman) and Governor William Lepetomane, one of two parts played by Brooks himself, the other being a brief role as a Yiddish-speaking Indian chief. Lepetomane has trouble walking and chewing gum at the same time, and the only thing that can hold his attention for more than ten seconds is his buxom and scantily clad secretary. Lamarr is clearly the power behind the throne, and he has no trouble obtaining Lepetomane's consent to commence the takeover of the town of Rock Ridge, which lies squarely in the proposed path of the railroad.

Rock Ridge, however, has other problems. The town is a parody of every Dodge City and Wichita that ever appeared on the screen. The place is so bucolic that cattle are as at home as the people in the town saloon. Rock Ridge is also terrorized by its violent element, which keeps murdering each successive sheriff appointed by the townsfolk. The solid citizens, all of whom seem to be named Johnson, including Howard Johnson, the owner of the new ice cream shop that boasts of its one flavor, decide to petition the governor for help.

Attorney General Lamarr sees his chance. He decides to appoint one of the troublemaking black convicts as sheriff of Rock Ridge. Bart (Cleavon Little), the man in question, learns of his dubious appointment as he is about to be hanged for assaulting Taggart (who, in addition to running the chain gang, is also one of Lamarr's henchmen) in an escape attempt. Lamarr figures that the people of Rock Ridge are so bigoted that they will leave town rather than live with a black sheriff, thus clearing the way for an easy takeover by Lamarr and the railroad interests.

Bart transforms himself into the gaudiest cowboy west of Bloomingdale's. Dressed in suede and leather from head to toe, he even has Gucci saddlebags. He rides across the prairie on a magnificent palomino as lush orchestral music swells in the background. The music grows louder the further Bart rides, until we see its source: the entire Count Basie band is playing out on the desolate plains for Bart's benefit.

One of the funniest scenes in the film occurs as Bart rides into Rock Ridge. The welcoming ceremony quickly deflates as the townspeople discover that their new sheriff is black, and he escapes a lynching only by putting a pistol to his own head and threatening to "shoot the nigger" unless he is allowed safe passage. Safely inside the jailhouse, Bart meets Jim, the Waco Kid (Gene Wilder), who will become his foremost ally. At the moment, however, the Waco Kid is being held prisoner until he sobers up. Once the terror of the West, the Kid is now an alcoholic. Dean Martin played a similar role in Howard Hawk's *Rio Bravo* (1959), but Gene Wilder's Waco Kid is cut from a more modern, absurdist cloth. Wilder gives the most effective performance in the film. By underplaying his part while everyone else is frantically overplaying theirs, he brings a bit of welcome subtlety to *Blazing Saddles*. Indeed, his sense of humor is all the more effective for being understated, and he and Cleavon Little work particularly well together.

While Bart helps the Waco Kid dry out, Lamarr and Taggart try another angle. They unleash the dreaded Mongo, played as a sort of hairless King Kong by ex-football player Alex Karras, on Rock Ridge. Mongo announces his arrival in town by knocking out a horse with one barefisted punch. Bart subdues Mongo by dressing up as a Western Union man with a candygram that turns out to be a bomb. Thus Bart saves the town from Mongo, and earns a measure of grudging respect from the citizens.

The beast having failed, Lamarr resolves to try the beauty. He asks his paramour, Lili Von Schtupp (Madeline Kahn), a luscious dance hall queen who is a parody of Marlene Dietrich in *Destry Rides Again* (1939), to seduce Bart and break his heart. The seduction is accomplished, but it is Lili who falls for Bart. He dismisses her the next morning with a cool "Auf Wiedersehen, baby."

Meanwhile, back at the jail, Mongo has developed a childlike affection for his captors, and decides to remain with Bart and the Waco Kid even though Hedley Lamarr has ordered his release. Mongo explains Lamarr's plot to his new friends, and his explanation is confirmed when Bart and the Kid secretly visit the railroad construction site. Suddenly Lamarr's machinations begin to make sense.

His other plans frustrated, Lamarr orders Taggart to round up a gang of the most vicious criminals in the West for a final assault on Rock Ridge. Taggart dutifully recruits a motley crew of Hell's Angels, Ku Klux Klansmen, Nazi stormtroopers, and Arab terrorists. When they learn of Lamarr's scheme, the craven citizens of Rock Ridge are ready to abandon their homes and shops immediately. Bart, however, pleads for twenty-four hours to save the town. "You'd do it for Randolph Scott," he argues, and they reluctantly consent. Armed with this grudging vote of confidence, Bart enlists the aid of the black railroad laborers. His plan is to build an exact replica of Rock Ridge and lure Taggart's gang into destroying it instead of the real thing.

With a herculean effort, they manage to duplicate the town overnight. As dawn breaks, however, they realize that something is missing—people. To delay Taggart's marauders, they set up a toll booth on the open prairie outside of the bogus town. It never occurs to Taggart to go around it. Instead, he sends one of the gang to get some dimes, and the men patiently file through the booth one at a time. The resultant delay allows Bart and his friends to place cardboard cutouts of the townspeople on the streets of the "town."

As Taggart's gang rides into the fake Rock Ridge to wreak their havoc, the Waco Kid detonates a cache of dynamite in the town, and Bart, the Kid, Mongo, the blacks, and the townspeople swoop into town to attack the remnants of the gang. At this point, the film abandons its burlesque of the Western genre and begins to parody itself. The camera pulls back to reveal the Hollywood set on which the film is being shot. The scene then shifts to another set on the same lot, where an effeminate director is attempting to stage a musical production number. The fighting from the *Blazing Saddles* set spills over into this one, and on into the studio commissary, where it degenerates into a food fight involving every actor and extra at Warner Bros. Studios. The melee then spills out of the studio into the streets of Los Angeles.

Harvey Korman, still dressed as Hedley Lamarr, jumps into a taxicab, pursued by Cleavon Little, still dressed as Bart. They run into a movie theater that is showing—what else?—*Blazing Saddles*, and there is a shootout in the lobby. Meanwhile, back on the screen, the film within a film within a film is at last winding down. Rock Ridge has been saved, and Bart and the Waco Kid clamber into a chauffeured limousine, in which they are driven off into the sunset.

Blazing Saddles, then, takes most of the conventions of the film Western and stands them on their head. The man in the white hat turns out to be black, and the townspeople he defends turn out to be as bigoted and crude as the bad guys. A movie cowboy is supposed to protect the womenfolk and kiss his horse; in *Blazing Saddles*, the horses get slugged, and everyone, womenfolk included, is consumed by lust.

The moviegoing public was clearly ready for such iconoclasm: *Blazing Saddles* was a huge success at the box office. Critics agreed that the film was often hilarious, but argued that it was also often out of control. The film's ending (or endings) exemplifies most of its strengths and its weaknesses. Brooks obviously had several different ideas on how to end the film. Instead of choosing among them, he simply shot them all.

If *Blazing Saddles* is a flawed film, however, it is one that is deliberately flawed, for Mel Brooks knew exactly what he was doing. Unlike some of his critics, he prefers bellylaughs to more cerebral humor. The acting reflected Brooks's preference for the blatant over the subtle. The cast of *Blazing Saddles* includes many fine actors and actresses, but, doubtless with Brooks's encouragement, most of them opt for broad rather than deep characterization. As noted above, Gene Wilder was an exception to this tendency. The result is quintessential Mel Brooks, take him or leave him. Obviously, millions of moviegoers were willing to take him and beg for more.

Robert Mitchell

BLITHE SPIRIT

Released: 1946
Production: Noel Coward for Cineguild/Two Cities/Rank; released by United
  Artists
Direction: David Lean
Screenplay: Noel Coward; based on David Lean's, Ronald Neame's, and An-
  thony Havelock-Allan's adaptation of the play of the same name by Noel
  Coward
Cinematography: Ronald Neame
Editing: Jack Harris
Special effects: Thomas Howard (AA)
Running time: 97 minutes

> *Principal characters:*
> Charles Condomine .... Rex Harrison
> Elvira Condomine .... Kay Hammond
> Ruth Condomine .... Constance Cummings
> Madame Arcati .... Margaret Rutherford
> Edith .... Jacqueline Clark

Blithe Spirit was the second coproduction of Two Cities (Noel Coward) and
Cineguild (David Lean, Ronald Neame, and Anthony Havelock-Allan) to
utilize one of Coward's stage successes. Coward subtitled his play "An Improbable Farce in Three Acts," but it might have been termed more accurately
a drawing-room comedy of the supernatural. The play's main characters are
the archetypal bored and snobbish members of the English petty aristocracy.
Since, as usual, Coward draws his effects from the wry exaggeration of those
archetypes, it becomes essential to the comedy of the film as much as it was
to that of the play that the twice-married novelist Charles Condomine (Rex
Harrison) and his wives Elvira (Kay Hammond) and Ruth (Constance Cummings), who die in that order, remain faithful to Coward's conception of them.

Charles, the main character of the play as well as the film, has been happily
married to Ruth for five years when the story begins. They live in a lovely,
sedate, "typically" British country home which was previously inhabited by
Charles and his late first wife, Elvira. In order to entertain themselves one
evening, Charles and Ruth decide to hold a seance under the auspices of a
local medium, Madame Arcati (Margaret Rutherford). During the course of
the seance, Charles's dead wife is conjured up, and from then on proceeds
to haunt him and wreck havoc on his new wife.

By this unique device of introducing the "blithe spirit" of Elvira, Coward
allows the more typical drawing-room comedy/battle of the sexes to take on
a new twist. The dead wife constantly interferes with Charles's domestic tranquility by teasing his new wife and making him doubt his current happiness.

His present wife attempts to exorcise the spirit in order to maintain the status quo which she has enjoyed with Charles for the past few years. In the course of their attempts to rid themselves of the spirit, however, Charles discovers that what he really wants is his freedom—both from his flirtatious, teasing first wife Elvira and from his domineering second wife Ruth. He thinks that he has finally found his freedom after his second wife is killed in a motor accident which was intended for him (arranged by Elvira who had wanted Charles to join her "on the other side"). When Ruth's restless spirit joins Elvira's in haunting him, he decides to take further measures to rid himself of them by arranging one final seance with Madame Arcati. However, after a marathon exorcism in which both of the spirits are finally banished from Charles's house forever, he is killed in an automobile accident as he is about to leave for a long vacation. The last scene of the film shows Charles in spirit form, ironically sitting on a fence between the spirits of both Elvira and Ruth.

Charles Condomine (Rex Harrison) is the sophisticated foil of Noel Coward's invention; he is adept at the well-turned, Wildesian phrase and is sublimely egotistical. When Madame Arcati, summoned to exorcise Elvira's ghost, complains that occasionally her premonitions do not come true, such as her feeling that she was going to have a puncture in her bicycle tire on the way to the Condomine house, Charles replies, "Perhaps you will on the way home," in characteristically gracious, but condescending fashion. At heart Charles is truest to a tradition of insensitive materialism, while his firmest belief is that the logical and regular order of things is not easily subverted. When a belief such as his feeling that there are no ghosts is finally and irrefutably contraverted, it can lead him to only one conclusion: that he must have gone mad.

In Coward's scheme, Charles is more prone to make the amusing "remark of a pompous ass" than an uproarious joke. Against what Elvira terms his "certainly seedy grandeur" are arrayed such ongoing standard devices as saying unpleasant things to a ghost and having other characters present think that the words are directed at them. Most of the comic conflict is provided by Madame Arcati, whose giddy naturalness and sensory awareness provide a sharp contrast to Charles's mannered artificiality. The cumulative result is a play that, with a few exceptions, is funny without being very imaginative. Still, the film manages here and there to inject a bit of the latter quality without compromising the former.

Lean adds some bits of visual humor, such as the comic dissolve from Arcati, saying "Oh, not red meat, I hope. I make it a rule never to eat red meat before I work" before dinner at Charles's and Ruth's house, to a close shot of a bloody slice of roast beef being carved and passed to her. Another example is the shot of the invisible Elvira driving Charles's roadster to the bewilderment of a traffic controller. These scenes are, however, few and peripheral, so that even the special effects are relatively restrained. The floating objects and doors opening by themselves are really nothing more than wired stagecraft. Even the transparent Elvira in her glowing green gown entering suddenly via the closed French windows, and having her hair disarranged as Ruth runs through her on the stairs, are simple movie illusions.

Lean makes fullest use of cinema techniques when Elvira demonstrates to Ruth that she is far from imaginary. Such details as flowers hovering in mid-air, Elvira menacingly raising a chair over her head, curtains pulled shut, an ornament hurled from the mantel, and a door thrown open are all flawlessly timed and gradually intercut with close shots of Elvira and Ruth. The feeling of confrontation is sharpened and concentrated until Ruth runs out screaming in capitulation, and Lean cuts to a long shot again which coincides with the release of tension.

The question of literary *versus* cinematic style is a complex one, and the Lean/Coward collaborations are typical. There is something of Lean present in *Blithe Spirit* which is more than the mere application of the director's craft. Yet, beyond certain aspects of Madame Arcati and her breathless entreaties, there is little in *Blithe Spirit* that thematically anticipates any of Lean's later work. The one major alteration of the play for the film version—the new ending in which Charles goes to meet his two wives in the "echoing vaults of eternity"—seems less to have been the personal inspiration of any of the adapters than a matter of rounding out the retribution for questionable motives and morals. This should not imply, however, that all the merit or lack of it in this picture was Coward's responsibility, or that credit or blame should not be divided with the members of Cineguild.

Certainly much of *Blithe's Spirit's* success was determined not only by the production unit, or by Rex Harrison's much-praised performance as Charles Condomine, but also by Kay Hammond's throaty Elvira and Margaret Rutherford's fatuous Madame Arcati, both practiced performances from the stage version. Constance Cummings' performance as the almost-bitchy second wife is also noteworthy. The real acting honors go to Margaret Rutherford, however. With her range of facial expressions, her wringing hands, and her manner of speaking as if she were eating a sandwich at the same time, Rutherford, as usual, is a gem. She has the ability to be lovable, clever, stupid, and exasperating all at once, and the scenes in which she appears are totally hers.

Although the production was well received and did well at the box office, it won only one major award: the Oscar for Best Special Effects for Thomas Howard, who provided the film with its visual tricks and techniques. Lean was nominated for an Oscar that year for Best Direction, but that nomination was for his film *Brief Encounter*.

Alain Silver

BLOW-UP

Released: 1966
Production: Carlo Ponti for Metro-Goldwyn-Mayer
Direction: Michelangelo Antonioni
Screenplay: Michelangelo Antonioni and Tonino Guerra, English dialogue in collaboration with Edward Bond
Cinematography: Carlo di Palma
Editing: Frank Clarke
Music: Herbert Hancock, with the song "Stroll On" written and performed by the Yardbirds
Running time: 110 minutes

Principal characters:

Thomas	David Hemmings
The Girl	Vanessa Redgrave
Patricia	Sarah Miles
Bill	John Castle
Ron	Peter Bowles
The Blonde	Jane Birkin
The Brunette	Gillian Hills

After international audiences had become accustomed to the somber relationships choreographed in his early work and had been awed by his brilliant and emotional study of a woman in *Red Desert* (1965), Antonioni left Italy and his wonderful star, Monica Vitti, seeking a more contemporary background for his studies of the human condition. Though the British culture and language were foreign to him, he decided upon London, the symbol and center of modern life in the mid-1960's, for his new setting. The resulting feature, *Blow-Up*, became his first international box-office success, his first film in English, and a forerunner of sexual expression in film. A tightly crafted, controlled masterpiece, *Blow-Up* is a study of modern man which has outlived the era it describes.

In his attempt to expand his audience, Antonioni mixed two genres popular at that time: the glossy world of youth fashion and the dramatic underworld of the murder mystery. Both were new to Antonioni's work. He uses a story by Julio Cortazar, set in Paris, about an anonymous character who witnesses a scene which he thinks is a moment of sensual intrigue, but which turns out to be tragically perverse. He creates a screen *persona*, a glamorous young photographer named Thomas (David Hemmings), who seems to have everything a man might desire: wealth, fame, youth, and beautiful women. His fashion photography shapes the fantasies of the public, yet Thomas is aware that something is lacking in the world he lives in and portrays through his camera.

   Bored with glamour and empty sexuality, he takes his camera outside the
studio in an attempt to discover reality and record it in documentary fashion.
He photographs flop houses, the aged, the poor—the seamy side of life—
believing them to reflect a reality that is missing in his world of high fashion.
Then one day Thomas accidentally witnesses a lovers' tryst in a park. Like
a voyeur, he photographs The Girl (Vanessa Redgrave) and her middle-aged
lover, thinking he has captured a moment of natural beauty totally unlike the
contrived beauty in the studio. The Girl catches him as he leaves the park,
demanding the negatives on grounds of privacy, but he refuses. As he tells
his writer-collaborator Ron (Peter Bowles), he wants to use the pictures as
an optimistic counterpoint in the documentary photobook they are planning.
   Meanwhile, a man searches Thomas' car, and The Girl mysteriously appears
at his studio demanding the negatives. Intrigued by her persistence, Thomas
sends her away with false film. He then processes and blows up the pictures
to poster size, pinning them in sequence around his living room, thus creating
the illusion of motion picture film ready to be cut into a scene. The blowups
reveal something he missed in the park; further enlargements reveal a gunman
in the bushes. Thomas realizes there was about to be a murder but that his
presence probably foiled it. Self-satisfied, he leaves the pictures and returns
to his fashion world, cavorting in a sexual romp with two would-be fashion
models (Jane Birkin and Gillian Hills).
   Soon, however, something draws him back to the pictures. A further blow-
up of the last picture which shows the grain of the film itself, reveals a mass
of dots that might be the prone body of the middle-aged man; when Thomas
returns to the park, he finds the body. He alone witnessed the murder, and
he has the proof. Stunned, Thomas returns to his studio to find that the blowups and negatives have been stolen; all that is left is the extreme blowup,
which is not proof: like the paintings of his neighbor, it is a picture of a body
only in the imagination. He rushes out to find Ron, but he spots The Girl
and chases her instead. Losing her in a rock-and-roll nightclub, he becomes
caught in a performance by the Yardbirds, who smash guitars and amplifiers
to arouse the mob instincts of their audience. Thomas finally finds Ron at a
fashionable party attended by "beautiful people." He wants Ron to return
to the park with him to photograph the body, but Ron either does not believe
or does not want to believe the story. The next morning, Thomas awakens
amid the wreckage of the party. He hurries to the park, but the body is gone,
along with any evidence that a murder ever happened. Thomas is left with
nothing.
   Antonioni continually upsets the viewer's sense of reality in *Blow-Up*. The
first time we see Thomas, he appears to be a bum leaving a flop house, until
this "bum" gets into his Rolls-Royce convertible with an expensive camera
hidden in a paper bag. He drives to his home, which turns out to be a
professional photographer's studio; there he erotically crawls over a model

(Verushka) while photographing her. Both Thomas and his model seem to attain sexual satisfaction, when in actuality they are merely performing a normal, mundane routine. Thomas himself goes through a three-stage process with his photographs: first, he interprets them as a lovers' rendezvous; second, as an attempted murder foiled by a photographer; and last, as the accidental recording of a murder. Thomas rises from artist to hero only to become a victim of the modern world because he is incapable of understanding, seeing, or controlling events. He has not been given the tools to view reality properly, and he does not know where to attain those tools. He is continually side-tracked from finding the truth or from having any part in shaping events. The world around him gets in his way: the young girls (sex), the party (drugs and peers), and the music and exploding emotions of youth all distract him from his purpose.

After discovering that the body has been removed, Thomas wanders around the park until he comes upon a group of students in white-face. Two students are miming a game of tennis without racket or ball, while the rest are playing the audience. Thomas stands near the court watching the charade. The persistent suspension of disbelief of the mimes attracts him. When the ball is knocked out of the court to the middle of a field, Thomas is coaxed by the students to retrieve it. He does, imagining its weight, believing the illusion, and throws it back. As he watches the game continue, the sound of an actual game fades in on the soundtrack. The final shot is from high above showing Thomas alone in the field of green. The camera rises, and Thomas fades away, leaving only green.

Until the final sequence, Antonioni has retained a straightforward sense of reality. The tennis sequence defies this reality by giving us a sound that does not exist except in Thomas' mind. This technique has been used earlier in the film, but never without matching the imagined sound or event to a real event or a real sound. By having Thomas vanish before our eyes, Antonioni has set a task for his audience, a symbolic puzzle that might either solve the film, explain Thomas' problems, or serve as the moral of the story. Many interpretations have been made; none is definitive. Each viewer must decide the meaning of the last image for himself.

Antonioni, unlike his neorealistic contemporaries, reworks reality for film. He omits mundane observations or any other elements that would distract from the sense of the story. Like a novelist streamlining language and grammar to create a compact reality that conforms only to the purpose of the novel, Antonioni controls film. He utilizes every element, from script and acting to lighting, art direction, color, and sound, as few directors have done. All elements take on symbolic qualities, describing the emotional states of the characters and the contrasts in the world around them, and centering attention on things and ideas that are immediate to the story. Thomas is defined as much by his studio, his friends, and his actions as by his words.

We follow his feelings and thoughts through the soundtrack as the record he puts on disappears when he forgets to listen, as an overhead jet signals his realization of the murder, and as the sounds of the park return as he studies the blowups. The colors green and purple take on symbolic contrasts within the film, as each is defined in relation to natural forces. Each character and prop becomes an editorial addition defining Thomas' (our) world and his (our) relation to it. We even see a symbol in the park that prepares us for the gun, a neon "F," the only element of the city to invade the park.

Antonioni is a master of filmmaking, an artist capable of using the medium to its peak efficiency. He is also a great humanist desiring only to provoke his audience into a better understanding of themselves. More than any of his other films, *Blow-Up* reaches the audience. Though the era of Swinging London has passed, the film still provokes and stimulates. The message touches a universal note in audiences because it relates to a need in each of us to see our world more clearly and to train ourselves to deal more effectively with the world.

John-Paul Ouellette

BODY AND SOUL

Released: 1947
Production: Bob Roberts for Enterprise Productions; released by United
 Artists
Direction: Robert Rossen
Screenplay: Abraham Polansky
Cinematography: James Wong Howe
Editing: Francis Lyon and Robert Parrish (AA)
Running time: 104 minutes

> *Principal characters:*
> Charlie Davis .... John Garfield
> Peg Born .... Lilli Palmer
> Anna Davis .... Anne Revere
> Ben Chaplin .... Canada Lee
> Roberts .... Lloyd Gouff
> Shorty Polaski .... Joseph Pevney
> Mr. David Davis .... Art Smith
> Quinn .... William Conrad

Hollywood has always been notoriously timid where controversy is concerned, particularly when such controversy suggests that all might not be well
in this best of all possible countries. Despite this fact, Enterprise Productions,
John Garfield's independent film company, was able to make two highly
powerful cinematic statements in the late 1940's before financial difficulty and
the burgeoning blacklist forced the company out of production.

The first film, which achieved high critical acclaim and garnered significant
box-office receipts, made the second film possible. Garfield, a powerhouse
talent, had often been thwarted by Warner Bros. during his seven-year stay
there. The studio bosses discovered early that audiences, especially women,
loved him most when he was playing a bloody-but-unbowed antihero battling
a world he never made. As a consequence he was cast in a succession of
monotonously similar roles, despite the fact that several of his films indicated
that when challenged, Garfield could act with the best.

Enterprise intended as its first production a biography of Barney Ross,
who had gone from middleweight champion to Marine hero to drug addict
and then fought his way back. Censorship at the time, however, forbade the
use of drug addiction as a theme, even though, as in the case of Ross, the
story ultimately dealt with his victory over drugs. This fact proved fortunate,
though, since it led Garfield to Abraham Polansky, who had written an original screenplay loosely based on Ross's life, which looked promising.

On the surface *Body and Soul* contains all the trappings of a typical Warner
Bros. social drama, but with a twist. Charlie Davis (John Garfield), the

protagonist, is a poor Jewish boy living in the depths of the Depression who wants to improve his desperate condition. The fastest way he knows to achieve success is to become a professional prizefighter. He first tries briefly to please his parents by looking for nonexistent jobs, but when his father (Art Smith) is accidentally killed and his mother Anna (Anne Revere) is forced to apply for welfare, his frustration turns into a determination never to be poor again.

With the help of his friend Shorty Polaski (Joseph Pevney), Charlie is able to turn professional. Fighting as if obsessed, his rage as much as his skill soon make him the leading contender to fight the middleweight champion. Big-time boxing is controlled by Roberts (Lloyd Gouff), an icy, thoroughly repellent gambler. He allows Charlie his title shot only after Charlie agrees to give him a large percentage of everything he earns. Shorty recognizes that what has transpired is more of a Satanic pact than a business arrangement and tries to warn Charlie, yet the blind drive which has brought him so near to the top of his profession also blinds him to the realization that he has sold himself, body and soul, to the "businessman," Roberts.

Ben Chaplin, the champion, brilliantly played by Canada Lee, has a blood clot; but, deeply in debt to Roberts, he too agrees to the proposed title bout with Charlie when Roberts assures him that he will not be hurt and that Charlie will "take it easy" on him. Charlie, unaware of this, fights to win and in the process of becoming the champion almost kills Ben. Shorty and Charlie's girl friend Peg Born (Lilli Palmer) learn about the blood clot, but when Shorty attempts to tell Charlie, he is beaten by one of Roberts' henchmen and stumbles in front of a speeding truck.

Charlie becomes a success. The price, however is the death of his childhood friend and the loss of his girl friend, who is repulsed by the evil which surrounds him. Trying to atone, Charlie makes Ben his trainer and continues his boxing career. To the world he is the champion, to Roberts he is a "money machine"; but to himself he is a haunted man, fighting because he does not know anything else. Once told by Peg that he reminded her of the "tyger" in William Blake's poem, years of soft living and easy fights have now turned him into a caricature of that image.

Finally, Roberts, seeing that Charlie's years at the top are nearing an end, decides to drop him after making a final large profit. He tells Charlie that he must throw his next fight. Despite the corruption which surrounds and taints him, Charlie essentially has remained the decent "street kid" he was in the beginning. He argues that he can beat his opponent, but Roberts is not interested. Charlie owes him money and he suggests that Charlie bet against himself and retire, assuring him that he does not have to lose by a knockout, but by a fifteen-round decison. Tired of it all, Charlie agrees and begins to go through the motions of training for the bout.

At the training camp Ben realizes what Charlie is doing. His muted rage explodes, and in a deeply moving scene, while lashing out at shadows his

blood clot bursts and he dies in the empty training ring, the dark shape of Charlies' exercise bag swaying like the silhouette of a hanged man against the canvas. Unable to live with his guilt, Charlie effects a reconciliation with Peg, assuring her that he is giving up boxing. But their reunion is shortlived when she learns that he intends to throw the fight. After the deaths of Shorty and Ben and Peg's rejection, Charlie is alone both in the world and in the ring.

As the sellout fifteen-round match begins, the audience learns that Roberts has betrayed Charlie just as he did Ben. Late in the fight the young contender is given a signal and opens up on the exhausted Charlie. Somehow managing to stay on his feet until the end of the round, Charlie is temporarily insane with rage. In these last few moments, all the compromises, all the pain he has thoughtlessly inflicted on those he loves turns Charlie into a killer. Charging back into the ring he demolishes his opponent in what is regarded as the most exciting boxing sequence ever filmed. The precision of the filming was due to James Wong Howe's superb camera work, which he did on roller skates with a camera strapped to his chest.

In the final scene, Peg, unable to stay away, breaks through the crowd to Charlie. As the two move up the aisle, Charlie is momentarily blocked by Roberts. But Charlie, as well as the audience, has been purged of fear after the catharsis in the ring, and Charlie's parting shot to the gambler is "What're you gonna do, kill me? Everybody dies!"

Directed by Robert Rossen, the film was a great commercial success and won Garfield an Oscar nomination. It was Abraham Polansky's script, with its lyric street poetry, which elevated the film above its essentially well-worn plot. Polansky might also be credited with saving the film by allowing Charlie Davis to live. An alternate ending by Rossen was filmed in which Charlie is shot by Roberts' henchmen and his body pushed head down in a garbage can, but this ending was rejected because it would have changed the sardonic impact of the film.

There was an obvious chemistry working between the star and his screen-writer; recognizing this, Garfield offered Polansky the opportunity to write and direct his next effort for Enterprise. It would be *Force of Evil* (1948), a film which only recently has come to be regarded as a neglected masterpiece.

Michael Shepler

THE BODY SNATCHER

Released: 1945
Production: Val Lewton for RKO/Radio
Direction: Robert Wise
Screenplay: Philip MacDonald and Carlos Keith (Val Lewton); based on a short story of the same name by Robert Louis Stevenson
Cinematography: Robert de Grasse
Editing: J. R. Whittredge
Running time: 77 minutes

Principal characters:
Gray	Boris Karloff
Dr. Macfarlane	Henry Daniell
Fettes	Russell Wade
Mrs. Marsh	Rita Corday
Georgina Marsh	Sharyn Moffett
Joseph	Bela Lugosi

The Body Snatcher is one of the last of producer Val Lewton's celebrated horror films. It may seem odd to discuss a film in terms of its producer, since conventional wisdom has long held that the authorship of a film belongs to its director, or, less frequently, to an actor or actress whose performance dominates the film. Val Lewton's films, however, are generally conceded to be an exception to this rule. Based on a short story by Robert Louis Stevenson and adapted by Lewton, the pseudonymous Carlos Keith, and Philip MacDonald, the film is set in Edinburgh in 1831. *The Body Snatcher* concerns "resurrectionists"—men who specialized in robbing graves to provide British medical schools with corpses to use in their research.

The Body Snatcher focuses on the personal confrontation between Dr. Macfarlane, a brilliant surgeon who is forced by the laws of the day to use extralegal methods to keep his medical school supplied with cadavers to be used for research, and Gray, a cabman who supplies the corpses by robbing fresh graves to get them. The story has all the makings of a conventional thriller—cemeteries in the dead of night, unsolved murders, and so forth—but Lewton added something more. By refusing to make his grave robbers altogether villainous, and by providing them with arguable, if not altogether convincing, reasons for their actions, Lewton forces the viewer to consider the question of ends *versus* means. In doing so, he transcends the limits of his genre.

Lewton introduces Gray (Boris Karloff) first. By all appearances a kindly old cabman, Gray is delivering Georgina Marsh (Sharyn Moffett), a crippled child, and Mrs. Marsh (Rita Corday), her widowed mother, to the office of Dr. Macfarlane (Henry Daniell). Touched by the child's plight, Gray immediately takes her up to sit with him on the driver's box. He solemnly introduces her to his horse and promises that they will be friends. While the grave robber is capable of inspiring instant affection from the young girl, the brilliant Dr. Macfarlane elicits precisely the opposite reaction. In the first of many ironies that Lewton introduces into the film, the child senses something evil about the doctor and refuses to answer any of his questions. Georgina's diagnosis proceeds only when Fettes (Russell Wade), one of Dr. Macfarlane's best students, enters the room and wins her trust.

With the help of his pupil, Macfarlane discovers that the girl's paralysis is caused by a tumor, which could be removed by means of a delicate operation. Macfarlane is the only surgeon skillful enough to perform the operation, but he declines to do so because he believes that his energies are best directed to the training of other skillful surgeons. Fettes and Mrs. Marsh are shocked. It is in this scene that Lewton begins to reveal Macfarlane's tragic flaw: he is so dedicated to medical science that it has become an end in itself, rather than a means to help people.

Dr. Macfarlane is impressed by Fettes' assistance in Georgina's diagnosis, and when Fettes reveals that financial difficulties may force him to leave medical school, Macfarlane makes him his chief assistant. He then reveals to his new protégé that the bodies his students use in their classes are obtained illegally. The next scene reveals exactly how the bodies are obtained. A shadowy figure is digging up a fresh grave. The figure turns out to be Gray, who delivers the body to Fettes at the medical school. His demeanor has changed markedly from that of a kindly cabbie, as he patronizingly instructs the stunned Fettes in the basics of paying for an illegal cadaver. Fettes threatens to resign, but he is dissuaded when Macfarlane convinces him that the only way medical science can advance is by experimentation, and that if bodies for experimentation cannot be obtained legally, they must be obtained illegally.

Fettes, at the same time, has developed a quiet attraction to Mrs. Marsh, who pleads with him to intercede with Macfarlane on Georgina's behalf, which he does. Rather more persuasive is Georgina's new friend Gray, who threatens to publicize the source of the school's corpses if Macfarlane declines to operate. Thus Lewton reveals the hold that Gray has over Macfarlane, and adds another irony: if Macfarlane is to help Georgina, he must replace her damaged tissue with healthy tissue, for which it will be necessary to acquire another illegal corpse.

This is no longer a simple matter, however, as Gray's recent depredations have resulted in a heavy guard being posted at the cemetery. Reluctantly, Gray decides to provide his own body; he murders a blind street singer. Lewton handles this murder particularly effectively. The street singer, a pretty young girl, walks down a dimly lit street singing as she vanishes into the mist. Then Gray's cab proceeds down the same street, also disappearing into the mist. Suddenly the girl's voice is cut off in mid-note. The murder thus occurs offstage, but there is no mistaking what has happened.

Although they try to convince themselves otherwise, both Macfarlane and Fettes realize what has happened. They are now accomplices in murder as well as grave robbing. Macfarlane tells Gray that he wants no more bodies, thinking to terminate the symbiotic relationship between the two men. Gray, however, replies sardonically that even though their business may be finished, they will always be "friends."

Dr. Macfarlane operates on Georgina, and although his performance is technically sound, the girl still cannot walk. Macfarlane is stunned by his failure. At this point, Gray begins to torment Macfarlane constantly, turning up at his house at odd times and delivering freshly murdered corpses, including that of Macfarlane's servant Joseph (Bela Lugosi). During one of their confrontations, it is revealed that long ago Gray went to prison for grave robbing and saved Macfarlane from a similar fate by declining to implicate him as a fellow conspirator. When Macfarlane tries to buy Gray off, Gray cuts him short. Gray hates his life, he says, and only one thing makes it bearable. "So long as the great Dr. Macfarlane jumps at my whistle, that long am I a man. And if I have not that, I have nothing."

Maddened by Gray's taunts, Macfarlane resolves to kill his tormentor. Once again, Lewton handles the killing cleverly. The actual fight is seen only as a series of shadows on a wall, and through the eyes of a witness to the battle. It is fairly commonplace for directors to indicate the ferocity of a fight by focusing not on the fight itself but on the reactions of spectators. Lewton gives this old technique a fresh twist by making Gray's cat the fight's only witness, and then focusing on its reactions.

Having killed his antagonist, Macfarlane takes the body to the medical school in Gray's cab. Ironically, his path leads past the Marsh residence, where Georgina hears the familiar clip-clop of the horse's hooves and unexpectedly runs to see her old friend Gray. Fettes and Mrs. Marsh are delighted at this recovery, and Fettes resolves to end his association with Macfarlane's sordid medical academy. He visits Macfarlane to break the news, but the doctor is fired up with enthusiasm for his research, and, incredibly, manages to persuade Fettes to accompany him to an out-of-the-way cemetery. With Gray out of the picture, Macfarlane intends to do his own dirty work.

The two men dig up the body of an old woman and return to Edinburgh in a driving rainstorm. Macfarlane loses control of the horses, and Fettes is thrown from the cab. The corpse lurches against Macfarlane, and it has Gray's face. Macfarlane screams in horror as the cab crashes. Naturally, when Fettes reaches the scene, "Gray" turns out to be the old woman, and Macfarlane is dead.

The Body Snatcher is not a perfect film. The confrontations between Gray and Macfarlane are truly inspired, but the subplot involving Fettes and Mrs.

Marsh is insipid by comparison; and the acting reflects this dichotomy.

Boris Karloff gives one of his best performances as Gray, a man whose self-loathing is so intense that he almost seems to take pride in despising himself. Karloff's expressive face, which Lewton uses effectively in repeated close-ups, conveys the horror of the sights he has seen and the deeds he has done; and his taunts, delivered in the patented Karloffian voice, are maddening. Henry Daniell as Macfarlane is almost as good. Without a strong performance in the second lead, Karloff's Gray would overwhelm the picture. Daniell brings subtlety and conviction to a role that could easily have deteriorated into a stereotyped mad scientist.

The performance of the rest of the cast is unexceptional. Bela Lugosi has only a small part as Macfarlane's servant, Joseph, and he is killed off by Gray midway through the film. Nonetheless, the vision of Val Lewton and the performances of Karloff and Daniell are more than enough to lift *The Body Snatcher* out of the ranks of the B-movie horror show and into the realm of film art.

Robert Mitchell

BOMBSHELL

Released: 1933
Production: Hunt Stromberg for Metro-Goldwyn-Mayer
Direction: Victor Fleming
Screenplay: Jules Furthman and John Lee Mahin; based on an unproduced
  play by Caroline Francke and Mack Crane
Cinematography: Chestor Lyons and Harold Rosson
Editing: Margaret Booth
Costume design: Adrian
Running time: 91 minutes

Principal characters:

Lola Burns	Jean Harlow
Space Hanlon	Lee Tracy
Pop Burns	Frank Morgan
Gifford Middleton	Franchot Tone
Mr. Middleton	C. Aubrey Smith
Mrs. Middleton	Mary Forbes
Jim Brogan	Pat O'Brien
Miss Mac	Una Merkel
Junior Burns	Ted Healy
Marquis di Binelli	Ivan Lebedeff

In 1933, no movie personality so symbolized the sensational aspects of
Hollywood stardom as did M-G-M's "Blonde Bombshell," Jean Harlow. Since
purring "Pardon me while I slip into something more comfortable" in *Hell's
Angels* (1930), the shapely, beauty-marked platinum blonde had become cinema's most sexually brazen star. Joining M-G-M in 1932, she had inspired an
aghast Hays Office to cinch the censorship code over her lascivious antics in
Red Headed Woman as the titian-wigged, garter-flashing vamp who bed-hops
her way to riches, and her role in *Red Dust* as Vantine, the jungle hooker
who tells Clark Gable "Scrub my back" while she is bathing nude in a rain
barrel. The actress had survived a grotesquely publicized scandal after her
second spouse, M-G-M producer Paul Bern, doused his naked body with her
perfume and shot himself, leaving the infamous "Dearest Dear" suicide note.
She lived above Bel Air's East Gate in a white, palatial hilltop mansion,
complete with a swimming pool, a lily pond, and her parasitic guardians,
"Mama Jean" and stepfather Marino Bello. She kept a bully agent, Arthur
Landau who, decades after her death, found solvency by providing the distortions for the ridiculous 1964 biography *Harlow*. During her days of stardom
raving fans grabbed at her hair and clothes, deviants swamped her with
pornographic fan mail, and personal happiness perversely eluded the sensitive, bewildered young woman.

Sadly enough, Jean Harlow was something of a joke within Hollywood circles, a joke that M-G-M festooned into one of Hollywood's most raucous self-spoofs, 1933's *Bombshell* sometimes titled *Blonde Bombshell* because some M-G-M executives feared the public would think it was a war movie. Many of the pathetic aspects of Harlow's quite miserable life, as well as gossip culled from the colorful lives of other cinema denizens, inspired this biting farce which, while manufacturing laughs at the star's personal expense, simultaneously provided the sterling comedienne the opportunity to play her most hilarious and touching performance.

Bombshell begins with a montage of exploitational advertisements for the sensual sagas of Lola Burns (Jean Harlow), sex queen of Monarch Studios, obviously modeled on M-G-M. Director Victor Fleming then sweeps the viewer into a white mansion similar to Harlow's own Beverly Glen palace and into Lola's ostentatious boudoir where her black maid Loretta (Louise Beavers) is awakening her. "What did you do that for?" quips the bleary-eyed Lola. "Something kind of cute was about to happen."

A gallery of Hollywood's leeches soon make their appearances. The first, Pop Burns (Frank Morgan), plays Lola's windbag father who has exploited her good fortune to forsake his livery stable and become a racehorse impresario. In real life, Harlow's own stepfather had drained her studio paychecks into his own get-rich-quick schemes and had harassed M-G-M personnel for investments. Next comes her loutish brother Junior (Ted Healy), and finally her secretary Miss Mac (Una Merkel), whose limited energies are largely reserved for looting Lola's wardrobe. The character of the secretary calls to mind a legal bout which silent star Clara Bow had had with her own secretary. Lola insults everyone, garbs herself in a luxurious white ensemble, tops it with a broad-brimmed chapeau, flanks herself with yelping white sheepdogs, and parades off into the dawn for another day at Monarch Studios.

On the lot, Lola prepares to jump into a rain barrel *á là Red Dust* for her latest sex epic, directed by Jim Brogan (Pat O'Brien). Brogan is smitten with her and casts aspersions on Lola's rumored fiancé, the Marquis di Binelli (Ivan Lebedeff). At this point the true bane of Lola's existence enters the picture: Space Hanlon (Lee Tracy), Monarch's ace press agent who is sworn to keep Lola a Monarch asset at any cost. The character was presumed by many at M-G-M to be a take-off on Arthur Landau, whom some have claimed was still collecting his ten percent commission from Harlow at the time even though he was no longer officially representing her. Hanlon gleefully destroys Lola's affair with the Marquis and, more brutally than humorously, manages to botch the star's dream to adopt a baby. Heartbroken, Lola flees for a vacation in Palm Springs.

At the desert resort, which was filmed on location in Arizona where the real Harlow fell in love with cameraman Hal Rosson, her subsequent husband of eight months, the fictional star Lola meets dapper Bostonian socialite Gifford Middleton (Franchot Tone) and his aristocratic parents (C. Aubrey

Smith and Mary Forbes). A love affair then develops. Lola is awed by their blue-blooded propriety, which is in refined contrast to her own gaudy existence. However, soon after Hanlon appears on the scene, with ever-gauche Pop Burns and Junior in tow, the Middletons reveal themselves to be the insufferable snobs that they are, and Lola fires a parting barrage at them: "You can take your Bostons and Bunker Hills and your bloodlines and stuff a codfish with them. And you know what you can do with the codfish!"

Lola learns on her return to the studio that the "Middletons" are actually aspiring bit players hired by Hanlon in another of his plots to convince Lola to remain a Monarch star. She explodes, but then realizes that Hanlon, in his own obnoxious way, cares for her. And, to her happy surprise, she realizes that she actually cares for him.

Bombshell does not exploit all the facets of the true Harlow *persona*. Ignored is her peculiarly close relationship with her mother, a potential embarrassment to which even the good-natured Harlow might have objected, nor was there any mention of a past husband who committed suicide. M-G-M later worked that topic into *Reckless* (1935), Harlow's only musical. Still, *Bombshell* is rich in both Harlow and Hollywood lore. The soundstages are shown as the cavernous, unglamorous barns that they are, and even the dressing room quarters appear rather seedy, predating the custom-built bungalows for such M-G-M deities as Greta Garbo, Jean Harlow, Myrna Loy, Jeanette MacDonald, *et al.* which Louis B. Mayer was to order. The film delights in inside M-G-M humor. After Tone recites some flowery verbiage to her, Harlow exclaims, "Not even Norma Shearer or Helen Hayes [both then contracted to the M-G-M pantheon] in their nicest pictures were ever spoken to like that." C. Aubrey Smith, after revealing himself to be a bit player, grumbles that he cannot understand why Lewis Stone, Metro's revered character star, gets all the meaty older parts. Dominating all, however, is Harlow's luminous presence. From the night of its premiere on September 30, 1933, at Grauman's Chinese Theatre where Jean had placed her hand and high heel prints and three lucky pennies in the fabled cement the day before, *Bombshell* was celebrated as the consummation of Jean Harlow's screen stardom. It was ". . . the first full-length portrait of the amazing young woman's increasingly impressive acting talent," the *New York Herald Tribune* stated.

In all the laughter that serenaded *Bombshell*, however, there was little sympathy for the ill-fated star. Perhaps there would have been had audiences known that, less than four years after *Bombshell*'s release, the corseted, bewigged, lacquered corpse of a twenty-six-year-old, yet long-dissipated Jean Harlow would lie on display for the very leeches so pungently satirized in this film.

Gregory William Mank

BONNIE AND CLYDE

Released: 1967
Production: Warren Beatty for Warner Bros.
Direction: Arthur Penn
Screenplay: David Newman and Robert Benton
Cinematography: Burnett Guffey (AA)
Editing: Dede Allen
Art direction: Dean Tavoularis
Costume design: Theodora Van Runkle
Music: Charles Strouse
Song: Lester Flatt and Earl Scruggs, "Foggie Mountain Breakdown"
Running time: 111 minutes

> *Principal characters:*
> Clyde Barrow .... Warren Beatty
> Bonnie Parker .... Faye Dunaway
> C. W. Moss .... Michael J. Pollard
> Buck Barrow .... Gene Hackman
> Blanche .... Estelle Parsons (AA)
> Frank Hamer .... Denver Pyle
> Ivan Moss .... Dub Taylor
> Velma Davis .... Evans Evans
> Eugene Grizzard .... Gene Wilder

"They're young. They're in love. And they kill people," proclaimed the publicity slogan for Arthur Penn's crime drama, *Bonnie and Clyde.* Loosely based on the actual accounts of two outlaws of the 1930's, Bonnie Parker and Clyde Barrow, the Depression-era saga combines comedy, violence, pathos, and love. Placing the legendary characters in historical perspective, the film begins with a succession of blurry period snapshots accompanied by period music that sounds as if it emanates from a wind-up phonograph. Set in the American Midwest in the early 1930's, the story concerns a bored waitress, Bonnie Parker (Faye Dunaway), who teams up with Clyde Barrow (Warren Beatty), a brazen ex-jailbird, after he attempts to steal her mother's car. Seeking excitement and thrills, the two create the Barrow Gang, which includes Clyde's brother Buck (Gene Hackman), his reluctant wife, a preacher's daughter named Blanche (Estelle Parsons), and C. W. Moss (Michael J. Pollard), a gas station attendant who becomes their getaway-driver.

As the quintet goes on a criminal spree, they become America's most feared and ruthless bankrobbers and killers. Although the police stage a statewide manhunt, the gang manages to escape the law. Eventually, however, the police surround the desperadoes in Dexter, Iowa. Buck, shot in the face, is killed, and Blanche is blinded and captured; the other three escape. After

Bonnie recovers from a shoulder wound in their hideout at C. W. Moss's father's Louisiana home, the three remaining partners move on. In order to obtain leniency for his son, however, Moss's father cooperates with the police in setting a trap, and the police finally ambush Bonnie and Clyde. In the film's brutal ending, the two are riddled with bullets.

A combination of murder and merriment, *Bonnie and Clyde* presents an ironically dramatic situation. The outlaws are portrayed as fun-loving, sympathetic heroes, while the law officers are seen as vengeful villains. The gangsters' grisly ventures have an aura of glamor; at the same time, the Barrow Gang members are depicted as down-home, good-natured folk. C. W. Moss bears a bluebird tatoo and has a penchant for Myrna Loy; All-American-type Buck Barrow carries a Kodak camera and tells corny jokes; and hysterically blithering Blanche keeps her fingers in her ears during the gunfire. The Barrow Gang is in many ways like a restless family of children out for a lark. Moreover, there is a touch of Robin Hood about the bunch. The Barrow Gang only robs banks that are foreclosing on poor farmers, and later, Clyde allows a laborer-depositor to keep his money during a bank robbery. Clyde also expresses his sorrow at killing people, and cannot understand why someone shoots at him: "Why'd he try to kill me?" he asks Bonnie with bewilderment and anguish.

The cohorts are made even more sympathetic because of their innocent belief in their own romantic fantasy and myth. Almost like children, they become fascinated with the legendary reputation growing around them; they seek even more celebrity and indulge in their urge to be theatrically remembered. They think of themselves as stars in a movie, and, as if playing the role of bankrobbers, they flaunt their big guns and dress in fancy clothes. Aware of their public image, Clyde enters a bank bragging, "Good afternoon. We're the Barrow Gang." As they depart, Buck proclaims with bravado, "Take a good look, old man, I'm Buck Barrow." Later, as Bonnie shoots a tire, Clyde gleefully says, "Ain't you something!" and in the midst of one escape, he happily sighs, "Ain't life grand!" Needing to feel they are someone special, the criminals enjoy their newspaper photos and keep a scrapbook of clippings about their adventures. At one point, they force a captured Texas ranger to pose with them for a picture, and Bonnie, with her sense of history, writes a ballad about their exploits and sends it to a Dallas newspaper.

Bonnie and Clyde contains many farcical interludes, as the inept gangsters hilariously bumble their way through hold-ups and engage in riotous, Mack Sennet-like getaways in stolen cars. "Straight" society, too, gets vicarious thrills and satisfaction from the group's adventures: awestruck migrant workers offer to share their food; a bank guard proudly recounts to reporters the drama of being captured by the Barrow Gang; and when the gang kidnaps a couple and jokingly asks them to join them, their response is, "What would Bill and Margaret say to that?" As Charles Stouse's lively twanging banjo music accompanies their escapades, the jazzy country-style tunes not only create a satiric edge to their ventures and produce a mood of laughter, but also punctuate the gang's need to be theatrical. At one point after a hold-up, the group seeks refuge in a movie theater; as they watch *Gold Diggers of 1933*, they listen to the song "We're in the Money."

Yet the cartoon-style comedy is juxtaposed with violence. Following a comical getaway, an innocent bystander is shot in the face; eventually, the gang kills eighteen people. In the film's final gruesome ambush, the cold-blooded violence is unsparing. On a country road, in the summer stillness, the trap has been set. To build the tension, editor Dede Allen cuts from the bushes behind which police hide, to the trees, to the flying birds, to the faces of several of the characters. Allen holds a beat while the doomed Bonnie and Clyde exchange a look of panic and love; then, in the fusillade of bullets, the two are gunned down in a slow-motion ballet of death. Their violently beautiful deaths underline and accentuate the romance of the Bonnie and Clyde myth.

Shot on location in northeast Texas, *Bonnie and Clyde* captures well the arid dustbowl country; and the barren, empty Southwest land serves as visual correlative for the bleak lives of the characters that propel them into a life of crime. Intelligently written by David Newman and Robert Benton with crisp dialogue and marvelous use of colloquialisms, and produced by a twenty-eight-year-old Warren Beatty, *Bonnie and Clyde* is sensitively directed by the gifted Arthur Penn. With a background in the Actors Studio, New York television, and Broadway theater (he directed *The Miracle Worker*, *Wait Until Dark*, *Golda*, and *Sly Fox* among many other stage productions), Penn was particularly qualified to direct this compellingly dramatic and well-observed study of two folk heroes. Penn's other movies also deal with myths and with outcasts of society: *The Left-Handed Gun* (1958), *The Chase* (1966), *Mickey One* (1965), *Night Moves* (1975), *Alice's Restaurant* (1969), *Little Big Man* (1970), and *Missouri Breaks* (1976).

Bonnie and Clyde boasts meticulous art direction, with its decor, antique cars, road houses, and farms; Faye Dunaway's costumes and hairstyle in *Bonnie and Clyde* had a great influence on fashions of the 1960's. The film also has evocative sound effects such as train whistles, crickets, and the wind, and a fine score of period music (Eddie Cantor, Rudy Vallee's "Deep Night," "The Shadow Waltz," and "One Hour with You"). *Bonnie and Clyde* also enjoys excellent, half-improvised, half-controlled performances by its stars. Warren Beatty as the debonair dandy in tight, wide-lapelled suits and fedora hats portrays Clyde as a confused neurotic. Clyde's outer ferocity and erratic behavior hides his inner weakness: he is impotent and sexually frustrated, and uses his gun in several scenes as a phallic symbol.

Faye Dunaway's role established her as a major screen personality. As the cigar-smoking poet-moll who later helps Clyde consummate his love for her, the actress is most affecting when she speaks about wanting to see her "Old Maw." In the homecoming scene, Bonnie does get to enjoy a clandestine family reunion; the scene, shot with a red filter to create a hazy softness, evokes a mood of warmth and American nostalgia.

The supporting cast is equally good. Michael J. Pollard is hilarious as the simpleton chauffeur with the squashed features who idolizes Clyde, and Gene Hackman as Clyde's hearty brother Buck is fine. In her screen debut, Estelle Parsons won an Academy Award for Best Supporting Actress for her portrayal of Blanche. Gene Wilder as mortician Eugene Grizzard and Evans Evans as his lady friend provide chuckles as the Barrow Gang kidnaps the couple and takes them for a joyride.

Nominated for ten Academy Awards, *Bonnie and Clyde* was one of the largest moneymakers in the history of American cinema. With its visual beauty and fantasy of violence, it was also a highly controversial picture. It not only reflected the 1960's anti-Establishment feelings, but also its anti-heroics were also a commentary on the mindless violence of the turbulent decade. A film of disturbing implications and stunning impact, *Bonnie and Clyde* far outshines earlier versions of the gangsters' story, such as *Gun Crazy* (1949) and the *Bonnie Parker Story* (1958).

Leslie Taubman

BORN YESTERDAY

Released: 1950
Production: S. Sylvan Simon for Columbia
Direction: George Cukor
Screenplay: Albert Mannheimer; based on the play of the same name by
   Garson Kanin
Cinematography: Joseph Walker
Editing: Charles Nelson
Costume design: Jean Louis
Running time: 103 minutes

Principal characters:
Billie Dawn .... Judy Holliday (AA)
Harry Brock .... Broderick Crawford
Paul Verrall .... William Holden
Jim Devery .... Howard St. John
Eddie .... Frank Otto
Norval Hedges .... Larry Oliver
Mrs. Hedges .... Barbara Brown

In the period immediately following World War II, both cinema and the
stage in the United States presented stories that treated the problems and
the changed conditions of the new postwar era. The film *The Best Years of
Our Lives* (1946), for example, dealt realistically with such issues as the new
social forces, readjustment to peacetime economic trends, and safeguards for
democracy. In the same year, the play *Born Yesterday* opened on Broadway;
the underlying concern of its comic, although equally valid, treatment is the
issue of adherence to democratic principles and vigilance to see that democracy is not thwarted. After the play enjoyed a successful run of 1,642 performances, the movie version of *Born Yesterday* appeared in 1950, with only
minor changes made to accommodate the story for the screen.

The movie opens with junk tycoon Harry Brock (Broderick Crawford)
arriving in Washington. Included in his entourage is his blonde companion-
mistress Billie Dawn (Judy Holliday). Paul Verrall (William Holden), a Washington journalist, observes their arrival and goes to Harry's hotel suite to get
an interview concerning the latter's business interests and political connections
in Washington; his initial attempt at uncovering information, however, is
unsuccessful. Meanwhile, Harry has been consulting with his Washington
lawyer Jim Devery (Howard St. John), who suggests that Billie must acquire
some polish and education so that Harry will not be ashamed of her in their
contact with important people in Washington. In the course of the story it is
revealed that Harry has been using Billie as an unwitting accomplice in his
suspect business ventures. Harry has placed his empire of interlocking junk-

yard businesses in Billie's name so that, even though Harry is actually controlling things, legally he cannot be held responsible for any of the activities of the business.

It transpires that Paul is hired as a tutor to give Billie the polish necessary to meet with congressmen and other influential people as a part of Harry's Washington dealings. Paul has his own reasons for accepting the assignment of educating Billie: he is secretly interested in exposing Harry's nefarious Washington maneuverings, and this position would give him a chance to find out more about the Brock operations. After some persuasion by Paul, Billie embarks on her education; Paul assigns a list of books she is to read and guides her around the monuments and public buildings of the capital. As she begins to acquire some education and social grace, the fundamentally bright Billie becomes imbued with a social consciousness and a respect for democratic views. Along with her enlightenment, Billie rebels against Harry's blatant corruption and arrogance. Harry now represents to her the menace of acquisitive power and greed against which democratic people must be alert. Billie refuses to sign any more of the papers involved in Harry's attempt to form a scrap iron cartel, and she tells Harry that she is leaving him. In order to prevent Harry from continuing to circumvent the democratic process, she will keep the companies in her name and release them back to him at the rate of only one per year; this means that it would take about eighty years for him to regain complete control of his companies. Meanwhile, Paul and Billie have fallen in love, and the story ends with the two married.

The serious moral of *Born Yesterday* is not slighted, but it was the humorous aspects of the film that made it the triumph it was. Much credit must be given to the performance of Judy Holliday as the comically ignorant blonde chorine with the pronounced New York accent, which won for her the Academy Award for Best Actress of 1950 and established her film career. The film gave Holliday the opportunity to demonstrate her great versatility as an actress. Particularly memorable is her voice, which can range from a plaintive squeak to a scream. There are several scenes in the film which have become "classics" because of her genius for comedy. One involves a gin rummy game between Billie and Harry in which Holliday combines quick manipulation of the cards with outrageously loud humming. In another scene, while Harry and Paul are trying to convince her to take lessons in culture, she defines the word peninsula as "the new wonder drug" so defiantly that the audience almost accepts her definition.

Broderick Crawford, who had recently won an Oscar for Best Actor for his performance in *All the King's Men* (1949), seems to parody his previous performance. His scenes with Billie are particularly noteworthy because he changes from a buffoon to a cold, calculating opportunist without detracting from the believability of either aspect of his character. William Holden gives a good performance, but his role does not require anything beyond a standard, journeymanlike job. The other actors in the film also give solid but unspectacular performances. The critical and financial success of the film was due to the marvelous appeal of Judy Holliday, with a large measure of assistance by Broderick Crawford and director George Cukor.

Mark Merbaum

THE BOY WITH GREEN HAIR

Released: 1948
Production: Stephen Ames for RKO/Radio
Direction: Joseph Losey
Screenplay: Ben Barzman and Alfred Lewis Levitt; based on a story by Betsy Beaton
Cinematography: George Barnes
Editing: Frank Doyle
Running time: 82 minutes

Principal characters:
Gramp .... Pat O'Brien
Peter Frye .... Dean Stockwell
Dr. Evans .... Robert Ryan
Miss Brand .... Barbara Hale
Michael .... Richard Lyon

The Boy with Green Hair was the first film directed by Joseph Losey, best-known for the films he made after emigrating to England as a result of being blacklisted in America. Losey started his career as a motion picture director under the most trying and difficult of conditions.

Initiated in 1946 by RKO studio head Dore Schary, *The Boy with Green Hair* became a pawn in the hands of The House Un-American Activities Committee. After some preparation, the project was cancelled when the original producer, Adrian Scott, was called before the Committee. Scott, one of the "Hollywood Ten," was eventually cited for contempt of court and was taken off the picture and effectively blacklisted for twenty years. The work that Losey, Schary, and Scott had done on the film was scrapped, and in 1947, Losey had to start again with a new producer and a new concept. The message of the film was both antiwar and antiracist—rather risky territory for those days of irrational fear in America. Losey felt that a combination of fantasy and realism would serve to get the film's point across, but he had his hands tied when RKO insisted on building sets for some all-important scenes that Losey felt should have been shot on location. The image of reality that Losey wanted to convey was diminished by the use of the same RKO standing set for a small town that had been seen in countless films before. For certain expressionistic effects, Losey had been working with designer John Hubley, but Hubley also had been blacklisted, and had no clout at the studio.

Coupled with these technical problems and ongoing budget difficulties was the sudden firing of Dore Schary by Howard Hughes, who actually owned RKO by 1948. Hughes tried to take over the film and inject into it anti-Russian propaganda. In an interview, Losey once said that he felt that the reason the film works at all now is because of the emotional context of the times in which we live. Since the film is avowedly antiwar, modern generations see in it a certain nobility. Still, Losey claims that the film falls far short of what he was trying to accomplish.

The picture opens in a room where a small boy is sitting, his head completely shaved. He refuses to identify himself until he wins the confidence of a psychiatrist, Dr. Evans (Robert Ryan), to whom he tells his strange story. The boy, Peter Frye (Dean Stockwell), lives with his grandfather (Pat O'Brien), an elderly ex-vaudevillian. He was sent to the old man after the war, after being shuttled from one relative to another. While helping his teacher, Miss Brand (Barbara Hale), to organize a clothing drive for war orphans, Peter learns that he too is a war orphan, for his parents were killed in England during the Blitz. Peter goes home and tries to talk to Gramps about his parents, but the old man just rambles on about his lost love Eileen, who always had something green around the house because it reminded her that no matter how foul the weather was, spring was sure to come.

The next morning Peter wakes up and finds that his hair has turned a bright green. It is from this point that Losey wanted to inject an element of fantasy, for the emphasis of the film changes from telling of an all-American boy in a small town to a symbolic tale in which Peter is a vehicle for a message of possible change. The townspeople shun the boy because of his hair; he becomes an outcast and wanders off to the woods outside of town. There, he finds a group of children who are identical to the ones depicted on the posters of the war orphans at school. Losey had visualized this critical scene as being possibly animated, or shot with the children static and composed in some way that could directly relate to the poster children. As it turned out, all of the children were portrayed standing in an ordinary glade behaving like ordinary children; Losey later felt that they came across as puppets rather than symbols. The scene is still moving, however, as the children tell Peter that *they* have turned his hair green so that he would attract attention to himself while telling the world that war is bad for children and must cease. Peter returns to the town and tries to carry out the children's mandate; but everyone still resents his changed appearance and he feels himself a failure. He goes to the barber and has his head shaved; then, feeling that he has betrayed the war orphans, he runs away.

As the flashback ends and the film switches back to Peter and the psychiatrist, Gramps comes into the room. The police had picked up Peter and sent the doctor to see him, later sending for Gramps. Gramps has brought with him a letter he received from friends of Peter's parents telling how bravely they had died in the fight against war, a struggle that the living must carry on. Peter is moved and decides to go on with his crusade, hoping that his hair will grow back green.

The film contains an amazing performance by Dean Stockwell as Peter, and by Pat O'Brien, completely winning as his lovable Gramps. If the film seems heavy-handed, it is because it is so obviously intended to convey a "message," and the tone of that message is at times ambivalent. Losey's concept of the film was as much antiracist as antiwar, but Schary fought him on this. Losey has stated that for him, the best scene in the film is the one in which the schoolteacher, as a result of a certain amount of persecution of Peter by the children, asks how many of the children have black hair, how many have blonde, how many have red; the director felt there should have been more such scenes, but he was overruled.

When the film first opened, its reception was mixed. As a concession to popular taste, the studio tacked on as a musical theme throughout the film the song "Nature Boy," a hit tune of the time written by a strange hermit named Eden Ahbez. Critics felt that the song and the film did not quite mesh, and Losey agreed. In retrospect, *The Boy with Green Hair* fits in with a group of Hollywood films made in the late 1940's that deal with social injustice— films such as *Gentlemen's Agreement* (1947) and *Crossfire* (1947), which tackled anti-Semitism; or *Pinky* (1949) and *Lost Boundaries* (1949), which were about racism in America.

With the rise of McCarthyism and the ever-growing popularity of television, the contents of films changed drastically in the late 1940's and early 1950's. Films with social messages were replaced with pictures that sought purely to entertain. *The Boy with Green Hair*, however, is more than a nostalgic period piece. In it one can see already the qualities that are immediately recognizable as belonging to Joseph Losey: his preoccupation with subjective truth; the way he presents a real, everyday world in a completely personal way; and his unique visual sense which became so fully realized in his later masterpieces, *Accident* (1967), *The Servant* (1963), and *The Go-Between* (1971).

Joan Cohen

BREAKFAST AT TIFFANY'S

Released: 1961
Production: Martin Jurow and Richard Shepherd for Paramount
Direction: Blake Edwards
Screenplay: George Axelrod; based on the novella of the same name by
   Truman Capote
Cinematography: Franz Planer
Editing: Howard Smith
Costume design: Edith Head
Music: Henry Mancini (AA)
Running time: 114 minutes

Principal characters:
Holly Golightly	Audrey Hepburn
Paul Varjak	George Peppard
"2-E"	Patricia Neal
O. J. Berman	Martin Balsam
Mr. Yunioshi	Mickey Rooney
Doc Golightly	Buddy Ebsen
José da Silva Perreira	Vilallonga
Mag Wildwood	Dorothy Whitney
Sally Tomato	Alan Reed
Tiffany's salesman	John McGiver
Stripper	Beverly Hills
Rusty Trawler	Stanley Adams
Librarian	Elvia Allman
Sid Arbuck	Claude Stroud

Upon its initial appearance in 1961, *Breakfast at Tiffany's* got good reviews and was well received by the public. The plot, the characters, the cinematography, and the music were all commented upon favorably, and the name of the main character, Holly Golightly, has since been used to describe a charming madcap, someone who is amoral but not hard, lovable but not saccharine.

The plot of the movie differs considerably from Truman Capote's novella of the same name. In the movie *Breakfast at Tiffany's*, Holly Golightly, formerly Lulamae Barnes from Tulip, Texas (Audrey Hepburn), lives in a brownstone in Manhattan's East Seventies. Totally *outré* and somewhat irresponsible, she has a partially furnished apartment (a sawed-in-half bathtub serves as her sofa), owns a cat with no name, keeps her perfume and lipstick in the mailbox, gets rid of the "mean reds" by visiting Tiffany's. She is constantly forgetting her front-door key and then buzzing her upstairs neighbor, a Japanese photographer named Mr. Yunioshi (Mickey Rooney), to open the front door. Holly supports herself in two ways: she requests fifty dollars from her gentlemen escorts whenever she needs powder-room money, and she is paid one hundred dollars for each weekly trip she makes to Sing-Sing Prison where she visits Sally Tomato (Alan Reed), a gangster serving time.

One day a new tenant moves into Holly's apartment building. He is Paul Varjak (George Peppard), a young writer who is being kept by a rich older woman nicknamed "2-E" (Patricia Neal). At the end of her visits to Paul's apartment, 2-E usually leaves two hundred dollars beside the bed before going home to her husband. As usual, not having her apartment key, Holly begins to buzz Paul's bell in addition to Mr. Yunioshi's. Holly and Paul strike up a neighborly friendship, and he comes to the cocktail party being held in Holly's apartment. The wild cocktail party is one of the memorable comic sequences of *Breakfast at Tiffany's*, containing a skillfully worked out routine in which, without her knowledge, one of the women at the cocktail party has her hat set on fire by another guest's cigarette. Without causing any interruption or calling attention to this accident, the drink held by one of the partygoers is inadvertently sloshed on the burning hat and the fire is put out.

The day after the cocktail party, Holly asks Paul to help her with Doc Golightly (Buddy Ebsen), an older Texan horse doctor whom Holly married when she was only fifteen. Now Doc wants Holly to go back to Texas with him; Holly explains to Paul that the marriage was annulled long ago, although Doc does not accept the fact of the annulment. With Paul's help, Holly puts Doc on a bus back to Texas. Following this event, Holly and Paul spend a day on the town together; they look at a copy of Paul's book in the public library, have a Crackerjack ring engraved at Tiffany's, and steal party masks from a five-and-ten-cent store. Paul realizes he is in love with Holly and proposes marriage, but Holly has decided to marry a Brazilian millionaire, José da Silva Perreira (Vilallonga). It is now publicly revealed that Holly has been innocently carrying narcotics ring information from Sally Tomato to his outside associates, and José leaves Holly. Because of these events, Holly is both depressed and furious at everything and everyone; she throws Cat into the rain and decides to leave New York. When Paul lectures her and then goes out to find Cat, Holly now realizes how much she is giving up and races through the streets for a happy reunion in the rain with Paul and Cat.

Most viewers were enchanted with *Breakfast at Tiffany's*, as reflected in the awards and nominations the film received: it won the Academy of Motion Picture Arts and Sciences Award for Best Musical Score, while the song "Moon River" with words by Johnny Mercer received the Academy Award as the Best Song first used in an eligible picture. *Breakfast at Tiffany's* was nominated for an Academy Award for Best Screenplay based on material from another medium; it also received a nomination for Best Art Direction of a color picture. In addition, Audrey Hepburn was nominated for the Best Actress award.

Mark Merbaum

BREAKING AWAY

Released: 1979
Production: Peter Yates for Twentieth Century-Fox
Direction: Peter Yates
Screenplay: Steve Tesich (AA)
Cinematography: Matthew F. Leonetti
Editing: Cynthia Scheider
Score: Patrick Williams
Running time: 100 minutes

> *Principal characters:*
> Dave Stoller .... Dennis Christopher
> Mike .... Dennis Quaid
> Cyril .... Daniel Stern
> Moocher .... Jackie Earle Haley
> Mrs. Stoller .... Barbara Barrie
> Mr. Stoller .... Paul Dooley
> Katherine .... Robyn Douglass
> Rod .... Hart Bochner
> Nancy .... Amy Wright
> President .... John W. Ryan

The Little 500 bicycle race is an annual competition at Indiana University. Patterned after the five-hundred-mile automobile race in Indianapolis, the Little 500 is a major event in the lives of the students at the University. Steve Tesich, an alumnus of the University, used the race and his memories of his adolescence in Bloomington as the basis for the screenplay of 1979's surprise hit, *Breaking Away.* Although the film concerns characters dealing with problems created by a specific place, the film is successful because audiences recognize and understand the underlying theme, which is the process of growing, of breaking away from adolescence into adulthood, a process everyone must endure.

Dave Stoller (Dennis Christopher) and his three closest friends have graduated from Bloomington High and are determined to preserve the life they have developed together during their high school years. Dave, although the brightest with the best prospects for success in the adult world, has retreated furthest from adult responsibilities. He is intensely committed to bicycle racing and to his heroes, the Italian racing team. His identification with the team has led him to construct a fantasy world in which he pretends to be Italian himself. He speaks Italian, sings Verdi arias, wishes his parents would have more children because Italians have large families, and calls the family cat Fellini, after the famous Italian director. Mike (Dennis Quaid) is the ex-quarterback of the football team. He knows he will never play college football and is angry that he lives in a town where he is constantly reminded of the achievements of the University teams. Cyril (Daniel Stern) is also an ex-athlete, aware of his unpromising future and burdened by a father who gains satisfaction from his son's failures. Moocher (Jackie Earle Haley), the smallest and poorest of the group, is also the most adult. Forced by circumstances to accept responsibility, Moocher makes a further commitment to the adult world by marrying his girl friend, Nancy (Amy Wright).

Dave's parents are baffled and bemused by Dave's fascination with Italy. Mrs. Stoller (Barbara Barrie) is supportive of Dave's desire for something beyond Bloomington, while also sympathizing with her husband's confusion and anger at this strange creature their son has become. Mr. Stoller (Paul Dooley) is a used-car salesman who is afraid that his son's behavior will adversely affect sales, as well as embarrass him in front of the neighbors. He is determined that Dave will act like everyone else in the town, while Dave is equally single-minded in his pursuit of bicycle racing and the allure of Italy.

Even though the four friends are aware of the cultural gap between the University students and the "cutters" (a contemptuous term for the citizens of Bloomington, so-called because many residents cut limestone in the quarries surrounding the city), Dave ventures onto the campus, where he encounters a lovely coed named Katherine (Robyn Douglass). He is wearing his racing gear, so he introduces himself as an Italian exchange student. Katherine is charmed, since he is unlike the fraternity men to whom she is accustomed. Dave and Cyril go to her sorority house to serenade her and her sisters with Italian arias. Touched by his song, Katherine goes for a walk with Dave, leaving Cyril to cope with Katherine's fraternity boyfriend Rod (Hart Bochner) and his fraternity brothers. Mike is determined to avenge Cyril's wounds, so he, Cyril, and Moocher invade the Student Union Building looking for the fraternity brothers. The confrontation quickly becomes a brawl and results in a disciplinary hearing in the University President's office.

The President (John W. Ryan) tells the fraternity men that relations between the town and the University must be improved, so he has decided to invite a team from the town to compete in the Little 500 bike race. Mike, Moocher, and Cyril are certain they can win the race if Dave will ride the entire fifty miles, but Dave is reluctant to enter the race because Katherine would discover his true identity. Also, he must train for the one-hundred-mile road race which will feature the touring Italian championship team.

Dave is now working for his father on the used-car lot. When a customer returns a car and asks for his money back, Dave agrees to the refund. Mr. Stoller's rage at Dave's gallantry causes a heart attack, and Dave decides to stay by his father's bedside instead of entering the one-hundred-mile race. His mother urges him to follow his dream, because it will not always be possible to do what he wants in life. Dave does enter the race after promising his mother to win for her, and he eventually catches up to the Italian team. He is thrilled to be able to ride with his heroes, and chatters excitedly with them in Italian. The Italians are less thrilled at the challenge of this Hoosier nobody, however, and deliberately run Dave off the road. Thoroughly disillusioned by his heroes and by things Italian, Dave cries in his father's arms, apologizes for refunding the money, saying "Everyone cheats, I just didn't know." Now determined to accept himself as he is, Dave tells Katherine the truth. She is as hurt by his deception as he has been by his heroes, and breaks off the friendship. Without her, Dave no longer has any reason to avoid the Little 500 race, so he enters with his friends.

Mr. Stoller takes Dave to the campus to see some of the buildings, for which he had cut the stone before he started selling cars. He explains that he had great pride in the workmanship, but he felt that the building did not belong to him, that the campus was an alien place. He urges Dave to enroll in the University, but Dave says he is just a cutter. Mr. Stoller replies, "No, you're not a cutter, I'm a cutter." Dave realizes that he is not trapped by his background, that he can be a student like Katherine and her friends.

Dave and the "Cutters" start the Little 500 race in the last position. The team led by Rod and his fraternity brothers is in first place. During the race, Dave steadily moves up until he is in the lead, while Mike, Moocher, and Cyril relax, enjoying the race which Dave will assuredly win for them. Dave has an accident, however, and the three friends must take over for him. Never having expected to ride in the race, they are not in good shape, and the lead passes back to Rod and his fraternity. Determined to win, however, Dave has his wounds bandaged, and is strapped onto the bicycle by his exhausted teammates. With great effort and determination, Dave overtakes the leaders and passes Rod at the finish line to win the race. Dave, Mike, Moocher, and Cyril can now face the adult world, having proven themselves the equal of the University students. They have earned their self-respect and can now move beyond the world of their high school days.

The success of *Breaking Away* is attributable in equal parts to the screenplay by Steve Tesich and the direction of Peter Yates. Tesich, who came to the United States from his native Yugoslavia, wrote a script which is a humorous, nostalgic examination of the growing pangs of four adolescents. Firmly sited in a specific place, the film nevertheless speaks to everyone because of its universal theme. Although British himself, Peter Yates enhances the sense of place through his attention to the details of Midwestern American life. Filmed entirely on location in Bloomington, Indiana, Yates uses the city to represent the home-town all Americans are familiar with in their mythic, if not their actual, lives. Yates's direction of Dennis Christopher in the central role ensures that Dave is admirable in his fierce commitment to Italy rather than silly and embarrassing, which the character could have so easily become. The biking sequences have an excitement and beauty that is solely due to Yates's sense of pacing and editing. The score, a potpourri of Italian operatic compositions, sections of Mendelssohn's Italian Symphony, and the Indiana

University fight song, adds immeasurably to the general ambience of the film, reinforcing Dave's obsession with Italy and adding tension to the visual beauty of the racing sequences.

While the young actors in the central roles, especially Dennis Christopher and Daniel Stern, are believable and affecting, the best performances in the film are those of Barbara Barrie and Paul Dooley playing Dave's parents. Barrie received an Academy Award nomination for Best Supporting Actress for her work as the understanding wife and mother who tries to reduce the conflicts between her husband and son. Paul Dooley was not nominated for his performance, but he is equally deserving of recognition. Dooley is amusing and touching as a man no better than he has to be who does not fully understand what has become of his life. He is even more frightened and angry by the eccentric behavior of his son. Mr. Stoller's movement towards acceptance of his son is invested by Dooley with humor and an inarticulate grace that solidly demonstrates his artistry. The film received four additional Oscar nominations, one each for Patrick Williams' scoring, Peter Yates's direction, Steve Tesich's original screenplay, and as Best Picture. Although Tesich received the film's only Academy Award, the very fact of receiving five nominations served to reinforce the success of the film. It proved once again that a low-budget, "little" film can be a critical as well as a financial success if it is well done. *Breaking Away* will most assuredly remain an excellent example of this type of filmmaking.

Don K Thompson

THE BRIDE OF FRANKENSTEIN

Released: 1935
Production: Universal
Direction: James Whale
Screenplay: John L. Balderston and William Hurlbut
Cinematography: John J. Mescall
Editing: Ted Kent
Sound: Gilbert Kurland
Running time: 75 minutes

Principal characters:
Henry Frankenstein	Colin Clive
The Monster	Boris Karloff
Dr. Pretorius	Ernest Thesiger
Mary Shelley/The Monster's Bride	Elsa Lanchester
Elizabeth	Valerie Hobson
Minnie	Una O'Connor
The Hermit	O. P. Heggie

The Bride of Frankenstein is perhaps the most famous, the least dated, and the most enjoyable of the classic horror films. It is the official sequel to Universal's 1931 *Frankenstein* (also directed by James Whale), a film whose most enduring qualities are Boris Karloff's performance as a sympathetic menace and the stylistic touches in the design and lighting of some of the sets. Otherwise the picture is stagebound and slow and dates badly. The sequel, however, does not suffer from these problems. Instead it plunges Dr. Frankenstein's long-suffering creation into a swift succession of bizarre events, paying little heed to the conventions of either stage or cinema.

The eccentricity begins with the prologue, in which Mary Shelley, the author of the original novel, tells her admirer Lord Byron that her famous monster did not perish in the climactic fire of the first film. Mrs. Shelley's story then continues with the murder of two peasants by the Monster (Boris Karloff) as he rises from the burned wreckage of an old mill. News of his escape reaches his creator Henry Frankenstein (Colin Clive) and his new bride Elizabeth (Valerie Hobson) as they recover from the events of the first film. The Monster then goes on something of a personal odyssey. After a peaceful encounter with a young shepherdess at a pool, he is captured by irate villagers and chained briefly in a dungeon. His next escape leads to an idyll in the cabin of a blind hermit (O. P. Heggie) who teaches him kindness and the simple pleasures of good food, good music, and a good cigar. The Hermit also encourages the Monster to talk, and together they establish for the audience that the Monster's greatest need is human compassion.

Finally, the Monster meets Dr. Pretorius (Ernest Thesiger), a grave robber whose conduct personifies the film's spirit. In a short discussion Pretorius interests the Monster in the possibility of having a mate created expressly for him. The doctor has already approached Henry Frankenstein with an offer to collaborate on a second creation but has been soundly refused. Using the Monster's power to intimidate Henry, Pretorius forces his cooperation, and, after a harrowing meeting between creator and creation, the stone-tower laboratory is reopened and work commences on a bride for the lovesick Monster.

The Monster's new bride is brought to life in a bravura sequence that surpasses the original. To the accompaniment of the driving beat of Franz Waxman's eerily romantic score, the mechanics of reviving the patchwork mate become a pounding montage of tilted camera angles, weird electrical devices, and an operating table that lifts the corpse into an electrical storm to receive the spark of life in the form of a lightning bolt. The cunning Pretorius has drugged the Monster to keep him from interfering and kidnaped Elizabeth as a further hold over Henry. Henry, however, has regained his old mad doctor spirit and forgets all about Elizabeth as he revels in his new success.

The Monster's Bride (Elsa Lanchester) is presented in a chillingly precise series of shots that accentuate her staring, uncomprehending eyes, huge fright wig, and stiffly angular stance. The Monster's introduction to his intended is a parody of a formal courtship, and the scene is perversely reminiscent of a classic painting when he takes her reptilian hand in his as the two doctors look on. The happy union, however, is short-lived; the bride-to-be can muster only a piercing scream or a bloodcurdling hiss in response to her paramour's romantic overtures. The Monster, seeing the utter hopelessness of it all, decides to destroy himself, his mate, and the whole lab. Sparing only Henry and Elizabeth Frankenstein, he tearfully voices his last screen words, "We belong dead," before pulling a lever that destroys the tower, Dr. Pretorius, and the two monsters in a series of explosions.

The Bride of Frankenstein exhibits a surprising sophistication that sets it far apart from most horror films of its time, including the original *Frankenstein*. There is little petty moralizing of the "man should not tamper in God's domain" variety; on the contrary, the authors seem to endorse the morbid events as much as do their crazed characters. This lack of apology surely added to the critics' labeling of the film as being in the worst of taste, a verdict, however, that had no effect on the film's popularity.

The most startlingly unapologetic thing about *The Bride of Frankenstein* is its sense of humor. A liberal helping of graveyard comedy keeps the film from taking itself too seriously, yet interferes with neither the film's fear content nor its sentimentality. The purity of emotion in the Hermit sequence is so sincerely touching that even the crudely superimposed cross at the end of the prayer scene has power. Besides the obvious anticlerical elements in the Frankenstein story, such as the nonholy life and the desecration of the dead, *The Bride of Frankenstein* toys with other concepts rather touchy for its time—necrophilia and similar forms of death worship. The Monster first embraces a skull while contemplating his future love, and at one point, enters a mausoleum to be where he feels most at home, with the dead.

The unorthodoxy of themes makes the film a favorite of Surrealists, who revel in the fact that its most normal character is an animated corpse whose profound alienation from society is expressed through a desire to die. The Surrealists see many of the images as having religious significance: when captured by the villagers, the lashing of the Monster to a pole resembles a crucifixion; in his rage he pushes over a number of stone-cross grave markers. Other images, such as the creation scene with its phallic and orgasmic symbols, have sexual undertones. Other scenes and details are even stranger; Pretorius displays for Henry his own experiments with life, a set of miniature homunculi in jars. John P. Fulton's special effects show the little Henry VIII figure escaping to join one of his Queens, only to be chastised by a diminutive Cardinal. Later, when Elizabeth is kidnaped, Pretorius suddenly produces a pre-Bell telephone to allow Henry to talk to her, but the anachronism is hardly noticed amid the other fantastic happenings.

The acting in *The Bride of Frankenstein* is as exaggerated as the rest of the film, sometimes approaching the limits of acceptability. Colin Clive as Henry Frankenstein is especially theatrical, and most of his speeches would be ludicrous if the whole film were not played at the same overemphatic pitch. Ernest Thesiger almost steals the show as Pretorius, a madman whose chilling but genteel manners cannot conceal his macabre derangement. Elsa Lanchester's stunningly brief appearance as the Bride (and also as Mary Shelley in the prologue) has established her as one of the most famous of screen monsters; her shriek is probably one of the most famous screams in cinema history, comparable to Fay Wray's wailing in *King Kong* (1933).

Boris Karloff played the Monster only three times, and each performance is different. *The Bride of Frankenstein* is the only film of the three in which the Monster talks, and although his lines are few, they have a riveting impact. For the first and only time on film the Monster becomes a full character, interacting with the others on an equal basis. Newfound speech aside, the Monster's essential *persona* is still instilled mainly by Karloff's brilliant pantomime: his yearning for a mate, his silly, childlike pleasure in smoking a cigar, and his dead-eyed scowls at his tormentors, show a range of emotion broader than any of the other players. Karloff's lasting genius is evident throughout in the depth of humanity he evokes from within the Monster's misshapen body. By the time *The Bride of Frankenstein* was released, Karloff was the top horror sensation in the country—a success which could be measured by the first title card that appeared on the screen. It contained the single word, Karloff.

Glenn Erickson

THE BRIDGE ON THE RIVER KWAI

Released: 1957
Production: Sam Spiegel for Horizon Pictures; released by Columbia (AA)
Direction: David Lean (AA)
Screenplay: Pierre Boulle (AA) and Carl Foreman (uncredited); based on
   the novel of the same name by Pierre Boulle
Cinematography: Jack Hilyard (AA)
Editing: Peter Taylor (AA)
Music: Malcolm Arnold (AA)
Running time: 161 minutes

Principal characters:
   Shears .... William Holden
   Colonel Nicholson .... Alec Guinness (AA)
   Major Warden .... Jack Hawkins
   Colonel Saito .... Sessue Hayakawa
   Major Clipton .... James Donald
   Lieutenant Joyce .... Geoffrey Horne

In 1957, both critics and the public looked forward to the release of David
Lean's *The Bridge on the River Kwai.* They had liked and respected Lean's
Brief Encounter (1946), *Great Expectations* (1947), and *Summertime* (1955),
and now the British director had become more ambitious: he was making a
multimillion-dollar spectacular. But this film was to be no ordinary spectacular. Instead, Lean planned to make "The Big Movie with Meaning." Certainly *The Bridge on the River Kwai* is a big movie. Its $3,000,000 budget
was a considerable one in 1957. Its filming required the housing and feeding
of a company of hundreds in the forests of distant Ceylon. And even today,
after so many more spectaculars, the 161-minute *The Bridge on the River
Kwai* still seems big.

From the beginning, Jack Hilyard's color camera tells the audience that
this is a big movie. It closes in on a single flying bird, then backs away to
reveal an aerial view of a vast tropical forest. Soon afterward, it closes in on
the feet of one marching soldier, then slowly backs off to show more and
more marching feet, finally revealing a large number of men marching into
a World War II Japanese prisoner of war camp. To further this sense of
bigness, the sound track parallels the camera's sweep. At the beginning of
a new scene, the music often starts out with restraint, as when the British
prisoners march into the camp. At first, the audience hears only the distant
whistling of the men. As the camera reveals more and more men, however,
a large orchestra joins in the film's march theme, and the audience soon feels
caught up in the crescendo.

The cast is as big and impressive as the camera work and the sound track.

At the top of the large company are big name actors, including William Holden as the American Shears, Alec Guinness as the British Colonel Nicholson, and Jack Hawkins as Major Warden, the British academic-turned-commando. The script also follows many rules of the Hollywood spectacular. It offers a tense, straight-line adventure story, a good deal of humor, and less successfully, a slice of Hollywood romance. The proud and determined Colonel Nicholson marches his men into the camp, which is supposed to be in Burma. Following his orders to the letter, he surrenders. Nicholson and the equally determined Japanese Colonel Saito (Sessue Hayakawa) immediately lock horns. Saito orders all the British men to build a bridge. Nicholson insists that, according to a military agreement, officers cannot do manual labor. Furious, Saito tries torture to change his mind. He sends the lesser officers to "The Hole," while Nicholson goes to the dreaded "Oven."

In contrast, the American prisoner Shears is cynical and acquiescent. He shakes his head at all the military singleness of purpose, and finally escapes through the almost impenetrable jungle. Back at the camp, Saito holds out, but even when he takes personal command of the bridge construction, the project still fails. In what is perhaps the most dramatic scene in the film, he orders Nicholson to his quarters. Seated directly across from Saito, Nicholson trembles from hunger as he watches the Japanese commander slowly savoring a dinner of fine food and wine. Then, finally realizing that his British counterpart will not bend, Saito admits that he will have to kill himself if the bridge is not finished on schedule, and asks Nicholson what he would do. In a wonderfully ironic moment, the British Colonel urges Saito to "please sit down"—at Saito's own dinner table. Suddenly, as the nearly starving Nicholson begins to describe his approach to construction, the power shifts. Not only will Nicholson be in charge of the bridge, but also, the audience knows, he will be in charge of Saito.

As Nicholson unsteadily but proudly leaves Saito's quarters, the tension is released as someone shouts, "He's done it!" The camera moves back to reveal more and more cheering men, and the sound track sweeps from near silence to another crescendo of a heavily orchestrated version of the march theme.

Up to this point, the film has been a war hero spectacular, and a fine one. Once Nicholson is in control, however, the film ironically—and, some critics think, rather confusingly—changes. The single-minded Nicholson's goal becomes the building of a perfect bridge, while, ironically, the escaped Shears is assigned to a commando team whose mission is to blow up the bridge. In keeping with his reputation of dramatic cutting, Lean juxtaposes scenes of the Colonel's tightly scheduled construction with scenes of the commandos' tortuous struggle to reach the bridge.

True to Hollywood form, *The Bridge on the River Kwai* interjects a bit of comic relief into the midst of the tension. The fine irony which holds the film together often has a comic edge. Not as successfully, there are a few touches of slapstick, as in the scene when British commando trainees attack Shears, and in the scenes of the British soldiers' early feeble attempts to build the bridge. Most out of place, however, are the romantic scenes, which were perhaps Lean's attempt to conform to Hollywood movie traditions. After Shears manages to escape the Japanese camp, the camera finds him sipping a mixed drink on the beach of a British base. Leaning next to him in the sand is a very pretty blonde nurse in a bathing suit that is rather revealing for 1957. Later, as Shears and two British soldiers struggle back through the jungle, their supply bearers are pretty, sarong-clad native women. Amidst the building tension, the camera lingers a few minutes on the women bathing beneath a beautiful waterfall. The cinematography is always excellent, but the romantic scenes themselves have a pasted-on effect.

In contrast to these scenes, most of the script is filled with tension and irony. Nicholson does a remarkable turnabout. In order to meet the deadline for his bridge, he finally orders manual labor not only for his own officers, but also for many of the sick men. Meanwhile, the commando team reaches the bridge site. During the night, they swim under the bridge and set up the explosives. They have learned that a train will be crossing the bridge in the morning, and they hope to destroy both the train and the bridge. Developing the tension of these scenes, the camera concentrates on darkened close-ups of the swimmers' faces. The sound track discloses only the lapping of the water against the bridge, the sporadic cries of birds, and then the sound of a celebration up above, where Nicholson and his men are celebrating the completion of the bridge and their imminent transfer to another camp. Most of the British men will cross the bridge at the same time as the train, and the sick men will be on the train. Shears and his team members, of course, know nothing about this.

When morning comes, the commandos see to their horror that the river level has fallen and the explosives' wires have become exposed. Nicholson and Saito discover the wires; soon there is the sound of the train whistle coming closer and closer. In a confusing series of events, Saito, a young Canadian commando, Shears, and Nicholson are killed. But before he dies, Nicholson wonders aloud: "What have I done?," and then he falls onto the detonator; the bridge and train go up in one of the grandest of movie explosions. It is unclear, however, whether Nicholson really meant to set off the explosion, or whether he fell accidentally.

As a spectacular, *The Bridge on the River Kwai* succeeds, but as "The Big Movie with Meaning," its success is less certain. Lean did not intend to make merely a good war movie; and, in fact, far from being a portrait of military heroism, the film turns out to be an antiwar movie. Much of the antiwar statement lies in the characterization of Nicholson himself. At first, the Colonel is seen as a man of great dignity and resolve who cares deeply for his men. Later, however, he is revealed as a man so controlled by rules that he loses all perspective, building a beautiful bridge for the enemy and sacrificing his rules and even his men in the process.

Peter Taylor's editing and Pierre Boulle's ironic script also help to underline the antiwar ideas. All the war efforts seem especially futile, as Nicholson determinedly builds the bridge and Shears struggles to reach and destroy it. Shears's personal situation brings another antiwar twist to the plot, and the comic presentation of his ludicrous situation seems to foreshadow later antiwar films such as *Dr. Strangelove* (1964) and *Catch-22* (1970). After Shears escapes from the camp, the American Navy learns that he is not an officer but merely an impostor. In a scene that suggests *Catch-22*, Major Warden informs Shears that the Navy has turned him over to the British. Apparently, the Americans feel that they cannot give an impostor a hero's welcome, and yet neither can they punish someone who has escaped so heroically.

Less effective aspects of Lean's antiwar statement are his sometimes heavy-handed use of visual symbolism and dialogue. For example, the early close-ups of a flying bird are beautiful and effective, but later the bird imagery too predictably follows each killing. With similar bluntness, Lean interjects a few antiwar diatribes into the usually restrained and witty script. Later in the film, Shears didactically describes Nicholson as "crazy with courage. For what? How to die like a gentleman, how to die by the rules—when the only important thing is how to live." After the explosion, the Red Cross major keeps saying "madness, madness, madness."

When *The Bridge on the River Kwai* was released in 1957, most critics seemed to agree that it was an excellent film; it was also a hit at the box office, and it earned seven Academy Awards. However, even at that time, its more favorable critics disagreed about many of its implications. Is Nicholson admirable but mistaken, or is he a narrow-minded fool? Does Shears ultimately gain satisfaction from working with the commando team, or does he just make the best of a bad situation? Most important, what actually happens during the last few minutes of the film? Lingering questions like these have recently turned many critics against the film and against Lean's other, later spectaculars, such as *Lawrence of Arabia* (1962), *Dr. Zhivago* (1965), and his weakest film, *Ryan's Daughter* (1970). Like Andrew Sarris, perhaps Lean's strongest and most influential critic, many critics now find *The Bridge on the River Kwai* self-consciously enigmatic and even foolishly obscure.

After such a long and tense film, the viewer does want a clearer ending. In the more introspective and impressionistic films of today, one does not always require such an ending, but because Lean offers a classic straight-line story, the ambiguous ending does not work. Lean tries to combine all the ingredients of the spectacular together with a strong thematic message. He uses the straight-line adventure story, sweeping color cinematography, a powerful sound track, and dramatic editing; then he mixes in heavy visual symbolism, enigmatic characterizations, and ambiguous twists in the plot.

The Bridge on the River Kwai has its flaws, but because of its beautiful camerawork, its impressive sound track, its ironic script, and its strong acting, it nevertheless remains powerful and provocative; and, unlike many of its antiwar successors, it is highly entertaining.

Elaine McCreight

BRIEF ENCOUNTER

Released: 1946
Production: Noel Coward for Cineguild; released by Prestige Pictures
Direction: David Lean
Screenplay: Noel Coward, David Lean, and Anthony Havelock-Allan; based
on the one-act play *Still Life* by Noel Coward
Cinematography: Robert Krasker
Editing: Jack Harris
Running time: 85 minutes

Principal characters:
Laura Jesson	Celia Johnson
Dr. Alec Harvey	Trevor Howard
Fred Jesson	Cyril Raymond
Myrtle Bagot	Joyce Carey
Albert Godby	Stanley Holloway
Dolly Messiter	Everley Gregg

Noel Coward continues to be known as a figure of wit and style. His specific contributions to the field of entertainment as an actor, composer, and director are equaled by his work as a playwright. Many of his plays continue to be performed, but it is his work in film which has captured for the public the essence of his diverse talent. Among Coward's works brought to the screen was his expansion of the one-act play *Still Life* for David Lean's film *Brief Encounter*. Although the sentiments of the public have changed considerably since 1946, this simple story of an extramarital affair between two happily married persons continues to find appreciative audiences in frequent screenings at revival theaters and on television. This film's ability to deal with one of the basic premises of the woman's film, while avoiding the maudlin sentimentality and artificial glamour characteristic of that film genre, supports Coward's reputation as one of the figures who captured the twentieth century in midstream and stylishly preserved its values for future generations.

When Laura Jesson (Celia Johnson), happily married wife and mother, departs for Milford Junction on her weekly shopping day, she does not suspect that a chance meeting will result in a relationship which will raise personal doubts and decisions. While waiting for a train to return home at the end of the day, she gets a cinder in her eye and retreats to the station refreshment bar where a kind stranger removes it for her. He is Alec Harvey (Trevor Howard), a doctor who travels to the town weekly to assist in the local clinic. They part company after enjoying a brief but pleasant conversation.

On Laura's next outing to town she again encounters the doctor, and they spend a refreshing afternoon together innocently becoming acquainted. Without second thoughts, they find themselves enjoying casual weekly encounters and the stimulation these meetings bring to their otherwise predictable lives. However, the relationship grows intimate, and each begins to feel guilty. They are both happily married, middle-class English citizens who have no intentions of disrupting their peaceful lives. In this context, they cannot justify these secret meetings with their moral code.

The situation is resolved when Alec tells Laura that he and his family are leaving for South Africa where he will join a medical clinic. Laura is both relieved and distraught. Having known that the relationship could not continue without bringing emotional pain to those she loves, she also knows that she will continue to bear the secret memory of this brief encounter which has so enriched her life.

The film opens as Laura and Alec part for the last time. The narration, provided by Laura, introduces the viewer to the story in reverse flashback. Whereas the standard cinematic technique recalls the past from the present in brief segments to illuminate the present action and advance the story, *Brief Encounter* both begins and ends in the past, bringing the viewer forward to round out the story. An out-of-focus, wavy shot acts as the transition which moves the action between the narrator's present and past. Were the film not so subtly and unself-consciously set in the England of the 1940's, this device would offend present-day audiences. Although now a clichéd device, it instead appears consistent with the elements which contribute to the story and setting.

The acting further provides the film with impact. Celia Johnson, one of Coward's favorite actresses, who starred with him in his earlier *In Which We Serve* (1942) and his later *The Astonished Heart* (1950), portrays Laura as a happy, thoughtful, sympathetic woman. She delivers dialogue in a straight-forward, staccato fashion, which prevents the viewer from dismissing her as a Hollywood-type character looking for adventure. Her appearance, while engaging, is average, enabling larger audiences to relate to her character. When Fred (Cyril Raymond), Laura's husband, interrupts her daydream one evening in the comfortable setting of their home, her caring voice expresses how she would like to tell him what she has experienced, but recognizes that he is the last person she could tell. Johnson's performance alone raises the sentiments of the film well above the level of soap opera.

As Alec Harvey, Trevor Howard presents the audience with a gentle, devoted man, yet one who also feels stereotyped male passions. He shows concern and responsibility for this friendship which has reached its limit and acts to protect his own interests, but more importantly Laura's. Howard, however, does not allow Alec to become the martyred male. Given social attitudes at the time the film was made, it is understandable that a gentleman would take action and protect the lady with whom he is involved. Howard's portrayal convinces the audience that his actions are beyond question; he is a true gentleman, not an idealized figure outside the experience of the film's audience.

In this story of two people, the supporting characters add fine contrast to support the central problem confronting Laura and Alec. Their partings at the train station include observing the working-class woman (Joyce Carey) who operates the station refreshment bar. Her pretensions and false proprieties, so transparent in her relationship with the station guard (Stanley Holloway), provide Alec and Laura with humorous moments. Yet to the audience, this adolescent behavior stands in sharp contrast to the mature relationship which is at the film's center. Likewise, Laura's encounter with Dolly Messiter (Everley Gregg), a gossiping woman from the village where she lives, with whom she must share a seat on the train as she returns from her final parting with Alec, strengthens the audience's understanding of Laura's need for stimulating relationships. And even Fred, the kind loving husband, is a rather dull counterpoint to Alec, in spite of his manner. The use of these situations to focus the central problem of the story rather than to divert attention from it adds warmth, contrast, and credibility, saving the film from becoming a manipulative, superficial tearjerker.

David Lean's even direction is evident in the smooth pace and emotional level maintained throughout the film. Although not visually striking, all elements of the film support the very solidly based English atmosphere. The unpretentious cinematography captures everyday moments, in both interior and exterior shots, with believability. When Laura and Fred sit at home in front of the fire listening to the radio, they appear at home, comfortable and believable. Laura's meeting with Alec in his friend's apartment also has a convincing quality which does not detract from the emotions which suddenly erupt. The sets, while simple, support the feeling that these are ordinary people whom one might encounter daily.

Brief Encounter was J. Arthur Rank's first import to the United States through Prestige Pictures, the company he organized to introduce quality British films to a select but appreciative American audience. Although British critics did not receive the film well, American critics recognized the broad appeal of the film to the general moviegoing public. The film offered then, as now, an honest alternative to glossy Hollywood glamour. Wisely set in prewar England, the production loyally portrays the middle-class values embraced by the central characters. While seemingly a low-budget film, the consistency gives it a quality that money alone could not have produced. Such realistic detail as background noises of traffic or trains further enhances the veneer of realism employed; this realism even allowed contemporary critics to appreciate rather than to scoff at such aspects of the film as the recurring Rachmaninoff "Concerto No. 2." When viewed today, this and other now-minor details are elevated by the well-balanced, tasteful presentation of adult emotion.

Brief Encounter combines those elements which contribute to a unified cinematic whole. The story, while limited, provides a framework to bring together such technical skills as acting, setting, costumes, cinematography, and sound with universal emotions to create a limited yet lasting impression which advantageously exploits the genre of the ill-fated love affair in a subtle and honest manner. The almost timeless appeal of the film was illustrated in the 1973 Melvin Frank film *A Touch of Class*, in which the two lovers, played by George Segal and Glenda Jackson, cry copiously while watching the parting scene of *Brief Encounter* on television and wonder if their parting will be so bittersweet.

The film received three Academy Award nominations, one for Celia Johnson as Best Actress, one for Lean's direction, and one for Noel Coward's screenplay. Although it won no Oscar, Celia Johnson did win the New York Film Critics' Best Actress Award that year. A 1975 television remake of the story starring Richard Burton and Sophia Loren proved a disastrous undertaking and further underlines the value of Lean's direction and the lasting appeal of the original principals, Trevor Howard and Celia Johnson.

Kenneth T. Burles

BRIGHT VICTORY

Released: 1951
Production: Robert Buckner for Universal
Direction: Mark Robson
Screenplay: Robert Buckner; based on the novel *Lights Out* by Baynard Kendrick
Cinematography: William Daniels
Editing: Russell Schoengarth
Music: Frank Skinner
Running time: 97 minutes

Principal characters:
Larry Nevins .... Arthur Kennedy
Judy Greene .... Peggy Dow
Joe Morgan ....James Edwards
Mr. Nevins .... Will Geer
Mrs. Nevins .... Nana Bryant
Chris Paterson ....Julie Adams

Bright Victory is a film that is highly representative of a body of films about disabled servicemen that began during World War II and which continued through the post-Korean War days of the 1950's. These films centered on the recuperation and the readjustment into society of American fighting men who returned from war not triumphant, but with limbs missing, bodies paralyzed, or eyes blinded. With varying amounts of either believable compassion or indulgent sentimentality, films such as *Pride of the Marines* (1945), *The Best Years of Our Lives* (1946), *The Men* (1950), and *Bright Victory* reflect this concern with the inevitable results of war.

Among these films, perhaps Mark Robson's *Bright Victory* and Fred Zinnemann's *The Men* (the latter marked Marlon Brando's screen debut) most directly explore the actual physical and mental stress of the disabled veteran's reentry into society. Yet, in all of the films dealing with this subject, from *Pride of the Marines* through *Bright Victory*, it is also apparent that the filmmakers could not resist the temptation of making the love of a good woman as important to the recovery of their protagonists as conventional medical treatment. Although these films do not completely avoid the harsh realities of readjustment for the disabled veteran, they do tend to give the subject the "Hollywood treatment" that makes happy endings imperative.

Bright Victory does not escape the problems of oversimplification or of sentimentality involved in a story of a blinded soldier, but it does manage to combine a rather sensitive presentation of the struggles of the newly handicapped with the kind of fledgling social consciousness that, although sometimes only minimally courageous in films of the 1940's and 1950's, was a positive step for the time.

The film concentrates upon the recuperation of a single blinded soldier, Larry Nevins (Arthur Kennedy), but it also touches upon the problem of racial prejudice through Nevins' resolution of his own prejudice. Admittedly, there is a contrived quality both to Nevins' rejection of his best friend when he discovers the latter is black, and to the convenient last-scene reconciliation between the two men. What is encouraging about the consideration of racial prejudice in *Bright Victory* is its indictment of prejudice as the result of ignorance and blindly accepted cultural conditioning, and its depiction of friendship between black and white not as a bloodless intellectual union, but as a relationship of close physical and emotional ties. Hollywood often showed friendship between black and white as something strangely devoid of close physical contact, but *Bright Victory* seems to use the blindness of the two friends as a welcome excuse to allow them a friendship that is fully expressed in talk, shared activities, and in the kind of affectionate physical camaraderie natural for close friends. The treatment of racial prejudice in *Bright Victory* is, however, limited to the part it plays in revealing Nevins' growing personal and social awareness.

Nevins is followed from the time he is wounded in North Africa until the final moments when, after accepting the woman who has come to love him, resolving his own prejudice, and discovering and accepting his potential for an independent life, he (and the audience) is assured of his bright future, in spite of his blindness.

The cause of Nevins' blindness is effectively presented in an opening scene of understatement and irony. Nevins is not a selfless war hero, but an overconfident technical sergeant who, with his comrades, fast-talks an M.P. into allowing them into restricted territory so that they can repair broken communication lines. When the men are caught in an ambush of sniper fire, Nevins is wounded as he sits helplessly in a jeep. One tiny hole in his helmet is the only outward indication of the irreversible damage to his sight. The film details Nevins' treatment from field ambulance to base hospital, from the plane carrying him back to the United States to his destination of Valley Forge General Hospital in Phoenixville, where Nevins' hopes of regaining his eyesight are ruined by a doctor's final verdict: the optic nerves are destroyed, and restoration of any sight at all is impossible.

Nevins' reaction to this news is an awkward attempt to slash his wrists in the ward bathroom. He is prevented from killing himself and is forced to embark on the unwelcome and frustrating process of learning to live with his blindness.

Arthur Kennedy's portrayal of Nevins succeeds in giving the character a depth of feeling that is not conveyed in the script, but which is essential to the film's effect. His portrayal of Nevins was the kind of performance that made Kennedy a respected actor, but which, unfortunately, did not assure him of stardom. A few short years later, Kennedy was gracing films, not as a leading man, but as an interesting secondary character or as a villain, as in the James Stewart-Anthony Mann cycle of Westerns. Even the Academy Award nomination for Best Actor that Kennedy earned for *Bright Victory* was not enough to make him a "star" personality, to overcome a screen *persona* that was a little too self-effacing, a little too ordinary. Kennedy's performance as Nevins brings into focus his ability, albeit one seemingly often unnecessary for stardom, to give a character credibility in weakness as well as in strength. The success of *Bright Victory* hinges upon Kennedy, for it is through him that the audience experiences the personal struggles of the disabled. Kennedy is convincing, not only in depicting the ways in which a newly blinded person learns to function in a seeing world, but also in the molding of a character who is an ordinary person, without glamour, and with some very typical if unpleasant human failings.

The sentimental tendency of the script, with its dependence upon a predictable love story and an incredibly optimistic denouement, are tempered not only by Kennedy's excellent acting, but also by that of the other principals, particularly Peggy Dow as Judy. Judy meets Nevins while he is recuperating at Valley Forge General, but her love for him is largely unrequited until Larry realizes the hopelessness of his continuing the relationship with his hometown fiancée, Chris Paterson (Julie Adams). Dow gives her characterization of Judy a warmth and intelligence often missing from such roles.

Will Geer and Nana Byrant are also effective in their roles as Larry's parents. The return home for Nevins is a bittersweet experience with a very tense first meeting with his parents. With the help of his father, however, Larry begins to understand the difficulties his parents experience in dealing with their only child's blindness. Larry's relationship with his parents is renewed on encouraging terms, but he is unprepared to face the attitude of pity and embarrassment evidenced by his fiancée and her parents. He realizes that, unlike the inhabitants of Phoenixville, where the hospital is located, people in his hometown are unaccustomed to being with the blind, and their preconceived notions of what he is capable of doing do not fulfill the ambitions that Judy had instilled in him while they were together in Phoenixville.

Bright Victory neatly ties up all loose ends by having Larry ask Judy to marry him after declaring his intention to become a lawyer. If *Bright Victory* does not avoid the pitfalls of sentimentality and simplification, it does offer a sympathetic and often touching presentation of the courageous struggle of one ordinary man, while dealing with some typical concerns of postwar America.

Gay Studlar

BRINGING UP BABY

Released: 1938
Production: Howard Hawks for RKO/Radio
Direction: Howard Hawks
Screenplay: Dudley Nichols and Hager Wilde; based on a story by Hager
  Wilde
Cinematography: Russell Metty
Editing: George Hively
Running time: 102 minutes

> *Principal characters:*
> David Huxley .... Cary Grant
> Susan Vance .... Katharine Hepburn
> Mrs. Carlton Random .... May Robson
> Major Applegate .... Charles Ruggles
> Alexander Peabody .... George Irving
> Alice Swallow .... Virginia Walker

A classic of screen comedy, *Bringing Up Baby* is a frantically funny film
with a breathless pace sustained by unflagging comic invention and constant
surprises. It is a creation of inspired lunacy whose comic perfection is orchestrated by director Howard Hawks and performed by a wonderfully adept
cast. Although Hawks is known primarily for his action films of male camaraderie, he proved here just as he had in *Twentieth Century* (1934) that he was
also an accomplished director of comedy.

Dr. David Huxley (Cary Grant) is a paleontologist who hopes to persuade
wealthy Mrs. Carlton Random (May Robson) to donate one million dollars
to the museum where he works. In pursuit of this goal he is playing golf with
her lawyer, Alexander Peabody (George Irving). During the game when he
goes to look for his golf ball, however, he discovers that madcap heiress Susan
Vance (Katharine Hepburn) mistakes his golf ball for hers and will not listen
to his attempted explanation. After David finally proves that the ball is his,
Susan dismisses the whole issue with the remark, "It's only a game." David's
troubles are not over, however, for just as he is about to resume his game,
he notices Susan trying to drive off in his car. When he tries to stop her, she
insists that it is her car and drives off with David standing on the running
board.

Later that evening David again encounters Susan, and again the results are
calamitous. Walking by her in a restaurant, he slips on an olive she has
dropped on the floor. David immediately tries to get as far away from her as
possible, but Susan begins to be intrigued by him. When a psychiatrist (at
whose table she stops to absent-mindedly pick up some more olives) explains
to her that "the love impulse frequently reveals itself in terms of conflict,"

Susan's feelings about David seem to crystallize. Always direct and candid, she immediately goes up to him and tells him that he has a fixation on her. David's supposed interest in her seems to spur Susan on to greater heights of absurd behavior, which are—from David's viewpoint—new outrages.

Bringing Up Baby builds its comic world with careful increments of absurdity. In the restaurant, for example, the series of comic happenings begins with David slipping on the olive and landing on his top hat. The progression continues as, through a mistake made by Susan, David is accused of stealing a woman's purse. Susan then accidentally rips David's coat. When he tells her to go away, refusing to listen to her apologies, it is her turn to be offended, and she starts to walk away, but as she does so, the back of her evening gown is torn away because David has inadvertently been standing on it. He sees what has happened, runs after her, and claps his battered top hat over her exposed posterior. Startled and offended, Susan, as usual, refuses to listen to his attempted explanations and orders him to leave her alone and stop his strange behavior. But when she discovers her predicament, she orders him to do something to help her. They leave the restaurant together with David walking closely behind Susan so her torn gown will not be noticed. The director and screenwriters have thus adroitly escalated a slip on the floor into a major comic scene in which David and Susan walk through the restaurant as if they were glued together, provoking laughter from all the patrons.

Later that evening, as she repairs David's torn coat, Susan learns that David is trying to see Alexander Peabody, whom she knows well. She offers to drive David to Peabody's home, overcoming his objections that he is supposed to meet Alice Swallow (Virginia Walker), whom he is going to marry the next day. Susan's plan to get David together with Peabody goes awry (as we might have expected, although the plan seems plausible at first), but she is determined not to let David disappear from her life. When she receives a tame leopard named Baby from her brother in Brazil, she telephones David for advice with the excuse that he is the only zoologist she knows. She then lures him to her apartment on the pretext that Baby has attacked her and next tricks him into accompanying her and Baby to the house of her aunt (who happens to be Mrs. Random) in Connecticut, even though it is the day he is to be married.

The accumulation of zany incidents begins to accelerate again as a further complication is now introduced. David has just received a package containing the intercostal clavicle bone that he needs to complete the reconstruction of a huge brontosaurus on which he has been working for four years. When he is tricked into accompanying Susan to Connecticut, he has no opportunity to leave the bone behind and takes it along with him.

After several misadventures during the trip to Connecticut, David and Susan arrive at her aunt's house with Baby. While David is taking a shower, Susan sees an opportunity to prevent him from returning to New York to be married by having his clothes sent to town to be pressed and cleaned. After discovering what Susan has done, David puts on the only available garment, a fur-trimmed negligee, to look for the gardener whose clothes he hopes to borrow, muttering that Susan is "spoiled, conceited, and scatterbrained." He is stopped in his search for suitable clothing by the ring of the doorbell. When he answers it, he finds himself confronting Susan's aunt, an imposing-looking elderly woman who demands to know who he is and what he is doing in such clothes. He replies despairingly that he is not quite himself, and her further questions push him past the breaking point—he leaps straight up in the air, shouting, "I just went gay all of a sudden."

Director Hawks does not, however, let this wacky sequence end here; he adds a barking dog, George, and the chattering presence of Susan to prevent David from getting in a word of explanation to the aunt. When David shouts for silence, Susan only looks at him indulgently and goes on talking to her aunt. Only after he stomps on her foot does she stop for a moment, and he stalks off to continue his search for clothes.

His departure leaves Susan's aunt momentarily overawed and Susan counting on her toes "He loves me, he loves me not," but Susan is soon brought back to reality by her aunt's questions. As she dashes off in breathless pursuit of David, she says, "If he gets some clothes he'll go away, and he's the only man I've ever loved." At this point David's feelings toward Susan are quite different: "Out of two million people why did I have to run into you?" he mutters to her as he emerges from the depths of a closet in the only clothes he can find, a too-small riding outfit. This sequence is not only one of inspired comic invention but also shows a side to David's character different from his surface conventionality which makes Susan's interest in him more believable. For the first time we realize that perhaps David and Susan are not so ill-matched after all, and for the first time we hear Susan explicitly state her love for David.

The film then reaches a new height of absurdity when David discovers that George has taken the precious intercostal clavicle and buried it somewhere on the grounds. Susan, trying to be encouraging and helpful, follows David around as he tries to persuade George to dig up the bone. "Isn't this fun, David? Just like a game," she comments brightly to a disgruntled, disheveled, and dirty David. After some time and many holes later she exclaims, "What we need is a plow."

That evening Susan and David dine with her aunt and a guest, Major Applegate (Charles Ruggles), a big game hunter. The dinner is complicated by the fact that David has learned that Susan's aunt is Mrs. Carlton Random, the prospective donor of one million dollars to his museum. He asks Susan not to reveal his identity, so she gives him a fictitious name, Mr. Bone. In addition, David is unable to concentrate on the dinner table conversation because his whole attention is centered on George, who he hopes will lead him to the intercostal clavicle.

In the middle of dinner a leopard's cry is heard, but Major Applegate, who claims to be an authority on animal cries, insists that it is the cry of a loon. Susan and David, however, realize instantly that it is Baby and that he has escaped. Susan decides that she and David will have to find Baby, but David joins in the search only after Susan threatens to reveal his identity to her aunt. Another twist to the already zany complications is added when—unknown to Susan and David—a circus in a nearby town dispatches a dangerous leopard to the zoo to be humanely killed. When Susan sees the circus truck parked by the side of the road, she assumes the leopard in the truck is Baby and releases the dangerous leopard, who promptly runs away.

After wandering around in the woods for a while Susan and David finally see Baby sitting on the roof of a house. They begin singing the leopard's favorite song, "I Can't Give You Anything But Love, Baby," which always calms him. The commotion brings to the window the owner of the house—who happens to be the stuffy psychiatrist Susan met in the restaurant. Susan calmly tells him that her leopard is on his roof and she has to get it to come down. The psychiatrist naturally think she is crazy and forces her into the house where he keeps her until the arrival of the local constable he has summoned. The constable finds David lurking outside and takes both him and Susan to jail. He refuses to believe that Susan is Mrs. Random's niece, and his suspicions seem to be confirmed when a telephone call to Mrs. Random elicits an irritated response that her niece is at home in bed.

Supported by the psychiatrist, the constable now believes he has two dangerous criminals under lock and key. Next, Mrs. Random and Major Applegate arrive, but the constable does not believe they are who they claim to be or their preposterous story that they are hunting for a leopard, and throws them into jail, too. At this point Susan, ever resourceful, assumes a nasal accent and identifies herself as "Swinging Door Susie." Saying that they are all members of a gang, she promises to reveal all their activities if she is released from her cell. During the questioning she manages to escape out the window and goes searching for the leopard just before the arrival of Peabody, Mrs. Random's lawyer, and David's fiancé Alice. Next the men from the circus come to report that their dangerous leopard is missing. The constable, now thoroughly bewildered and uneasy, realizes that these absurd people may actually be who they claim they are.

Adding to the confusion is the appearance of Baby and George, which causes everyone to realize that there are two leopards, one of them dangerous and on the loose. David's first thought is for Susan's safety. "She's in danger and she's helpless without me," he exclaims, but Susan immediately appears with the snarling, untamed leopard at the end of a rope. When it is explained to her that the leopard she is dragging along is not Baby, she momentarily panics, and it is up to David to take command of the situation, which he promptly does. Stepping in front of Susan he defends her with a chair until the leopard has been maneuvered into an empty cell. He then faints while Susan maintains her usual breathless flow of chatter.

Alice's assessment of the situation is that David is "just a butterfly" and not the man for her, thus clearing the way for David and Susan to get together. But David, although he may be in love with Susan, is also afraid of her; and when she comes to see him at the Museum, he promptly runs up a ladder to a platform behind the huge brontosaurus skeleton on which he is working. Susan climbs another ladder on the opposite side of the skeleton to tell him that the Museum will receive the one million dollar gift after all—Mrs. Random is giving the money to Susan, and she wants to give it to David. As they talk, Susan begins swaying back and forth on her tall ladder, and we can see that disaster is imminent. During the ensuing conversation David finally confesses that he has never had a better time than the day he spent with her. At the same moment Susan finally overbalances on her ladder but manages to climb onto the skeleton to save herself from falling. As the giant skeleton begins to collapse, David grabs her hand, barely rescuing her. The two embrace above the ruins as the film ends.

The charm and humor of *Bringing Up Baby* lies partly in the comic situations that result from the diametrically opposed characters and personalities of David Huxley and Susan Vance. In 1930's romantic comedies, one of the protagonists is nearly always in love with a prim, conventional partner at the beginning of the film and has to be rescued and changed by an unconventional free spirit. In *Bringing Up Baby* Cary Grant is a stiff, bespectacled, dedicated paleontologist rescued by madcap heiress Katharine Hepburn. Director Howard Hawks has commented that Grant's role was intended to be a caricature of a scientist. At the beginning of the film, David is absentminded, awkward, and over-disciplined. He has devoted four years of his professional career to assembling the skeleton of a brontosaurus, but he is so inept that he tries to put one bone in the same wrong place that he tried the day before. Near the end of the film he finds himself in jail after a series of adventures which are just the opposite of his normal way of life, including assuming a false name, wearing a woman's negligee, singing to a leopard on a rooftop, and following a dog about to find a lost brontosaurus bone. Though he complains of the chaos Susan has involved him in, he does admit that she and her way of living have some attraction for him. At one time he says to her, "During quiet moments I feel a certain attraction for you—only there haven't been any quiet moments." Grant plays the stodgy scientist to perfection, using his voice and facial expressions both to convey a wooden exterior and to suggest that underneath there is a vital, fun-loving person.

The madcap, wacky heiress was a popular character in screwball comedies of the 1930's, but seldom was it so well acted and brought to such vivid, restless life as in this performance by Katharine Hepburn. She is a study in perpetual motion—always breathlessly talking and moving. Using a different expression, pose, or walk for each scene, she gives a variety and interest to her performance which keeps it both fresh and charming. Sometimes, for example, she does not merely laugh, she winnies. In the middle of the confusion, however, there are oases of calm and feeling that contrast subtly and tellingly with the frenzied activities that surround the characters. After David tells Susan that he is engaged, a close-up of her face shows that she is momentarily taken aback and more affected than we might have expected. Indeed, director Hawks uses close-ups sparingly in the film, and most are used to emphasize a moment of tranquility or deep emotion. Susan first learns of David's engagement when she offers to drive him to Peabody's house. While her face reveals to the audience her true feelings for David, her reply to him is both flippant and revealing: "Then she won't mind waiting will she?" Susan says. "If I were engaged to you I wouldn't mind waiting at all. I'd wait forever."

Another moment of deep emotion occurs when David, tired and disheveled from wandering through the woods in search of Baby, is accidentally knocked down by Susan and breaks his spectacles. He blames Susan for the accident and for embroiling him in the whole affair, making it clear that he does not want her help. There is a close-up of Susan's face—she is hurt and crushed— and she begins to cry, saying "You mean you don't want me to help you any more—after all the fun we've had?"

Hawks's achievement in the film is the creation of a complete comic world in which the absurd becomes rational and the normal becomes ridiculous. He has also created a film of almost constant comic invention and surprise that moves rapidly toward unexpected climaxes and unforeseen twists. At the beginning of some of the zaniest scenes there is no reason to suppose that they will culminate in absolute absurdity. David does not see where his actions will lead him and neither does the audience. The deft direction of Howard Hawks, the impeccable performances of the stars, and the inspired lunacy of the script make *Bringing Up Baby* a classic comedy which remains as fresh and vivid today as when it was first released

Julia Johnson

THE BROADWAY MELODY

Released: 1929
Production: Metro-Goldwyn-Mayer (AA)
Direction: Harry Beaumont
Screenplay: Edmund Goulding, with additional dialogue by James Gleason
  and Norman Houston; based on a screen story by Edmund Goulding
Cinematography: John Arnold
Editing: Sam Zimbalist
Music: Arthur Freed and Nacio Herb Brown, with additional songs by George
  M. Cohan and Willard Robison
Running time: 110 minutes

> *Principal characters:*
> Queenie Mahoney .... Anita Page
> Hank Mahoney .... Bessie Love
> Eddie Kearns .... Charles King

M-G-M's "all-talking, all-singing, all-dancing" motion picture *The Broadway Melody* heralded a new era in cinema history. It set the entire attitude toward filmmaking in that year, and in 1929 alone no fewer than seventy-five musicals were released, as well as countless additional dramas and comedies containing musical numbers. *The Broadway Melody* carried with it a real threat to the producers of live stage musicals, because it offered the chance to see a musical extravaganza from a better vantage point than live theater at a fraction of the cost to the audience. In any major American city the cost of admission to a stage musical was approximately $4.40, while the price of a movie ticket was a mere 75¢.

The plot of *The Broadway Melody* introduced all the basic clichés for the musicals to follow. Bessie Love and Anita Page played a vaudeville sister team, who, finding moderate success in their home town, decide to give Broadway a chance to appreciate their talents. Hank (Bessie Love), the elder sister, is engaged to a song-and-dance man on Broadway, Eddie (Charles King). But Eddie starts falling for the younger sister, Queenie (Anita Page), who is now grown up and beautiful. Queenie, aware of Eddie's burgeoning feelings towards her and also of her own feelings when he is around, starts encouraging one of the show's wealthy backers in order to discourage Eddie and save her sister from heartbreak. In between plot and dialogue, there is music. A landmark song is "You Were Meant for Me," which Eddie sings to Queenie. It is notable not so much for its pleasant melody or lyrics but because it is an early example of a song especially written to further the story. It is a harbinger of the more sophisticated "integrated" musical numbers of both stage and screen musicals that were to follow in the next decade.

Becoming successful is not easy for the sisters, but Queenie finally pulls them through with her ravishing good looks. There is still the unrequited love of Eddie for Queenie, however, to be resolved. In order to put an end to his thoughts of her, Queenie accepts money from her wealthy suitor and gives the impression that she has been bought. When Eddie, in an uncontrollable outburst, makes it clear that it is Queenie rather than Hank that he loves, Hank berates him into following and saving her sister by telling him that she has only been using him as a means of breaking into the revue. Hank, in a moving scene in her dressing room, reveals more depth of character than expected.

The Broadway Melody enjoys a surprisingly crisp tempo that is unusual for early "talkies," which were, for the most part, characterized by the exasperatingly laborious enunciation of the actors. The film did not have the static quality that most talkies displayed. Much of what we take for granted in films today, when first introduced to the audiences in the 1920's, was astoundingly innovative and daring. For example, during one scene in which Queenie and her partner are dancing, the microphone and camera move with them, picking up their conversation and expressions as they glide across the floor. This was a novelty of production at the time, and gave electrifying hints of what further possibilities lay ahead for the talkies.

The number "Wedding of the Painted Doll" was cleverly shot in two-strip Technicolor, a process in which for every frame of film shot, two frames were split by a prism and exposed through a red filter and a green filter. Not every primary color could be captured, naturally, but flesh tones were remarkably accurate even though the costumes tended to be either red or green. In spite of the fact that audience response to this color discovery was overwhelmingly enthusiastic, the studios were slow to move ahead with the color process. Lacking any foresight of its future importance, the studio let the color negatives disintegrate; today there is no example of this early color sequence known to exist.

There is much surprising sophistication to be found in this early film musical. The patter concocted by James Gleason and Norman Houston is clever and provides many intended laughs. The stars are likable and more than adequately prepared to handle their various chores. The story, by today's standards, is hokey and predictable, but one can see why fifty years ago it was considered modern, and was justifiably awarded the Oscar for Best Picture of the Year.

Juliette Friedgen

BROADWAY MELODY OF 1940

Released: 1940
Production: Jack Cummings for Metro-Goldwyn-Mayer
Direction: Norman Taurog
Screenplay: Leon Gordon and George Oppenheimer; based on a screen story
  by Jack McGowan and Dore Schary
Cinematography: Oliver T. Marsh
Editing: Blanche Sewell
Music: Cole Porter
Running time: 96 minutes

Principal characters:
Johnny Brett .... Fred Astaire
Clare Bennett .... Eleanor Powell
King Shaw .... George Murphy
Bob Casey .... Frank Morgan

Broadway Melody of 1940 is a prime example of the type of musical film which became popular based solely on the talents of the stars and the composer. Unlike some films of the 1930's which boasted half a dozen expensively produced numbers staged by choreographers such as Busby Berkeley, or musicals of the 1950's such as *Oklahoma!* (1955) and *Gigi* (1958), which had important stories and settings, *Broadway Melody of 1940* has a simple plot held together by good dancers and a good score.

The rather mundane story concerns Johnny Brett (Fred Astaire) and King Shaw (George Murphy), who comprise a dance team. In the absence of bookings, they take temporary jobs as professional hosts in New York's Dawnland Ballroom. Johnny finally prevails upon the manager to allow them to do their specialty act as an added attraction. They are an instant success, and a well-known musical show author is impressed by Johnny's dancing. Later, however, it is King who gets the call to appear at the theater for an audition as dancing partner for stage star Clare Bennett (Eleanor Powell). With the intense coaching of Johnny, the brains of the team, King manages to land the spot in the show. The success, however, goes to his head.

The day before the show opens Clare begs the producer (Frank Morgan) to speak to King. As they approach his dressing room, they hear faultless taps coming from within and decide to wait for the confrontation. The producer leaves but Clare discovers, without King knowing it, that Johnny has been doing the dancing in the dressing room. They meet and find each other excellent company because of their mutual interest in dancing.

The night the show opens King reports late and drunk. Johnny fails in his efforts to sober him up and dons King's costume and mask for the opening number. Clare recognizes his voice but he cautions her to keep the secret.

King is able to go on for the rest of the show. The rave reviews in the morning's paper give King more reason for his growing conceit. Johnny takes as much as he can then finally walks out. After he has gone, Clare comes to the apartment and tells King that Johnny saved both his job and his reputation; King then realizes that it is Johnny she loves. That night he again shows up for the performance in a drunken stupor and tells Clare to go and get Johnny, who has returned to his old job at the Dawnland Ballroom. Clare races after Johnny and brings him back to the theater in time to make the first curtain. The finale finds all three reconciled and happy as they dance to Cole Porter's "Begin the Beguine."

This was Astaire's first film at M-G-M after his contract had expired with RKO, and consequently his first chance to dance with that studio's queen of tap dancing, Eleanor Powell. Unfortunately the showcase for these two amazing performers does not measure up to their talents and abilities. It is a rather mundane effort on the part of the writers, and instead of becoming a grand musical, it has the appearance of another conveyor-belt song-and-dance film, with the notable exception being the finale number. This is not to detract from the film's elaborate production numbers which M-G-M did better than anyone else, or the dancing of the three stars, which they did better than anyone else; it is simply the case of the parts being great when viewed individually, but the sum of the parts not making an overall great film.

The success of the pairing of Astaire and Powell is, and has been all along, a matter of personal opinion. There seem to be two definite camps on this issue. On one side there are those who are adamant that without Ginger Rogers, Fred Astaire was half a dancer, half a personality; that it was that magic spark of their personalities that made them a legend. On the other hand, Astaire fans contend that with or without a partner, Astaire is magic enough and that it is he who imparts to whomever his partner may be the rarefied essence of success. It is a matter of record that Astaire was a demanding drillmaster, rehearsing a routine over and over again until the combinations came as naturally as walking, and he insisted that his partners keep up with him. Anyone familiar with the dance realizes that until a routine becomes second nature through endless hours of practice, no spark or electrifying personal touch can be imparted to it.

It did not matter with whom Astaire danced, the sparks did fly. A stunning example of this is the grand finale number, "Begin the Beguine." Dressed in elegant white and dancing on a floor of black mirrors against a backdrop of mirrors, Astaire and Powell whirl like pinwheels around each other, tapping out messages in swing-rhythmed code. They are a single entity, moving in perfect syncopation and balance, sensuously involved in each other and the throbbing of the already familiar Cole Porter melody. It is a number that almost forty years later still seems electrifying. It was used almost in its entirety to illustrate Astaire's (and Powell's) dancing magnetism in the film *That's Entertainment* (1974). It is also a beautiful example of two great tap dancers performing magnificently without heavy reliance on gala sets, costumes, or dozens of chorus girls.

Juliette Friedgen

BROKEN ARROW

Released: 1950
Production: Julian Blaustein for Twentieth Century-Fox
Direction: Delmer Daves
Screenplay: Michael Blankfort; based on the novel *Blood Brother* by Elliott Arnold
Cinematography: Ernest Palmer
Editing: J. Watson Webb, Jr.
Running time: 93 minutes

Principal characters:
Tom Jeffords	James Stewart
Cochise	Jeff Chandler
Sonseeahray	Debra Paget
Slade	Will Geer
General Howard	Basil Ruysdael

Broken Arrow is the first of a cycle of Western films that appeared during the 1950's in which previously employed caricatures of Native Americans were discarded. The Indians here are depicted as intelligent men with a culture of their own which is as worthy of respect as that of the whites. Every aspect of this beautifully produced film, from the glorious Technicolor cinematography to the poetic dialogue, is designed to be an expression of the humanistic concerns of the filmmaker. Though attacked in its time for being condescending to the Indians by portraying them as more than perfect men, *Broken Arrow* honors the American cinema and is a harbinger of the great reexamination of the racial question which preoccupied the nation over the next two decades. It is a plea for love and understanding between peoples, as well as a cry of despair for a world which leaves little room for such feelings.

The story is set in 1871, ten years after the beginning of a war between the United States and the Apache nation which has been punctuated by immense atrocities on both sides. The narrator is Tom Jeffords (James Stewart), a former army officer and prospector who is en route to Tucson to act as a scout for the military. In the Arizona desert he encounters a wounded Apache adolescent whose life he saves. They spend several days together while the boy recuperates, and when they are discovered by an Apache war party, the boy talks them into sparing Jeffords' life. Nonetheless, Jeffords is tied to a tree and forced to watch them ambush a party of prospectors who have intruded on Indian territory. Some of the survivors are tortured to death after Apache scalps are found in their possession.

This prelude sets the tone for the film. Jeffords informs us in his narration that everything we see in the picture will be just as it happened, except that the Indians will speak English "so that you can understand them." Thus the dialogue in most scenes involving characters of different races is extremely simple, with few words of more than two syllables, to emphasize the fact that the audience is hearing a translation. The invocation of reason, not passion, in interracial relations, and the need for empathy between people of different cultures, is beautifully demonstrated by this opening sequence. The example of every individual motivated by courage and honesty is needed to put an end to the senseless killing which pollutes the inspiring landscapes of the film. Jeffords tells the Indians he would kill an Apache only in battle, not for the bounty his scalp would bring. In turn, they let him live out of respect for his mercy to the boy.

Jeffords arrives in Tucson where he discovers that a survivor of the ambush he witnessed is staying at his rooming house. At the dinner table one evening, the man makes exaggerated claims about the number of Indians he killed in the attack, though in reality there were only five or six Apaches involved in the fight. When Jeffords attempts to set the record straight, he only arouses the suspicions of the townspeople, who wonder at the fact that he lived through Indian captivity. Jeffords is shown in this instance and throughout the film as being exceptional in his ability to relate to both races. He treats the Indians with the same respect he offers whites. Yet the fact that he does not share the prejudices of his own people sets him apart. They consider the Indians to be savages, little better than wild animals, and have never attempted to understand their motivations or, in fact, to realize that they have minds like other men.

Jeffords declines the army's offer of a job as a scout, instead hiring an Apache to teach him not only the language, but also the folklore and customs of the tribe. Armed with this knowledge, he sends smoke signals to Cochise (Jeff Chandler), chief of the Apache, and sets off alone to visit his stronghold. In spite of the poor record of whites in honoring previous treaties, he talks Cochise into accepting a temporary truce of a sort: the Indians will allow mail riders to pass through their territory unmolested. The two men hope that if this small step proves viable, it will lead to a comprehensive peace treaty.

When he announces this accomplishment to the people of Tucson, they are skeptical and place bets as to the outcome of this small glimmer of hope that has been offered them. Several riders arrive unharmed, but when Cochise's warriors attack and destroy a wagon train, the townspeople turn on Jeffords and are about to lynch him. He is saved only through the intervention of the newly arrived General Howard (Basil Ruysdael). The General has been sent to Arizona by President Grant to attempt to arrange a treaty with Cochise. Jeffords agrees to take him to the Indian camp. Howard is presented in the film as an evangelical Christian—"Bible-reading Howard," they call him—who wants to extend Christian principles to the Indians.

During his first visit to the camp of the Apache, Jeffords also meets the maiden Sonseeahray (Debra Paget). He asks her to marry him when he meets her a second time. This is the ultimate expression of his belief that there must be peace between the races. Although this element of the plot has been criticized as being just another formula love story put in by the studio to provide a role for a rising young starlet, it becomes much more in the hands of director Delmer Daves. The importance which Daves gives to the love relationships in his films sets him apart from other directors of the period. His love stories contain a lyricism best exemplified by the ending he gave his 1947 film *Dark Passage*, in which lovers Humphrey Bogart and Lauren Bacall are reunited by having her simply walk into a nightclub in Peru where he waits. As the band strikes up the melody associated with their love affair, they silently begin dancing, erasing with this gesture the fact that he is a fugitive from a murder charge in the United States.

Since the dialogue in *Broken Arrow* is extemely stylized, it lends a certain poetic cadence to the love scenes which makes them unique. The lovers' words to each other are simple and direct, spoken honestly and with feeling by Debra Paget and Jimmy Stewart. The wedding scene, in which they mingle their blood and ride off on white horses, is mysterious and poignant. Their honeymoon in the wilderness is a beautiful expression of the strength they gain through their love. The issue of the authenticity of the ceremony in terms of actual Indian practices is not really relevant here. The sequences must be taken as a poetic expression of emotions between two people who have made their own rules about love.

The meeting between Cochise and General Howard results in a ninety-day armistice, attached to a promise concerning the establishment of a homeland for the Apache nation. Dissident Indians led by Geronimo leave the Indian encampment to continue the war against the whites. But Cochise has decided that it is unrealistic for the tribe to continue a fight in which they are so hopelessly outnumbered.

As a historical fact, this treaty led the way to the destruction of the Apache way of life. Daves does not deal with this unpleasant reality in the film, however. He concludes with a sequence in which dissident whites set up an ambush for Cochise and Jeffords. Interestingly, their leader Slade is played by Will Geer, in a role which resembles a preliminary sketch of the racist sheriff he would play in the classic *Salt of the Earth* three years later. During the skirmish, Sonseeahray is killed defending the wounded Jeffords, when she grabs his knife and charges at the gun-toting whites. When Jeffords regains consciousness, he wants to slit the throat of the one member of the ambush gang who has been captured; but Cochise insists that the man be turned over to the justice of the whites, as provided for in the armistice agreement. After a few pious words about how Sonseeahray's death has united the two sides in a determination to make the truce work, the film closes with a shot of Jeffords riding off alone into the wilderness. His voice-over narration says that the memory of his wife will live with him forever.

There is a lack of real resolution to the ending of the story. Even so, the greatness of *Broken Arrow* lies in its beautiful presentation of the nature of love between people and races.

Rodger Nadelman

BUCK PRIVATES

Released: 1941
Production: Alex Gottlieb for Universal
Direction: Arthur Lubin
Screenplay: Arthur T. Horman, with special material written for Abbott and Costello by John Grant
Cinematography: Milton Krasner
Editing: Philip Cahn
Running time: 82 minutes

Principal characters:
Slicker Smith	Bud Abbott
Herbie Brown	Lou Costello
The Andrews Sisters	Themselves
Randolph Parker III	Lee Bowman
Bob Martin	Alan Curtis
Judy Gray	Jane Frazee
Sergeant Michael Collins	Nat Pendleton

Buck Privates was not Bud Abbott and Lou Costello's first film together: they had appeared briefly in a film entitled *One Night in the Tropics* in 1940. Nevertheless, it was the first film produced and written entirely for them, and it was the film that made them stars. To say that the film was a success would be an understatement; it eventually grossed four million dollars, making it Universal's biggest money-maker to that date, and establishing Abbott and Costello as the third-ranking box-office attraction of the year.

In any Abbott and Costello film the story is merely a device to support their comedy routines, and *Buck Privates* is no exception. In this story, Abbott and Costello play Slicker Smith and Herbie Brown, respectively, two street merchants who hustle dollar neckties. A tough cop, Michael Collins (Nat Pendleton), not one to appreciate their efforts to make an honest buck, chases them off the street into an army recruiting center which they mistakenly believe is a movie theater. Before they can order their popcorn they have enlisted, thinking they are signing up for a raffle.

Unfortunately, Universal was not particularly confident of the pair's ability to sustain an entire feature with their comedy, so a romantic story line was introduced to supplement the comedy routines. Randolph Parker III (Lee Bowman) gets drafted into the same regiment with his former chauffeur Bob Martin (Alan Curtis). Parker figures that his connections on the outside will soon free him of this slight inconvenience, but his plans change after he meets pretty army hostess Judy Gray (Jane Frazee). Unfortunately, his ex-chauffeur has also met Judy, and the two men become embroiled in a fight for her affections. The army, however, proves to be the great equalizer; Parker eventually becomes a hero and the two men become friends by the end of the film.

Universal also decided that the film could use some music, and wisely chose the Andrews Sisters. The film provided the trio with three of their most famous hits, "Boogie Woogie Bugle Boy," "I'll Be with You in Apple Blossom Time" and "You're a Lucky Fellow, Mr. Smith." A specialty number performed by Costello called "When Private Brown Becomes a Captain" is also quite good.

Nonetheless, it was Abbott and Costello and their style of comedy which made *Buck Privates* a hit. Even so, the material was not really fresh; all the routines and jokes came from old vaudeville material which had been passed on from one entertainer to the next for years. The success of the script lay in the fact that it provided Abbott and Costello with ample opportunities for ad-libbing, a practice so prevalent that director Arthur Lubin claims never to have witnessed a scene performed the same way twice. Costello would constantly toss out *non sequiturs* in an effort to throw Abbott off. Such is the case in the dice game scene when Costello suddenly says, for no apparent reason, "Starting Tuesday I'm going out with girls," to which Abbott calmly responds "I don't blame you." Or in the drill scene when Costello turns to Abbott and asks "What time is it?" and Abbott shouts back "None of your business!" Yet it was not so much what the two said, as how they said it. Abbott was an exceptional straight man whose timing provided Costello with the perfect foil for his lines and antics. Costello, on the other hand, had an incredibly cherubic face which made him seem even more innocent and vulnerable than his lines and actions suggested.

As the years passed, Abbott and Costello became bored with moviemaking; once the routines, gags, skits, and lines were all memorized and down pat, much of the challenge was gone. As a result, many of their later films lacked the energy and enthusiasm so evident in *Buck Privates*. Nevertheless, in 1941 there was an entire generation which was unfamiliar with the old treasures of vaudeville; to them, the routines were fresh and funny, and the humor was simple and uncomplicated. Abbott and Costello were not cerebral comics: their comedy was fast and physical. If Abbott was hard to understand, it was because he was supposed to be; the audience could always depend on Costello to be just a little bit slower than they were. He captured audience's sympathies by making them feel secure; his frustrations were their frustrations, and audiences loved him. Costello was a child released into a world of grown-ups; adults felt protective of him, and children identified with him.

However, from time to time, it was Costello who seemed in control of the world around him. He knew how to use his apparent naïveté and innocence to hide the imp within him. This is well demonstrated in a scene from *Buck Privates* in which he stumbles onto a crap game while riding the troop train. Claiming never to have played the game before, he asks Abbott to teach him how to play. Believing he has a real "sucker" in tow and eager to relieve Costello of his pay, Abbott agrees to show him how to play the game. Costello, however, soon begins to show a great deal of knowledge of the game, using such gambling slang as "Fade that" and "Let it ride." He is also winning, much to the chagrin of Abbott, who repeatedly asks, "You sure you never played this game before?"

Recognizing the potential of Abbott and Costello demonstrated in this film, Universal set out to exploit them to the fullest. In their first year, they made five features: *Buck Privates*, *Hold That Ghost*, *In the Navy*, *Ride 'Em Cowboy* and *Keep 'Em Flying*, all directed by Arthur Lubin. The energy demonstrated in these early films was never equaled in the films that followed. The team remained popular and occasionally produced an entertaining film like *Abbott and Costello Meet Frankenstein* (1948) and *The Time of Their Lives* (1946), but on the whole, the quality of their product diminished over the years as they duplicated routines and performed them with more proficiency than love.

In retrospect, it is easy to understand why Abbott and Costello became so popular. By 1941, the Marx Brothers were fading, and Laurel and Hardy were long past their prime. There were no other comedy teams to fill the gap. Furthermore, the country was coming out of the Depression and war was looming. Audiences were eager for something light to take their minds off their troubles. Abbott and Costello were perfect: simple but direct, light but energetic.

Critics and historians have not been overly kind to Abbott and Costello. For the most part they have been either overlooked or passed off as a wartime diversion. Nonetheless, their popularity was unmistakable and their influence on the country was remarkable. During the 1940's they were the kings of comedy, and *Buck Privates* is an excellent example of their talent.

James J. Desmarais

BULLITT

Released: 1968
Production: Philip D'Antoni for Solar Productions; released by Warner Bros.
Direction: Peter Yates
Screenplay: Alan R. Trustman and Harry Kleiner; based on the novel *Mute Witness* by Robert L. Pike
Cinematography: William A. Fraker
Editing: Frank P. Keller (AA)
Running time: 114 minutes

Principal characters:

Frank Bullitt	Steve McQueen
Walter Chalmers	Robert Vaughn
Cathy	Jacqueline Bisset
Delgetti	Don Gordon
Weissberg	Robert Duvall
Captain Bennett	Simon Oakland
Captain Baker	Norman Fell
Dr. Willard	Georg Stanford Brown
Renick	Felice Orlandi
Johnny Ross	Pat Renella

In 1967, British filmmaker Peter Yates directed a picture based on the much-publicized hijacking of a London night-mail train, a daring theft which had netted its participants more than two million pounds in 1963. Entitled *Robbery*, the film was a tense, action-filled, yet only partially satisfying melodrama that was greeted with universal indifference by audiences on both sides of the Atlantic. Fortunately for Yates, however, one man was impressed enough by *Robbery*'s spine-tingling auto chases to ask the thirty-eight-year-old Englishman to guide his next project, a detective-thriller based on Robert Pike's best-selling novel, *Mute Witness*.

In 1968, Steve McQueen was one of the screen's foremost stars. His prominent position in the motion picture industry had allowed him a degree of freedom reserved for Hollywood's elite and had even enabled him to form his own production company, Solar Productions. McQueen brought Yates to the United States to direct the adaptation of *Mute Witness*, and the resulting film, *Bullitt*, was released to great acclaim. *Bullitt* further solidified McQueen's screen *persona* and commercial stature, while establishing Peter Yates as an action-adventure director of international caliber.

As he was a director unknown to American audiences, Yates correctly surmised that he would have to make *Bullitt*, given its conventional story line and familiar character types, a thoroughly distinctive motion picture. Consequently, he decided to film entirely on location in San Francisco, using the bay city's picturesque streets in such a way as to make the city itself become an essential character, a vital participant in the action taking place within its bounds. In addition, Yates felt that by taking to the streets he could effectively use the thriller format to convey his own impressions of the United States; to bring the detective genre up to date; and, most significantly, to assure that *Bullitt* would possess a realistic veneer that would set the film apart from the dozens of cop and private-eye programs which dominated America's television screens at the time.

Bullitt's complicated plot starts to unravel in the film's dazzling opening credit sequence. Here Yates creates a brilliant series of images orchestrated by a jazzy music track that gives the viewer the impression of having seen something quite significant without knowing exactly what has taken place. It is not until much later that the implications outlined in these opening minutes become clear.

The story begins in Chicago where a group of Mafia killers are trying to murder mob figure Johnny Ross (Pat Renella). As they break into his office, Ross delays them with a smoke bomb and makes his getaway with his brother's assistance. After Ross's car careens out of an underground garage amid a hail of bullets, his brother returns to his henchmen, contritely phones in to report their failure, and agrees to continue pursuit. This sequence is paced at lightning speed, followed by the film's credits zooming up to display the next image as the previous one fades away.

The scene then shifts to San Francisco. Ross has made good his escape after having defrauded his former associates out of two million dollars. He has also, oddly enough, agreed to testify before a Senate subcommittee headed by an ambitious, calculating politician named Walter Chalmers (Robert Vaughn). At Chalmers' request, Detective Lieutenant Frank Bullitt (Steve McQueen) is assigned to protect Ross, who has holed-up in a skid-row hotel. Before long, however, two gunmen manage to enter his room (with some ambiguous aid from Ross himself), and seriously wound the gangster with a shotgun blast in the chest. Ross dies later that evening and Bullitt persuades the attending physician (Georg Stanford Brown) to conceal the death, thus enabling the detective to investigate the case in his own fashion. Although Bullitt is now under great pressure from Chalmers to account for the shooting, he brushes the politician off, warning him to stay out of the way and let him do his job as he sees fit.

Bullitt soon encounters Ross's killers, and in the high-speed car chase that follows, his skillful driving causes the gangsters to crash into a gas station pump; they are burned beyond recognition. Despite the objections of his girl friend, Cathy (Jacqueline Bisset), the anxious concern of his superiors, and Chalmers' constant badgering, Bullitt retraces Ross's movements. He soon learns that the dead man was merely a decoy planted by Ross and his friends, and that the real Ross plans to leave the country under an assumed name with the money he stole from the mob. Bullitt traces a phone call placed by the phony Ross to a San Mateo motel, but arrives there only to find a murdered woman and $30,000 in traveler's checks made out to Albert and Dorothy Renick. Bullitt concludes that Ross had set the Renicks up, had them killed, and now has booked a seat on a night flight out of the country in the dead man's name. He speeds to the airport and chases Ross from his departing plane and onto the runway. Another harrowing chase ensues, this time around and under rumbling airliners on the tarmac. Ross finally runs into the terminal, and there, amid hundreds of terrified travelers, he is gunned down by the persistent police detective.

As laid out in the above paragraphs, *Bullitt*'s story line is strictly conventional, falling easily within the confines of the modern crime-detective genre. But what elevates *Bullitt* above the more routine films of its type is not that Yates has made a statement on the genre (for he has not), and not that the director and his screenwriters have significantly inverted standard genre elements (their alterations along this line are minimal). What makes *Bullitt* a unique and compelling visual experience is its marvelous pacing and editing, combined with William A. Fraker's wonderful cinematography. Every shot and cut is correctly placed. The overall effect is a story of heightening tensions that ranks in every way with the classics of the genre.

The heart of *Bullitt* is its spectacular car chase through San Francisco, a visual delight that places the viewer in the driver's seat, sweeping him along convoluted streets and towering hills, and careening through alleys at a furious pace. This chase is placed in the exact center of the film. Yates has prepared the viewer for it by developing the pent-up tension in Bullitt's character and by constantly providing scenes of cars driving through the city. The first shot after the credits is a bird's-eye view of a taxicab carrying Johnny Ross up a steep hill. After Ross/Renick dies in the hospital, Bullitt drives home in his sleek black Mustang, and the drive is dramatized by low camera angles. To replace the inevitable letdown after the conclusion of the chase, and to keep viewer interest up, Yates and his writers now begin the elaborate plot twists which maintain our interest in the action as it winds toward its bloody conclusion. The film becomes a series of sharp climaxes carefully spaced by informational scenes which enable the viewer to draw momentary breaths.

Yates reveals a fine eye for detail and an ability to use locations effectively. To one familiar with San Francisco, *Bullitt* often takes on the appearance of a travelogue. The famous landmarks which figure throughout—from the Golden Gate Bridge to North Beach's striptease clubs—all remind the viewer that he is watching a true-to-life story being played out in real settings.

The director's documentary style is further enhanced by Fraker's camerawork, which often appears haphazard and hand-held. Scenes of hospital operating rooms, police procedures, modern machinery in action, and coroners' techniques are depicted with an unemotional detachment that deromanticizes rather than sentimentalizes. Bullitt's world is not a pretty one, and the viewer is forced to confront his seedy environment at every turn. Yates refuses to cut away from the gruesome scenes and the dull routines of those who trade in death, always making the viewer see more than he would ordinarily desire. Except for the action scenes, which are tightly cut, the film has a loose quality not normally associated with others of its type. By allowing scenes to run longer than usual, Yates is playing with the rules of the genre, subverting our expectations ever so slightly.

Bullitt is filled with in-jokes and instances of black humor which can slip by an unsuspecting viewer. When Bullitt meets an informant in front of Enrico's North Beach restaurant, a sign on an adjoining building announces it to be "The Galaxy Club . . . Where The Stars Meet." An ambulance bears the notice "SPEED KILLS," which is visible just as the race to the hospital begins. After Chalmers berates Bullitt for allowing Ross to die, he climbs into his limousine which is emblazened with a bumper sticker that reads, "Support Your Local Police."

The actors' performances are first-rate. McQueen plays his role with an ease that is deceptively casual. He performed all of his own stunts, including lying under a jet airliner as it taxied down the runway. Yates, however, was taking no chances when it came to the car chase. Although his star was to do the driving, the director cautiously decided to film that dangerous sequence only after everything else was completed.

The secondary performances are, on the whole, quite well played. Robert Vaughn sweeps through *Bullitt* with an icy assurance that has a decidedly gangsterlike tone. Don Gordon works admirably to make believable the thankless role of Delgetti, foil to Bullitt's hero. Only Jacqueline Bisset seems inadequate here, not because of her acting ability but because her part is superfluous. Bisset's only major scene, one in which she chastizes Bullitt for remaining in his dirty world, seems ridiculous, and one senses that no actress could have made it not seem so.

Bullitt is more than merely a conventional genre film. Although every essential element is present—the steely-eyed professional cop, the ambitious politician, the long-suffering girl friend, the helpless superiors, the brutal violence, and senseless death—these components are glued together by a beautifully integrated combination of adventurous cinematography, precise editing, restrained performances, a good script, and finely crafted direction to make *Bullitt* one of the finest detective-thriller films America has yet produced.

Daniel Einstein

BUS STOP

Released: 1956
Production: Buddy Adler for Twentieth Century-Fox
Direction: Joshua Logan
Screenplay: George Axelrod; based on the play of the same name by William
    Inge
Cinematography: Milton Krasner
Editing: William Reynolds
Music: Alfred Newman and Cyril J. Mockridge
Running time: 96 minutes

> *Principal characters:*
> Cherie .... Marilyn Monroe
> Bo Decker .... Don Murray
> Virgil "Virge" Blessing .... Arthur O'Connell
> Elma Duckworth .... Hope Lange
> Vera .... Eileen Heckart
> Grace .... Betty Field
> Carl .... Robert Bray

Bus Stop marked a turning point in Marilyn Monroe's career. Released on
August 31, 1956, it terminated her fourteen-month absence from films, and
signified the beginning of her greater control over her material as Marilyn
Monroe, Inc. The year away from Hollywood not only saw her relationship
with Arthur Miller develop, but more important professionally, it gave her
a chance to work at the Actors Studio with Lee Strasberg. Early in her career
critics had commented favorably on her acting, but as she evolved into a sex
goddess, they became increasingly skeptical. With *Bus Stop*, however, Monroe emerged unquestionably as an actress of great talent, though some reviewers acknowledged the fact grudgingly, if at all.

Bosley Crowther, reviewing the film in the *New York Times*, commented
that Monroe "finally proved herself an actress"; and Arthur Knight in *Saturday Review* went even further, stating that her performance in *Bus Stop*
"effectively dispels once and for all the notion that she is merely a glamour
personality." But in other reviews the patronizing, sexist bias with which
many viewed her attempts to establish herself as a serious actress is evident.
Tom Armstrong, reviewing *Will Acting Spoil Marilyn Monroe?* in the *Hollywood Reporter*, preferred the sex goddess, saying that "If Marilyn, the
mortal girl, wishes to learn to act for her own extra-mural amusement, that
is her privilege." And *Life*, though praising her acting, reassured moviegoers
that "as soon as she steps through the beaded curtain of a Phoenix honky-
tonk in Twentieth Century-Fox's *Bus Stop*, it becomes evident that all this
intellectual activity has done Marilyn absolutely no harm whatsoever."

Interestingly, though some commented that she was perfectly cast, there was little or no comment that she had been "typecast" as Cherie, though the character has much in common with her own. Briefly, *Bus Stop* concerns the efforts of a rambunctious cowboy, Bo Decker (Don Murray), fresh off the ranch and unused to civilized company, to find a girl, an "angel," to accompany him back to his ranch in Montana. The "angel," of course, is Monroe, a "chantooze" named Cherie, or "Cherry," as Bo persists in calling her, a singer and a hustler of drinks at a cheap Phoenix bar. Cherie, seeking from a man not only "all the lovin' part" but also respect, fights desperately throughout the film to maintain her self-respect and dignity.

Under Joshua Logan's expert direction, Monroe gave a performance of great sensitivity and range. Logan, in fact, compared her facial expressiveness to that of Garbo, and her ability to play the tragicomic to that of Chaplin— high praise indeed. Logan also gave her credit, according to Maurice Zolotow, for the basic interpretation of Cherie. Logan, in addition to having directed William Inge's *Picnic* for the screen the year before, was a friend of Lee Strasberg's and had studied with Stanislavsky in Moscow, and was therefore sympathetic to the way Monroe approached the role.

George Axelrod's script improved vastly upon the original, which now seems somewhat pedestrian and dated, though it was a Broadway hit just before it was filmed. Axelrod's approach was to open up William Inge's play considerably, and, more importantly, to strip away nonessentials in order to focus on the two principals. Inge's original version took place entirely in the bus stop itself, where a group of passengers comprising Bo, his sidekick Virgil Blessing, a drunken English professor, Cherie, and Carl, the bus driver are stranded in a blizzard. Also present are Grace, the owner of the bus stop, Elma Duckworth, the waitress, and the sheriff. Cherie and Bo's meeting is narrated rather than seen, and there is a rather tasteless subplot regarding Elma and the professor, a lecherous Vitamin Flintheart caricature of an academic. Axelrod dropped the professor and the sheriff and added two children who are being sent to their grandmother's. They are equally obnoxious but fortunately less in evidence. He also added Vera, a waitress in the Blue Dragon Cafe, who is Cherie's confidante.

The result is a lively script which shows us Bo Decker from the moment he leaves his ranch for the rodeo. It was Don Murray's first leading role. From the very opening, when we see Bo practicing for the rodeo, up to the conclusion, the character's physical strength, his ego, his brashness, and his appealing naïveté, are powerfully expressed. From the moment Bo boards the bus, oblivious to the needs and feelings of anyone else, it is clear that he has a great deal to learn before he will successfully woo the "angel" he is determined to bring back from the Phoenix rodeo. There is a great deal of frontier humor in the film, based on the tall-tale, country-boy *versus* city-slicker motif. Bo is nearly run down because he ignores traffic signals; he luxuriates in the tub, taking a bath and a shower at the same time; and he interprets all of the television and magazine ads for preparing to go out with a girl literally, with painful results. There are, as well, some humorous glimpses of the "professional" cowboy on the rodeo circuit. Because the film was so much Monroe's, it is easy in retrospect to overlook the care the scriptwriter and director took in delineating Bo's character, and the skill with which Murray portrayed him.

Cherie is a waitress at the Blue Dragon, a cheap cafe where she sings, and more importantly, from the management's view, cons customers into buying her drinks of whiskey, which are in reality shot glasses of tea. Our first glimpse of her is through the eyes of Virge (Arthur O'Connell), who observes, from his hotel window, the manager berating her and treating her roughly. His sympathy changes to disgust when he meets her in the cafe, buys her a drink, and discovers that she is cheating him. Though he has the unsympathetic role of trying to keep Bo and Cherie apart, O'Connell brought his usual warmth and skill to his performance.

As she tells her friend and confidante, Vera (Eileen Heckart), about the fight with the manager, Cherie also reveals her plans to leave. Disgusted with being exploited and handled, and not being treated with the respect an "artist" deserves, she pulls out a map and shows Vera where she has come from— River Gulch, Missouri—and where she is going—Hollywood and Vine, the magical corner where everyone is "discovered." Her naïveté and a sort of innocence are a complement for Bo's similar traits.

Monroe chose her own costumes for the film, rejecting most of the first designs as too grandiose to suit the character. She selected the tawdry coat of lamé and monkey fur in which Cherie leaves the café. It resembles the one Kim Stanley wore in the original production, which Monroe studied. She also carefully ripped and mended the fishnet stockings in which Cherie appears for her big number, "That Old Black Magic." She imitates Hildegarde and many other torch singers in a performance that manages to be a very skillful burlesque of the style without becoming ridiculous enough to lose the appeal of the character. She is singing against the uproar of the crowd, who ignore her, and desperately kicking the switches of the spotlights for the effects when Bo bursts in with his friend Virge and quiets the crowd with some ear-splitting whistles and a few well-directed punches. He listens in rapt attention as she finishes the number.

From that point, over Virge's protests, Bo moves quickly. He invites Cherie to go outside with him, or rather, insists that she go, and they quickly progress to their first kiss. Bo assumes that this means they are to be married, but Cherie does not share his assumption, and Virge is only too willing to help her get away from his friend. But Bo, hauling her out of bed at nine o'clock the next morning (an unheard-of hour for Cherie), insists on taking her to breakfast and the rodeo. The scene in her bedroom, which Monroe played nude under the sheet, was a daring one for the 1950's, and left the impression that there was much more between them than a single kiss.

Night is Cherie's element, as day is Bo's. For breakfast, Bo orders raw hamburgers, and Cherie, with a shudder, black coffee. Monroe's makeup, giving her a marvelous pallor that suggests that she is totally a creature of the evening, was one thing a number of critics disliked or found somewhat exaggerated. But the effect works. So does the contrast of Monroe's fragility to Murray's strong, healthy vitality, as he easily places her up on his shoulder to watch the parade. As she watches Bo's prowess at the rodeo, she discovers a grudging admiration for him; but she panics when she realizes that he means to marry her that afternoon, and she tries to flee. She almost gets away, but stops with a pathetic eagerness to pose for a team of *Life* photographers covering the rodeo, who catch her in an unflattering pose. Back at the cafe, Virge gives her bus fare to Los Angeles, but Bo follows her to the bus station. Just as she is about to make her escape to Hollywood and Vine, he ropes her and forces her onto the bus to Montana with him and Virge.

From there, things move predictably to the end. Elma, the waitress (Hope Lange), returning from a weekend in the city, and two children are the only other passengers remaining as they approach a bus stop somewhere in the mountains. Cherie, in a wistful monologue, explains to Elma what she is looking for in a man. Beyond the bus stop, however, the road is impassable because of a blizzard and the bus must halt. Cherie seizes the opportunity to enlist the help of Elma and of Carl, the bus driver (Robert Bray), to escape from Bo. She also finds a sympathetic ally in Virge, who by this time is completely disgusted with Bo's behavior. Carl gives Bo the beating of his life, egged on by Virge and cheered by Grace, the bus stop owner (Betty Field). The scene is beautifully filmed in what is obviously good genuine snow (Sun Valley location). Jokingly referred to as the longest fight sequence ever filmed, the shooting occupied two days while Monroe was in the hospital with bronchitis.

Humiliated, Bo is forced to apologize to all concerned, and in apologizing to Cherie, he wins for the first time her grudging respect and admiration. Shamefaced, he asks to kiss her goodbye. In this kiss their love and its essential innocence is evident. They reconcile and Virge gives them a paternal blessing, having finally realized that it is now a case of Bo having to prove he is good enough for Cherie rather than the other way around.

As Cherie and Bo again board the bus for Montana, he steps back to allow her to get on first, and realizing that she must be freezing in her thin coat, offers her his heavy coat with the sheepskin collar. The blissfully ecstatic look on Monroe's face as she snuggles into the heavy coat, rubbing her face against the wooly fur almost as though she were making love to it, reveals a glimpse of the Monroe image, a bit out of character for Cherie and the relationship she has established with Bo, but possibly considered necessary by director

Logan. Virge bids the two good-bye, and Bo, in a brief relapse, tries to force him to stay with them; but Cherie helps him to see Virge's point of view. Bo is grown up now, and no longer needs his friend.

The film has a folk quality, reinforced by the musical score of Alfred Newman and Cyril J. Mockridge, which exploits the possibilities of Virge's guitar, Monroe's singing, and also effectively uses "Paper of Pins" at the opening to state subtly the theme of the story. The location and setting are authentic. The rodeo scenes were filmed during a Phoenix rodeo, the hotel is suitably unpretentious as is the bus stop, and the Blue Dragon is the ultimate cheap bar—claustrophobic, dark, hazy with smoke and alcohol. These elements, as well as possibly the best performances of Monroe's and Murray's careers, make *Bus Stop* a minor classic.

Katharine M. Morsberger

BUTCH CASSIDY AND THE SUNDANCE KID

Released: 1969
Production: John Foreman for Twentieth Century-Fox
Direction: George Roy Hill
Screenplay: William Goldman (AA)
Cinematography: Conrad Hall (AA)
Editing: John C. Howard and Richard C. Meyer
Art direction: Jack Martin Smith and Phillip Jeffries; set decoration, Walter M. Scott and Chester L. Bayhi
Costume design: Edith Head
Sound: William E. Edmondson and David E. Dockendorf
Music: Burt Bacharach (AA)
Song: Burt Bacharach and Hal David, "Raindrops Keep Fallin' on My Head" (AA)
Running time: 112 minutes

Principal characters:
Butch Cassidy	Paul Newman
The Sundance Kid	Robert Redford
Etta Place	Katharine Ross
Bike Salesman	Henry Jones
Sheriff Bledsoe	Jeff Corey
Woodcock	George Furth
Agnes	Cloris Leachman
Harvey Logan	Ted Cassidy
Marshal	Kenneth Mars

Butch Cassidy and the Sundance Kid is a whimsical Western based on the purportedly true daring adventures of outlaws Robert LeRoy Parker, known as "Butch Cassidy," and Harry Longbaugh, known as "The Sundance Kid." The colorful duo flourished at the turn of the century, years after such notorious desperadoes as Jessie James and his brother Frank; thus they were the last in the tradition of highwaymen and bank and train robbers. Their mode of life, in fact, had already become preposterous, an anachronism in the twentieth century. The film is a high-spirited comedy-drama which presents a strange mixture of the present and the past: the hero-bandits' historic misadventures are conveyed in a joyous contemporary spirit, reflected in the comedy, the characterizations, the bantering dialogue, the music, and the cinematic effects.

Sundance (Robert Redford) is a conventional Western character—a cardsharp, a wanderer, and a killer if necessary. Although we discover that he is deathly afraid to swim, he is nevertheless depicted as the strong and silent sort. Butch Cassidy (Paul Newman), on the other hand, is a modern, spunky, talkative romantic. Both men are engaging, appealing criminals; and Butch's quixotic notions are balanced by Sundance's earthbound realism.

The film is set around 1905 to 1909. It opens with a film within a film; on a small black-and-white screen, like an old silent flicker, we see a (simulated) newsreel, circa 1905, of the outlaws' criminal team. "The Wild Bunch," also known as "The Hole in the Wall Gang," are seen holding up a train. Already, Butch and Sundance are fabled, legends living in their own time.

After spending time in Macon's saloon, Butch and Sundance ride back to their lair amidst the rugged hills. As Butch exclaims of their hideout, "Y'know, everytime I see 'Hole in the Wall' again, it's like seeing it fresh for the very first time, and whenever that happens, I ask myself the same question, 'How can I be so damn stupid as to keep coming back here?'"

Quickly suppressing the brief uprising of one of their gang members, Harvey Logan (Ted Cassidy), the two then come up with an audacious method of train robbery. They plan to overtake the Union Pacific Railroad twice—once on the going trip and once on the return trip. They expect the railroad to be shipping back large sums of money since they reason that the railroad authorities will not suspect robbers to be so ingenious as to plan a second hold-up.

The first train hold-up is a success, and while Butch takes time off to visit his favorite brothel, Sundance spends time with his renegade schoolteacher girl friend, hot-blooded Etta Place (Katharine Ross). The second robbery, however, is not so successful. The railroad president has anticipated another hold-up, and following the train, a second locomotive arrives with a boxcar loaded with horses and a posse. Using all their wiles and attempting to avoid capture, Butch and Sundance take an enormous leap from a high cliff into the raging mountain stream below.

With the help of Etta, who teaches them phonetic Spanish, the two decide to go to Bolivia, where the silver, tin, and gold mines make for better picking. Though Etta refuses to remain with them there as she feels they will be killed, the two, for a while, attempt to reform. But their legitimate posts as payroll guards are thwarted when Bolivian bandits attempt to rob them. For the first time in his life, Butch is forced to kill; the two conclude that the past is irrevocable and they take off with the money.

Though they have several successful heists, they also have problems with language and unfamiliar terrain. Ambushed by Bolivian soldiers, the two find themselves cornered in a small stucco structure. The badly wounded but ever-optimistic Butch buoyantly talks about starting a new life in Australia. With this fantasy of new capers in mind and unaware that the entire Bolivian cavalry awaits them outside, Butch and Sundance rush out of the building, only to face an onrushing barrage of bullets.

We never see the likable criminals die, however. With one of the most appropriate uses of the final freeze-frame since Truffaut's *The 400 Blows* (1959), and at the same time reminiscent of a similar scene in Arthur Penn's

Bonnie and Clyde (1967), the camera captures the men's last bravura moments; the action is frozen into a photograph and the color is drained to look like an antiquated sepia still. Rather than witness their deaths, the legend is preserved for the audience.

Directed with great flair, George Roy Hill's film is not a traditional Western. Instead, the genre is turned upside down, and what results is an easygoing film full of reversals, twists, and revisions of the classic Western clichés, such as when the inept train robbers dynamite the loot and the boxcar along with the safe, or the picture of the old prospector who cannot spit straight. Unlike the mythologized Westerns of the past, such as those of John Ford, *Butch Cassidy and the Sundance Kid* does not idealize; unlike the harsh, violent Westerns of the present, such as those of Sam Peckinpah, it is not overly cynical either. With comic realism, the film presents social misfits who do not mean any harm; because of their innate humanity and goodwill, we not only forgive their criminal actions, but end up rooting for them as well.

The spontaneity and freshness of the film is immensely enhanced by its musical score. One example is the scene (which does not advance the plot, but is included for its own intrinsic charm) in which a carefree Butch and Etta try out a new-fangled bicycle in an idyllic woody area; underscoring the feeling of celebration is the lazy Bacharach/David pop tune "Raindrops Keep Fallin' on My Head," sung by B. J. Thomas. Another example occurs when Butch, Etta, and Sundance, on their way to take the boat to Bolivia, spend time in New York. As we watch a series of fast, amusing green-gold tinted period stills of old-time Manhattan and Coney Island, the light and lilting music adds to the mood, blending perfectly with Conrad Hall's cinematography with its luxurious landscapes filled with lush colors and sunlight.

The endearing chemistry of Redford and Newman creates much of the fun. One of many male "buddy films" made in 1969-1970 (among them *Easy Rider*, *M*A*S*H*, and *Midnight Cowboy*), *Butch Cassidy and the Sundance Kid* (as well as George Roy Hill's later movie *The Sting*, 1973) makes wonderful use of the two actors' boyish charms, as both Redford and Newman bring a suave and twinkling urbanity to the wild and wicked West.

Leslie Taubman

CABARET

Released: 1972
Production: Cy Feuer for Allied Artists
Direction: Bob Fosse (AA)
Screenplay: Jay Presson Allen; based on the musical play of the same name
  by Joe Masterhoff, adapted from the play *I Am a Camera* by John Van
  Druten
Cinematography: Geoffrey Unsworth (AA)
Editing: David Bretherton (AA)
Art direction: Jurgen Kiebach and Rolf Zehetbauer (AA); set decoration,
  Herbert Strabel (AA)
Costume design: Charlotte Flemming
Music direction: Ralph Burns (AA)
Music: John Kander and Fred Ebb
Running time: 123 minutes

Principal characters:
Sally Bowles	Liza Minnelli (AA)
Brian Roberts	Michael York
Maximilian von Heune	Helmut Griem
Master of Ceremonies	Joel Grey (AA)
Fritz Wendel	Fritz Wepper
Natalia Landauer	Marisa Berenson
Fraulein Schneider	Elisabeth Neumann-Viertel

"Willkommen, bienvenue, welcome," invites the macabre, androgynous Master of Ceremonies (Joel Grey) of the Kit Kat Klub, beginning one of the most brilliant musicals ever made. Based upon Christopher Isherwood's Berlin stories, the play *I Am a Camera*, and the Broadway stage musical of the same name, *Cabaret*, shot on location in West Germany, is a perfect wedding of script, music, performances, and direction. No mere bit of superficial fluff, the film is an adult musical, a bawdy social commentary rich with psychological insight and thematic depth.

Like Vittorio DeSica's *The Garden of the Finzi-Continis* (1972) and Visconti's *The Damned* (1969), *Cabaret* deals with the psychology of a decaying society, 1930's pre-World War II Germany, at a time when the old order was being supplanted by the new, when the collapsing Weimar Republic was being replaced by the rising tide of Nazism. Set in Berlin, a hotbed of vice, depravity, and anti-Semitism, the electrifying musical drama revolves around the smoky, seedy, synthetically gay café, the Kit Kat Klub, which serves as a microcosm of Germany in transition. There, musical numbers are performed which, fully integrated into the story, ultimately reflect and reinforce events happening in the film.

A young, upright English language instructor and writer, Brian Roberts

(Michael York), arrives at the boardinghouse owned by Fraulein Schneider (Elizabeth Neumann-Viertel). There he meets the "divinely decadent" Sally Bowles (Liza Minnelli), his free-living-and-loving next-door neighbor who is an American singer at the Kit Kat Klub. After the two spend some happy time together, Sally is pleased with their relationship, despite Brian's homosexual past. Although Brian is well aware of the growing turmoil in Germany, the romantic and impractical Sally completely ignores it.

Entanglements ensue when the two meet the wealthy and handsome baron Maximilian von Heune (Helmut Griem). Following a weekend at Max's luxurious country mansion, tensions between Sally and Brian erupt as a result of the manipulative Max. After discussing the baron, Brian angrily shouts, "Screw Max." To which the hurt Sally retorts, "I do." With an ironic smile, Brian replies, "So do I." Soon after, Sally learns that she is pregnant, though she does not know if Brian or Max is the father. Though Brian volunteers to marry her, Sally realizes that it would be better for both of them if she got an abortion. Eventually, because of the decline of their relationship, and because the sweep of Nazism is more and more apparent, Brian decides it is time to leave Berlin and return once again to Britain.

Cabaret also has a subplot involving a romance between another couple. In the course of Brian's giving speech lessons, two of his pupils meet: Fritz Wendel (Fritz Wepper), a fortune hunter, and Natalia Landauer (Marisa Berenson), a beautiful Jewish young lady whose father owns the biggest department store in Berlin. In the course of the film, Fritz truly falls in love with Natalia and asks her to marry him; she declines, however, because she is Jewish and he is not. With Brian's prodding, Fritz is compelled to reveal the truth: he is Jewish, but because of the prevailing mood of anti-Semitism and his fear of persecution, he has chosen to hide his background and masquerade as an Aryan. When he explains this to Natalia, she decides to marry him.

The musical numbers performed in the Kit Kat Klub are marvelously staged and choreographed with dazzling inventiveness. The Master of Ceremonies opens the film with "Willkommen," as he tells the audience of lustful old men, frumpy middle-aged ladies, and pseudosophisticates, "Leave your troubles outside. So, life is disappointing? Forget it! In here, life is beautiful. The girls are beautiful. Even the orchestra is beautiful." We see, however, that the female musicians and dancers are sleazy, frizzy-haired, and overly painted; one of them is even a transvestite.

When Brian visits the cabaret early in the film, Sally describes the breaking-off of one of her madcap affairs with her song "Mein Herr," as if to let Brian know she is now available for him. Later, when the two become involved, the hopeful Sally sings "Maybe This Time"; and when the wealthy Max comes into their lives, Sally and the Master of Ceremonies perform a rousing rendition of "Money." As if to underline the relationship of Sally, Max, and

Brian, the Master of Ceremonies sings "Two Ladies"; then, to underscore the relationship between Fritz and Natalia, he also sings the satirical "If You Could See Her Through My Eyes," a mock love duet with a pink-tulled gorilla, suggesting that Jews are a subhuman species. At the end of the movie, when Brian leaves Berlin, he and Sally embrace for the last time; then we see Sally back at the nightclub singing the philosophical "Life Is a Cabaret."

Liza Minnelli is wonderful in the role of politically innocent Sally Bowles, the raffish spirit in the tatty kimono with green eyeshadow, green nail polish, false eyelashes, and red lipstick. Though seemingly an amoral character and a *femme fatale* with an oh-so-wicked surface, Minnelli projects the good-hearted innocence and vulnerability under Sally's worldly façade. Only twenty-five when she made the film, Liza Minnelli established herself as a major actress and star and a consummate professional—a vibrant and powerful deliverer of songs, a remarkable dancer, and an accomplished dramatic actress. The daughter of Judy Garland and director Vincente Minnelli, master of such film musicals as *Meet Me in St. Louis* (1944), *The Band Wagon* (1953), *An American in Paris* (1951), and *Gigi* (1958), Liza Minnelli manifests her show-business blood magnificently.

Michael York is superb as the blond, fresh-faced, slightly effete Brian; his character is believed to have been based upon Christopher Isherwood himself. An understated performer, he, too, projects a fully dimensioned character—intelligent and charming, wise and sad, fearful and strong, understanding and humane. Joel Grey, son of comedian Mickey Katz, re-creates his Tony Award-winning role of the diminutive, mocking, nasty, and slick Master of Ceremonies who introduces such tawdry acts as female wrestlers rolling in mud while a tuxedoed male entertainer in whiteface, dark lipstick, rouge, and slicked-down patent-leather hair comments on the story's action. Evil, leering, mischievous, sly, the sardonic and raucous Master of Ceremonies is decadence incarnate—a living symbol of Berlin in the 1930's.

Cinematically, the celebrated film is brilliantly innovative. Expressionistic in its distortions and exaggerations, *Cabaret*'s *mise-en-scène* is a perfect blend of acting, makeup, costume, setting, and lighting. With its garish colors and opulent sets, the glittering film is a visual feast. The use of editing is unusually imaginative. Inside the Kit Kat Klub in the glaring spotlight, the Master of Ceremonies and cabaret dancers are performing a musical Bavarian slap-dance; the overly lit stage is contrasted with the harsh brutality occuring in the darkened alleyway outside, where Nazi hoodlums are seen beating up the manager of the Kit Kat Klub because he has ejected them from the cabaret. At another time, Sally is onstage singing "Maybe This Time," and the number is juxtaposed with scenes of Brian and Sally making love.

One chilling use of camera movement occurs when Sally, Brian, and Max are visiting a country beer garden where a blond, angelic, and handsome youth sings "Tomorrow Belongs to Me." As the camera moves downward and his voice grows more strong, the audience sees that the youth is wearing a Nazi uniform and armband. As the camera moves back, we see more and more Nazis joining in the song, until the group is aroused and singing with militant fervor. The film's final cinematic frieze leaves us equally stunned. With the use of a distorted mirror device, the cabaret's audience sees itself, and soon, several Nazis, who were heretofore forbidden in the club, are also seen. The soft, menacing drum roll sounds and then ceases. The screen goes silent and black.

Cabaret is beautifully directed by Bob Fosse. Originally a Broadway and film choreographer for *Pajama Game* (1957) and *Damn Yankees* (1958), the extraordinarily talented Fosse has danced and acted; directed and choreographed the film adaptation of *Sweet Charity* (1969); and directed dramatic films such as *Lenny* (1974).

Although some may say the film has imperfections (the close physical resemblance between Helmut Griem and Fritz Wepper is confusing; the Freudian explanation of Sally's father's rejection of her causing her to be promiscuous is pat; the overwhelmingly talented Sally Bowles is too good for the third-rate Kit Kat Klub and therefore unbelievable), *Cabaret* is now considered a classic. A popular entertainment as well as innovative art, the film even initiated the revival of the American musical genre. A spectacular landmark film, *Cabaret* was the winner of eight Academy Awards including Best Director, Best Actress, Best Supporting Actor, Cinematography, Art Direction, Film Editing, Musical Score, and Sound.

Leslie Taubman

CABIN IN THE SKY

Released: 1943
Production: Arthur Freed for Metro-Goldwyn-Mayer
Direction: Vincente Minnelli
Screenplay: Joseph Schrank; based on the musical play with book of the same
  name by Lynn Root
Cinematography: Sidney Wagner
Editing: Harold F. Kress
Music: Vernon Duke and John Latouche, with additional songs by Harold
  Arlen, E. Y. Harburg, and Duke Ellington
Running time: 99 minutes

> *Principal characters:*
> Petunia Jackson .... Ethel Waters
> Little Joe Jackson .... Eddie "Rochester" Anderson
> Georgia Brown .... Lena Horne
> The Trumpeter .... Louis Armstrong
> Lucifer, Jr. .... Rex Ingram
> The General .... Kenneth Spencer
> Domino Johnson .... "Bubbles" (John W. Sublett)

Black musicals are for the most part a historical footnote to the Hollywood musicals of the 1930's and 1940's. By and large, the image of blacks they convey is stereotypic, condescending, and ridiculous. M-G-M's *Cabin in the Sky* is an exception among the few all-black musicals produced during those decades. The 1942 production is a comedy with a hilarious script, and many of its songs are now standards. Its stars are performers familiar to generations of audiences: Ethel Waters, Eddie "Rochester" Anderson, Lena Horne, Duke Ellington, and even, in a small part, Louis Armstrong. The roles these stars play are indeed roles, not the stereotypic walk-ons often given black actors in other Hollywood films of the time. And the story told by *Cabin in the Sky* is a fable which might be set in any American locale.

The movie concerns characters in a small rural town. Little Joe Jackson (Eddie "Rochester" Anderson) and his wife Petunia (Ethel Waters) are poor and honest. If Petunia had her way, they would be hardworking, but Little Joe loves gambling, and he has a weakness for a sexy nightclub singer named Georgia Brown (Lena Horne). His problems begin when he sneaks away from church one night to shoot dice down at Jim Henry's nightclub. Domino Johnson ("Bubbles"), a crooked gambler, shoots Little Joe in an argument. Seriously wounded, he is brought home. As Petunia keeps an anxious bedside watch, a delirious Little Joe begins to dream. His dream makes up the rest of the movie.

Little Joe creates an amusing set of characters who represent the forces of Heaven and Hell, or the best and worst of his intentions. "The General" (Kenneth Spencer) and his troops, in beautiful brocaded uniforms, are sent down from Heaven to keep him on his best behavior. But temptations are also close at hand, as Lucifer, Jr., (Rex Ingram) and his troublemaking assistants work hard to lead him astray. But first, Little Joe dreams that he dies and faces a day of reckoning. Both Heaven and Hell send messengers to claim his immortal soul. To his consternation, the claim is decided in favor of the Fires Below. But strenuous prayer by Petunia, still installed at his bedside in the dream, sways the Lord. Little Joe is given a six-month extension on his life, a second chance to prove worthy of admittance to Heaven.

At this point, we are deliberately misled by the movie. Little Joe dreams that he wakes up, and, because we see him wake up, we believe the dream is over. Only at the film's end do we learn that the entire series of events has been a dream.

For a while, it looks as though Little Joe's second chance has set him on the path to Heaven. He gets a job, works around the house, and even remembers Petunia's birthday by giving her a washing machine. But Lucifer, Jr., is determined to see Little Joe down below. The top "idea men" in Hell are called together to consider various temptations to send to Little Joe. They decide on a powerful invitation to sin: sudden riches and the irresistible attentions of Georgia Brown.

That day, the sexy singer brings Little Joe the news that he has won a fortune in the Irish Sweepstakes. His new wealth has helped to make Little Joe very attractive to Georgia, and she takes up a provocative position in Little Joe's hammock. After an amusing duet, "That Ole Debbil Consequence," in which Little Joe debates the outcome of the seduction, he resists Georgia's advances. The money, he tells her, will go to the church. But as he thanks Georgia, Petunia comes home, takes one look at Georgia, and throws her husband out of the house; hence, Little Joe's new wealth goes to gambling and sinning after all.

Matters are brought to a head one night at Jim Henry's, site of Little Joe's initial gunshot wound. Domino Jackson, just out of jail, shows up, and after singing a boasting "Just Because," inquires after Georgia Brown. A nervous management hustles Domino off to the gambling room. Soon, a marvelously elegant Little Joe and feather-bedecked Georgia Brown arrive. She sings a come hither number, "There's Honey in the Honeycomb." As we wait for the inevitable confrontation between Domino and Little Joe over Georgia, a kink is thrown into the plot: Petunia shows up dressed to kill. Her ample figure draped in yards of satin, she steals Georgia's number, "There's Honey in the Honeycomb," and uses it to enflame Domino. So the confrontation between Little Joe and Domino proves to be over Petunia. During the brawl, Petunia prays for help, and Heaven provides a tornado. But Domino has drawn a gun, and hits both Little Joe and Petunia as the nightclub is destroyed by the winds.

Once again Little Joe faces the day of judgment, this time with Petunia. The books are balanced on them both. Hell seems inevitable for Little Joe until Petunia offers to sacrifice her own passage to Heaven for him. The stairway to Heaven suddenly appears, and the two start the long climb together. At that point, having gained the Pearly Gates both for himself and Petunia, Little Joe awakens with a new resolve to give up gambling.

Originally a show on Broadway, *Cabin in the Sky*, lost money and M-G-M picked up the rights to the musical rather cheaply; a new man on the lot, Vincente Minnelli, was given his first chance to direct. Minnelli, an extremely successful and experienced director of stage revues and musicals, was in some ways a natural to transfer *Cabin in the Sky* to film. His stage background makes the lack of staginess of his first film all the more impressive. Hallmarks of Minnelli's style are visible here in his use of boom and tracking shots in long takes rather than frequent cutting. The neutral medium-shot camera length, also typical of Minnelli's later films, is in evidence here. Minnelli's first film was not only a critical success, but it made money for the studio.

Several changes were made in the musical when it was transferred to film. Most important of these involved a change in the score. Additional songs by Harold Arlen and E. Y. Harburg including "Happiness Is Just a Thing Called Joe," "L'il Black Sheep," "That Ole Debbil Consequence," as well as the Ellington numbers "Going Up" and "Things Ain't What They Used to Be," added luster to the original score by Vernon Duke and John Latouche. A major character change was decided upon for Georgia Brown. Originally a dancer in the stage version, she bacame a singer in a part tailor-made for Lena Horne.

The film is a showcase for Ethel Waters' talents in particular, and she takes full advantage of its very strong score. Some idea of her earlier stage career as a dancer is given when she cuts loose in her nightclub finery, managing high kicks despite a sizable figure. Lena Horne does not have songs comparable to those she was given in other M-G-M musicals, or the other all-black musical for which she is known, *Stormy Weather* (1943). Neither "That Old Debbil Consequence" nor "There's Honey in the Honeycomb" has the strength of Waters' numbers, such as "Taking a Chance on Love" or "Happiness Is Just a Thing Called Joe." A third Horne number, "Ain't It the Truth," sung during a bubblebath, was cut by censors. Eddie Anderson manages his songs with a comic bravado and blustery, bad-boy performance which proved fortunate, as he is not a strong singer.

The structure of *Cabin in the Sky* resembles that of *The Wizard of Oz* (1939). After a prologue which introduces the principle characters in reality, the hero brings about a traumatic separation from home and family. Dorothy runs away from home; Little Joe sneaks off from church to Jim Henry's nightclub. The transgression puts the hero near death, permitting a dream sequence. The dream makes up the body of the movie, in which the hero works through problems of "getting home." Finally, a waking conclusion repeats the solutions arrived at in the dream. In the light of similarity between the two movies, it is ironic that the tornado scene in which Jim Henry's club is destroyed, is footage taken from the earlier *Wizard of Oz*.

Cabin in the Sky was the first all-black musical to be mounted by a studio since Warners' *Green Pastures* (1936), which had been attacked in the press for presenting a ridiculous image of blacks, and M-G-M was anxious to avoid similar criticism. With a story of rural innocents caught between a storybook heaven and hell, the movie might have had "happy darky" overtones, but this possibility was not realized. *Cabin in the Sky* has the strength and simplicity of a child's fable. It happens to be set within a black, rural cultural and musical tradition, a setting which adds to its charm.

Leslie Donaldson

THE CAINE MUTINY

Released: 1954
Production: Stanley Kramer for Columbia
Direction: Edward Dmytryk
Screenplay: Stanley Roberts; based on the novel of the same name by Herman Wouk
Cinematography: Franz Planer
Editing: William A. Lyon
Running time: 125 minutes

Principal characters:

Captain Queeg	Humphrey Bogart
Lieutenant Steve Maryk	Van Johnson
Lieutenant Tom Keefer	Fred MacMurray
Lieutenant Barney Greenwald	José Ferrer
Ensign Willie Keith	Robert Francis
Captain DeVriess	Tom Tully
Mrs. Keith	Katharine Warren
May Wynn	May Wynn
Ensign Harding	Jerry Paris
Meatball	Lee Marvin
Horrible	Claude Akins

Immediately following the credits in *The Caine Mutiny*, there is a statement advising the audience that there has never been a mutiny in the United States Navy, or a trial for a mutiny, and that this film deals with the way in which men respond to certain crises. At issue is the relief of the captain of the *U.S.S. Caine* by his executive officer during a typhoon. Herman Wouk's novel won the Pulitzer Prize in 1951 and then became a successful Broadway play, *The Caine Mutiny Court Martial*, with Lloyd Nolan taking wide acclaim for his role as Captain Queeg. The Navy, however, publicly objected to the filming of this novel because it makes the obvious point that a mentally disturbed man not only could remain a naval officer but also could be put in command of a ship. The Navy also objected to the word "mutiny" in the title, and suggested it be replaced by a word such as "incident." With opposition to the filming worked out, producer Stanley Kramer in the end won the full cooperation of the naval authorities to film at Pearl Harbor. Edward Dmytryk, one of the famous "Hollywood Ten," was chosen as director. Dymtryk had made a reputation in the 1940's as an original stylist with tough-guy thrillers such as *Murder, My Sweet* (1944) and the murky, conscientious exposé of anti-Semitism, *Crossfire* (1947). His direction of *The Caine Mutiny* is not distinguished but is always appropriate, managing to give a fair amount of tautness and consistency to a diverse story line.

Set in the Pacific during World War II, the story follows the experiences

of Ensign Willie Keith (Robert Francis), a young, clean-cut Princeton graduate involved in numerous conflicts with authority. He defies his overly protective mother (Katharine Warren), a society matron, to become engaged to
a nightclub singer, May (May Wynn). Assigned to the *U.S.S. Caine*, a shabby
backwater minesweeper-destroyer, he earns a mediocre fitness report from
Captain DeVriess (Tom Tully). Captain Queeg (Humphrey Bogart) soon replaces DeVriess and in time antagonizes all his officers, particularly Lieutenant Keefer (Fred MacMurray), a writer and pseudointellectual who suggests
that the Captain might be unbalanced. Willie agrees with Keefer's diagnosis
of Queeg's erratic behavior. The executive officer, Lieutenant Maryk (Van
Johnson), at first spiritedly defends Queeg, but, after repeated incidents of
faulty seamanship and poor command, he joins Willie and Keefer on an
abortive visit to Admiral Halsey about Queeg. The issue of Queeg's com-
petency climaxes in an incident when Maryk, with Willie's support, mutinies
and takes over the ship when it appears to be foundering in a typhoon. At
the court martial brought about by this incident, Maryk fares badly until
Queeg, cornered on the stand by Maryk's defense counsel, Lieutenant Greenwald (José Ferrer), proves through his reactions to Greenwald's probings that
Maryk's charges of instability have been justified. Maryk is thus cleared; but
at the celebration afterwards Greenwald upbraids him and the other officers
for not backing Queeg when he needed their loyalty. Greenwald admits that
he took the case and destroyed Queeg only because he realized that the
wrong man was on trial: Keefer was the real "author" of the *Caine* mutiny.

The film's action centers on Queeg's deterioration, both on the *U.S.S.
Caine* and in the witness chair. Queeg has replaced the lax and popular captain
of a weary vessel. When he announces to his officers that he is a disciplinarian
who runs things "by the book," and that he intends to turn the *U.S.S. Caine*
into a smart ship, he evokes a kind of bemused tolerance in them, since they
know the *U.S.S. Caine* and her crew. Keefer's hostile charges about Queeg's
behavior subsequently move Maryk to start a medical log on Queeg. The
charges involve two major blunders. Once, while the *U.S.S. Caine* tows
targets for gunnery practice, Queeg becomes so enraged with a seaman for
leaving his shirttail out that he allows the ship to steam in a circle over its
own tow cable. A second, more telling incident occurs when the *U.S.S. Caine*
has to lead some Marine landing barges within a thousand yards of the shore.
Queeg, distraught over the fire from the Japanese batteries, outruns the
barges, then orders the ship back before it can come close to the shore and
has a yellow dye marker thrown over to guide the stranded barges.

The meeting following the dye marker incident defines the break between
Queeg and his officers. As Greenwald rightly charges the men after the trial,
Queeg comes to his officers for help and they turn him down. Queeg, greatly
discomfited, tries to apologize, but immediately afterwards Keefer charges
to Maryk and Willie that Queeg is obviously a paranoid, "crawling with

clues"—for example, his fixation on the pair of steel ball bearings he absently rolls in his palm. Although Maryk again defends Queeg, he is bothered enough to begin keeping a record on him.

The narrative now moves to Maryk's relation of three incidents, entered in his record, that lead to his relieving Queeg of command. On questionable grounds Queeg first bans movies for thirty days, then, a little later, cancels liberties for three months. During the final incident Queeg enjoys two petty victories. He demonstrates with a gallon can of sand that the officers could not have eaten a gallon of strawberries at dinner, and after a futile, all-night investigation, proudly announces that someone therefore has made a duplicate key to the pantry. He orders the men stripped, has all their keys collected, and then has the ship turned upside down for the nonexistent key.

After this episode Maryk admits that Keefer's analysis of the Captain is correct. When Ensign Harding (Jerry Paris) departs on emergency leave, he tells Maryk that the mess boys ate the strawberries, and that he has already informed Queeg, who has called him a liar, threatening to hold up his leave. Convinced of Queeg's imbalance, Maryk, accompanied by Willie and Keefer, takes his record on Queeg to Halsey's flagship, but never sees the Admiral because Keefer, calling himself "too smart to be brave," refuses to go through with the interview. During a typhoon that night in which Queeg insists on maintaining the fleet course into the wind, Maryk assumes command by the authority of Article 184 of Naval Regulations.

Had Queeg been able to retain his initial composure in the witness chair, Maryk presumably would have been convicted of mutiny. A psychologist declares Queeg competent; Keefer slyly distorts his own part in the affair, stressing how he dissuaded Maryk from seeing Halsey; and Maryk proves that he is unqualified to talk sensibly about mental disorders since he cannot even distinguish "paranoid" from "paranoia." Queeg's façade of normalcy, however, quickly shatters under Greenwald's interrogation. When Greenwald threatens to produce Ensign Harding in order to solve the problem of the missing strawberries, Queeg becomes almost hysterical in his condemnation of his officers' disloyalty and in his attempt to justify his behavior. Here follows the strongest scene in the film, shot in a steadily encroaching close-up. Suddenly Queeg stops, looks hurriedly at the faces that surround him, and realizes that he has trapped himself, that all have seen his fears and his shame at his sense of inferiority. The court martial is closed.

Dmytryk draws convincing performances from a first-rate cast. Queeg was Bogart's last good role (he died in 1957), one that he requested and, because of the big-name cast, accepted less money for playing. As Queeg, Bogart does not recapture the genius of his characterization of the demented Fred C. Dobbs in *The Treasure of the Sierra Madre* (1948) although he portrays well a man incapable of acknowledging, much less handling, his dread that his defenses will be exposed. Johnson, playing the steadfast Maryk, shows the right amount of indecision about Queeg; he is caught between his duty to uphold his superior and, as second in command, his responsibility to the ship. Francis, who would die the following year in an air crash at the age of twenty-five, makes a notable film debut as the determined but untried Willie. MacMurray's ambiguous Keefer balances intellectual superiority with an almost fanatical aversion to military authority. It is he rather than Maryk who is the real antagonist of Queeg, whose vulnerability Keefer instinctively perceives. Yet, in the end, Keefer owns up to his cowardice and submits with some embarrassment both to Greenwald's recriminations and to a glass of champagne in his face. Ferrer, underplaying the brusque, sneering Greenwald, proceeds from an inviolable sense of duty. He defends Maryk ably, while never condoning his actions; and at the appropriate time he shows compassion for Queeg, whom he sees as a victim of both combat fatigue and his officers' lack of understanding.

The Caine Mutiny, in keeping with the themes of other war films of the 1950's such as Robert Aldrich's *Attack!* (1956) and Stanley Kubrick's *Paths of Glory* (1957), focuses not on war but on the military hierarchy and its workings. Stanley Roberts' screenplay successfully molds audience sympathies to give the film a smoothly changing point of view. At first Keefer's response to Queeg and his harsh discipline appears to be justified; however, Keefer soon reveals himself to be a treacherous opportunist, just as Maryk, despite his sincere, well-intentioned actions, emerges as less than a model officer—a man of good instincts but limited intelligence, never able to control any situation that involves Keefer. The reversal occurs plainly after the trial, as Greenwald excuses Queeg's irrationality because of his service record (he has spent seven years in the Atlantic, the last few fighting U-Boats) and the necessity for preserving the integrity of command. Greenwald argues that Navy regulars like Queeg, who admittedly broke under the strain, protected their "fat, dumb, happy country" while the others, including himself, were too busy elsewhere to care.

Dmytryk maintains a good pace throughout the film. He integrates in comfortable proportions the numerous tensions and hostilities among his characters with the lightness that comes from the events of Willie's collisions with his mother and the two captains of the *U.S.S. Caine*, supplemented by the antics of the ship's clowns, Meatball (Lee Marvin) and Horrible (Claude Akins). The dark humor that surrounds Queeg's attempts to mask his shallowness, especially the hunt for the imaginary key, gives way to the pathetic as all his credibility evaporates in the witness chair. On the other hand, the story's diffused nature undermines its power to explore the conditions of the individual within the system. Willie's drawn-out romance with May, to be sure, breaks up the monotony of a story about men at war; however, it adds nothing to the issues the film purports to treat. A more serious flaw in the film is the poorly defined perspective in the end. Greenwald's attempt to salvage the deportment of an obvious neurotic by appeal to his patriotism does not make Maryk's action seem any less necessary. The concluding frames show Willie, reassigned under Captain DeVriess, taking a ship back to the Pacific theater as May, now a bride, watches from the dock. Love has won out over class barriers, the system is reaffirmed in the tacit reconciliation of DeVriess' equanimity and salt water astuteness with Willie's youthful idealism. The questions of legitimate responsibilities raised at the court martial in turn fade away as the ship steams under the Golden Gate Bridge.

William H. Brown, Jr.

CALL NORTHSIDE 777

Released: 1948
Production: Otto Lang for Twentieth Century-Fox
Direction: Henry Hathaway
Screenplay: Jerome Cady and Jay Dratler; based on Leonard Hoffman's and Quentin Reynolds' adaptation of the newspaper articles by James P. McGuire and John McPaul
Cinematography: Joe MacDonald
Editing: J. Watson Webb, Jr.
Running time: 110 minutes

> *Principal characters:*
> P. J. McNeal .... James Stewart
> Frank Wiecek .... Richard Conte
> Brian Kelly .... Lee J. Cobb
> Laura McNeal .... Helen Walker
> Wanda Skutnik .... Betty Garde
> Tillie Wiecek .... Kasia Orzazewski
> Helen Wiecek-Rayska .... Joanne de Bergh
> Leonarde Keeler .... Himself
> Tomek Zaleska .... George Tyne

On December 9, 1932, Chicago police officer William D. Lundy was shot and killed by two unidentified gunmen in a Southwest Side speakeasy owned by a woman named Vera Walush. Lundy was the eighth policeman killed in the line of duty that year; and Mayor Anton Cermak, anxious to clean up Chicago's reputation as the nation's crime capitol before the World's Fair opened there in 1933, pressed hard for the arrest and conviction of the murderers. (Cermak was himself to be the victim of an assassin's bullet a few months later.) The police had one lead: Bessie Barron, a wholesaler who supplied Vera Walush with alcohol, had heard a young Polish-American named Ted Marcinkiewicz threaten to "make Vera's joint." On December 22, the police interviewed Ted's friend Joe Majczek, who said he knew nothing about the killing but admitted that Marcinkiewicz had spent the night of December 9 at his house. Joe had a minor police record, and the police took him in for further questioning. When first asked to identify him, Vera said he was not one of the men she had seen kill Officer Lundy. An hour later, she changed her testimony and identified Joe and—after he had turned himself in—Ted Marcinkiewicz as the two gunmen.

On the strength of Vera's identification, Joe and Ted were brought to trial, convicted, and sentenced to serve ninety-nine years apiece in Stateville Penitentiary. John Zageta, the only other witness to Lundy's murder, refused to identify Joe and Ted as the men he had seen entering Vera's place. After he had passed sentence, the judge called Vera into his chambers and threatened her with a perjury indictment. He told Joe and Ted that he would try to get them a new trial but the State Attorney refused, and Joe became Convict No. 8356E with no possibility of parole until 1966. At his insistence, his wife divorced him and eventually married a man who promised her and Joe's young son a better chance in life.

Tillie Majczek, Joe's mother, never lost faith in her son's innocence. For eleven years she scrubbed floors, trying to accumulate enough money to buy evidence and pay attorneys' fees for a new trial. After Pearl Harbor, Joe's brother sent his family allotment to be put into Tillie's defense fund. Finally, on October 10, 1944, Tillie placed the following ad in the classified section of the Chicago *Times*, a picture tabloid: "$5,000 reward for killers of Officer Lundy on Dec. 9, 1932. Call GRO. 1758, 12-7 P. M." Tillie's ad caught the eye of *Times* city editor Karin Walsh, who assigned a former private detective-turned-newspaperman named James P. McGuire to interview Mrs. Majczek for a possible human interest story. McGuire was impressed by Tillie's determination and, after driving down to Stateville to interview Joe, set to work in earnest gathering evidence that would force the State Attorney to reopen the case.

Over the next ten months McGuire and *Times* rewrite man John McPaul wrote thirty-five articles pointing out the questionable validity of Vera Walush's identification and the probability that Joe and Ted had not received a fair trial. (Vera reportedly told friends that the police had threatened to close her down if she refused to cooperate by fingering Joe and Ted; Joe's family had hired an alcoholic gangland attorney named William O'Brien who never challenged Vera's testimony and kept Joe from testifying on his own behalf. O'Brien was disbarred three years after Joe's conviction.) On August 15, 1945, Joe Majczek was granted an unconditional pardon by the Illinois State Pardon Board and released from prison. McGuire was robbed of his headline by the circumstance that Joe was released on V-J Day; but he and the *Times*, which was soon to become the Chicago *Sun-Times*, won the Sigma Delta Chi Award for best general reporting and the National Headliners Club Award for outstanding public service of 1945.

Ted Marcinkiewicz was not pardoned with Joe because of Bessie Barron's testimony that she had heard him threatening to rob Vera's speakeasy. McGuire uncovered evidence that Bessie harbored a grudge against Ted because he had once stolen some alcohol from her. In November, 1949, he secured a writ of *habeas corpus* to force the Pardon Board to reopen Ted's case, and three months later Ted, too, was released after serving seventeen years for a crime that he almost certainly did not commit. Vera Walush never admitted that she had lied about Joe and Ted, but stayed in her dingy LaSalle Street walk-up apartment, refusing all requests for interviews.

McGuire's crusade on Joe's behalf was widely covered in the national press. Twentieth Century-Fox, which had become an industry leader since the war in a new school of filmmaking that emphasized shooting true stories in the original locations in a semidocumentary style, paid Joe Majczek $1,000 for the rights to his story and McGuire $2,500 to use his research. Fox's previous efforts in the semidocumentary field included *The House on 92nd Street* (1945), *13 Rue Madeleine* (1946), and *Boomerang!* (1947).

When *Call Northside 777* (the title refers to the telephone number the studio invented to take the place of Tillie Majczek's number as listed in her original ad) was released early in 1948, it was widely praised as the best semidocumentary to date. United States movie audiences, who were accustomed to seeing real people and places on the screen in the many documentaries that were released during World War II, welcomed dramatic films that also depicted real settings, even if the "real" people of the wartime documentaries were replaced by well-known actors. Most Hollywood films of the day were shot in a studio, whether it was feasible to go on location or not; now, thirty years later, when movies of every description are routinely shot on location, the most impressive quality about a film like *Call Northside 777* is the careful craftsmanship with which it was made. In his *Time* magazine review, James Agee praised Joe MacDonald's "cleanly intelligent" camera work, but, in point of fact, the black-and-white cinematography in all of the postwar semidocumentaries was handsome and exciting, and a stunning rebuke to modern filmmakers who equate truth with grainy cinematography.

Although the names of the principal characters were changed, the screenplay that was fashioned from McGuire's articles follows Joe Majczek's story quite faithfully. Newspaperman P. J. McNeal (James Stewart) is assigned by his editor, Brian Kelly (Lee J. Cobb), to write a story based on the ad that Tillie Wiecek (Kasia Orzazewski) has placed, offering a reward for information that will clear her son Frank (Richard Conte). At first, McNeal is inclined to believe that Frank really must have been guilty, even though the Stateville warden tells him: "Up here, *every* man claims to be innocent. But the prisoners are the harshest judges of themselves, and they believe we have only two men who don't belong here: Tomek Zaleska [the film's name for Ted Marcinkiewicz] and Frank Wiecek." Even after Frank's former wife (Joanne de Bergh) tells him that she still believes her husband to be innocent, McNeal goes only so far as to promise Frank that he will dig up every bit of information about his case that he can.

In one of the film's most dramatic scenes, McNeal arranges for Frank to take a lie-detector test under the supervision of polygraph expert Leonarde Keeler. Keeler was the only person connected with Joe Majczek's case who played himself in the film. His calm professionalism as he explains the polygraph procedure to James Stewart and attaches his apparatus to Richard Conte makes his performance a welcome exception to the rule that it is usually impossible to mix professional and nonprofessional actors in the same scene without sacrificing dramatic credibility. The person who appears most nervous—and it works very well as a re-creation of Joe Majczek's probable nervousness in real life—is Conte, who was purposely told very little about the nature of the test he would be given on camera, thereby making him anxious about doing something to spoil the scene. Only after the results of the test indicate that Frank Wiecek has been telling the truth does McNeal accept his story unequivocally.

McNeal's decision to believe in Frank's innocence comes after a late-night conversation between McNeal and his understanding wife (Helen Walker). The unconvincing nature of this and of all of James Stewart's scenes with Walker may point up a fundamental pitfall in the semidocumentary method: so long as we can watch McNeal busy in the newsroom or in the city streets, our knowledge that we are watching Jimmy Stewart, movie star, does not seriously hamper our belief in the story. But when we see McNeal fussing with a jigsaw puzzle, or hear his wife offer to fix him a sandwich—when we watch this attractive couple in the sterile, "tasteful" apartment the studio decorators have furnished for them and listen to their contrived domestic small talk—they seem as phony in their ordinariness as the folksy celebrities who appear on television talk shows.

The evidence of the magazine accounts of Joe Majczek's pardon suggests that he was freed as a result of the cumulative effect of McGuire's newspaper articles on public opinion in the State of Illinois. The filmmakers must have felt that something more dramatic was required for the movie, however: the State Attorney's office, embarrassed by McNeal's charges that it is in a conspiracy with the Chicago Police Department to supress evidence that might point to their mishandling of Wiecek's case eleven years before, offers McNeal's publisher a bargain. A special meeting of the State Pardon Board will be convened in one week's time. McNeal will appear before the Board and present all the evidence he has uncovered relating to Wiecek's innocence. If the Board still refuses to grant Wiecek a pardon, McNeal will drop his crusade and the *Times* will admit that justice has been served. McNeal accepts the challenge, even though he is warned that his evidence is valueless unless he can find Wanda Skutnik, the film's name for Vera Walush, and get her to confess that she lied on the witness stand. McNeal finally tracks down the slatternly Wanda (Betty Garde) in her shabby Back of the Yards apartment. She refuses to change her story, however, and McNeal is left with no alternative but to withdraw the *Times*'s petition to the Board.

At the last possible minute, however, with the paper's attorney about to go before the Board, McNeal reads a newsstory about a police technique for enlarging sections of a photograph up to one thousand times. Earlier, when McNeal had been attempting to prove that Wanda Skutnik saw Frank Wiecek between the time of his arrest and before she supposedly picked him out of a police lineup, he had found an old news photograph showing Wanda as she watched the handcuffed Frank enter a precinct house. Frank was arrested on

December 22, 1932 (the presumed date of the photo), but was not identified by Wanda until December 23. The problem is that until now McNeal has had no way of proving that the news photo was not taken sometime after Frank was booked on the twenty-third. In the background of the photograph is a newsboy with a stand full of papers. McNeal arranges to have the police lab blow up that section of the picture several hundred times, and to have the result wired in to the State capitol in Springfield, where the Board is meeting. It is difficult to believe that in such an extraordinary circumstance the Pardon Board would have been unwilling to wait the hour or two required for the enlarged wirephoto to be received; but the script requires James Stewart to plead for their forbearance in his best Mr. Smith manner. The enlargement comes through; and the camera watches closely as the date on one of the newsboy's papers is revealed: December 22, 1932, one full day before Wanda Skutnik made the identification that resulted in Frank Wiecek's and Tomek Zaleska's (George Tyne) being sentenced to prison for ninety-nine years. Frank gets his pardon and McNeal is waiting at the gate to tell him: "It's a big thing when a sovereign state admits an error. And remember this: there aren't many governments in the world that would do it." Frank agrees: "Yes, it's a good world—outside."

A better resolution to the drama than this overwrought and unconvincing hokum was reported in the same issue of *Time* (February 16, 1948) that carried Agee's review of the movie. After Joe Majczek's release, a Chicago assemblyman named Ragnar Nelson (who liked to be called Rags) campaigned in the legislature for a cash award to be given Joe as partial compensation for the dozen years he had spent behind bars. The legislature finally voted Joe the sum of twenty-four thousand dollars, which was presented in a special ceremony in the governor's office with the beaming Rags standing in the background. Then, a short time later, Rags got Joe alone and demanded five thousand dollars as his cut of the award. Joe gave him the money but he also told McGuire, who broke the story in the *Sun-Times*. Because Rags had had the foresight to ask for his money in unmarked bills, the Chicago Grand Jury refused to indict him. By this time, Joe had already had fourteen years of experience with the Illinois judicial system. He refused to comment on the Grand Jury's decision, and instead quietly took his mother to the Chicago opening of *Call Northside 777*.

Charles Hopkins

CAMILLE

Released: 1936
Production: David Lewis for Metro-Goldwyn-Mayer
Direction: George Cukor
Screenplay: Zoe Akins, Frances Marion, and James Hilton; based on the novel and play *La Dame aux camélias* by Alexandre Dumas, *fils*
Cinematography: William Daniels
Editing: Margaret Booth
Running time: 115 minutes

Principal characters:

Marguerite Gautier (Camille)	Greta Garbo
Armand Duval	Robert Taylor
Monsieur Duval	Lionel Barrymore
Baron de Varville	Henry Daniell
Olympe	Lenore Ulric
Nanine	Jessie Ralph
Prudence Duvernoy	Laura Hope Crews
Nichette	Elizabeth Allan
Gustave	Russell Hardie

For over a century the romance that Alexandre Dumas, *fils*, wrote as a novel and then as a play, *La Dame aux camélias*, has held its audiences spellbound. Its heroine, Marguerite Gautier, was based upon a real *demi-mondaine*, Marie (*née* Alphonsine) Plessis, whom Dumas knew in Paris, a youthful courtesan who had crowded a lifetime into her brief twenty-three years. Dumas made Marie immortal when he created Marguerite Gautier; and many an actress since has yearned to play her, because the role is such a challenge. In the theater, great dramatic stars such as Sarah Bernhardt and Eleanora Duse triumphed in the role. From 1915 to 1927 there were at least four well-remembered silent film productions of *Camille*, as the story was known in the English-speaking world, starring such actresses as Clara Kimball Young, Theda Bara, Nazimova, and Norma Talmadge.

In 1936, the first talking film production of *Camille* was released, starring Greta Garbo. It remains the definitive version, for it represents a perfect melding of all the talents concerned in its making. Garbo was never more moving, never so much the mistress of the camera. "She's never been so unguarded," noted Irving Thalberg, head of production at M-G-M. An actress playing the role of Camille must appear to be unguarded, for Camille slips moodily from one emotion to another, revealing every extreme, relishing every delight, tasting every sorrow. She was guided by her director, George Cukor, into sheer perfection, the realization of every nuance of her character, looking and moving always as if she had stepped directly from the mid-nineteenth century.

Paris was never so light-hearted as it was in 1847, when its citizens dictated the taste of the European world. Every night theaters were crowded with women in silks and diamonds attracting new lovers, for Paris was the city of love, and every Parisian lived for love, even though it lasted but a single night. It is in the early hours of such a night that the film's story begins. A carriage pauses at a florist's shop run by Madame Buyon, who hurries out with a handsome nosegay of camellias. A gloved hand emerges from the open window of the carriage. The old florist smiles happily and with a proud little bow presents the flowers. "For the lady of the camellias," she says—and as the carriage starts up again, the camera moves inside for a first view of the lady, beautifully gowned in fine velvets and silks, with jewels reflecting the radiance of her exquisite face. This is Marguerite Gautier (Greta Garbo), known familiarly to all in her world as "Camille," because she always wears camellias. She is with her elderly companion, Prudence Duvernoy (Laura Hope Crews), a greedy, well-dressed bawd who knows her way around. She scolds Camille for her extravagances; she should make better use of her extraordinary charms and conserve her delicate health only for those lovers who will shower her with gifts that count—a lover such as the Baron de Varville (Henry Daniell), for example, to whom Prudence intends to introduce her that night.

At the theater, Camille lingers at the head of the double staircase, looking down upon the well-dressed crowds thronging the main lobby. At the foot of the stairs a young man looks up at her with frank adoration. She is pleased and amused by his youth and sincerity, and flirts with him audaciously. She takes her place beside Prudence in the box as the entertainment begins. Prudence, directing her opera glasses over the house, is excited when she spies the Baron de Varville, middle-aged, cynical, and one of the richest and most desirable men in Paris. She gives the glasses to Camille, pointing out the Baron, but by mistake Camille focuses upon the young man she had seen in the foyer, and is both delighted and surprised that a real baron can be so young, handsome, and available. She agrees to be introduced to him, and it is only during the meeting that she realizes, with some embarrassment, that he is not de Varville but a young man recently come to Paris named Armand Duval (Robert Taylor). He is disappointed, thinking that she was interested in him only for a wealth he does not possess, but she puts him at ease and sends him to the confectioner's for some bonbons. In the meantime, Olympe (Lenore Ulric), a jealous rival of Camille, has snagged the Baron de Varville into her box; but Camille smiles enticingly at him, and by the time Armand returns breathlessly with the sweets, Camille has departed with the Baron. Armand finds a glove she has carelessly left behind and clutches it longingly as the scene fades out.

And so the stage is set, with all but one of the principal characters introduced in a single superbly written sequence. The one remaining character is Monsieur Duval (Lionel Barrymore), Armand's father, and he does not come into the action until later when his character becomes pivotal. This introductory scene is completely original, the creative device of the three screenwriters, used to establish the colorful Parisian *demi-monde* of the period. All other versions of the movie were modeled after the novel or directly upon the play. The novel begins with Marguerite Gautier already deceased and a sale of her private effects in progress to satisfy her creditors; this provides a frame for the romance itself, which is told in flashback. Some theater productions used this device in introducing Armand, who reads Camille's diary under a full-length portrait of her, as the lights dim and the first act begins. The Norma Talmadge silent screen version, modern but not stylized, used this prologue frame, dissolving into an introductory sequence wherein Camille is washing windows in the shop where she works, and as she clears a clean circle of glass, she looks out to see the Baron de Varville "discovering" her.

But in this M-G-M talking version, the entire scene is boldly played as straight narrative, with a haunting musical background, and all the characters coming into the picture as flesh-and-blood people with humors and passions of their own. They may owe their being to Dumas, *fils*, but their separate lives, personalities, and dialogue are the creation of Zoe Akins, Frances Marion, and James Hilton, who dramatized the old story with a new verve and true professional skill.

The pattern of the screen story thereafter more closely follows that of the novel and play, but even so, the approach is fresh and, above all, the romance of Camille and Armand is both accurate and believable. The story of a courtesan and the youth she loves outside the bonds of matrimony was scarcely proper film fare for the mid-1930's, when censorship ruled the screen mercilessly; but a remarkably clever device was manufactured to satisfy the Puritanical whims of those who guard the public morals. Camille and Armand realize their love in the country at her cottage, even though he is supposed to be sleeping in a nearby inn. Camille has an old friend, Nichette (Elizabeth Allan), from the days when she worked as a shopgirl, and Nichette is to be married to a respectable young man, Gustave (Russell Hardie). Camille begs to be allowed to give the wedding party in her garden. The marriage ceremony has a special significance for Camille and Armand. Later he tells her that every word the priest spoke was meant for them and that in his heart he made all the vows—to her; she responds glowingly, "And I to you." The censors chose to look the other way.

In a crucial scene that shortly follows, Armand has gone to Paris for business reasons, and in his absence, Monsieur Duval, his father, comes to the cottage to plead with Camille to give up the love she and Armand share, for that love is ruining Armand's chances for success in a diplomatic career. This has always been a crucial scene in any dramatization of *Camille*, for it allows the actress to run the full gamut of emotion, promising finally to send Armand back to his father, and then pretending convincingly to renounce her love, making Armand believe that she has wearied of him and is returning to de Varville. Garbo plays this scene with heartbreaking sincerity made all the more dramatic because the Armand of Robert Taylor is so innocently confused, so desperate with youthful unhappiness.

The story line continues after the established pattern, with the famous gambling scene wherein Armand wins a fortune from de Varville, only to throw it at Camille's feet, denouncing her as a woman who can be bought, who has a price for everything. De Varville challenges him to a duel, which Camille cannot prevent. Armand wounds de Varville, and has to leave Paris for a few months until the scandal of the affair dies.

The last reel of the Garbo picture is superb. Armand returns to Paris to find that Camille is dying. He takes her in his arms, but even as they plan a happy future together, she grows limp, saying that she has lived for love, and now she is dying for it. He puts her on a chaise longue and kneels at her side. She looks at him with ecstatic happiness, and her eyes close in death, while he buries his face on her breast, weeping.

As a film, the Cukor-Garbo version was not only an enormous success critically, but it was also well received by international audiences. The picture is constantly being revived, both as a theatrical release and as a television classic. Garbo's performance gained her a nomination by the Motion Picture Academy as Best Actress of the Year, but she lost to Luise Rainer in *The Good Earth*. Today, the name of Luise Rainer is scarcely remembered, while *The Good Earth* is a film more often read about than seen. In 1955, the Academy awarded Garbo an overdue honorary Oscar for her many unforgettable screen performances. And the one that is the most unforgettable is the one she gave in *Camille*.

DeWitt Bodeen

CAPTAINS COURAGEOUS

Released: 1937
Production: Louis D. Lighton for Metro-Goldwyn-Mayer
Direction: Victor Fleming
Screenplay: John Lee Mahin, Marc Connelly, and Dale Van Every; based on
    the novel of the same name by Rudyard Kipling
Cinematography: Harold Rosson
Editing: Elmo Vernon
Running time: 116 minutes

Principal characters:
    Harvey .... Freddie Bartholomew
    Manuel .... Spencer Tracy (AA)
    Captain Disko .... Lionel Barrymore
    Mr. Cheyne .... Melvyn Douglas
    Uncle Salters .... Charley Grapewin
    Dan .... Mickey Rooney
    "Long Jack" .... John Carradine

If Rudyard Kipling had found himself at M-G-M during the 1930's, he probably would have been one of the studios most prized screenwriters. Kipling's work is filled with the type of stories M-G-M sought for its audience: great tales of adventure and danger in tropical climes and on the high seas. These stories depict white men facing both the perils of nature and the often treacherous pagan natives, and usually convey a moral message, often through the hero's own learning process. In 1937, director Victor Fleming adapted such a Kipling story, *Captains Courageous.* Although the film was notable for its excellent cinematography and its use of several of M-G-M's major stars—Spencer Tracy, Lionel Barrymore, and Melvyn Douglas—most critics focused their attention on the rising child star Freddie Bartholomew, who, playing the character of a spoiled, obnoxious millionaire's son sent away to sea to learn the arts of manhood, manages to dominate the action.

Captains Courageous is a classic Kipling story of a youth learning to understand adversity. Ten-year-old Harvey Cheyne (Freddie Bartholomew) is a materialistic, pampered boy neglected by his industrialist father; he believes money can buy him anything he wants: social acceptance, power, and love. Denied acceptance into an exclusive club at his boarding school, young Harvey accuses the school's administration and its instructors of assisting the club's members in discriminating against him. Harvey is accused of lying and is socially ostracized by the other students, who dislike his snobbishness. Unable to endure such humiliating treatment, Harvey runs away from school and seeks out his father (Melvyn Douglas) who decides to take the boy to Europe. Mr. Cheyne and his son board a luxurious ship en route to Europe where, true to form, Harvey engages in his usual false bravado for the benefit of the ship's passengers. During a storm at sea, Harvey goes to the rail, bends over too far, and falls into the ocean. As luck would have it, he is picked up by a Gloucester fishing boat, aptly named *We're Here*. When Harvey recovers consciousness, he finds himself in a world he has never experienced, surrounded by men who are, in the tradition of Hollywood character actors, gruff yet kind, demanding but benevolent. Particularly kind and understanding is one of the schooner's mates, Manuel (Spencer Tracy).

The young snob, dressed in his neatly pressed tweed suit, is forced to adapt to his new circumstances. The schooner's Captain (Lionel Barrymore) tells the boy that he will have to stay with the schooner for several months. The boy sulks and is increasingly disliked by the crew. Forced to work as a member of the crew for three dollars a month, Harvey soon comes to idolize the Portuguese sailor, Manuel. Manuel is tender with the boy, yet demands the loyalty and strength that all men must bring to the world if they hope to survive. Introduced to the world of simple virtues and quiet bravery, Harvey learns and grows, and his metamorphosis astounds the captain and crew. He thus becomes part of the crew, although his universe is now centered around Manuel. The real test of how much he has learned, however, remains for the film's climactic scenes.

Harvey begs Manuel to take him along in his dory to fish, knowing, as Manuel has told him many times, that he prefers to be alone when he is in his small boat. Meanwhile, Manuel accepts a challenge, based on a long-standing rivalry, from "Long Jack," another fisherman (John Carradine). The two men will compete to see who can catch more fish. True to his code of honor, Manuel seeks to win only by fair means. Harvey, however, who has persuaded Manuel to let him go along, secretly snarls Long Jack's net because he wants his idol to win. The boy has still not learned the lesson of honor, and when the crew discovers what has happened, they once again snub him, referring to him as a "Jonah." Manuel, however, understands and patiently continues to teach the boy.

Tempered by Manuel's honorable teachings and kind words, Harvey is about to embark on the final stage of his initiation. He has discovered virtue, kindness, and humility, and now he must experience tragedy and loss. During a race to port, Captain Disko calls for more sail. Manuel volunteers to climb the topsail, and, when the mast begins to crack, the entire crew is horrified to see Manuel fall into the water, entangled by mast and dangling ropes. The sailor is aware of his hopeless situation and knows that he is gravely injured, but he suffers quietly. He shouts to Disko to cut the ropes of the mast, for he knows all is lost. With Harvey weeping at the ship's rail, Disko cuts the rope and the final waves crash over Manuel's head.

When the fishing schooner reaches port, the now-strengthened Harvey, devoid of his earlier pretensions and snobbishness, takes part in a memorial service to the departed Manuel. Joined by his father, who has arrived and is ecstatic at his son's complete change of heart and appearance, Harvey is presented with Manuel's beloved vielle, the musical instrument the dead fisherman played so often aboard ship. As the wreaths to the dead are placed in the water, Harvey turns to his father for comfort, and, their glances meeting, both father and son know that a new life has begun for them. The music fades out as the two characters lovingly embrace.

Captains Courageous was a typical M-G-M product of the late 1930's. The studio had always believed in releasing films with straightforward story lines, uncomplicated by subtle plot devices or experimental cinematic affectations. The characters in *Captains Courageous* are clearly defined, and, despite the fact that the dialogue is often strained and the contrast between Bartholomew as the naïve young snob and Mickey Rooney as the poor but worldly-wise captain's son is heavy-handed, Victor Fleming has managed to stay true to the basic Kipling story. Young Harvey Cheyne learns about the world of men because he is thrust into a place where sturdy, honorable, yet poor souls rule the day. Generally well-received by critics when it was first released in 1937, *Captains Courageous* was the perfect vehicle through which director Fleming could explore the values Hollywood believed in: strength, redemption through suffering, and moral virtue molded out of adversity. The film also brought Spencer Tracy his first Academy Award for Best Actor, to be followed the next year by another for *Boys Town*.

Lawrence J. Rudner

CAREFREE

Released: 1938
Production: Pandro S. Berman for RKO/Radio
Direction: Mark Sandrich
Screenplay: Allan Scott and Ernest Pagano; based on the story of the same
 name by Dudley Nichols and Hager Wilde, adapted from an idea of Marian
 Ainslee and Guy Endore
Cinematography: Robert de Grasse
Editing: William Hamilton
Choreography: Hermes Pan
Music: Irving Berlin
Running time: 83 minutes

> *Principal characters:*
> Dr. Tony Flagg .... Fred Astaire
> Amanda Cooper .... Ginger Rogers
> Stephen Arden .... Ralph Bellamy
> Aunt Cora .... Luella Gear
> Connors .... Jack Carson

Called the twilight movie of the Astaire-Rogers cycle, *Carefree* is really
anything but carefree. However it remains difficult to find fault with any
Astaire-Rogers film since they were not intended to be taken seriously.

Astaire and Rogers were the screen's most alluring couple during the 1930's
and were much more interesting than the plots of the vehicles in which they
starred. *Carefree* was the first film the duo made after a fifteen-month separation. In the film, a number of traditions were broken and new routes
explored. *Carefree* is the first picture in which Astaire does not play a professional entertainer. It is also the first in which Rogers plays the aggressor in
the relationship; this time it is she who is consumed with the desire to dance
with Astaire. The story reverses their usual plot of boy meets girl, boy pursues
girl, boy dances his way into girl's heart. Also, this film presents the onscreen
kiss which had been promised in all their prior films but never had been
consummated. There is a wonderful lightness and innocence in their other
films that is less evident in *Carefree*. The magic the two could conjure up
simply by walking in tempo together happens only once during the film, yet
when it does happen it is as powerful and enrapturing as ever.

The plot of *Carefree* takes an analyst's couch for its setting rather than a
dance floor or rehearsal hall. Stephen Arden (Ralph Bellamy) is a rather
simple young lawyer with a love problem. His own true heart's desire Amanda
Cooper (Ginger Rogers) is a radio star who cannot make up her mind whether
to accept his proposal of marriage, so he turns to his good friend, psychiatrist
Dr. Tony Flagg (Fred Astaire), and persuades him to analyze Amanda. Waiting in the reception area for her appointment, Amanda overhears Tony refer

to a patient as a "pampered, maladjusted female" and assumes he is referring to her, so she is less than cooperative as he tries to treat her. Stephen, confident that everything will work out perfectly, takes them both out to his country club, where, before dinner, Tony does the incredible number "Since They Turned 'Loch Lomond' into Swing." Believing his patient needs to dream to release her inhibitions, Tony orders for her the most dreadful combination of foods, confident that it will cause visions of Stephen to dance in her head. Visions do dance, but they are of Tony, and Amanda wakes up in love with her doctor. The next morning Tony pronounces that there is nothing wrong with Amanda, so, not wanting him to stop the treatment, she fabricates a dream that fascinates him, and he diagnoses her as the most "beautiful case of complex maladjustment."

To relieve her of any lingering inhibitions, Tony administers an anesthetic and leaves his patient to rest. But with her subconscious freed, Amanda goes wild, and in a hilarious sequence wreaks havoc on Manhattan, starting with the elevator operators in the doctor's building. She hurls a wrench through a plate glass window ready for installation, and ends up at her radio broadcast telling the audience what she really thinks of the sponsors' products. That night at the country club she threatens to do more damage if Tony will not dance with her (a good plot counterpoint to the later number "Change Partners"). They do the Yam, a number with plenty of good intentions and energy which is nevertheless forgettable as soon as the music ends.

Soon after, Tony compassionately tells Amanda that it is natural for a patient to think she is in love with her doctor, and he promises that he will hypnotize her into loving Stephen and hating him. It is a surprisingly tender and touching scene and reveals a facet of the team's acting that unfortunately was never developed, perhaps for fear it would detract from their dancing. The hypnosis is a success, and now Amanda truly hates the doctor; she cannot stand the sight of him and even tries to shoot him when he shows up at a skeet match. Meanwhile, Tony has had to admit to himself (in a conversation with his image in a two-way mirror) that, as much as he has tried to resist, he really is in love with Amanda. That night at the country club he tries to win her back during the number "Change Partners." He manages to get her alone out on the balcony, and before she can protest, he puts her under a trance and is ready to work another metamorphosis when Stephen rushes in to save her. In the final minutes of the film, of course, there is a switch at the wedding, and the right guy and the right girl say their vows.

In the late 1930's, psychoanalysis was considered *de rigueur* for the well-heeled and the movers of society, and the writers and the studio probably felt that a plot poking fun at it would be a rousing success; but it was not. The film made less money at the box-office than the other Astaire/Rogers films, and it was a definite sign that the team's partnership had nearly run its course.

The dance numbers of *Carefree* for the most part were professional but uninspiring, with the exception of "Since They Turned 'Loch Lomond' into Swing" and "Change Partners." Tony performs the former on the tee at the country club in order to impress Amanda. It is one of Astaire's most astounding routines. He dances, swings his club, tees off perfectly, and plays a harmonica without giving up an ounce of precision in any movement. It is an exacting example of the master at work.

"I Used To Be Color Blind," the number in which Amanda dreams she is dancing with the doctor, is innovative insomuch as it utilizes slow motion and makes the dancers appear to be dancing in the air. The lyrics for this number were written for color (the red in your cheeks, the gold in your hair, the blue in your eyes), and at one point in the dance the image was supposed to go from black-and-white into color, but when the studio money manager realized how much it would cost to splice in color inserts in release printing, the idea was dropped.

The only song and dance number that stands out as an unmistakable Astaire/Rogers routine is "Change Partners." It is a magnificent song and somehow saves the entire film from embarrassment. When Astaire lures Ginger out onto the balcony in order to try to reverse his hypnotic suggestion that she hate him, he momentarily places her under a trance, and it is electrifying to see the way she responds to the mere ripple of his fingers as he silently bids her to him. That he is Merlin, there is no doubt, and this scene underscores how sensuous their dancing was. When the music was right, the time right, the place right, there was nothing else like it. It is watching Astaire and Rogers do what made them legendary.

Carefree was an ironic title for this film, since it marked a change in the styles of both stars. Rogers showed a deft handling of comedy and gave an indication that her goals were to take on more than a new dance step. Astaire played a mellower, more mature character than the flippant man-about-town audiences had come to expect and love. What *Carefree* did, unfortunately, was to bring Astaire and Rogers down from the clouds and make them real people. It was a film with a less trivial plot than before, but a less memorable one. Still, it was Astaire and Rogers, and no matter how good or bad the story, how tame or same the dances, there was always that indefinable quality that made them very special.

Juliette Friedgen

CARNAL KNOWLEDGE

Released: 1971
Production: Mike Nichols for Icarus; released by Avco Embassy
Direction: Mike Nichols
Screenplay: Jules Feiffer
Cinematography: Giussepe Rotunno
Editing: Sam O'Steen
Running time: 96 minutes

> *Principal characters:*
> Jonathan .... Jack Nicholson
> Sandy .... Arthur Garfunkel
> Bobbie .... Ann-Margret
> Susan .... Candice Bergen

Carnal Knowledge, as the title might imply, is one of the frankest cinematic explorations of contemporary sexual mores yet filmed. But the title is also bitterly ironic, because the story reveals the characters' pathetic inability ever really to understand what goes into a healthy sexual and romantic relationship. By the film's depressing conclusion, we are made to realize that "carnal knowledge" is a misnomer—it is really no knowledge at all.

The story opens in the mid-1940's at Amherst, where Jonathan (Jack Nicholson) and Sandy (Arthur Garfunkel) are students. When we first meet them, although both are still virgins, the die is cast regarding their orientations toward the opposite sex. Jonathan is a good-natured, aspiring "make-out artist." For him, women are not much more than potential ciphers on a cosmic scorecard; Sandy, on the other hand, clings to an old-fashioned notion of almost Platonic adoration of women, and spends a lot of time mooning over a beautiful Smith coed named Susan (Candice Bergen). Not surprisingly, Jonathan is the one who finally scores with her, although he is still a good enough friend to Sandy (who by this time has started dating her) that he never reveals the betrayal.

After the initial exposition of the characters' sexual awakening, the story jumps ahead, periodically stopping off at various points in Jonathan's and Sandy's lives to examine the current status of their relations with women. The story chronicles their romantic downfalls, presumably because of their male conditioning, concluding with Sandy's hopeless attempts to maintain a youthful "swinger" pose deep into middle age, and Jonathan's ultimate humiliation in having to resort to a prostitute as the only remedy for almost total impotence—the result of a long, miserable affair with Bobbie (Ann-Margret), a sexy but finally emasculating partner. The film contains a fair amount of barbed humor, particularly in the early part, but assumes an increasingly bleak tone as the protagonists' lives become more and more hollow and joyless. The concluding shot—Jonathan's rapturous face dissolving into his fantasy image of a beautiful ice skater as the prostitute hypnotically drones on—represents the most crushingly final indictment of American male sexual attitudes to be shown in a major motion picture.

While the film's disapproval of its male characters' behavior is clear, its depiction of the women's positions in the relationship is more ambiguous. One reviewer simplified the identities as "man the vaginal raider, woman the castrator." Were this the case, it would certainly reflect an unhealthy attitude on the part of the scenarist, Jules Feiffer, as well as on that of his dramatic creations. But it seems that such a facile description hardly does the script full justice.

While Feiffer often depicts in his regular cartoon column—and has often indicated in interviews—a basically paranoid and pessimistic attitude about what each partner in a relationship intends to give and get from the other, his characters in *Carnal Knowledge* at least give the impression of trying for something lasting and important. That they never accomplish this is due as much to their upbringing and acculturation as to any latent personality flaw. In fact, one of the film's ironic motifs is the ever-shifting sexual fashions with which the characters breathlessly try to keep up. We recognize in their struggle something of our own insecurities in the face of society's pressures to remain youthful, desirable, sexually active—in short, to remain viable in the ongoing biological competition.

Whether one agrees with the cynical view of the filmmakers on sex and the likelihood of finding a genuine, unselfish love, there can be little doubt that the film is an excellent artistic expression of this view. In fact, the film's characters were so convincing in their attitudes that many critics assumed the positions taken by Jonathan and Sandy toward women actually reflected those of Nichols and Feiffer. This is, of course, a misinterpretation, but it is indicative of the dramatic skills of the actors, the writer, and the director.

Feiffer's dialogue has the sharpness, perception, and wit that typifies Woody Allen's but there is a cold, bitter edge to it that the more sentimental Allen lacks. While Feiffer's characters in both his cartoon strips and prose all share a common bond of obsessive self-analysis in every aspect of their behavior, their concern is essentially nonproductive; they have learned enough to realize that nothing can be done about anything, and this knowledge only deepens their, and our, sense of despair about the human condition. Still, this grim truth is undercut with enough humor to keep the whole work digestible.

Mike Nichols' work with actors has never been better than in *Carnal Knowledge*. Jack Nicholson is unforgettable as a man robbed of the one elusive quality he has spent his life trying to cultivate—his sexuality. Arthur Garfunkel's Sandy is likewise a realistic and depressing portrait of the type of man doomed to remain a boy forever; Sandy proceeds from adolescent naïveté to adolescent sophistication (bragging about his techniques and experiences), but is never able to get beyond this basic, restricted framework.

Ann-Margret's Bobbie was her first completely serious role, and her very real involvement in it (the woman abused as nothing more than a sex object has many unfortunate parallels with her own acting career) brought a new dimension to her performance. She earned an Oscar nomination for Best Supporting Actress.

In addition to the fine work with actors, *Carnal Knowledge* also showcased Nichols' increasing control in maneuvering the camera around the action. This was most evident in the many held shots that simply showed the characters engaged in dialogue, or the continuous trucking shots gliding along with them from one place to another. Like many European directors, Nichols has enough confidence in his cast to let them carry a scene, and he renders the camera a dispassionate observer rather than an active participant. This glacial style was augmented by the fine cinematography of Giussepe Rotunno; the look of the film was naturalistic to a fault, with people often disappearing into protective shadows with an air of doomed placidity, or smiling in the soft romantic glows with an innocent happiness that belies the tragedy.

Despite the often bitter tone of *Carnal Knowledge*, our sympathies remain with the characters; they are victims as well as victimizers. The social context from which they emerged has crippled them, the film seems to be saying, and for this they deserve our pity and understanding. It is this aspect of the film that makes the ending so disturbing and poignant. *Carnal Knowledge* is not an easy film to deal with; numerous obscenity suits (all eventually dismissed) indicated that the public was not really ready in 1971 to face up to such a straightforward examination of this "forbidden" part of our physical and psychological makeup.

Joel Bellman

CAROUSEL

Released: 1956
Production: Henry Ephron for Twentieth Century-Fox
Direction: Henry King
Screenplay: Phoebe Ephron and Henry Ephron; based on Benjamin F. Glazer's adaptation of the play *Liliom* by Ferenc Molnar and the book *Carousel* by Oscar Hammerstein II
Cinematography: Charles G. Clarke
Editing: William Reynolds
Choreography: Rod Alexander
Music: Oscar Hammerstein II and Richard Rodgers
Running time: 128 minutes

Principal characters:
Billy .... Gordon MacRae
Julie .... Shirley Jones
Mrs. Mullin .... Audrey Christie
Jigger .... Cameron Mitchell
Cousin Nettie .... Claramae Turner
Carrie .... Barbara Ruick
Louise .... Susan Luckey
Mr. Snow .... Robert Rounseville
Starkeeper .... Gene Lockhart

Film musicals which have antiheroes as main characters can be counted on the fingers of one hand, and two of those have music by Richard Rodgers. The title character in *Pal Joey* (1957), which Rodgers wrote with Lorenz Hart in the 1930's, is a likable heel, a ladies' man, a rogue. Billy (Gordon MacRae), however, the drifter and carousel operator in *Carousel*, written with Oscar Hammerstein, II, is not quite like Joey. Billy is also likable and charms both hardened women and less worldly town girls. Like Joey, Billy does not mind being kept by women: he is supported first by his boss, Mrs. Mullin (Audrey Christie), owner of the carousel, and then by her rival, his wife Julie (Shirley Jones). His character is rigidly defined by his inability to support himself, and when he tries to make some money in a robbery, he bungles the job and loses his life. Yet Billy is more than the engaging womanizer and con man familiar to many film musicals; instead, he belongs more to the melodrama or the "woman's picture."

Billy's main interest as a character arises from his relationship with Julie. Her love for Billy survives all tests of faith, including the unhappiness of their daughter as she nears high school graduation; it even survives his death. As a transcendent love story, *Carousel* is an optimistic, extremely positive musical with a twist most musicals lack. Its love story is based upon a faith which suffering and loss cannot damage. Billy cannot be reformed by the women who love him; but he can be redeemed by them. Despite a framework borrowed from the melodrama, however, *Carousel* is by no means a tragedy. All of its points are made lightly, with a beautiful score including "If I Loved You," "June Is Bustin' Out All Over," and "You'll Never Walk Alone."

The triangle of Billy, Mrs. Mullin, and Julie is counterpointed with a humorous second couple: Mr. Snow (Robert Rounseville) and Carrie (Barbara Ruick). Carrie is a giggling romantic; her beau is very respectable, although because of his profession he often smells like fish. Billy's cracks about Mr. Snow's smell only prove how out of touch he is with small-town life; his own social drawbacks are much more serious. He does not work; he has a job when Julie meets him, but not a respectable one—he runs the carousel at a carnival. The scene in which Julie buys a ticket to the carousel beautifully conveys Billy's and Julie's love at first sight. Julie's ride is dizzying, a whirl of colors and lights; it is also clearly sexual, as Billy steadies her on the rapidly rising and falling pony. After a short flirtation in which they sing the duet "If I Loved You," the couple elopes. Julie then brings her new husband back to live with her cousin Nettie (Claramae Turner) on Nettie's boat.

After Billy has given up his carousel job, he shows no interest in finding a respectable job. He is out of place in Julie's small fishing community and feels awkward with her friends. Julie is soon defending his inability to find work, which is more painful to her than it is to Billy. For her sake, the audience hopes that things will work out; but when Mrs. Mullin appears, Billy quickly yields to temptation. When he goes to Julie to tell her of Mrs. Mullin's job offer and his decision to return to the carousel, she first tells him that she is pregnant, thus winning Billy back. Even as an expectant father, however, Billy remains true to character. He declines to attend a clambake with Julie and her friends, and instead attempts a payroll robbery planned by a blackguard friend; he sees himself rich and able to take Julie away from her small town. Instead, the robbery fails, and Billy, trying to outrun a constable, falls off a pile of crates on the dock and lands on his own knife. As he lies dying, Julie returns with her friends from the clambake in time to hold him for a last good-bye, and to forgive him. Nettie then comforts her with the song "You'll Never Walk Alone."

The story of Billy and Julie's romance is framed in flashback. The movie opens with Billy in heaven; even there he is a reprobate prone to exaggerate the facts. A friend tips him off that his daughter, now grown to high-school age, is in trouble. Billy is worried and asks to have one day back on earth. To get permission, he must tell his story to the Starkeeper (Gene Lockhart). After the flashback story, permission is granted and Billy returns to earth, where he watches his daughter, Louise (Susan Lucky), on the beach. Her character is established and developed not by dialogue, but in a ballet choreographed by Agnes de Mille, which reveals Louise to be a social outsider as he once was, eager for fun and scorned by her more respectable peers.

Billy follows his daughter home and speaks to her, but she is confused by the stranger's offer of a "star." He loses his patience and slaps her. Louise cries out, and Julie comes to the front porch, but Billy is unseen again, as Louise shows the star to Julie. "Can a man slap you so that it doesn't hurt?" Louise asks. Julie knows the feeling, and says that he can; thus, mother and daughter share the experience of a transcendent love for Billy. Louise goes to her graduation less defiant, joining her classmates in the ceremony as Billy looks on unseen. The movie ends as the entire community joins together in song.

Carousel was a big success for Rodgers and Hammerstein on the stage, and the film took no chances by altering a proven product. The film was also a success, following the stage version closely as it does, differing primarily in its location shooting. Seen today, *Carousel* lacks the visual interest of other musicals made in the period just prior to its release in 1956. Henry King also directed some of the classics of melodrama, including *Stella Dallas* (1937) and *Love Is a Many Splendored Thing* (1955). For *Carousel*, King adapted his style to CinemaScope, then popular at the box office. In addition to wide panoramas, however, the movie includes scenes which are quite stagey. The opening scenes in Heaven make no attempt to avoid a theatrical look, while subsequent shots capitalize on the genuine Maine harbor and dock locations of "June Is Bustin' Out All Over." A similarly uneasy match is the actual beach setting of Billy's soliloquy when he learns he is to be a father, followed by the obvious soundstage set for the clambake scenes.

The pairing of Shirley Jones and Gordon MacRae in the main roles of Julie and Billy repeated their successful partnership in the previous year's Rodgers and Hammerstein musical, *Oklahoma!* (1955), which, like *Carousel*, included a ballet choreographed by Agnes de Mille.

Leslie Donaldson

CARRY ON NURSE

Released: 1960
Production: Peter Rogers for Anglo Amalgamated/Governor Films
Direction: Gerald Thomas
Screenplay: Norman Hudis; based on an idea by Patrick Cargill and Jack Searle
Cinematography: Reginald H. Wyer
Editing: John Shirley
Running time: 86 minutes

Principal characters:

Dorothy Denton	Shirley Eaton
Bernie Bishop	Kenneth Connor
Hinton	Charles Hawtrey
Matron	Hattie Jacques
Ted York	Terence Longdon
Percy Hickson	Bill Owen
Jack Bell	Leslie Phillips
Stella Dawson	Joan Sims
Oliver Reckitt	Kenneth Williams
The Colonel	Wilfrid Hyde-White

The British "Carry On" series, which began in 1958 with *Carry on Sergeant* and the most recent release of which has been *Carry on Emanuelle* (1978), is in the tradition of the British Music Hall. Its ancestry lies in the comedy sketches of the Crazy Gang, a group of zany performers who delighted music hall audiences from the 1930's through the 1950's, and in the vulgar, risque patter of Max Miller, who, with good reason, was known by the title of "The Cheeky Chappie." The comedies could never have been produced in the United States; they have a peculiar vulgar style, both in terms of dialogue and purely visual routines, and a type of "toilet humor" which is exclusively British. One of the leading actors, Jim Dale, who appeared in ten films of the series, perhaps summed it up best when he commented:

> If on screen you see the front of a home and somebody opens a door and there's a field behind it, that's American humor. If, when the door is opened, there's a field with a lavatory in it, that's French humor. If there's a field with a lavatory and somebody sat on it, using it, that's a "Carry On" film.

The "Carry On" series is a unique phenomenom. Twenty-nine "Carry On" films have been produced to date, plus one compilation, *That's Carry*, released in 1978. All produced by Peter Rogers and all directed by Gerald Thomas, the films were cheaply made, generally for less than $150,000, and they have been the major British box-office hits of their respective years, earning more than a million dollars apiece. From time to time, the Carry On team has also appeared on British television in Christmas specials and the like. The series has even been the subject of a book-length study, *The Carry On Book* by Kenneth Eastaugh. The films are very much a family affair, with the same players—Charles Hawtrey, Kenneth Williams, Sidney James, Barbara Windsor, Joan Sims, Kenneth Connor, Peter Butterworth, Hattie Jacques, Terry Scott, Jack Douglas, and Bernard Bresslaw—appearing in most, and Talbot Bothwell or Norman Hudis preparing the scripts.

The story line is not of great importance in the "Carry On" series, but the humor is, and it must never vary from a certain low level; and when a nonvulgar joke is thrown in, it is usually of a vintage and corny nature. Even some of the titles smack of vulgarity: *Carry on Cruising* (1962), *Carry on Camping* (1968), *Carry on Dick* (1974), *Carry on Behind* (1975), and *Carry on at Your Convenience* (1971), a title which is lost on American viewers unless they are aware that public lavatories in England are referred to as "conveniences."

Character names also smack of vulgarity. In *Carry on Teacher* (1959), Joan Sims plays Sarah Allcock. In *Carry on Jack* (1963), Bernard Cribbins plays Albert Poop-Decker. In *Carry on . . . Don't Lose Your Head* (1966), Peter Butterworth plays Citizen Bidet. In *Carry on . . . Follow That Camel* (1967), Phil Silvers plays Sergeant Nocker. In *Carry on Again Doctor* (1969), Sidney James plays Gladstone Screwer, and Florence Knight, Nurse Willing. In *Carry on at Your Convenience*, there is much British humor, with Kenneth Williams portraying W. C. Boggs, a reference to lavatories in England being called water closets, or W. C.'s, and, in slang, "bogs." In *Carry on Dick*, Jack Douglas plays Sergeant Jock Strapp.

Verbal humor in the "Carry on" series is best illustrated by the following random examples: "Are you satisfied with your equipment, Miss Allcock?" "Well! I've had no complaints so far. . . ." "Your birds . . . what sort are they? Blue tits?" "No, my place is centrally heated. . . ." "Psst." "What?" "Psst!" "Don't be ridiculous. I've only had a couple. All men talk nonsense in their cups, Bidet. It's what we call coq-au-vin." For connoisseurs of visual humor, the "Carry On" series can offer an unwilling victim having a hypodermic needle jabbed in his rear, the bosomy Barbara Windsor losing her bra, Kenneth Cope in drag visiting the men's room, or Dick Turpin stripping every stitch of clothing from the passengers on the coach he is robbing.

One of the most popular of the "Carry On" films, and the most successful in the United States, was *Carry on Nurse*, the second film in the series and one of six written by Norman Hudis. Not only did the film gross more than any other British production released in England up to that time, but it was also one of the highest-grossing English films to be released in the United States, playing fifteen weeks at one New York theater and more than thirty weeks in Los Angeles, and eventually becoming something of a cult movie on college campuses and on television. Most American critics loved it, with the *Los Angeles Times* insisting that it would inspire Aristotle to rewrite his treatise on the essence of comedy.

Carry on Nurse is set in the men's wing of a large public hospital, providing plenty of opportunities for coy male nudity as nurses busily strip their patients, not to mention endless jokes concerning bedpans and enemas. As two nurses prepare to remove a patient's underwear, he protests to no avail, "I'll do it myself if you don't mind." After unceremoniously being derobed and flung on the bed, one of the nurses remarks to him, "What a fuss—about such a little thing."

Presiding over the nurses is the stern and solidly built matron, played by Hattie Jacques, who looks as if she would be more at home as the commandant of a German concentration camp. Her staff includes the clumsy Nurse Dawson (Joan Sims) and the appropriately named Nurse Nightie Nightingale. The patients include a boxer (Kenneth Connor) who has broken his wrist in a fight, a building worker (Bill Owen) with a broken leg, a reporter (Terence Longdon) who is gathering material on hospital life for his newspaper and who falls in love with an attractive nurse played by Shirley Eaton, a prissy little eccentric man (Charles Hawtrey), a bookworm (Kenneth Williams), and the Colonel (Wilfrid Hyde-White), who, from his private ward, directs the nurses to place bets for him.

The film is really nothing more than a series of episodic adventures, varying from a group of doctors getting inebriated and, in a drunken stupor, attempting an operation to remove a patient's bunion, to scenes in which toilet paper becomes streamers, to the shaving of pubic hair prior to an operation, and, in another scene, the insertion of a suppository.

The classic gag in *Carry on Nurse* occurs at the end of the film. The nurses have become tired of the Colonel's constant demands on them to run his errands, and two of them—Joan Sims and Susan Stephen—decide on revenge. They tell the Colonel that one final test is needed before his release. Although the Colonel's naked rear end is never seen, it is obvious that the nurses have inserted a daffodil therein. As they are about to photograph the daffodil in position, matron enters. "Colonel, whatever's going on?" she demands. "Surely you've seen a temperature taken like this before," responds the Colonel. "Oh, yes, Colonel, many times," replies matron, "but never with a daffodil." And she thereupon plucks it out. That one scene is the essence of the humor in the "Carry On" series, with outrageous behavior implied rather than actually witnessed in graphic detail.

The medical profession obviously offered ample opportunities for comedy to the Carry on team, such as *Carry on Doctor* (1972) and *Carry on Again Doctor*. Today, the future of the series is somewhat in doubt, with most of its original performers showing signs of age, and two of them, Peter Butterworth and Sidney James, having died. However, regardless of whether any further films are produced, one thing is certain: so long as the series continues to be revived, audiences will continue to carry on laughing, and in so doing, will continue to carry on paying tribute to a unique group of actors.

Anthony Slide

CASABLANCA

Released: 1942
Production: Hal B. Wallis for Warner Bros. (AA)
Direction: Michael Curtiz (AA)
Screenplay: Julius J. Epstein, Philip G. Epstein, and Howard Koch (AA);
   based on the play *Everybody Comes to Rick's* by Murray Burnett and Jean
   Alison
Cinematography: Arthur Edeson
Editing: Owen Marks
Running time: 102 minutes

> *Principal characters:*
> Rick Blaine .... Humphrey Bogart
> Ilsa Lund .... Ingrid Bergman
> Victor Laszlo .... Paul Henreid
> Captain Louis Renault .... Claude Rains
> Major Strasser .... Conrad Veidt
> Senor Ferrari .... Sydney Greenstreet
> Ugarte .... Peter Lorre
> Sam .... Dooley Wilson

Casablanca, which opened to mixed reviews in 1942, has successfully weathered the perspective of time and achieved the designation of "classic." Though created under somewhat adverse conditions of confusion and haste, with the script being written from day to day as the shooting progressed and the actors uncertain as to the final outcome, it still displays the look of a thoroughly prepared, well-crafted masterpiece. In fact, it has become a cult film among successive generations of filmgoers through its successful fusion of the major qualities of the Hollywood romantic melodrama at its finest. These characteristics include a surprisingly tightly constructed plot that never wastes a second under Michael Curtiz's direction, a well-balanced cast, superb cinematography and music, and the polish of a well-knit studio team working together.

It is due primarily to the efforts of this studio team that the basic flaws in the screenplay were surmounted to make the film into the legend that it has become. The story, based on a forgotten drama entitled *Everybody Comes to Rick's*, is riddled with improbable situations and awkward dialogue that would normally seal a picture's doom—yet in *Casablanca*, everything works. The result remains a richly satisfying film, both of its own time as a stirring piece of anti-Nazi propaganda and of all time in its feeling for the drama of love.

Michael Curtiz directed this Hal B. Wallis production with primary emphasis on atmosphere and characterization. Although the motion picture does not drip with the sin and the local color of the North African city where the refugees "wait and wait and wait," it does reproduce the tense thrill of a strange foreign place in which all types of unconventional people are gathered. The focal point of the film is Rick's Café Americaine, where refugees from Hitler's Europe gather anxiously in search of exit visas to Lisbon while Nazi agents plot their capture.

As portrayed by Humphrey Bogart, Rick Blaine is the American who has continuously fought for the underdog, but who is out for no one. He is not the classic hero but a touchy, stubborn, self-centered figure who could not be totally counted on to do the right thing. Yet he is a man who has flung himself deeply into love and who demonstrates an immense vulnerability to emotional upsets.

Casablanca, by means of flashback, presents a picture of a Parisian romance. Rick, or Richard Blaine, as he was known then, is gloriously happy in his whirlwind romance with Ilsa (Ingrid Bergman), and is so absorbed in an attempt to rush her into marriage that he ignores the troubled look in her eyes and the note of hesitation in her voice. Expecting her to flee Paris with him ahead of the German invaders, Richard is stunned by Ilsa's cryptic note of farewell. It is a stunning blow to his self-esteem, and the flashback ends as the rain symbolically wipes out the episode by smudging Ilsa's writing on the letter in Richard's hand.

By 1941, Richard Blaine has become "Rick" of Rick's Café Americaine in Casablanca. He has hardened, like his name, and withdrawn into himself. Rick's professed attitude—"I stick my neck out for no one,"—is, however, a case of self-deception. He has fought the Fascists in Spain and left Paris because the Germans would have been after him. Even in Casablanca he indicates a dislike for Germans, ordering one away from his gambling tables and allowing the band to play "La Marseillaise" to drown out the Germans singing "Wacht am Rhein." He aids Ugarte (Peter Lorre), who has killed two Germans and stolen their Weygand-signed visas, by hiding the visas for him. He later refuses to help Ugarte evade capture by the police because it is too late to assist him and not because he is unsympathetic. Rick is also notably impressed at the mention of resistance leader Victor Laszlo.

When Laszlo (Paul Henreid) shows up at Rick's cafe, it could be assumed that Rick would be predisposed to aid his escape to America. Laszlo, however, is accompanied by his wife, Ilsa, and Bogart superbly conveys the impact of her unexpected return both by his angry stride to stop Sam the piano player from playing the tune that recalls Paris, "As Time Goes By," and by his startled, dumbfounded reaction to the sight of Ilsa sitting there. He surprises himself by having a casual drink with her and Laszlo. Then late that night, drinking gin in a fog of cigarette smoke, he relives the past to help him resist the explanation that he knows she will bring for her betrayal of him in Paris. He is also suspicious that she will be interested only in the passports he has hidden. It is a losing battle. Ilsa comes to plead for forgiveness and help, but ultimately attempts to take the precious letters of transit at gunpoint. When she breaks down and cannot do it, Rick is forced to admire her once again, and then to accept her complete submission to his will.

Ingrid Bergman plays this strange role with subtlety and conviction, but the character of Ilsa is not entirely clear because of its continual vacillation. Paul Henreid superbly portrays Laszlo as a poor lover in comparison with Bogart's Rick. The qualities of aloofness and diplomacy that make him a great statesman deny him the spontaneity of feeling and the recklessness of passionate love, although it is clear that he indeed loves Ilsa and is dependent upon her support. At the film's end, his noble offer to sacrifice his own freedom for hers is admirable, but also cold and calculated.

For Rick, the time has come to act, and his imaginative solution to everyone's problems teases the audience with the possibility that he has betrayed the resistance leader to the police. This ploy enables him to restage the earlier heartbreaking departure from Paris in a similarly urgent departure scene at Casablanca airport. He again is separated from Ilsa, but this time it is by his choice and he maintains his self-esteem. He has betrayed her by putting her on the plane with her husband when she expects to stay with him. Rick's betrayal of Ilsa is based on the same reasons as her earlier betrayal of him—the greater cause represented by Laszlo. The climax is made more satisfactory to the audience by providing the opportunity for Rick to kill the Nazi leader, Major Strasser (Conrad Veidt), after he has allowed the German to get off the first shot. The hazards represented by Rick's love for Ilsa are supplanted by the more stable, less competitive friendship that appears possible between two men such as Rick and Police Captain Renault (Claude Rains), who discover that they are fellow patriots who thoroughly enjoy each other's company.

The major characters in this film are given support by a striking group of minor actors such as Sydney Greenstreet, S.Z. Sakall, Leonid Kinskey, and Marcel Dalio. Another excellent actor of the supporting cast is Dooley Wilson as Sam the pianist—a man devoted to Rick, his boss. Wilson's fine singing and piano playing contribute much to the film's effectiveness.

Casablanca won the Oscar for Best Picture of 1943. Michael Curtiz also won the award that year for Best Direction, as did the team of writers for Best Screenplay. Oddly enough, however, the haunting musical theme of the picture, "As Time Goes By," did not win the award, since it was written and published previous to the film. The acting in the film, although excellent, also went unawarded when Humphrey Bogart and Ingrid Bergman were passed over that year in favor of Paul Lukas and Jennifer Jones.

Stephen L. Hanson

CAT ON A HOT TIN ROOF

Released: 1958
Production: Lawrence Weingarten for Metro-Goldwyn-Mayer
Direction: Richard Brooks
Screenplay: Richard Brooks and James Poe; based on the play of the same name by Tennessee Williams
Cinematography: William Daniels
Editing: Ferris Webster
Art direction: William A. Horning and Urie McCleary; set decoration, Henry Grace and Robert Priestley
Running time: 108 minutes

Principal characters:
Maggie .... Elizabeth Taylor
Brick .... Paul Newman
Big Daddy .... Burl Ives
Gooper .... Jack Carson
Big Mama .... Judith Anderson
Mae .... Madeleine Sherwood

Produced in wide screen and Metrocolor under the superlative direction of Richard Brooks, *Cat on a Hot Tin Roof* preserves all the shocking, high-voltage atmosphere of the original Pulitzer Prize-winning play by Tennessee Williams. Richard Brooks, who had previously written and directed such films as *Blackboard Jungle* (1955), has exacted a cinematic tribute to Williams' genius as a playwright. His screenplay, which was cowritten with James Poe, adds individual lines and entire scenes to the play, while it deletes all of the original four-letter words as well as all references to homosexuality. Despite these alterations, however, the script remains remarkably faithful to the original, retaining the play's atmosphere of highly charged emotion.

Cat on a Hot Tin Roof is the intense story of twelve harrowing hours in the life of a family in conflict. Here, on a lush, fertile plantation in the Mississippi delta, greed, jealousy, love, and hate run rampant.

The story opens on the eve of the sixty-fifth birthday of Big Daddy (Burl Ives), a blustering bull of a man who expresses his love toward his family in the only way he knows—by bestowing upon them an abundance of material possessions. This habit is to be his undoing and theirs. Ives, a veteran character actor with immense stage and screen presence who has appeared in such films as *East of Eden* (1955) and *The Big Country* (1958) (the latter won him an Academy Award as Best Supporting Actor), is perfect as Big Daddy. He created the role for the stage and, under Brooks's inspired direction in the film, he fleshes out every facet of this crotchety old millionaire's indomitable character.

Safely ensconced in his lavishly appointed mansion, having just returned from an Eastern clinic where he believes he has been given a clean bill of health, Big Daddy is prepared to accept the fawning idolatry of his family, which has assembled to celebrate his birthday. Only his two sons and the family doctor know the true story; Big Daddy is dying of cancer.

Jack Carson as Gooper, the older son, reveals a degree of dramatic talent unseen in his previous roles. As in the stage version, greed is Gooper's most obvious trait, but Carson's Gooper is less one-dimensional and more sympathetic. He is the good, conscientious son who, in addition to establishing a successful law practice of his own, has worked diligently to keep the plantation viable. Knowing that he is not, and has never been, Big Daddy's favorite, he fears that his hard work and loyalty will go unrewarded.

Madeleine Sherwood re-creates her Broadway role as Gooper's wife Mae, and her brilliant performance as Gooper's mewing, favor-currying, back-biting wife loses nothing in its transition from stage to screen. Gooper's driving ambition for wealth is surpassed only by that of his wife, who will use any weapon, including her ability to provide heirs, to secure her husband's inheritance. Mae and Gooper's brood of five children, unaffectionately called the "no-neck monsters" by the rest of the family, are nearly as big an aggravation to the audience as they obviously are to the family.

Brick, ably portrayed by Paul Newman, recoils from the sexual attentions of his beautiful wife Maggie because he believes she is somehow responsible for the suicide of a best friend whom Brick had idolized. This case of peer worship is a radical departure from the original script, in which the implication of a homosexual attachment is made quite clear. Newman is excellent as the bitter, brooding young husband, for he conveys a kind of dormant virility which smolders just beneath the surface, refusing to be stoked into the white-hot heat of passion. Sullenly, he hobbles around his and Maggie's bedroom on crutches, having broken his ankle while drunkenly trying to jump hurdles in an attempt to relive the athletic days of his youth. In direct contrast to Gooper's avariciousness, Brick, the favorite son, recoils from the old man's money with nearly the same repugnance with which he greets his wife's advances.

Maggie, perceptively played by Elizabeth Taylor, is the beautiful kitten-turned-cat who fights tooth and nail to save both her marriage and her husband's share of his inheritance. She is obsessed with passion for a husband who refuses to touch her; at the same time, she is vilified by her in-laws because she is childless. Taylor, who had appeared previously in such successful films as *Giant* (1956) and *Raintree County* (1958), both of which garnered her Academy Award nominations, emphatically proves in her sensitive portrayal of Maggie that her talents can match her renowned beauty.

The lines of battle are drawn early in the film: Maggie "the Cat" is pitted against Gooper, Mae, and their children, with Brick refusing to take responsibility for his part of the inheritance. In the background is Big Daddy's wife, "Big Mama," a shadowy, sentimental figure whose opinions are virtually ignored. Judith Anderson's interpretation of Big Mama is that of a mindless, silly woman who is completely overshadowed and awed by her husband's bellowing intensity and moneymaking ability.

When fatherly love finally prompts Big Daddy to force Brick into a no-holds-barred discussion about his drinking and total lack of responsibility for either his marriage or the family's fortunes, he is adamant. Never a subtle man, he hammers away at Brick, probing and searching for what went wrong in his son's life. Goaded beyond the point of reason, Brick involuntarily discloses to the old man that Big Daddy does not have long to live. For several long minutes, Big Daddy is devastated; the truth is all the more shattering because he has been led to believe by the clinic that he is in good health.

The enormity of the terrible pain he has caused cuts through Brick's thick veil of self-pity, and he watches in helpless shame as the broken old man slowly begins to gather up the pieces. In one of the most electrifying scenes in the movie, Big Daddy turns on his son and shouts: "I've got the guts to die, boy . . . have you got the guts to live?"

Later, when Maggie is again taunted by Mae because of her inability to produce heirs, Maggie plays her last card: she tells Big Daddy that she *is* going to bear a child and that she had wanted it to be a birthday surprise for him. She has gambled, but this time she does not lose, for Brick, sobered into facing reality by the harrowing confrontation with his father, goes to her and stoutly backs up her stunning proclamation. Perhaps he has finally discovered that he does, indeed, have the "guts to live."

Cat on a Hot Tin Roof, one of the top ten moneymaking films of 1958, received six Academy Award nominations: for Best Picture, Best Actor, Best Actress, Best Direction, Best Screenplay, and Best Color Cinematography. Also worthy of note is the excellent contribution of art directors William A. Horning and Urie McCleary in their creation of the rambling plantation mansion, and of set directors Henry Grace and Robert Priestley, for the lavish furnishings. The lush background of the Deep South, with its hazy tranquillity, is ably captured in the cinematography of William Daniels.

In addition to being one of the best interpretations of Tennessee Williams' material ever to be transferred to the screen, *Cat on a Hot Tin Roof* was noteworthy for its effect on the careers of both Elizabeth Taylor and Paul Newman. Both actors' careers were to rise to the level of "superstardom" and to remain there for more than twenty years. Taylor followed her success in this film with such pictures as *Suddenly Last Summer* (1959), *Butterfield 8* (1960), and *Who's Afraid of Virginia Woolf?* (1966), the latter two winning Academy Awards for her performances. Paul Newman, who was relatively unsuccessful until his outstanding performance here, went on to star in *The*

Hustler (1961), *Hud* (1963), and *Cool Hand Luke* (1967). All three of these films resulted in Academy Award nominations for him.

Richard Brooks, who was already an established director, went on to work on a wide variety of successful films, both dramas—such as *Elmer Gantry* (1960), for which his screenplay won an Academy Award—and comedies, such as the Pink Panther series.

D. Gail Huskins

CAT PEOPLE

Released: 1942
Production: Val Lewton for RKO/Radio
Direction: Jacques Tourneur
Screenplay: DeWitt Bodeen
Cinematography: Nicholas Musuraca
Editing: Mark Robson
Running time: 73 minutes

Principal characters:
Irena Dubrovna .... Simone Simon
Oliver Reed .... Kent Smith
Dr. Louis Judd .... Tom Conway
Alice Moore .... Jane Randolph
The Commodore .... Jack Holt
The Cat Woman .... Elizabeth Russell

In 1941, Charles Koerner, then head of production at RKO, decided to create a new unit at the studio devoted to the filming of a series of high-class horror pictures. From David O. Selznick, for whom he had been employed for nine years as story editor, Koerner brought over Val Lewton to head the new unit as producer. Lewton hired writer DeWitt Bodeen, who was instructed to write a story with the title *Cat People*, which had been chosen by Koerner for its potential appeal to audiences. Vampires, monsters, and werewolves had had a thorough working over among horror filmmakers, but few had done anything with cats. Yet cats formed a good part of lycanthropy and related legends, going back as far as ancient Egypt and India, where the superstition still existed that under certain conditions human beings could change into feline form and destroy those they love. Bodeen next worked the story into screenplay form; Jacques Tourneur was chosen as director; and filming began in the summer of 1942.

Cat People is a simple story based upon fear of the unknown; it centers on a Yugoslavian girl, Irena Dubrovna (Simone Simon) who left her native village under mysterious circumstances. Her father had died mysteriously in the forest, and her mother had been looked upon by the villagers as one of the cat people, women who can change into leopard form and destroy any man who possesses them sexually. Irena has come to New York, where she works successfully as a costume designer, living a lonely, solitary life in the midst of the great Manhattan jungle. The story begins one day in late summer when Irena meets Oliver Reed (Kent Smith) in the outdoor zoo at Central Park. Oliver is working with a maritime design office, and he is intrigued by Irena, who is idly sketching the big cats in their cages. She agrees to let him walk her home, and throws away the drawing she had been working on. It depicts a rampant black panther, pierced by a heavy silver sword.

Oliver learns more about Irena, whose kittenlike personality fascinates him. Everything about her is feline and adorable, yet she has inexplicable idiosyncrasies. On a second visit to her apartment, Oliver tries to bring her a gift of a pet kitten, but when the kitten snarls and withdraws from Irena's touch, she explains that domestic cats have always borne her a strange antagonism. She and Oliver go to the pet store to exchange the kitten for a bird, and Irena's mere presence in the store causes pandemonium among the animals in their cages. Nevertheless, they take home a canary in a cage, and Irena is happy until one day, in playing with the bird, she literally frightens it to death, and it falls to the floor of the cage lifeless. She puts the body of the dead bird in a little box and takes it to the zoo, where, fascinated, she stands watching the pacing black panther; then, with a curious cruel smile, she tosses the panther the body of the bird. The panther snarls, placing one paw possessively upon the feathered gift, glaring upon her with new interest.

Oliver asks Irena to marry him, and although she confesses her fears, he laughs them away, convincing her that she is torturing herself with fears brought on by loneliness. In the midst of the gaieties of their wedding party, held in a Balkan restaurant in Greenwich Village, a smartly dressed woman (Elizabeth Russell) passes by the table on her way to the door. The eyes of the woman are slanted mysteriously, the face heart-shaped; she looks with a beguiling smile upon the happy bride, and says, *"Moia sestra,"* then smiles knowingly, and leaves. Irena is distraught; the woman has called her "sister." Why? The fears and superstitions that have ruled her life are called back, and that night the marriage is not consummated; Oliver agrees to wait, to help her rid herself of her fears with the help of a psychiatrist.

Previous horror movies had been basically of two kinds. The more popular variety, usually favored by Universal, began with an opening reel of sheer, monstrous terror that could scarcely be topped later in the film. The more European variety began slowly and subtly, building mood and developing character, and then struck suddenly with the first of three horror sequences, culminating in an action-filled climax and quick finale. The latter type of story is the type used in *Cat People*. There is to be no supernatural violence; the fears that the characters suffer are of the mind. Man can only really fear what he does not know and understand. What may lurk in the dark is far more fearsome than what can be seen in the light of day. Of all the fears besieging man, that of the unknown is the most potent, for it is the most destructive. Fortunately, the depiction of such fears lends itself well to cinematographic interpretation.

In the maritime office where Oliver works there is a girl named Alice Moore (Jane Randolph). She and Oliver have not only been coworkers but also close friends. He tells her of the problems besetting him and Irena, and she suggests a psychiatrist who might be of assistance—Dr. Louis Judd (Tom

Conway). When Judd meets Irena, he puts her under hypnosis and is intrigued by what he learns; yet it is so fantastic a pattern that he cannot believe it. Irena, meanwhile, becomes jealous of the growing intimacy between Oliver and Alice, and is aware of, and annoyed by, Dr. Judd's desire to possess her.

The stage is now set for the three horror sequences. First, Irena spies upon Oliver and Alice when they are dining together after working late. Oliver walks Alice to the park transverse, where they part. Unafraid, Alice begins to walk home, and then is aware that something she cannot see is following her. She heard footsteps on the concrete walk at first, but now there is nothing—only a little night wind and the softness of silence. Frightened, Alice runs from one lighted lamppost to the next, lingering in each circle of light. An angry roar bears down upon her, and she clings in terror to the post, only to have a bus come to a stop at the curb, and the door open for her to enter.

This is Irena's first attempt upon Alice. A few nights later, the second attempt is made, when Irena follows Alice to the residential hotel in which she lives. Alice has gone down to the deserted indoor swimming pool. Suddenly, the shadows move menacingly; there is a warning snarl; and Alice, frightened, leaps into the pool. The shadows move around her with darker shadows within them; the eerie light makes curious, unnatural patterns upon the ceiling; and Alice is confident that some unknown danger is pacing the periphery of the pool on cat feet. She screams for help and suddenly the room is flooded with light; Irena is there, amused, smiling down upon her, while two female night clerks come in answer to the scream. There is a natural explanation for everything until Alice finds her robe torn to shreds, as if a savage beast had deliberately ripped it.

A third attempt is made in the drafting-rooms of the office at night, this time upon both Oliver and Alice. They then try to close in on Irena before she can harm Dr. Judd, for he is the only one who does not believe in her as a fearsome threat to his own life. But it is too late. They find Dr. Judd clawed to death, and Irena's body pierced by the protective sword he always carries in his cane. Wounded, Irena makes her way to the zoo, and, with a stolen key, unlocks the leopard's cage. The leopard springs out and destroys her with one savage blow. In death, Irena's body seems to reassume its feline shape, and Oliver and Alice, who have rushed to the park, leave whispering, "She never lied to us."

Cat People was released early in December of 1942. Many of the first reviews dismissed it as just another horror film, but the public was attracted, and the picture started doing a tremendous box-office business. Later reviews reevaluated the film when it played thirteen consecutive weeks in Hollywood at the Hawaii, breaking all records. It had been made on a budget of $134,000, which was a modest-to-average sum for a "B" picture at that time. Today *Cat People* has grossed more than four million dollars in domestic and foreign releases; along with another film, *Hitler's Children* (1942), it helped to pull RKO out of the red, and for the first time in a long while the Studio was solvent.

Because of wartime emergencies *Cat People* was filmed almost entirely on studio stages, either at RKO/Radio in Hollywood, or on the RKO-Pathe lot in Culver City. Only one sequence, the swimming pool scene, was shot off the lot, at a swimming pool in a once-swank residential hotel in the Alvarado district of Los Angeles; the cat cages at Central Park Zoo, the transverse walk through the park, and the street scenes were all filmed on studio stages. The largest interior setting, Alice's apartment, was the upper floor of the same brownstone front building that had been used in *The Magnificent Ambersons* (1942). The four-storied stairway in the entrance hall was redressed to lend the film a richness it could not otherwise have afforded on its limited budget.

Today, *Cat People* is known as a cult film. It plays regularly throughout the world and is a standard television attraction. Simone Simon considers it the best picture she made in Hollywood. Ideally cast, she brought a special feline charm to the role of Irena. Her individual mystique contrasted admirably with the more mundane characters played by Kent Smith and Jane Randolph as Oliver and Alice. Due to the film's popularity, the cast was called back to do a sequel, *The Curse of the Cat People* (1944), which drew strong critical notices from reviewers such as James Agee and Tom Milne, but which did not enjoy the enormous box-office receipts of *Cat People*.

DeWitt Bodeen

CAVALCADE

Released: 1933
Production: Frank Lloyd for Fox Films (AA)
Direction: Frank Lloyd (AA)
Screenplay: Reginald Berkeley; based on the play of the same name by Noel Coward
Cinematography: Ernest Palmer
Editing: Margaret Clancey
Art direction: William Darling (AA)
War scenes: William Cameron Menzies
Running time: 110 minutes

Principal characters:
Jane Marryot	Diana Wynyard
Robert Marryot	Clive Brook
Fanny Bridges	Ursula Jeans
Alfred Bridges	Herbert Mundin
Ellen Bridges	Una O'Connor
Annie	Merle Tottenham
Margaret Harris	Irene Browne
Cook	Beryl Mercer
Joe Marryot	Frank Lawton
Edward Marryot	John Warburton
Edith Harris	Margaret Lindsay

In January of 1931, soon after arriving in New York for the Broadway production of *Private Lives*, Noel Coward began research for *Cavalcade*, a vast spectacular drama far removed from the intimacy of his previous play. Returning to England in May, Coward spent the summer writing the play, which opened at London's Theatre Royal, Drury Lane, on October 31, 1931, with a cast that included Mary Clare, Edward Sinclair, and John Mills.

The success of both the London production of *Cavalcade* and M-G-M's film version of *Private Lives* (1931), with Norma Shearer and Robert Montgomery, persuaded the Fox Film Corporation to put up $100,000 for the screen rights to *Cavalcade*, *Hay Fever*, and *Bitter Sweet*. *Hay Fever* was never filmed; *Bitter Sweet* was eventually filmed by Herbert Wilcox (1933) and later M-G-M (1940). But Fox, after some perfunctory discussion as to whether the film should be shot in England, put *Cavalcade* into production in August of 1932 at the present Twentieth Century-Fox studios, then called Movietone City. The direction was assigned to Frank Lloyd, who, in answer to criticism that *Cavalcade* should be directed by an Englishman, claimed that he was "especially sympathetic to British themes." Coward apparently took little interest in the production, aside from insisting that Una O'Connor should re-create the role of Ellen Bridges, which she had played in the London production. Una O'Connor became one of the American film industry's best character actresses, and serves as a reminder that much of the success of *Cavalcade* rests in the casting of the character roles, particularly Merle Tottenham as Annie, the Marryot's maid, and Tempe Piggott, the tired old matriarch of the servant's hall, with her continual expressions of gloom and despondency.

Cavalcade is concerned with three basic themes: family life as it is affected by international events, the British class structure and its subconscious favoring of the educated upper classes, and the continuing futility of war with its tragic after-effects. It is an episodic historical drama, covering a period of thirty-two years in the lives of a British family. As a historical epic, contemporary critics compared it favorably to D. W. Griffith's *Intolerance* (1916) and Rex Ingram's *The Four Horsemen of the Apocalypse* (1921). It is still a distinguished and impressive production, deeply patriotic and profoundly moving, although it is, perhaps, hard not to be cynical towards the film's hopes and aspirations in view of all that has passed since its release.

The story begins just before midnight on December 31, 1899, the dawn of a new century, and introduces the Marryot family: the mother, Jane (Diana Wynyard), the father, Robert (Clive Brook), and their two sons, Edward (John Warburton) and Joe (Frank Lawton). Attending the Marryots are their servants, and in particular Ellen, the maid (Una O'Connor) and Bridges, the butler (Herbert Mundin). The entire family and their staff are together to drink their toast to 1900, but both the family and their servants must face an immediate threat to their happiness. Robert Marryot and Bridges are about to leave for South Africa to relieve the British troops at Mafeking. In one of the most impressive jobs of art direction ever tackled by a Hollywood studio, a complete dock is re-created, peopled with thousands of extras as departing soldiers, and the Catalina Island ferry standing in as a troop ship. Yet, despite the epic nature of this scene, the simple, moving farewell of the womenfolk to their men remains the focal point of the action. In the next scene, war and what it can mean to a family is driven home by having the mother cry out in anguish as she sees her children playing soldier; her nerves are shattered by the constant playing of "Soldiers of the Queen."

Events move briskly. As Jane and her best friend attend a musical comedy— a brilliant re-creation by Noel Coward of a turn-of-the-century musical—the manager rushes onstage to announce the relief of Mafeking. The soldiers return, but as they do, drastic changes occur in both the family circle and on a national scale. Bridges and Ellen purchase a "pub" and leave the Marryots, while Queen Victoria's death affects the entire nation. Victoria's funeral procession is seen only through the eyes of the Marryots as they stand at attention on the balcony of their home, and Jane Marryot points out the five Kings riding together in the procession.

Life moves on; Robert Marryot is elevated to the peerage; Bridges has become an alcoholic, and, in a drunken stupor, is knocked down and killed by a fire engine. His daughter, Fanny (Ursula Jeans), shows promise as a dancer, and wins a prize while vacationing at a seaside resort where her family renews acquaintance with their former employers, the Marryots. In all these scenes, there is unquestioned authenticity, a perfect re-creation of English life in the Edwardian era, a mixture of personal happenings and historical incidents, such as Bleriot, who has just crossed the English Channel, flying over the family on the beach below.

More years pass, but the viewer's interest never wanes. Director-producer Frank Lloyd is able to jump several years at a time in the story without the audience being aware of any awkwardness in editing or plot. In one of those hauntingly, tragically happy moments at which Noel Coward seemed to excel, Edward Marryot and his new bride, Edith (Margaret Lindsay), are on board ship on their honeymoon. As Edith tells Edward of her love for him—that this is their moment and that the world may end tonight for them and she will be satisfied as they have known love and happiness—the couple moves away from the rail of the ship, and we see one of the life buoys, on which is printed "S.S. Titanic." This scene touches the heart more than any other in *Cavalcade*.

War begins again in August of 1914, and in one of the toasts which appear as signposts throughout the production, Sir Robert asks that the family drink to England's success against Germany, but his wife demurs, crying:

> Drink to the war, then! I'm not going to. I can't. Rule Britannia! Send us victorious, happy and glorious! Drink Joey, you're only a baby, still, but you're old enough for war. Drink as the Germans are drinking tonight, to victory and defeat, and stupid, tragic, sorrow. But don't ask me to do it, please!

World War I causes the final disintegration of the Marryot clan. Joe enlists and falls in love with Fanny Bridges. Her mother, Ellen, comes to see Lady Jane, feeling that it is not proper for the couple to "carry on" without marriage, but even as they talk a telegram comes with the message that Joe has been killed. Lady Jane bravely tries to cheer with the others in Trafalgar Square on Armistice Night. It is in scenes such as this that Diana Wynyard excels. Her voice and her bearing are those of an English gentlewoman, and, with the possible exception of Celia Johnson—who was a favorite Noel Coward film actress—it is doubtful anyone has been able to portray the British middle class with such sympathy and sincerity.

As if not wishing to concern itself with modern history, the production embarks on a montage of scenes to cover the 1920's, including the Geneva disarmament conference and an anarchist insisting that God is a mere superstition. As the music becomes more and more discordant and raucous, as church pews are shown empty, and gangsters seen mowing down innocent passersby with machine guns, *Cavalcade* arrives at December 31, 1932. Fanny Bridges, one of the "survivors," sings a doleful Noel Coward song titled "Twentieth Century Blues," which, with the earlier musical comedy sequence, was the only original number written by Coward for *Cavalcade*.

In direct contrast to the modernity of the song, the scene changes to the Marryot home, where Sir Robert and Lady Jane, the bastions of the old order, and the only other "survivors," end the film as it began—with a toast. It is a toast for a better England and for a better world, and audiences from 1932 to the present can join Lady Jane in echoing its sentiments: "Let's drink to the spirit of gallantry and courage that made a strange heaven out of an unbelievable hell, and let's drink to the hope that one day this country of ours, which we love so much, will find dignity and greatness and peace again."

In an America which has experienced the Korean War, Vietnam, Watergate, and a loss of moral values, *Cavalcade* still has much to teach and to preach to us.

Anthony Slide

CHAMPAGNE FOR CAESAR

Released: 1950
Production: George Moskov for United Artists
Direction: Richard B. Whorf
Screenplay: Hans Jacoby and Fred Brady
Cinematography: Paul Ivano
Editing: Hugh Bennett
Running time: 99 minutes

Principal characters:
Beauregard Bottomley .... Ronald Colman
Flame O'Neill .... Celeste Holm
Burnbridge Waters .... Vincent Price
Gwenn Bottomley .... Barbara Britton
Happy Hogan .... Art Linkletter

In the early 1950's Hollywood suddenly found itself losing much of its audience to the new medium of television. Its main response was to emphasize all the things television could not bring its viewers: wide screens, color, spectacle, and for a brief time, 3-D. Hollywood, however, seldom used any aspect of television as the subject of a film. One exception is *Champagne for Caesar*, a modest but likable comedy which centers on a television quiz program.

The hero of the film is Beauregard Bottomley (Ronald Colman), who is called by the narrator "the last scholar" and spends most of his time reading everything from Schopenhauer's philosophy to atomic physics. He lives with his sister, Gwenn (Barbara Britton), and a parrot, Caesar, who likes champagne. The piano lessons Gwenn gives are apparently their primary means of support, since Bottomley cannot find a job despite his encyclopedic knowledge. "I know everything," he says, "but what is commonly known as how to make a buck."

Willing to try anything, he applies for a forty-dollar-a-week job on a research survey for Milady Soap Company, which makes "the soap that sanctifies." Bottomley is interviewed by the president of the company, Burnbridge Waters (Vincent Price), who despises intellectual types because they are dreamers, not doers. He almost gets the job anyway until he makes a small joke about the soap. (Waters does not like humorous types either.) Smarting from that rejection, he gets the idea of bankrupting Milady Soap by appearing on the television quiz show it sponsors. Another motive for his plan of revenge is that he regards the program as "the forerunner of the intellectual destruction of America."

His chance for revenge makes Bottomley bend his dignity to appear on the quiz program dressed as a volume of an encyclopedia and to endure the sarcasm of Happy Hogan (Art Linkletter), the silly "host" of the program.

After winning the evening's prize money, Bottomley goads the soap company into allowing him to return for another game of "double or nothing" by appealing to the audience for support. Although no previous contestant has been on the program more than once, Bottomley's popularity forces the company to allow him to continue. Confident in his ability to answer any question given to him, he assumes that it is merely a matter of time before he wins the company's entire net worth of $40,000,000.

Once Bottomley begins winning large sums of money, Milady Soap begins to take him seriously. Waters' first idea is to promote interest in Bottomley and the show for six weeks, and then, when Bottomley reaches the $40,000 level, ask him an impossibly difficult question to get rid of him. The strategy is successful up to a point. The show becomes more and more popular and the sales of Milady Soap increase greatly, but Bottomley easily answers the question which is supposed to defeat him.

A number of other tactics are then tried. Happy Hogan pretends to be interested in Gwenn in order to find out if Bottomley has a weakness they can use against him. Despite the fact that she realizes his purpose, Gwenn is surprisingly flattered by his attentions, but Hogan finds no helpful information. Waters tries canceling the program, but then the sales of Milady Soap plummet. Finally Waters conceives a scheme which he calls "a shining example of foul play in our time." He hires an attractive and treacherous woman, Flame O'Neill (Celeste Holm), to get Bottomley to fall in love with her so that she can manipulate him for the benefit of Milady Soap.

Flame arrives at Bottomley's house saying she is a nurse sent by the Billings, Montana, Beauregard Bottomley Fan Club to care for him while he is bedridden with a cold. She also says she is familiar with the book he is reading, and Bottomley, who has been so intelligent and level-headed about everything else, falls for her immediately. Indeed, he sees no parallel between his romance with Flame and Gwenn's with Hogan. Hogan is a "wise-cracking, treacherous moron," he tells Gwenn. But Flame is a "charming, cultivated, lovely lady." Flame's plan is to use the days before the next quiz program to get Bottomley so upset and confused that he will be unable to concentrate on the question when it is asked. She uses such devices as failing to show up for a dinner date and then the next day refusing to explain; she even gets him to apologize to her. On the day of the program, Bottomley finally gets a bit suspicious and casually mentions that he does not fully understand Einstein's space-time continuum. Thus when he is asked a question on that subject, he knows of her deceit, but he still loves her. Meanwhile, it takes an on-the-air telephone call from Einstein to Hogan to confirm that Bottomley's answer to the question is correct.

The week finally arrives when Bottomley will either win the whole soap company or nothing. He and Flame, and his sister and Hogan are planning to marry the day after the program, but he suspects that Flame and Hogan are only after his money. In addition, two men from the Internal Revenue Service have told him that taxes will take most of his winnings.

At a specially staged program in the Hollywood Bowl, Bottomley is asked the final question: What is his social security number? When his answer is judged "absolutely wrong" and he and Gwenn go back to their modest bungalow without Flame or Hogan, we think all is lost; but soon both Flame and Hogan arrive still intending to marry. As Bottomley and Flame drive to Nevada for their wedding, Bottomley tells her that he had discussed with Waters deliberately missing the final question if the Milady Soap Company would give him his own radio show, a car, and some stock in the company. He confesses, however, that he really did not know his social security number. So the film ends with everyone happy; the last shot shows Flame throwing his books out of the car.

It must be admitted that characterizations and credibility begin to crumble in the last part of the film as we are asked to accept the fact that both Flame and Hogan have turned into sympathetic characters and that both Bottomley and his sister are made completely irrational by love. Indeed, the strength of the film lies chiefly in the first part, in the presentation without condescension of the character of Beauregard Bottomley, a man who lives for ideas and finds his satisfaction in thinking and reading. Played by a cultured Ronald Colman, Bottomley is an interesting and sympathetic character.

Art Linkletter is so appropriately obnoxious as Happy Hogan that we fail to see why Gwenn is interested in him, and Vincent Price gives a delightfully flamboyant performance as Burnbridge Waters, the soap company president who alternates between wild tirades and trances in which he can neither see nor hear anyone. Celeste Holm and Barbara Britton merely do the best they can with the roles of Flame O'Neill and Gwenn Bottomley.

Released more than a year before there were nationwide television broadcasts and long before such programs as "The $64,000 Question" made some intellectuals into household names, *Champagne for Caesar* is remarkably perceptive in its depiction of the power of the media in general and television in particular.

Timothy W. Johnson

CHARADE

Released: 1963
Production: Stanley Donen for Universal
Direction: Stanley Donen
Screenplay: Peter Stone; based on the story "The Unsuspecting Wife" by Peter Stone and Marc Behm
Cinematography: Charles Lang
Editing: James B. Clark
Music: Henry Mancini
Running time: 113 minutes

Principal characters:
Peter Joshua/Alexander Dyle/ Adam Canfield/Brian Cruikshank	Cary Grant
Regina (Reggie) Lambert	Audrey Hepburn
Hamilton Bartholomew/ Carson Dyle	Walter Matthau
Tex Panthollow	James Coburn
Herman Scobie	George Kennedy
Leopold Gideon	Ned Glass

Charade is one of the best of the many Hitchcock-style suspense thrillers which have appeared over the years. Directed by Stanley Donen, and starring Cary Grant and Audrey Hepburn, the film is a sophisticated blend of romance, comedy, and mystery.

The film's plot follows a convoluted course through a series of rapid-fire twists and surprises. The suspense begins in the first scene, as the stillness of a morning in the French countryside is broken by a body being hurled from a passing train. The body is that of Charles Lampert, a wealthy, mysterious figure whose wife, Reggie (Audrey Hepburn) knows little about him. At Charles's funeral, three men appear, each one checking the coffin to make certain Charles is dead. Soon, Reggie is summoned to the American Embassy by Mr. Bartholomew (Walter Matthau), who tells her that he is with the CIA and has been trying to find her husband to recover $250,000 which Charles and four of his friends had stolen from the government during the war. He identifies the men at the funeral as Tex (James Coburn), Gideon (Ned Glass), and Scobie (George Kennedy), three of Charles's accomplices whom he had double-crossed. Bartholomew insists that Charles must have had the $250,000 with him on the train when he was murdered, but there is no clue to the money's whereabouts.

Peter Joshua (Cary Grant), whom Reggie has met at a mountain resort, arrives in Paris and comes to see her when he reads of her husband's death. Reggie is threatened by Tex and Gideon, and Peter appears to be protecting her, but when Scobie attacks her, Peter gives chase and the audience discovers that he is working with the three criminals to find the money. Reggie learns that Peter is not who he claims to be. He tells her that his real name is Alexander Dyle and that he is the brother of Carson Dyle, the fifth member of the robbery plot who was left to die by Charles and the others. He convinces her that he is only working with the men to learn what they know and to see that they are brought to justice so that his brother is avenged. Reggie is rapidly falling in love with Peter/Alexander, but when she checks his story with Mr. Bartholomew, she learns that Carson Dyle had no brother. She confronts him with this information, and he tells her that he is actually a thief named Adam Canfield and that he is after the $250,000.

Scobie is drowned in Adam's bathtub and Gideon is strangled in the hotel elevator, leaving only Tex and Adam as the possible murderers. An entry in Charles's appointment book leads Reggie and Adam to the park, where they see Tex. Spotting the weekly stamp market, first Tex, then Adam, realize that Charles had used the money to purchase three rare and valuable stamps, which he then pasted on an envelope and placed in his travel bag. The two men race back to the hotel only to discover that Reggie has removed the stamps. They believe she has known their value all along, but in reality she has given them to the son of a friend who collects stamps. She recovers them from the dealer to whom the boy has sold them, and returns to the hotel. There she finds Tex murdered and, believing Adam to be responsible, phones Bartholomew and arranges to meet him outside the Palais Royale. She leaves the hotel just as Adam returns, and a harrowing chase ensues through the Paris subways. Just as Reggie reaches Bartholomew, Adam shouts to her that Bartholomew is really Carson Dyle, the fifth robber whom the others had believed dead, and that it is Bartholomew who has murdered Charles, Tex, Scobie and Gideon. Bartholomew chases Reggie into the theater, where she hides inside the prompter's box on the stage. Bartholomew sees her, and as he crosses the stage to shoot her, Adam, who is on the level below, opens the trapdoor under Bartholomew's feet and he falls to his death.

The next day, Reggie and Adam go to the American Embassy, where Adam reluctantly agrees to let her turn over the stamps. She enters the office alone and finds Adam seated at the desk inside. He tells her he is really Brian Cruikshank, the head of the Treasury Office, and says he will prove it to her by writing it on their marriage license. Reggie accepts his proposal, saying she hopes they have several sons so she can name them all for him.

Charade's outstanding characteristic is its stylish wit and sophistication. The film's mystery-and-suspense elements are enhanced by the developing romance between Reggie and the Cary Grant character in all of its aliases, and both of these themes are handled with Stanley Donen's light, humorous touch. Donen is best known for such musicals as *On the Town* (1949), *Singin' in the Rain* (1952), and *Funny Face* (1957), all of which share the same carefree tone that dominates *Charade*. Even moments of the highest suspense, such as the chase through the subway or the terrifying fight between the Grant character and Scobie, are laced with whimsical incidents and light-hearted banter. The romance between Grant and Hepburn includes a great deal of playful sparring in which the traditional roles are reversed, with Hepburn pursuing a seemingly reluctant Grant.

Donen's directing is greatly assisted by Henry Mancini's remarkable score, which consists primarily of variations on the film's famous title song. The music serves to underscore both the romance and the suspense in *Charade*, and it remains one of the best examples of the effective use of music in film.

The performance of both Cary Grant and Audrey Hepburn are central to the film's success. Grant's screen *persona* is ideally suited to *Charade*'s overall tone, as well as to the character he plays. Throughout his career, Grant has been known for his portrayals of witty, romantically handsome men in any number of screen comedies, as well as for his performances in such Hitchcock classics as *Notorious* (1946) and *North by Northwest* (1959). In *Charade*, the constantly shifting guilt or innocence of his character might easily have led to a loss of believability in the hands of another actor; but with Grant in the role, it is not difficult to understand Reggie's willingness to trust him.

Audrey Hepburn is also perfectly cast as Reggie. Her mixture of wide-eyed innocence and chic sophistication is exactly right both for her part and for her pairing with Grant. She is fragile without being helpless, and she brings a kind of wistful romanticism to her pursuit of Grant which makes his apparent treachery all the more painful.

The supporting cast of *Charade* is excellent. Walter Matthau is first hilarious, then menacing as Bartholomew/Dyle, and the switch is so abrupt and convincing that the effect is chilling. Ned Glass's Gideon is a tired, middle-aged man who would simply like to get his share of the money and go home. James Coburn as Tex seems coolly capable of anything, yet uneasy and wary of the Grant character.

It is George Kennedy as Scobie, however, who creates the most memorable villain. With a hook replacing his left hand, and a violent temper apparent from the moment he appears on the screen, Scobie is a terrifying man who remains in the viewer's mind long after the picture has ended. Yet Donen manages to use even Scobie for comic effect. The rooftop struggle between Scobie and the Grant character is tense and frightening, but when Scobie finally loses the fight and falls onto the sloping portion of the roof, his hook strikes sparks on the tiles as he slides into the darkness below. This touch of bizarre humor brings an added dimension to the fight, and the scene stands as a perfect example of the combination of suspense and wit which makes *Charade* such a delight to watch.

Janet E. Lorenz

CHARLY

Released: 1968
Production: Ralph Nelson for Selmur Pictures
Direction: Ralph Nelson
Screenplay: Stirling Silliphant; based on the short story and novel *Flowers for Algernon* by Daniel Keyes
Cinematography: Arthur J. Ornitz
Editing: Fredric Steinkamp
Running time: 106 minutes

Principal characters:
Charly Gordon	Cliff Robertson (AA)
Alice Kinian	Claire Bloom
Dr. Anna Strauss	Lilia Skala
Dr. Richard Nemur	Leon Janney
Bert	Dick Van Patten
Joey	William Dwyer
Gimpy	Ed McNally
Convention speaker	Ralph Nelson

In 1968, Cliff Robertson was a man with a most aggravating problem. Since the early 1950's, the forty-three-year-old actor had been widely regarded as one of television's premiere talents and had even received an Emmy in 1965 for his performance in the "Chrysler Theater" production of *The Game.* He had appeared in nearly every major dramatic anthology series, had starred in a series of his own, and had proven himself a multitalented, thoroughly professional actor with every performance.

However, like a great many television stars then and now, Robertson was for some unknown reason unable to transfer this success into the prestigious world of motion pictures. He had distinguished himself in a few films, most notably *Picnic* (1955), *PT-109* (1963), and *The Best Man* (1964); but the majority of his twenty-two screen roles had been mired in a collection of B-pictures and uninspired exploitation films on the order of *Gidget* (1959) and *The Interns* (1962).

Robertson was also in the unenviable position of having starred in two major teleplays which were later turned into highly successful motion pictures without his participation. He had played the lead in both *The Hustler* and *Days of Wine and Roses* on television, but had been overlooked by the producers of the film versions. Insult was added to injury when both Paul Newman in *The Hustler* (1961) and Jack Lemmon in *Days of Wine and Roses* (1962) received Oscar nominations for their performances in the roles that Robertson had originated on television.

In 1961, Robertson had starred in a "United States Steel Hour" production based on Daniel Keyes's moving story "Flowers for Algernon." He received an Emmy nomination for his performance in the program entitled "The Two Worlds of Charly Gordon," and hoped eventually to re-create the title role on the screen. Consequently, he personally purchased the motion picture rights to the story and steadfastly refused to release his grip on the property until he was given the opportunity to star in the film. After seven long and frustrating years, *Charly* finally arrived on the screen, and Robertson's touching performance in this, his first major film endeavor, at last enabled him to rise to genuine stardom.

As Charly Gordon, Robertson portrays a thirty-year-old retarded man, with the mental capacity of a small child. He works as a sweeper in a bakery where he is often the victim of cruel practical jokes perpetrated by coworkers whom he naïvely regards as his best friends. Charly has a burning desire to better himself and to become a functioning member of a society that has forced him to remain an outsider. He attends special evening classes taught by a pretty young idealist, Alice Kinian (Claire Bloom), but cannot grasp even the most elementary concepts. Alice, however, is touched by Charly's kind, diligent spirit and arranges for him to be examined by a team of neurosurgeons who have surgically cured mentally defective mice and are now looking for a suitable human subject.

Charly is given a barrage of tests, the most important of which concerns a white mouse named Algernon who is placed inside a maze. Charly is told to race Algernon by using a blueprint replica of the puzzle. Initially, Algernon consistently beats Charly, but after the experimental surgery, Charly rapidly begins to improve. In the film's most moving scene, Charly, still frustrated by Algernon and the maze, finally wins a race. Immediately, he realizes that his intelligence has grown and that it will continue to increase as time goes on.

Charly's improvement is so rapid that his "friends" at the bakery find they cannot tolerate his presence any longer, even as the butt of their jokes. They have him fired, and Charly discovers that instead of enabling him to enter normal society, his new intelligence has provoked an even greater separation. Although his mental capacity continues to rise to the genius level, his emotional growth does not accelerate at the same pace. He misinterprets Alice's platonic kindness as love, forcibly tries to make love to her, and is violently rebuffed.

Shamed by this rejection, Charly runs away and briefly lives the carefree life of a hippie. When he returns to his studies, he has clearly become a mature adult. Alice finally realizes her love for her pupil, and he in turn has learned the value of genuine affection. The two lovers spend an idyllic holiday together and return only when the secret of Charly's amazing progress is to be revealed to the scientific community. Before Charly goes on stage to speak to a distinguished gathering, Algernon is discovered dead in his cage. In

addition, all the other experimental mice have begun to revert to their retarded states. Charly painfully realizes that the operation's effects will also
be temporary for him. An awareness of modern society's technological horrors suddenly overcomes him, and when called upon to speak he delivers a
scathing attack on civilization's evils to the shocked scientists.

Soon Charly's own regression begins. Despite the best efforts of all concerned, it is evident that nothing can be done. Charly recognizes defeat and
returns to his lonely room to await the inevitable. Alice pleads with him to
marry her anyway, but to no avail. As the end credits roll, we see Charly as
we saw him during the film's initial scenes, frolicking on a playground swing
amid a sea of children, an idiotic grin once again on his simple face.

Robertson's performance was a revelation to both critics and the public.
With uncanny accuracy, he affected the mannerisms, facial expressions, and
movements of the mentally retarded. He brought to this difficult role a sense
of discipline, continuity, and an ability to change expression and mood with
chameleonlike subtlety. Robertson's persistence had finally paid off, and the
Academy Award for Best Actor of 1968 became his ultimate vindication.

The rest of the film unfortunately does not achieve the same level of
excellence. While Claire Bloom reveals a warmth that recalls her performance
in Charles Chaplin's *Limelight* (1952), the rest of the cast members are simply
not up to the demands of their roles. The story itself has become, from our
current vantage point, a dated, overly sentimental look at the Frankenstein
myth, toned with a naïve liberalism that does not stand the test of time. Ralph
Nelson's direction is filled with special effects and pseudopsychedelic optical
techniques that border on the self-conscious. His frequent use of "op-mon-
tage" devices of split-screen and frame-within-frame sequences often effectively dissects events and reveals the mechanics of the filmmaking process,
but does not in the long run work successfully to create an adequate whole.
The overall impression is one of elaborate gaudiness with no apparent purpose
or cohesion.

Despite these structural and ideological flaws, *Charly* remains an interesting
reflection of its era, an overview of liberal attitudes prevalent in American
thought in the late 1960's. It tells us in no uncertain terms that modern society
has become horribly impersonal, that unchecked scientific and technological
progress can bring only pain and loss of individuality, that people are better
off when left alone, and that one should never try to be anything other than
what he or she already is.

Charly is severely flawed, but Cliff Robertson's wonderful performance is
so finely hewn and so carefully drawn that the film ultimately rises above its
faults. It can stand on its own as the testament of one actor's persistence and
intense desire to play a part for which he was ideally suited.

Daniel Einstein

THE CHILDREN'S HOUR

Released: 1961
Production: William Wyler for United Artists
Direction: William Wyler
Screenplay: John Michael Hayes; based on Lillian Hellman's adaptation of
 her play of the same name
Cinematography: Franz Planer
Editing: Robert Swink
Art direction: Fernando Carrere; set decoration, Edward G. Boyle
Music: Alex North
Running time: 109 minutes

Principal characters:
Karen Wright .... Audrey Hepburn
Martha Dobie .... Shirley MacLaine
Dr. Joe Cardin .... James Garner
Mrs. Lily Mortar .... Miriam Hopkins
Mrs. Amelia Tilford .... Fay Bainter
Mary Tilford .... Karen Balkin
Rosalie .... Veronica Cartwright

In 1933-1934, Lillian Hellman's prizewinning play about slander and lesbianism, *The Children's Hour*, was a sensational shocker. When Sam Goldwyn's film adaptation of the drama, entitled *These Three*, was released in
1936, it was considerably altered from the stage production. Directed by
William Wyler and starring Miriam Hopkins, Merle Oberon, and Joel
McCrea, the milder and "safe" screen version had a child accuse a woman
of having an affair with a man rather than with a woman.

In 1961, William Wyler again directed an adaptation of Hellman's powerful
play, but this time the version was faithful to the original story. Although the
theme of slander and lesbianism was still controversial, it was no longer a
forbidden subject; but if *The Children's Hour* did not shock audiences of
1961, it was nevertheless a candid and effective drama.

Ironically set in New England, the supposed cradle of liberty and free
thought, and entitled *The Children's Hour* (the title of one of Longfellow's
best-known poems), this psychological drama deals with two women, Karen
Wright (Audrey Hepburn) and Martha Dobie (Shirley MacLaine), who have
invested their life savings in an exclusive private all-girls school. As the
headmistresses of the Wright-Dobie School, the two find themselves subjected to the lies of one of their students. When twelve-year-old Mary Tilford
(Karen Balkin) receives a well-deserved punishment, the evil girl spitefully
and irresponsibly accuses the teachers of "unnatural affection" for each other.
In spreading the rumor, Mary tells her dowager grandmother, Mrs. Amelia

Tilford (Fay Bainter), one of the town's most influential citizens. The mis-
informed woman believes the malicious child, and at Mrs. Tilford's urging,
the pupils' parents withdraw their children from the school. Soon Martha
and Karen are in financial ruin and are forced to close their school.

At the same time, Karen's fiancé, Joe Cardin (James Garner), a promising
doctor, begins to doubt his betrothed's word. As their tangled lives and
emotions turn into a nightmare, the two women are forced to take drastic
action. They bring a slander lawsuit against Mrs. Tilford; but they are unable
to prove their innocence in court, and the judge finds them guilty of "a certain
kind of repressive moral transgression."

The most tragic ramification of the shattering ordeal is Martha's self-doubt
and tortured recognition that she subconsciously did have "those feelings"
toward her friend. Feeling guilty in mind, if not in deed, Martha is severely
shocked. Though the lie is ultimately exposed and the error acknowledged
with pleas for forgiveness, it is too late; the devastated Martha commits
suicide by hanging herself. In the funeral scene of the film's bitter conclusion,
Karen walks silently past Joe, Mrs. Tilford, and all of the other townspeople.

A provocative study sensitively directed by William Wyler, *The Children's
Hour* is well acted by its leading players, Audrey Hepburn and Shirley
MacLaine, whose personalities and screen presences strongly complement
each other. As Karen, Audrey Hepburn is strong and assertive beneath her
deceptive softness and frailty. As she walks past the townspeople in the final
scene, we know she will survive.

With depth and substance, Shirley MacLaine gains our pity and understanding. Though perhaps Martha's homosexual feelings are exaggerated as
a result of the scandal, there are moments in the film where her latent lesbianism is indicated, as in her response to the news that Karen is to be
married. Later, Martha says "I never loved a man," and admits that she does
love Karen "in the way they said," and "that's what's the matter with me."
(Actually, the word "lesbian" is never mentioned during the film; instead,
such expressions as "sinful sexual knowledge" are used.)

Young Karen Balkin is fine in her performance as Mary, the child responsible for defamation of character who only dimly understands what she has
done; and Veronica Cartwright is well cast as Mary's puppet Rosalie. Fay
Bainter is equally good as the well-meaning, if ignorant, grandmother who
sets the destruction in motion. Miriam Hopkins (who played the role of
Martha in *These Three*) is appropriately despicable as Mrs. Lily Mortar,
Martha's simple-minded aunt, the chief court witness who deserts the teachers
by refusing to testify in their behalf.

The film, however, does have problems. Written originally as a play, the
dialogue-oriented drama is often too wordy for the film medium; and occasionally, its dramatics are too heavy-handed. At times the story strains the
viewer's credulity: just what is it, for example, that the twelve-year-old child

whispers to her startled, indignant grandmother that causes her to rush to the telephone? Why does no one suspect that the child is lying? Why would parents pull their children out of the school so fast? Why does the court not protect the innocent women? Why does it accept as sole evidence the word of one little girl and the failure of a key witness to appear?

Although *The Children's Hour* is really about malicious gossip and false accusations more than it is about lesbianism, William Wyler did not submit the script to the Johnston Office. Because of the Production Code taboo against any discussion of sexual deviation, the office would not have given its seal of approval. Ironically, however, just after the picture was finished, the Johnston Office reversed itself on the sexual deviation clause. *The Children's Hour* was therefore one of the first films to be released under the relaxed provision of the Production Code Administration.

Leslie Taubman

CHINATOWN

Released: 1974
Production: Robert Evans for Paramount
Direction: Roman Polanski
Screenplay: Robert Towne (AA)
Cinematography: John A. Alonzo
Editing: Sam O'Steen
Art direction: Richard Sylbert and W. Stewart Campbell
Music: Jerry Goldsmith
Running time: 131 minutes

Principal characters:
J. J. (Jake) Gittes .... Jack Nicholson
Evelyn Mulwray .... Faye Dunaway
Noah Cross .... John Huston
Yelburton .... John Hillerman
Lieutenant Escobar .... Perry Lopez
Curly .... Burt Young

One of the most interesting trends in Hollywood film production during the 1970's has been the rash of films which take the movie past as a touchstone for personal expression about contemporary life. Directors as diverse as Brian de Palma, Peter Bogdanovich, Clint Eastwood, and Mel Brooks have drawn on the styles, directors, and genres of a bygone era in filmmaking for inspiration. *Chinatown* is representative of this trend. The Polish-born director Roman Polanski interweaves elements of the classic detective thriller with his unique world view. In the best tradition of Hollywood *film noir*, Polanski skillfully blends a mixture of romance, mystery, and cool cynicism while adding several contemporary variations. The result is the best of these "touchstone" films. Polanski is aided by the topnotch original screenplay of Robert Towne, an expert and attractive cast, and overall production values (especially with regard to music, cinematography, and set decoration) which are among the most outstanding in modern film history.

Chinatown concerns Jake Gittes (Jack Nicholson), a private detective who is duped into discrediting Hollis Mulwray, an engineer involved in an important water project. When Mulwray is a victim of an apparent suicide, Gittes decides to dig deeper into the case. He soon finds himself piecing together an elaborate puzzle composed of murder, the monopolization of drought-stricken Los Angeles' water supply, a land swindle, and Mulwray's mysteriously beautiful wife Evelyn (Faye Dunaway). Gittes and Evelyn become romantically involved, but the woman's dark past eventually leads to her death while Gittes himself is rendered powerless in the face of widespread political corruption.

This plot is generated by the traditional private-eye formula of literature and film. Gittes is a cool, wisecracking lone operator much like Raymond Chandler's Phillip Marlowe. The film is by and large Chandleresque in its structure and outlook. As in the Marlowe novels, *Chinatown* is set in Los Angeles during the late 1930's and involves the stripping away of façades to reveal secrets. Like Marlowe, Gittes operates under a self-imposed code of honor and is undeterred by warnings from the police to mind his own business or by threats on his life.

Crucial to *Chinatown* is the metaphorical depiction of Los Angeles as a moral wasteland. The drought-ravaged Los Angeles of the film is shown as intensely arid, a near desert. This is a land where life is cheap, where the money and power of opportunists sap the energy of the city's inhabitants. Like Chandler, Polanski and Towne give us a city whose glamorous allure masks anguish and despair.

As in the hard-boiled detective tradition, *Chinatown* places its detective in the center of the action. Gittes has the largest amount of onscreen time, and it is his perception of events which is relayed to the audience. In this sense, the film approximates the first-person narration typical of Chandler's lean prose. 1940's versions of Chandler's Marlowe novels, such as *Murder, my Sweet* (1944) and *Lady in the Lake* (1946), tried to duplicate this narrative style as closely as possible. *Lady in the Lake* employs a subjective camera throughout the film to approximate Marlowe's point of view. In *Murder, my Sweet*, Marlowe relates events through flashback, which allows certain visual effects to become the equivalent of his mental state. Notable among these is the darkening of the screen with an inky substance when Marlowe is knocked unconscious (as his voice-over explains that he felt darkness descending over him). While *Chinatown* eschews stylistic devices such as this, the film nevertheless gives us a perception of events and details which approximates Gittes's own idea of them. We see clues (the obituary column, Mulwray's glasses) when he does, and we are never allowed to have more information than he does. Thus, we become sharers in Gittes's search for truth amidst a maze of deceptive appearances. A crucial scene in this regard occurs when Gittes follows Evelyn to a house and watches her through a window. Here, Evelyn appears to be abusing the distraught "mistress" of her late husband. Gittes concludes that Evelyn is holding the girl prisoner (a conclusion that turns out to be incorrect), but at this point he and the audience share a voyeuristic perspective of misleading appearances. It is this perspective that is at the core of *Chinatown*. As Gittes says at one point, "You can't always tell what's going on." This line serves as an indicator of Gittes's predicament as well as our own.

While *Chinatown* is faithful to its generic source in terms of plot, formula, and character, it is more than just a nostalgic homage. Polanski and Towne have added a number of variations on the standard structure. Among these is Evelyn's sensational revelation that she had incestuous relations with her father, the villainous Noah Cross (John Huston). Mulwray's "mistress" is, in fact, the offspring of this liaison. In addition, the film's subtext of political corruption clearly has echoes of a Watergate type of coverup and is depicted as the kind of corruption that permeates every level of government. Finally, the criminals are not apprehended at the conclusion of the film. Gittes's powerlessness and failure to effect successfully the private eye's code establishes the film's vision as bleak and uncompromising. The private eye's code is shown as no longer operable. In short, the film re-creates a fictional universe of the past to displace its pessimistic view of a decadent present.

All of Polanski's work generates from the director's pessimistic vision of a decadent world. As in *Chinatown*, a key element in his films is faulty perception. For example, in *Repulsion* (1965), *Rosemary's Baby* (1968), and *Macbeth* (1971), Polanski presents distraught female protagonists whose mental conditions gradually deteriorate. As a result, they become uncertain as to whether their experience of events is real or illusory. In *Repulsion* and *Macbeth*, certain of the females' visions (the hands reaching from the wall in the former film, the blood on the hands in the latter) turn out to be manifestations of unbalanced minds. But in *Rosemary's Baby*, the female protagonist's nightmares become realized. Thus, Polanski's work can be seen as centering on characters who tread the line between what they believe to be real and what is in fact real. In other words, appearances become the basic structural problem in Polanski's cinema, and *Chinatown* is certainly relevant in this regard. Moreover, *Chinatown*, like *Cul-de-Sac* (1966) and *Macbeth*, concerns a male protagonist who becomes embroiled in events which get out of control and finally overcome him in some way. And like all of Polanski's work, *Chinatown* contains scenes of grisly, blood-soaked violence. Polanski himself appears in the film as a vicious hoodlum who slices off part of Gittes's nose. This is a reworking of a scene from one of Polanski's Polish film shorts, *Two Men and a Wardrobe* (1958), in which Polanski also plays a menacing hoodlum.

It is Polanski's overall personal vision that clarifies *Chinatown*'s position as a "touchstone" film of the 1970's. On the one hand, he takes the Hollywood *film noir* and the hard-boiled detective novel as a point of contact. For example, the casting of John Huston as Noah Cross has considerable resonance—Huston directed *The Maltese Falcon* (1941), one of the first classics of *film noir*. Jerry Goldsmith's haunting score calls to mind the films of Hollywood's past, as do *Chinatown*'s opening credits: they are shot in black and white and appear in the old 1:33 screen format. On the other hand, Polanski works to subvert the genre once we enter this fictional universe. Indeed, the very first scene, in which Curly (Burt Young) frantically gnaws on Gittes's Venetian blinds, hints at the subversion to follow. In a sense, Curly's action functions as an assault on this familiar visual motif from the *film noir*. What we are finally left with is a world where values of individual honor and effective action are sadly out of place.

Both Polanski's Polish films and his English-language features have generally earned critical acclaim in this country, but at the box office he has not fared so well. *Chinatown* is an exception to this, as was *Rosemary's Baby*. Both films are among the two hundred top-grossing films of all time. According to a 1977 survey conducted by the American Film Institute, *Chinatown* appeared on the list of the fifty most popular films ever made in Hollywood. One reason for *Chinatown*'s popularity is the potent teaming of Jack Nicholson and Faye Dunaway. Gittes is yet another of Nicholson's volatile but essentially vulnerable screen characters. With his flashy suits and gold cigarette case, Gittes is himself all surface and appearance; the autographed portrait of Adolphe Menjou on the wall of his office reinforces Gittes's aura of artificial glamour. Like other Nicholson portrayals, Gittes's façade begins to crack once he comes to care for others. Nicholson won much acclaim for this performance. He received the National Society of Film Critics and the New York Film Critics awards as Best Actor of 1974 (in both cases, he was honored for his roles in *Chinatown* and *The Last Detail*), as well as the Golden Globe award as Best Actor in a Drama. For her role as a woman coming apart at the seams, Dunaway received an Academy Award nomination as Best Actress. Both stars would have to wait for their Oscars, however. Nicholson won his in 1975 for *One Flew Over the Cukoo's Nest*, while Dunaway received hers in 1976 for *Network*.

Ironically, *Chinatown*, one of the most critically acclaimed films of 1974, was overshadowed by another Paramount-produced "touchstone" film, *The Godfather, Part Two*, which won the lion's share of Academy Awards and critical accolades that year. Still, *Chinatown* was nominated in several major categories in addition to its acting nominees (John Huston's scene-stealing performance is also worthy of honors, but was unaccountably ignored), including Best Picture, Best Director, and Best Cinematography. Robert Towne, who had labored anonymously for many years as a script doctor, received the film's only Oscar for his original screenplay. Towne also won the Writer's Guild Award for Best Written Drama (written directly for the screen). The film also appeared on the "ten best" lists of the National Board of Review and *Time* magazine.

Chinatown richly deserves this critical acclaim, for it is in every way an exemplary film. It powerfully holds up the movie past as a mirror to reflect a modern world in which old values are no longer functional.

Charles Albright, Jr.

A CHRISTMAS CAROL
(SCROOGE)

Released: 1951
Production: Brian Desmond Hurst for Renown-United Artists
Direction: Brian Desmond Hurst
Screenplay: Noel Langley; based on the novella of the same name by Charles
   Dickens
Cinematography: C. Pennington-Richards
Editing: Clive Donner
Running time: 86 minutes

Principal characters:

Scrooge	Alastair Sim
Bob Cratchit	Mervyn Johns
Mrs. Cratchit	Hermione Baddeley
Tiny Tim	Glyn Dearman
Scrooge (younger)	George Cole
Fan	Carol Marsh
Jacob Marley	Michael Hordern
Alice	Rona Anderson
Fred	Brian Worth
Fred's Wife	Olga Edwardes
Mr. Jorkins	Jack Warner
Mrs. Dilber	Kathleen Harrison
Fezziwig	Roddy Hughes
Spirit of Christmas Past	Michael Dolan
Spirit of Christmas Present	Francis De Wolff
Spirit of Christman Future	C. Konarski

A Christmas Carol by Charles Dickens is one of the most popular Christmas stories ever written. Every child in the English-speaking world grows up knowing intimately the tale of the curmudgeon Scrooge and the brave cripple Tiny Tim, of Scrooge's sudden conversion and of Tiny Tim's redemption. So ingrained is this story in our cultural consciousness that, through the years, "Scrooge" has become an epithet used to describe any cantankerous, penny-pinching old man.

A Christmas Carol is not a conventional Christmas story by any means: it dwells far more on the dark side of life than the light. Social injustice, personal betrayals, and lost ideals permeate the story, only periodically brightened by the presence of such characters as Fezziwig, Scrooge's jovial former employer, and Fred, Scrooge's congenial nephew. But even Fezziwig ends his days penniless and sad in a Dickensian world colored by gloomy fatalism. The black humor of the story also reflects this mood. Humor such as that surrounding

Scrooge's "imagined" death; sadistic gibes such as those aimed at Christmas ("Every idiot who goes about with 'Merry Christmas' on his lips should be boiled with his own pudding and buried with a stake of holly through his heart. . . ."); and barbs such as those thrown at the overworked, underpaid Bob Cratchit are typical of the comic style of the piece.

The 1951 British adaptation of *A Christmas Carol* is the most literal translation of the story to date as well as the best at re-creating the mood and feel of the original. Dickens is, of course, among the easiest novelists to adapt to film. He had a strong visual sense in his writings, creating the totality of scene through pithy, descriptive passages and exploiting in a precinematic era cinematic devices such as the flashback and parallel editing between stories. The film opens on Christmas Eve in a picture-postcard re-creation of a Victorian Christmas scene: snow-covered streets, sleigh bells, carriages laden with presents racing through the streets, gas lamps being lit, children caroling from door to door. The spirit of Christmas overpowers everyone—everyone except the bitter, cynical Ebenezer Scrooge (Alastair Sims) who even refuses to let his employee, Bob Cratchit (Mervyn Johns), go home early on this holiday eve. He rebukes a group of philanthropic gentlemen raising money for orphans, caroling children, and his own nephew (Brian Worth) who has come to invite his uncle to his house for Christmas dinner. Instead Scrooge returns to his own home alone. There he begins experiencing hallucinations: a door ornament turns into the head of his deceased partner Jacob Marley (Michael Hordern), followed by the appearance of Marley himself dragging a long and ponderous chain which represents the sins he has committed. He has come to warn Scrooge of the punishment which awaits him and of his chance for redemption. The disbelieving Scrooge is to be visited by three spirits: one of the past, one of the present, and one of the future.

The visitations come, one after the other. Through the Spirit of Christmas Past (Michael Dolan) in the form of a benevolent old man, we learn of Scrooge's background, of the incidents which created this cynical old man. His lonely years away from home at school; his love for his sister Fan (Carol Marsh) and her death in childbirth; his later love for Alice (Rona Anderson) and their parting over his greed for money; and his gradual hardening against the world are shown progressively. The Spirit of Christmas Present (Francis De Wolff), in the form of a Dionysian god, gives him a taste of Victorian Christmas among the rich and poor alike, ending with a visit, invisibly, of course, to the home of the Cratchits and their crippled son, Tiny Tim (Glyn Dearman). The last spirit is the most frightening of all. Dressed in a monk's habit with blackness where a face should be, the Spirit of Christmas Future (C. Konarski) is the revealer of "what may be." Scrooge witnesses his own death, friendless, his belongings sold out from underneath his corpse, his grave unattended. He also sees the Cratchit family minus Tiny Tim, and their bereavement and pain. Returned to the present, Scrooge awakens from his visions a changed man. Resolving to alter his apparent destiny, he visits his nephew and is reconciled with him, and becomes the benefactor of Tiny Tim and his family, providing them with money and moral support. And as the film closes, the narrator describes the new Scrooge: "He knew how to keep Christmas well, if any man alive possessed the knowledge."

A great deal could be said about Alastair Sim's performance as Scrooge; in many viewers' minds he is the defintive Ebenezer Scrooge. He has the ability to emphasize the idiosyncrasies of the character without exaggerating them and to maintain, at all times, the "humanness" of Scrooge even when he is behaving outrageously.

The film version of *A Christmas Carol* is full of visually stunning moments. The vision shown to Ebenezer by Marley of damned souls floating through the air, encircling a beggar woman and child, trying futilely in death to give her the assistance they refused to extend to her kind in life, and the sight of Ebenezer transfixed before his own grave, forced by the deathlike Spirit of Christmas Future to gaze at his own final resting place, are both examples of brilliant visual transliterations of scenes Dickens brought to life verbally. The art direction is also admirable, re-creating Victorian England in all its quaintness as well as sumptuous banquets, plush interiors, and ponderous architecture. Much of this look, along with the makeup of the actors, is drawn from the nineteenth century sketches used for various publications of the Dickens story.

James Ursini

CIMARRON

Released: 1931
Production: William Le Baron for RKO/Radio (AA)
Direction: Wesley Ruggles
Screenplay: Howard Estabrook (AA); based on the novel of the same name
  by Edna Ferber
Cinematography: Edward Cronjager
Editing: William Hamilton
Art direction: Max Ree (AA)
Running time: 131 minutes

>*Principal characters:*
>Yancey Cravat .... Richard Dix
>Sabra Cravat .... Irene Dunne
>Dixie Lee .... Estelle Taylor
>Felice Venable .... Nance O'Neil
>The Kid .... William Collier, Jr.
>Mrs. Tracy Wyatt .... Edna May Oliver
>Jess Rickey .... Roscoe Ates

The era of the Hollywood Western is gone, perhaps never to return. Nobody is making Westerns the way John Ford, Howard Hawks, Raoul Walsh, and other major directors did when the Western was a staple commodity in film production. The reason for the decline in their popularity as regular film fare can probably be traced to television, where the Western has thrived in the form of highly popular weekly series.

Even when Hollywood Westerns were at the peak of their popularity, only one Western ever earned an Academy Award for Best Picture: *Cimarron*, RKO's biggest entry in the 1930-1931 Academy Award race. *Cimarron* also won two additional Academy Awards out of its total of five nominations. With a Best Picture Oscar, RKO/Radio, a relatively young studio, took its place among the major companies and became fully competitive with them.

Cimarron had been a popular best-selling novel. Its author, Edna Ferber, was at that time the most successful woman fiction writer in the United States. American critics were prone to disparage her talent, but in England and Europe she has always been looked upon with the same respect accorded Edith Wharton and Willa Cather. Ferber, like Wharton and Cather, was a Pulitzer Prize-winner, and, moreover, she was a lover of American history. *Cimarron* is a rousing action story that could have happened only in the American West, for it is a story of Oklahoma, beginning with the big land rush on April 22, 1889, and continuing through its emergence as an important, rich state. Ferber populated that history with a vast array of characters, fictional and real, who act out their destinies over a period of forty years.

The picture opens with a brief introduction to the main characters and sets the scene for the land rush; Oklahoma is a territory about to be opened to homesteaders. They gather in wagons and carriages, on horseback, and even on foot at the starting line in Osage to wait for the cannon to sound at noon, when they can race westward to claim their part of the two million acres being released by the government. It is one of the most exciting action scenes ever filmed, and footage from it has reappeared in almost every movie made thereafter that has anything to do with the Oklahoma land rush.

Among those gathered is Yancey Cravat (Richard Dix), a pioneer adventurer who has come to the West with his bride, Sabra (Irene Dunne). He races to stake out the Bear Creek claim and also aids Dixie Lee (Estelle Taylor), a young adventuress, in staking her claim. The overnight camp of Osage, which had been the starting point of the land rush, grows gradually into a large but respectable town. Yancey Cravat establishes his home with Sabra, and she bears him children. He is a fighter who even engages in a gun battle with Billy the Kid. When the bank is robbed, it is he who stops the two bandits. He defends Dixie Lee over Sabra's protestations in a courtroom battle when she is on trial as a harlot, and his defense is so able that Dixie is acquitted. He becomes one of the town's pioneer citizens when he establishes himself as editor of the liberal weekly newspaper, *The Oklahoma Wigwam*. Although his influence is wide, he is secretly infected with wanderlust. When Osage has grown from an early wild wilderness to a young city, he finds himself looking westward to further horizons. His wife is aware of his desire to move on, but there is little she can do about it, for she is busy establishing herself as a leader in her own right among the townswomen.

Overnight, Yancey quietly disappears from Osage, and Sabra, instead of grieving, takes over the editorship of the paper. Soon it grows into a daily, and then into one of the leading newspapers of the West. The great oil boom begins and everybody, especially the Indians, becomes wealthy. The Cravat children grow up, and Sabra becomes a dominant force in civic and then statewide activities. Tragedy strikes, however, when her best-loved son is killed in a railroad accident, but she perseveres in the strength of her belief and faith in the land and successfully runs for Congress to represent her state.

The years pass. Sabra becomes a grandmother, a matriarch in the town. Yancey is only a beloved memory to her, but he is remembered also by the Osage elders for his work in establishing the early town, and a monument is erected to him. On the day of its unveiling, there is an accident in the nearby newly discovered oilfield, and an old worker is fatally injured in a heroic rescue. Something about the stranger strikes a chord in Sabra's memory, and she rushes to the scene of the accident. She recognizes the old stranger at once and kneels in the dust to take him in her arms. It is Yancey, who dies with her kiss upon him; the wanderer has returned home as the monument to him is unveiled.

The action of the film covers forty years, and the actors age accordingly. Irene Dunne, in her second screen appearance, aged from sixteen to fifty-six and captured an Academy Award nomination as Best Actress, the first of five she was to receive during her brilliant screen career. She is seen first as a pretty, gently reared Kansas girl, swept off her feet by an adventurer whom she marries and with whom she goes to the Oklahoma Territory. She begins as a teen-age bride in 1889, and at the final fade-out she is a greying grand-mother and senior congresswoman in 1929.

Dunne had to fight a game of wits to get the part of Sabra. RKO/Radio had signed her to a contract when she was appearing on the stage as another Ferber heroine, Magnolia Hawks, in the Chicago company of *Show Boat*. She moved to Hollywood, and her first appearance in films was as the female lead in the musical *Leathernecking* (1930). But musicals fell out of favor for several years, and the picture's songs were cut and the film ignored. At first, Fay Bainter was chosen to play Sabra, but she lost favor with producer William Le Baron. Dunne then realized that the part of Sabra would go to the actress who earned it, and she knew that she also had Richard Dix, who was going to play Yancey, on her side. She persuaded makeup artist Ernest Westmore and still cameraman Ernest Bracken to work with her one Saturday afternoon, making a series of photographs showing how she could age ac-ceptably from sixteen to fifty-six. Those photographs were on Le Baron's desk Monday morning with a note from Westmore—"This is Irene Dunne, the girl who should play the lead in *Cimarron*." Le Baron was impressed and ordered a screen test, which Richard Dix is alleged to have made with her. Director Wesley Ruggles, who had resisted the idea of her playing Sabra because he thought her too young and inexperienced, was convinced, and Dunne got the part.

There was no question about Richard Dix's playing Yancey. He was a longtime friend of Le Baron, and anybody who had read the Ferber novel knew he was perfect for the part. In fact, RKO supposedly acquired the property because they had him under contract as a star. He worked well with Dunne, and he won a nomination as Best Actor at Academy Award time. Wesley Ruggles won a nomination as Best Director, and *Cimarron* became not only his finest directorial job, but it has remained a genuine Western epic. Ruggles took on Edward Cronjager as cinematographer, and he too won an Oscar nomination that year for his thrilling camerawork. The supporting roles were brilliantly cast by Ruggles and included Estelle Taylor as a seductive Dixie Lee; Edna May Oliver as a onetime belle, Mrs. Tracy Wyatt; Roscoe Ates playing Jess Rickey, a stuttering painter; and William Collier, Jr., as Billy the Kid in a spirited sequence of conflict with Dix.

As a Western, *Cimarron* remains an epic movie with giant sweep. Any film that begins with so magnificent an action sequence as the land rush and then continues to build interest so that every one of its 131 minutes is suspenseful could only be listed as a landmark in motion picture history. In spite of its early appearance in talking film history, it remains unsurpassed, even by the unsuccessful 1960 remake.

DeWitt Bodeen

THE CITADEL

Released: 1938
Production: Victor Saville for Metro-Goldwyn-Mayer
Direction: King Vidor
Screenplay: Ian Dalrymple, Frank Wead, and Elizabeth Hill, with additional
   dialogue by Emlyn Williams; based on the novel of the same name by A. J.
   Cronin
Cinematography: Harry Stradling
Editing: Charles Frend
Running time: 110 minutes

Principal characters:
Andrew Manson .... Robert Donat
Christine Manson .... Rosalind Russell
Denny .... Ralph Richardson
Ben Chenkin .... Francis L. Sullivan
Lawford .... Rex Harrison
Charles Every .... Cecil Parker

Victor Saville's production of A. J. Cronin's *The Citadel* is one of Hollywood's rare ventures into medical drama in support of a populist theme. The citadel of the title is a symbolic rather than a literal one: it signifies a kingdom of truth, honesty, and integrity within the medical profession. These are goals pursued by Dr. Andrew Manson with idealistic determination despite the enemies they make and the barrier they ironically put between him and professional success. The screenplay by Ian Dalrymple, Frank Wead, Elizabeth Hill, and Emlyn Williams compresses the novel to a manageable, smoothly flowing series of episodes. In so doing, it lends an urgency of which the stars take full advantage despite a weak ending.

Andrew Manson (Robert Donat) arrives in a poor Welsh mining village where he is expected to tolerate filthy working conditions, ignorance, illiteracy, and a populace indifferent to the plight of those afflicted with black lung disease. The man he is to replace is an endearing eccentric named Denny (Ralph Richardson) with his own ideas about helping the miners, such as blowing up the town's disgraceful sewer system so that officials will be forced to build a new one. Manson takes an interest in Denny's daring methods while dealing with the miners on an individual basis. A heart-rending scene occurs when Manson has to deliver a baby from a middle-aged woman whose last chance this is to bear a child. She gives up the seemingly stillborn baby for dead, but Manson persists, dipping it in cold water and slapping it into wailing life. Donat later remarked that of all the scenes he had ever performed, this was the most satisfying personally.

This act, however, is only an interlude in a life devoted to mining-related illnesses, black lung disease chief among them. Yet the miners distrust Manson's prying into their lives, even if it is in their own best interests. Led by a burly veteran miner named Ben Chenkin (Frances L. Sullivan), they force Manson to move elsewhere. He relocates, marries a schoolteacher named Christine (Rosalind Russell), and settles down to life as an idealistic but poor research scientist. A rich woman given to fits of hysteria changes his life after Manson is called upon to slap her back into sanity one day. She takes a liking to his bedside manner, spurring him on to forsake his research for a lucrative private practice. The patients he treats are generally rich, overfed hypochondriacs rather than needy people. In this practice he loses sight of the principles with which he began his medical career.

The Citadel, made at M-G-M's British studio, marked King Vidor's return to the earthy drama of such films as *The Big Parade* (1925) and *The Crowd* (1928) after several years of glossy melodramas. His strongly naturalistic touches are evident throughout, leading one to feel that Vidor too seldom found material worthy of his talent.

As Andrew Manson, Robert Donat gave one of the finest performances of his regrettably limited career as a film actor. As in *The Count of Monte Cristo* (1934), *The 39 Steps* (1935), and *The Ghost Goes West* (1936), he projects an aura of warmth, sincerity, humor, and idealism. When one thinks of Donat, one recalls his melodious voice and handsome, reassuring countenance; but what Donat brought to the role of Manson was innate sensitivity and moral strength. Watching him deliver the baby or tend to dying miners or give an impassioned speech before priggish doctors, one is convinced that he *is* a doctor who cares and struggles on behalf of the unfortunate. This sort of personal conviction lends poignancy to that section of the film in which he has become a medical quack. He makes us hope that he will return to his real calling, research science.

The death of Denny is what brings Manson to his senses. In his few scenes as Denny, Richardson steals the show, mainly because of the charming eccentricity he brings to the part. He refuses to sacrifice idealism for what he sees as the deadening smugness of material success. When we last see Denny, he is drunk, trying to persuade Manson to give up his practice in order to join forces with him. Manson politely refuses, leaving Denny to hobble into the street, where he is run over by a car. Denny later dies on an operating table, a victim of malpractice at the hands of an affluent but incompetent surgeon named Charles Every (Cecil Parker). It is this event which convinces Manson to return to his real work.

The film ends with Manson pleading before a tribunal of distinguished surgeons on behalf of a skilled but unlicensed peer. The scene works splendidly up to the point at which Manson finishes his speech. It is the second time in the film that Donat is allowed the full potential of his magnificent voice, recalling a similar oration in *The Count of Monte Cristo*. However, when he and Christine leave the courtroom, their faces beaming, the viewer may experience a letdown, feeling that there should have been more to the ending than this. It is as though the picture inexplicably stops instead of building to a conclusion with the impact we have been led to expect. Nor is this the film's only flaw. Though Rosalind Russell does her best with the role of Christine, it is too thinly written. We want to know more about her; she is not given enough to do as Donat's helpmate, making their relationship a lopsided one. Despite these faults, what matters most is that King Vidor was able to fashion an eloquently meaningful movie from an equally eloquent book. As film critic Ernest B. Ferguson noted, the picture sags somewhat in the second half, but its overall strength is what counts. That the book should have been transferred to the screen without the sentimental clichés and cloying sweetness common to most M-G-M films at that time is an accomplishment in itself.

The only other similar medical drama released during the decade of the 1930's was *Arrowsmith* (1931), directed by John Ford and starring Ronald Colman. Of the two films, *The Citadel* is better, largely because sound techniques had considerably improved in the seven-year interim and because Donat was physically better suited to his role as an English doctor than the equally British Colman was to his role as an American one. Temperamentally, however, both actors shared a humanistic approach to their work, making their portrayals all the more convincing. One could conceivably argue that *The Citadel*'s view of material success at the expense of integrity is a naïve, simplistic one, yet there are too many real doctors similar to Andrew Manson to allow us to deny the validity of the film's theme.

Though *The Citadel* holds up beautifully, it has not been revived in recent years except on television, and then only in badly edited form. The version discussed here is a composite of two differently edited ninety-five-minute prints of the original one hundred and ten minutes. Even so, Vidor's masterful direction, the star performances of Donat and Richardson, and Harry Stradling's exquisite black and white cinematography retain their power to uplift. It is regrettable that no one has revived this film, preferably on a double bill with Donat's Oscar-winning performance for M-G-M in *Goodbye, Mr. Chips* (1939).

Sam Frank

CITIZEN KANE

Released: 1941
Production: Orson Welles for RKO/Radio
Direction: Orson Welles
Screenplay: Herman J. Mankiewicz and Orson Welles (AA)
Cinematography: Gregg Toland
Editing: Robert Wise
Running time: 119 minutes

Principal characters:

Charles Foster Kane	Orson Welles
Jedediah Leland	Joseph Cotten
Susan Alexander	Dorothy Comingore
Emily Norton Kane	Ruth Warrick
Mr. Bernstein	Everett Sloane
Mrs. Kane	Agnes Moorehead
Walter Parks Thatcher	George Coulouris
Raymond	Paul Stewart
Thompson	William Alland
James W. Gettys	Ray Collins
Herbert Carter	Erskine Sanford

Citizen Kane, widely regarded as one of the best films ever made, is a triumph of technique, storytelling, and acting. From the opening shot to the end of the film we are impressed and intrigued by this powerful and complex examination of a complicated man's life. Orson Welles was producer, director, and star of the film, so it is to a great extent his film, but he owes a great deal to his collaborators—particularly Herman Mankiewicz, with whom he worked on the script, and Gregg Toland, his extremely talented cinematographer.

Citizen Kane is the story of Charles Foster Kane. His mother becomes unexpectedly wealthy when he is a child and appoints the firm of Thatcher and Company as trustees of the fortune and guardian of her son Charles, who is sent east to be reared and educated. Upon reaching the age of twenty-one, Charles assumes control of what has become the world's sixth-largest private fortune, but only one part of his holdings interests him—a small New York newspaper, *The Inquirer*. He takes personal charge of the paper and eventually builds it into a powerful publishing empire of thirty-seven newspapers. Two men are associated with him throughout, Bernstein (Everett Sloane), his business manager, and Jedediah Leland (Joseph Cotten), his closest friend and the drama critic for two of his newspapers.

During his rise to power, Kane marries the niece of the President of the United States, Emily Norton (Ruth Warrick), but many years later begins an affair with Susan Alexander (Dorothy Comingore). Once he achieves power through his newspaper empire, he becomes politically ambitious and runs for governor, but during the campaign his affair with Susan is revealed and he loses the race. After his divorce from Emily and marriage to Susan, Kane's political career is over, so he tries to use his wealth and influence to establish Susan as a successful opera singer. He builds an opera house for her and insists that his newspapers give her glowing reviews even though her voice teacher says she has no talent and Susan herself wants to stop. Not until she attempts suicide, however, does he allow her to do so. He then builds her a castle in Florida, called Xanadu, into which they withdraw. But Susan does not like their isolated, lonely life there and finally summons up the courage to leave him. At his death, Kane is a wealthy but friendless old man.

Perhaps the most notable feature of *Citizen Kane* is its intricate structure. The film begins with night shots of a mysterious castle, then goes inside to witness the last moment of Kane, the castle's owner. Next we are suddenly watching a newsreel covering Kane's life, and are thus given a brief look at the public side of the man. The producer of the newsreel, however, does not think the film reveals enough about Kane because it does not show how he was different from other men, so he sends Thompson (William Alland), one of his reporters, to find out more about Kane's life. Specifically, he wants to find the meaning of the single word Kane spoke just before he died, "Rosebud." He feels that finding out what the word meant to Kane might explain his life.

The rest of the film is the story of what Thompson discovers. After an unsuccessful attempt to interview Kane's second wife, Susan Alexander Kane, he reads a chapter on Kane from the memoirs of the late Walter Thatcher (George Coulouris), who was Kane's guardian; he then interviews Bernstein and Jedediah Leland. Thompson then returns to Susan and is able to persuade her to tell her part of the story. After talking to Susan he goes to Kane's castle, Xanadu, and talks briefly with Raymond, the butler (Paul Stewart). Only after Thompson leaves do we learn the "answer" to the riddle: as workers burn an accumulation of Kane's possessions, including his mother's belongings and his own boyhood mementos, we briefly see the name "Rosebud" on a child's sled before it is consumed by the flames. It is the sled with which we saw Kane playing just before he was sent away from his parents' home. The camera then takes us outside to watch the smoke rising from the chimney of the castle as the film ends.

The film uses its unusual structure as a way of introducing various parts of the story rather than as a device to give us different points of view about Kane. The five sources from which Thompson, the reporter, gets his information serve to introduce separate sections of the film rather than to present different points of view. Although we do learn something of each person's opinion of Kane, the story each ostensibly tells is not limited to what he or she knows from actual experience or even has heard about. The opening sequence showing the night shrouded castle and the dying man with the word

"Rosebud" on his lips tantalizes and mystifies. Next we are given a brief, superficial report of the man's life in a newsreel, followed by a more detailed investigation, and a short ending in which the "meaning" of the mysterious word is revealed. After he finishes his investigation without discovering the meaning of "Rosebud," Thompson says, "I don't think any word can explain a man's life," and once we see the word on the sled, we realize that Thompson is right; there is no simple explanation of a person's life.

Two themes predominate in *Citizen Kane*: power and love. The two are inextricably linked in the mind and psyche of Charles Foster Kane. The fact that his first wife, Emily, is the niece of the President of the United States suggests a connection between power and love, but an even more complex interlocking of the two themes is seen in his relationship with Susan Alexander.

Kane first meets Susan in a chance encounter on a street corner and is delighted that she likes him even though she does not know who he is. He describes her to Leland as "a cross-section of the American public," suggesting that he believes this proves that he can be loved by the people. When he runs for governor, love and power are again linked. He wants the power of the office, but he also sees the election as an opportunity for the people of the state to demonstrate their love for him. After the preelection revelation of his affair with Susan deprives him of the love of the people, he decides to use his power and money for Susan, to give her a career as an opera singer, but however generous or noble that impulse might have been at the start, her career soon becomes a test of his power and judgment. He realizes that if Susan does not become a successful opera singer, both his power to influence events and his judgment will be in question. Her feelings mean nothing to him as he forces her to practice her singing though her voice teacher tells him she has no talent. Susan begs Kane to let her stop until finally, unable to stand appearing before audiences who scorn her, she attempts suicide, forcing Kane to realize he can push her no further. He then builds her a castle, but we quickly see that power rather than love is his motivation because he insists that she stay in the castle even though she comes to regard it as a joyless prison. The marriage ends when Susan can no longer tolerate Kane's not-so-benevolent despotism. As she tells Thompson, "Everything was his idea, except my leaving him."

Enhancing the complex presentation of Kane's character is the distinctive visual style of the film, which arises from its unconventional lighting in which shadows play an important part, its use of the entire area of the picture from the foreground to the background, and its frequent use of long uninterrupted shots to portray an action or an encounter. All these techniques effectively hold and direct the attention of the audience. To understand the complexity and innovation of *Citizen Kane* it is necessary to understand the conventional method of presenting a scene in a film (particularly a Hollywood film) in the 1930's, the decade before *Citizen Kane*. A standard presentation first shows an overall view of the setting and then separate closer views of whatever is important in the scene. Each character is fully lighted, and anything significant happens close to the camera rather than in the background. For example, a standard presentation of a conversation between two people in a room would first show the room with the two people in it, then would cut to a closer view of one person speaking, then to the other person listening or answering. In *Citizen Kane*, however, Welles frequently shows such a scene in one long unbroken shot with the camera showing both the characters and their surroundings for the entire scene rather than dividing it into separate segments.

A good example of Welles's directorial technique is the scene which occurs after political boss James W. Gettys (Ray Collins) discovers Kane's affair with Susan Alexander and tries to use his information to get Kane to withdraw from the race for governor. It is a dramatic confrontation at Susan's apartment between Gettys, Susan, Kane, and Kane's wife, Emily. The heart of the scene is one long shot (nearly two full minutes) in which the dramatic emphasis is made subtly but effectively by lighting and the movement of the characters. The lighting is so arranged that at any one time only one character is fully lighted, and the emphasis shifts dramatically from character to character during the shot. As the shot begins, Kane and Emily are talking when Susan comes into the picture. Then the camera moves slightly to the right, leaving Emily in the foreground and showing Gettys in the background where there is little light. After Kane approaches Gettys in the background and begins speaking to him, Gettys turns and walks toward Emily, stopping in the middleground where his face is fully lighted. While Gettys addresses Emily, Susan joins Kane in the background, but as she becomes concerned about her fate should the affair become known to the public, she comes toward the camera and Gettys also. When at the end of the shot the other three characters look back at Kane, the turning of their heads shifts all the emphasis to him, even though he is in the background and his face is not lighted. The entire scene, particularly this long crucial shot, perfectly demonstrates the ability of Welles to use all areas of the picture—foreground, middleground, and background—for dramatic effect. Most of these techniques had been used before, mainly by foreign directors, but their creative combination in *Citizen Kane* was unprecedented in a Hollywood film.

Of the many virtuoso scenes and techniques in *Citizen Kane*, two are particularly noteworthy. In one, the deterioration of Kane's marriage to his first wife, Emily, is conveyed in a short but telling sequence. At the beginning of the sequence we see the two at the breakfast table talking affectionately, although Emily does lament the time he devotes to the newspaper. Then the camera suddenly swings to the right so fast that the image blurs (a swish pan), and when it stops, we see Emily again, but it is obvious that some time has passed. She is now complaining more strongly about the time Kane spends at the newspaper. As the sequence continues with additional scenes separated by swish pans, we see that they are becoming more and more distant from each other both physically and emotionally until they are sitting silently at opposite ends of the table and Emily is reading the rival newspaper. A great deal of information is thus conveyed about their relationship with a minimum of dialogue, and the swish pans imaginatively convey the passage of time.

Also visually imaginative is the prelude to Thompson's first attempt to interview Susan. We first see a billboard picture of Susan in a thunderstorm. Then the camera moves to show a neon sign on an old building announcing "Susan Alexander Kane/Twice Nightly," and the camera continues, seemingly going through the skylight in the roof of the building down to a table inside the nightclub where Susan sits, her head on the table. Thompson then enters the shot to interview her, but she will not talk to him. It is on a later visit that Thompson gets her story.

Although *Citizen Kane* is always praised for its technical and stylistic innovations, the acting in the film should not be underrated, since it gives the film much of its power. Each member of the cast, most of whom had stage and radio experience but were appearing in their first film, is excellent; four, however, must be singled out for special mention. Orson Welles is compelling and convincing as the bright and ambitious young Charles Foster Kane and also as the sixty-year-old Kane who has lost most of his idealism and sense of humor. Joseph Cotten ably conveys the inner dignity and devotion to principles which Jedediah Leland retains throughout his sometimes acrimonious relationship with Kane. Everett Sloane gives a quietly supportive performance as Bernstein, and Dorothy Comingore as Susan Alexander is appropriately common and vulnerable.

At the time of its release, *Citizen Kane* aroused considerable controversy because of Charles Foster Kane's resemblance to the powerful newspaper magnate William Randolph Hearst. Time has proven, however, that whether or not Hearst was the original inspiration for the character has nothing to do with the power and artistry of the film. As years go by, the original controversy has been forgotten, and *Citizen Kane* stands on its own merits as one of the greatest masterpieces of cinema. A more recent controversy about the film was ignited in 1970, when critic Pauline Kael published two long articles on the film (which were later incorporated into a book), in which she argued that Orson Welles was given too much credit for *Citizen Kane*, and Herman Mankiewicz, credited as coauthor (with Welles) of the script, was given too little. Once again the controversy has little or nothing to contribute to one's understanding or enjoyment of the film. Film is the most collaborative of art forms, and even a feature film requires for its completion the efforts of hundreds of people at various levels of creativity. Any attempt to ascertain the exact contribution of any one of these people can only be of very limited success, involving as it must memories, egos, and controversies. What is important is the film itself.

   Citizen Kane is a true masterpiece. From its overall design to its smallest detail, it displays an imaginative use of the film medium which gives it a striking visual and emotional impact. Especially impressive is the fact that it was the film debut of Orson Welles, who had made his reputation in the theater and radio as an actor and director for the Mercury Theater, which he and John Housman founded in 1937. The Hearst controversy, the daring novelty of the film in its structure and techniques, and the resentment and jealousy Welles aroused in Hollywood limited the film's popular and critical success when it was first released. The only Academy Award it received was for the screenplay, but *Citizen Kane* fairly soon gained its current high critical reputation and was a great influence on many filmmakers who followed.

Timothy W. Johnson

CITY LIGHTS

Released: 1931
Production: Charles Chaplin for United Artists
Direction: Charles Chaplin
Screenplay: Charles Chaplin, with assistance from Harry Crocker, Henry Bergman, and Albert Austin
Cinematography: Rollie Totheroh, Gordon Pollock, and Mark Marklatt
Editing: Charles Chaplin
Art direction: Charles D. Hall
Music: Charles Chaplin
Running time: 87 minutes

Principal characters:
The Little Tramp .... Charles Chaplin
The Blind Girl .... Virginia Cherrill
The Eccentric Millionaire .... Harry Myers

City Lights is a perfectly balanced mixture of comedy and pathos and is considered by many to be Charles Chaplin's finest film. It was released in 1931, three years into the era of motion picture talkies, yet for all intents and purposes, it is a silent film. In making it, there was the fear that the public, having become accustomed to the talking motion picture, would balk at a newly made silent film, considering it to be a *passé* and regressive genre. Chaplin, however, was audacious and a purist in his decision to make *City Lights* nonverbal—or, as the elegant subtitle proclaims, "A Comedy Romance in Pantomime." Chaplin considered pantomine to be a valid and important artistic expression with a universal appeal, and he considered himself a master of the art. He also was somewhat apprehensive about having the famous Tramp speak for the first time. Audiences had come to know the "little fellow" from physical actions, through his exquisite smirks and shrugs and delightful movements; the danger existed that if he talked, his endearing quality would be destroyed. A belief in the silent film as a superior and transcendent art form was something of an ethos with Chaplin, so he took the gamble. He spent two to three years making *City Lights*, which became an overwhelming critical and popular success and made a profit of five million dollars in its first release.

A "silent" movie with a complete musical soundtrack is the least silent of all movies. The music of *City Lights*, composed by Chaplin, is perfectly synchronized and based on the idea of the *leitmotif*: specific tunes are used as themes for certain characters. In his autobiography, Chaplin remarks that he "wanted the music to be a counterpoint of grace and charm, to express sentiment without which . . . a work of art is incomplete." Certainly, the music serves a larger purpose than that of simple accompaniment. Not only does it add dimension and spice to the visuals, but it also serves as an emotional signpost, giving definitive momentum to the scenes through fanfares and sudden transitions. Furthermore, in *City Lights* Chaplin makes a unique use of cinema sound by incorporating an assortment of engaging effects. One example occurs in a party scene halfway through the film when the blithe and tipsy Tramp mistakenly swallows a whistle. Beset by an attack of hiccoughs, he whistles with each spasm. When he steps outside to allow his malady to subside, he first attracts a taxi cab and then is descended upon by a horde of dogs.

The opening of the film is renowned for a scene of comic satire which employs an impeccable aural gag. A listless and dignified civic group assembled for the dramatic unveiling of a statue is listening to a series of boring presentation speeches. While the man at the microphone is fastidiously speaking, a grossly quacking saxophone parodies his voice. When a woman takes the podium, the same hilarious garble is heard, only in a higher register. When the shroud is lifted from the statue, the crowd is taken aback as it beholds the Little Tramp napping in the lap of one of the figures. As he embarrassedly tries to climb down, his baggy pants become impaled on the statue's sword, and he is desperately trying to extricate himself when the national anthem begins. Being the gentleman that he is, he respectfully takes off his hat and holds it to his chest while trying to remain in a half-standing position. After escaping the mighty sword, he continues to grope his way over the hills and valleys of the statue's body until finally, his profile juxtaposed against a huge outspread hand creates a consummate nose-thumbing gesture. Such wit and irreverence is characteristic of Chaplin at his best.

The film continues as the dignified Little Tramp saunters down the street, stopping along the way to examine aesthetically a nude statue in a shop window; he rebukes two newspaper boys for their insensitivity in making fun of his tattered clothes, and removes the ragged tips of his gloves to snap his fingers in their faces. When he ducks through a parked limousine to avoid a policeman, he comes upon a beautiful blind flower girl (Virginia Cherrill) who mistakes him for a millionaire. He is smitten and gives his only coin to her. When, after walking away, he tiptoes back to gaze tenderly upon her, she unwittingly throws a bucket of water in his face. Just when we think that gushing sentimentality is going to prevail, our hero gets a pail of water in his face or a flower pot on his head, and we find ourselves laughing at our own human vulnerability. It is a wonderful moment. The emotional and humanistic resonance of the film as a whole makes it transcend mere slapstick; the moment is sentimental without being maudlin. Although some claim that the scene is too self-indulgently romantic, it is certainly not as much so as similar scenes in some of Chaplin's later films.

The Little Tramp next happens upon a drunk clumsily trying to drown himself by tying a weighted rope around his neck. The Tramp rushes valiantly to save him, and after about three minutes of physical convolutions, they both end up in the water. They become buddies, and when the Tramp escorts his new friend home, he finds that he is the inhabitant of an elegant mansion. They drink a few champagne toasts to life, with half the bottle going down our hero's pants, and dress to go out on the town. Later, a series of unfortunate incidents occurs at a crowded dinner and dance club, resulting in a lady being squirted with seltzer water, a waiter being passionately swung around the dance floor by the fervid and drunken Tramp, and a spaghetti-confetti sequence wherein a noodle from the Tramp's plate becomes entangled with a string of confetti falling from above and he finds himself helplessly sucking ever-upward on an endless strand.

We soon discover that the Eccentric Millionaire (Harry Myers) has to be drunk to recognize the Little Tramp as his friend. When sober, he is icy and stern and wants nothing to do with the lowly creature. The "little fellow," of course, is adaptable and used to falling in and out of fortune, so he enjoys the pleasures his friend has to offer whenever the opportunity arises. It is this optimistic resourcefulness in the Tramp which gives him his winsome charm. Chaplin described the Tramp as "a gentleman, a poet, a dreamer— always hopeful of romance." At once vulnerable and triumphant, he is a "universal little man" whose pathos is not pathetic but heartwarming. His guileless innocence and naïveté enchant us as he trips through the vagaries of life tipping his hat to everybody and everything.

As the film progresses, the Tramp becomes the lovely flower girl's benefactor. She, of course, still thinks he is wealthy. Wanting to send her for an operation to cure her blindness, he gets a job as a streetsweeper, but immediately runs into trouble. As he shuffles along in his white uniform, broom and trash barrel in tow, he is overwhelmed by a menagerie of animals ambling down the street—first a string of donkeys, then a trio of elephants. He finally loses his job for being late once too often, so he decides to make some money boxing. However, things go awry when the crook who enticed him to fight by promising that they would take it easy on each other and split the purse, runs off to avoid the police. The poor Tramp is left to face a sour-puss palooka whom he nearly dances to death in the ring before being knocked cold.

Finally, the drunk Millionaire offers to give his friend $1,000 for the Blind Girl; robbers attack, knocking him on the head but not getting the money. The police then arrive and mistake the Tramp for the thief. The schizophrenic Millionaire, sobered by the blow, does not recognize him, so the Tramp snatches the money and runs, giving it to the girl for the operation and bidding her farewell. Then, in a brief scene so characteristic of the Tramp, he is escorted to the door of the prison, where he takes a last puff of his cigar and tosses it over his shoulder, giving it a devil-may-care kick with his heel.

The melancholy epilogue is one of the most memorable and touching endings in cinema. Autumn has arrived and the bereft, bedraggled Little Tramp, just released from prison, shuffles along the city streets dispiritedly, his mettle and sauciness all but gone. When he sees the now cured flower girl giggling at him through the window of a flower shop that she and her grandmother own, he is transfixed with wonder and joy. He tries to evade her, but she calls him back to give him a rose. When she takes his hand, she recognizes his touch and with the timeless wistfulness of all broken dreams tremulously asks, "You?" The final close-up of the Little Tramp, an ethereal expression of bliss and pain etched in his face as he holds the rose to his mouth, is frozen forever in our minds.

Lynn Woods

CLEOPATRA

Released: 1934
Production: Cecil B. De Mille for Paramount
Direction: Cecil B. De Mille
Screenplay: Waldemar Young and Vincent Lawrence; based on an adaptation of historical material by Barlett Cormack
Cinematography: Victor Milner (AA)
Editing: Anne Bauchens
Costume design: Travis Banton
Running time: 103 minutes

> *Principal characters:*
> Cleopatra .... Claudette Colbert
> Julius Caesar .... Warren William
> Marc Antony .... Henry Wilcoxon
> Calpurnia .... Gertrude Michael
> Herod .... Joseph Schildkraut
> Octavian .... Ian Keith
> Enobarbus .... C. Aubrey Smith
> Pothinos .... Leonard Mudie
> Appollodorus .... Irving Pichel
> Octavia .... Claudia Dell
> Charmian .... Eleanor Phelps
> Iras .... Grace Durkin

According to Charles Higham's biography, Cecil B. De Mille had not originally wanted to make *Cleopatra* at all. His last film, a sophisticated comedy-adventure called *Four Frightened People* (1934), had failed at the box office, however; and Paramount studio chief Adolph Zukor suggested that De Mille return to the field of costume spectacle for which the public knew him best. De Mille at first began preparing a science fiction story, "When Worlds Collide," about a scientist who launches a rocket ship into space containing a hand-picked colony of human beings, animals, and plants after he discovers that the earth is on a collision course with another planet. A reissue of Warner Bros.' *Noah's Ark* (1929), with its similar theme, forced De Mille to cancel this project (which was eventually filmed by Paramount and special effects wizard George Pal in 1951); and De Mille reluctantly turned to a film biography of the most famous seductress in history. To play Cleopatra, he selected Paramount star Claudette Colbert, who had been his leading lady in *Four Frightened People* and had made a nicely lascivious Poppaea, Nero's wife, in his last historical epic, *The Sign of the Cross* (1932). Charles Laughton had turned in a magnificent, high camp performance as Nero; but De Mille rejected him as too soft and effeminate to play Julius Caesar, Cleopatra's first lover. The role finally went to Warren William, a well-known actor with a commanding presence who is best remembered today for his portrayal of the Lone Wolf in a popular B-picture mystery series of the 1940's.

The crucial role of Marc Antony proved more difficult to cast. Fredric March, who had played the heroic Roman tribune in *The Sign of the Cross,* would have been ideal; but he had another commitment. None of the other available leading men with established reputations suited De Mille's conception of the hero; and he decided to search the ranks of beginning actors for his Antony.

On January 6, 1934, as De Mille was waiting to enter a Paramount screening room to run test footage of some likely prospects, his attention was caught by the sound of a deep, thrilling voice coming from the sound track of the picture that was then being shown. The voice belonged to Henry Wilcoxon, a young British actor who had been signed by the studio on the strength of his success as Robert Browning in the London stage production of *The Barretts of Wimpole Street.* Wilcoxon was twenty-eight years old, six feet tall, and the possessor of a superb physique. De Mille knew as soon as he saw him that he had found the perfect Antony. Like De Mille, Wilcoxon was, in Higham's words, "uncomplicatedly masculine, straight-backed and fearless," and the two men became fast friends. Wilcoxon starred as Richard the Lion-Hearted in De Mille's next film, *The Crusades* (1935), and, after his acting career waned, he became an executive in De Mille's production company and continued to play small roles in most of his later films.

By the early 1930's, De Mille had perfected a method of preplanning every detail of his productions, so that by the time shooting got under way, he could leave the work of setting up a scene to an associate, arriving on the set himself only to conduct a final rehearsal before the cameras started rolling. For *Cleopatra,* months were spent in research verifying such details as the design of Egyptian hairpins and the correct pronunciation of the heroine's name. In point of fact, De Mille was as meticulous about the historical background of his epics as he was about correct visual detail. But he was also committed to an ideal of film narrative that had its roots in nineteenth century popular theater (where his father had functioned as a successful playwright and where he himself, like D. W. Griffith, had started his career intending to be an actor). The plot of a De Mille film was constructed around simple well-defined characters, a heaping dose of spectacle, and as much sex as the censors would allow. De Mille did not hesitate to turn the meandering stream of historical record into a straight channel if by so doing he made his films more exciting and comprehensible to a general audience; but if he simplified history, he was seldom guilty of conscious distortion. His Western *The Plainsman* (1936), which tells a largely fictional story about such historical figures as Wild Bill Hickok, Calamity Jane, and Buffalo Bill Cody, opens with a title frankly admitting that characters and events separated by many years have been brought together in an attempt to be faithful to the "spirit" of the era.

The career of Cleopatra, as recounted by Suetonius and Plutarch, hardly needed dramatic embellishment; on the contrary, De Mille's problem in retelling her life story was to decide which exciting events to leave out, if he did not want to end up with what, by the standards of the time, would have been an impossibly long film. Although De Mille never took a writer's credit on any of his films, he sat in on every story conference and frequently dictated whole scenes and lines of dialogue.

The film opens in 48 B.C., when Julius Caesar, having, as a title says, "conquered half the world," turned his attention to the tangled affairs of Egypt, which had become almost a Roman province. The ancient kingdom was nominally ruled by Ptolemy XII and his sister Cleopatra; but real power lay in the hands of the prime minister, Pothinos. Ptolemy was still only a boy, but Cleopatra was twenty when Caesar arrived in Egypt; and Pothinos rightly feared that she would try to influence Caesar to help her seize control of the kingdom for herself.

In the film, Pothinos (Leonard Mudie) kidnaps Cleopatra and sets her down at the border with Syria, telling her that it means certain death if she ever attempts to return to Alexandria, the Egyptian capital. With the help of her teacher and counselor, Appollodorus (Irving Pichel), Cleopatra makes her way back to Alexandria, where Appollodorus smuggles her into Caesar's presence in a Persian rug. Caesar is amused by her effrontery; but he is still about to sign a treaty recognizing Ptolemy's claim to be sole ruler when Cleopatra stops him with one word: "India!" She reminds him that the road to that fabled realm lies through Egypt, and invites him to her private apartments that evening to discuss a possible alliance between them. Pothinos sneaks into Cleopatra's rooms intending to kill both Caesar and the queen; but Cleopatra stabs him herself when she spots him hiding behind a curtain. Caesar, now impressed by Cleopatra's courage and ruthlessness as well as by her beauty, takes the queen as his mistress, telling his staff that he will be staying in Egypt longer than he had originally planned. (According to Suetonius, Caesar learned that Pothinos was plotting against him from his barber, and arranged for his assassination himself.)

In Rome, Caesar's friends gossip about his affair with the Egyptian queen behind the back of his wife, Calpurnia (Gertrude Michael). Octavian (Ian Keith), Caesar's nephew and heir, also feels that his uncle has been neglecting him. Why is it that Caesar can always find time to write letters to Marc Antony, he asks his sister, Octavia (Claudia Dell), but not to him? Octavia teasingly reminds him that Antony is her husband and that she herself would rather write to Antony than to her brother. (At the time Caesar's affair with Cleopatra began, the historical Octavian was barely into his teens. Octavia, his sister, did not become Antony's wife until 40 B.C., six years after Caesar's assassination.) When Caesar finally returns in triumph to Rome, Cleopatra is with him. Caesar installs her in a house near the capitol and tells her that he will announce his intention to divorce Calpurnia and marry her on the same day that he expects the Senate to crown him king: March 15, 44 B.C.—the Ides of March. The news of Caesar's murder by Brutus and his fellow conspirators reaches Cleopatra just as she is about to leave for the Senate. Appollodorus prevents her from going to Caesar's body by brutally telling her that it was not herself Caesar loved, but the power she represented. Cleopatra broken-heartedly realizes the truth of this and escapes with Appollodorus and her court in a boat down the Tiber.

De Mille now compresses the decade of the Second Triumvirate (43-33 B.C.) into what seems, on the screen, a year or two at most. Passing over the defeat of the conspirators in Caesar's murder at Philippi, De Mille shows Antony eagerly accepting a commission to bring Cleopatra back to Rome and justice. Sure of himself against the wiles of the woman who had snared Caesar, Antony sends messengers ordering Cleopatra to present herself before him in the public square of Tarsus. Cleopatra dutifully arrives in her imperial barge, but keeps Antony waiting while her handmaidens prepare an elaborate feast. Enobarbus (C. Aubrey Smith), Antony's gruff second-in-command, reports that the citizens of Tarsus, impressed by the splendor of Cleopatra's barge, have flocked to the water's edge to gape. At nightfall, Antony goes by himself to confront the rebellious queen. Sizing him up, Cleopatra confesses to Antony that she had hoped to seduce him as she seduced Caesar, but that now she recognizes the hopelessness of her situation. This puts Antony in a better humor, and he graciously decides to stay for dinner after all. Many drinks later, Cleopatra has the hiccups, which leads to Antony pounding her on the back to rid her of them, which leads to Cleopatra getting angry with him for his *lèse-majesté* until she realizes that, indeed, the hiccups are gone. Drunkenness as a metaphor for desire was a common device in the romantic comedies of the 1930's. Hero and heroine, their inhibitions freed by alcohol, could express their attraction for each other without, presumably, being able to do anything about it until they had sobered up, at least. De Mille was as straight-jacketed by the restrictions of the Production Code as any other Hollywood director of his time. Still, it is distressing to see two of the world's legendary star-crossed lovers behaving like a playboy and a spoiled heiress in a Lubitsch farce.

In Rome, the jealous Octavian takes advantage of the news of Antony's sudden infatuation to stir up the Senate and the people against their former hero. King Herod (Joseph Schildkraut), on his way home to Judea after a state visit to Rome, stops in Alexandria to advise Cleopatra that Octavian would look on her with favor if she poisoned Antony. Appollodorus reminds her of her duty to Egypt; and Cleopatra is just about to commit the deed when Enobarbus bursts in with news that Octavian, unable to wait, has launched an expedition against his faithless ally. Antony's determination to fight alone, if necessary, against the legions of imperial Rome (even the loyal

Enobarbus has left him) kindles Cleopatra's love in earnest; and she rides at his side to do battle with Octavian's troops. Helped by a liberal use of stock footage from his own 1923 production of *The Ten Commandments*, De Mille and his editor, Anne Bauchens, compress the events leading to Antony and Cleopatra's downfall—including the Battle of Actium, the greatest sea battle ever fought up to that time—into one brilliantly executed montage. The Battle of Actium was fought with models; and the scenes of hand-to-combat, put together out of close-ups only a few frames long, may not have called for even fifty extras.

The lovers fight valiantly; but finally Octavian has them trapped behind the walls of Alexandria. Cleopatra goes to Octavian to offer him Egypt's crown in exchange for Antony's life; and Antony, thinking she means to betray him, falls on his sword in her absence. Octavian sensibly refuses Cleopatra's offer but gives her safe conduct back to her palace, where she finds the mortally wounded Antony. "I am dying, Egypt, dying," he whispers in one of De Mille's few borrowings from Shakespeare's version of the story. Assisted by her handmaids, Charmian (Eleanor Phelps) and Iras (Grace Durkin), Cleopatra makes the last of her many costume changes in the film and, dressed in black with a cut-out décolletage, holds the fatal asp to her bosom. In rehearsals, Claudette Colbert made it clear to De Mille that she would not handle a real snake. On the day of shooting, he came onto the set with a huge snake wrapped around his whole arm. When Colbert screamed, De Mille produced a smaller snake that was the same size as an Egyptian asp and asked is she minded handling that instead. "Oh, that little thing?" she cried with relief. "Give it to me."

Cleopatra was a huge success; and De Mille was never tempted to stray from the proven ground of costume spectacle again. His skill at covering in 103 minutes the same number of years that Shaw covered in *Caesar and Cleopatra* and Shakespeare in *Julius Caesar* and *Antony and Cleopatra*—without making the audience feel that it has been cheated by getting only the bare bones of the story—is impressive even today. For all his pedantry about hairpins, De Mille never creates a single image that looks like a convincing replica of life in ancient Egypt and Rome. Travis Banton's costumes for Cleopatra—only vaguely Egyptian, only vaguely 1934—are nonetheless effective because they are completely timeless, their sole purpose being to display Colbert's considerable charms as alluringly as possible. In the same way, De Mille's staging of the banquet on Cleopatra's barge—an affair of dancing girls, exotic dishes, silken draperies, and falling rose petals that passes beyond considerations of good taste, beyond kitsch, almost into the realm of genuine art—is proof of Nabokov's dictum that there is nothing so exhilarating as Philistine vulgarity.

The film was nominated for Academy Awards for Best Picture, Best Cinematography, Best Sound Recording, and Best Editing (a new category that year), although only Victor Milner won for his shimmering black-and-white cinematography. Claudette Colbert did win the Oscar for Best Actress of 1934, but it was for her performance in a cheaply shot comedy, made in only four weeks, that was about as different from *Cleopatra* as any film could be: Frank Capra's *It Happened One Night*, which swept all the major Academy Awards.

Charles Hopkins

CLOSE ENCOUNTERS OF THE THIRD KIND

Released: 1977
Production: Julia Phillips and Michael Phillips—Steven Spielberg Film Productions for Columbia
Direction: Steven Spielberg
Screenplay: Steven Spielberg
Cinematography: Vilmos Zsigmond
Editing: Michael Kahn
Special effects: Douglas Trumbull
Running time: 134 minutes

> *Principal characters:*
> Roy Neary .... Richard Dreyfuss
> Jillian Guiler .... Melinda Dillon
> Claude Lacombe .... François Truffaut
> Barry Guiler .... Cary Guffey
> Ronnie Neary .... Teri Garr
> David Laughlin .... Bob Balaban

Director Steven Spielberg's career in films has been phenomenal. Although very young, he has brought two of the most spectacular financial successes of the 1970's to the screen, *Jaws* (1975) and *Close Encounters of the Third Kind*. The latter film is impossible to ignore in cinema history on the basis of its special effects alone. An ambitious and technically brilliant film, it is also one of the top-grossing films of all time. Critically it received eight Academy Award nominations as well as accolades from a majority of reviewers. As is true of all other forms of art, the art of cinema, dependent though it may be upon the variables of the contemporary culture in which it is formed, must also outlive its own generation and endure in meaning for future ones. In its childlike innocence, *Close Encounters of the Third Kind* seems to captivate the audience through the images, fantasies, and magic involved in man's primal, universal quests for identity, meaning, and divinity. It is a film of beautifully integrated fantasy and reality, partially because of its two-year gestation period of almost organic growth and change. The changes were often necessitated by such practicalities as time and money, but just as often they reflected a refinement of vision and an attempt by director/writer Spielberg to clarify his intergalactic fable of a visitation by aliens to planet Earth.

The title of the film refers to physical contact between beings from outer space and people on Earth. In Spielberg's film, the visitation of the aliens is preceded by a series of bizarre worldwide occurrences: the discovery in the Sonora Desert of a squadron of abandoned airplanes dating from the time of their disappearance in the 1940's; power blackouts throughout the world;

UFO sightings accompanied by harmonic signals; and the mental "calling" of various individuals to the proposed location of the aliens' visitation, Devil's Tower, Wyoming. It is around these "callings" that the film centers. The film traces the development of two seemingly normal, middle-class characters, Roy Neary (Richard Dreyfuss), a power company employee, and Jillian Guiler (Melinda Dillon), a working mother, who are mentally impressed with a vision of monolithic Devil's Tower, to which they are being called to come. It is a vision which obsesses them, making their behavior so erratic to their families and society as to literally divorce them from humanity: Neary ends up estranged from his family, sculpting a massive mud image of the mountain in his living room, and Jillian, whose son Barry (Cary Guffey) has been kidnaped by the aliens, shuts herself up in a motel, sketching her version of the vision. It is only after their independent discoveries of Devil's Tower and the base camp—which the government and scientists, headed by researcher Claude Lacombe (François Truffaut), have set up to greet the alien visitors—that they discover their obsessions to be otherworldly, and are thus freed to follow their individual fates.

The film draws its power and uniqueness from a number of sources based both in reality and fantasy. It incorporates man's universal desire to believe in higher beings, whether they be gods or aliens, and in such concepts as revelation, epiphany, and magic. The presentation of such concepts in the film produces a sense of wonder and innocence which is granted by both admirers and detractors to be the film's chief asset. It is galaxies away from the fear and paranoia of science fiction films of the 1950's. It almost mimicks such films as *The Thing* (1951), *Them* (1954), and *Invaders from Mars* (1953) in aspects of plot in order to demonstrate that the confrontation between Earth and aliens did not have to be violent and end in destruction as it had in the films of an earlier generation. In the final scenes of the film, the alien ships arrive in a flurry of harmonious colors and sounds, first treating the dumbfounded humans to a light show without rival and then to a concert which introduces earthlings to the universal language of tones. When the aliens themselves do finally appear, they are not hypertrophic monsters or other grotesque science fiction fantasies, but rather appear as somewhat embryonic children. With this magical finale, the film replaces fear with awe, paranoia with wonder, violence with joy, and confrontation itself with revelation.

More than any other science fiction film before it, *Close Encounters of the Third Kind* is a gentle film aligned emphatically on the side of creativity, imagination, and inspiration. Music is the mode of the aliens' communication and is indicative, in some way, of their ability to infuse artistic creativity into those whom they have called: Neary becomes alienated from his family, his suburban milieu, and his dull and mindless job and develops into a passionate, eccentric sculptor. It is as if these unearthly visitors are actually muses who can inspire, or, more accurately in the case of Neary, who is locked into his bourgeois existence, force out that creative passion which resides somewhere in each human spirit. Jillian's son Barry, prior to his abduction, plays a tune over and over again on his xylophone picking up the musical communication of the aliens, while his mother draws sketch after sketch. It is as if the arts must be infused into those with whom the aliens come in contact as a process of the communicative experience. *Close Encounters of the Third Kind* belongs more to the magical world of Walt Disney than to the fear-ridden world of cinema science fiction. Just as there are allusions to science fiction films, there are also allusions to Disney films: the Tinkerbell-like spaceship which follows a few feet behind the larger ships; the *Pinocchio* (1940) motifs; and the final title shots of the film as the members of the base camp watch Neary, who has chosen to be among the new space pioneers, fly away aboard the alien mothership, much like the children in *Peter Pan* (1952) watch their hero return to his "Never-Never Land."

Spielberg reaches deep down into our collective childhood memory for these images, and it may be these very images, more than any of the other admittedly brilliant special effects, which convince us to suspend disbelief for a time in order to allow the child in each of us to emerge for a few moments and wonder at the magic of it all.

James Ursini

COAL MINER'S DAUGHTER

Released: 1980
Production: Bernard Schwartz Productions; released by Universal
Direction: Michael Apted
Screenplay: Tom Rickman; based on the autobiography of the same name by
   Loretta Vecsey and George Vecsey
Cinematography: Ralf D. Bode
Editing: Arthur Schmidt
Running time: 125 minutes

> *Principal characters:*
> Loretta Lynn .... Sissy Spacek
> Doolittle "Mooney" Lynn .... Tommy Lee Jones
> Patsy Cline .... Beverly D'Angelo
> Ted Webb .... Levon Helm
> Clara Webb .... Phyllis Boyens

Country music superstar Loretta Lynn has never forgotten her simple beginnings and her heritage. Hers is the quintessential rags to riches tale—a climb from a childhood of poverty in Appalachia to a regal position as queen of country music. *Coal Miner's Daughter*, which is also the name of Lynn's most popular song, and her best-selling autobiography (coauthored with George Vecsey), details Lynn's story.

Told in straightforward fashion, the film is marked by a feeling of sincerity— that quality which distinguishes so much of country music. In fact, with its chronicle of one couple's determined goals, set against the backdrop of country music, this film evokes a sturdy sense of Americana. Country music has long been the subject of much humor; but, bouffant hair-dos, cowboy hats, Dolly Parton's bustline, and rhinestone-studded paraphernalia aside, this music form has roots which extend into America's heritage. In addition to telling Loretta Lynn's story, *Coal Miner's Daughter* underlines that legacy.

Actually, Lynn's own story seems as far-fetched as a tall tale. Married at the age of fourteen, she was the mother of four at age eighteen. Yet with the support and guidance of her husband "Mooney" (a one-time Moonshiner), she was propelled toward fame. She got her start in run-down honky-tonks and wound up a Grand Ole Opry regular, ultimately taking country music's top honor as Entertainer of the Year. In the realm of country music, Loretta Lynn reigns as first lady. Attaining that position, as this film details, was not easy.

The film opens against a breathtaking backdrop of the smoky Kentucky mountains, then moves quickly to the coal mining town of Butcher's Holler. Loretta Lynn (Sissy Spacek), who is thirteen, is accompanying her father, Ted Webb (Levon Helm), as he picks up his paycheck, then heads off for the company store to buy much-needed supplies. As Webb makes his purchases (and the grim observation that his hard-earned money flows right back to his employers), Loretta wanders outside. She witnesses a lively scene, as a brash man named Mooney (Tommy Lee Jones), just returned home from an Army stint, takes bets on whether his jeep can make it to the top of a slag heap. Loretta is wide-eyed over the stranger's cocky demeanor, and Mooney also glances her way. Moments later, we see her delighted gleam as the daring Mooney successfully scales the heap. This fast-talking red-headed man has caught her fancy. Immediately, we sense that this scrawny girl is on the verge of womanhood.

Her father also senses Loretta's impending maturity. When the annual package from Sears Roebuck arrives, each of the seven Webb youngsters receives a new pair of shoes, and Loretta also gets a blue floral print dress with lace trim. "Loretta is a woman now; she needs a woman's dress," says her father. The film portrays a dirt-poor but loving family. Home is a ramshackle cabin; Ted Webb's graveyard shift hours are long and hard. Nonetheless, the family does enjoy some high-spirited moments. On a Saturday night, with the family gathered around the radio, a Nashville broadcast delivers a rousing "Blue Moon of Kentucky." Lifting her skirts, Loretta's usually dour-faced mother, Clara (Phyllis Boyens), delights the family by doing a lively country dance.

The relationship between Loretta and Mooney begins to develop at a church social, where Mooney dramatically outbids all others at five dollars for Loretta's chocolate pie. Loretta is both pleased and uneasy at this display of aggressiveness; clearly, this man has more on his mind than just a pie. The sequence ends humorously when Mooney bites into the pie, and promptly spits it out. Loretta, who knows next to nothing about cooking, used salt where the recipe called for sugar.

Later, Loretta thrills to a sense of freedom as she rides about, against her father's wishes, with Mooney in his jeep. Her parents watch with some remorse as their daughter is wooed by this man who is so much older (almost twice her age) and more experienced than Loretta. Moreover, they do not think that Mooney, with his "wild ways," will make a responsible husband. But Loretta thinks otherwise, and her parents, with some prodding from Mooney, at last reluctantly give their permission for the marriage. First, however, Mooney promises Ted Webb that he will never hit Loretta and that he will never take her far from home.

Though the marriage gets off to a shaky start, the film details the problems with humor. Loretta, who knows nothing about sex, is so upset on her wedding night that she comes to bed with her new nightgown pulled over all her clothes. Mooney promptly orders her to the bathroom to get rid of the clothes underneath. The next morning, an angry Loretta will not accompany Mooney into a restaurant for breakfast "because they'll know what we've been doing in here."

Forced to work in the mines, an unhappy Mooney comes home to an unkept house and an unkempt wife. Loretta cannot cook, and she will not read the sex manual Mooney has bought for her. The two argue, and following an emotional outburst, Loretta leaves her husband and returns home.

Later, following a trip to the town doctor, Loretta discovers Mooney flirting with another girl. In a sequence which highlights her strong-willed, sassy streak, she picks up a stick and, flailing it about, goes after the interloping girl. Mooney, who is both surprised and amused by his child-bride's outburst, is also unruffled by the news that she is pregnant. At last, he tells her, she may have found something that she is good at.

Too ambitious to remain a miner, Mooney migrates to Washington, where he hopes to find work. After getting a job on a logging crew, he sends for Loretta. In the film's most touching moment, a seven-months-pregnant Loretta bids good-bye to her father at the railway station. "I feel like a thief has stolen your young years," laments her father, declaring, "I'll never see my little girl again." When Loretta insists she will return home one day, he sadly replies, "Yes, but you won't be a little girl." The memorable father-daughter farewell bisects this film; Loretta's early days are over, and the climb to the top follows.

The second half of the film is not so sharply detailed as the first. In fact, what ensues is fairly standard treatment of the star-on-the-rise theme. Loretta receives a second-hand guitar from Mooney as an anniversary gift. (What she really wanted was a wedding ring.) Encouraged by Mooney, who admires her singing voice, Loretta practices the guitar and begins writing her own lyrics. One night, Mooney takes her out and pushes her onstage in a small, noisy club. It is Loretta's first public appearance, and the surprised crowd is receptive. Convinced of his wife's musical talents, Mooney arranges for Loretta to cut her first record, "Honky Tonk Girl." He sends copies of the record, along with a photo of Loretta (taken by Mooney, in their home, using a bedspread as a backdrop), to music stations across the country.

Following a brief, guilt-ridden trip home to Butcher's Holler for her father's funeral, Loretta—guided by Mooney—begins the exhausting, but familiar, climb to fame. Leaving their children with Loretta's mother, the couple endures an odyssey of radio stations, sleeping in the car, eating baloney sandwiches, and covering endless miles of roadway in an effort to get "Honky Tonk Girl" on the air. During one of their station stops they are shocked to learn that the record is number fourteen on the national charts. Upon hearing this, Mooney is insistent that they head for Nashville, heart of the country music industry.

Once there, Loretta makes it to the stage of the revered Grand Ole Opry (she is introduced to the crowds by Ernest Tubb, playing himself). She goes on to play the Opry for seventeen straight weeks. She also performs on Tubb's radio show, where she sings Patsy Cline's hit song, "I Fall to Pieces." The song is meant as a gift to Cline, who has been hospitalized following a car accident. Still, Loretta is stunned and uneasy when Cline summons her to her hospital room; but the meeting results in a sturdy friendship. Following Cline's recuperation, the two even tour together. They become fast friends, and Cline helps to show Loretta the ropes where touring is concerned.

The more Loretta learns and the more she accomplishes, the angrier Mooney becomes. He feels less needed and, in retaliation, takes to drinking and carousing with other women. Loretta, however, will not tolerate such behavior. The girl from Butcher's Holler, who once chased away her competition with a stick, now goes at her own husband, clobbering him with her purse, in a fit of hysterics, in a Nashville parking lot. She is infuriated, but she is also determined to keep her marriage going. Hers is a strong temperament, reflected in her simple, but message-laden songs.

Loretta and Mooney stick it out, but it is not easy. They endure career changes (for a while, Mooney bows out of his wife's career and concentrates on raising horses). There are two more babies—twin girls, reared mostly by Mooney while Loretta tours. Loretta is despondent when Patsy Cline is killed in a plane crash. Eventually, Loretta is also battered by the high-pressure entertainment industry. One night, in front of a capacity crowd, she reaches a breaking point. After a rambling monologue, she collapses and is carried offstage by Mooney.

Ultimately, as the film details, Loretta makes a triumphant recovery, both in her professional and her personal lives. She and Mooney are still bickering, to be sure (as the film ends, she finds he has decided without consulting her to have a new house built), but they are also devoted to each other. Loretta's fans also remain devoted, and enthusiastically applaud her return to the stage. It is an upbeat finale to the story of an unlikely marital team and the legendary rise of a country music favorite.

The much-lauded film (praised, at the time of its release, as the first important film of 1980) is directed by England's Michael Apted, who first achieved prominence by directing British television productions. He later directed feature films, including the well-received *Stardust* (1975, the story of a rock music performer) and the stylish mystery *Agatha* (1979). Apted's direction of *Coal Miner's Daughter* is frank and concise. There is no camera trickery here, unless one counts the lush Kentucky and Tennessee locales. Mostly, the film is dominated by story and characters.

The casting is nearly impeccable. Sissy Spacek achieved national prominence with her portrayal of Loretta. Known mostly for her portrayals in cult films such as *Carrie* (1976), in which she was Oscar-nominated for her role as the telekinetic teen, or *Badlands* (1973), in which she was an accomplice on a senseless murder spree, Spacek displays a remarkable affinity for the earthy role of Loretta. In fact, Spacek initially set out to be a singer herself, rather than an actress, which accounts for the fact that she does a fine job of performing Lynn's songs, which make up the soundtrack for this film. Spacek's wispy appearance also enables her to portray credibly Lynn through the years. Tommy Lee Jones, who first captured industry attention with his moody portrayal of a loser in the exploitation film *Jackson County Jail* (1976), portrays the colorful Mooney. Like Spacek, he seems well suited for the role. Both principal performers, incidentally, have Southern origins.

Among the supporting players, Beverly D'Angelo is effective as Patsy Cline; not only does D'Angelo bear an uncanny resemblance to Cline, but she also sounds amazingly like her. The casting of Levon Helm and Phyllis Boyens as Loretta's parents also drew much critical praise. Helm, drummer and founder of the famed music group The Band (which backed Bob Dylan), makes his acting debut in the role of Ted Webb. Boyens, herself the daughter of a coal miner (who was also a well-known folk singer), is a folk singer and songwriter who appeared in the Academy Award-winning film *Harlan County, U.S.A.* (1977). Both Helm and Boyens have physical appearances and mannerisms which suggest a quiet strength and dignity. Their film moments reflect the painful struggle of Appalachia's working people.

Screenwriter Tom Rickman, who interned at the American Film Institute, also has country origins. The Kentucky native's credits include Burt Reynold's action pictures, *W. W. and the Dixie Dancekings* (1975) and *Hooper* (1978).

To date, *Coal Miner's Daughter* has proved to be a commercial as well as a critical success. Its popularity underlines the fact that screen biographies, long a Hollywood staple, can still entice audiences. The film also speaks well of Nashville, the legendary country music capital, which received a rather rough going-over in the Robert Altman country music epic, *Nashville* (1975). The character portrayed by Ronee Blakley in that film was based on Loretta Lynn. It was a largely unsympathetic portrayal (much of Altman's film angered the country music world). In *Coal Miner's Daughter*, the story line is told with a decidedly pro-country slant.

Pat H. Broeske

COME BACK, LITTLE SHEBA

Released: 1952
Production: Hal B. Wallis for Paramount
Direction: Daniel Mann
Screenplay: Ketti Frings; based on the play of the same name by William Inge
Cinematography: James Wong Howe
Editing: Warren Low
Running time: 99 minutes

Principal characters:
Doc Delaney	Burt Lancaster
Lola Delaney	Shirley Booth (AA)
Marie Buckholder	Terry Moore
Turk Fisher	Richard Jaeckel
Ed Anderson	Philip Ober
Mrs. Coffman	Liza Golm
Bruce	Walter Kelley

Come Back, Little Sheba is a poignant and compelling screen version of William Inge's highly acclaimed play of the same name. Although it was produced in 1952, it is still acknowledged as a fine and sensitive film portrayal of a couple's heart-rending struggle against the bondage of alcoholism and the destruction it has wrought in their lives.

Doc Delaney, played by Burt Lancaster, and Lola Delaney, portrayed by Shirley Booth in her first screen appearance, are a lower-middle-class couple with no children and the best years of their lives behind them. We sense, almost immediately, the pervasive air of defeatism that permeates their existence. Doc Delaney, a small-town chiropractor with a meager roster of patients, cannot forget that twenty years earlier he was a promising young medical student, a Phi Beta Kappa with a dazzling career before him. Then he got a woman pregnant and married her in order to "do the right thing." But the child died—he had thrown away his career for nothing. He now lives in the past, his frustration and anger feeding on the shattered dreams of his youth. Fueled by alcohol, his feelings periodically erupt into violence, causing him to hurl blame and scathing words of vilification upon his hapless wife, Lola.

The character of Doc Delaney is a demanding role and is a far cry from Lancaster's usual swashbuckling, muscle-flexing parts. Lancaster rises to that demand, displaying a hitherto unsuspected depth of talent and, in the process, establishing himself as a dramatic actor of considerable merit. There is no stereotyping here; with the sure touch of a fine artist, Lancaster invokes a whole range of emotions in the character of Doc Delaney. We feel his pain, his frustration, his helplessness, even his anger. We do not condone his actions or his solutions to problems, but we understand them.

However, it is Broadway star Shirley Booth who, with the consummate skill and sensitivity of a great actress, makes the screen version of *Come Back, Little Sheba* one of the most compelling adult dramas in the history of cinema. Acclaimed for her portrayal of Lola Delaney on the stage, she surpasses that performance in the screen version. With disarming honesty and disquieting realism, she portrays the inept, frowsy housewife who has allowed both herself and her house to go to seed. She is no martyr, no long-suffering saint, but she has had her share of pain and she bears it with dignity. Her fearful, overanxious, anything-to-please attitude is in sharp contrast to that of the silent, moody Doc, who holds his anger in tight rein.

The setting of the story is a nondescript, middle-class home in a small university town. Screenwriter Ketti Frings and first-time director Daniel Mann have the good sense to remain faithful to the William Inge play and stage much of the drama within the four walls of the Delaney home, for therein lies the secret of the film's power and emotional impact. With paramount skill and sureness, Mann develops his characters, showing the increasing interaction between them and the chain of events that builds inexorably toward the climax.

The film opens as Lola Delaney has rented a room to a young college art student, Marie Buckholder (Terry Moore). Grieving over the disappearance of a small pet, Little Sheba, Lola is almost pathetic in her eagerness to rent to the young woman, for she needs the presence of someone or something to help her cope with the boredom and futility that fill her days. Doc Delaney, however, is apprehensive that Marie may find out about his history of alcoholism. Although he has not touched a drop for a year, he is acutely aware of the social stigma that surrounds his problem. Perhaps he also senses that a crisis, a time of testing, is in the offing, for in Marie he sees the daughter he never had.

Marie and her current boyfriend, Turk Fisher (Richard Jaeckel), are stereotypes of American youth: naïve adolescents who lack compassion for the hardships of others and blithely toy with affections and emotions they do not yet fully understand. Jaeckel is excellent as the egotistical young man eager to make a conquest. Marie, although she has a fiancé who loves her, is filled with sexual curiosity; she courts Turk's attentions and revels in his desire for her.

In Marie and Turk, we see images of the young Doc and Lola. Marie's presence and her romantic involvement with Turk open old wounds and release memories long buried but not forgotten. Lola remembers her youth, when she too was pretty, vivacious, and sought after. Doc remembers his setbacks, the crippling blows fate has dealt him, and can see the pattern repeating itself in Marie's life. She will give up her innocence and her career and throw herself away on a man who is unworthy of her, while the young man will be forced to marry before he is ready and will blame her for destroying his future.

Little Sheba, the lost pet, is the symbol of the past in which the Delaneys dwell. She is gone but they cannot forget her. She had been the buffer, the neutral ground between them that allowed them to maintain their relationship without facing its emptiness. She had accepted their love and repaid it in good measure, never demanding or needing the personal involvement or parental guidance that a child would require. She made no judgments. Little Sheba is gone, however, replaced by Marie, who is catapulting herself toward disaster. As Doc watches Marie and Turk once more act out the scenario of his and Lola's youth, moving slowly, inexorably toward the final scene, his feelings of frustration and helplessness mount to the breaking point, for he can no more change the course of Marie's life than he can go back and rewrite that of his own.

It is near the end of the film before we meet Marie's fiancé, a staunch, hard-working young man who lives in another city. Bruce (Walter Kelley) is a symbol of the better side of American youth. He is devoted and loyal to his fiancée, unlike Turk. Throughout the film, Marie's affections are torn between the excitement and adventure offered by Turk and the solidarity and enduring love of Bruce.

The crisis occurs when Doc sees Marie enter her darkened bedroom late at night accompanied by Turk. Not knowing that they have had a spat and that Turk is leaving, Doc believes that Marie has decided to give herself to Turk. Upon leaving for work the following morning, Doc conceals a bottle of whiskey beneath his raincoat, the same bottle that had remained untouched on the kitchen shelf for one long year. Preparing to serve drinks to Marie and her fiancé, who has just arrived for a short visit, Lola opens the kitchen cupboard and discovers that the whiskey bottle is missing. The audience is completely caught up in Lola's dismay and fear as the nightmare which has been looming for the entire duration of the film is finally set in motion.

When Doc returns late that night, an ugly scene ensues, finally culminating in a physical, life-threatening attack upon Lola when she dares to reach out for help. When Doc collapses, she calls his friend Ed Anderson, played most believingly by Philip Ober. Ed is a man who has been there, a staunch pillar of Alcoholics Anonymous. He and another A.A. member come to Lola's rescue and escort Doc to City Hospital. With all her hopes in ruins, Lola now turns in the only direction left—inward. Finding a strength she did not know she possessed, she finally faces reality.

In the final scene, Doc Delaney returns home with the realization that the woman he thought had destroyed his life has, in fact, become, over the years, his impetus to go on living. She has believed in him more than he has believed in himself.

During Doc's absence, Lola has made a sincere and honest effort to improve both herself and her surroundings. As she fixes breakfast, she tells him that Marie has married her fiancé and credits Doc with opening her eyes about Turk. Then Lola recounts a dream in which she and Doc are at the Olympics watching Turk perform. Lola's father, who is refereeing the event, disqualifies Turk and Doc takes his place. He picks up the javelin Turk has discarded and throws it. It soars upward toward the sun and never comes down. But as they leave the arena, Lola sees Little Sheba lying dead in the middle of the field. Doc pulls her away, telling her they must go on. "I don't think Little Sheba's ever coming back, Doc," Lola says, "I'm not going to call her any more." The past is dead, but the Delaneys will survive and prevail.

Director Daniel Mann has executed an artistic triumph in this moving, emotional interpretation of an irrationally feared, and grossly misunderstood social problem. Each scene is a delicate balance of sensitive interpretation and stark realism. Warren Low did an expert job of editing, and received an Academy Award nomination for his fine contribution. Burt Lancaster's characterization matches, if not surpasses, such memorable performances as Ray Milland's in *The Lost Weekend* (1945) and Jack Lemmon's in *Days of Wine and Roses* (1962). Terry Moore received an Academy Award nomination as Best Supporting Actress for her realistic portrayal of Marie Buckholder as the naïve, impulsive teenager who precipitates such havoc in the Delaney household. Shirley Booth, however, gives the most memorable performance of this tense drama. Her portrayal of Lola Delaney earned her an Academy Award as Best Actress, an honor she richly deserved.

D. Gail Huskins

COMING HOME

Released: 1978
Production: Jerome Hellman for United Artists
Direction: Hal Ashby
Screenplay: Waldo Salt and Robert C. Jones (AA); based on a story by Nancy Dowd
Cinematography: Haskell Wexler
Editing: Don Zimmerman
Running time: 127 minutes

Principal characters:
Luke Martin	Jon Voight (AA)
Sally Hyde	Jane Fonda (AA)
Captain Bob Hyde	Bruce Dern
Vi Munson	Penelope Milford
Bill Munson	Robert Carradine
Sergeant Dink Mobley	Robert Ginty

Like Hal Ashby's *Shampoo* (1975), *Coming Home* is also set in 1968. However, unlike *Shampoo*, in which the events of the day serve only as a backdrop to the story line, *Coming Home* is about people whose daily lives are intimately affected by the decade-long war in Vietnam. Although American military involvement in Vietnam officially ended in 1975, the war left its mark on the lives of most Americans. Not since the Civil War had any military conflict aroused so much controversy, and never before had America's foreign policy seemed so morally ambiguous. Perhaps for this reason, the film industry was never able to deal successfully with the war while it was being waged—John Wayne's *Green Berets* (1968), for example, seemed partisan and simplistic. As time passed and perspective developed, however, all this changed. The year 1978 brought the release of several realistic war films (among them *Go Tell the Spartans*, *The Deer Hunter*), and *Apocalypse Now* (1979) managed to deal with Vietnam and its effect on American lives without being merely propagandistic and to make some sense out of an American tragedy. *Coming Home* is among this group of films.

Coming Home is a special film in a number of ways, not the least of which is that Hal Ashby and his writers, Waldo Salt and Robert C. Jones, deal with the effect of the war not only upon the hearts and minds of the participants, but also upon their bodies: one of the film's major characters is a paraplegic whose war wounds have left him paralyzed from the waist down.

Ashby opens the film with a scene of a group of young disabled veterans, some bedridden and some in wheelchairs, who are discussing their part in the war. They talk of their urgent need to make some sense of what happened to them. Ultimately, all of the major characters in *Coming Home* will be forced to redefine themselves in the light of the changes wrought upon them or their loved ones by the Vietnam experience.

In the next scene, the filmmakers present an ironic contrast to the men who have had their bodies and spirits broken by the war through the introduction of two men who are about to be sent overseas and cannot wait to get to Vietnam. Marine Bob Hyde (Bruce Dern) and his buddy Dink (Robert Ginty) exchange macho comments about combat and about their women; subsequent events make it clear that they understand neither.

More ironic commentary is provided by the music on the soundtrack. The song is "Out of Time" by the Rolling Stones, and it suggests that time is running out for Bob and Dink. Ashby uses rock music from 1968 not only to solidify the audience's identification with the era, but also to underline and comment on the action in front of the camera. He frequently uses songs as bridges between two scenes, with the lyrics taking on new meaning as the context shifts. "Out of Time" is a song about a woman, and as it continues to play in the background, we meet two more characters in the film whose lives will soon change dramatically. Dink's girlfriend, Vi Munson (Penelope Milford), is a young and uninhibited nurse at the local Veterans Administration hospital. Sally Hyde (Jane Fonda) is a bit older, much more conventional, and slightly uncomfortable in Vi's company as the two couples share a farewell drink. Later that night, Sally and Bob make love for the last time before he leaves for war. From the expression on Sally's face, we can tell that her participation is more sympathetic than enthusiastic. Despite their apparent sexual incompatibility, however, Sally loves her husband.

After Bob and Dink leave, Vi invites Sally to her house for a drink; when Sally accepts, the two are on their way to becoming close friends. We learn that Vi's younger brother Billy (Robert Carradine) is a patient at the Veterans Administration hospital; he was sent home from Vietnam after suffering a nervous breakdown. Luke Martin (Jon Voight) is also a patient at this hospital. He has not yet reconciled himself to life as a cripple and spends much of his time raging against any handy target. One such target is Sally Hyde, who comes to the hospital to do volunteer work (the Rolling Stones' "No Expectations" plays in the background for this sequence) and accidentally bumps into Luke's bed, breaking his urine bag. Luke is so beside himself with anger and embarrassment that he has to be forcibly subdued by the hospital staff. The scene is a graphic illustration of the petty humiliations that become a part of everyday life for Luke and the other patients.

It develops that Luke and Sally went to the same high school, where he was the captain of the football team and she was a cheerleader. She mentions this to Luke, whose only reaction is to begin calling her "Bender," her maiden name. Full of self-pity, he has nothing but abuse for Sally, whom he accuses of patronizing him because he is crippled. She persists in visiting him, however, and gradually his insults take on a friendlier, more bantering tone. Sally, meanwhile, is undergoing a gradual but perceptible personality change. Free from her husband's influence for the first time, she begins, very slowly, to exert some independence. She moves off the military base into a house on the beach, buys a sports car, and stops straightening her hair—none of which she mentions in her letters to Bob. She also becomes more concerned with the plight of the men in the hospital, and is outraged when the officers' wives who run the base newspaper decline to write about their problems, favoring instead gossip columns and little league scores.

As Luke learns to live with his paralysis, he begins to relax somewhat. His relationship with Sally deepens into friendship; and he also becomes friendly with Billy Munson. When he gets a wheelchair and thus is no longer bound to the hospital, Sally invites him to her house for dinner. The dinner scene is one of the film's most moving. Both Sally and Luke are nervous. Sally apologizes for her taste in music by saying "I don't think you're going to like my records very much." "You probably won't like the way I dance, either," replies Luke, who has become almost shy. "I'm just very happy to be here," he says haltingly. In an easy and intimate conversation, they drop their banter for the first time and talk to each other of their feelings about life and personal relationships. Abruptly, Luke confesses to Sally that he spends much of his time thinking about making love to her. She is confused but not repelled by the thought, and after she drives him back to the hospital, they kiss goodnight. Their relationship is interrupted, however, by a letter from Sally's husband, asking her to join him on leave in Hong Kong. She feels obligated to go, and breaks the news to Luke just as he has received word that he is being released from the hospital. The Rolling Stones' version of "My Girl" on the sound track provides an ironic bridge between this scene and the next, in which Sally, with her hair once again straightened and bouffant, is reunited with Bob in Hong Kong. Obviously, it is not yet clear just whose girl she is.

Ashby reinforces Sally's conflict through a series of intercut scenes in which a happy Luke Martin is contrasted with a disintegrating Bob Hyde. These scenes, similar to so many in the film, are also connected by Rolling Stones songs. As their time together in Hong Kong reveals to Sally, Vietnam has had a traumatic effect on Bob. He seems distracted, and tells her of a chilling incident in which his men calmly asked him for permission to behead the enemy dead. He has passed beyond disillusionment into incomprehension, and, indeed, is so shaken by his war experiences that he is not even interested in sex with Sally.

Back in the States, Luke is rapidly adjusting to life outside the hospital: he has a house of his own, a specially outfitted car to drive, and, unlike Bob, is definitely interested in sex. He is entertaining a prostitute when he gets a phone call from the hospital; Billy Munson has committed suicide. The death of his friend does what his own injuries did not—it turns him into an antiwar activist. He chains himself to the gate of a Marine Corps recruiting station, where he is arrested. Sally and Vi bail Luke out of jail, and Sally takes him home. In a tastefully handled scene, Sally and Luke make love. Despite his handicap, Sally enjoys sex with Luke, and responds to him as she never could with Bob. As the Beatles' "Strawberry Fields Forever" comments on the action, director Ashby permits the new lovers to enjoy their idyll. The scenes of domestic bliss—puttering around the house, romping on the beach—are brought to a jarring halt, however, when we learn that we are seeing these events through the eyes of the FBI, who have kept Luke under surveillance since his arrest.

Inevitably, Bob Hyde comes home. In a freak accident, he has shot himself in the leg, ironically being awarded a medal for bravery by the Marines as a result, and is shipped back to California. Luke, in a scene that typifies the transformation that has come over him, takes the news of Bob's impending return calmly. Although he admits to being jealous, he is confident that he and Sally will always be friends, and his serenity in this scene is in marked contrast to the uncontrollable rage and self-pity that characterized his behavior when the film opened. He has become an almost saintly figure. Sally is a good deal more confused about her relationships with the two men in her life, but resolves to go back to being Bob's wife, albeit on her own terms: symbolically, she refuses to straighten her hair.

The scene in which Sally and Bob are reunited abounds with ironies. Most of the men leaving the plane are so severely hurt that they have to be carried off, but Bob is only limping slightly. His first words to Sally are hardly auspicious: "What the hell did you do to your hair?" he snaps, and the emotional distance between them is underlined by the chain link fence that separates them as they both walk toward the exit. Bob is still as unstrung by the war as he had been in Hong Kong, and Sally's new Porsche and the beach house, additional evidence of her growing independence, unnerve him further. He bolts from the welcome home celebration that Sally and Vi have arranged and heads for the nearest bar.

With "Time Has Come Today" by the Chambers Brothers providing the musical commentary in the background, *Coming Home* hurries toward its denouement. The FBI tells Bob of the relationship between Sally and Luke. He appears to take the news calmly, and even goes to Luke to tell him about the FBI surveillance. When he returns home, however, it is clear that something in him has snapped. He loads his combat rifle and confronts Sally. In a taut scene, he attempts to explain the confusion that has overcome him. His macho world has crumbled. All he has wanted to do was be a war hero, and he has found nothing heroic about Vietnam. His wife is in love with the very antithesis of a war hero, and the medal which might have bolstered his self-esteem mocks him instead. He is on the verge of killing Sally when Luke arrives. Luke's presence has a miraculously calming effect on Bob, perhaps because he senses that Luke has wrestled with the same demons that are torturing him.

In the next scene, Luke addresses a group of high school students, and although his words are simple—almost banal—the emotion he puts into them makes him eloquent. He impresses upon them the fact that the experience of war is not what it might seem from movies or comic books, and that the scars it can leave on the soul are worse than those they leave on the body.

Ashby reinforces Luke's words by intercutting this scene with that of Bob's suicide. Unable to reconcile the difference between his expectations—of himself, of Sally, and of the war—and reality, Bob runs into the ocean and drowns. Ashby uses Sally and Vi to offer a final comment. They are shopping in a Lucky's supermarket; and as they leave, the camera fixes upon a sign on the door: "Lucky Out." This ending is surprisingly unsatisfactory. In addition to the too-pat "Lucky Out," Ashby's failure to integrate Sally Hyde meaningfully into the film's resolution weakens it. All through the film, Sally has been the center of the story, the character through whom the other characters interact; shunting her off to the periphery at the end is a disappointment.

There is no denying, however, that *Coming Home* is a powerful and important film. The dialogue is superb; writers Salt and Jones have captured the manner in which real people talk, and there is no false or pedantic note in any character's lines. On the other hand, some of the characters are one-dimensional. Had the character of Bob Hyde been a bit more sympathetic, Sally's emotional conflict would have seemed more genuine, but as it is, one can hardly imagine Sally's preferring Bob to Luke.

Aside from the flawed ending and the occasional overuse of rock music to comment on the action (the Rolling Stones had more lines than most of the actors), Ashby's direction is controlled and to the point. His tactful handling of the sexual relationship between Sally and Luke is masterful in a scene where the slightest hint of sensationalism would have ruined the film. His subtlety in allowing the characters their awkward dignity only intensifies the impact of the scene.

Each of the four major actors in the film garnered Academy Award nominations for their work. In the supporting roles, Penelope Milford is perfect as the warm, open, try-anything-once Vi Munson; and Bruce Dern, whose film career seems based on playing psychotics like Bob Hyde, capably depicts a man watching his world crumble around him. Jane Fonda and Jon Voight, however, are the stars of the film, and it is difficult to decide whose job was the more difficult. Widely known as an outspoken critic of the war, Fonda faced the task of making the early, straight-haired Sally Hyde as believable and likable as the later, more natural one; in other words, she had to make the audience see Sally Hyde on the screen, and not Jane Fonda, and she succeeds admirably. There is not a hint of irony in her portrayal of the unliberated Sally, and her growth throughout the film seems organic rather than preordained.

Jon Voight had no such image problems, but the role of Luke Martin presented tremendous physical difficulties. His portrayal of Luke's rage and frustration at no longer being in control of his body is utterly convincing. With his physical mobility severely limited by the part, Voight makes effective use of facial expressions and vocal inflections to convey Luke's gradual acceptance of his handicap. By the end of the film, Voight seems almost to radiate serenity.

Coming Home, then, is a war film that is not about combat, but about the effects of combat—both upon those who do the fighting and upon their loved ones. It is only when they have dropped out or been forced out of the war that they can come home and begin the process of redefining themselves in the light of their experience. Ashby, Salt, Jones, Fonda, Voight, Dern, and Milford make this painful process come alive; and, despite its flaws, *Coming Home* is a vital and important film.

James P. Girard

COMPULSION

Released: 1959
Production: Richard D. Zanuck for Twentieth Century-Fox
Direction: Richard Fleischer
Screenplay: Richard Murphy; based on the novel of the same name by Meyer Levin
Cinematography: William C. Mellor
Editing: William Reynolds
Running time: 103 minutes

Principal characters:
Judd Steiner	Dean Stockwell
Artie Straus	Bradford Dillman
Jonathan Wilk	Orson Welles
Ruth Evans	Diane Varsi
D. A. Horn	E. G. Marshall
Sid Brooks	Martin Milner

Compulsion is a fictional thriller suggested by the Leopold and Loeb case, one of the most famous murder trials in American legal history.

On May 21, 1924, two law students at the University of Chicago, Nathan Leopold, age nineteen, and Richard Loeb, age eighteen, attempted to commit the "perfect crime" by murdering fourteen-year-old Robert Franks. There was no motive. Arrested and brought to trial, Leopold and Loeb were defended by Clarence Darrow, the crusading lawyer who had devoted much of his life to campaigning against capital punishment. As a result of Darrow's efforts, the youths, who pleaded guilty, did not receive the death sentence but were instead sentenced, on September 10, 1924, to "99 years plus life." In the fall of 1956, Meyer Levin, a campus contemporary of the two murderers and, like the character of Sid Brooks in *Compulsion*, a journalist on the college newspaper, published a best-selling novel based on the case. The novel was swiftly turned into a Broadway play and the screen rights were acquired by Darryl F. Zanuck in December, 1957.

Compulsion, which went into production in October, 1958, in the slightly unusual combination of black-and-white and CinemaScope, was twenty-three-year-old Richard D. Zanuck's first production for his father's company. It was adapted for the screen by Richard Murphy, whose previous credits include such realist social melodramas as *Boomerang* (1947) and *Panic in the Streets* (1950); his screenplay is at its best in the earlier, pretrial scenes, where it has a sparseness and energy not always found in the trial itself. One casting anecdote is worth relating with regard to the trial scene. Zanuck's original plan was to get a real judge: he failed, but the actor who finally got the part, Voltaire Perkins, was not only an ex-lawyer and one-time protem judge, but also a family friend of Clarence Darrow and the latter's guest at the original Leopold and Loeb trial. Television audiences also had come to know him as the familiar presiding judge in the long running series *Divorce Court*.

Compulsion concerns two wealthy Chicago teenagers, Judd Steiner (Dean Stockwell) and Artie Straus (Bradford Dillman), students of law and of Nietzsche, who are determined to prove their intellectual superiority not only by confronting their professors (Artie faces down one of his supposed mentors on the question of evolution and the survival of the fittest), but also by commiting a series of petty crimes without getting caught. The movie opens with a precredit sequence which fairly accurately sums up Fleischer's ability to create a sense of menace without the use of overt violence (an achievement repeated in the early scenes of his British-made thriller *Blind Terror*, released in the United States as *See No Evil*, 1971). The boys steal a typewriter and then attempt to run down a drunk casually encountered on the road home. The sequence is genuinely disturbing in its random, uncommented vicious-ness. Shortly afterwards, the drowned body of a boy is found in a local park. Covering the story as part-time reporter for the Chicago *Globe*, student Sid Brooks (Martin Milner) visits the morgue to find that the child has been battered to death, and that a pair of glasses has been found near the body. The police trace the glasses to, among others, Judd because of a specially designed hinge, and he is questioned by District Attorney Horn (E. G. Marshall). He sticks to the alibi earlier agreed to with Artie, and although Horn calls in the latter to check the story, he is on the point of letting them go when the Steiner family chauffeur arrives with an overnight case for Judd and inadvertently destroys the alibi. By the time the brilliant lawyer Jonathan Wilk (Orson Welles) has been engaged to defend the pair, their guilt is established beyond all doubt (as indeed happened in the Leopold and Loeb case, where the families thought the idea of their sons committing murder so preposterous that they did not engage Darrow until confessions had been obtained).

Rather than face a jury trial in a case in which public hostility has been raised to fever pitch, Wilk (who has already had a burning cross planted on his lawn by the local Ku Klux Klan) enters a plea of guilty, claiming that the boys, though not technically insane, were "sick" and could not be held entirely responsible. In the course of a rousing summing-up, Wilk (Welles was aged for the role by means of a shaved hairline, body padding, latex bags under his eyes, and dyed hair) pulls out all the stops. Slightly improbably reducing E. G. Marshall to respectful silence in what is "believed to be the longest speech ever delivered on screen" (although at fifteen minutes, rather less than Darrow's two-day, sixty-thousand-word original), Wilk successfully swings the judge away from the almost certain death penalty, ending with a rousing call for: "Life! Any more goes back to the hyena!"

Though the producers were at pains to stress that "the picture is no way a documentary," the parallels with the Leopold and Loeb case—already fictionalized on stage and screen in *Rope* (1948)—were lost on nobody, and certainly not on Nathan Leopold. He filed suit in the Chicago Circuit Court in October, 1959, for $1,500,000 damages on the grounds that Levin had "appropriated his name, likeness and personality for profit." *Variety*, which commented on the story, cynically remarked that the lawsuit would not do any harm to the film's box-office potential. *Compulsion* received generally favorable reviews and did brisk business, grossing about $1,500,000 million and ending up a respectable though not spectacular 48th on *Variety*'s 1959 box-office charts.

On screen for only the last third of the movie in what is almost a guest part, Welles inevitably got the lion's share of the reviews, and his concluding speech was even issued as a phonograph record. The less flamboyant but more subtly impressive performances of Bradford Dillman and Dean Stockwell were also widely praised, however, and the three male leads shared the Best Actor Award at the Cannes Film Festival. Only Diane Varsi in a part with very little substance—a kind of middle-class redeeming angel whom Judd tries to rape and who ends up comforting him—got poor reviews. Fleischer's direction was justly praised for its tension and restraint, particularly in avoiding sensationalism while dealing with a sensational crime (something which he repeated ten years later in his version of the even more horrific Christie case in *Ten Rillington Place*).

In retrospect, *Compulsion* is very much a film of the late 1950's—a cautious but honest return to the treatment of social issues generally absent from American cinema screens for a decade. The movie is unequivocally against capital punishment, and Wilk's concluding speech is as eloquent an attack on it as the commercial cinema has seen. In this respect, the script is a combination of objectivity and special pleading. No attempt is made to make Straus and Steiner sympathetic characters or to obscure the calculating callousness of their crime; Dillman's Straus is all calm menace gradually shading into imbalance (a role in which the actor has tended to be type-cast ever since). On the other hand, the possibility of our sympathy is kept open since we are not shown the murder, and, despite a number of heavy hints, we do not "discover" who the murderers are much in advance of Horn. The emphasis throughout is on the psychology of the criminals and on the machinery of justice when faced with a crime of this kind. Fleischer adopts much the same approach to his theme as in *The Boston Strangler* (1968), where the point at issue is not *who* the Strangler is but his coming to terms with his own schizophrenia and the fact that he *is* the Strangler.

The question of capital punishment aside, however, *Compulsion* is a finely paced thriller every bit as impressive in its way as Fleischer's masterful 1951 film *The Narrow Margin*. Particularly impressive is the suppressed hysteria of such scenes as the assault on the drunk, Horn's cat-and-mouse cross-examination of Judd and Artie and Judd's attempted rape of Ruth at the spot of the original murder. At the same time, the hysteria of the scenes never develops into melodramatic rhetoric, even allowing for the discreet and highly effective use of tilted camera angles and ominous compositions during, for example, the cross-examination. Tilted angles in CinemaScope are a risky proposition but Fleischer's use of them in *Compulsion* is a tribute to his tight, thoughtful control of the film as a whole.

One way in which the film has not aged well, however, is in its cautious treatment of the homosexuality of its two central protagonists. Hailed as courageous at the time, the film in fact portrays Judd's and Artie's homosexuality as very little more than an adjunct to their psychopathic behavior, every bit as sinister and even, perhaps, as dangerous. In almost all other respects, however, *Compulsion* is an intelligent, committed thriller, using the devices of investigative and courtroom drama to register a strong argument in favor of abolishing capital punishment.

Nick Roddick

COOL HAND LUKE

Released: 1967
Production: Gordon Carroll for Jalem Productions; released by Warner Bros.
Direction: Stuart Rosenberg
Screenplay: Donn Pearce and Frank R. Pierson; based on the novel of the same name by Donn Pearce
Cinematography: Conrad Hall
Editing: Sam O'Steen
Running time: 129 minutes

> *Principal characters:*
> Lucas (Luke) Jackson .... Paul Newman
> Dragline .... George Kennedy (AA)
> Society Red .... J. D. Cannon
> Koko .... Lou Antonio
> Captain .... Strother Martin
> Arletta .... Jo Van Fleet

The 1960's provided a springboard for countless films about the individual at odds with society. *Cool Hand Luke* is among the best of them, with Luke Jackson (Paul Newman) personifying one of the decade's most popular character types, the antihero. *Cool Hand Luke* is about a man alienated from the Establishment. A chain-gang loner with more nerve than brains, Luke refuses to bow to authority. To his comrades he becomes a symbol of individuality, a man they idolize, but Luke, who wants only to be his own man, rejects the adulation. "Stop feedin' off me. Get out there yourself," he tells the men.

We meet Luke during a summer night in the South in 1948. He is on a drunken spree and is cutting the heads off parking meters. When a police car arrives at the scene, Luke grins broadly, lifting his bottle in salute. He receives a stiff sentence of two years with a chain gang, Road Company Number 36. The camp is presented as an isolated world of sadistic guards and regimentation, into which comes Luke, a man with an unbreakable cool and a fiercely independent spirit.

Luke refuses to let his cool slip, even when he is assigned to the toughest, most back-breaking road work and must endure the cruel terrain and penetrating sun. The eagle-eyed guards keep their eyes on Luke; and the road-gang men mumble about him among themselves. Dragline (George Kennedy), a leader among the men, takes a particular disliking to Luke. Angered by Luke's flippant spirit, Dragline grows more hostile until the two men fight it out in front of the other men. It's a knock-down, drag-out fight; although he is no match for the hulking Dragline, Luke, beaten and bloody, will not give up, despite Dragline's urgings that he stay down. At last, Luke's rebelliousness commands even Dragline's respect, and Luke becomes a hero in the eyes of the prisoners.

Cool Hand Luke embraces a wide range of emotions. There is comedy, such as the scene in which Luke, for want of anything better to do, declares that he can eat fifty hardboiled eggs; as ever, he sees the bet through. In another funny sequence, Luke, who is attempting to escape, outsmarts the camp dogs. There is also pathos, particularly in the scenes involving Luke's dying mother (Jo Van Fleet), who comes to the prison to visit her son. Propped-up in the bed of a truck, she has come to bid Luke good-bye. "You was boring the hell out of us, trying to be respectable," she tells him. Later, when Luke receives a telegram informing him of his mother's death, his cool finally cracks, sending him to his bunk where he sings a teary parody of an old-time hymn in the hushed silence of the prisoner quarters.

A week later, Luke escapes and is recaptured and brought back. A new battle of will power has begun. The guards (who are all called "Boss") are determined to break Luke. "What we have here is a failure to communicate," admonishes (the guard) Captain (Strother Martin). His words sum up the dilemma of society's antihero, since for the enigmatic Luke there can be no communication. He is a valiant loser.

Luke can no longer endure confinement, and his escape attempts continue; the guards respond by mistreating him. Ultimately, Luke cannot face isolation in the hot-box pen. When he begs the guards for mercy in front of the other prisoners, his comrades turn away from him; he is no longer the man they idolize. But Luke's defeat is brief, and he soon tries to escape again, in a dump truck, with Dragline following. Later, Luke takes refuge in a church, for a talk with God, having sent Dragline away. When the prison authorities capture Dragline, he leads them to the church in return for a promise of clemency. Luke is shot to death; he dies in a crucifixion pose, a symbolic modern-day savior. Several other sequences serve as religious symbolism— an approach that riled a number of critics.

With its pertinent theme, Stuart Rosenberg's taunt direction, and Paul Newman's fine performance, *Cool Hand Luke* was a big box-office success. Newman was nominated for an Oscar, but the award went to Rod Steiger for *In the Heat of the Night*. Nevertheless, Newman's performance in a role which seems tailor-made for him ranks as one of the best in his career. Luke has an easy-going demeanor, a will of iron, and a decidedly engaging quality. He has always fought the system (we learn that he once fought a private war with the Army), although the odds have never been in his favor. While Newman's abilities have not been taxed by many demanding roles, his amiable style and likable presence have allowed him to portray effectively both heels and heroes in films such as *The Hustler* (1961) and *Hud* (1963)—for both of which he also received Oscar nominations.

Cool Hand Luke also showcases George Kennedy's talent. He is convincing as Luke's illiterate, well-meaning buddy, and received an Oscar for Best Supporting Actor for his performance. The film is a sturdy piece of ensemble work. With the exception of Luke's mother and a sexy blonde woman who taunts the road workers while she washes her car, the film has an all-male cast. Among those appearing as prisoners in brief roles are Luke Askew, Dennis Hopper, Wayne Rogers, (Harry) Dean Stanton, Ralph Waite, and Anthony Zerbe—all of whom have gone on to do noteworthy work in television and film.

Cool Hand Luke is a successful character study, but in terms of social significance, *I Am a Fugitive from a Chain Gang* (1932) remains the most powerful and frightening look at life on a chain gang. *Cool Hand Luke* nevertheless enjoys an air of authenticity—probably owing to the fact that Donn Pearce, who coscripted the film and authored the novel on which it is based, had personally experienced the horrors of Southern prison camps.

Director Stuart Rosenberg, who came to the project after extensive television credits (including *The Defenders*), displays a terse, easy-flowing style. With the exception of Luke's rambling monologue in the church, *Cool Hand Luke* is a tidy effort boasting memorable characterizations. The film is also visually powerful. An impassive guard, wearing reflective sunglasses to hide his searching eyes, cooly tampers with the prisoners' sensibilities. It is Strother Martin, however, cast as Captain, who best captures the tension and uneasiness of an all-powerful authority figure. A longtime character actor, Martin's work in *Cool Hand Luke* propelled him into a career of supporting roles, including those in such Newman vehicles as *Butch Cassidy and the Sundance Kid* (1969) and *Slap Shot* (1977). With his wry observation about the inability to communicate, Captain predicts that Luke is foredoomed; and with his comment ". . . some men you just can't reach," Luke's fate comes sharply into focus. It is an ironic fate, since Luke, a man who always shirked responsibility, dies a martyr; and he probably would not have wanted his legend to live on.

Pat H. Broeske

THE CORN IS GREEN

Released: 1945
Production: Jack Chertok for Warner Bros.
Direction: Irving Rapper
Screenplay: Casey Robinson and Frank Cavett; based on the play of the same
   name by Emlyn Williams
Cinematography: Sol Polito
Editing: Frederick Richards
Art direction: Carl Jules Weyl
Music: Max Steiner
Running time: 115 minutes

> *Principal characters:*
> Miss Lilly Moffat .... Bette Davis
> Morgan Evans .... John Dall
> Bessie Watty .... Joan Lorring
> The Squire .... Nigel Bruce
> Mr. Jones .... Rhys Williams
> Miss Ronberry .... Mildred Dunnock
> Mrs. Watty .... Rosalind Ivan

When sparked by the love of learning, the association between teacher and student can be the most intimate and rewarding of relationships. Such communion of spirit is the subject of Emlyn Williams' autobiographical play, *The Corn Is Green.* First produced in England with Dame Sybil Thorndike playing the English schoolteacher, Miss Moffat, and later staged on Broadway with Ethel Barrymore, the play became a classic of the modern theater. When Warners' bought the property, four members of the Broadway cast were signed to repeat their stage roles in the film version: Rhys Williams, Gwenyth Hughes, Mildred Dunnock, and Rosalind Ivan.

Bette Davis was to play the Barrymore role of Miss Lilly Moffat. She had already made *The Little Foxes* (1941) and *Watch on the Rhine* (1943), both filmed versions of stage plays with original cast members, and she capably demonstrated her ability to fit into ensemble playing. In *The Corn Is Green,* she plays a fifty-year-old Englishwoman, necessitating heavy makeup, padded clothing, and an elaborate wig; and she succeeds brilliantly. Davis makes this film of Miss Moffat's story her own.

Miss Moffat arrives in the Welsh mining village of Glensarno to live in a house she has inherited. A very proper English schoolteacher, she is shocked at the poverty and ignorance in which the miners live. She determines to aid the community by establishing a school to teach basic education to any of the locals who wish to learn. Her project is scorned in colorful language by her housekeeper, Mrs. Watty (Rosalind Ivan), a reformed petty criminal who is now a vocal member of a fundamentalist religious group. Mrs. Watty is noisy, opinionated, and narrow-minded, as only reformed sinners can be, and her character puts its stamp on her pretty daughter Bessie (Joan Lorring), a cheap little flirt whose sly tricks are thwarted at every turn by the redoubtable Miss Moffat.

The teacher recruits Miss Ronberry (Mildred Dunnock), a local gentlewoman, and Mr. Jones, a shop clerk, who are fired by Miss Moffat's sense of mission. Mildred Dunnock as the gentle, timid Ronberry and Rhys Williams as the stalwart Jones are delightful as the oddly matched lieutenants in Moffat's army. These three crusaders face the open opposition of the Squire, a local landowner who views the school as a threat to his economic interests. He does not want his cheap labor spoiled with notions beyond their station, and he refuses to lease Miss Moffat the village location most suitable for the school. Nigel Bruce is suitably pompous as the blustering Squire who laughs at Moffat's intentions.

Ridicule from the Squire and truculent hostility from the suspicious villagers she seeks to aid do not dampen Moffat's spirit. She converts part of her house into classrooms, structures lessons with Ronberry, Jones, and herself as teachers; and, with Mrs. Watty and Bessie acting as an unwilling support group, she declares her school open for business.

Success and satisfaction do not immediately ensue. The miners are not quick to place their trust in an educated outsider, and they cannot immediately see the benefit of schooling. Education has no place in their lives. They toil in the earth from childhood until they are no longer fit. Long hours at an arduous trade under inhuman working conditions have deadened them to the delights of learning. Their sense of beauty is expressed only in song, the beautiful Welsh folk music sung as the men trudge homeward from the mines. While the singing is beautiful it is misplaced in the film, since no audience will believe that the tired miners can sing like the Saint Luke Choristers. Excepting the use of this professional group where untrained voices would have served better, however, Max Steiner's score is one of his best. He makes use of many Welsh folk songs in a successful attempt to evoke time and place.

This is a particular achievement as there was no location filming for *The Corn Is Green*. Rhys Williams doubled as technical director and worked with Carl Jules Weyl on the monumental task of converting a studio sound stage into a Welsh mining town *circa* the early 1900's. All interior and exterior shots were done on the Warner sound stage. Meadows were created with grass sod, trees planted, a bridge built, scores of goats, and a thousand props brought in to create Glensarno in Burbank. Wind machines moved smoke and Britt solution clouds against a cyclorama of blue sky. There are moments in the film when the sets are obvious but the overall effect is a spectacular achievement for Weyl and his crew.

The school is established but not progressing. Miss Moffat is nearly defeated by the unrewarding task of drumming elementary education into slow and unresponsive students when she uncovers the prize she has unconsciously sought. One of her pupils is Morgan Evans (John Dall), an insolent, swaggering young miner. When Miss Moffat is totally demoralized and near surrender, she reads his essay in which he speaks of what he sees in the wet, black hell of the mines. He looks around him and envisions a flowering world in which "the corn is green." Moffat takes Morgan Evans in hand and for two years she teaches him all his mind will accept. As he progresses she studies herself to keep ahead of him. Together they embark on a great adventure: intellectual discovery.

It is in her work with John Dall that Bette Davis really shines. He is transformed from a rude bully into a bright, inquisitive young man. They share love, but it is the love of learning; Davis resists any temptation to lace the relationship with sexual overtones, while she also rejects the kindly old lady image. She is no Mr. Chips but a prickly, difficult taskmaster who drives Morgan so hard he breaks away from her and spends a drunken night in Bessie Watty's arms. He returns repentant to study for the scholarship examinations that will enable him to attend Oxford. On examination day Bessie tells Miss Moffat she is to have Morgan's child. The teacher pays Bessie to leave the village, saying nothing to Morgan. With the whole village supporting him and the Squire as sponsor, Morgan passes his examination and prepares for Oxford when Bessie returns with her baby. Morgan is willing to give up his scholarship and marry her, but Miss Moffat offers to adopt the child. Bessie willingly rids herself of an unwanted baby and Morgan departs for the University leaving his son in the care of his great friend and teacher.

Their work in *The Corn Is Green* gave film newcomers Joan Lorring and John Dall Best Supporting Actress and Actor nominations from the Academy but they both lost to veteran character actors in other films. Davis did not receive a nomination and her performance was unfavorably compared by many to that of Ethel Barrymore. Nevertheless, the film remains a classic thanks to Emlyn Williams' beautiful and realistic story and Davis' brilliantly conceived portrayal of the difficult and determined Miss Moffat.

Cheryl Karnes

THE COUNTRY GIRL

Released: 1954
Production: William Perlberg and George Seaton for Paramount
Direction: George Seaton
Screenplay: George Seaton (AA); based on the play *Winter Journey* by Clifford Odets
Cinematography: John F. Warren
Editing: Ellsworth Hoagland
Running time: 104 minutes

Principal characters:
Frank Elgin .... Bing Crosby
Georgie Elgin .... Grace Kelly (AA)
Bernie Dodd .... William Holden

Clifford Odets' *Winter Journey* is one of those tried and true, talky vehicles which is constantly being revived by repertory companies because it has three marvelous parts. Odets' themes about the war of the sexes, ambition, and sublimation are a bit naïve, to say the least, but each of the three roles in this essentially three-character play is a *tour de force*.

Winter Journey is the kind of play which very often suffers when translated to the screen simply because of its talkative nature. But screenwriter/director George Seaton does away with Odets' grandiloquent dialogue, bringing the characterizations and the words the characters speak down to earth. This avoidance of Odets' innate pretentiousness and sometimes even smugness, plus the impeccable casting of the three leads, make the 1954 screen version of *Winter Journey, The Country Girl*, a major cinematic event.

The plot of *The Country Girl* involves the efforts of stage director Bernie Dodd (William Holden) to revive the waning career of alcoholic actor/singer Frank Elgin (Bing Crosby), by casting him in a play entitled *The Land Around Us* against the wishes of the play's backers. The play's third character is Elgin's mousy wife, Georgie (Grace Kelly). The success of any production of *The Country Girl* depends upon the ability of the actors to convey the multiple aspects of their characters singly and collectively. Dodd, recently divorced, regards women as a necessary evil. At one point he says, "They all start out as Juliets and wind up as Lady Macbeths." Frank Elgin is the most unsympathetic of the three characters. He must show the despair and vulnerability of the male who cannot make it on his own, as well as the deviousness of an alcoholic. The catalyst of these two roles is Georgie, who must simultaneously appear domineering and self-sacrificing. *The Country Girl* is a story in which very little action takes place. The characters reveal their innermost thoughts and desires by exposition. Using this device, Seaton's production and his fine cast succeed admirably.

Bernie Dodd is convinced that the only actor who can bring theatrical life to *The Land Around Us* is "has-been" Frank Elgin, who has ruined his career through alcohol. Dodd convinces the play's backers to allow Elgin to read for the part, but Elgin leaves the audition upon learning that the part is the male lead. When the backers still agree to go along with Dodd's belief that Elgin is the only actor for the part, Dodd seeks out Elgin at his apartment, a dismal, furnished room over a restaurant in the dingy Times Square area of New York City.

Elgin is not at home when Dodd arrives, but his wife Georgie is. She is a plain, weary woman who looks older than her years and who appears to be a domineering burden to her husband. Dodd takes an immediate dislike to her. At one point he chastises her by saying, "You try to look like an old lady and you're not. You shouldn't wear your hair like that. There are two kinds of women. Those who pay too much attention to themselves, and those who don't pay enough." Then he asks her if she was ever in the theater, and she responds with, "I'm just a girl from the country. The theater and the people in it have always been a complete mystery to me. They still are."

Elgin finally arrives home, and Dodd insists that he can do the role, that it is a part made for him, but only if he stays completely away from alcohol. Elgin explains that his drinking is a result of the death of his son. Through the device of flashback we learn that it was Elgin's fault that the child was hit by an automobile. However, Georgie insists that the only reason Elgin ever drank, both before and after the death of his son, was his fear of responsibility. This is the key weakness in Odets' plot. We know that Elgin uses his son's death as an excuse for his drinking, but we never learn the initial cause of his alcoholism. Odets never clarified this point, which is crucial to understanding an alcoholic.

Nonetheless, Elgin gets the job. Dodd continues to regard Georgie as an unloving shrew who is responsible for her husband's self-destructive behavior. The play opens in Boston to bad reviews, and believing that Georgie is the negative influence on his star, Dodd sends her back to New York City. Before she leaves, she warns him that Frank is on the brink of a binge.

Predictably, the binge takes place. Frank lands in jail and blames his condition on his wife by fabricating a story of her infidelity, her own drinking, her suicide attempt, and a fire she set in the apartment, all of which resulted from *her* remorse over the death of their child. Finally Georgie reveals to Dodd that the story of the unfaithful, drinking wife, the suicide attempt, and the fire are fictional—straight out of a play in which Frank had once appeared. Now both Dodd and the audience see Georgie for what she really is—a faithful, loving, supportive wife. She has suppressed her own personality and desires in order to encourage and nurture her neurotic husband long enough for him to regain his self-confidence so that she might free herself from his stranglehold and live a life of her own.

With Elgin's devious motivations out in the open, Dodd and Georgie join forces to bolster his self-esteem and assure his success in the play's New York opening. At the opening night party we find Dodd in love with the "loyal, steadfast," and devoted Georgie, trying to persuade her to leave Elgin and go away with him. For the first time we see Georgie as the attractive, feminine, desirable woman she really is, and for a moment it appears that she may consider leaving her husband. Elgin is aware that his wife must choose between him and Dodd, so he leaves the party. Georgie hesitates briefly, then follows him. On the street they meet and walk away together, Dodd watching from the window of the apartment above where the party is still in progress.

Seaton's excellent script earned him an Academy Award, but the real prize-winning element of *The Country Girl* was the excellent acting ensemble of Crosby, Holden, and Kelly. Crosby's performance as Frank Elgin is considered by many to be the best of his long career. It was a role which did not allow him to fall back on the easygoing charm that had characterized his many previous screen roles and his public image. Instead, he revealed acting skill far beyond that which the public had seen from him before. His Frank Elgin is a complex, restrained, and powerful character. His performance won him the Best Actor Award from the National Board of Review of Motion Pictures, but he lost the Oscar to Marlon Brando for *On the Waterfront*. Holden's portrayal of Bernie Dodd was a further indication of his ability to portray the all-American hero with just the right touch of cynicism to transcend the image of the hero, as he had done earlier in *Sunset Boulevard* (1950) and would do again in *Network* (1976).

Grace Kelly's role as Georgie Elgin turned out to be a personal triumph. Kelly's star build-up was so enmeshed in the "patrician beauty" mold that it frequently overshadowed her considerable acting abilities. She once exclaimed that "I went to Hollywood and became a star to get on the stage." When she learned that Jennifer Jones, who had been set to star in *The Country Girl*, was pregnant, she delivered an ultimatum to her agent to have her studio, M-G-M, loan her to Paramount for the part. "You have got to let Metro release me to play this part," she demanded. "If you don't, I'm going to quit the picture business and go back to the theater in New York." Her tenacity paid off, and her portrayal of Georgie Elgin won her the Academy Award, the New York Film Critics Award, and the National Board of Review of Motion Pictures Award.

Ronald Bowers

THE COURT JESTER

Released: 1956
Production: Norman Panama and Melvin Frank for Dena Enterprises; released by Paramount
Direction: Norman Panama and Melvin Frank
Screenplay: Norman Panama and Melvin Frank
Cinematography: Ray June
Editing: Tom McAdoo
Song: Sylvia Fine and Sammy Cahn
Running time: 101 minutes

Principal characters:
Hawkins .... Danny Kaye
Maid Jean .... Glynis Johns
Sir Ravenhurst .... Basil Rathbone
Princess Gwendolyn .... Angela Lansbury
King Roderick .... Cecil Parker
Griselda .... Mildred Natwick
Sir Griswold .... Robert Middleton
Black Fox .... Edward Ashley
Giacomo .... John Carradine

In a long line of screen comedians, Danny Kaye was probably the one with the most impact in the 1940's and early 1950's. During that period, he made a short but impressive series of movies, many of which contained little of value other than Kaye's comic talents. *The Court Jester* is probably the best of this series.

Born Daniel David Kaminsky in Brooklyn, Kaye had his first success on Broadway in 1940 in *Lady in the Dark* with Gertrude Lawrence. A number entitled "Tchaikovsky" in which Kaye named fifty-four Russian composers in thirty-nine seconds, brought him attention and typified the verbal alacrity and rubber-faced delivery which were to become Danny Kaye's trademark.

Soon after this success, Samuel Goldwyn put Kaye under contract. Agonizing over Kaye's features, Goldwyn recommended a nose job. Kaye refused, but did become a blond on Goldwyn's advice. Kaye's wife, Sylvia Fine, who wrote his specialty songs, was also signed.

Unbeknownst to Goldwyn, Danny Kaye had already done some film work in two-reel comedies for Educational Pictures in Astoria, with actors Imogene Coca, June Allyson, and Hank Henry. Under contract, however, Goldwyn produced a series of vehicles for Kaye, among them *Wonder Man* (1945), *A Song Is Born* (1948), and *The Secret Life of Walter Mitty* (1947). Kaye's character was generally patterned after Harold Lloyd—shy and inept, but nevertheless winning the girl, usually played by Virginia Mayo, in the end.

Unfortunately, these early films were, for the most part, merely showcases for Danny Kaye's musical spoofery. Logic was not their strong point, as the naïve Kaye was set into unusual situations and forced to make the best of them. General weaknesses in plot and characterization caused a lack of audience empathy for Kaye's character.

After an erratic film career, which added *The Inspector General* (1949), *On the Riviera* (1951), and *Hans Christian Andersen* (1952) to his list of earlier credits, Danny Kaye and Sylvia Fine formed their own production company for the purpose of creating films which would be more tailored to Kaye's talents. The writing/directing/producing team of Norman Panama and Melvin Frank, comedy writers for Goldwyn, whose combined efforts would produce such successes as *My Favorite Blonde* (1942), *Mr. Blandings Builds His Dream House* (1948), and several of the Bob Hope/Bing Crosby "Road" pictures, were hired. Individually, Norman Panama would go on to do *The Maltese Bippy* (1969), a "Laugh-In" product, while Melvin Frank would direct *A Funny Thing Happened on the Way to the Forum* (1966), and, continuing his tradition as a writer/director/producer, would create *A Touch of Class* (1973).

Under Panama and Frank's careful handling, Kaye's character achieved something it had not had before: believability. Comedy was combined with a realistic character, one who could be credible as a romantic lead or a hero, while retaining his clownish aspect. The first efforts of the new production team yielded Kaye's two best pictures, *Knock on Wood* (1954) and *The Court Jester* (1956). This period, from 1954 to 1956, marked the highlight of Danny Kaye's career.

The critics were wildly enthusiastic about *The Court Jester*; in praising the film, a spoof on swashbucklers and Robin Hood types, they were quick to comment on the expertise and talent of the film's creators. The most expensive screen comedy of that time, filmed at a cost of four million dollars, *The Court Jester* was a lavish costume spectacle. Kaye is cast as Hawkins, the inept pot boy for a raffish band of Merry Men type outlaws and nursemaid to an infant deposed king, the Purple Pimpernel. Trying hard to earn the admiration of his hero, the Black Fox (Edward Ashley), leader of this underground movement, Hawkins becomes involved with a plot to return the Purple Pimpernel to his throne.

Involved also is Maid Jean (Glynis Johns), tough but lovely leader in the absence of the Black Fox, and a tender and credible romance begins to develop between Hawkins and her. While trying to smuggle the royal baby into the castle, Maid Jean is caught and carried off to the unlawful King Roderick (Cecil Parker). Hawkins, meanwhile, has donned the costume of Giacomo (John Carradine), "King of Jesters and Jester to the King," in order to establish contact with the king and steal the key to an underground passage allowing for the entry of the Black Fox's men. Hawkins is unwittingly thrown into an impossible and seemingly hopeless situation, but his character is believable and sympathetic, and carries along the film's overabundant plot.

Sylvia Fine's specialty songs are an additional benefit.

Once inside the castle, Hawkins falls prey to the advances of Princess Gwendolyn (Angela Lansbury), whose old nursemaid, the witch Griselda, is trying to prevent the forced marriage of Gwendolyn and Sir Griswold. Spying Hawkins as the solution to the dilemma, Griselda (Mildred Natwick) casts a spell on him, whereby, at the snap of a finger, he becomes a dashing, courageous lover. An additional snap, however, changes him back to his usual cautious and inept self. Thus, the stage for comedy is set. The twists and turns which the plot now takes, in attempting to reunite Hawkins and Maid Jean and to restore the Purple Pimpernel, are numerous to the point of absurdity. The film handles these convolutions with wit and sparkle, as the plot moves at a breathtaking pace.

Among the highlights is Hawkins' duel with Sir Ravenhurst, played by Basil Rathbone with his usual elegance and wit in a gentle spoof of the characters he played so well throughout the 1940's. The dual is a hilarious contrast between Hawkins as himself and as a bold swordsman, as these two natures are rapidly alternated by the continual snapping of fingers. In what must surely be a take-off on *The Mark of Zorro* (1940), and suggested, perhaps, by Rathbone, who also appeared in that film, Ravenhurst slices off the tip of a candle with his saber and challenges Hawkins to match him. Hawkins, with a marvelously smug countenance, strides cooly over to an entire candelabra and slashes at it. As the candles continue to burn, Ravenhurst emits a derisive laugh, but is soon silenced as Hawkins blows at the candelabra, whereupon all the tips fall off and he laughs derisively in his turn.

Other occurences befalling the unhappy Hawkins are his incredibly swift induction into knighthood in order to qualify to fight a duel against Sir Griswold (Robert Middleton) and the duel itself. Customarily, the contestants are required to drink a preliminary toast on the field of battle, but one is poisoned, and Hawkins is warned beforehand that, "The pellet with the poison's in the vessel with the pestle; the chalice with the palace has the brew that is true." As a flagon with a dragon is introduced, Hawkins' panic and confusion increase. Having successfully eluded the toast, Hawkins is faced with combat with the enormous and powerful Sir Griswold. Nervously arming himself with every weapon available, Hawkins enters the arena. A fortuitous lightning bolt strikes him, magnetizes his armor, and saves the day. Eventually, an army of dwarfs enters the palace, catapulting the enemies out, restoring the Purple Pimpernel to his throne, and bringing the film to a happy close.

Primarily notable for Kaye's comic qualities, *The Court Jester* also contains the polished performances of an illustrious supporting cast, including Rathbone, Angela Lansbury, Cecil Parker, Mildred Natwick, Robert Middleton, John Carradine, and Glynis Johns.

Rathbone, himself considered Hollywood's best swordsman, was greatly impressed by Kaye's talent. Commenting that he combined this talent with a prodigious amount of work, Rathbone stated that Kaye could as easily make an audience cry as laugh, and that this was the mark of a truly great comedian. With his quick reflexes and his extraordinary sense of mime, which enabled him to imitate easily anything seen once, Kaye could outfence Rathbone after a few weeks of instruction. Trusting to his own talent, Kaye refused to have anything doubled for him, and even went so far as to learn to play the cornet for the film *The Five Pennies* (1959), a musical biography of Red Nichols.

The number of Kaye's films is small, as Kaye has refused to make more than one film a year in order to leave time for recording and for radio and stage performances; he always has been more concerned with the performance than with becoming a star. Although many of his films have been enormously popular, it generally has been felt that Kaye is a stage performer and entertainer rather than a screen performer, and he comes across to audiences much more vibrantly in person. Because of his incredible rapport with his audiences, Kaye has enjoyed great success on the London stage, which has led to a Royal Command performance. Kaye was recognized with a special Academy Award in 1954 "for his unique talents, his service to the industry and the American people." *The Court Jester* remains a prime example of Danny Kaye at his best.

Grace Anne Morsberger

CRAIG'S WIFE

Released: 1936
Production: Edward Chodorov for Columbia
Direction: Dorothy Arzner
Screenplay: Mary C. McCall, Jr.; based on the play of the same name by
   George Kelly
Cinematography: Lucian Ballard
Editing: Viola Lawrence
Running time: 85 minutes

> *Principal characters:*
> Harriet Craig .... Rosalind Russell
> Walter Craig .... John Boles
> Mrs. Harold .... Jane Darwell
> Mrs. Frazier .... Billie Burke
> Miss Austen .... Alma Kruger
> Ethel Landreth .... Dorothy Wilson
> Professor Gene Fredericks .... Robert Allen

Originally a Pulitzer Prize-winning play, *Craig's Wife* has been successfully
filmed three times. The first version was a silent film starring the beautiful
and sadly forgotten Irene Rich. In 1936, Rosalind Russell appeared for Columbia in what is considered the definitive version; and in 1952, Joan Crawford
turned Craig's wife into a total villain who thinks more of her carpets than
of her husband. The Crawford version, entitled *Harriet Craig*, depicted the
original play's disturbed yet human heroine without a trace of sympathy.

Craig's Wife is the ultimate woman's picture. Rather than a typical soap-
opera like most pictures made specifically for female audiences, it is an intelligent analysis of the social and economic aspects of the institution of
marriage. Although written in 1925, the film's message is still appropriate
today: marriage should be for love, not for financial security. Harriet Craig
married her husband so that she could have a beautiful home; once she had
her home, she found her husband merely a necessary nuisance.

The film opens with Harriet Craig, against her better judgment, having left
the home she loves to go to Albany because she has received word that her
sister is seriously ill, a fact which Mrs. Craig will not believe. In her absence
the servants breath easier, but Mrs. Harold (Jane Darwell), the housekeeper,
keeps everything immaculate and ready for her mistress, in case she might
suddenly return. It is Mrs. Harold's opinion that if Mrs. Craig should get an
idea that there is a pin out of place, she will take the first train out of Albany.
Mrs. Harold has long ago learned that the only way to live peacefully is to
keep at least a day ahead of a woman like Mrs. Craig. There is more than
a pin out of place, however, for the newspaper headlines announce a recent

scandalous murder mystery in which the bodies of the J. Fergus Passmores have been discovered dead in the Passmore library—and Fergus Passmore and Walter Craig (John Boles) have always been the best and closest of friends.

Mrs. Harold and a maid are gossiping about what a long-suffering husband Walter Craig is when Mrs. Harold's worst fears are realized: Mrs. Craig suddenly returns home, bringing her niece, Ethel Landreth (Dorothy Wilson), with her. Mrs. Craig has arranged things in Albany so that her sister and her sister's doctor have advised her to go home and take Ethel with her. Ethel, nineteen years old, is distressed, for she has not had a chance to tell her mother that she has virtually promised Professor Gene Fredericks (Robert Allen) to marry him, and it might comfort her mother, who likes Professor Fredericks, to know that her daughter is in good hands. Mrs. Craig is not so sure about that; a college professor does not make very much money. Mrs. Craig has no romantic illusions; she has seen to it that her marriage is an emancipation for her. She has not been exactly dishonest in her marriage, but she has cleverly connived a kind of independence and authority over the man she married, which has made her actually independent of everybody. It is evident that Mrs. Craig values her home more than she does her husband; in fact, she is obsessed by her home. She had seen her own mother dispossessed of her house when her husband, Mrs. Craig's father, abandoned her for another woman; and Mrs. Craig has long ago determined that such a thing will never happen to her.

After sending Ethel upstairs to rest, Mrs. Craig inspects her house and finds fresh scratches on the polished stairs. Also, there are fresh roses in the room, and fresh flowers have shed their petals on the carpets. It is even more irksome for her to know that at this very moment Miss Austen (Alma Kruger), Mr. Craig's aunt who lives in the house, is upstairs in her room entertaining the neighbor, Mrs. Frazier (Billie Burke), who had brought the roses from her own garden. Mrs. Craig is certain that Mrs. Frazier is a busybody who has used the roses as an excuse to get inside the house, which she has been dying to see. Because of these circumstances, Mrs. Craig's homecoming is not a particularly happy one. The scene is set, and the remainder of the action takes place in a single night and the following morning. In less than sixteen hours, the destiny of Mrs. Craig is plotted and resolved.

Insecure and overly cautious, Mrs. Craig has made it clear that she wishes to live to herself, and, as Miss Austen notes, "People who live to themselves are generally left to themselves." One by one, the people close to Mrs. Craig see her clearly for what she is and abandon her. Unwittingly, she involves her husband as a suspect in the murder of Fergus Passmore and his wife; and, had Passmore not left a letter taking blame for his own suicide and the murder of his wife because she had betrayed him, Walter Craig could have been looked upon by the police as a suspect. She has called her husband "a romantic fool," and Walter Craig, his eyes opened to her dishonesties, prepares to desert her. Then, Professor Gene Fredericks arrives, disconcerted, and persuades Ethel to return to Albany with him. Miss Austen announces that she has long wanted to travel extensively, and packs her bags, taking not only her personal possessions but Mrs. Harold, the housekeeper, with her.

Alone at last in the house, Mrs. Craig receives a telegram: her sister in Albany has died. Stunned, she cannot give way to grief. When Mrs. Frazier, the kindly neighbor, comes by with more roses, Mrs. Craig accepts them numbly and confides, because she must tell somebody, that she has just received word that her sister has died. Mrs. Frazier is sympathetic, but withdraws. Mrs. Craig stands alone on the stairs, her arms laden with fresh roses, unmindful that their petals are falling softly onto her beloved carpet.

The brilliance of this 1936 version comes from the star, Rosalind Russell, who was borrowed for the picture from M-G-M, and from the director, Dorothy Arzner. Russell always had a talent for bringing warmth to the many cold and calculating characters she portrayed in films. *Craig's Wife* made her a star in her own right and opened producers' eyes to that rare gift she had for making unsympathetic parts acceptable to audiences; afterwards she made a career of playing hard-headed business women. For her part, director Dorothy Arzner was ideal. At that time she was the only woman in Hollywood working as a director. This smart, mannish-looking woman had worked her way up from the editing department to the position of director through hard work and a no-nonsense attitude. *Craig's Wife* is certainly the best film Arzner ever directed. She brought to it an awareness and sympathy for the plight of women. Her own personal experiences in her career gave Arzner insight into the character of Harriet Craig; whereas the establishment saw Harriet as a bad woman, Arzner saw her as a victim of society.

Craig's Wife was very well received by critics. *Photoplay* magazine named it one of the best of the month, and it is generally acknowledged to be the picture that opened up Russell's career.

Larry Lee Holland

CYRANO DE BERGERAC

Released: 1950
Production: Stanley Kramer for the Stanley Kramer Company; released by
    United Artists
Direction: Michael Gordon
Screenplay: Carl Foreman; based on the play of the same name by Edmond
    Rostand
Cinematography: Franz Planer
Editing: Harry Gerstad
Running time: 112 minutes

> *Principal characters:*
> Cyrano de Bergerac .... José Ferrer (AA)
> Roxane .... Mala Powers
> Christian de Neuvillette .... William Prince
> Le Bret .... Morris Carnovsky
> Comte de Guiche .... Ralph Clanton
> Ragueneau .... Lloyd Corrigan

Cyrano-Savinien-Hercule de Bergerac (José Ferrer) is a seventeenth century French soldier and poet as much feared for his ready wit and satires in
the press as he is for his skilled sword arm. He has also written a play; but
he rejects an offer from Cardinal Richelieu to have it produced under his
sponsorship because the Cardinal insists on changing a few lines.

Cyrano is secretly in love with his cousin, the beautiful Roxane (Mala
Powers); but Roxane loves the Baron Christian de Neuvillette (William
Prince), a handsome new member of Cyrano's regiment, the elite Cadets of
Gascoyne. Cyrano, whose nose is overly large, is miserably aware of his ugly
countenance and goes out of his way to become friends with de Neuvillette,
as his cousin has asked. Christian confesses that he loves Roxane in return,
but is much too shy to speak the things that are in his heart. Cyrano eagerly
proposes that he write Christian's love letters to Roxane for him. She is
thrilled by the letters, and by the pretty speeches that Cyrano puts into
Christian's mouth; but the ardent young Baron grows uneasy when he suspects
that it is Cyrano's words Roxane loves, and not himself. He attempts to woo
her in his own words, but can manage no more than a stammered "I love
you . . . very much" before retreating to beg Cyrano to come to his rescue.

The night is dark; Roxane is waiting on her balcony; and from the shadows
Cyrano can at last pour out in his own voice the words of love he would never
dare speak for himself. With Cyrano's help, Christian and Roxane are secretly
married that same night, just before the Comte de Guiche (Ralph Clanton)
arrives with news that their regiment has been posted to the front and that
they march at once. Even during the worst of the subsequent fighting (France

is at war with Spain), Cyrano manages to slip through the lines every night with a fresh love letter ostensibly written by Christian. His eloquence has never burned higher; and Roxane makes her way to where the Cadets are besieged before Arras to tell her husband that whereas she married him for his outward good looks, his letters have made her love him for his soul.

Christian finally realizes that Cyrano has loved Roxane too, and confronts Cyrano to demand that he tell Roxane everything and make her choose between them. But, before Cyrano can comply, Christian is mortally wounded on a scouting mission behind the enemy lines. He is carried back to the French camp, where Cyrano, in Roxane's presence, tells Christian that he alone has been the man she loved. After Christian's death, Roxane withdraws to a convent, where for fourteen years she cherishes his memory and what she believes to have been his last letter to her. Her only contacts with the outside world are the occasional visits she receives from a few old friends, including Cyrano, who comes every Saturday to amuse her with the latest gossip from the Court and to please her by talking about Christian.

One Friday night, as Cyrano is leaving the pastry shop owned by his friend Ragueneau (Lloyd Corrigan), an amateur poet as well as a cook, Cyrano is set upon and wounded by a gang of assassins hired by a nobleman he has angered with his published satires. Although the doctor warns him that to leave his bed means death, Cyrano painfully makes his way to the convent the next afternoon for his weekly visit with Roxane. He asks to be allowed to see Christian's last letter ("Farewell, Roxane, because today I die"); and his impassioned reading reminds her of the voice that had spoken to her out of the darkness beneath her balcony on her wedding night. She tells Cyrano that now she realizes he has been the man whose soul she loved, but it is too late: Cyrano dies of his wounds, proclaiming that when he meets God he will salute Him with the emblem of the Cadets of Gascoyne and the symbol of his own proudly maintained independence, "my white plume!"

Such is the story of Stanley Kramer's film and the play by Edmond Rostand (1868-1918) on which it was based. One would hardly guess from Rostand's melodramatic plot that Cyrano was a real person, whose dates were 1619-1655. He was, indeed, well-known in his own time as a soldier, poet, satirist, and playwright; and he was reputed to have had a long nose (although it could not have been as long as the magnificent proboscis makeup artists Gustaf and Josef Norin created for José Ferrer in the film). Cyrano's accomplishments, when one looks them up, are quite impressive: he was a pioneer in the field of science fiction (his series of proposals to Guiche, at one point in the play, for breaking free of the earth's gravity were taken from Cyrano's *Histoire comique des états et empires de la lune*); and his plays *Le Pédant joué* and *La Mort d'Agrippine* are still highly regarded in France. He undoubtedly deserved better than Rostand's portrait of him as a self-loathing masochist and, by virtue of his fourteen years' deference to Roxane's mistaken memory of Christian, one of the greatest chumps in dramatic literature.

The reason that *Cyrano de Bergerac*, for all its shameless hokum, has held the boards since it was first performed by the great French actor Coquelin in 1897 is that Rostand disguised the banality of his dramatic conception in verse of a rich sonorousness that is as satisfying for actors to speak as it is for audiences to hear. The play was performed in English by Richard Mansfield as early as 1899; but the translation by Brian Hooker that American and British audiences are familiar with today (and on which Carl Foreman's screenplay was based) was commissioned by Walter Hampden and first performed in 1923. As Brooks Atkinson has written, "the Brian Hooker translation is not only so distinguished but also so familiar that we have almost forgotten that Rostand did not write it himself." Hooker was a Broadway lyricist whose only other notable work was the libretto he cowrote with William H. Post for *The Vagabond King*. There would seem to be no explanation other than clairvoyance for the skill with which he found equivalents for Rostand's Alexandrines in the iambic pentameter of English dramatic verse. Had Hampden, when he decided to revive the play, stuck with the translation used by Mansfield (in which the familiar line that Hooker rendered "And then as I end the refrain, thrust home!" had emerged as "And then at the envoi's end, *touché!*"), *Cyrano de Bergerac* in English might long ago have entered the same limbo as such once-popular works by Rostand as *La Princesse Lointaine*, *La Samaritaine*, and *L'Aiglon*.

In recent years, the more ridiculous aspects of the story (such as Roxane's arrival at Arras with Ragueneau in a coach and four just as the beleaguered Cadets are bracing themselves for a ferocious Spanish assault) have usually been played for their value as comedy, without detracting from the seriousness of such moments as Cyrano's great speech rejecting Guiche's offer of patronage or Guiche's avowal of dissatisfaction in the last act.

Michael Gordon, the director of the film version, later demonstrated a flair for comedy in *Pillow Talk* (1959)—one of the first and best of the Doris Day vehicles of the late 1950's and early 1960's—and in such subsequent trifles as *Boys' Night Out* (1962) and *Move Over Darling* (1963). His treatment of *Cyrano de Bergerac* is squarely (in both senses of the word, as Dwight Macdonald once said) in the solemn tradition of the typical Hollywood "prestige" picture, however. The few notes of levity that creep in—such as the sudden disappearance of the actor Montfleury when Cyrano orders him off the stage in midperformance and all that is left is his handkerchief floating in the air, or Cyrano's impatience when he is coaching Christian in his speeches to Roxane—are obvious bits of comedy relief inserted into a story that needs none. Most of the principal actors—Mala Powers, William Prince, Ralph Clanton, and Morris Carnovsky (who plays Le Bret, the captain of Cyrano's regiment)—intone their lines as if Rostand and Hooker were Shakespeare and they were afraid they might not measure up. Only José Ferrer, who had already played Cyrano on the stage, seems to have been in on the joke of the story: Cyrano's masochism and self-pity are fascinating because of the delight he himself takes in the spectacle of his own suffering. Ferrer is not a "great" actor in the sense that Olivier or John Gielgud is great, but then great acting in a superior potboiler like *Cyrano de Bergerac* is not what is required for the film's success. Ferrer's witty performance, which makes watching the film pleasurable in spite of the generally mediocre acting of the supporting cast and Rudolph Sternad's *papier-mâché* sets, was recognized by the members of the Academy of Motion Picture Arts and Sciences when they voted him the film's only Oscar nomination and he won the Award for Best Actor of 1950.

Cyrano de Bergerac on the screen has an interesting history as a vehicle for testing technical innovations: Coquelin himself performed the first-act duel scene for the camera and phonograph in one of the earliest experiments with talking pictures; and an Italian production of 1925 was photographed throughout in a primitive color process. Kramer in 1950 was not willing to go to the expense of Technicolor (a mistake, for the story cries out for color and it might have diverted the eye a little from the overall cheapness of the production); but his black-and-white film was photographed with the new Garutso Balanced Lens, which allowed a greater depth of focus than was possible with most camera lenses of the day. This meant that the spectators in the duel scene, for instance, could now be photographed as clearly as Cyrano and his opponent. The result was an illusion of seeing in three dimensions what was otherwise difficult to achieve in the days of the narrow screen.

Charles Hopkins

DADDY LONG LEGS

Released: 1955
Production: Samuel G. Engel for Twentieth Century-Fox
Direction: Jean Negulesco
Screenplay: Phoebe Ephron and Henry Ephron; based on the novel and play
  of the same name by Jean Webster
Cinematography: Leon Shamroy
Editing: William Reynolds
Music: Johnny Mercer and Alex North
Running time: 126 minutes

Principal characters:
Jervis Pendleton III	Fred Astaire
Julie André	Leslie Caron
Linda Pendleton	Terry Moore
Miss Prichard	Thelma Ritter
Griggs	Fred Clark
Sally McBride	Charlotte Austin
Ambassador Alexander Williamson	Larry Keating
Gertrude Pendleton	Kathryn Givney
Jimmy McBride	Kelly Brown
Madame Sevanne	Ann Codee

According to Stanley Green and Burt Goldblatt's book *Starring Fred Astaire*, Twentieth Century-Fox studio chief Darryl Zanuck had originally conceived a musical version of *Daddy Long Legs*, Jean Webster's sentimental 1912 novel, as a vehicle for Mitzi Gaynor in 1951. The story had a longer history as a movie property than that, however: Mary Pickford had starred in the first screen *Daddy Long Legs* in 1919; and there had also been an early talkie version with Janet Gaynor and Warner Baxter in 1931. When Zanuck revived the project early in 1954, it was as a showcase for the young French star Leslie Caron, who had been well received by American audiences in the M-G-M musicals *An American in Paris* (1951) and *Lili* (1953). Miss Caron's training had been in ballet; and it was planned that the film would include two lengthy dream sequences in the manner of the elaborate ballet Gene Kelly had devised for *An American in Paris*.

Fox had not been in the forefront of the postwar development of the big Hollywood musical. Instead, M-G-M had that honor, with producers Arthur Freed and Joe Pasternak, directors Vincente Minnelli, Gene Kelly, and Stanley Donen, and such stars as Kelly, Judy Garland, Frank Sinatra, Fred Astaire, Jane Powell, Ann Miller, and Howard Keel all under contract. Fox's biggest musical star during those years was the pretty but not notably talented Betty Grable, followed closely by the "South American bombshell," Carmen Miranda. Zanuck's decision to commit his studio's resources to so costly a project as an original musical at a time when even M-G-M was curtailing production of these expensive entertainments may seem paradoxical; but it should be remembered that Fox was then in the process of introducing CinemaScope and stereophonic sound, and that the musical form was ideally suited to show off these new developments in screen technology.

Jean Webster's original story described the May-December romance of a vivacious, intelligent orphan girl and the wealthy bachelor who has been anonymously sponsoring her education at an exclusive women's college. Caron's partner in the musical version would obviously have to be a dancer. Zanuck offered the role to a man who, as it happened, had never worked for Fox before but who had long since become the twentieth century's leading exponent of the traditional art of the song and dance man. Fred Astaire was fifty-four years old when *Daddy Long Legs* went into rehearsal. His contract with M-G-M had expired after the release of *The Band Wagon* (1953); and he had been contemplating retirement when Fox unexpectedly sent him the script he later described as "one of the best ever to come my way."

Screenwriters Phoebe and Henry Ephron used only the bare outline of Webster's story as a frame on which to hang the different elements that would have to be integrated into Zanuck's musical. To begin with, a way had to be found to reconcile Caron's French origin and accent with the character of Judy Abbot, the very American heroine of the original novel. The solution was simple enough: Judy Abbot became Julie André, an eighteen-year-old foundling who has lived since infancy in an orphanage outside Paris. Astaire plays Jervis Pendleton III (the same name as the character in the novel), a breezy American industrialist who goes to France on an economic mission for the State Department. When the limousine in which he and his fellow "experts" are traveling gets stuck in the mud of a French country lane, Jervis hikes over to the orphanage to see if they have a car he can borrow.

While waiting to speak to the woman in charge, Madame Sevanne (Ann Codee), he catches sight of Julie through a window as she guides the younger children through an English lesson in song. Jervis is captivated by her intelligence and joyful spirit; and, when he reaches Paris, he asks the American ambassador how he can adopt her. The ambassador (played to stuffy perfection by Larry Keating) is horrified at the thought of helping Jervis adopt an eighteen-year-old girl. "Do you have any idea how easy it is to lose a job in the State Department these days?," he asks, in what for a light entertainment is a pretty straightforward reference to the McCarthy-inspired paranoia of the early 1950's. Jervis agrees merely to sponsor Julie anonymously at a United States women's college; and, when the arrangements have been completed, he motors back to the orphanage to tell the good news to Madame Sevanne. Julie is overjoyed at her good fortune, but disappointed that her only contact with her benefactor, whom she has been told to address as "John Smith," is to be through the monthly letter she must write reporting her progress in school. When she returns to her dormitory, the children tell her that they have seen the long-legged shadow (like a *faucheux*, or daddy long legs) of an American visitor leaving Madame Sevanne's office. Jervis had hidden himself during Julie's interview with Madame Sevanne, and Julie had not seen him during his previous visit to the orphanage; so the children's meager description is all the information she has about the physical appearance of "John Smith."

In America, Julie easily adjusts to the routine of college life. She gets along well with her roommates, Sally McBride (Charlotte Austin) and Linda Pendleton, Jervis' niece (Terry Moore), who knows nothing about her uncle's connection with this mysterious French girl. Soon, Julie even has a beau, Sally's brother Jimmy (Kelly Brown); but she is lonely for someone she can think of as family, and pours her heart out in her monthly letter to "John Smith," whom she fondly addresses as "Daddy Long Legs." Jervis, meanwhile, has forgotten all about Miss André.

The only people who have read Julie's letters are Jervis' associate, Griggs (Fred Clark), and his warm-hearted secretary Miss Prichard (Thelma Ritter). As time passes, Julie writes of her growing despondency at the failure of "John Smith" to reply to anything she asks or tells him, until finally Griggs, at Miss Prichard's urging, marches into Jervis' office and lays the whole voluminous file of Julie's correspondence in his lap. Jervis is at first taken aback at the amount of stationery Julie has gone through in just two years; but, as he reads, he finds himself becoming captivated by her all over again. (The form of the novel *Daddy Long Legs* is epistolary: except for a brief opening chapter, the whole of the story is told in Judy Abbot's letters to Jervis—whose identity as her secret benefactor is not revealed until the end.)

Jervis phones his sister-in-law Gertrude (Kathryn Givney) to suggest that the two of them drive up to the college to visit his niece Linda, whom Jervis has not seen since she was a baby. Mrs. Pendleton is puzzled by Jervis' sudden rush of family feeling, but tells him that he can be her escort when she chaperones the spring dance, if he wishes. At the dance, as Jervis had hoped, Linda introduces him to her roommate, Miss André. In spite of the difference in their ages, Jervis and Julie are attracted to each other at once, and even distinguish themselves among the other couples with their stylish footwork in a novelty dance step, the Sluefoot.

Jervis invites Linda and Julie to be his guests for a weekend in New York. When Linda catches a cold at the last minute and is unable to come, Julie decides to go anyway. Jervis is at first embarrassed to take Julie to the hotel suite he has booked without Linda; but that evening, after dinner, he finally confesses to Julie that he has fallen in love with her. The song Astaire sings at this point, "Something's Gotta Give," was the film's one big hit. It was nominated for the Academy Award for Best Song of 1955, but lost to "Love Is a Many Splendored Thing." Jervis chastely deposits Julie back at the door of her suite after a romantic night out on the town; and the next morning, he arrives for breakfast with an engagement ring in his pocket.

While they are talking out on the terrace, their words of love are overheard by Jervis' friend the American ambassador (Larry Keating), who has come back to the States on official business and has spent the night in the adjoining suite before going on to Washington. The ambassador telephones Julie's suite and tells Jervis to come next door at once. When they are sitting together, Jervis protests that, whatever his friend may think, he has kept his guardianship of Julie a secret from her. Jervis finally agrees that even if Julie does not know exactly how much she owes him, her apparent love may be only a young girl's natural gratitude for the attention shown her by an older, obviously sophisticated man; and that she would probably be happier with Jimmy McBride, who is at least her own age. Without going back to her suite, Jervis telephones Julie and tells her that he has been suddenly called out of the country on a mysterious government mission, from which he will not return for some time.

Julie brokenheartedly follows Jervis' progress from one world capital to the next in the gossip columns, which link him with a succession of beautiful women. When, on the eve of her graduation, Julie writes "John Smith" a letter pleading for his advice, Miss Prichard takes matters into her own hands and sends Jervis a cablegram telling him that Griggs is not expected to live and that he has to return to New York at once. Jervis is furious when he arrives and discovers the trick that has been played on him. He is about to make Griggs impersonate "John Smith" for Julie's benefit when Linda bursts in with news that she and Jimmy McBride are in love with each other and to ask his help in persuading her mother to give them a big wedding. Jervis, his conscience now clear, is waiting when Julie drives up with Miss Prichard to confess that he has been "John Smith"—alias Daddy Long Legs—and to ask her to marry him. As Jervis and Julie waltz happily together, Griggs and Miss Prichard slip back into the office for a well-deserved drink.

Daddy Long Legs opened to good reviews and received Academy Award nominations in two other categories—Color Art Direction and Best Scoring of a Musical Picture—in addition to Best Song. Arthur Knight spoke for many reviewers when he wrote in the *Saturday Review* that the film "gives Fred Astaire one of his best opportunities in ages to display both his peculiar charm and his dancing skill." Why then, if the film was generally well received when it opened, is it so little seen today? It is revived much less often than such Astaire musicals as *The Band Wagon*, *Easter Parade* (1948), or almost any of the films he made with Ginger Rogers. Johnny Mercer's original score (a rarity in an era when film musicals were increasingly based on works that had been popular on the stage) included no other new songs on the level of "Something's Gotta Give"; but "History of the Beat," "C-A-T Spells Cat," and "Sluefoot" were nicely calculated to display the "peculiar charm and

. . . dancing skill" of both Caron and Astaire. At Astaire's suggestion, an eleven-year-old Mercer ballad, "Dream," was used as a motif for Julie's musings about the identity of her mysterious benefactor. The film's chief distinction, in fact, may lie in its quality as a late specimen of the musical conceived as a vehicle for the talents of a few star performers.

Every objection the audience could make to the improbable romantic pairing of the two leads and to the contrived story was anticipated in the script of *Daddy Long Legs*. Is Astaire obviously at least thirty years older than Caron? Jervis' sister-in-law is on hand at the occasion of his first meeting with Julie to remind him that he is "a well-traveled piece of luggage." Is it patently incredible that the American ambassador should be right next door on the morning Jervis intends to propose to Julie? As Jervis storms out after their interview, he yells over his shoulder: "Do you have any idea how many hotel rooms there are in New York?" "But, Jervis," the ambassador pleads, "I *always* stop at this hotel."

Even the circumstance that the film includes *two* dream ballets is explained when one sees them and realizes that the first—in which Jervis imagines himself as Julie had described him in three favorite daydreams: as a Texas oil millionaire, as an international playboy, and, literally, as her guardian angel—is tailored to show off Astaire's ballroom-*cum*-tap style of dancing; and that the second—in which Julie imagines herself vainly pursuing Jervis after their breakup to Paris, Hong Kong, and Rio at carnival time—has been designed to show off Caron's training in ballet. The music for this second sequence was composed by Alex North, and includes the score for an original ballet, *Le Papilon*, which Caron dances while imagining herself as a member of the corps de ballet of the Paris Opera. That the filmmakers were unable to devise a sequence that would showcase the talents of both performers at the same time points up the fundamental weakness in *Daddy Long Legs* that has kept it from being considered one of the great movie musicals. That elusive quality that makes us care about the protagonists of a musical drama has sometimes been called chemistry, sometimes heart; and it is just this quality that *Daddy Long Legs* painfully lacks. Both Astaire and Caron are likable performers; but we never for a minute believe that they are two people in love. Astaire not only looks like Caron's uncle, but seems to have an uncle's affection for her; that special warmth that animated his scenes with Ginger Rogers is missing from his scenes with Caron. In the final dream ballet, when Julie is dancing her heart out in *Le Papilon*, Jervis is shown coldly observing her performance from a stage box. Not only is this a long way from the closeness of "Cheek to Cheek," it is even further removed from the performing philosophy of the man who, asked to sum up his career, replied, "I just dance."

Charles Hopkins

DARK VICTORY

Released: 1939
Production: Hal B. Wallis for Warner Bros.
Direction: Edmund Goulding
Screenplay: Casey Robinson; based on the play of the same name by George Emerson Brewer, Jr., and Bertram Bloch
Cinematography: Ernest Haller
Editing: William Holmes
Running time: 106 minutes

Principal characters:
Judith Traherne	Bette Davis
Dr. Frederick Steele	George Brent
Ann King	Geraldine Fitzgerald
Michael O'Leary	Humphrey Bogart
Alec Hamin	Ronald Reagan

One of the most famous films of the 1930's, *Dark Victory* features a memorable Bette Davis performance. As Judith Traherne, a rich young socialite dying of a brain tumor, Davis proves through the integrity of her acting that it is not necessary to be sentimental or banal in this kind of role and lifts the film above mere melodrama. So sincere and compelling is her performance that it is difficult to imagine any other interpretation of the role, though two versions of the story were filmed later.

Before they meet, the film's two main characters are complete opposites. Judith Traherne is rich, young, and attractive—the center of attention wherever she goes. She plays bridge, trains and shows her horses, sails, fishes, and travels. She feels that she is so young and strong that nothing can touch her. Dr. Frederick Steele (George Brent), on the other hand, is a mature and skillful brain surgeon, respected by his colleagues and completely dedicated to his work. He has little time or inclination to engage in the pursuit of pleasure. He is more interested in discovering the causes of brain tumors and is giving up his practice to spend all of his time on research.

When the two first meet, therefore, they are contemptuous and hostile. Judith comes to Steele's office as he is moving out of it, because her doctor thinks she needs to see a specialist. She has been having severe headaches and occasional attacks of double vision. We have already seen her fail to take her horse over a jump because she saw two of them. She wants to ignore her illness and is very antagonistic to the surgeon. Steele wants to finish moving out and at first thinks she is just a "Long Island nitwit" with a silly complaint.

The scene in the doctor's office is one of the best-written, acted, and directed in the entire film. Scarcely a word is wasted as the dialogue reveals the characters of Judith and Steele while it advances the story. Through her nervous movements and rapid delivery of her lines, Bette Davis conveys how frightened and vulnerable Judith is beneath her surface bravado. When she tries to light her cigarette, Steele must guide her hand. Instead of the conventional static shots of two people talking, director Edmund Goulding uses Judith's nervous movements to show the two characters from every angle. In this cinematic way, Goulding shows Judith and Steele literally, as well as figuratively, circling around each other. Steele probes, trying by means of exploratory questions and simple tests to discover the nature and extent of Judith's illness. Judith tries desperately to keep her poise and prevent her fear from surfacing. By the end of the scene Steele recognizes the seriousness of her illness and postpones his plans to abandon his practice for research. He decides, instead, to operate on Judith.

He performs the operation but finds the tumor inoperable. According to his own diagnosis and that of all the doctors he consults, Judith will live normally for a few months and then die quickly. Her only warning will be a loss of vision shortly before she dies. Steele decides to keep this information from Judith and let her think that the operation has cured her.

Since their first meeting, Judith and Steele have changed their opinions of each other. Steele's contempt turns to curiosity and then to liking. Judith begins to respect Steele, then to trust him, and finally to love him. She has begun to feel that her life is empty and self-centered, and she tells Steele that it must be good to believe in what one is doing. She finds that her love for him gives her, for the first time, something to think of besides "horses and hats and food." On his part, Steele, who has never before been interested in women, realizes that he too has fallen in love. They plan to marry, and Judith is eager to share his life and help with his research, visualizing herself as the wife of a famous scientist—a Mrs. Louis Pasteur. Although the conventions of the romantic melodrama dictate that Judith fall in love with her doctor and he with her, it is perfectly believable that she should fall in love with the man who has apparently saved her life, and that he would be attracted to such a vibrantly alive woman as Judith.

When Judith accidentally discovers the truth about her illness, her dream world is shattered. She is enraged and overwhelmed by the knowledge and by Steele's deception, and she refuses to see him again. Beginning a frenzied, unceasing round of partying and drinking, she refuses to rest or sleep because it is a "waste of time; time doesn't sleep." At the horse show she takes enormous risks to win first prize because she knows it is her last chance. All the time she presents a bitter, cynical front to the world. At last, however, she realizes that she must seek her peace with Steele; she calls him to apologize, saying that she does not know what to do. "It's the waiting, day and night," she tells him, asking for his help. They decide to marry and go to Vermont as they originally had planned.

The poignance of the final sequence is a result of Goulding's sensitive direction and the restraint and sincerity of Davis' performance. Steele and Judith are planning a trip to New York where he is to present a paper on the progress of his research. But as Judith's sight begins to fail, she realizes that death is only a few hours away. Because his research is so important, she conceals this fact from Steele and sends him off to New York. After his departure, she reveals the truth to her best friend, Ann King (Geraldine Fitzgerald), who is visiting them, before also sending her away, saying that she must show Steele that she can face death alone. Judith's victory is that she is able to face death with dignity—"beautifully, finely, peacefully"—as Steele had wished her to.

In the final scene the camera follows Judith as she haltingly climbs the stairs to her room, saying good-bye to her dogs on the way. She lies down on the bed, telling her maid Martha that she does not want to be disturbed. Martha pulls down the blinds, covers Judith with a quilt, and leaves the room, carefully closing the door. The final shot shows Judith blindly gazing into space as the camera slowly goes out of focus. No description of the scene can avoid making it sound too melodramatic, but because of Davis' compelling performance it is completely believable and touching.

Indeed, the acting in the entire film is outstanding except for that of Humphrey Bogart, who is miscast in the minor role of Judith's horse trainer. Geraldine Fitzgerald gives an excellent performance as Judith's secretary-companion and best friend, and George Brent is equally deserving of praise. As Frederick Steele, he gives a quiet performance entirely appropriate to his role, investing the character of the doctor with the charm to make believable Judith's attraction to him, and the strength to justify her trust. However, in the final analysis *Dark Victory* is Bette Davis' film, and it is her performance that dominates it and makes it truly memorable.

Julia Johnson

DARLING

Released: 1965
Production: Joseph Janni for Embassy
Direction: John Schlesinger
Screenplay: Frederic Raphael (AA)
Cinematography: Kenneth Higgins
Editing: James B. Clark
Costume design: Julie Harris (AA)
Running time: 122 minutes

Principal characters:
Diana Scott .... Julie Christie (AA)
Miles Brand .... Laurence Harvey
Robert Gold .... Dirk Bogarde
Malcolm .... Roland Curram
Cesare .... Vilallonga

Darling is John Schlesinger's jaundiced look at swinging London in the mid-1960's. It was a period in which the British pop music explosion spearheaded by the Beatles, the brief ascendancy of the Carnaby Street look in the world of fashion, and the surge of interest in the James Bond books and films combined to give England, and London in particular, an indelible aura of the *avante garde*. Schlesinger's sardonic film, however, suggests that there was less to the whole scene than met the eye. The medium for Schlesinger's message is one Diana Scott (Julie Christie), a London model who drifts aimlessly through the fringes of the jet set, ostensibly looking for love, but all too willing to settle merely for thrills. The film's strength, however, resides in its refusal to turn Diana into a villain. Frederic Raphael's fine script makes it clear that Diana is altogether average in most respects; only her looks are extraordinary. Her physical beauty, however, brings with it temptations that she can recognize but never quite resist, and the result is a spectacular professional career that cannot compensate for the emptiness in her personal life.

As the film opens, Diana Scott is, outwardly at least, at the pinnacle of success. The former bra model has become a "beautiful person," rich, famous, married to a real Prince, and reciting the story of her life and times to a magazine writer. Schlesinger and Raphael use her recollections as a springboard for a series of flashbacks through which they paint their own portrait of Diana. The two images of Diana—her own as she relates it, and the point of view of the filmmakers—are often ironically juxtaposed, as Schlesinger contradicts Diana's blithe narration by presenting the dark side of life that her glossy success story omits: the wrong choices, the broken promises, and the failed dreams that help explain the sadness in her eyes.

Early in the film while she is a model for bras, Diana meets Robert Gold

(Dirk Bogarde), who interviews her for a BBC documentary. She is taken by his depth and his obvious intelligence, and he is attracted to her vitality, as well as being flattered by the open admiration of a pretty girl. Although the two are polar opposites, Robert being a sober intellectual who, though only a few years older than Diana, radiates a calm maturity that she will never achieve regardless of age, they fall in love. It is a credit to Schlesinger and Raphael that they make this couple believable and effective. The couple begins to spend time together, with Diana tagging along while Robert conducts interviews for his documentaries. The subject of one of these programs is an eminent poet; Diana is dazzled by the older man's brilliance, and even more delighted when the poet deigns to talk to her. As she describes the encounter later, she cannot remember what they discussed; her dominant recollection is of being "pleased to be accepted."

Only one thing appears to stand in the way of Diana's happiness. The courtship takes on a nervous, almost furtive edge, as Diana voices what will become her frequent plaint during the course of the film: "It should be the easiest thing in the world to be happy." The problem, as the filmmakers finally reveal, is that both Diana and Robert are already married. They spend a weekend together, leaving town "on business" and taking turns phoning their respective spouses with an excuse about being delayed. Characteristically, Diana enjoys perpetrating the rendezvous since it is a game to her; Robert, however, is a reluctant liar, if not a reluctant adulterer. As Diana voices her horror at the very idea of breaking up Robert's happy home, we see her on screen spying on his family; and indeed, both Diana and Robert ultimately leave their spouses to move in together. "Your books have arrived," a bubbly Diana announces as they unpack; "and your records," replies a considerably more subdued Robert. This brief scene is a brilliantly succinct summary of the differences between the attitudes of the two lovers and neatly foreshadows their eventual breakup.

Diana grows increasingly bored with the loving, earnest, but, to her taste, dull Robert; and temptation, in the form of an old lover, Miles Brand (Laurence Harvey), once again proves irresistible. Miles, a shallow sybarite, takes Diana to Paris to introduce her to its decadent jet set. Her descent into this demimonde is preceded by a reprise of the "deception by telephone" scene, which Schlesinger uses as a clear signal to the audience that Diana's relationship with Robert is dead. Ostensibly in Paris to pursue a film career, Diana instead plunges into a Felliniesque world of existential amorality and casual debauchery. Oddly, the scenes in Paris are among the film's weakest; the "orgies" are astonishingly mundane, characterized by background jazz, a hint of polymorphous perversity, and sleeping around. Schlesinger's catalogue of iniquities seems a bit stuffy, not to mention unimaginative. Although the decadent life does not bring Diana happiness, she at least is not bored, and a formal break with Robert soon follows, severing Diana's last ties with normality, and, as Schlesinger illustrates, happiness.

A chillingly amusing scene, maps out the next stage of Diana's life. A candy manufacturing company is trying to select a "Happiness Girl" to project its corporate image in its advertising. Although childishly playful in some respects as they giggle and bounce a balloon around the table, the board of directors are absolutely cold-blooded about selecting their Happiness Girl, and Diana Scott is chosen, finally, for her "Aryan qualities." Directed with surgical precision by Schlesinger, the scene is a perfect example of the film-maker's mordant wit. It also effectively foreshadows Diana's future; the world's Happiness Girl will be surrounded by cold-blooded manipulators, and the irony of her title will increase as the film nears its climax.

While filming a candy commercial in Italy, Diana abstains from sex, although only temporarily, as it turns out. Malcolm (Roland Curram), her homosexual companion, violates their mutual vow of celibacy when he spends a night with a handsome young waiter, whereupon Diana retaliates by seducing the same young man. Then, she meets a wealthy Italian prince, Cesare (Vilallonga), who asks her to marry him, and almost indifferently, she consents. Schlesinger utilizes a newsreel documentary film about the "New English Princess" to show the audience the truth about Diana's marriage. The hearty narration waxes enthusiastic about Diana's new life, but the scenes on the screen tell an entirely different story as they show an awkward and vaguely bewildered woman mingling uncomfortably among Cesare's servants and family. A vacant, slightly worried look on Diana's face as the newsreel ends presages the fate of her marriage. Cesare, an older man, is distant, both emotionally and physically, and Diana predictably grows lonely, bored, and restless. She flies to London to seek a reconciliation with Robert, who takes her to bed, but then, with uncharacteristic, although not unmotivated, cruelty, throws her out.

The film ends with Diana, back in Italy, out of options, and concluding the recitation of her magazine autobiography. The last scene portrays an old crone, as ugly as Diana is beautiful, hawking copies of the magazine containing Diana's life story, entitled "Ideal Woman."

The acting in *Darling* is first-rate. Dirk Bogarde is particularly effective as Robert Gold, whose only sin is being a bit too dull for Diana Scott. Laurence Harvey is also good as sleazy Miles Brand, who starts the unresisting Diana on her road to, if not exactly ruin, at least emptiness. The top acting honors in the film, however, go to Julie Christie, who won an Academy Award for her portrayal of Diana Scott. Christie obviously had the physical beauty to play Diana, but she also had the talent to make this childish woman seem hapless rather than evil. The dominant tone of the film is irony, and this is perhaps *Darling*'s ultimate irony—that Diana Scott is not really a bad person; she is simply neither bright enough nor strong enough to make the correct moral choice at critical times. The distinction is a delicate one, but it is altogether vital to the success of the film, and it is a tribute to Christie's skill as an actress that she conveys the distinction.

Although not universally acclaimed, since some critics felt that the film was a bit too slick and a bit too obvious, *Darling* was a critical and financial success. The film and its director were both nominated for Academy Awards, and Frederic Raphael won an Academy Award for his screenplay. The film's success is merited: *Darling* is a sharp, clear-eyed look at a woman and a life style that could resist everything but temptation.

James P. Girard

DAWN PATROL

Released: 1938
Production: Hal B. Wallis for Warner Bros.
Direction: Edmund Goulding
Screenplay: Seton I. Miller and Dan Totheroh; based on the story "Flight Commander" by John Monk Saunders and Howard Hawks
Cinematography: Tony Gaudio
Editing: Ralph Dawson
Running time: 107 minutes

Principal characters:
Captain Courtney .... Errol Flynn
Lieutenant Scott .... David Niven
Major Brand .... Basil Rathbone
Phipps .... Donald Crisp

War is "a great big stupid game," an insane fact of life; but perhaps a man may find meaning in his life by the way in which he faces death. This is the view expressed in the 1930 Howard Hawks film *The Dawn Patrol.* When Warner Bros. decided to remake this cinema classic in 1938, the philosophical slant remained the same, and, although dialogue was revised and an all-British cast was selected, the original was faithfully repeated in all other respects; even the spectacular flying footage of the earlier film was used in the remake. Both versions are excellent films, but the 1938 production has the advantage that Errol Flynn and David Niven play the doomed comrades.

The 59th Squadron of the British Royal Flying Corps is in France in 1915. With obsolete equipment, this undermanned squadron confronts a superior force of German flyers led by ace pilot, Richter. Captain Courtney (Errol Flynn) is the flamboyant and courageous leader of "A" Flight, supported by his friend, Lieutenant Scott (David Niven). We see their great affection for each other when Scott is shot down while attempting to aid another pilot in trouble. As Courtney grieves for his friend, Scott appears, drunk and waving champagne bottles, to turn his wake into a victory celebration. Sophomoric pranks and joyful drinking bouts add to the lighthearted tone which dominates the early scenes.

Flynn and Niven are very effective as the dashing comrades Courtney and Scott. They exhibit a sincere friendship and regard for each other that is impossible to doubt, and Niven displays a particular charm as the tipsy, irreverent Scott. However, the warmth and humor of these scenes is played against a menacing backdrop. Brandy and soda are liberally dispensed in the officers' club bar, and the flyers drink while the names of their dead comrades are struck from the roster and a phonograph plays "Poor Butterfly."

While this sense of doom begins to shadow every scene on the ground, the air battles continue as exhausted men risk their lives in patched-up aircraft. The flying sequences in the *Dawn Patrol* remain breathtaking even today. Diving and spinning, the vintage fighters engage in dogfights above a peaceful countryside. Close-ups of Niven and Flynn were intergrated into the original footage, and the result is a beautiful, flawless piece of filmmaking.

Basil Rathbone plays the unsympathetic role of Major Brand, Squadron Commander. It is he who must send young men up to die, unable to furnish them with sufficient training or adequate equipment. We first view Brand as a rather stern headmaster trying to curb the undergraduate antics of Courtney and Scott. When they disobey orders and fly off in a daring raid on the German command post, he upbraids them with a vehemence that seems unnecessary. But Brand is a man on the verge of cracking. His voice breaks as he agonizes to Phipps, his *aide-de-camp*, "It's a slaughterhouse, that's what it is, and I'm the executioner." The edge of hysteria in Rathbone's performance prepares us for what happens to Courtney when he assumes command of the squadron. Brand takes an insane delight in turning over command to Courtney. The captain has called him a butcher for sending untried pilots to their deaths, and now Brand fairly gloats over the prospect of Courtney having that responsibility.

The captain is a commander now. No longer Scott's devil-may-care drinking companion, he drinks alone as his nerve buckles under the weight of his responsibilities. Donald Crisp as Phipps watches the change, displaying a marvelous sympathy as the older man who has seen it all before.

Faced with the chronic shortage of manpower, Courtney must order Scott's inexperienced younger brother into action. The boy is killed and the friends argue bitterly. The shift in mood from gallant gaiety to agonized despair brings the futility of war, especially this war, into sharp relief. Scott next volunteers for what amounts to a suicide mission, a lone attack on a German munitions dump; but before he leaves, the two old friends are reconciled over drinks. Courtney gets Scott thoroughly drunk and flies the mission himself. In a spectacular action sequence he blows up the munitions dump but is shot down and killed by Richter. It is left to Scott to assume the burdens of command.

The futility expressed in the *Dawn Patrol* is matched only by its fatalism. The flyers sing as they stand in the bar:

> So stand by your glasses steady.
> This world is a world of lies.
> Here's to the dead already—
> Hurrah for the next man who dies!

Cheryl Karnes

DAYS OF WINE AND ROSES

Released: 1962
Production: Martin Manulis for Warner Bros.
Direction: Blake Edwards
Screenplay: J P Miller; based on his teleplay of the same name
Cinematography: Philip H. Lathrop
Editing: Patrick McCormack
Art direction: Joseph Wright; set decoration, George James Hopkins
Song: Henry Mancini and Johnny Mercer, "Days of Wine and Roses" (AA)
Running time: 117 minutes

> *Principal characters:*
> Joe Clay ....Jack Lemmon
> Kirsten Arnesen Clay ....Lee Remick
> Ellis Arnesen ....Charles Bickford
> Debbie Clay ....Debbie Megowan
> Jim Hungerford .... Jack Klugman

Days of Wine and Roses, a Martin Manulis production for Warner Bros., is the most graphic and sensitive film treatment of the subject of alcoholism since the inspired performances given by Ray Milland in *The Lost Weekend* (1945), and by Burt Lancaster and Shirley Booth in *Come Back Little Sheba* (1952). Manulis, well-known for his production of the outstanding television shows *Climax* and *Playhouse 90*, hired Blake Edwards to direct the film version of J P Miller's highly acclaimed television drama. Edwards, a top television and motion picture director, was responsible for the creation of the *Peter Gunn* and *Mr. Lucky* series for television, and his film credits include *Operation Petticoat* (1959) and *Breakfast at Tiffany's* (1961). Miller's powerful drama tells the story of Joe Clay (Jack Lemmon) and Kirsten Arnesen (Lee Remick), who, while very much in love, also share an irresistible attraction to alcohol. Under Edwards' sensitive and taut direction, the film compassionately yet honestly follows the couple's gradual decline into alcoholism, and it is with mounting anxiety and increased involvement that the audience watches the pair struggle to work out their problem.

The story is set in San Francisco, which is captured in all its diverse beauty through Philip H. Lathrop's cinematography. The opening scene of the film takes place in a San Francisco bar where Joe Clay, a hard-drinking public relations man, is busy plying his trade. A very important friend of Joe's client, Prince Aben el Sud, is holding a party aboard the Prince's yacht, and, as the Prince's public relations man, it is Joe's job to stock the party with beautiful girls. Lemmon is entirely believable as the fast-talking, hard-drinking, slightly cynical Joe; he brings the character alive as a competitive individual suffering from the unhealthy stress brought to bear on him by society's complex business structure. Joe meets Kirsten Arnesen at the party aboard the Prince's yacht. This first encounter is a disaster for Joe, who, muddled by too much alcohol, mistakes Kirsten, who is actually the client's secretary, for one of the party girls he has invited. Lee Remick plays Kirsten as a wholesome, assertive woman who is tinged with a certain sadness that makes her both appealing and memorable. In an effort to atone for his blunder, Joe visits Kirsten at her office and begs to make amends by taking her to dinner. The couple's future is foreshadowed during their first date, when Joe induces Kirsten, a chocolate addict, to try her first drink, a chocolate Brandy Alexander. It is not long before Kirsten loses her initial distaste for alcohol and learns to appreciate the feeling of well-being that it instills.

We first meet Kirsten's father, Ellis Arnesen (Charles Bickford), when the exuberant young couple arrive at his home late one night to break the news that they were married that evening. Bickford, who is a fine actor, is given a rather ambiguous role in this film. His initially impassive reaction to Joe and Kirsten's marriage seems to be more a device to advance the plot than anything else. Later he helps them, but again he is not important *per se*, but merely because he causes them to act.

Joe and Kirsten's slide into alcoholism is barely perceptible at first, since the couple has a fashionable apartment on Pacific Street, a beautiful baby daughter, and a mutual love and concern for each other. After eight years have passed, however, Joe and Kirsten have become totally dependent on alcohol, and their world is disintegrating rapidly. Joe's career is floundering after having lost half a dozen jobs because of his drinking; and Kirsten has embraced alcohol with the same zeal she had previously shown for life. The story has the mood of relentless inevitability as Joe and Kirsten's marriage begins to fall apart, their child becomes neglected and withdrawn, and they are reduced to living in the slums. Particularly in this portion of the film, Lemmon (as did Burt Lancaster in 1952's *Come Back Little Sheba*) displays a depth and range of emotion unequaled in his previous acting experience; he is at all times entirely believable, and compels a profound involvement on the part of the audience. Remick, likewise, shows how Kirsten can sink to the depths of despair and degradation while still maintaining some last vestige of misplaced pride and integrity, thus making her condition all the more heartbreaking. Edwards' direction is at times brilliant, for he develops the full potential of Miller's story without preaching or resorting to clichés.

In a desperate attempt to save themselves, the couple moves in with Kirsten's father at his nursery, and, after a few weeks of abstinence and hard work, they appear healthy once again. Joe, however, convincing himself that he has gained back his self-control, sneaks two pints of whiskey into his and Kirsten's room. After the two bottles are finished, Joe goes in search of a bottle he had hidden in the greenhouse. His brain fogged by alcohol, he is unable to remember its exact location, and growing more distraught and violent by the minute, he practically destroys the greenhouse in his search. Following his total collapse, Joe is placed in the violent ward of a hospital where, through his befuddled brain and physical agony, he begins to realize the depths to which he has fallen. In this hospital scene, Lemmon gives one of the most demanding performances of his acting career; his intensity is almost terrifying. After his physical torment subsides, Joe meets Jim Hungerford (Jack Klugman), who offers him help through Alcoholics Anonymous. Having finally faced the reality of his condition, Joe attends one of the group's meetings. Kirsten, however, refuses to accompany him, adamantly denying that she is an alcoholic. When Joe returns from the meeting, Kirsten is gone.

Through Jim's continued support and encouragement, Joe begins a tenuous journey to recovery; and, while holding down a full-time job, he also takes on the responsibility of his daughter Debbie (Debbie Megowan), giving her the care and love she has lacked for so long. Almost a year later, Kirsten appears at Joe's apartment, pleading to be taken back. Much to his dismay, however, she still refuses to admit she is an alcoholic and informs him that she could never stop drinking entirely. He knows he can never take her back under her conditions, although for one moment as she turns to leave, his love for her nearly destroys his resolve. The final scene of the film shows Joe looking at Kirsten through his window after telling their daughter that someday perhaps she will return.

The Days of Wine and Roses, while presenting a poignant love story with great emotional impact, also makes an enlightened and compelling statement about alcoholism. The film received six Academy Award nominations: for Best Actor, Best Actress, Best Art Direction, Best Set Decoration, Best Costume Design, and Best Song. Henry Mancini and Johnny Mercer went on to receive the Academy Award for Best Song. In addition to being a great film, *Days of Wine and Roses* had an accelerating effect on the careers of its principal characters. Jack Lemmon went on to star in such diverse films as *Save the Tiger* (1973), for which he received an Academy Award, *The Front Page* (1974), and, more recently, *The China Syndrome* (1979). Lee Remick has given fine performances in a number of films including *Hallelujah Trail* (1965) and *The Europeans* (1979). Jack Klugman gravitated to television and earned an Emmy award in 1971 and 1973 for his costarring role in *The Odd Couple*. Charles Bickford, whose film career spanned nearly forty years, acted in only one more film, *A Big Hand for the Little Lady* (1966), before his death in 1967.

D. Gail Huskins

DEATH OF A SALESMAN

Released: 1952
Production: Stanley Kramer for Columbia
Direction: Laslo Benedek
Screenplay: Stanley Roberts; based on the play of the same name by Arthur Miller
Cinematography: Franz Planer
Editing: William A. Lyon
Running time: 115 minutes

Principal characters:
Willy Loman	Fredric March
Linda Loman	Mildred Dunnock
Biff	Kevin McCarthy
Happy	Cameron Mitchell
Charley	Howard Smith
Ben	Royal Beal

Arthur Miller's *Death of a Salesman* is frequently regarded as the best modern American tragedy, although it is not a Classical tragedy because its hero does not suffer a fall from grace. In fact, its protagonist is no hero in the usual sense of the word, nor is he a man who has ever achieved greatness or a state of grace in any aspect of his life.

Willy Loman (Fredric March) is a pathetic traveling salesman who has spent his life worshiping success and popularity, a man living a life of delusion and never really facing up to reality. But the key to Willy is that he is a human being to whom we respond with compassion because the fate he suffers touches us all. *Death of a Salesman* is an indictment of the American economic system which rates the individual only by what he has achieved, or how much money he has made, and then tosses him aside just like any other dispensable commodity when he can no longer produce at peak level.

Miller's play opened at the Morosco Theatre in New York City on February 10, 1949, starred Lee J. Cobb, and ran for 742 performances. It became one of the most praised and honored of American plays, winning almost every award available: the Pulitzer Prize, the New York Drama Circle Critics Award, the Theatre Club's Gold Medal, the Newspaper Guild's Front Page Award, the Donaldson Award, and the Antoinette Perry (Tony) Award as best drama of the year.

In translating the play to the screen, producer Stanley Kramer, director Laslo Benedek, and screenwriter Stanley Roberts made every effort to remain faithful to the original. Those changes that were necessary were achieved without cinematic tricks. For many, the screen version is regarded as better than the stage play, largely because of the strong sense of intuition and humanity brought to the role of Willy Loman by Fredric March.

Willy Loman is a man in his early sixties who has spent his life as a traveling salesman covering the New England territory. Selling has been the all-consuming passion of his life, and success and popularity are his gods. What Willy cannot admit is that he has never been very good at his job, and time and life have passed him by. He has never faced up to the reality of life; in fact, his "tragedy" is that his life has been wasted on delusions of success. He has always been a braggart who was determined to be well-liked. His philosophy of selling was based on false hopes and appearances: "It's not what you say, it's how you say it—personality always wins the day. Start big and you'll end up big. It's important not only to be liked, but to be well-liked."

In his prime, a good week in New England meant one hundred dollars but there are no more good weeks and Willy's world is closing in on him. Miller has constructed the play as if Willy is trapped in the prison he has built around himself. This same sense of claustrophobia is maintained brilliantly in the film. He is now sixty-three and at the end of his tether. He is a mentally tired and physically exhausted man with thirty years of frustration behind him and nothing to which he can look forward. He is often confused, and his mind frequently wanders back to the "good old days." He is unable to drive his car, and not to drive is not to sell. When he seeks a transfer to his company's New York office, Willy is fired. He is no longer useful in the competitive business world and is as dispensable as the wares he has sold for thirty years.

Miller wrote the play using a series of flashbacks in Willy's memory to illustrate his past life. As his past unravels before us through his reveries, we see that Willy's ambitions have eroded all of his personal relationships. He has one good friend, Charley (Howard Smith), who now looks at him with pity. His life of deceit and mediocrity has undermined his relationship with his two grown sons, who are disappointments to their father.

The older son, Biff (Kevin McCarthy), has become a worthless drifter since he discovered his father in a hotel room with another woman years before. Though Biff has lost respect for his father, he does make an effort to force Willy to abandon the false pretenses of his life and face reality, but to no avail. The younger son, Happy (Cameron Mitchell), while fairly successful in business, is a chauvinistic womanizer who likewise fails to face reality. Willy's loyal and long-suffering wife, Linda (Mildred Dunnock), realizes that her husband's fate is sealed, but she is steadfast in her efforts to be supportive. She knows that he is only a shell of the man he once was, and that he has given up hope and wants to die.

Willy refuses an offer of a job made by his friend Charley. In one of his mental "wanderings," he listens to the advice of his dead brother, Ben (Royal Beal), and realizes that once dead, because of his twenty-thousand-dollar insurance policy, he will be worth more to his family than he is alive. Resolute that this is what fate has dealt him, Willy drives away in his car to commit suicide. Willy had bragged that his funeral would be attended by all his business colleagues and clients, attesting to his success and popularity, but the only mourner besides his family is his friend Charley, who says, "Nobody ought to blame him. A salesman has got to dream. It comes with the territory."

Death of a Salesman is a devastating portrait of the frustrations of the little man in a society that worships success. Willy is neither an attractive nor a likable man, and onstage his character was criticized for being removed from the audience, too cold to elicit sympathy. Most critics agree that in the film version, Fredric March's inner resources as an actor reveal an understanding of Willy far beyond that delineated by the script.

March is regarded by many as America's finest screen actor. Romano Tozzi wrote in *Films in Review* in 1958: "The essence of March's excellence is his integrity. He is a skilled craftsman, is blessed with an exceptionally fine speaking voice, and is a well-informed and intelligent man. But beyond these priceless assets is the more valuable one of sincerity." Many admirers consider March's portrayal of Willy Loman as the crowning achievement of his remarkable career, although his performance failed to capture an Academy Award.

In addition to March's performance in *Death of a Salesman*, the other performances were also first-rate. Cameron Mitchell as Happy and Howard Smith as Charley had come from the Broadway version, and Kevin McCarthy as Biff gives an impressive performance as the older son. The wonderful Mildred Dunnock, also from the stage version, gives as luminous and subtle a performance as any on the screen that year. She is an actress of merit whose talent has rarely been utilized to the fullest on film.

In bringing the play to the screen, Laslo Benedek took Willy's "wanderings" and turned them into internal monologues. These transitions in time and place suited the film medium perfectly, and the film is strengthened by presenting these as realistic rather than dream sequences. Though not often seen on television or in revival houses, this screen version of *Death of a Salesman* remains one of the best film adaptations of an American stage play, and Fredric March's acting ranks with the best.

Ronald Bowers

DEATH TAKES A HOLIDAY

Released: 1934
Production: E. Lloyd Sheldon for Paramount
Direction: Mitchell Leisen
Screenplay: Maxwell Anderson, Gladys Lehman, and Walter Ferris; based on the play of the same name by Alberto Casella, adapted from the Italian by Walter Ferris
Cinematography: Charles Lang
Editing: no listing
Art direction: Ernst Fegte
Costume design: Travis Banton and Edith Head
Running time: 78 minutes

Principal characters:
Prince Sirki .... Fredric March
Grazia .... Evelyn Venable
Duke Lambert .... Sir Guy Standing
Alda .... Katherine Alexander
Rhoda .... Gail Patrick

Speculations about death and the prospects of the hereafter had already been popular subjects for the theater by the time motion pictures came into being at the beginning of the twentieth century. Some of the earliest films made in the United States and Europe continued this line of thought, utilizing crude double exposure techniques to create ghosts. By the mid-1930's, when horror movies such as *Dracula* (1931) had presented a terrifying view of the afterlife, Mitchell Leisen's film *Death Takes a Holiday* was unique in that it presented a view of death which was reasonable and ultimately comforting.

The script by Maxwell Anderson, Gladys Lehman, and Walter Ferris closely followed the story line of Anderson's popular play of the same title, which in turn had been derived from an old play by Alberto Casella. The story begins as Duke Lambert (Sir Guy Standing) and his various house guests return to Lambert's palazzo after a happy afternoon's drive to await the arrival of another guest, Prince Sirki (Fredric March). One member of the party, the Princess Grazia (Evelyn Venable), seems oblivious to the merriment of the others. Walking out into the garden, she feels an indescribable sensation pass over her and she faints. The others take her inside, and when she is revived, she cannot explain what happened. "An icy wind seemed to touch me, only it wasn't a wind," she says.

Late that night as he is putting out the lights, Duke Lambert is confronted with a black apparition. The apparition gradually becomes more opaque until it assumes the human form of the long-awaited Prince Sirki, who has actually just died. The Duke attempts to shoot the apparition with his gun but without effect. It reveals that it is Death, come to earth in the guise of the handsome Prince Sirki to try to discover why humanity fears him so and to learn what earthly pleasures could be so great as to cause a desire to prolong life. Hearing the shots, the alarmed guests come downstairs and are introduced to the strange Prince Sirki. Only the radiant Grazia is unafraid of him.

For the next three days, as Death takes his "holiday," no person, animal, or plant on earth dies. Death enjoys all earthly pleasures: the life of luxury in the Duke's palazzo, constant winnings at the race track and in the casino, and the attentions of two seductive women (Gail Patrick and Katherine Alexander). Despite all this, he fails to find any quality in human life as profound as death.

At the end of the third day, the Duke throws a lavish party. As his time on earth draws to a close, Death lets his true identity become more and more obvious, and the two seductive women run in terror as they begin to perceive it. Only Grazia remains unafraid of Sirki, and quietly they slip into the garden where their love is consummated.

Returning, they console Grazia's terrified mother and the other party guests. As the clock strikes twelve, Death relinquishes his human form and once again becomes the black apparition. He tells Grazia, "Now you see me as I really am," and she replies, "I've always seen you that way. I love you." His final statement is, "Now I know that Love is stronger than Death," and Grazia joins him. As they disappear, a breeze scatters newly fallen leaves across their path. Death's holiday is over.

A mood piece depending on a careful mixture of sentimentality, sophistication, and complex visual imagery as a background for the intricate drama, *Death Takes a Holiday* was an assignment tailor-made for Mitchell Leisen. Having risen through the ranks as costume designer and art director for many Cecil B. De Mille productions, and later serving as associate director on *The Sign of the Cross* (1932), *Tonight Is Ours* (1933), and *The Eagle and the Hawk* (1933), all of which starred Fredric March, Leisen had a broad background in many phases of the motion picture business. His first solo directorial effort, a religious story entitled *Cradle Song* (1933), proved to Paramount that he could handle serious story material with taste and sensitivity. When *Cradle Song* was released while *Death Takes a Holiday* was in production, its success with the critics and at the box office confirmed the faith the studio had in its new director.

Leisen had already undergone eight years of psychoanalysis when he started the film, and this experience helped him when Maxwell Anderson said he worried that he had never found a motivation for Grazia's inexplicable behavior in following Death. Leisen later recalled, "I said to Max, 'She simply does not want to live; just take the attitude that she has gone out into the garden and caught pneumonia and does not have the will to live.' "

Leisen and the writers agreed to retain the existentialistic viewpoint of the play. Although it takes place in Spain, there is no mention of Catholicism except for a brief moment in the opening sequence when Grazia is seen praying in a cathedral. The hereafter to which she goes is not that of the traditional Christian heaven, but rather a simple state of peace and quiet.

The casting of all the leading roles was very fortunate. Fredric March's theatrical style of delivery undermined some of his roles, but is perfectly appropriate for Death, whose inexperience in behaving like a human causes him to overact somewhat. Evelyn Venable's interpretation of the difficult role of Grazia is sublime. It was only her second screen part (the first had been *Cradle Song*). In person she was vivacious, robust, and almost as large as March, but Leisen was able to elicit from her a dreamy, ethereal quality which made Grazia believable. *Death Takes a Holiday*'s first preview was held in Pasadena while Venable was working on *David Harum*, and she invited the whole *David Harum* company to attend the preview with her. Hal Mohr, the cinematographer on *David Harum*, would later remember, "I thought she was a cute kid, but I never paid much attention to her until I saw her coming down the stairs to meet Grazia for the first time and that was it, I really fell." Venable and Mohr were married, and she retired from the screen. Leisen decided to cast Kent Taylor as Grazia's fiancé, Corrado, because he resembled Fredric March.

Paramount executives were afraid of releasing a film with the word "death" in the title, so they arranged for a one-week test run in Fresno, California, under the alternative title, *Strange Holiday*. Then they ran it in Sacramento for a week under the original title, and did much greater business, so that the title *Death Takes a Holiday* was retained. The film opened in March, 1934, to excellent reviews and box-office success. *Photoplay* wrote, ". . . this picture is an experience no intelligent person should miss. "We were right behind Mae West," Mitchell Leisen would later recall proudly.

David Chierichetti

THE DEER HUNTER

Released: 1978
Production: John Peverall for EMI Films; released by Universal (AA)
Direction: Michael Cimino (AA)
Screenplay: Deric Washburn; based on a story by Michael Cimino, Deric Washburn, Louis Garfinkle, and Quinn K. Redeker
Cinematography: Vilmos Zsigmond
Editing: Peter Zinner (AA)
Sound: Richard Portman, William McCaughey, Aaron Rochin, and Darin Knight (AA)
Running time: 180 minutes

Principal characters:
Michael .... Robert De Niro
Nick .... Christopher Walken (AA)
Steven .... John Savage
Stan .... John Cazale
Linda .... Meryl Streep
Axel .... Chuck Aspegren

In a year that was in many ways dominated by quality cinematic reflections of the war in Vietnam such as *Coming Home* and *Go Tell the Spartans*, *The Deer Hunter* won two of the most prestigious and coveted awards of 1978: the New York Film Critics' Circle Award for best English-language film of the year and the Academy Award for the Best Picture of the Year. Among the film's four other Academy Awards was one given to Michael Cimino for Best Director.

The film is epic in scope. Unlike *Coming Home*, in which the war takes place offscreen, and in which we are shown relatively little of the protagonists' lives before they begin to be affected by Vietnam, Cimino in *The Deer Hunter* provides the audience with a substantial amount of detail about his characters' lives both before they go to war and during combat, as well as about their lives in the aftermath of the war. The result is a long film that occasionally seems to lose its way, particularly during the first third, in which Cimino concentrates on character development at the expense of furthering the plot. Once the action moves to Vietnam, however, *The Deer Hunter* becomes a taut, compelling narrative in which Cimino is able to reveal the purgative as well as the destructive effects of war at its worst.

The Deer Hunter is a film of metaphors and images, and opens with an image that is to recur frequently—an awesome blast of fire. In the film's Vietnam sequences, fire signifies destruction and terror; at the beginning, however, the image is less malignant. The flames come from a blast furnace

in the Pennsylvania steel mill in which the film's Ukrainian-American protagonists work. This is the last day on the job for Michael (Robert De Niro),
Nick (Christopher Walken), and Steven (John Savage). Steven is to be married, and all three are soon to be sent to Vietnam.

As they leave work, the three men, accompanied by their friends Stan
(John Cazale) and Axel, head for their neighborhood bar. Cimino demonstrates the camaraderie and affection the men have for one another as they
sing along with Frankie Valli on the jukebox, engage in boisterous banter,
shoot pool, and down endless bottles of beer. For the most part these are
simple, uncomplicated men who clearly revel in one another's company. The
only hint of discomfort is provided, not by the imminent departure of three
of them, but by Steven's impending marriage, which threatens to interfere
with a farewell deer hunt that Michael has suggested.

As they dress for the wedding, Michael and Nick discuss deer hunting.
Nick enjoys the aesthetic aspects of the hunt—the mountains and the trees.
Michael, on the other hand, is the complete hunter and takes pains to impart
his philosophy to Nick: the deer must be killed "with one shot," he emphasizes, "one shot."

Michael, the eldest of his group and its natural leader, is, however, painfully
shy and inarticulate around women. Cimino first reveals this side of Michael's
personality at Steven's wedding reception. All of his companions are paired
off with their girl friends, but Michael stands alone at the bar drinking beer.
He is clearly infatuated with Nick's girl friend Linda (Meryl Streep), but
cannot bring himself to do more than offer her beer and lurch hesitantly in
her direction.

The wedding reception and its aftermath, which are depicted in seemingly
endless scenes that could have been shortened without damaging the film in
the least, bring out complicated emotions in the three friends. Steven is
confused and unhappy because Angela, his bride, is pregnant by another
man. The normally inhibited Michael, affected by both the emotion of the
occasion and the vast quantity of beer he has consumed, responds by shedding
his clothes and running alongside the wedding party. Nick is forced to
acknowledge that he loves his hometown, and makes Michael promise that
he will bring his body back to Pennsylvania should he die in Vietnam.

Michael leads his friends on a deer hunt before going overseas. Although
the hunt is successful, Michael is unhappy because the others refuse to take
the endeavor seriously. To Michael, deer hunting is almost a religious rite,
and he appears to respect his quarry more than he does his friends. At this
point in the film, however, he does not respect the deer enough to spare its
life. As evidenced by its title, the film's central metaphor is the deer hunt,
and Michael is "the Deer Hunter." He soon learns, however, what it is like
to be the game rather than the hunter.

In another blaze of fire, this time rockets, grenades, and flame throwers, the scene shifts to Vietnam. An American unit, including Michael, Nick, and Steven, has been captured by the Viet Cong, who use their prisoners in a bizarre and deadly form of entertainment. The captives are forced to play Russian roulette while their brutal captors wager on who will be the first to die. Cimino directs the scene with a sure hand, and the effect is riveting. The terror and the tension snap something inside both Steven, who eventually recovers, and Nick, who never does; but they bring out the best in Michael, who persuades his captors to put not one but three bullets in the gun, which he then uses on them. The scene is graphic without being sensational. The real violence is that of the spirit—the look on the faces of the sadistically portrayed Viet Cong is far more horrifying than the sight of spurting blood.

The three men escape, but are soon separated. Nick is taken to a hospital in Saigon where he begins to put himself together after his ordeal. He roams the streets in search of his friends, and, hearing the sound of gunfire, discovers that he has stumbled onto a civilian version of the Russian roulette game he endured as a POW. Willing contestants play against one another for a share of the gambling proceeds. Ironically, one of the spectators at the game is Michael, although Nick does not see him. As all of the horror of his own captivity floods back into his mind, Nick snatches a revolver, puts it to his head, and pulls the trigger. The chamber is empty, but something within Nick snaps again, this time for good. He staggers from the room and is taken in tow by the game's proprietor, who promises to make him rich by entering him as a contestant in the suicidal "sport." Michael pursues, but is unable to overtake the pair.

The film follows Michael back to Pennsylvania. He is clearly a changed man. He avoids a welcome home party arranged by his friends, choosing instead to visit Linda, whose picture he has carried throughout the war. She is glad to see him, but the thought of Nick, coupled with Michael's natural reticence, makes communication awkward. They continue seeing each other, however, and Linda finally suggests that they go to bed to "comfort each other." Michael does not want to lose Linda, but he cannot bring himself to respond to her. In addition, he learns that Steven is somewhere in town, although his exact whereabouts is unknown. Michael cannot bring himself to seek out his friend. Cimino thus paints a picture of a man tied in knots by his own suppressed emotions.

That knot is untied during the film's second symbolic deer hunt. While his friends carouse, Michael stalks a magnificent buck. When he gets the animal in his sights, however, he deliberately aims high and fires. "OK?" he shouts, "OK?" It is both a question and an affirmation. Having been both the hunter and the hunted, he discovers within himself the strength *not* to kill. This discovery unlocks a number of doors for Michael. He is able to make love to Linda, and he contacts Steven, who is in a local veteran's hospital, having lost an arm and both legs to the war. He persuades the reluctant Steven to rejoin his family, and, remembering his promise, returns to Vietnam to reclaim his friend Nick.

The next sequences, set in Vietnam, are the most effective and the most harrowing of the film. It is mid-1975, and Vietnam is about to fall to the Communists. Michael arrives in Saigon amid the desperate eleventh-hour attempts of most to flee the country. Overloaded helicopters buck and crash to the ground, and terrified would-be refugees stage full-scale riots as they attempt to board anything moving out of the city. Fires burn out of control, and the river itself seems to be aflame.

Michael locates Nick at the gambling house where the Russian roulette game still flourishes even as the city disintegrates. He attempts to persuade Nick to leave with him, but Nick's eyes are blank; he has spent two years staring death in the face, and he no longer recognizes his best friend. Desperate, Michael buys his way into the game. He will risk suicide to shock Nick back to his senses. As the wrenching tension mounts, both men raise the gun to their heads and pull the trigger. Both survive the first round. As an extra bullet is added to the gun before Nick's next turn, Michael asks Nick to remember their deer hunts in the mountains. Nick smiles in recognition. "One shot," he recalls. He puts the gun to his temple and kills himself.

The film concludes back in Pennsylvania after Nick's funeral. His friends gather in their favorite bar. Though Nick's death grieves them, it seems to signal the end of their ordeal. Steven is reconciled with Angela, and Michael and Linda are together. After an awkward silence, someone begins to hum "God Bless America," and everyone joins in, bringing the film to a close. By ending the film in this way, Cimino reaffirms the sense of community that has pervaded the entire story. Together, they have survived.

Cimino draws first-rate performances from virtually every member of the cast. Christopher Walken won an Academy Award as Best Supporting Actor for his portrayal of Nick, and the performances of John Savage and John Cazale are on a par with Walken's. Walken's transformation of Nick from a bright, sensitive young man into a compulsively suicidal zombie is as convincing as it is horrifying. Savage brings a mixture of nervous energy and sweetness to the character of Steven; and Cazale plays Stan much as he did the part of Fredo Corleone in *The Godfather, Part II* (1974)—as a basically weak man given to macho posturing as compensation. Meryl Streep is likewise excellent as Linda, the film's only major female character. Linda is an island of sanity amidst the physical and psychic chaos of the film.

The Deer Hunter, however, is anchored by the performance of Robert De Niro. His portrayal of Michael is a masterpiece of subtlety and understatement. The dialogue he is given is spare; even more than the rest of the characters in the film, Michael is inarticulate. De Niro compensates by acting with his face—he has never been as expressive. From his explosive rage at his Vietnamese captors to the tenderness he exhibits towards Linda and Nick,

De Niro's performance is flawless.

The film itself, however, is not without flaws, primarily in the first third, which tends to drag. Cimino seems to enjoy the macho camaraderie and the Ukrainian wedding so much that he forgets to keep the plot moving. In addition, some critics have charged Cimino with racism, claiming that he has portrayed all Vietnamese as venal, sadistic killers, and that *The Deer Hunter* represents the Pentagon's version of the war. This is surely a misreading of the film. It was clearly never Cimino's intention to present a balanced, politically "correct" analysis of the war in Vietnam. The director has been quoted as saying that his protagonists are simply "trying to support each other. They are not endorsing anything except their common humanity—their common frailty, their need for each other." While liberals or conservatives who are in search of propaganda are bound to be disappointed in *The Deer Hunter*, viewers who are willing to settle for a gripping story directed with verve and vision and acted with skill and passion will find *The Deer Hunter* a richly rewarding cinematic experience.

Robert Mitchell

DELIVERANCE

Released: 1972
Production: John Boorman and Elmer Enterprises Films for Warner Bros.
Direction: John Boorman
Screenplay: James Dickey; based on his novel of the same name
Cinematography: Vilmos Zsigmond
Editing: Tom Priestley
Running time: 109 minutes

Principal characters:
Ed Gentry .... Jon Voight
Lewis Medlock .... Burt Reynolds
Bobby Trippe .... Ned Beatty
Drew Ballinger .... Ronny Cox
Sheriff Bullard .... James Dickey

Deliverance is, at first glance, an exciting but obvious mix of fairly standard themes: the rape of nature by "progress," the city men who find their own "heart of darkness" in the dangerous rapids, the horrifying degeneracy of backwoods folk, and the breakdown of civilized morality under survival conditions. Along with these literary themes, biblical allusions, primarily to the flood which will cleanse a sinful world, add to the first-glance impression of obvious allegory; but this impression is deceptive.

In-depth critical articles demonstrate this deceptiveness in their contradictory interpretations of the film. Some call it a "boyish adventure turned sour," others bemoan the *macho* cliches which Lewis Medlock (Burt Reynolds) both voices and stands for, while still others see a rejection of these values in Lewis' fate. Jon Voight's performance as Ed Gentry, the timid but curious city-dweller who eventually is thrust into a leadership role, elicited particularly diverse comment. Some praised his convincing transformation, others found his mild-mannered personality hard to believe. Actually, this early part of his performance is compromised by too-obvious symbols: he clutches a pipe in his teeth in awkward moments and is given ridiculous lines which ring hollow even when he is supposed to be drunk. Worst of all, he continues to treat the brutally sadistic mountain men who torment him and Bobby Trippe (Ned Beatty) like fellow board members, repeating "Gentlemen, there must be some misunderstanding" long after it is an appropriate response. The very diversity of serious reactions to *Deliverance* indicates its strongest quality: it remains a richly ambiguous film from viewing to viewing.

Deliverance won five major prizes at the Fifth Annual Atlanta Film Festival and was nominated for three Academy Awards: Best Picture, Best Direction, and Best Editing. Adapted by James Dickey from his critically successful novel, the story concerns four city men who decide to canoe down the Cahulawassee River, which is about to be flooded in a "progressive" measure to dam the river and put the entire area at the bottom of a lake. Lewis is the *machismo*-driven leader of the group who wants the "machines and the system to break down," leaving only "survival." Bobby is an overweight salesman, and Drew Ballinger (Ronnie Cox) is a gentle, decent, guitar-playing soul who is least able to cope with the events of their odyssey.

The four men first have to deal with the mountain folk to hire someone to drive their cars down to their landing point, and their different reactions are clues to their characters. Bobby finds the people repulsive in their genetic inbreeding; Drew makes musical contact with a seemingly retarded boy in the film's famous "dueling banjoes" sequence; Lewis bargains with the men; and Ed looks on, curious but uninvolved.

Once on the river, the men experience the exuberant thrill of the wild rapids, and camp at night in boozy comradeship. The next day Ed and Bobby stop in the thick wilderness and are attacked by two degenerate mountain men. Ed is tied while one rapes Bobby, then just as the other prepares to force Ed to perform fellatio on him, Lewis shoots an arrow through the first man with his powerful bow. The four argue over what they should do next: Lewis urges that they bury the body, while Drew thinks they should take it with them and report the incident to the police. Lewis wins out, and they bury the man, whose outstretched arm will not willingly stay underground.

They leave in a near panic, and a shaken Drew fails to put his lifejacket on. Just before they reach the dangerous rapids, Drew falls (or jumps) overboard, and in the ensuing confusion, both canoes capsize and the men are swept down the rocky rapids. Lewis' leg is badly broken, and Drew, the audience learns later, is killed. Thinking that Drew was shot by the murdered rapist's companion, Ed scales the difficult cliff and kills the man he finds there. Similar to the question of whether Drew was actually shot, the certainty of the second man's identity is not clear. The three men continue on to town, where Sheriff Bullard (James Dickey) does not quite believe their story but lets them go, telling them never to do anything like this again, and not to return. At home in bed with his wife, Ed wakes in fear at his dream of a stiff hand breaking through the smooth surface of the lake.

Ambiguities abound. Is man raping the river by damming it, as Lewis claims in his voice-over at the beginning of the film, or is the flood represented by the lake cleansing the evil of the town? Is the virgin river and dense wilderness surrounding it pure and ennobling or evil? Are the backwoods people an affront to nature in their genetic deficiencies, or do they only appear horrible from the city men's point of view? Who is innocent? Some reviewers called the poverty-stricken natives "simpletons," but we have to agree with the man who tells the four, "you don't know nothin'" in response to their plan to canoe down the river. When asked why they are doing it, Lewis answers, "Because it's there," and a mountain man sensibly replies:

"It's there alright. You get in there and can't get out, you gonna wish it wasn't."

The teasing homosexual quality of Ed and Lewis' relationship is restricted almost entirely to visual elements in the film (it is more extensive in the book), although Lewis does pointedly ask Ed why he comes on these trips with him. Lewis is photographed sensuously, especially from Ed's point of view. The homosexual element is another flirtation for Ed and Lewis, just as is the danger of the river. The men seem titillated by the possibilities, until both sexual and danger attractions turn ugly as they become real during the rape and the later injuries and death. Special mention must be made of the rape scene, which is one of the most honest rape sequences ever filmed. Neither character involved is attractive, so that perverse erotic appeal does not exist. Instead of being sexy, the rape is violent, repulsive, humiliating, and ugly. No attempt is made to glamorize it; actors and filmmakers are to be congratulated for showing the true nature of this violent act that so much fiction makes attractive.

During Ed's transformation from a passive observer to a man of action, his voyeurism, a central element of his character, is destroyed. He is forced to watch Bobby's rape, then to see his hero Lewis nearly helpless after his leg is injured. Ed, who earlier could not shoot a deer, kills a man. The change in him is a key to the title of the film; but here too is fertile ambiguity. Is Ed "delivered," and if so, from what state and to what state? He has become a killer, a leader, a man of responsibility and of guilt. His deliverance is from naïveté, security, and innocence to liberating yet incriminating responsibility. Never again will any of the men see "civilization" and "nature" as simple dichotomies. They came looking for momentary deliverance from boredom, tame technology, and security, but found the necessary correlative to what they were seeking: deliverance from comfort and from innocence into complexity. The mountain men who daily face the "survival" conditions Lewis romantically longs for are not ennobled, but rather become sadistic brutes. The river is not a symbol for virgin purity or for degeneracy; it is a potent force which can push men farther in the direction in which they are already headed.

The visual style of *Deliverance* is a major factor in the rich ambiguity the film poses. Under extremely difficult conditions, the film was shot in sequence (an unusual and expensive method), using U.S. Navy Underwater Demolition team rafts outfitted with cameras. Director of cinematography Vilmos Zsigmond used long lenses to keep characters in close-up, abstracting them from their environment. There are extremely long takes throughout the film, unusual for such fast action, which create an impression of a sensuous, dreamy flow. The intimacy of close-ups and tight frame also gives the film an impressive immediacy, seeming to draw the viewer right into the river.

Deliverance is an excellent example of Hollywood's "new wave" of location shooting. The mix of literary themes and realistic visual style is particularly fruitful when easy answers are refused, and the complex tangle of causes and effects are left up to the viewer to unravel.

Janey Place

DESTRY RIDES AGAIN

Released: 1939
Production: Joe Pasternak for Universal
Direction: George Marshall
Screenplay: Felix Jackson, Gertrude Purcell, and Henry Myers; based on Felix Jackson's screen story, adapted from the novel of the same name by Max Brand
Cinematography: Hal Mohr
Editing: Milton Carruth
Running time: 94 minutes

Principal characters:
Frenchy	Marlene Dietrich
Tom Destry, Jr.	James Stewart
Washington Dimsdale	Charles Winninger
Boris Callahan	Mischa Auer
Kent	Brian Donlevy
Lily Belle Callahan	Una Merkel
Judge Slade	Samuel S. Hinds

A brisk comedy-Western, *Destry Rides Again* successfully combines laughter and action, and, because of several key decisions, the film transcends its genre. Marlene Dietrich, who usually played elegant and glamorous roles, was cast as a tawdry hostess in a saloon, and James Stewart, who had never appeared in a Western, was cast as a young lawman. The unexpected pairing of the two in a genre unfamiliar to both proved to be inspired. Dietrich and Stewart work well together, and the script, which treats the conventional Western situation with affectionate humor, allows them to display their considerable comedic abilities.

In the opening scene, the camera, moving smoothly and continuously from one part of the saloon to another, introduces all the important characters. By the time the scene ends, the situation which will confront Tom Destry (James Stewart) is completely understood. A typical brawling and lawless Western town, Bottleneck is dominated by Kent (Brian Donlevy), the owner of the Last Chance Saloon. Aided by Frenchy (Marlene Dietrich), the hostess for his saloon, he cheats at card games in order to gain control of a strip of land that will prevent ranchers from driving their herds to market unless they pay him a handsome toll for the privilege. The town's corrupt, tobacco-chewing Mayor, Judge Slade (Samuel S. Hinds), is also part of Kent's gang, but Bottleneck's sheriff is not. When he confronts Kent with evidence of his land-grab schemes, the sheriff is killed, and the venal Mayor appoints the town drunk, Washington Dimsdale (Charles Winninger), to the now-vacant office.

Wash takes his job seriously, however, and sends for Tom Destry, son of the famous but now deceased Marshall Destry under whom Wash once served as a deputy. Having prepared the townspeople for a tough lawman, Wash is embarrassed by the mild-mannered, unarmed man whom they first see holding a frilly parasol and a birdcage for a lady alighting from the stagecoach. Although Wash tells him that everyone is laughing at him, Destry shrugs and says first impressions are foolish anyway. Wash then introduces Destry to Frenchy, "the real boss of Bottleneck," but Destry barely has time to murmur politely that he "always likes to know who's boss," before Kent approaches, determined to establish his domination of Destry. He demands Destry's gun, but finds he cannot provoke a fight because Destry does not carry a gun. The crowd laughs uproariously at this lanky buffoon who does not seem to have enough spirit to stand up to Kent. Mockingly, Frenchy hands him a mop and a pail of water so that he can clean up the town.

A comic set-piece is the fight which follows between Frenchy and an angry townswoman, Lily Belle Callahan (Una Merkel), while the crowd and Kent are still laughing at Destry. Mrs. Callahan is angry because Frenchy has won the pants of her husband, Boris (Mischa Auer), in a poker game. They engage in a kicking, scratching, wrestling fight that Destry stops by pouring a pail of water over them. Furious, Frenchy begins punching, kicking, and clawing Destry, then works up to throwing glasses at him, and finally grabs a six-gun and starts shooting at him. Escaping, Destry tells her she has a "knack for making a stranger feel right at home."

Destry persuades a now-dubious Wash to swear him in as a deputy by explaining that, although his father did things the old way, he is going to do them the new way: "If you shoot it out with 'em it makes 'em heroes. Put 'em behind bars and they look little and cheap." He does not carry a gun because his father had one when he was shot in the back, which is why he believes in "law and order—without guns."

It becomes quickly apparent that Destry also believes in the educational value of storytelling. He starts each story with the words, "I once had a friend," and is seldom without an appropriate anecdote to illustrate a principle or point out a moral. His slow, sometimes exasperating drawl and his fondness for storytelling also give hot tempers time to cool and Destry time to think. Although his chief weapon in taming Bottleneck is his cool temper and sense of humor, he knows there is a time for action and does not hesitate to demonstrate his skill with a six-gun to overawe some rowdy troublemakers.

He uses his brains to trick Kent and his gang into leading Wash and Boris, whose dream has always been to become a cowboy, to the body of the murdered sheriff. He then arrests one of the gang members and sends for a federal judge to keep the crooked Mayor from trying the case. Kent's men, however, raid the jail, kill Wash, and rescue the prisoner, but Destry is saved by Frenchy, who lures him away from the jail because she does not want him killed.

Under her tough façade, Frenchy has the proverbial heart of gold, at least where Destry is concerned. She gives him her lucky rabbit's foot to carry and tries to smooth over any friction between him and Kent. Frenchy also attempts to persuade Destry to come to New Orleans to see her, but after Destry learns what has happened at the jail, he is interested only in bringing Wash's murderers to justice.

As Destry and the townsmen attack Kent and his men, who have barricaded themselves in the saloon, Frenchy desperately tries to rally the respectable women of the town to his aid. At first hostile and resentful, at her suggestion, they eventually form themselves into a band armed with pitchforks and gardening implements. Forcing themselves between the two opposing sides, they march into the saloon where they engage in hand-to-hand combat with the gang.

Destry, meanwhile, has forced his way into the saloon's second story and begins searching for Kent in the wild melee below him. As Destry descends into the surging crowd, Kent stalks him from behind. At the last moment, Frenchy sees Kent and forces her way to Destry's side, throwing her arms around him in time to take Kent's bullet in the back. Destry immediately shoots Kent, and Frenchy dies in his arms.

In the film's last sequence, Destry strolls down the street whittling industriously, accompanied by an admiring youngster who copies his drawl and other mannerisms. Our last glimpse of Destry is similar to our first; he is telling a story about marriage to an admiring young woman.

Exceptionally well-paced and well-written, *Destry Rides Again* shows director George Marshall's talent for both comedy and action, and the performances of James Stewart and Marlene Dietrich add the final polish to an almost perfect Western spoof. James Stewart as Destry is pleasant, likable, easygoing, and humorous. But underneath this mild-mannered façade is the soul of a true town-tamer, which emerges when the action requires it. His sure, deft characterization adds immeasurably to the likableness and depth of Destry.

Destry Rides Again revived Marlene Dietrich's faded film career. As Frenchy, the tough, brazen saloon singer who seems impervious to everything but Destry's charm and has a sense of humor to match his own, she has a role similar to her famous screen debut in *The Blue Angel* (1930). She sings two songs, "Little Joe" and "See What the Boys in the Back Room Will Have," with robust vitality and a twinkle in her eye in the inimitable, throaty Dietrich manner. Uncertain about the role, Dietrich took it only after being advised to do so by her mentor, director Josef von Sternberg. After *Destry Rides Again* she frequently was cast in roles that were variations on the part of Frenchy just as she had previously been cast in variations of her Sternberg-directed roles.

The achievement of *Destry Rides Again* is that it nicely balances the serious elements of the Max Brand novel from which it was adapted against the comic elements of the script to produce a film which is funny but not a burlesque. The 1954 remake, *Destry*, with Audie Murphy, is merely ordinary.

Julia Johnson

DIAL M FOR MURDER

Released: 1954
Production: Alfred Hitchcock for Warner Bros.
Direction: Alfred Hitchcock
Screenplay: Frederick Knott; based on his play of the same name
Cinematography: Robert Burks
Editing: Rudi Fehr
Running time: 105 minutes

Principal characters:
Tony Wendice .... Ray Milland
Margot Wendice .... Grace Kelly
Mark Halliday .... Robert Cummings
Inspector Hubbard .... John Williams
Captain Lesgate .... Anthony Dawson

Alfred Hitchcock, the undisputed master of suspense, retains the theatrical origins of this lovely melodrama by confining most of the action to one room. The result is an intellectual chase scene for the mind rather than the body, as the audience watches the police inspector unravel the puzzle of the keys. The success of the film rests with the sound plotting of the script, the fine pacing, and the cinematography. Since there is only one action scene, a stabbing which occurs halfway through the movie, most of the tension is derived from the way Hitchcock first involves the audience in the murder scheme, and then in the efforts to entrap the murderer.

From the beginning it is clear that charming tennis pro Tony Wendice (Ray Milland), is planning to have his beautiful but unfaithful wife, Margot (Grace Kelly), murdered. Tony, who is nothing if not thorough, has been planning her demise for more than a year, ever since he discovered that she was having an affair with Mark Halliday (Robert Cummings), an American television mystery writer. Having married Margot for her money, Tony is now afraid that she will seek a divorce, thereby depriving him of his luxurious life style.

In the first scenes, Margot, seeing Mark for the first time in a year, explains that she had stopped their correspondence after the one love letter she had saved had been stolen from her purse at Victoria Station six months before. After that she had received two extortion letters, but the money she had sent in payment had never been collected by the blackmailer. She is convinced that Tony knows nothing of their affair.

The audience soon learns that Tony not only knows about the liaison, but that he is also her extortionist. Furthermore, Margot is not the only person he is going to blackmail. Pleading a heavy workload, Tony backs out of the theater engagement he and Margot have planned with Mark. Playing the role of the congenial, unsuspecting husband, he invites Mark to join him at a banquet being held at his club the following night. After Margot and Mark leave, Tony lures Captain Lesgate (Anthony Dawson), a disreputable rogue, over to the apartment. Lesgate, whose real name is Swann, was at Cambridge at the same time as Tony, who even then recognized a soul as unscrupulous as his own. Having followed Lesgate's activities for several months, Tony has now amassed a portfolio of crimes sufficient to convince Lesgate that he must carry out Tony's well-conceived plan, or he will go to jail.

Throughout the film Hitchcock uses a ground-level camera to capture the interaction between the players. As Tony outlines the perfect murder, however, the camera shifts overhead to give the audience a godlike perspective. Lesgate is to arrive at 10:37 the following night, take the key from under the carpet of the fifth step of the stairway just outside the apartment door, enter the flat, and hide behind the draperies behind the desk. Tony will excuse himself from the dinner at 10:40 to call his boss, but first will call home. When the phone rings, Margot will get out of bed and come to the desk, where Lesgate will strangle her. He will then whistle into the phone, at which point Tony will hang up and call his boss to support his alibi. When the deed is done, Tony will pay Lesgate a thousand pounds, which he has unobtrusively been saving at the rate of twenty pounds per week.

The next night the camera is returned to the human, fallible level to watch the drama unfold. Much of Hitchcock's brilliance is revealed in the way he manipulates the audience's involvement. When Margot suddenly announces her intention to go to a movie, thereby ruining all of Tony's masterful planning, the audience roots for him as he persuades her to stay home. Ironically, his vain suggestion that she clip articles for his scrapbook results in the ultimate failure of his plan, by providing her with the weapon she needs for her own defense. Tony unobtrusively removes her latchkey from her purse and places it under the carpet in the stairway before he and Mark leave for dinner.

When Lesgate enters the apartment that night, Hitchcock uses the technique of "film time" to stretch out action which normally would take only a few seconds. The result is an increase in the level of tension as the importance of the events is emphasized. In one of the few cuts outside the apartment, the audience sees that Tony's watch is slow and that Lesgate is about to leave. To the audience's relief, the call comes through just in time, and as Margot answers the phone, Lesgate slips a knotted stocking around her neck and begins violently choking her. The dim lighting creates an ominous atmosphere which emphasizes her agony as she struggles against his superior strength. Suddenly, however, she is able to grasp the scissors on the desk and plunge them into her assailant. In the one truly gruesome shot, Lesgate falls on his back, driving the scissors in deeper.

Tony, realizing that the plan has gone awry, now comes on the line to tell Margot not to call the police until he gets home. Panic-stricken and grateful to hear his voice, Margot follows his instructions. Clever as well as diabolical, Tony quickly alters the plan to make it appear that Lesgate had been black-mailing Margot, who in turn killed him. Tony plants Mark's love letter on Lesgate, removes the latchkey from the victim's pocket and places it in Mar-got's purse, and hides a knotted silk stocking in the wastebasket before calling the police.

From here on the tension is derived from a cat-and-mouse game between Tony and Inspector Hubbard (John Williams), an investigator who is the epitome of the British detective. The audience now begins to identify with the inquisitive, perceptive Inspector.

The bewildered Margot is amazed to find that all the evidence is suddenly distorted against her. Tony, as her loyal husband, staunchly defends her on the surface, while subtly providing all the evidence needed to convict her of first-degree murder. He informs the Inspector that he is sure that Margot does not know Lesgate (that is, Swann), but that he had known him briefly in college; he had only seen Swann once since, and that was at Victoria Station six months before. This, together with the love letter found in Les-gate's pocket, makes the blackmail motive for murder very plausible. When the silk stocking is found in the wastebasket, it appears likely that Margot's neck bruises were self-inflicted. The most damning piece of evidence, how-ever, is the fact that the carpet and the condition of Lesgate's shoes prove that he must have come in through the front door, and that she must have let him in.

For the trial, Hitchcock maintains a claustrophobic intensity by using an effective series of close-ups of Margot's face illuminated with colored lights against a neutral backdrop. She is convicted of first-degree murder and sen-tenced to death. Wiley Inspector Hubbard, however, is bothered by the fact that Lesgate carried no latchkey, so the day before the sentence is to be carried out, he devises a scheme to unearth new evidence. Hubbard goes to the apartment purportedly to question Tony about the large sums of money he has been spending lately, but during the course of the interview the In-spector manages to switch raincoats with Tony. He suggests Tony drop by the station to pick up some of Margot's possessions. After Tony goes out, Hub-bard uses the key inside Tony's raincoat to enter the apartment. Upon re-turning, he finds that Mark has broken in hoping to find evidence to save Margot.

Inspector Hubbard then initiates step one. Margot is driven to the front door and told to go inside the apartment. The Inspector and Mark wait quietly inside the darkened flat and listen as she enters the building, walks down the hallway, and tries to open the door with the key from her purse. When she is unable to open the door, she walks back outside. Hitchcock heightens the effectiveness of this scene with the use of real tiles in the hallway which emphasize the drama as the footsteps echo and recede.

The police then rush Margot's purse back to the station where Tony soon picks it up. Inspector Hubbard explains to Mark and Margot that the key in her purse was Lesgate's own latchkey and that he has Tony's key. The Inspector has located Margot's key under the carpet on the fifth step of the stairway; she has proven that she did not know it was there; her fate now rests on proving that Tony does know. The tension mounts as Tony's footsteps are heard in the hallway. He tries the key from Margot's purse; it does not work; he starts out, then stops. Suddenly, he realizes that Lesgate must have returned the key to the step before entering the apartment. He retrieves it, unlocks the door, and turns on the light, illuminating the scene.

Though Hitchcock maintains the theatricality of the production by confining the action to one room, he uses close-ups to capture the terror on the actors' faces which would be missed on stage. Changes in lighting, from the dimly lit attack scene to the symbolic illumination of the villain at the end, add to the atmosphere. Hitchcock's use of color also helps set the mood. Margot is first dressed in lovely colors, she is wearing white when attacked, and as her plight becomes desperate she wears black.

Though most audiences saw *Dial M for Murder* in the traditional format, it was filmed in Naturalvision, Warner Bros.' version of 3-D. The 3-D format was useful in this case, not for special effects, but for giving the film additional depth and intimacy within the confining set.

Hitchcock, always noted for his inconspicuous appearances in his films, has cleverly worked himself into a reunion picture which Tony shows to Lesgate during their interview.

The performances are generally good. John Williams and Anthony Dawson reenacted their Broadway roles. Williams is well cast as the Scotland Yard-type detective who enjoys unraveling clues. Dawson has made a career out of playing snakelike villain roles. Ray Milland is convincingly pathological as the venal Tony, and Grace Kelly is good at conveying bewilderment and terror. All in all, Hitchcock's talent for creating suspense blends with Frederick Knott's well-crafted plot to provide an interesting and diverting mystery.

Anne Louise Lynch

DINNER AT EIGHT

Released: 1933
Production: David O. Selznick for Metro-Goldwyn-Mayer
Direction: George Cukor
Screenplay: Frances Marion and Herman J. Mankiewicz, with additional dialogue by Donald Ogden Stewart; based on the play of the same name by George S. Kaufman and Edna Ferber
Cinematography: William Daniels
Editing: Ben Lewis
Running time: 110 minutes

Principal characters:
Carlotta Vance	Marie Dressler
Larry Renault	John Barrymore
Dan Packard	Wallace Beery
Kitty Packard	Jean Harlow
Oliver Jordan	Lionel Barrymore
Max Kane	Lee Tracy
Dr. Wayne Talbot	Edmund Lowe
Mrs. Talbot	Karen Morley
Mrs. Oliver Jordan	Billie Burke
Paula Jordan	Madge Evans
Jo Stengel	Jean Hersholt

When *Dinner at Eight* opened on Broadway in October of 1932, it was an instant success. It ran for 232 performances at the Music Box Theatre, and the rights to film it were acquired by M-G-M, where Irving Thalberg, who never received screen credit on any picture he personally supervised, planned it as one of his own productions for 1933. Thalberg, however, fell seriously ill and was forced to take a vacation from filmmaking. Louis B. Mayer turned over production to his son-in-law, David O. Selznick, who gave *Dinner at Eight* preferential treatment, bringing over his friend, George Cukor, from RKO.

The two men established the film as an all-star feature presenting ten stars in the leading roles. M-G-M had done very well during the 1930's with a series of productions that were truly all-star, starting in 1932 with *Grand Hotel*. Now, with ten players featured in *Dinner at Eight*, all of whom rated top billing, even the subsidiary roles were filled by performers who were known at the box office, such as Karen Morley, Louise Closser Hale, Phillips Holmes, and May Robson. The film proved to be one of M-G-M's biggest moneymakers, although it did not earn a single Academy Award nomination, perhaps because it was slick, glamorous, sophisticated, and had almost no real heart. Selznick gave the production his own touch of glitter, and Cukor, with the help of a very smartly written screenplay, made the story move smoothly, with all episodes leading up to the final scene in the Jordan drawing-room.

Dinner at Eight is basically the story of a fashionable dinner party given by a socialite wife, Mrs. Oliver Jordan (Billie Burke). Unknown to her, not only is the Jordan Steamship Line on the verge of financial disaster, but her husband (Lionel Barrymore) is on the brink of a physical breakdown. A week before the dinner party, Mrs. Jordan has acquired Lord and Lady Ferncliffe as honored guests, and she is building her guest list around them. She is having Dr. Wayne Talbot (Edmund Lowe) and his wife (Karen Morley), and Carlotta Vance (Marie Dressler), who had once been a great star in the theater. Oliver asks her also to invite Dan Packard (Wallace Beery) and his wife Kitty (Jean Harlow). Packard, who lives somewhere out West and owns freight lines, might be able to do Jordan some good. What Jordan does not know is that Packard plans to acquire the ailing Jordan line for as small a sum as possible.

When Kitty tells her husband that they have been invited to dinner at the Jordans on the coming Friday, he says they are not going. When he learns that Lord and Lady Ferncliffe will be there, however, he admits that he has been trying for years to meet the Ferncliffes and changes his mind. He leaves his wife's boudoir before Dr. Talbot arrives. Almost at once the relationship between Kitty and Dr. Talbot is established. He is a Park Avenue doctor with a "bedside manner," and already Kitty is becoming one of his most demanding patients.

Millicent Jordan has all her guests' acceptances, but she needs an extra man because Carlotta Vance is coming by herself. She decides to invite Larry Renault (John Barrymore), a stage star who had gone into the movies and made a big hit, until he began drinking. As a result of liquor and his advancing years, he can no longer get film roles. Now he is in New York seeking a play that will put him back in circulation. What Millicent does not know is that her daughter Paula (Madge Evans), engaged to marry the socially prominent Ernest DeGraff within a month, has caught the fancy of Renault, and Paula and Renault are enjoying a secret, if somewhat indiscreet, love affair. Larry tries to talk Paula out of the crush she has developed on him, pointing out that she is nineteen, while he is in his forties and burned out; but Paula is determined that nothing shall hurt their lovely affair.

On the day of his wife's dinner party, Oliver Jordan suffers an acute heart attack and is taken to Dr. Talbot's office. The doctor recognizes that Jordan will not live more than a few months, and mildly suggests that he skip his wife's dinner party that night and get a little rest. Jordan is not fooled by the doctor's demeanor, but he also will not disappoint Millicent; he will be the host as usual.

It does not take long for Jordan to learn the worst about his failing steamship line. Although he has asked Carlotta to hold onto her stock, she has sold it that afternoon, because of her own financial problems, to a man named James K. Baldridge. Jordan learns that another block of stock has been sold by other friends to the same man. He knows that Baldridge is a front name to cover the identity of the real buyer, who is Dan Packard.

The Packards have an argument as they are dressing for the Jordans' dinner, and Dan accuses Kitty of cheating on him. Kitty denies it; she has seen no other man except the doctor, and her maid verifies that. When she threatens him with her knowledge of his crooked deals, the argument is stalemated, with Kitty forcing Dan to make good on the Jordan stock in exchange for her silence.

Larry Renault's fate is more tragic. He has insulted the one Broadway producer who might have given him a choice supporting role, insisting that he will accept nothing but the lead; this causes his hitherto faithful agent to turn on him. Alone and half-drunk, Larry realizes that he is going nowhere; he is financially broke and virtually friendless. He locks the door, stuffs pillows and clothing at the door and window cracks, turns on the gas, and sits in front of the heater in his dinner clothes, waiting.

The guests begin to arrive at the Jordans' home for dinner. At the last minute, the secretary to Lord and Lady Ferncliffe, who were the *raison d'être* for the dinner, has called to say that they are sorry, but they are in Florida and unable to attend the party. Millicent, who is distraught over the preparations for the party, has gotten her cousins to substitute at the last moment. Because Millicent is so caught up in her own petty little world, she fails to realize how ill her husband is and chastizes him for wishing to go to bed early. She also refuses to listen to her daughter as Paula tries to tell her mother of her love for Renault.

The stories are neatly wrapped up before the guests sit down to dinner. Oliver is told by Packard that his company has been saved, shortly after Millicent tearfully tells her husband that their life will be "happier than ever" when she learns of his financial and physical worries. She admits to her frivolousness and promises to change. The Jordans' daughter decides to marry her fiancé after all when Carlotta informs her that Renault has killed himself; Paula realizes the hopelessness of that love and she walks into dinner on Ernest DeGraff's arm.

Thus, all the plots and subplots of the story are resolved just before the guests sit down to their dinner. The final lines of the film are a classically funny interchange between Carlotta and Kitty. Kitty observes brightly, "I was reading a book the other day," an admission that brings an incredulous look to Carlotta's face, but Kitty goes on blithely: "It's about civilization or something. Do you know, the guy said machinery is going to take the place of every profession." Carlotta grunts to herself with a meaningful look at the sensuous Kitty, "Oh, my dear. That's something you'll never have to worry about."

Top billing went to Marie Dressler, who played her part as legitimately as she could; Cukor somehow managed to get her to soft pedal her usual mugging. Carlotta Vance, the actress played by Dressler, was supposed to have been an intimate of Somerset Maugham, Michael Arlen, and Charlie Chaplin. There are elements of famous socialite and actress Maxine Elliott in the background of Carlotta as written by Kaufman and Ferber, but there is never anything of the upper crust society woman in Dressler's characterization.

John Barrymore and Wallace Beery got second and third billing. Barrymore brings elegance to his role of Larry Renault, and Beery, who had been co-starring in several films with Dressler, manages some mugging of his own as the uncouth Westerner, Dan Packard. Fourth billing went to Jean Harlow, who positively blooms under Cukor's experienced direction. The role of Kitty Packard is so well-written as to be almost actress-proof, and Harlow plays it with the innocent but nonetheless malevolent joyousness that she first displayed in *Red-Headed Woman* (1932).

Lionel Barrymore is sympathetic as the dying Oliver, underplaying the part effectively; Lee Tracy gives one of his best performances as the faithful actor's agent, Max Kane. Edmund Lowe has just the right virility and polish for the society doctor, Wayne Talbot; and Billie Burke, who had been annoyingly saccharine in her first talking roles, is perfect as a fluttering matron unaware that her fine house is tumbling down. Madge Evans brings youthful beauty and sincerity to her role as the daughter, Paula Jordan, and Jean Hersholt is perfect as Jo Stengel, the producer willing to give the fading Larry Renault a second chance.

The play had boasted a series of subplots devoted to the servants who prepared and served the dinner, but the downstairs part of the play was cut and the upstairs emphasized in the movie version. *Dinner at Eight* marked David O. Selznick's debut as a producer at M-G-M (he followed it with another 1933 all-star production that is forgotten today: *Night Flight*, with both John and Lionel Barrymore, Helen Hayes, Clark Gable, Robert Montgomery, Myrna Loy, and William Gargan). *Dinner at Eight* remains a top favorite and is certain to be included in every retrospective of the best from M-G-M in the 1930's.

DeWitt Bodeen

THE DIRTY DOZEN

Released: 1967
Production: Kenneth Hyman for Metro-Goldwyn-Mayer
Direction: Robert Aldrich
Screenplay: Nunnally Johnson and Lukas Heller; based on the novel of the same name by E. M. Nathanson
Cinematography: Edward Scaife
Editing: Michael Luciano
Sound effects: John Poyner (AA)
Running time: 149 minutes

Principal characters:
Major Reisman	Lee Marvin
General Worden	Ernest Borgnine
Joseph Wladislaw	Charles Bronson
Robert Jefferson	Jim Brown
Victor Franko	John Cassavetes
Sergeant Bowren	Richard Jaeckel
Major Max Armbruster	George Kennedy
Colonel Everett Dasher Breed	Robert Ryan
Archer Maggott	Telly Savalas
Vernon Pinkley	Donald Sutherland
Samson Posey	Clint Walker

In *The Dirty Dozen*, a box-office sensation in 1967, Lee Marvin led a band of murderers, psychopaths, and sex maniacs on a violent suicide mission during which the misfits acquitted themselves as military heroes. Released at a time when the United States antiwar movement was nearing its most passionate level, it fascinated "dove" moviegoers who were totally ready to accept the delineation of top soldiers as manic slaughterers, as well as "hawkish" audiences who applauded the Dozen's brutal combat. *The Dirty Dozen* became one of the greatest box-office successes in M-G-M's history.

Based on E. M. Nathanson's novel and directed by Robert Aldrich, *The Dirty Dozen* tells the story of Major Reisman (Lee Marvin), who is assigned by General Worden (Ernest Borgnine) to train twelve convicted G. I.'s for a suicide mission. The task: parachute into Nazi-infested France, attack a chateau retreat for top Nazi officers, and completely destroy it. Reisman thinks the plan "stinks" but reluctantly accepts, and soon meets his troops: Chicago hoodlum and psychopath Victor Franko (John Cassavetes); murderer Joseph Wladislaw (Charles Bronson); white-hating black Robert Jefferson (Jim Brown); moronic Vernon Pinkley (Donald Sutherland); and Southern bigot, religious fanatic, and sex fiend Archer Maggott (Telly Savalas) among them. The odd group accepts the proposal, hoping they may win pardons if they survive. At first they all resent Reisman, but he, with the aid of Sergeant

Bowren (Richard Jaeckel), eventually wins their respect by controlling them with browbeating, bullying, and leadership.

Reisman's greatest aid in producing a fighting unit comes when pompous Colonel Everett Dasher Breed (Robert Ryan), of West Point distinction, pits his highly disciplined troops against the Dozen in war games. The Dirty Dozen, who ironically earn that nickname not because of their morals but because they are at one point deprived of soap, triumph in the contest, capturing the entire staff of the abashed Breed and winning the go-ahead for their mission. Here the theme of the film is pungently conveyed, as Breed's men, full of discipline, training, and military logic, prove no match for the Dozen and their crafty, underhanded tactics.

The plane carrying Reisman, Bowren, and the Dozen is soon over France, and they parachute to the site of their mission. Wladislaw, who speaks fluent German, and Reisman, who speaks not a word of it, disguise themselves as German officers and penetrate the chalet as the soldiers take their various stations outside. Director Aldrich ingeniously presents the very proper, well-groomed, aristocratic German officers, their lovely concubines, and the beautiful accoutrements of the retreat, creating a marvelous contrast to the grimy conspirators who lurk outside, waiting to destroy such representations of impeccable civilization.

The mission is proceeding well when Maggott cracks. The deranged maniac crawls into a posh bedroom, snares the young lover of an officer, sadistically taunts her with knife play, and slays her. Then, seemingly enjoying a perverted sexual release, the madly grinning Maggott begins shooting off his machine gun, betraying the plot. He is killed by Jefferson, and in the ensuing horror of grenade explosions and machine gun bursts, the Allies corral the officers and girls into the cellars, pour gasoline-soaked grenades down the ventilator shafts, and totally destroy the chateau.

The final scene takes place in a hospital; only Reisman, Wladislaw, and Bowren are still alive. The survivors hear General Worden's news that the dead criminals will be listed in the annals as gallant soldiers who honorably gave their lives for love of country.

Predominately rave reviews greeted *The Dirty Dozen* when it was released in the summer of 1967: *Variety* called it "An exciting, well-mounted, and grimly realistic World War II drama. . . ." Judith Crist of NBC's "Today Show" said it was ". . . one of the best and least compromising he-man adventure films. . . ." There was, however, a very vocal minority who despised the film, such as Bosley Crowther of the *New York Times*, who found the film ", . . . astonishingly wanton . . . downright preposterous." Decrying the violence and the grim moral, such critics did, however, affect the movie's reception at the box office. *The Dirty Dozen* soared into the top ten money-makers of M-G-M's forty-year history, grossing $20,170,000. It did not succeed, however, in persuading the Motion Picture Academy of its merits at awards time. *The Dirty Dozen* won only one Oscar; John Poyner for his Sound effects; and reaped only one major nomination, John Cassavetes for Best Supporting Actor. He lost, ironically, to *Cool Hand Luke*'s George Kennedy, who appeared in *The Dirty Dozen* as sympathetic Major Armbruster, Worden's cohort. The film placed fifth in the *Film Daily* 1967 "Ten Best" roster.

The Dirty Dozen remains a riveting, exciting film; it scored powerful ratings when first shown on television, although it was considerably edited, and it continues to fascinate not only because of its plot, but also because of the several small parts played by future "superstars," such as Charles Bronson, Donald Sutherland, and Telly Savalas. Marvin is superbly taut as Reisman, and all of the Dozen, with the exception of singer Trini Lopez as Pedro Jiminez, obviously revel in their grotesquely picaresque roles. Topping the lot for the acting honors are Cassavetes, who plays his part of the psychotic Franko with morsels of sardonic humor, and Telly Savalas, whose bug-eyed, Dixie-drawling, maniacal Maggott appears a very distant relation to his more familiar role as television's lollipop-sucking Kojack.

Many antiwar pictures followed *The Dirty Dozen*. In most however, the military denizens were caricatured as bloodthirsty buffoons, as in *M*A*S*H* (1970) and *Alice's Restaurant* (1969). None, however, took the compelling slant of *The Dirty Dozen*: that war, a horrible event, can only be truly ended by horrible means, most effectively concocted and executed by horrible men.

Gregory William Mank

DIRTY HARRY

Released: 1971
Production: Don Siegel for Malpaso Company Productions; released by
Warner Bros.
Direction: Don Siegel
Screenplay: Harry Julian Fink, R. M. Fink, and Dean Riesner; based on a
story by Harry Julian Fink and R. M. Fink
Cinematography: Bruce Surtees
Editing: Carl Pingitore
Running time: 103 minutes

Principal characters:
Harry Callahan .... Clint Eastwood
Bressler .... Harry Guardino
Chico .... Reni Santoni
Killer (Scorpio) .... Andy Robinson
Chief .... John Larch
Mayor .... John Vernon

Dirty Harry is the first in a series of three movies (including *Magnum
Force*, 1973; and *The Enforcer*, 1976) about the adventures of Detective Harry
Callahan of the San Francisco Police Department. All three films star Clint
Eastwood as Harry, all are controversial, and all were very successful, each
one earning more at the box office than its predecessor. They all depend on
intense action and graphic violence to lure the audiences. The appeal of the
Eastwood *persona* also draws people to the theater, as does the more dubious
attraction of the Callahan character. While the two sequels are not without
merit, *Dirty Harry* is the most successful in terms of cinematic artistry and
deserves a close examination.

The film opens with a sniper on a rooftop in San Francisco shooting a girl
in a nearby swimming pool. The killer leaves a note demanding money and
threatening to kill a priest or a black person next. The note is signed
"Scorpio." Detective Harry Callahan is called in to investigate and apprehend
the murderer.

Harry (Clint Eastwood), both coolly professional and rudely contemptuous
of authority, is assigned a partner by the Police Chief (John Larch). Harry
is dismayed to discover that the partner is a rookie, a Mexican-American,
and college-educated, all serious liabilities. Chico (Reni Santoni) is eager to
learn and to prove himself to the man widely known in the department as
Dirty Harry. As they begin their investigation, they accidentally interrupt a
bank robbery in progress. In a spectacular sequence, Harry quickly and
violently captures the robbers. His methods are brutal and extralegal and
clearly explain his nickname.

Scorpio (Andy Robinson) is spotted on another rooftop, and Harry and Chico attempt to capture him, but he escapes. After a young black man is killed, Harry sets a trap using a policeman disguised as a priest. Scorpio takes the bait, but once again escapes before Harry can capture him. Scorpio next sends the police a note informing them that he has buried a young girl alive with only a little oxygen to sustain her. He will tell the police where she is if they give him $200,000. The Mayor (John Vernon) assigns Harry to deliver the ransom and instructs him not to attempt to capture the killer. Chico shadows Harry as Scorpio leads him on a chase across the city, ending finally in a park, where Harry and Chico are shot in their attempt to capture Scorpio, although Harry manages to stab Scorpio in the leg.

After being treated for his gunshot wound, Harry learns from a doctor in the hospital emergency room that the groundskeeper at Kezar Stadium has just been treated for a stab wound in the leg. Harry goes to the stadium, kicks in the door of the room where Scorpio lives, and wounds him in the ensuing struggle. He tortures the killer into revealing the location of the kidnaped girl, but it is too late—the girl is dead.

Harry next discovers that the District Attorney has released Scorpio. Because Harry used illegal means to capture and coerce a confession from the killer, the case against Scorpio would be defeated in court. Harry is incensed, and, disobeying orders, determines to capture Scorpio again. He begins to follow and harass the killer all over the city. Scorpio then pays a black man to beat him, and complains to the Police Chief that Harry had done the beating. Harry is called off the case.

Next Scorpio robs a liquor store, hijacks a school bus with a woman driver and six children as passengers, and calls the police demanding money and an escape plane. Harry is told to deliver the ransom to the airport, but instead, he leaps on the bus as it passes under a railway trestle. The driver faints, and the bus veers into a quarry yard. Harry chases Scorpio to the edge of a pond where he is cornered. Scorpio grabs a boy as a shield. Harry shoots Scorpio, narrowly missing the boy, and Scorpio falls into the muddy water. Harry tosses his police badge into the water, turns and walks down the road away from the approaching police cars as the film ends.

American society is based on a system of laws, but there is something in the American character that admires the anarchic hero who functions successfully regardless of the law. Whether frontiersman or soldier, America relied upon men willing to go beyond the law to protect society from the savages and outlaws encountered in the wilderness. Competence and success were more important than observance of the law, even though the advance of the law was a measure of the advance of civilization. Dirty Harry is a direct descendant of those mythological heroes of our past. Confronted with the savage, he is prepared to use extralegal means to eliminate the pathological threat to society. While the film audience may deplore the illegality of Harry's methods, they applaud his success in eliminating the threat. Harry, like the heroes of the past, functions primarily as a mythological hero. The real world of the San Francisco Police Department is much more complex than the world depicted in the film. The audience admires Harry precisely because he provides simple solutions to problems that are very complex in reality. It is easy to believe that Harry has the answers to society's ills; it is very satisfying, even cathartic, to cheer him on to the ultimate elimination of the villain. Through Harry, the audience can experience vicariously his coping with a frustrating and difficult existence.

The controversy surrounding the film centered on Harry's use of extralegal methods to capture the killer, and the film's criticism of the Supreme Court's criminal rights decisions. Harry certainly does not like the decisions. But it is less clear that the director, Don Siegel, and the writers share Harry's beliefs. The film asks how society should respond to the monster in its midst, but provides no answers. Harry's response is characteristic, but society cannot allow him simply to dispose of a badge and walk away from the problem.

Siegel maintains suspense and swift action throughout the film. He works against the San Francisco image as a pretty, picturesque city to convey a more sinister urban aspect. In his first film role, Andy Robinson as the killer is extremely effective. He displays the cunning and the pathology of the character without becoming a grotesque caricature. Clint Eastwood goes beyond his usual screen image to portray a character whose obsession matches his quarry's pathology. Harry becomes more like Scorpio as the film progresses. When he realizes what is happening to him, he despises Scorpio for pushing him to the brink.

Dirty Harry is a superb example of the police genre; it is also one of the best films Don Siegel has directed, and Clint Eastwood gives one of his best performances. It is one of a trio of highly popular films which speak to conditions in America in the early 1970's. Finally, *Dirty Harry* raises serious questions about law enforcement in America. Its audience can choose to be satisfied with the solution Harry provides, but the filmmakers suggest that their hero may be wrong.

Don K Thompson

DR. EHRLICH'S MAGIC BULLET

Released: 1940
Production: Hal B. Wallis for Warner Bros.
Direction: William Dieterle
Screenplay: John Huston, Heinz Herald, and Norman Burnside; based on an idea by Norman Burnside and biographical material in the possession of Dr. Ehrlich's family
Cinematography: James Wong Howe
Editing: Warren Low
Running time: 103 minutes

Principal characters:
Dr. Paul Ehrlich .... Edward G. Robinson
Dr. Emil Von Behring .... Otto Kruger
Mrs. Ehrlich .... Ruth Gordon

The quest for knowledge is a difficult subject to present effectively on film. It is usually romanticized or oversimplified to make it palatable to filmgoers. *Dr. Ehrlich's Magic Bullet* is one of the few Hollywood films that treats such a theme with dignity and power while remaining absorbing and entertaining. It is the story of Paul Ehrlich, the turn-of-the-century German scientist who searched for what he called "magic bullets" to cure disease.

As the film opens the viewer sees Ehrlich (Edward G. Robinson) as a young doctor frustrated that he must prescribe meaningless treatments for diseases that medical science does not understand. When a young patient whom Ehrlich is treating for syphilis realizes that there is no cure for his disease and kills himself, Ehrlich wants to quit his position at the hospital and devote all his time to research in an attempt to understand and cure disease. Because he has a family to support, however, he compromises by keeping his post at the hospital and doing research at night.

One night he goes to a medical meeting when he is supposed to be on duty at the hospital. He is fired and must continue his research at home. His success in staining the tubercle bacillus then earns him an appointment to the prestigious Koch Institute, where he is allowed to study whatever he wishes. His work at the Institute, however, is delayed because he has contracted tuberculosis in his earlier research. Forced to spend nearly a year in Egypt recuperating, he becomes frustrated by the enforced idleness. He tells his wife that rest, sunshine, and milk are the three things he hates most. Upon returning to Germany he begins work on immunization, based on an idea he developed after an experience with a snake-bite victim in Egypt. He combines his knowledge with that of his colleague and friend Dr. Emil Von Behring (Otto Kruger) to produce a serum which cures diphtheria. Later, he conducts a long series of experiments which finally lead to a cure for syphilis.

When the cure is used before being fully tested, thousands of others are cured, although a few people die; the medical establishment accuses Ehrlich of neglectfully causing the deaths of these people. Ehrlich charges his opponents with libel, and the issue is brought to trial. At the climax of the trial, Behring, with whom Ehrlich has had a falling-out, is brought in to testify against him. Unexpectedly, he testifies in Ehrlich's favor, saying that Ehrlich has caused the death of syphilis itself. This statement brings tears to Ehrlich's eyes and assures his victory in the trial, but the physical strain has been too much and he dies soon afterward.

Dr. Ehrlich's Magic Bullet does a good job of conveying on film the process and method of scientific research. It makes the principles involved clear to the average viewer without undue simplification or overdramatization. There are no discoveries made by a lucky guess or a dramatic development at midnight. The scriptwriters do perhaps stretch things a bit when they have Ehrlich berate his wife for ruining an experiment by lighting his stove, only to find the heat was exactly what was needed for success. However, that is the only serious concession to the usual tendency of Hollywood to sentimentalize or romanticize scientific endeavor. Particularly effective is the use of color in the otherwise black-and-white film to show the microscope slides. The artistry of the filmmakers is also exhibited in the sequence showing a cure for syphilis from the patient's point of view. Blind before the treatment begins, the patient is visited daily by Ehrlich. We see the doctor through the patient's eyes, as each day he appears less blurry.

Ehrlich's scientific research, as presented by the film, is in three stages. First he works on dyes that will stain one microscopic substance but no other. His first practical application of this work is to find a way to stain the bacillus of tuberculosis so that it can be easily seen and identified, thus making diagnosis of tuberculosis a simple matter. Then, while in Egypt recuperating from the tuberculosis he contracted during the research, he is called to treat a man and a boy who have been bitten by a poisonous snake. The boy dies, but the man, who has been bitten four times before, is scarcely affected. Ehrlich finds that each time the man is bitten he suffers less, and when he returns to Germany he decides to pursue this phenomenon of immunity. This work, too, soon has a practical use as he combines his work with that of his friend and colleague Behring to produce a serum to treat diphtheria. His third major project is finding a cure for syphilis by developing a substance which combines arsenic with the spirochaete of syphilis to cure the illness without the arsenic injuring the cells of the body. He expects that it may require nearly one hundred experiments to find just the right substance, but it is not until the 606th that success is reached.

While Ehrlich was working on his cure for syphilis early in this century, there was great opposition to his work. Many people considered the disease a punishment for sin and thought it should not be cured, a fact which is touched upon in the film. Since the disease was still seldom discussed publicly in 1940, the filmmakers were required by the censorship board to use the word "syphilis" as few times as possible and to avoid any sensationalism. Also barely mentioned in the film is the fact that some of the opposition to Ehrlich was anti-Semitic.

The conflict between research and healing is a serious theme of the film. When Ehrlich wants to quit practicing medicine in order to do research, it is not because he is insensitive to people but because he sees that helping patients requires more knowledge than medical science possesses, and he cannot be content with prescribing useless remedies. After he starts working on the theory of immunity, however, he becomes more removed from people. Behring comes to him for help in developing a serum for diphtheria while an epidemic of the disease is ravaging the country, but Ehrlich is not interested in helping him. Only after an emotional outburst by Behring does Ehrlich begin to help Behring with the work on the diphtheria cure. Once they have developed the serum and are given permission to test it on a group of sick children, Ehrlich comes into contact with patients again and his scientific objectivity disappears. When he sees the mothers of the children, he cannot withhold the medicine from the control group no matter how experimentally sound that procedure might be for testing the effectiveness of the serum. Despite protests from the hospital administration, he injects all the children. Later, the issue arises again when he develops the cure for syphilis but wants to do extensive testing for a year before the medicine is released for use. Again he is persuaded that people suffering from the disease should be helped as soon as possible. As a result a few people die after being treated, but balanced against the thousands who are cured the few are, as Behring says at the trial, "martyrs to the public good." In addition, Ehrlich does not hesitate to take personal risks in his research. Once the syphilis cure is perfected in animal studies, he plans to innoculate himself in order to be the first human on which it is tested.

Though the script is not a perfectly accurate picture of Ehrlich's life, it skillfully condenses and engrossingly presents the essence of his career. It is the outstanding achievement of Edward G. Robinson and director William Dieterle that they make Ehrlich a believable figure. Indeed, domestic scenes are interwoven with the scientific to show that though he is dedicated to his research, he is still human in his emotions and feelings. Tired of playing the two-dimensional gangster roles for which he is best known, Robinson fought for the role of Ehrlich; and once he got the role, he proved his acting skill and range in a fine performance which makes us remember Dr. Ehrlich and forget who is playing him. *Dr. Ehrlich's Magic Bullet* is serious Hollywood screen biography at its best.

Timothy W. Johnson

DR. JEKYLL AND MR. HYDE

Released: 1932
Production: Rouben Mamoulian for Paramount
Direction: Rouben Mamoulian
Screenplay: Samuel Hoffenstein and Percy Heath; based on the novel of the same name by Robert Louis Stevenson
Cinematography: Karl Struss
Editing: William Shea
Running time: 90 minutes

> *Principal characters:*
> Dr. Henry Jekyll/Mr. Hyde .... Fredric March (AA)
> Ivy Pearson .... Miriam Hopkins
> Muriel Carew .... Rose Hobart
> Brigadier General Carew .... Halliwell Hobbes
> Dr. Lanyan .... Holmes Herbert
> Poole .... Edgar Norton

Very few characters have struck the chord of man's imagination with more resonance than Robert Louis Stevenson's Dr. Jekyll, for in his duality he represents the struggle of good and evil within the individual. It is a struggle that has always intrigued, puzzled, and preoccupied men. As early as 1908, Hollywood's fledgling filmmakers recognized the potential box-office appeal of Stevenson's spine-chilling classic. It was a story that possessed all the winning ingredients: horror, suspense, romance, and morality. Only three of the Jekyll and Hyde films have done justice to Stevenson's literary master-piece—the inspired performance given by John Barrymore in 1920, the 1932 version starring Fredric March as the infamous doctor, and the Victor Fleming 1941 production starring Spencer Tracy. The 1932 film was produced and directed by Rouben Mamoulian, who was acknowledged and esteemed as one of the most inspired and innovative Broadway directors during the 1930's. Although *Dr. Jekyll and Mr. Hyde* was only Mamoulian's third film, he infused this stunning melodrama with a theatrical virtuosity which perfectly expressed the brooding, bizarre quality of Stevenson's character.

Dr. Jekyll (Fredric March), is a man unshackled by the taboos of convention. As Karl Struss's camera pans a filled-to-capacity auditorium of students and distinguished medical men, Dr. Jekyll leans on his dais and elaborates on his theory of the dualistic nature of the human psyche. "I have found," he explains, "that certain agents, certain chemicals have the power to disturb the trembling immateriality of the seemingly solid body in which we walk." The reaction to this heretical proclamation is immediate and sharply divided, some believing the doctor to be a savior, others convinced that he is in league with the devil.

In addition to his research and lectures, Jekyll unselfishly devotes long hours of his time to a free medical clinic, causing him, on this particular evening, to arrive late at a dinner party held at the home of Brigadier General Carew (Halliwell Hobbes), Jekyll's future father-in-law. However, Muriel Carew (Rose Hobart), Jekyll's fiancée, forgives the good doctor for his tardiness, and as they stroll in the garden, they discuss their impending marriage on which the general has imposed an eight-month waiting period. Jekyll leaves the Carew home in the company of his good friend, Dr. Lanyan (Holmes Herbert). Suddenly their reverie is broken by a noisy scuffle between a man and a woman in the dimly lit street ahead. Rushing forward, Jekyll drives off the assailant and helps the manhandled young woman upstairs to her rooms. Encouraged by his solicitous ministrations, the cockney woman, Ivy Pearson (Miriam Hopkins), becomes coquettish and attempts to seduce him. However, she fails, and with the scene rather abruptly ended, the audience realizes that Ivy will reappear later in the film.

Following this is a scene which takes place in Jekyll's laboratory where, after three days of unflagging experimentation, Jekyll has produced a bubbling elixir which awaits its final test. The doctor hesitates for one long moment, then raises the flask and drinks the foaming potion. Suddenly, a spasm convulses his body, and he writhes in pain, his face horribly contorted. This scene portraying the initial transformation from Dr. Jekyll to Mr. Hyde is a cinemagraphic masterpiece since it was done without the usual series of dissolves to accommodate makeup changes. The use of a number of colored gelatin filters caused March's makeup to appear to change and, as Struss's camera relentlessly focuses on Jekyll's face, the audience watches in horror as the evil in his soul permeates and contorts his features into a dark and loathsome mask of wickedness and malice before their very eyes. Moving with an animal's quick grace, Hyde grins savagely in the mirror and then, throwing a cape around his shoulders, leaves the lab by the back door.

In a later scene, the doctor restlessly paces his lab, his life in limbo. General Carew, concerned over Jekyll's refusal to give up his research, has taken his daughter to Bath on an extended holiday. A telegram from Bath informing the doctor that Muriel will not be returning for at least another month incites Jekyll to action. Downing a draft of the potion, he changes quickly to Hyde and slinks off into the foggy London streets. After making inquiries at Ivy Pearson's boarding house about her whereabouts, Hyde proceeds to the Blue Boar dance hall where, amidst the bacchanalian revelry, he observes Ivy flitting about with debauched abandon. Hyde snatches up a broken glass and with a savage, threatening gesture, chases away Ivy's escort. Then, with a wolfish, terrifying intensity, he turns to Ivy and says, "You'll come with me, eh?"

From this point on, the pace of the movie quickens dramatically; time lapses are effected through a series of dissolves and slow fades as Jekyll catapults, through the character of Mr. Hyde, toward an abyss from which there is no escape. The sound effects, including the use of quickening heartbeats, builds suspense throughout the ensuing scenes to a raw, nerve-jangling level of intensity. Having been informed of the recent return to London of General Carew and his daughter, Jekyll is deeply disturbed and full of remorse over his recent indulgences. Deciding to end his double life, he sends his butler, Poole (Edgar Norton), with a fifty-pound note and a message to be delivered to Ivy. In addition, he gives his butler the key to the rear door of his lab, stating that he will no longer have need of it.

Later, Ivy arrives at the doctor's home to return his money and beg his assistance in freeing herself from Hyde's sadistic attentions. Jekyll, remorseful over the anguish which he has caused her, promises that she will never see Hyde again. However, Jekyll has unleashed the licentious Mr. Hyde once too often. The fragile chain of conscious control has been irrevocably broken and the beast lurks ever-present, unshackled, and ready to claw its way into the upper consciousness of Jekyll's mind. Totally unaware of this irreversible change that has occurred within himself, Jekyll strolls happily through the park on his way to the Carew home. Following their return from Bath, the General has undergone a change of heart and agreed to an early marriage between Dr. Jekyll and his daughter, and this is the night the formal wedding announcement is to be made. Suddenly, with dynamic primitive force, Hyde takes over Jekyll's body and walks towards Ivy's flat. Here, he informs the terrified Ivy that he is the wonderful Dr. Jekyll in which she has believed; then, with a pagan enjoyment, he wantonly takes her life. Smashing his way through the curious onlookers who have heard Ivy's screams and gathered on the stairs, Hyde escapes into the safety of the darkness.

Unable to return to his laboratory and no longer being in possession of the rear door key, Hyde sends a message by porter to his friend Lanyan, instructing him to retrieve certain chemicals from his lab and give them to a messenger whom Jekyll will send to Lanyan's home at midnight. Lanyan, however, refuses to release the package to the suspicious-looking Mr. Hyde. Having no choice, Hyde mixes and drinks the potion, reverting to Dr. Jekyll before the disbelieving, horrified eyes of his friend. Jekyll swears Lanyan to secrecy, promising that in return for his trust, he will give up Muriel and never again take the potion.

With a heavy heart, Jekyll arrives at the Carew home and informs Muriel that he is releasing her from her marriage commitment. However, as he leaves the house, Hyde again takes possession of Jekyll's mind and body. Reentering the house, he pursues Muriel, who screams at the sight of this horrifying stranger. General Carew comes to his daughter's rescue, but Hyde savagely beats the old man with his cane and escapes into the night. Two constables, alerted by the General's cries for help, take up the chase, tracking their suspect to the home of Dr. Jekyll. Frantically Hyde mixes his potion with the constables pounding on the door. At the last second, as the door finally succumbs to their persistent barrage, Hyde changes back to Jekyll and convinces the officers who have burst into the room that the murderer, Hyde, has been there but has escaped by the back door. At this moment, Lanyan appears and reveals to the constables that Jekyll himself is the ruthless, cold-blooded killer whom they seek. Shock and anger at Lanyan's betrayal brings the ever-present Hyde back to the surface. He attacks Lanyan and then the police until his frenzy of unbridled hatred is finally halted by a bullet; and, as the formless evil power slowly dissipates, Jekyll emerges to claim his dying and desecrated body.

Mamoulian's finely etched, visual interpretation of *Dr. Jekyll and Mr. Hyde* possesses the timeless elegance of the Stevenson classic. Each scene is a hand-carved cameo, perfect in lighting and composition. The characters of Jekyll and Hyde allowed Mamoulian to draw upon the full range of his theatrical genius, to portray the elemental struggle of man's emotions against a background of rich symbolic imagery. In one scene, violence is juxtaposed against a lyric view of romantic statuary, and in another, a bubbling cauldron flickers in the flames of a fireplace, providing a fleeting symbolic glimpse of the hell lurking in man's soul. March is stunning in his portrayal of Jekyll and Hyde, a role which earned him an Academy Award for Best Actor. His interpretation of Hyde's unsheathed wickedness pares Jekyll's civilized veneer in one clean, devastating stroke, stupefying audiences with its raw and savage intensity, and making the Mamoulian production of *Dr. Jekyll and Mr. Hyde* a classic of the horror film genre.

D. Gail Huskins

DR. JEKYLL AND MR. HYDE

Released: 1941
Production: Victor Saville for Metro-Goldwyn-Mayer
Direction: Victor Fleming
Screenplay: John Lee Mahin; based on the novel of the same name by Robert Louis Stevenson
Cinematography: Joseph Ruttenberg
Editing: Harold F. Kress
Special effects: Warren Newcombe
Montage effects: Peter Ballbusch
Music: Franz Waxman
Running time: 127 minutes

Principal characters:

Dr. Henry Jekyll/Mr. Hyde	Spencer Tracy
Ivy Peterson	Ingrid Bergman
Beatrix Emery	Lana Turner
Sir Charles Emery	Donald Crisp
Dr. John Lanyon	Ian Hunter
Sam Higgins	Barton MacLane
The Bishop	C. Aubrey Smith
Poole	Peter Godfrey

In 1885, Robert Louis Stevenson, the celebrated Scottish novelist, had a strange nightmare in which he envisioned man's personality as being split into two diametrically opposed aspects; this strange dream provided the inspiration for his immortal novel, *Dr. Jekyll and Mr. Hyde*. The dual nature of mankind was a chilling but intriguing premise, one that was to engage the creative imaginations of numerous film producers. Of the many films which handle this theme, only the three versions of Stevenson's classic story are worthy of note: the 1920 production starring John Barrymore; the 1932 version with Fredric March; and the 1941 Victor Saville production. Saville's film starred Spencer Tracy, who had won Oscars for Best Actor two years in a row: for *Captains Courageous* in 1937 and *Boys' Town* in 1938. Saville spared no expense in this production; Victor Fleming, acclaimed for *The Wizard of Oz* (1939) and *Gone with the Wind* (1939), was named as director.

The film opens on a quiet Sunday morning in London as the camera, under Joseph Ruttenberg's expert direction, pans a church steeple while bells toll melodiously in the background. Inside one of London's most prestigious churches, the bishop is delivering a eulogy in honor of Queen Victoria's Golden Jubilee. Suddenly the derisive voice of a distraught parishioner, Sam Higgins (Barton MacLane), pierces the tranquillity of the service. As he is being subdued, the noted mental health specialist Dr. Henry Jekyll (Spencer

Tracy) intervenes and orders the man taken to Camden Hospital for observation and treatment. Here, Jekyll importunes the heads of the hospital to allow him to test his theory that the evil in a man's soul can be separated and, consequently, eliminated or expelled. However, the distinguished doctors frown on his request, believing that his proposal trespasses into the domain of religion.

In the scene that follows, Dr. Jekyll arrives late at a dinner party and takes his seat beside his fiancée, Beatrix Emery (Lana Turner). Close-ups focus on individual guests or groups of guests, painting intimate portraits and establishing the relationships between the members of the dinner party. Jekyll, stung by his rejection at the hospital, elaborates on his theory of man's dual nature, seeking a glimmer of understanding and support from the distinguished medical men attending the dinner. His discourse, however, is met with both fear and rejection.

On the way home from the party, Jekyll, accompanied by his friend Dr. John Lanyon (Ian Hunter), comes upon a young woman in distress. The two men scare off her assailant and escort her to her lodgings. Feigning a sprained ankle, the woman, an amoral barmaid named Ivy Peterson (Ingrid Bergman), tricks Jekyll into carrying her up to her flat, where she openly flirts with him. Jekyll, both mesmerized and shocked by her behavior, forgets himself for a moment and kisses her. Bergman manages to infuse an air of realism into the essentially stereotyped and poorly written role of Ivy.

The scene shifts to Jekyll's laboratory, where, posed against a backdrop of test tube racks and bubbling flasks, he drinks a foaming potion. The change is immediate and horrifying to behold, as Jekyll's features become coarse and primitive, his eyebrows shaggy, his hair disheveled, and his voice low and guttural. In addition to these outward changes, a montage of dreamlike sequences by technical expert Peter Ballbusch visually indicates the inward, mental changes as Jekyll's inhibitions slip silently beneath the surface of his conscious mind and evil bubbles up out of the depths to claim precedence. This physical personification of Jekyll's baser nature gives himself the name of Mr. Hyde.

Much later, after the drug has lost its effect, Jekyll is treated to an unexpected visit by Beatrix, who is in a state of distress because she has dreamed that he is slipping away from her. As the lovers embrace, Beatrix's father, Sir Charles Emery (Donald Crisp), arrives. Angered at finding his unchaperoned daughter in Jekyll's company and upset by Jekyll's previous refusal to give up his unorthodox research, he announces his intention of taking his daughter to the Continent, far away from Jekyll's influence.

During a subsequent transformation, Hyde goes in search of Ivy until he finds her, singing and laughing, serving drinks in a sleazy music hall. After paying the bar manager to fire her, he gives her money and sends her home in a cab. Without her job, she is now completely dependent on him for her survival. Fleming uses a number of imaginative techniques to magnify the ongoing struggle between good and evil in the story. For example, he uses the concept of light and dark to mirror the difference between the two women in Jekyll's life. Beatrix, symbolizing good, has blond hair, wears light, airy clothing, and is usually presented in brightly lit surroundings; Ivy, by contrast, has dark hair and generally wears dark, somber clothing. She is a nocturnal creature who frequents dark alleys and dimly lit rooms. Franz Waxman's musical score accentuates further the differences between the two women: the light, airy waltz is repeatedly associated with Beatrix, and the earthy rhythm of the dance hall polka with Ivy.

Jekyll returns home from one of his clandestine visits to find a telegram informing him that his fiancée is returning home. Resolving to give up his indulgences, Jekyll sends Ivy fifty pounds to enable her to leave London for good. The meeting between Jekyll and Beatrix following their long, enforced separation is a most happy affair, for Sir Charles has relented and agreed to an early marriage. However, upon his return home from the joyful reunion, the doctor is stunned to find Ivy waiting in his consulting room. Remembering his previous kindness to her, the distraught Ivy, bewildered by Hyde's cruel treatment of her and believing the fifty pounds to be merely a ploy to trap her into trying to escape, has sought the assistance of Dr. Jekyll in a last effort to retain her sanity.

The night that follows begins on a light note with Jekyll on his way to a reception where his forthcoming marriage will be announced. However, the night soon turns sinister as Jekyll finds himself uncontrollably reverting to Hyde. He arrives at Ivy's flat, where he sadistically discloses that he is the kind doctor whose help she had sought. Horrified, Ivy becomes hysterical and attempts to escape; Hyde kills her and flees into the dark, fog-shrouded streets.

Unable to enter his home because he is no longer in possession of the back door key to his laboratory, Hyde leaves a note for his friend, Dr. Lanyon, asking him to obtain the crucial vials from his laboratory and give them to a messenger whom Jekyll says he will send. However, Lanyon is suspicious and refuses to give the vials to the bogus messenger, Hyde, without some assurance that Dr. Jekyll is safe. Having no recourse, Jekyll drinks the potion, and after reverting to his normal state, he confides to his friend that he can no longer control his transformations. Knowing there is no chance now that he can marry Beatrix, Jekyll goes to her and tells her that he can never see her again. However, as he turns to leave, he reverts again to the monstrous Hyde, the sight of which causes Beatrix to swoon. Sir Charles hurries to her rescue but Hyde strikes him a killing blow and rushes off. His cape billowing and flapping like great black wings, he flees through the murky London streets. Breaking into his house, he knocks down his servant and locks himself in the laboratory.

Meanwhile, Dr. Lanyon, who has joined the police at the scene of the crime, recognizes the cane lying by Sir Charles' lifeless body as belonging to Dr. Jekyll. They arrive at Jekyll's house, where Jekyll attempts to deny the accusations of his friend, but the horrifying transformation begins again. Hyde goes beserk and attacks Lanyon, leaving his friend no option but to shoot him. With death approaching, Jekyll's soul returns to him and Hyde gives up the body he has abused and destroyed. As in the opening scene, the camera pans the church steeple and bells toll, signifying tranquillity and the return of normalcy.

Fleming's *Dr. Jekyll and Mr. Hyde* is a superlative example of what Hollywood's technology can accomplish; this 1941 version of Stevenson's classic has a polish and flow unmatched in March's 1932 version. The film received three Academy Award nominations, for the black-and-white cinematography by Joseph Ruttenberg; the film editing by Harold F. Kress; and the music score by Franz Waxman. In addition, Ingrid Bergman won the critics' acclaim for her laudable performance as the tormented Ivy Peterson; the actress has gone on to win three Academy Awards during her career: two for Best Actress (*Gaslight*, 1944; *Anastasia*, 1956) and one for Best Supporting Actress (*Murder on the Orient Express*, 1974).

D. Gail Huskins

DR. STRANGELOVE, OR: HOW I LEARNED TO STOP WORRYING AND LOVE THE BOMB

Released: 1964
Production: Stanley Kubrick for Hawk Films; released by Columbia
Direction: Stanley Kubrick
Screenplay: Stanley Kubrick, Terry Southern, and Peter George; based on the novel *Red Alert* by Peter George
Cinematography: Gilbert Taylor
Editing: Anthony Harvey
Art direction: Ken Adam
Special effects: Wally Veevers
Running time: 93 minutes

Principal characters:
Group Captain Lionel Mandrake/President
Muffley/Dr. Strangelove .... Peter Sellers
General "Buck" Turgidson .... George C. Scott
General Jack D. Ripper .... Sterling Hayden
Colonel "Bat" Guano .... Keenan Wynn
Major T. J. "King" Kong .... Slim Pickens
Ambassador de Sadesky .... Peter Bull
Miss Scott .... Tracy Reed
Lieutenant Lothar Zogg .... James Earl Jones

The films of Stanley Kubrick are most illuminating when they deal with ideas and issues. Some, notably *2001: A Space Odyssey* (1968), *A Clockwork Orange* (1971), and *Dr. Strangelove, Or: How I Learned to Stop Worrying and Love the Bomb*, are scathing, controversial chronicles of a society gone haywire, its technology dominating and ultimately triumphing over humanity. His *Paths of Glory* (1957) is one of the most eloquent of all antiwar films. Kubrick's films, however, are also entertaining: even his *The Killing* (1956), a nonmessage movie with a standard racetrack rip-off plot, is transformed by the director into a slick, taut thriller. Kubrick's most personal film to date is *Dr. Strangelove*, a ninety-three-minute joke about the atom bomb that is as comical and entertaining as it is terrifying. It is one of the best films of the 1960's, and one of the most biting satires ever produced.

The story line of *Dr. Strangelove* is frightening. Strategic Air Command General Jack D. Ripper (Sterling Hayden), a right-wing fanatic, sends a squadron of nuclear bombers to attack the Soviet Union. He seals off his base so that Muffley (Peter Sellers), the President of the United States, will be unable to contact him or reverse the order, which has been given in a secret code known only to the General. The scenario then shifts between Ripper, the flight deck of one of the B-52 Bombers en route to Russia, and the Pentagon's War Room. The design of Ken Adam, the War Room is an awesome, surreal set with an intricate map overhead; when lit up, the position of the planes nearing their target is revealed.

Among the characters are General "Buck" Turgidson (George C. Scott), a hawkish Pentagon Chief of Staff who argues for the bombing; Group Captain Lionel Mandrake (Sellers again), a level-headed RAF officer who attempts to dissuade Ripper; Colonel "Bat" Guano (Keenan Wynn), a cretinous combat officer ordered by Muffley to attack Ripper's base; Major T. J. "King" Kong (Slim Pickens), a simple-minded bomber commander; Ambassador de Sadesky (Peter Bull), the puffy Russian bureaucrat summoned by Muffley to the War Room; and Dr. Strangelove (Sellers, playing a third role), a Nazilike scientist with an alias of Merkwuerdigichiliebe who is now in the employ of the United States.

One's personal response to *Dr. Strangelove* will depend not so much on an appreciation of good cinema as on one's own politics and sense of propriety. From its inception, the film is bitingly satiric. At the onset, the camera zooms over a cloud protruding over a mountain peak. A narrator ominously explains that the Russians are creating the ultimate atomic weapon, a doomsday bomb. Two planes are flying by; one refuels another in an act of aerial copulation to the sugary background musical arrangement of "Try a Little Tenderness." All of the military and political leaders who possess unlimited power over the continued existence of the world are as imbecilic as their names: the President is Merkin Muffley; the Russian head of state is Dimitri Kissof; military men are "Buck" Turgidson, "Bat" Guano, Jack D. Ripper. Ripper's command post is called Burpelson Air Force Base.

The script, written by Kubrick, Terry Southern, and Peter George (from George's suspense novel, *Red Alert*), is loaded with coarse, pungent dialogue. General Ripper is paranoid that the Russians are planning to fluoridate America's drinking water to "sap and impurify all of our precious bodily fluids." "Buck" Turgidson explains the risks of nuclear retaliation by the Russians: "Mr. President, I'm not saying we wouldn't get our hair mussed, but I do say not more than ten or twenty million killed tops, depending on the breaks." Muffley phones Kissof (who is never seen on camera) on the hot line; after several minutes of hilarious small talk, he blubbers that "one of our generals went and did a silly thing." Muffley and Kissof argue about who is sorrier for the blunder. Mandrake learns the code which will halt the destruction, but he has no telephone change, so he phones the White House collect and is told that his call will not be accepted because he is an unknown group captain. He requests Guano to shoot off the lock of a Coke machine so that he can complete his urgent call; Guano, who is convinced that Mandrake is either a spy or a "deviated prevert," rebuffs the group captain because he will be destroying private property. Indeed, the audience should be cringing in its seats at what it is viewing: the obliteration of civilization, the result of a general, empowered to push *the* ultimate button, going mad and deciding to play with his deadly toy. Kubrick, nevertheless, succeeds in making us laugh, but, even more telling, he succeeds in making us think. Beyond this, the film is a terrific thriller: will the bombers be halted in time, or will they complete their mission and thus blast us all to oblivion?

The performances are all appropriately broad. Peter Sellers is superb in his trio of roles. Dr. Strangelove is the most outrageous of the three: his alias is Merkwuerdigichiliebe and his artificial arm, with a mind all its own, repeatedly shoots up in a Nazi salute, then sometimes punches and strangles him. Slim Pickens is all "shucks" and "heck" as "King" Kong; the image of Pickens straddling the middle of the bomb as if it were a bucking bronco, waving his ten-gallon Stetson and yelling "Yippee" as he rides to his doom, is equally horrific and hilarious. George C. Scott is brilliant and bullish as the fiery Turgidson, and Bull and Wynn are solid in their roles. The best performance is by Sterling Hayden in what is effortlessly the finest role of his career. Hayden, who also starred for Kubrick in *The Killing*, is superb as Ripper. As he chomps on his cigar and blusters on about the "Commie plot," he is the epitome of the right-wing fanatic caught up in his own paranoia.

On its release, *Dr. Strangelove* sparked controversy. The question of accidental nuclear war was debated in Europe; detractors in America argued that the film was anti-American, and that Kubrick—and the makers of *Fail Safe* (1964), a drama with a plot line similar to *Dr. Strangelove*—had betrayed their country. However, most film reviewers were ecstatic in their praise of *Dr. Strangelove*. The film was nominated for an Oscar for Best Picture, Actor (Sellers), Director, and Screenplay, but lost in all categories, but it was named on the *New York Times* "ten best" list. The New York Film Critics named Kubrick the year's best director. The Writers Guild of America cited Kubrick, Peter George, and Terry Southern for their screenplay, and George for his original story.

The film was also listed by *Time* magazine as among the top films of its decade, and in an American Film Institute survey it ranked among the fifty all-time greatest American films. The financial success of *Dr. Strangelove* is proof that the American public is not content solely with mindless comedies, romances, and thrillers. Since its release, the film has earned a respectable $5,000,000 on an original investment of $1,500,000. It was the fourteenth-highest grossing film of its year.

After Pickens and his bomb plummet towards Russia, the doomsday device is triggered and nuclear explosions are set off around the world. *Dr. Strangelove* ends with a shot of an H-bomb exploding; on the sound track is a syrupy rendition of "We'll Meet Again." This finale is funny, but painfully so, for *Dr. Strangelove* is not merely a gruesome fairy tale. The viewer—if he is willing to accept Kubrick's message—is made uncomfortably aware that the madness of the film's scenario could indeed actually come to pass.

Rob Edelman

DR. ZHIVAGO

Released: 1965
Production: Carlo Ponti for Metro-Goldwyn-Mayer
Direction: David Lean
Screenplay: Robert Bolt (AA); based on the novel of the same name by Boris Pasternak
Cinematography: Freddie A. Young (AA)
Editing: Norman Savage
Music: Maurice Jarre (AA)
Art direction: John Box and Terry March (AA); set decoration, Dario Simon (AA)
Costume design: Phyllis Dalton (AA)
Running time: 197 minutes

Principal characters:
Yuri .... Omar Sharif
Tonya .... Geraldine Chaplin
Lara .... Julie Christie
Pasha .... Tom Courtenay
Yevgraf .... Alec Guinness
Anna .... Siobhan McKenna
Alexander .... Ralph Richardson
Komarovsky .... Rod Steiger
The Girl .... Rita Tushingham

Dr. Zhivago is a radiant film, combining deep passion, art, and social commentary with stunning cinematography and an electrifying musical score. These and other qualities make *Dr. Zhivago* excellent cinema as all elements are skillfully incorporated into an epic historical saga. One of the most powerfully engrossing films ever made, *Dr. Zhivago* could very well have been successful solely on the original Boris Pasternak story, skillfully adapted to the screen by Robert Bolt. Set in Russia during the tumultuous years between 1905 and 1935, *Dr. Zhivago* chronicles the intense, rich, always heroic, but often tragic life of Yuri Zhivago (Omar Sharif). Zhivago, the orphaned son of an impoverished Russian nobleman, is reared by a gentle, aristocratic family wealthy enough to divide its days between living in St. Petersburg, the capital city of tsarist Russia, and in a lavish family estate in the provinces. Nurtured in this caring environment, Zhivago matures into a sensitive poet and physician; and, as his emotions ripen, he turns his affections toward the family's daughter Tonya (Geraldine Chaplin), whom he ultimately marries. Their lives, sheltered by love, cultural refinement, and professional stability, insulate the Zhivagos from the seamier side of life which was the lot of most Russians living before 1917.

The film is not about harmonious domesticity, however. Rather, it deals with human reactions to cataclysmic events which disrupt this insulated domesticity. The Russian Revolution of 1905, the horrors of World War I, the Bolshevik Revolution of 1917, and the subsequent civil war of 1918-1920 snare the Zhivagos into a social disruption perhaps unequaled in the twentieth century.

As a physician, Zhivago is pressed into service during World War I, and his life is never the same afterwards. There he meets the selfless chief nurse Lara (Julie Christie) whom Zhivago grows to respect for her gentle strength and capacity to nurture unbendingly in the middle of extraordinary suffering. Respect turns to love, yet Zhivago returns at the end of the war to Tonya and his family, adjusting to the dramatic new social milieu created by the new Bolshevik government. While stripped of most of their prewar riches, Zhivago's family still retains the habits of refinement, if not the actual substance. At their now commandeered country estate, Zhivago again meets Lara. Their love based on respect now spawns into a full-fledged romance; but events disrupt their passionate relationship.

On one visit to the estate, Zhivago is kidnaped by a band of Bolshevik soldiers, now entrenched in a tragic civil war; he never sees his family again since they are forced to flee to Paris because of their previous aristocratic connections. After traveling with the Bolshevik forces for the winter, Zhivago escapes, wandering half-crazed back to Lara. They live briefly together, and it is a time during which Zhivago produces his best and most intense poetry. This brief emotional and aesthetic coupling, however, does not last. Lara is forced to leave Russia because her husband, Pasha (Tom Courtenay), from whom she has been long estranged, is now deemed dangerous to the new state because he had once been a leader of the revolution. Now all of Pasha's contacts are in danger as well, and after he is found dead near Lara's house, she decides to leave Russia with the help of the unscrupulous Boris Komarovsky (Rod Steiger) with whom she had an affair as a girl. Komarovsky slithers his way through the film as an amoral, self-serving, lecherous survivor with many contacts. He is the antithesis of Zhivago, as detestable as Zhivago is admirable; still, his connections save Lara from a certain death. Escape means that Lara will never see Zhivago again, but should she stay, Zhivago also might die because of her relationship to Pasha.

Dr. Zhivago is Boris Pasternak's most passionate work. Elaborate and intricate, the novel commands intense emotional responses from the audience. Robert Bolt takes some liberties with the novel without harming the essential story. One such change is the manner in which the tale is related. In the novel, an absent third person relates the story; in the film, however, the story is told by Yevgraf (Alec Guinness), Yuri's brother, who relates Zhivago's story to a girl (Rita Tushingham) whom we suspect may be the daughter of Lara and Zhivago, who had been lost since childhood.

The success of the film rests largely with the story line; *Dr. Zhivago* is an excellent example of a writer's film. The acting is also of a universally high caliber. Omar Sharif offers one of his strongest performances; he is thoroughly convincing as the intensely passionate, sensitive, and generous Zhivago. He is boldly committed to his profession, his family, his lover, and his poetry; these commitments, pursued without reservation, complicate his life and create both his strengths and weaknesses. Geraldine Chaplin as Tonya, the gentle, accepting, always loving wife, is equally convincing. Rod Steiger and Tom Courtenay convey perfectly the qualities of their respective characters. The film is further enhanced by an unforgettable Oscar-winning score by Maurice Jarre—who had previously earned an Academy Award for his orchestration of *Lawrence of Arabia* (1962)—and by the breathtaking cinematography. The landscape photographs are meticulously composed and emphasize the enormous majesty of the Russian environment, an environment which, similar to the social forces at work in the film, reiterate the broader, uncontrollable elements in life which shape and often overwhelm the main characters.

Dr. Zhivago is a lavish, expansive film, and one which, although produced in America, captures the Russian tradition of epic works of art, whether they be historic films or novels. It is rich in strong characters who act forcefully, at times heroically, yet who are always subject to the upheavals of society. Repeatedly in and out of harmony with society but never estranged from it, the characters' lives are complexly interwoven with those of the individuals around them. This is the stuff from which great films are made, and *Dr. Zhivago* is a film that will not be quickly forgotten.

The film fared extremely well at the box office both initially and in later re-releases. It also had one of the largest viewing audiences to date when it appeared on television. The film ultimately won five Academy Awards: for Jarre's musical score, Freddie A. Young's cinematography, Robert Bolt's screenplay, Phyllis Dalton's costumes, the art direction of John Box and Terry March, and set decorations of Dario Simon. Additional nominations were earned in other categories; however, the big Oscar-winner that year was *The Sound of Music*, an all-time audience favorite. *Dr. Zhivago*'s only nomination in an acting category went to Tom Courtenay for Best Supporting Actor; he lost to Martin Balsam for *A Thousand Clowns*. Julie Christie won the Oscar that year for Best Actress, but it was for her work in *Darling* rather than *Dr. Zhivago*.

John G. Tomlinson, Jr.

DODSWORTH

Released: 1936
Production: Samuel Goldwyn for United Artists
Direction: William Wyler
Screenplay: Sidney Howard; based on the novel and play of the same name
  by Sinclair Lewis
Cinematography: Rudolph Maté
Editing: Daniel Mandell
Art direction: Richard Day (AA)
Running time: 90 minutes

Principal characters:

Sam Dodsworth	Walter Huston
Fran Dodsworth	Ruth Chatterton
Edith Cortright	Mary Astor
Arnold Iselin	Paul Lukas
Major Clyde Lockert	David Niven
Baroness Von Obersdorf	Mme. Maria Ouspenskaya

It is fortunate for filmgoing audiences that Sam Goldwyn was a stubborn man, for without his obstinacy, *Dodsworth* might never have been made. Even though his studio turned out many entertaining products year after year, Goldwyn wanted very much to do movies of importance, and the highly successful Broadway play of Sinclair Lewis' novel was one in which he was particularly interested. Against the recommendations of his advisers, who told him that *Dodsworth* would not have any appeal because it was about middle-aged people, Goldwyn proceeded to pay $160,000 for the film rights and brought Walter Huston, who had played Dodsworth on the New York stage, to Hollywood to star in the film.

Part of the appeal of *Dodsworth* lies in its uncomplicated story. Sam Dodsworth (Walter Huston) is an automobile industry magnate who has retired. At the urging of his wife Fran (Ruth Chatterton), he takes his first trip to Europe aboard the Queen Mary because she wants him to see the world. He is not particularly enthusiastic, and goes more to please her than anything else. The trip, however, becomes a psychologically fatal voyage: after much pain, anguish, revelations of true character, and selfish upheaval, their marriage is ruined. Fran Dodsworth is caught up with the desire to experience "life" before life leaves her behind. She wants the party to go on forever, without her getting old. Because of this, her husband becomes a constantly distasteful reminder that the years are passing; so she turns to younger men, first on the ship and then in cities throughout Europe.

Sam Dodsworth is an uncultured but devoted husband who is ready to

stand almost anything once, even adultery, and who cannot rid himself of the
deep sense of responsibility he has accumulated in twenty years of marriage.
However, he is also human, and while his wife is pursuing various younger
men with exotic accents, he meets a genteel, understanding widow, Edith
Cortright (Mary Astor), who is capable and willing to give him the affection
and company his wife will not. Their relationship is based on living life for
the day without expectations on the future, but their idyll is shattered by a
phone call from Fran. Rejected by her last suitor and his baroness mother,
Fran says that she is ready to go home and settle down. Sam's sense of loyalty
and honor leave him no alternative but to go with her; she is his wife,
representing the life he has known. As their ship prepares to leave port,
however, Fran's shallow repentence for what she has done quickly evaporates
and her mean self-centeredness surfaces. It takes only moments for Sam to
realize that his wife and the life back home are no longer what he wants. As
Edith Cortright stands watching the luxury ship pull out to sea, a small dinghy
ties up at the dock with a beaming Sam aboard, returning to the new life he
has chosen.

Dodsworth is an extremely well-made and well-acted film. Sam Dodsworth
is a man we understand and respect, if not altogether believe for there is a
basic improbability inherent in the story, and therefore, in Sam's character;
how could he and Fran have been married for twenty years before he realized
what a priggish, selfish, vain woman she was? Perhaps all his years spent
building his automobile business kept him from really knowing his wife; or
perhaps he simply cannot believe that she is the woman he married.

Dodsworth is a very personal story which gives the impression of a film of
large scope, mainly because of Walter Huston's portrayal. Since he commanded the role on Broadway for two years prior to the movie, it was a role
in which he was as comfortable as any actor could be, and yet the acting is
entirely fresh. Huston's Dodsworth is a man of sympathy, humor, irony, and
delicacy, and it is sometimes impossible to tell what in Dodsworth is Huston
and what is Sinclair Lewis, since the actor fits the character perfectly.

As Fran Dodsworth, Ruth Chatterton creates one of film's most despicable
women; her dialogue spews forth venomously and she is consummate in
displaying the character's embittered egotism through the way she holds her
body, tight and self-conscious, like someone always on display. The character
of Edith Cortright is as far removed as possible from the usual "other woman,"
and Mary Astor plays her with remarkable grace and intelligence. Also adding
to the character of the film is the casting of a young man named David Niven
as Major Clive Lockert in his first role for Goldwyn, although he had had
a contract with the studio for some time.

Although *Dodsworth* is essentially a static and talky film, William Wyler
has directed it skillfully in cinematic terms. It easily could have been a visually
confining piece, but it is not; the pace flows evenly and is dramatically bal-

anced to sustain the impact of important scenes, then eases naturally back into the expository. The look of the film is grand, expensive, and very Continental, although most of the major shooting took place at the Goldwyn studios in Hollywood. Only a small second-unit was sent to Europe to film the exteriors which give the film such a colorful background.

Goldwyn's insistence that *Dodsworth* was important and thus had to be perfect almost kept *Dodsworth* from ultimately being filmed. Sidney Howard's dramatization of the novel was submitted; according to those involved, it was well-constructed and, in fact, expertly concealed some of the story's basic flaws. Goldwyn, however, brought in another writer, who was then embarrassed because he could find no way to improve upon Howard's adaptation. Over the next two years, Goldwyn hired and fired five more writers and accepted, then rejected, eight different drafts before he finally realized that he could not improve on Howard's version, and that adaptation at last became the official screenplay.

Juliette Friedgen

DOG DAY AFTERNOON

Released: 1975
Production: Martin Bregman and Martin Elfand for Warner Bros.
Direction: Sidney Lumet
Screenplay: Frank Pierson (AA); based on a *Life* magazine article "The Boys in the Bank" by P. F. Kluge and Thomas Moore
Cinematography: Victor J. Kemper
Editing: Dede Allen
Running time: 130 minutes

Principal characters:
Sonny .... Al Pacino
Sal .... John Cazale
Leon .... Chris Sarandon
Sheldon .... James Broderick
Moretti .... Charles Durning
Mulvaney .... Sully Boyar
Angie .... Susan Peretz
Sylvia .... Penny Allen
Jenny .... Carol Kane
Miriam .... Marcia Jean Kurtz
Bobby .... Gary Springer

In August, 1972, two gunmen attempted to rob a Chase Manhattan Bank branch office in Brooklyn, New York. Caught in the act, the pair held nine bank employees hostage for a period of fourteen hours, turning the robbery into an event worthy of live television coverage. One of the perpetrators, an admitted bisexual and former bank teller named John Wojtowicz, claimed he needed money to finance a sex change operation for his "girl friend." This bizarre scenario ended in disaster: while attempting to board a jet at Kennedy Airport to fly out of the country, Wojtowicz was captured and his cohort killed. These events are re-created in *Dog Day Afternoon*, a perceptive blend of comedy and pathos.

Although the robbers and their caper are fictionalized for the film, the events remain just as bizarre as they were in reality. The robbery begins in the manner of a comedy routine as Sonny (Al Pacino), the homosexual desperado, hops around and issues orders to those in the bank as if he is directing a three-ring circus. After their initial shock, the bank hostages become part of the show. They watch themselves on television and take a pizza break; women vainly primp their hair in anticipation of their appearance on the nightly news. Sonny even shows one of the young girls drill and ceremony techniques with his rifle.

Sal (John Cazale), Sonny's partner in crime, says little and appears to be in a constant fog; thus, most of the action centers around Sonny, who is portrayed as an outcast, a man who has been pushed and tormented from birth. His mother has refused to acknowledge that he is an adult and manages his life in spite of his wishes. In the midst of his troubles, all she can murmur is, "How beautiful you were as a baby." Angie (Susan Peretz), his overweight wife, carries on about her problems and refuses to let him complete a sentence when she talks to him over the telephone. She has grown to resemble a pig, and defensively explains that she is not at the bank site because she is unable to hire a babysitter.

It is no wonder, then, that Sonny has turned to Leon (Chris Sarandon), a woman trapped in a man's body. In an extremely well-played telephone scene between the two—which compares favorably with the Luise Rainer soliloquy in *The Great Ziegfeld* (1936)—it is revealed that Leon is the only person who has ever made an honest effort to listen to what is on Sonny's mind. Despite the rather shallow reference that Sonny's homosexuality is the result of the emasculating women in his life, it is to the filmmakers' credit that homosexuals are portrayed as human beings with complex lives and emotions. Although Sonny and Leon are not typical, everyday citizens, neither are they one-dimensional limp-wristed stereotypes. Before filming commenced, the script was carefully scrutinized by the National Gay Task Force, an image-conscious homosexual organization.

Certainly, while Sonny is unemployed and anonymous, a mere speck in the sea of eight million New York faces, he is also an individual, a man desperately trying to define himself. He is compassionate and evinces a genuine sympathy for the inconvenience he is causing the hostages. In a scene in which he dictates his will, he expresses his love for both his wife and mother in spite of their personalities. It is clear that his motive for robbing the bank is not merely monetary; the act is his way of lashing out at a society which has dehumanized him. It is his moment in the spotlight as he struts out in front of the bank, performs for the crowd to win their support, and, in an ultimate irony, throws a bundle of paper bills at his audience.

However, after his capture, with the gun of an FBI agent pointed at his head, Sonny is the portrait of the consummate loser. He appears bewildered as he is read his rights, with the thunder of jet planes taking off and landing in the background. His day of glory has ended, and he knows that all he has left is the anonymity of a jail cell.

Whether comically hopping around the bank and waving his rifle or stoically reading his will, Al Pacino is perfectly cast as Sonny and gives a bravura performance. His voice rises when he is nervous; his tongue lashes out, he shrugs his shoulders, twitches his eyes, and his fingers nervously crumple a paper ball. From his screen debut as a junkie in *The Panic in Needle Park* (1971) through his roles as the honest cop bucking the corrupt system in *Serpico* (1973) and as Michael Corleone in *The Godfather* (1971) and *The*

Godfather, Part II (1974), Pacino has proved to be one of the more durable ethnic antiheroes of the 1970's.

Pacino is ably assisted by a hand-picked cast of character types, notably Chris Sarandon as Leon and Penny Allen as a bold bank teller. Sarandon brings a special humanity to a character who could easily have been played as a caricature; Allen is appropriately mouthy as a hostage who will not sit back and accept her fate. Charles Durning and James Broderick are cast as police officers (Durning was inexplicably selected over Sarandon as the year's Best Supporting Actor by the National Board of Review), while a pre-*Hester Street* (1975) Carol Kane may be seen as one of the prisoners. John Cazale is adequate as Sal, rivaling his best film role as the wormy Fredo Corleone in *The Godfather* and *The Godfather, Part II*.

Frank Pierson's screenplay is both funny and touching, and the film is crisply directed by Sidney Lumet. Over the past two decades, Lumet has consistently utilized New York City exteriors more creatively than any other director. The streets and neighborhoods of the city are the on-location sets of *The Pawnbroker* (1965), *A View from the Bridge* (1961), *The Anderson Tapes* (1971), *Bye Bye Braverman* (1968), and *Serpico*, among others. In *The Pawnbroker* and *Serpico*, he most successfully captures the grit and soul of the city; in *The Wiz* (1978), he transforms locations from the Brooklyn Bridge to the subways, the ghetto streets to the World Trade Center, into a majestic fairyland. *Dog Day Afternoon* was shot outside a warehouse in the Park Slope section of Brooklyn since Lumet was unable to film on the site of the actual robbery, several miles away, on Avenue P in Midwood.

Dog Day Afternoon's one glaring weakness is that it is too much of a comedy with dramatic touches in the first half, then a drama with comic bits in the second. While Sonny's personality is completely explored, very little is revealed about his partner. Overall, though, *Dog Day Afternoon* is an entertaining and insightful re-creation of reality. The film, which cost $3,500,000 to produce, was a box-office smash. It has earned $22,500,000 since its release, and was the seventh-highest grossing film of 1975. *Dog Day Afternoon* was Oscar-nominated for Best Picture, Best Actor (Al Pacino), Best Supporting Actor (Chris Sarandon, in his screen debut), Best Director, and Best Screenplay. All were losers: only Frank Pierson was honored for his script, as he also was by the Writers Guild of America. However, the Union of Film Critics in Athens voted the film the best to be released in Greece for the year, the National Board of Review named it to its Ten Best List, and Pacino was cited as Best Actor at the San Sebastian Film Festival and by the British Academy, the latter for both *Dog Day Afternoon* and *The Godfather, Part II*.

John Wojtowicz, the actual lead robber, was sentenced to a twenty-year prison term for his part in the robbery. He received $7,500 and a percentage of the net profit for his permission to be depicted in the film. Under a New

York State law passed in 1977, the state Crime Victims Compensation Board made available to the original hostages monies from *Dog Day Afternoon*'s earnings owed to Wojtowicz. After its release, Wojtowicz called *Dog Day Afternoon* "only thirty percent true." The filmmakers, however, claimed from the outset that it was only "based on a true incident." Wojtowicz was paroled in November, 1978.

In 1975, Wojtowicz's wife Carmen filed a lawsuit in New York State Supreme Court against Warner Bros., the film's distributor, and Dell Publishing and Delacorte Press, publishers of the follow-up novel. Mrs. Wojtowicz claimed the depiction of her character in the film constituted an invasion of her privacy. In turn, the Authors League of America, fearing costly legal actions if "unidentified" persons could sue filmmakers or novelists whose works were based on fact (Mrs. Wojtowicz was not actually named or pictured in the film), filed an Amicus Curiae brief in favor of the defendants. The case was dismissed in 1978.

Rob Edelman

DOUBLE INDEMNITY

Released: 1944
Production: Joseph Sistrom for Paramount
Direction: Billy Wilder
Screenplay: Billy Wilder and Raymond Chandler; based on the novel *Three of a Kind* by James M. Cain
Cinematography: John F. Seitz
Editing: Doane Harrison
Costume design: Edith Head
Music: Miklos Rozsa
Running time: 107 minutes

Principal characters:
Walter Neff .... Fred MacMurray
Phyllis Dietrichson .... Barbara Stanwyck
Barton Keyes .... Edward G. Robinson
Mr. Jackson .... Porter Hall
Lola Dietrichson .... Jean Heather

It is difficult to believe that such a brilliant film as *Double Indemnity* was only Billy Wilder's second directorial assignment. An immensely talented and volatile Austrian who left Europe in the 1930's to escape from Hitler, Wilder had a long and successful career as a screenwriter, both in Europe and the United States, but often made studio producers uneasy because of his ability to expose human weakness on the screen. Wilder has a sardonic wit and the ability to turn bad taste into good box office, as demonstrated in his first film directed in the United States—*The Major and the Minor* (1942), a pre-Lolita comedy in which Ray Milland is attracted to Ginger Rogers disguised as a twelve-year-old child.

In spite of the fact that *Double Indemnity* is now firmly established as a classic, it was a difficult project for Wilder. Paramount producer Joe Sistrom discovered James M. Cain's novella "Double Indemnity," which had appeared as a serial in Liberty magazine in 1936. The plot appealed immediately to Wilder but Charles Brackett, his long-time collaborator, hated the story so much that he refused either to work on the screenplay or to produce the film. This refusal terminated a working relationship that had lasted for seven years, and another writer had to be found. James M. Cain was the obvious choice to help adapt the story, but he was at that time working at Twentieth Century-Fox on *Western Union* (1941). Sistrom then suggested Raymond Chandler, since he thought that his writing style was rather similar to Cain's—a comparison that never failed to annoy Chandler.

Sistrom was partly right: although Chandler was a better writer than Cain, both men were particularly responsive to the ambience of California. Chandler's style was quite unique, however; and after reading a copy of *The Big Sleep* at one sitting, Wilder realized that its author was an ideal partner for this film. Unfortunately, Chandler had a severe drinking problem and no experience at writing screenplays (it was his first assignment); he did not seem much interested in moviemaking, had never collaborated with another writer, and hated Wilder on sight (the feeling was mutual). Chandler had hoped to finish the screenplay quickly, and he produced his version in five weeks. Wilder was not satisfied, and they worked together on the script for six months; Chandler was also forced to stay around the studio during filming.

Then came the problem of casting, although in retrospect it seems strange that any problems arose at all. The screenplay was touted around Hollywood, and not one of the leading actors of the day wanted to play the part of Walter Neff; *Double Indemnity* was considered to be a distasteful and immoral film. Wilder wanted Fred MacMurray to play the role—a strange choice, since the role of Neff required him to play a likable insurance agent who commits a brutal murder. The murder was not a crime of passion which the audience could understand, nor an accidental murder, but a calculated crime for lust and gain. Until then, MacMurray's career had been in light comedy, but Wilder finally persuaded him to accept the part; MacMurray thought it would end his career, but instead it was the best role he ever had in films.

Double Indemnity has an unusual plot in that the killer is identified in the opening scenes, a technique used repeatedly since then but uncommon at the time. Walter Neff (Fred MacMurray) is dictating an office memo to his boss. Neff is clearly dying from gunshot wounds but has returned late at night to the offices of the large insurance company for which he works. The dictation allows Neff's voice to change subtly from that of confessor to narrator and leads us into the flashback. This device is almost always effective but works exceptionally well in this case for it allows Chandler's descriptive linking passages to be spoken by a narrator, using language which would have been too literary as spoken dialogue.

The events related in the flashback begin as Walter Neff makes a seemingly routine call on a customer about auto insurance. The house he visits is a Spanish-style and slightly run down house in Glendale, California; the customer is out but Neff asks to see the man's wife instead. It would be difficult to forget Barbara Stanwyck's first appearance as Phyllis Dietrichson: she has been taking a sunbath and appears at the top of the staircase wearing only a bathtowel and a look of cool appraisal. Stanwyck is a gifted and intelligent actress, not strictly beautiful in the Hollywood style of Lana Turner or Heddy Lamarr, and her career has been that of an actress rather than a sex symbol. In this role, however, she conveys superbly a kind of sluttish sexuality. It is clear that there is a mutual attraction between Neff and Phyllis. His is a purely physical one, but she has a strangely calculating look. Neff is invited back to the house, Dietrichson is again out, and this time the maid is significantly absent as well.

Phyllis is wearing a dress this time, sexy but not blatantly so, and as she descends the staircase, the camera tracks along focusing on her chain anklet. She is, of course, unhappily married to an older man (his second wife), and is desperate to escape the boredom of life with a husband she hates, a resentful stepdaughter, and an allowance that does not begin to buy all the things she wants. She married for a kind of security and now finds herself a prisoner; but she does not intend to walk out empty-handed. She is obviously an experienced predator, and after conveying her interest in Neff, she warily outlines her plan to take out a large insurance policy on her husband's life. She wishes to have the policy signed as though it were for auto insurance, and she wishes her husband to know nothing about the arrangement. The conversation is like a chess game. Neff is responsive to her, but too astute to be fooled by an insurance deal which is obviously a prologue to murder. He rejects the whole idea and leaves, but the attraction is too strong; they meet again and he is drawn into her plan. Perhaps he also feels that as an insurance agent he is in an ideal position to plan and execute a fool-proof insurance fraud.

Like all murders planned so that two people can be together, the planning and aftermath of the crime inevitably mean that from the beginning, the parties concerned cannot meet without arousing suspicion. Most of their meetings take place in the very mundane atmosphere of a supermarket (Chandler used Jerry's Market on Melrose Avenue in Los Angeles for the locale), and these scenes are stunningly effective. Phyllis methodically selects groceries and at the same time coolly outlines the murder plan. It is in these scenes particularly that Stanwyck's acting is so strong, as she convinces us not only that Phyllis is capable of getting rid of her husband, but also that she is capable of persuading her lover not only to be an accomplice but also actually to commit the crime. The murder is carried out, while the camera rests on Phyllis Dietrichson's face as she remains virtually unmoved by the brutal killing taking place beside her. After the body has been carefully placed near the railway tracks (the policy now includes a double indemnity clause to include a rail accident), they must now wait for the insurance company to pay. The authorities seem to accept a verdict of accidental death, but the insurance company is more suspicious and throws out the claim.

Neff's boss at the insurance company is Burton Keyes (Edward G. Robinson), and he and Neff are friends as well as colleagues. Keyes loves the insurance business and seemingly has no private life at all. It is significant that at one time he was engaged, but this was abruptly terminated after he had the insurance company investigate his prospective wife. Keyes looks upon the insurance company business not as a collection of files and claims but as an endlessly fascinating series of case histories, constantly challenging him. When Keyes gets a phony claim, his dyspepsia gives him no peace; and the

Dietrichson claim gives his digestion a very hard time indeed.

The role of Burton Keyes could have been a rather colorless one had it not been for the magnetic presence of Edward G. Robinson. In one scene he reels off a long list of insurance company statistics on different types of death, with subdivisions for each section, to illustrate the improbability of the Dietrichson claim. Very few actors could have brought that kind of dialogue to life, but Robinson succeeds.

As the story draws to a close, the lovers continue to meet only in the supermarket, but now Neff is very nervous and wants to get out. Phyllis takes off her dark glasses, and, over a display of canned goods, informs him with chilling calm that people who commit murders cannot get off the trolley car when they choose but must stay together "all the way down the line." Neff finally kills Phyllis, and the film ends as he painfully makes his way to Keyes's office and, while dying of gunshot wounds himself, confesses his crime to his boss. The ending of *Double Indemnity* was changed after filming the original ending showing Neff in the gas chamber at Folsom. Wilder, against all advice, insisted on scrapping the footage and writing and filming a different ending. His decision was a fortunate one: the final scene between Keyes and Neff is beautifully done and manages to convince the audience that Walter Neff, although a murderer, does deserve some sympathy.

Elizabeth Leese

DRACULA

Released: 1931
Production: Universal
Direction: Tod Browning
Screenplay: Garrett Fort; based on Hamilton Deane's and John L. Balderston's stage adaptation of the novel of the same name by Bram Stoker
Cinematography: Karl Freund
Editing: Milton Carruth
Running time: 84 minutes

Principal characters:
Count Dracula .... Bela Lugosi
Mina .... Helen Chandler
Jonathan Harker .... David Manners
Renfield .... Dwight Frye
Professor Van Helsing .... Edward Van Sloan

Bram Stoker's *Dracula*, published in 1897, is an outstanding gothic novel. It is a long tale, replete with the conventions of its day—sentimental subplots, the letter format of the opening chapters, lengthy reported conversations—yet it remains eminently readable even in an age of novelettes and journalistic prose. It has been subjected to Freudian analysis, interpreted as a metaphor for the repression of female sexuality, and dismissed as a hack writer's "penny dreadful." Yet *Dracula* has never been out of print, and since the early days of the cinema the tale of an aristocratic vampire who travels from Eastern Europe to Victorian London in pursuit of human blood has fascinated filmmakers throughout the world. The United States, Great Britain, France, Germany, Japan, and Mexico have all produced distinctive Draculas of their own.

The first film version, produced independently of any of the stage versions circulating in the early years of this century, was a German silent film released in 1922. Directed by F. W. Murnau, *Nosferatu: A Symphony in Terror* features the extraordinary character actor, Max Schreck (whose name means "Terror" in German), as the undead count. Though Murnau, who was unwilling to pay for the rights to Stoker's novel, gave his film a different title, he drew heavily on the original work for his screenplay. The transition from novel to film is most assured. Of all the screen versions, *Nosferatu* is perhaps the truest to the spirit of the book. It is a masterpiece of narrative in its own right, weeding out the longer, less exotic sections and stretching the boundaries of the medium with unsettling use of negative images and fast-motion. A court action brought by Stoker's widow resulted in the destruction of many prints of Murnau's film (though *Nosferatu* survives in a variety of versions), and it was not until almost ten years later that an "official" *Dracula* film was undertaken. The director was Tod Browning, veteran of macabre silent films such as *The Unknown* (1927) and *London after Midnight* (1927), and the production company was Carl Laemmle's Universal Pictures.

Renfield (Dwight Frye), an English businessman, is on the last stage of his coach journey to the castle of Count Dracula (Bela Lugosi), a Transylvanian nobleman who plans to purchase property in London. The locals, a sullen and suspicious crew, mysteriously cross themselves at the mention of the Count's name, and urge Renfield to abandon his trip. He presses on, only to be abandoned by his driver at a bleak crossroads. Here he is met by a mute coachman and conducted at a frantic pace into the Count's abode. Dracula, who appears only between sunset and sunrise, proves a refined, almost congenial host; but as the days pass, Renfield realizes that he is being kept a prisoner, and worse, that he is in danger of losing his immortal soul. For Dracula is a vampire—a reanimated corpse who feeds off the blood of the living, turning his victims into vampires in the process. A cunning fiend, the Count plans to take up residence in a land where the prevailing skepticism will enable him to pursue his career undetected.

Once he decides that he has learned enough about England from his unwilling guest, Dracula sets sail for the White Cliffs ensconsed within a casket containing his native earth. Ever-hungry, he decimates the cargo vessel's crew en route. For a while after arriving in England he finds his strange need for blood satisfied, until he encounters Professor Van Helsing (Edward Van Sloan), a middle-European doctor who has dedicated his life to battling the undead. Van Helsing recognizes Dracula as a vampire as he does not cast a shadow nor a reflection, and henceforth the battlelines are drawn. The Count pits his creatures, among them Renfield, now the dessicated inmate of a lunatic asylum, against Van Helsing and his allies. Their prize is the soul of his latest victim, Mina (Helen Chandler). After a savage struggle the forces of light triumph, and Van Helsing destroys the vampire in time-honored fashion, with a wooden stake through the heart.

The most obvious problem with Universal's *Dracula* is its script: even a first-rate cast and high production values cannot compensate for the mediocre screenplay, adapted not from Stoker's novel but from a hacked-out melodrama in which the most interesting occurrences take place offstage. Dracula's skill at metamorphosis; his control over bats, rats, and wolves; his phenomenal strength; and the scene in which he crawls head-first down the castle wall are dropped in favor of Garrett Fort's trite dialogue. Even the Count's demise is depicted by an offscreen groan—a tragically insipid end for evil incarnate. And despite his distinguished career in silent pictures, Tod Browning's *mise-en-scene* is rather tedious. The fact that *Dracula* was an early talking picture, constrained by cumbrous equipment, does not excuse sloppy pace and poor staging. In contrast, *Frankenstein*, directed the same year by James

Whale, is visually innovative and cohesive. Unlike Browning's film it stands the test of time remarkably well.

What saves *Dracula* from mediocrity is its cast. Some of the supporting players, particularly Edward Van Sloan and Dwight Frye (who also played the sadistic dwarf in *Frankenstein*), are excellent; while in the title role Bela Lugosi established himself as the definitive screen vampire. Born in Hungary, Lugosi had worked with Murnau (*Der Januskopf*, 1920) before emigrating to the United States. After a diverse stage and film career, he played Dracula on Broadway and was invited to portray the Count in pictures following the death of Browning's first choice, silent horror-star Lon Chaney. Aquiline and perhaps too exotic to be cast as a "straight" leading man, Lugosi was instantly identified with Stoker's character. Without a doubt, he is at his best when saying Stoker's lines: "I never drink . . . wine," or "Wolves . . . children of the night . . . what music they make." Such dialogue, immaculately delivered, stands many stories above the vapid verbalizing of playwrights Deane and Balderston. And today, with subsequent competition from powerful presences such as Christopher Lee, John Carradine, and Klaus Kinski, Lugosi's performance has not been bettered.

Without Lugosi's unique contribution, the history of Universal Pictures might have been quite different. *Dracula*, released on Valentine's Day of 1931, was the company's largest grossing film in years. It launched the most celebrated of all the horror-picture cycles, a series which included the individual adventures of Dracula, Frankenstein's monster, the Mummy, the Wolf Man, and the Invisible Man, and which, in its declining years, incorporated them all into such formula potboilers as *Abbott and Costello Meet Frankenstein* (1948). Despite its less inventive latter days, the Universal cycle boasted a distinguished repertory of actors and distinctive cinematography and production design, the art direction being fashioned after the dusty vaults and dark interiors created by Charles Hall for *Dracula*.

Lugosi himself auditioned for the monster's role in *Frankenstein*, but decided not to take the part (which, unlike the simple makeup job on *Dracula*, demanded four hours of preparation daily). Instead, the role went to an English actor named William Henry Pratt, better known as Boris Karloff. Between them, the two men cornered the market on the best horror roles for almost twenty years, and both men went on acting up until their deaths. Despite sequels and imitations, Lugosi and Karloff remain in the popular imagination and critical esteem alike the definitive Dracula and Frankenstein, and their portrayals kept the candle of supernatural unease burning well into the all-too-real twentieth century.

V. I. Huxner

DRUMS ALONG THE MOHAWK

Released: 1939
Production: Raymond Griffith for Twentieth Century-Fox
Direction: John Ford
Screenplay: Lamar Trotti and Sonya Levien; based on the novel of the same
name by Walter D. Edmonds
Cinematography: Bert Glennon
Editing: Robert Simpson
Running time: 130 minutes

Principal characters:
Gilbert Martin	Henry Fonda
Lana (Magdelana) Martin	Claudette Colbert
Mrs. McKlennar	Edna May Oliver
Caldwell	John Carradine
Reverend Rosenkrantz	Arthur Shields
General Nicholas Herkimer	Roger Imhof
Adam Helmer	Ward Bond
Blue Back	Chief Big Tree

In the twelve-month period from March 2, 1939, through March 15, 1940, John Ford released four films: *Stagecoach* (1939), *Young Mr. Lincoln* (1939), *Drums Along the Mohawk*, and *The Grapes of Wrath* (1940). There is general agreement among film scholars that *Stagecoach*, *Young Mr. Lincoln*, and *The Grapes of Wrath* are major achievements in Ford's fifty-year film career. It is generally conceded that *Drums Along the Mohawk*, does not quite match the astonishing creativity of the other three films of this highly productive period; this is not to suggest, however, that the film is not without significant merit. It is an exciting and vivid film—Ford's first in color—and is directly concerned with a theme which Ford would examine many times in the next thirty-five years—that of Americans settling the frontier.

The film begins in Albany, New York, just before the Revolutionary War at the wedding of Lana Borst (Claudette Colbert) to Gilbert Martin (Henry Fonda). Lana, the daughter of a wealthy Dutch burgher, is accustomed to the comforts and pleasures of a settled town; her husband, a yeoman farmer, will take her to his frontier homestead in the Mohawk Valley. After the wedding, they leave her father's home in a wagon leading a cow and proceed west into the wilderness. They spend their wedding night at an inn, where they have a troubling encounter with a sinister man named Caldwell (John Carradine) who is most interested in Gil's political views on the crisis between the colonies and England.

The next evening they arrive at the cabin Gil has constructed for his bride. It is a small, stark hovel compared to her father's brick mansion in Albany, and Lana is shocked, thoroughly frightened, and drenched by the fierce thunderstorm through which they have driven; but when an Indian invades the cabin, she collapses in total hysteria. Gil slaps her back to sensibility, and when Lana calms down, he introduces the Indian as Blue Back (Chief Big Tree), a friend and "a better Christian than you or I."

In a series of short scenes, Lana is shown slowly adjusting to the life of a farm wife. Gil takes her to the fort, which is the center of community life; here she meets the other farm wives and watches the men drill as militia in order to defend themselves against a possible attack by the English and the Indians. That attack comes swiftly, and Lana and Gil are forced to abandon the farm and flee to the fort. The Indians are driven back by the militia at the fort, but in the process, the Martins have lost everything including the baby Lana was carrying.

Without either home or money, Gil hires himself out to work the farm of Mrs. McKlennar (Edna May Oliver), a robust and willful woman who is steadfast in her love for her late husband, Barney. She is also kind and motherly and soon looks upon Gil and Lana as her children. She waits with Lana when Gil is called to go off to fight with the militia, and when the soldiers finally return, she sets up a hospital in her kitchen. Gil, however, does not return with the militia, and Lana sets out to search for him, finding him ultimately in a ditch, unable to walk. Lana manages to bring him back to the house to tend to his wounds. As Gil awakens after a recuperative period, Lana tells him that she is expecting another child. Meanwhile, downstairs in the kitchen, General Nicholas Herkimer (Roger Imhof), the leader of the successful campaign, dies of his wounds.

In the spring, amid much drunken celebration by the father's friends, Gil and Lana's baby is born. Just as life seems to be improving for the Martins, the Indians attack once more, led by Caldwell, the Tory agent whom the Martins had met on their wedding night. During this attack, the Indians invade Mrs. McKlennar's bedroom, and in a comic battle of wills, she forces them to carry her bed out of the house which they have set on fire. Although the Martins manage to escape to the fort with the feisty widow, Mrs. McKlennar is killed in the ensuing attack on the fort.

With the fort in grave danger and the women helping the men defend it, a farmer volunteers to go for help by night. When he is quickly captured and tied to a burning haywagon by the Indians, Reverend Rosenkrantz (Arthur Shields), a militant minister, shoots him to save him from the more painful death by fire. Gil, volunteering to run for help, gets away from the fort, but is soon discovered by three Indians who start pursuing him in an epic foot race that lasts past daybreak. Gil finally is victorious in outdistancing his pursuers and returns with the soldiers, who break the siege and enter the fort to raise the new American flag—a symbol which seems to promise the settlers a new era of peace in which they can raise their families in the fertile valley.

John Ford would never again be quite so positive about the settling of the American continent; in his very next film, *The Grapes of Wrath*, he would deal with the failure of America to care for all her people, and World War II would further challenge his belief in the morality of America's past. But in 1939, he was convinced that taking the land from the Indians was both necessary and proper, and the Indians in the film are portrayed as truly savage, with no evidence of humanity. They are more like demons than men, with the only good Indian being a Christian, an emasculated comic figure who has no real function in the community.

The white settlers are portrayed as decent, moral people who yearn only for peace in order to farm their rich valley and to rear their families; they are the people who will make America great, and there is no sense that they have committed any wrong in driving the Indians from the land. Ford here presents good and evil only in shades of black and white whereas in his later films, the grays would predominate. *Drums Along the Mohawk* was Ford's last film in which everything was simple and clear-cut.

Ford was always to prefer the look of black-and-white cinematography to color, but he worked easily with color from the beginning, and his sense of color composition in *Drums Along the Mohawk* is superb. He uses color to enhance the mood of the story; the Indians, for example, are associated with fire, like demons from hell. In the foot race sequence, while the Indians seem strongest at night, Gil grows stronger as day breaks, and the arrival of a glorious Technicolor dawn signals his triumph.

Henry Fonda starred in three of the four films Ford directed during this period, but there is very little similarity in the three characters Fonda plays: Abraham Lincoln in *Young Mr. Lincoln*, Tom Joad in *The Grapes of Wrath*, and Gil Martin in *Drums Along the Mohawk*. Fonda demonstrates the depth and power of his skill and talent in all three roles, and his Gil Martin characterization portrays a stalwart young farmer sure of himself and his young country as he and his wife begin their life together. The scene in which Gil holds his newborn child for the first time is a model of acting as Fonda conveys excitement, awe, pride, embarrassment, and the burden of responsibility, in a charmingly comic manner. Edna May Oliver was nominated for Best Supporting Actress in her role as Mrs. McKlennar; her superb performance is full of nuance as well as the bolder strokes of an endearing and broadly comic character. Arthur Shields is memorable in his small role as the fighting parson, a character Ford would return to again in *The Searchers* (1956). Although Ford would return to the theme of settlers confronting the wilderness many times during his career, he never again would view their efforts with quite the same equanimity as he does in *Drums Along the Mohawk*.

Don K Thompson

EAST OF EDEN

Released: 1955
Production: Elia Kazan for Warner Bros.
Direction: Elia Kazan
Screenplay: Paul Osborn; based on the novel of the same name by John Steinbeck
Cinematography: Ted McCord
Editing: Owen Marks
Running time: 115 minutes

Principal characters:
Cal Trask	James Dean
Abra	Julie Harris
Adam Trask	Raymond Massey
Aron Trask	Richard Davalos
Kate	Jo Van Fleet (AA)

The film *East of Eden* is a period piece, an attempt to reconstruct faithfully Monterey and Salinas, California, in 1917. The title and basic story are both taken from the 1952 novel by John Steinbeck, an American author who was born in Salinas in 1902 and who devoted much of his writing to stories set in this same locale. Popular at the time of the film's casting, the novel proved a superb vehicle to begin the all too brief, dazzling career of James Dean, whose performance dominates the film and provides a large degree of its power and critical interest.

While the film's director, Elia Kazan, remains an accomplished *auteur*, Dean's three extant films—*East of Eden*, *Rebel Without a Cause* (1955), and the less successful *Giant* (1956)—all under different directors, are united more by the young star's acting style and skill than by any *auteur* considerations. His accidental death on September 30, 1955 (at age twenty-four, while driving his Porsche sportscar to the Salinas road races), began a posthumous, cultlike recognition, perhaps matched only by the death of Valentino in 1926. To this day, his moody, introspective, sometimes mumbled, often method performances capture audience interest; and he is as well known in Tokyo or London as he is in Indiana, where he grew up. His acting style has been judged imitative, especially in comparison to early Marlon Brando performances. Still, his unique charisma makes otherwise modest films such as *East of Eden* and *Rebel Without a Cause* very special artifacts.

Steinbeck's novel was in part intended to modernize the Biblical myth of Cain and Abel. Spanning two generations, it concentrates on the figures of Adam Trask (the favorite son) and his Cainlike brother Charles. Further, Adam's twin sons, the adored Aron and the misunderstood Caleb, are parallel Abel-Cain figures. Steinbeck's vision of Caleb as more misunderstood than malevolent, more neurotic than evil, seems today an uncanny match for the very *persona* Dean was developing in early television and theatrical performances. And while Dean's national and international fame came primarily from the later *Rebel Without a Cause*, released close to the time of his death, his dominance as Cal Trask in *East of Eden* was assurance of stardom.

Appropriately, the screenplay focuses more on the second generation, especially on the character of Cal and on his clumsy search both to give and to receive love. The film, in fact, begins with a love triangle. The respected and conservative Aron (Richard Davalos) is close to marriage with the girl Abra (Julie Harris); the rejected and moody Cal is puzzled by his (to his own mind evil) attraction to the same girl. Throughout the film, the mutual love between Cal and Abra progresses at extraordinary expense to Cal's brother and father (Raymond Massey). But, ironically, that same growing love provides index to Cal's psychological metamorphosis. The hurt, halting incompetence of Cal's early emotions are replaced by rich, mature relationships at the film's end.

Such progress is not without cost. Beyond Cal's reluctant courting of Abra are two actions, one springing from kindness, the other from hate, that together result in much evil for Cal's family. First, Cal's father is an idealistic man who exhausts his small funds in an attempt to develop a method for shipping ice-packed produce. Although he cares for his son, he neither understands him nor expresses his love for him. In the hope of gaining that love, Cal secretly borrows five thousand dollars to take advantage of a coming wartime market for beans. When the profits from this successful venture are presented to the father, the money is rejected; the ensuing heated dialogue causes the father to become paralyzed by an apparent stroke. Second, Aron naïvely believes his mother is dead, while in fact she is Kate (Jo Van Fleet), the madam of a nearby brothel. Cal, in contrast, knows this (in fact, he borrows his capital from her). Feeling guilty as a result of his father's stroke, Cal brings Aron to the brothel, destroying his brother's illusions and, apparently, his sanity as well.

The slender credibility of these strange situations is mitigated only by Dean's credible performance. His shy, sly, and very brave meeting with his mother to borrow a then vast sum is successful in part because we are made to believe the genetic bond of similar personalities; but more important is Dean's amalgam of boyish charm and an uncanny understanding of the world's ways. And Dean's *persona* always seems barely to contain, barely to hide a capability for anger and violence that allows the terrible argument with his father or the devilish vengeance that has him bring together harlot mother with angelic son. The film's rather abrupt ending makes the eventual reconciliations and Cal's transformed characterization ring untrue.

Beyond Dean's legendary acting, as well as good supporting performances by Julie Harris, Raymond Massey, and Jo Van Fleet, the film is also interesting from two separate perspectives. First, a classic concern for film theory and criticism has been the comparison between novels and their cinematic translations. A number of Steinbeck's works (for example, *Grapes of Wrath*, 1940) have enjoyed such translation, and *East of Eden* is an interesting example. Second, the film remains true to Steinbeck's fine attention to local color, offering enough historical accuracy to provide a fictionalized yet valuable insight into an America of decades past.

Perhaps future generations will come to view Dean's acting in a comparable manner: of historical interest, as an example of a fashion that differs from contemporary taste. For the present, however, his art has survived a quarter century of cinematic change and evolution, continuing to please diverse, ever more sophisticated audiences.

Edward S. Small